HER
MAJESTY'S
SECRET
SERVICE

# HER MAJESTY'S SECRET SERVICE

## The Making of the British Intelligence Community

CHRISTOPHER ANDREW

ELISABETH SIFTON BOOKS
VIKING

ELISABETH SIFTON BOOKS • VIKING
Viking Penguin Inc.
40 West 23rd Street,
New York, New York 10010, U.S.A.

First American Edition
Published in 1986

First published in Great Britain under
the title *Secret Service: The Making of
the British Intelligence Community.*

LIBRARY OF CONGRESS CATALOGING IN PUBLICATION DATA
Andrew, Christopher M.
   Her Majesty's Secret Service.
   Previously published as: Secret Service. 1985.
   "Elisabeth Sifton books."
   Bibliography: p.
   Includes index.
   1. Great Britain. Secret Intelligence Service—
History. 2. Intelligence service—Great Britain—
History. I. Title.
JN329.I6A53   1986      327.1′2′0941      85-40574
ISBN 0-670-80941-1

Printed in the United States of America by
R. R. Donnelley & Sons Company, Harrisonburg, Virginia
Set in Ehrhardt

FOR BRANDON

# CONTENTS

# ILLUSTRATIONS

# ABBREVIATIONS

| | |
|---|---|
| ACSS | Assistant Chief of the Secret Service |
| AI | Air Intelligence |
| AOER | Army Officers Emergency Reserve |
| APS | Axis Planning Staff |
| BAOR | British Army on the Rhine |
| BEF | British Expeditionary Force |
| BSC | British Security Coordination (New York) |
| BUF | British Union of Fascists |
| C | Head of the Secret Service (also known as CSS) |
| CF | Cameron, Folkestone (First World War military intelligence network) |
| Cheka | Predecessor of the KGB (1917–22) |
| CIA | Central Intelligence Agency (USA) |
| CID | Committee of Imperial Defence |
| CID | Criminal Investigation Department (Scotland Yard) |
| CIG | Central Intelligence Group (USA) |
| CIGS | Chief of the Imperial General Staff |
| CIU | Central Interpretation Unit |
| COS | Chief(s) of Staff |
| CPGB | Communist Party of Great Britain |
| CPI | Communist Party of India |
| CRPO | Combined Research and Planning Office (Middle East) |
| DCI | Director of Central Intelligence (USA) |
| DCSS | Deputy Chief of the Secret Service |
| DIB | Delhi Intelligence Bureau |
| DID | Director of the Naval Intelligence Division/Department (also known as DNI) |
| DMI | Director of Military Intelligence |
| DMO | Director of Military Operations |
| DMO & I | Director of Military Operations and Intelligence |

| | |
|---|---|
| DMP | Dublin Metropolitan Police |
| DNI | Director of Naval Intelligence |
| DORA | Defence of the Realm Act |
| DRC | Defence Requirements Sub-Committee (of CID) |
| FB | Fenian Brotherhood |
| FCI | Industrial Intelligence in Foreign Countries Sub-Committee (of CID) |
| FO | Foreign Office |
| FOES | Future Operations (Enemy) Section |
| GC & CS | Government Code and Cypher School |
| GCHQ | Government Communications Head-Quarters |
| GPU | Predecessor of KGB (1922–3) |
| GRU | Soviet Military Intelligence |
| GS(R) | General Staff Research Unit |
| IB | Intelligence Branch (War Office) |
| IBS | Intelligence Branch Simla |
| ID | Intelligence Division/Department (War Office) |
| ID25 | Cryptographic unit in Admiralty (successor to Room 40) |
| IIC | Industrial Intelligence Centre |
| ILP | Independent Labour Party |
| IPI | Indian Political Intelligence |
| IRA | Irish Republican Army |
| IRB | Irish Revolutionary/Republican Brotherhood |
| ISIC | Inter-Service Intelligence Committee |
| ISLD | Inter-Service Liaison Department |
| JIC | Joint Intelligence (Sub-) Committee (of COS) |
| JIO | Joint Intelligence Organisation |
| JIS | Joint Intelligence Staff |
| JPS | Joint Planning Staff (of COS) |
| KGB | Soviet Intelligence Service |
| MEW | Ministry of Economic Warfare |
| MI1b | Cryptographic unit in War Office |
| MI1c | Predecessor, later military section, of SIS |
| MI5 | Security Service |
| MI6 | Successor to MI1c as military section of, later alternative designation for, SIS |
| MID | Military Intelligence Department/Division |
| MOD | Ministry of Defence |
| NID | Naval Intelligence Department/Division |
| NKVD | Predecessor of KGB (1934–41) |
| NSA | National Security Agency (USA) |
| OIC | Operational Intelligence Centre (Admiralty) |
| OGPU | Predecessor of KGB (1923–34) |

| | |
|---|---|
| OSS | Office of Strategic Services (USA) |
| PCO | Passport Control Officer |
| PDU | Photographic Development Unit |
| PIU | Photographic Interpretation Unit |
| PMS 2 | Intelligence section of Ministry of Munitions |
| PR | Photographic Reconnaissance |
| Profintern | See RILU |
| PRU | Photographic Reconnaissance Unit |
| PSIS | Permanent Secretaries Steering Group on Intelligence |
| P Squad | Section of Italian Intelligence specialising in removal (prevelamento) of secret documents |
| RFC | Royal Flying Corps |
| RIC | Royal Irish Constabulary |
| RILU | Red International of Labour Unions (Profintern) |
| SD | Sicherheitsdienst (SS Security Service) |
| Section D | SIS sabotage Section (1938–40) |
| Sigint | Signals Intelligence |
| SIS | Secret Intelligence Service |
| SOE | Special Operations Executive |
| Sovnarkom | Soviet Council of People's Commissars |
| SRC | Situation Report Centre |
| STC | Supply and Transport Committee |
| STO | Supply and Transport Organisation |
| T & S | Topographical and Statistical Department (War Office) |
| U2 | American spyplane |
| UDC | Union of Democratic Control |
| WL | Wallinger, London (First World War military intelligence network) |
| Z Organisation | SIS network headed by Colonel Dansey ('Z') |

# PREFACE

Whitehall has done what it can to discourage serious study of the making of the British intelligence community. The government continues improbably to insist that in the interests of national security the entire archives of the intelligence services must remain closed indefinitely. It has authorised the publication of a distinguished official history of *British Intelligence in the Second World War*[1] and has released to the Public Record Office some of the wartime intelligence reports which reached Whitehall ministries and commanders in the field. But it refuses to release many of the same sort of documents (notably intercepted communications) for earlier years on the dotty grounds that intelligence-gathering before the war must remain more secret than during the war.[2]

There are, of course, excellent reasons for protecting the secrecy of current and recent intelligence operations. There are good grounds also for protecting the identity of some intelligence officers (such as penetration agents) throughout their lifetime. But the present government follows all its predecessors in taking these sensible arguments to preposterous lengths. The proposition that the release of documents on British intelligence operations in Germany during the Agadir crisis of 1911 or in Russia before the Bolshevik Revolution of 1917 might threaten national security in the 1980s is so absurd that probably only Whitehall is capable of defending it. The judgment of those ministers and officials who take this extraordinary view has, I believe, been sadly warped by ancient and irrational taboos. Malcolm Muggeridge derived from his years in British intelligence the lesson that 'nothing should ever be done simply if there are devious ways of doing it ... Secrecy is as essential to intelligence as vestments to a Mass, or darkness to a spiritualist séance, and must at all costs be maintained, quite irrespective of whether or not it serves any purpose'.[3] The arguments in favour of such exaggerated secrecy even about intelligence operations before the First World War would be unlikely to withstand serious public debate. But they do not have to. The taboos remain so strong that even the tenuous justification for them is usually considered too secret for public discussion.

Official attempts to conceal most of the intelligence archive have inevitably complicated my research. But, on balance, they have probably hastened this book's completion. Had I been able to consult the whole of the intelligence archive, *Secret Service* would have been even longer in the making. As it is, the number of intelligence-related twentieth-century documents which have slipped through the censorship net is larger than is available to many historians of less sensitive subjects in earlier periods or of closed societies in modern times. Careless or kindly 'weeders' have allowed a surprising amount of intelligence material into the Public Record Office, though its distribution is erratic and often difficult to trace. A document weeded from, say, a Foreign Office file may sometimes be found in a Treasury file (or vice versa). A substantial number of private papers in a variety of archives also contain intelligence documents which Whitehall would never willingly have allowed out; happily, it is nowadays reluctant to make itself ridiculous by reclaiming them.

Academic historians, discouraged by the difficulty of researching the intelligence record and repelled by the inaccurate sensationalism of many best-selling accounts of espionage, have usually tended either to ignore intelligence altogether or to treat it as of little importance. Many excellent biographies of British prime ministers, foreign secretaries and other senior ministers do not even mention the heads of their intelligence services. Such omissions are understandable but mistaken. Secret intelligence in twentieth-century Britain has varied greatly in both quantity and quality but the historian of national and international politics can never afford to ignore it. Any analysis of government policy, particularly on foreign affairs and defence, which leaves intelligence out of account is bound to be incomplete. It may also be distorted as a result.[4]

*Secret Service* is chiefly concerned with the secret intelligence services rather than with the publicly acknowledged service intelligence departments, and with strategic rather than tactical intelligence. In practice, however, these distinctions have often been blurred. During the First World War, for example, the Director of Naval Intelligence, Admiral 'Blinker' Hall, also presided over the revival of British codebreaking; his successor, 'Quex' Sinclair, later became chief of SIS. Chapter 1 therefore traces the emergence of the Victorian Military and Naval Intelligence Departments and of the Special Branch. Chapter 2 analyses the creation of the Edwardian Secret Service Bureau, the forerunner of MI5 and SIS. Chapters 3, 4 and 5 consider three aspects of the great expansion of the intelligence services produced by the First World War: the renaissance of British codebreaking, intelligence gathering on the Western Front, and the growth of counter-espionage and counter-subversion. Chapters 6 and 7 discuss the intelligence response to the Bolshevik Revolution within Soviet Russia itself and in combating the 'Red Menace' at home. Chapter 8 analyses the intelligence débâcle in Ireland which preceded the founding of the Free State. Chapters 9 and 10 are chiefly concerned with intelligence operations against the two main targets of the 1920s: Soviet Russia and Communist 'subversion'. Chapter 11 reviews the state of the intelligence services during the interwar depression as, with inadequate resources, they begin to change their main target from Soviet Russia to Nazi Germany. Chapters 12 and 13 concentrate on intelligence operations against Germany and the confusion of Whitehall as it attempts, often unsuccessfully, to distinguish good from bad intelligence during the pre-war crises and the Phoney War. Chapter 14 analyses the remarkable renaissance of the intelligence services during the first two years of the Second World War and their emergence as, for the first time, an intelligence community. An epilogue considers some of the main elements of postwar continuity and change since the community's finest hour in hastening victory over Germany.

There is space in the crowded story which follows only for those intelligence services based in the United Kingdom itself. I have been unable to provide more than a few glimpses of the imperial intelligence network linked to the British intelligence community. That is a subject to which I hope to return in the future.

During the years of research which have led up to this volume and the long searches for often elusive documents I have incurred too many debts of gratitude to friends, colleagues, former intelligence officers and their families, to fit decently into a brief preface. Some of these debts cannot, in any case, be publicly recorded. I must, however, record my grateful thanks to those who have allowed me to make use of papers to which they own the copyright and have given me other valuable assistance: Colonel J.A. Aylmer (for the Spears MSS), Vice-Admiral B.B. Schofield, Mr Robin Denniston, Mr and Mrs Robin Frost (for the Kell MSS), Mrs J.H. Godfrey, Colonel Richard Kirke, General Marshall-Cornwall, Miss Diana Pares (great-niece of Sir Mansfield Cumming), Mrs Bridget Payne Best, Mr Walter L. Pforzheimer (for the A.E.W. Mason MSS), Mrs Shearer, Mr John Spottiswoode, Mrs Pippa Temple (great-great niece of Sir Mansfield Cumming) and Mrs Ivy Vincent. Some further debts are acknowledged in the notes. I should also like to thank the Birmingham and Cambridge University Libraries, the Churchill College Archive Centre, the House of Lords Record Office, the Imperial War Museum, the India Office Library and Records, the Intelligence Corps Museum, the Liddell Hart Centre for Military Archives, the National Maritime Museum and the Wiltshire Record Office for permission to consult and, where appropriate, to quote from the papers listed in the bibliography. Documents in the Public Record Office and other Crown copyright material are quoted by permission of the Controller of HM Stationery Office.

Detailed references to my sources are given in notes. I shall be very grateful to readers who are kind enough to let me know of additional sources which I have overlooked.

*Christopher Andrew*
Cambridge, March 1985

# HER
# MAJESTY'S
# SECRET
# SERVICE

# 1 | VICTORIAN PROLOGUE: MID, NID AND THE SPECIAL BRANCH

Intelligence gathering is one of the world's oldest professions. Unlike the oldest it can claim scriptural authority. In about 1250 BC the Lord instructed Moses to send secret agents 'to spy out the land of Canaan', and gave him valuable advice on intelligence recruitment.[1] On this occasion, as so often since, good intelligence was badly used, and the children of Israel were condemned to forty years in the wilderness. But their final descent into the Promised Land was preceded by another successful intelligence operation which, with secret assistance from Rahab the harlot in the enemy camp, prepared the way for the conquest of Jericho by Joshua, one of the agents who had spied out the land forty years before.[2] Three millennia later the Victorian intelligence officer, Sir George Aston, was first attracted to secret service work by a picture in a children's book of Bible stories which showed two of Moses's agents on their way back from the land of Canaan, staggering under the weight of a huge bunch of grapes hanging from a pole carried on their shoulders.[3]

The progress of intelligence work in Britain during the three millennia between Moses and Queen Victoria was slow and erratic. From the Tudors onwards, however, there were intermittently some striking intelligence coups. Elizabeth I's secretary of state, Sir Francis Walsingham, ran and largely financed a small, underpaid secret service which uncovered the Ridolfi and Babbington plots, provided the evidence which sent Mary Queen of Scots to the scaffold, and finally drove Walsingham himself to the verge of bankruptcy. During the Interregnum Oliver Cromwell was kept well informed about royalist plots by a network of agents run by his secretary John Thurloe who, unlike Walsingham, was suspected of making a private profit out of secret service and subsequently offered his services to Charles II. The Cambridge mathematician, the Reverend John Wallis, who had decrypted some of Charles I's coded despatches for Parliament during the Civil War, was also re-employed by Charles II both as codebreaker and as royal chaplain.

From the Restoration there was a Secret Service Fund and, from 1797, an annual Secret Service Vote in parliament which continues to this day. But the pre-Victorian Secret Service Fund did not provide for an established Secret Service. It was used instead to finance British propaganda on the Continent, an assortment of part-time informants, a variety of secret operations by freelance agents, and an elaborate system of political and diplomatic bribery. During Walpole's twenty-one years as Britain's first prime minister (1721–42) the Secret Fund was probably used more for political bribes at home than for diplomatic bribes abroad. About £40,000 was spent on the 1734 election campaign alone. Walpole boasted that bribes by the Tory opposition could never match those of his Whig administration 'for 100,000 [pounds] a year spent by the Crown will in a little time drain the gentry's pockets'.[4] After his resignation in 1742 a Secret Committee of the Commons tried to intimidate John Scrope, the secretary to the Treasury, into giving evidence of Walpole's abuse of Secret Service Funds:

> But this old man, firm against all threats, had formerly braved a sterner tyranny than theirs. As a stripling he had fought under Monmouth at Sedge Moor, and carried intelligence to Holland in woman's clothes. He now, with as bold a spirit, answered the Committee that 'he was fourscore years of age, and did not care whether he spent the few months he had to live in the Tower or not, but that the last thing he would do was to betray the King, and, next to the King, the Earl of Orford [Walpole].'

Scrope escaped 'without further molestation', and went on to serve ten more years at the Treasury. As prime minister from 1743 to 1753, Henry Pelham used methods quite similar to Walpole's. One of his secretaries later recalled how he distributed banknotes to Pelham's parliamentary supporters at the end of each session:

> The sums, which varied according to the merits, ability, and attendance of the respective individuals, amounted usually to from 500 1. to 800 1. per annum; this largess I distributed in the Court of Requests on the day of the prorogation of Parliament. I took my stand there, and as the gentlemen passed me in going to or returning from the House, I conveyed the money in a squeeze of the hand. Whatever person received the ministerial bounty in the manner thus related, I entered his name in a book which was preserved in the deepest secrecy, it being never inspected by any one except the King and Mr Pelham.

The Tory prime minister, Lord Bute, allegedly set aside £80,000 from 'Secret Service' to ensure the passage of the Treaty of Paris through the Commons at the end of the Seven Years War in 1763. His secretary to the Treasury, Ross Mackay, claimed to have paid forty M.P.s £1,000 each and eighty others £500.[5]

By the time Pitt the Younger became prime minister in 1783, most bribes went abroad where they were satirically entitled 'the cavalry of St George' after the sovereigns which bore the likeness of the British patron saint. Unlike their twentieth-century counterparts, eighteenth-century heads of British diplomatic missions were often expected to distribute bribes and pay secret informants themselves. Some, perhaps most, disliked it. 'I abhor this dirty work', wrote Sir James Harris (later Earl of Malmesbury) while minister at the Hague in 1785, 'but when one is employed to sweep chimneys one must black one's fingers.' A few diplomats refused all direct contact with such 'dirty work'. Sir Robert Keith claimed virtuously in 1792 that he had 'never charged a *single shilling* for Secret Service' during his twenty-five year diplomatic career. How far eighteenth-century British diplomacy got value for its Secret Service money remains problematical. William Eden, the ambassador in Paris, paid informants in the American mission to France in 1777 to keep him informed of the progress of French negotiations with the American rebels. But the American mission discovered Eden's intelligence sources and turned them to their own advantage in negotiating an alliance with the French. Harris's lavish use of the 'cavalry of St George' in Holland during the 1780s did much to secure British, and undermine French, influence. But the large sums spent by William Wickham, the envoy in Switzerland, to promote French counter-revolution during the 1790s produced little return. Over Europe as a whole the gains from eighteenth-century espionage and covert action were probably smaller than the time and money expended on them.[6]

The department funded by the pre-Victorian Secret Service Fund which came closest to a professional intelligence service was the tiny 'Decyphering Branch' created in 1703, which the Oxford don, the Reverend Edward Willes, had by 1716 turned virtually into a family firm. By the 1750s Willes, now Bishop of Bath and Wells, had three sons working with him. The Willes family were, however, only part-time intelligence officers who combined cryptanalysis with lives as squires and clerics, and did almost all their secret work in the comfort of their country homes. By the beginning of the Victorian era the Decyphering Branch, still run by the Willes family, had fallen into decay as the general use of couriers rather than the post for diplomatic despatches reduced the flow of intercepted messages to a trickle. The Branch was formally abolished in 1844 after a Commons row over the opening of correspondence of the exiled Italian nationalist Giuseppe Mazzini. The decypherer, Francis Willes, and his nephew and assistant, John Lovell, were pensioned off with secret service money.[7]

Only a fraction of the Secret Service Fund, however, was spent on any form of intelligence gathering. Much of the Fund had nothing to do with intelligence. During the later seventeenth century, for example, the Fund was used to relieve distress among both the former mistresses of Charles II and the starving prisoners of Chester gaol. At the beginning of the nineteenth century Secret Service money was similarly used to provide a £4,000 annual pension for the Cardinal of York, the last survivor of the House of Stuart, and to support French royalist refugees on a scale ranging, according to rank, from two shillings a day to £20 a month. Lord Aberdeen concluded while foreign secretary in the 1840s that over half the purposes to which Secret Service money was put had 'nothing whatever secret' about them. On second thoughts he concluded that the Fund might not be a bad system after all 'for although there are many charges upon it which ought not to be there, they at least remain secret'.

The Civil List Act of 1782 restricted Secret Service expenditure to the principal secretaries of state for home and foreign affairs and to the first commissioner of the admiralty, each of whom had to render annual accounts to the Treasury. Secret Service, said George Canning in 1808, remained 'the only fund which has not been pried into by Parliament'. As foreign secretary in 1824, Canning tightened up supervision of Secret Service expenditure by the Foreign Office, its main consumer, and paid the permanent under-secretary an extra £500 a year for keeping full accounts. It was discovered ten years later, however, that all detailed accounts up to 1831 had disappeared.[8]

The early Victorian Foreign Office continued to dabble in covert action. In 1855, for example, Palmerston, the prime minister, and Clarendon, his foreign secretary, jointly agreed to supply £600 Secret Service money to help finance a secret attempt by Antonio Panizzi, principal librarian at the British Museum, to free six political prisoners from gaols in the Kingdom of Naples. Mr and Mrs Gladstone provided £100 of their own money and raised £200 from their friends for the same covert operation. Sadly the expedition failed. On its first outing Panizzi's rescue steamer was damaged in a storm and had to return for repairs to Hull. At its second attempt it sank near Great Yarmouth.[9]

Like Panizzi, the informants paid by the Foreign Office from the Secret Service Vote were invariably freelance amateurs rather than professional intelligence gatherers. One of the most celebrated mid-Victorian agents was the author, mystic, entrepreneur and wit, Laurence Oliphant, who was already an experienced traveller in India, Russia, America, Turkey, China and Japan by the time he was thirty. In January 1862, at the age of thirty-two, he was asked by the foreign secretary, Lord John Russell, to undertake at short notice an extensive intelligence-gathering mission in Italy to check on reports that a reaction had set in against further national unification. Over the next two years Oliphant was sent on further assorted confidential missions to investigate Austrian policy to the kingdom of Italy, the progress of the Polish rebellion, the confiscation of ecclesiastical property in Moldavia, and the dispute over the Schleswig-Holstein succession. Though Oliphant's biographer refers to him throughout these missions as a 'secret agent', he was scarcely inconspicuous. He travelled to Venice and Trieste in the suite of the Prince of Wales with whom he struck up a continuing friendship. At the town of Salmona he was wrongly identified as Palmerston's nephew, welcomed by a band playing 'God Save the Queen', and given a civic reception. In Poland he wore coloured trousers and a distinctive hat in order not to be mistaken for a Pole. Oliphant's intelligence career came to an abrupt end in March 1864 when he published details in *Blackwood's Magazine* of his secret inspection of the Danish defences and publicly denounced the Foreign Office for betraying nationalist aspirations the length and breadth of Europe. 'I am', he complained, 'in tremendous hot water, cut right and left by members of the Government.'[10]

The decline of intelligence gathering and covert action financed by the Victorian Foreign Office was reflected in the fall of the Secret Service Vote. Throughout the Napoleonic Wars the Vote had remained at over £100,000 a year, reaching a peak of £172,830 in 1805. After Waterloo it fell rapidly to £40,000 in 1822, and fluctuated at about that level for the next twenty years. It then declined gradually again to a low point of £23,000 a year in the early 1880s. Though the vote increased as a result of the Fenian bombing campaign in London of 1883–5, the Foreign Office share of it probably never exceeded £17,000 before the Boer War. It was symptomatic of the declining Foreign Office use of Secret Service money that the permanent under-secretary's annual fee for keeping the accounts, fixed at £500 in 1824, was cut to £300 in 1873 at the suggestion of the permanent under-secretary himself and remained at that level until the First World War. In most years large unexpended surpluses from the Secret Vote were returned to the Treasury.[11]

The dwindling intelligence effort financed by the late Victorian Foreign Office was increasingly focused on imperial rivalries in areas overseas where traditional forms of bribery and espionage worked more effectively and aroused fewer moral scruples than in the more modern states of continental Europe. The long drawn-out 'Great Game' with Tsarist Russia on India's North-West Frontier, which reached its peak in the later nineteenth century, gave rise to an equally long drawn-out series of intelligence operations – conducted, however, on nothing like the scale and with nothing like the sophistication suggested by Rudyard Kipling's *Kim*.[12] Though the main player on the British side was the Raj, the Foreign Office had a supporting role, particularly in Persia which acquired growing importance in British eyes as a buffer state between India and the expanding Russian Empire in Central Asia. By the 1890s, the buffer was visibly crumbling. When a British mission arrived to present the Shah with the Order of the Garter in 1903, a palace sentry presented arms with a broken table leg. The mullahs, who were the main authority within the country, proved vulnerable, however, to the 'Cavalry of St George'. Sir Charles (later Baron) Hardinge, who became British minister at Teheran in 1900, quickly concluded there were few Persian clerics 'whose religious zeal is proof against bribes'. The bribes to both mullahs and civil officials sometimes took unusual forms: among them hyacinth bulbs, cigars, coloured spectacles, silver clocks and – on one occasion – an artificial limb presented to a Persian brigand who had lost an arm in an attack on a caravan. The Marquess of Lansdowne, the foreign secretary, would scarcely have run the risk of distributing such eccentric largesse in the great powers of Europe. But in Persia, he acknowledged, he had 'not hesitated to use secret service money'.[13]

In almost every way except their handling of secret intelligence, the nineteenth-century Foreign Office and Diplomatic Service (administratively distinct until 1919) became decisively more professional. Palmerston's reforms turned the Foreign Office from a scrivener's office into a relatively up-to-date secretarial department. By the time it moved into its present building on Whitehall in 1868 it was handling more than eight times as many despatches as forty years before. The reforms of the 1850s similarly gave the Diplomatic Service, hitherto organised around the households of heads of mission, a professional, if still socially exclusive, career structure.[14] But the Victorian Foreign Office made no serious attempt to professionalise its secret intelligence system. Instead, at least in Europe, the old amateur system of intelligence gathering and covert operations fell into decay. Envoys to the great powers at the end of the nineteenth century shunned the personal involvement with spies and bribery often expected of their eighteenth-century predecessors. They were probably right to believe that the risks of such activities outweighed any potential advantage to be gained from them.

The closure of the Decyphering Branch in 1844, however, had much more serious consequences. By abandoning cryptanalysis at a time when the electric telegraph – which already linked the Admiralty to Portsmouth – was about to make both the transmission and interception of diplomatic messages much easier, the Foreign Office deprived itself of what was to become the most valuable form of diplomatic intelligence gathering. Victorian statesmen sometimes showed themselves woefully ignorant of all forms of communications intelligence. Gladstone found it difficult to believe that even the French were capable of such infamous behaviour as to open his correspondence during his foreign travels. When finally persuaded that they were, he proved hopelessly naive in his efforts to outwit them. On one occasion, when writing to his foreign secretary, Lord Granville, from Cannes, Gladstone asked a friend to write the address for him, confident, he told Granville, that if the French authorities failed to recognise his handwriting on the envelope they would not bother to open it. As Granville replied in some exasperation, the fact that the letter was addressed to the Foreign Office was, in itself, sufficient to attract the attention of the *Cabinet noir*. 'You would', he told Gladstone, 'have been a good clergyman, a first-rate lawyer and the greatest of generals, but you would have been an indifferent Fouché [police chief] in dealing with the post office.' When Lord Lansdowne became foreign secretary in 1900, he proved almost as incautious as Gladstone. 'I think it right to tell you', wrote his ambassador in Paris 1902, 'that your recent letters by post have been palpably opened by the bureau noir....'[15] By now, though the Foreign Office seems not to have realised it, the French and, probably, the Russians were able, at least intermittently, to break British diplomatic codes.[16]

The first hesitant steps towards the creation of a professional intelligence community were taken not by the Foreign Office but by the Victorian War Office.

During the Napoleonic Wars the Quarter Master General's Department at Horse Guards on Whitehall had acquired a rudimentary responsibility for strategic intelligence. As well as continuing his traditional duties of moving and quartering troops, the Quarter Master General established in 1803 a Depot of Military Knowledge to collect, mostly from overt sources, maps and information on the military resources and topography of foreign powers. But during the forty years of comparative European peace which followed the defeat of Napoleon at Waterloo in 1815, the Depot, like much else in the British Army, withered away. Renamed the Topographical Department, it became a neglected appendage of the run-down Quarter Master General's Department, doing little either to collect military information or produce new maps. Military manuals ignored strategic intelligence and confined themselves to problems of tactical or field intelligence such as cavalry reconnaissance. During 'the long peace' the British Army as a whole concerned itself with tactics rather than with strategy. As the army became for the first time in its history largely a colonial army, fighting far-flung campaigns in Southern Africa, India, Burma, Malaya, China and New Zealand, it had to contend with an often chronic shortage of intelligence from the War Office on its theatres of operations and the native forces ranged against it. The commander-in-chief at the Horse Guards had no authority over the colonial troops or expeditionary forces fighting at the frontiers of the Empire. The Duke of Wellington, during his final term as commander-in-chief from 1842 to 1852, claimed to rely on the newspapers for information on the progress of colonial conflicts. He wrote sourly in 1851, when asked by the secretary of state for war and colonies for advice on the conduct of the Kaffir War:

> I have never had any information of the causes of the War in the Cape Colonies, or the objects of the Government in carrying it on, or the views of the Government in relation to a frontier at its termination.[17]

The improbable progenitor of strategic intelligence in the Victorian War Office was Thomas Best Jervis, a retired major from the Bombay Sappers and Miners. Jervis's devoted son was deeply impressed by the 'resemblance between the well-ordered heads and noble foreheads' of his father and 'the immortal Cicero':

Thomas Best Jervis also had a head of large dimensions, moulded with exquisite symmetry – all the better seen since he was bald – scantily ornamented behind with a few locks of curly, silkily gray hair, a capacious forehead, an open countenance, bespeaking genuine candour, and illuminated by far-sighted, limpid, grayish-blue Saxon eyes, unmistakably revealing sincerity and a warm, loving soul of the most expansive nature, no less than a lucid mathematical and linguistic mind of exceptional beauty.[18]

Jervis made less of an impression on the Bombay Sappers and Miners. Handicapped by what his son considered a 'great humility of disposition' (which must sometimes have seemed a tedious moral earnestness to his fellow sappers), Jervis took seven and a half years to rise from ensign to lieutenant. Though not a distinguished soldier, he made a reputation as cartographer and topographer which led to his selection in 1837 as the next surveyor-general of India to succeed Colonel Everest (who gave his name to the world's highest mountain). But by 1841 Jervis had grown tired of waiting for the ailing Everest to retire, resigned his post in India and returned to England. Back home, he threw himself into a wide range of scholarly and philanthropic pursuits. He was elected Fellow of the Royal Astronomical, Royal Geographical, Royal Geological, Royal Asiatic and Royal Societies. He was active also in the British and Foreign Bible Society, the Association for the Discouragement of Duelling, the Evangelical Alliance, and many other worthy British and Indian causes. Jervis bombarded the government and East India Company with advice and exhortation on an extraordinary variety of topics: among them native education, 'moral destitution' on emigrant ships, the use of dromedaries, the introduction of silkworms, slate roofing and Chinese labour. By far his most influential lobbying, however, was on the subject of cartography. In 1846 he wrote to Lord Aberdeen, the foreign secretary, to complain of the 'acknowledged want of geographical information in many well-known and recent cases' ranging from Borneo to South America. This want, said Jervis, could 'now be supplied' and, his letter clearly implied, he was the man to do it. The Foreign Office was not convinced.[19]

The beginning of the Crimean War against Tsarist Russia in 1854 quickly proved Jervis's point. The British commander-in-chief, Field Marshal Lord Raglan, left for the Crimea without not merely secret intelligence on the enemy but also much basic information. He complained when setting out for Sebastopol that it was as much a mystery to him as to Jason and the Argonauts two and a half millennia before. Once in the Crimea British commanders frequently also lacked elementary tactical intelligence. After the charge of the Heavy Brigade at Balaclava, Lord Lucan, the commander of the ill-fated Light Brigade, was brought the brief, urgent message: 'Attack and prevent the enemy carrying away the guns'. But Lucan had no scouts posted, no idea what lay beyond the surrounding hills, and could only reply in bewilderment: 'Attack, Sir? Attack what? What guns, Sir?'[20]

The early débâcles of the war gave Jervis a new opportunity to urge his case. On the outbreak of war he managed to obtain in Belgium both a map of the Crimea prepared by the Russian general staff and a twenty-one sheet Austrian military map of Turkey in Europe. As soon as he returned to England a friend gained him an audience with the secretary of state for war, the Duke of Newcastle. Although, according to Jervis's son, 'it then transpired that the Government had no knowledge whatever of the maps, which did not exist in the great public or military libraries', Newcastle remained unwilling to disturb War Office routine by setting up a map-making department. But he told Jervis that if he were willing to prepare suitable maps at his own expense, 'the Government were willing to purchase of him as many copies as they might feel it desirable to obtain'.

Jervis lost no time in producing a ten-sheet map of the Crimea: probably the first printed in England to delineate marine contours in blue, the hills in brown, and the rest in black. Simultaneously, according to his son, he assailed 'all the leading men of the day' with demands for 'an efficient department for the construction of maps', basing his case not merely on the lack of maps but also on the general shortage of Russian intelligence resulting from 'our overweening presumption, inattention to due precautions, sheer ignorance and contempt of an enemy by no means contemptible'. On 2 February 1885 Lord Panmure, the Duke of Newcastle's successor at the War Office, finally wilted under the pressure and announced the creation of the Topographical and Statistical Department (T & S) under the direction of Jervis who was shortly afterwards promoted lieutenant-colonel.[21]

T & S eventually developed into the War Office's first intelligence department. But its progress was painfully slow. During the Crimean War it was mainly occupied by preparing maps. After the war ended in 1856 and Jervis died in the following year even its cartography declined. By the mid-1860s T & S was being given such trivial tasks as preparing illustrations for army dress regulations. When Captain (later Major-General Sir) Charles Wilson became director of the department on 1 April 1870 he reported that its foreign map collection was 'very incomplete', its intelligence on foreign armies shamefully deficient, and the 'means for keeping the office supplied with information from abroad' non-existent. On the last point Wilson overstated his case. Since the Crimean War military attachés had been posted for the first time at Berlin, Paris, St Petersburg, Turin and Vienna (together with a solitary naval attaché in Paris). But the outbreak of the Franco-Prussian War in July 1870 provided further evidence of the general poverty of British military intelligence. 'Had any complications arisen with France ... and had we been asked for information', Wilson later told a friend, 'we should have had to translate a German work on the French army as giving a better account of it than we could prepare ourselves'.[22]

Though Wilson had a much larger vision of military intelligence than Thomas Jervis, he had a good deal in common with him. Like Jervis, he was a devout, scholarly man, who had made a reputation as cartographer and topographer, and had been elected a Fellow of both the Royal and Royal Geographical Societies. Wilson helped to found the Palestine Exploration Fund in 1865 and retained a life-long passion for the excavation and survey of the Holy Land, above all for Jerusalem which he believed not even 'any infidel or any atheist could view without emotion'. He was not, however, an ideal propagandist for an enlarged T & S Department. Wilson had a taciturn manner and, as his official biographer tactfully puts it, was 'not what he called a society man'. But he had the great advantage of the active support of Edward Cardwell, Gladstone's reforming secretary of state for war.[23]

Shortly after Wilson became director of the T & S Department, Cardwell asked him for a report analysing its main weaknesses and proposing remedies. Wilson's report was submitted to a committee which included himself as secretary and Lord Northbrook, under-secretary for war, as chairman. The Northbrook committee's findings, published on 24 January 1871 and formally approved by Cardwell only two days later, endorsed Wilson's report virtually in its entirety and gave a scathing analysis of the cumbrous bureaucracy to which T & S was subject:

> Captain Wilson prepares a minute requesting that a map may be purchased. This passes to the Chief Clerk, who, after approving it, forwards the request to 'C' Division in which a demand on the Stationery Office is made out. The Stationery Office order the map from the mapseller, who send it to 'C' Division who forward it to the Chief Clerk who passes it to Captain Wilson.

As a result of the Northbrook report, military intelligence ceased at last to be regarded as an offshoot of map-making. The T & S was divided into two sections, one topographical, the other statistical. The Topographical Section remained responsible for collecting foreign military maps and plans (as well as photographs, when available), but its work was simplified by the removal of the Ordnance Survey to the Office of Works. The Statistical Section was made responsible for gathering and collating intelligence on foreign armed forces, and divided into three subsections responsible for different geographic areas. Its officers were required to know at least two foreign languages and were equipped with an improved library. The military intelligence with which they dealt was, however, scarcely secret intelligence. Their two main sources were foreign publications and the reports of military attachés with whom, for the first time, they were authorised to correspond directly. The only reference to covert (or almost covert) intelligence collection was a recommendation that 'soldiers should be encouraged to obtain plans of foreign fortresses and that sailors should be encouraged to do sketches of foreign ports'. Limited funds were allocated to the department to support such semi-covert activities by its officers abroad 'on condition that the officer worked and made a useful report'. In June 1871 Sir Edward Lugard, the permanent under-secretary at the War Office, gave the reorganised and strengthened T & S a statement of its duties which for the first time approximated to those of a modern military intelligence department:

> to collect and classify all possible information relating to the strength, organisation, etc, of foreign armies; to keep themselves acquainted with the progress made by foreign countries in military art and science, and to preserve the information in such a form that it can readily be consulted, and made available for any purposes for which it may be required.

In 1872, at Cardwell's request, Wilson submitted a second report on the T & S, proposed a further expansion of its work, and modestly proposed that, in order to emphasise its importance, he be replaced as director by 'an officer of high rank and position'. In February 1873 Cardwell announced the transformation of T & S into 'a real Intelligence Department' to be known as the Intelligence Branch (IB) and directed by Major-General Sir Patrick MacDougall, formerly first commandant of the Staff College at Camberley, with 'that most excellent officer Captain Wilson' as his deputy. The new IB was formally instituted on April Fools Day 1873 with a staff of 27 (15 more than the old T & S). Its founders intended it not merely as an intelligence department but as the embryo of a British General Staff along the lines pioneered in Prussia (and not finally established in Britain until 1904). Its duties were defined not merely as the collection and collation of military intelligence but also as planning for war in the light of that intelligence.[24]

MacDougall and Wilson intended that the IB should take a major role in defence planning. They were not, however, thinking mainly of war in Europe. The preoccupations of Victorian soldiers and statesmen during the years of 'splendid isolation' from the Continent were imperial rather than European: above all the defence of India and the routes to it. The first major IB concern was the Russian threat to India's North-West frontier. It provided the inspiration for the Indian Intelligence Branch at Simla (IBS), formally constituted in 1878, which assumed primary responsibility for intelligence gathering on India's borders. The IB also became heavily involved in the Scramble for Africa. The British expeditionary force to Egypt took with it copies of a 400 page IB 'Handbook on Egypt' which contained compendious information on everything from Egyptian battle order to the output of Egyptian bakeries.[25]

But though the IB quickly made itself a reputation among the civilian administrators in the War Office, it was viewed with suspicion by the high command at Horse Guards and in particular by Field-Marshal the Duke of Cambridge, cousin to Queen Victoria, a vigorous opponent of Cardwell's reforms, and commander-in-chief from 1856 to 1895. One IB officer later recalled how at Staff College dinners the Duke, 'a great favourite with the Army ... always spoke most scornfully of "Pwogress"' and was always 'cheered to the echo'.[26] The IB was more quickly appreciated by the Foreign and India Offices than by the army. Its most influential early friend was the future prime minister, the Marquess of Salisbury, who as secretary for India (1874–8) and then as foreign secretary (1878–80) in Disraeli's second government, read IB reports with great attention. After the British diplomatic triumph at the Congress of Berlin in 1878 when Disraeli returned home announcing 'peace with honour', Salisbury wrote to express his warm appreciation

> for the assistance which has been so frequently and so ably rendered to the Foreign Office on many occasions during the recent Congress, and the preceding diplomatic negotiations, by the Intelligence Department of the War Office.[27]

Lacking a Cardwell to disturb its venerable inertia, the Admiralty took over a decade to catch up with the establishment of the IB at the War Office. For a generation after the Crimean War little stirred within its walls. As in the pre-Cardwellian War Office, peacetime intelligence gathering was treated largely as an offshoot of mapmaking. The Hydrographic Department was expected to pick up what information it could while surveying. Not much came its way; even the coastal topography on most of its charts was too inaccurate to assist either defenders or attackers.[28] The threat of war with Russia during the Russo-Turkish conflict of 1877–8 provoked the first mid-Victorian rumblings of discontent at the lack of naval intelligence. The rumblings grew in volume as the result of a vigorous campaign by the leading naval publicist, Captain (later Sir) John Colomb, against the threat to Britain's expanding overseas trade and possessions from the growing Russian and French fleets. The protection of British commerce, he argued, made urgently necessary 'an organised and far-reaching system of naval intelligence'.[29] In a remarkable lecture at the Royal United Service Institution in 1881 Colomb challenged the Admiralty 'to determine the question whether systematic organised naval intelligence is or is not a great national necessity' by means of a simple experiment:

> Take the *Hecla* [a torpedo school ship], or hire a merchant steamer, give her a roving commission, such armament as she can carry, and a plentiful supply of red or white paint. Let her put to sea and disappear. Give notice to the Admirals abroad, and allow them ample time to make their

arrangements to protect commerce from this pretended hostile cruizer, which, instead of capturing and burning, might be authorized to paint on the side of any British vessel boarded at discretion, either a large C for capture, or a B for burnt.

As soon as the raider came within the range of a warship with superior gunpower the experiment would end. But Colomb expected that, because of the lack of a naval intelligence department to keep track of the raider's movements, the experiment would continue until 'C's and B's crowd our ports'.[30]

Colomb's challenge was predictably declined. But his pressure helped to persuade the Admiralty early in 1883, after lengthy hearings by a Royal Commission on the Defence of British Possessions and Commerce Abroad, to found its first intelligence department, the Foreign Intelligence Committee (FIC) under the direction of Captain William Hall, with a staff of one marine officer, two clerks and a copyist.[31] The FIC was housed in the Secretary's Department at the Admiralty, whose civilian staff had striven (usually successfully) to resist all intrusions by naval officers. When George Aston joined the FIC as a young marine in 1886, he found that it was still accepted in the Secretary's Department 'only on sufferance'. Aston freely confessed that he himself had no qualifications for an intelligence appointment other than a reputation for tact and sobriety (neither taken for granted in the Victorian navy). He was, by his own admission, 'abysmally' ignorant of geography, foreign affairs and foreign languages.[32] Though a powerful personality with strong, if misguided, views on the protection of commerce, Hall lacked the resources to run the FIC effectively. W.T. Stead, the influential editor of the *Pall Mall Gazette*, wrote scornfully that Hall was a 'mere compiler of information, a contemporary gazeteer in breeches'. There was, he claimed, still 'no Intelligence Department at the Admiralty' worthy of the name.[33]

Hall's fortunes improved when the excitable Captain (later Admiral) Lord Charles Beresford M.P. became junior naval lord in August 1886, indignant at the Admiralty's unpreparedness for war. His indignation, as Beresford acknowledged, impressed his friends as a 'Craze' or 'amiable form of lunacy', and his enemies as a condition bordering on hysteria. 'No doubt you'll try to do a number of things', his predecessor warned him, 'but you'll run up against a dead wall. Your sole business will be to sign papers.' Beresford was not deterred. Within six weeks of taking office he had submitted to the Board of Admiralty a memorandum arguing that the country was faced with 'the gravest and most certain danger', insisting that '*immediate steps* be taken to minimise the danger', and demanding the creation of a Naval Intelligence Department. 'My colleagues,' wrote Beresford, 'came to the unanimous conclusion that my statements were exaggerated; and also that, as a junior, I was meddling with high matters which were not my business; as indeed I was.' Still undeterred, Beresford took his memorandum to the prime minister, Lord Salisbury:

> ... He observed that, practically, what I was asking him to do, was to set my opinion above the opinion of my senior officers at the Admiralty and their predecessors.
>
> I replied that, since he put the matter in that way, although it might sound egotistical, I did ask him to do that very thing; but I begged him, before deciding that I was in the wrong, to consult with three admirals, whom I named.

Salisbury had already been impressed by the Intelligence Branch at the War Office. He consulted the three admirals, they supported Beresford, the Board of Admiralty yielded to pressure from the prime minister, and the Naval Intelligence Department (NID) was established with Captain Hall as its first director (DNI).[34]

The Board of Admiralty did not take their defeat lightly. To Beresford's fury, they cut the salaries of the new department by £950 at the end of 1887, leaving the DNI worse paid than the director of transports. Hall, wrote his deputy Custance, achieved 'wonders by sheer force of character and of *knowing*' and was 'quite in the van of naval thinkers', but lacked 'sufficient standing to hold his own' in the Admiralty.[35]

The first minor crisis with which Hall had to deal quickly demonstrated the continuing difficulty of obtaining even basic information on the movements of foreign fleets. The crisis followed sensational revelations in the London *Standard* on 21 January 1888 of the mobilisation of the French fleet, still the Royal Navy's main rival, at Toulon. 'Everything', it claimed, 'is being done to place a squadron of ironclads and all available cruisers in readiness to sail.' Since the British naval attaché at Paris was absent in Italy (to which he was accredited as well as France), the Admiralty had to ask the military attaché to investigate. He reported via the Foreign Office on 30 January that there were no abnormal naval preparations at Toulon. Three days later, however, the prime minister, Lord Salisbury, was told by the Italian chargé d'affaires that most of the French fleet *was* being mobilised in the Mediterranean. On 22 February the British ambassador in Paris reported that both the Italian and German embassies were satisfied that, on the contrary, 'there is no unusual armament at either Cherbourg or Toulon. The German embassy here is certain to have immediate intelligence of any change in this respect and has promised to communicate to me any such intelligence as soon as received.' As a Foreign Office official told Hall, the whole episode revealed a system of intelligence gathering 'which would be ludicrous were it not of vital importance to this country to be kept accurately informed of French naval affairs':

... It appears that all the F.O. can gather through our representatives is obtained second hand from the German and Italian Governments. We ought surely to be able to obtain as good information as the Germans in regard to naval movements.[36]

The NID's own ability to collect intelligence remained very limited. Not long after the Toulon scare Hall received a report that new harbour works under construction at Dunkirk with railway lines along the quays were intended to embark troops for the invasion of England. George Aston was sent on his first foreign mission as an NID officer to investigate. Still unsure 'what the ethics of espionage were', he 'made no secret of being a British officer'. Once at Dunkirk, Aston was quickly offered the plans of a new fort but concluded that the vendor was 'an obvious *agent provocateur*'. Aston's fractured schoolboy French caused further problems. He later recalled particular difficulty in distinguishing the French for 'sea' and 'mother': 'I remember asking my way to the sea, and being understood to want my mother'. But even Aston's inept investigation was sufficient to establish that the Dunkirk report received by Hall was the work of 'some imaginative panic-monger'.

Aston took some time to learn his trade. On a visit to the Paris Exhibition in 1889 he reported on a huge gun constructed with remarkable speed by a new French factory, only to discover later 'that the wretched gun was made of *papier-mâché*'. Intelligence collection improved as naval stations gradually established their own intelligence departments to report to NID, beginning with the Mediterranean station in 1892. Even in 1914, however, there was still no intelligence officer in the flagship of the Australian squadron. Soon after the outbreak of war the squadron was ordered to destroy the German wireless station at Rabaul in New Guinea, failed to find Rabaul, and returned without completing its mission.[37]

Like MID and NID, domestic intelligence gathering was slow to become institutionalised. Informers and spies had regularly preyed on pre-Victorian radical and working-class movements, 'debilitating their strength and distorting their image in the eyes of successive governments'.[38] The authorities in early Victorian England also used informers when dealing with agitation by the Chartists, but they established no organised system of political surveillance. 'We have no political police, no police over opinion', boasted Charles Dickens's *Household Words* in the 1850s: 'The most rabid demagogue can say in this free country what he chooses ... He speaks not under the terror of an organised spy system'. The Metropolitan Police Force, founded by Sir Robert Peel in 1829, originally contained no plain-clothes officers at all. The detective department, established in 1842, still had only fifteen men a quarter of a century later. Despite the founding of the Criminal Investigation Department (CID) in 1877, Superintendent

Adolphus 'Dolly' Williamson complained in 1880 that detective work remained unpopular within the Met:

> ... The uncertainty and irregularity of the duties ... are ... no doubt in many cases very distasteful and repugnant to the better class of men in the service, as their duties constantly bring them into contact with the worst classes, frequently cause unnecessary drinking, and compel them at times to resort to trickey [*sic*] practices which they dislike.[39]

Both undercover detectives and political surveillance developed more rapidly in Dublin than in London, spurred on by the growth of a republican underground from mid-century onwards. 1858 saw the foundation of the Fenian Brotherhood among Irish emigrants in the United States and of the Irish Revolutionary (later Republican) Brotherhood in Dublin. Both the FB and the IRB, collectively known as the Fenians, planned the violent overthrow of British rule. The IRB, however, was quickly penetrated by undercover agents of the government in Dublin Castle. In 1865 the Dublin Metropolitan Police (DMP) swooped on the IRB headquarters and arrested most of its leaders who were convicted of treason felony and sentenced to penal servitude. Forewarned by its spies and informers, Dublin Castle was able to crush a Fenian rising in March 1867 without difficulty.[40]

During the autumn and winter of 1867 Fenian violence spilled over into England. In September a police van carrying Fenian prisoners in Manchester was ambushed and a police sergeant killed. In December a bomb explosion at Clerkenwell House of Detention, where Richard Burke, leader of the Manchester ambush, was imprisoned, killed twelve people and injured 120. The following day, fearing that the Clerkenwell explosion was only the beginning of a Fenian bombing campaign, the cabinet set up a 'Secret Service Department' independent of the Met under a law officer from Dublin Castle, Robert Anderson (later knighted), who was charged with masterminding the defence of London. But the bombing campaign never materialised and the new department was wound up only four months later. Anderson, however, stayed on at the Home Office for the next fifteen years to liaise with Dublin Castle on the Fenian threat. He found life in London more leisurely than in Dublin, working in the Home Office from 11 a.m. to 5 p.m. 'It was', he later recalled, 'a nominal 11 and a punctual 5'. Anderson also recruited a remarkable agent, Thomas Billis Beach, alias Henri Le Caron, who successfully penetrated the Fenian movement in America and was commissioned in August 1868 as 'Major and Military Organizer in the Service of the Irish Republic'. Le Caron provided regular intelligence on Fenian activities, mostly in the United States, for over twenty years. When he died in 1894, five years after revealing himself in his 'true colours, as an Englishman, proud of his country', the American-Fenian leader John Devoy called him, with some exaggeration, 'the champion spy of the century', and complained that, with the Irish nation 'thirsting for his blood', he had been allowed to die peacefully in his bed.[41]

The short-lived Fenian scare of 1867–8 which led to Le Caron's recruitment did little to accustom the Metropolitan Police to political surveillance. When the Home Office was faced with urgent requests from foreign governments to investigate the activities of French 'Communist' refugees after the bloodthirsty suppression of the Paris Commune in 1871, it had little idea how to go about it. Its first, remarkably naive, reaction was to write to Britain's most celebrated political exile, Karl Marx, who obligingly provided information on the activities of the Workingmen's International. In May 1872 a sergeant from Scotland Yard was sent to investigate a meeting of French 'Communist refugees' at the Canonbury Arms in Islington. On his way into the meeting the sergeant was asked if he was a Communist himself, replied that he was not, but insisted on his right to stay:

Upon that a person (whom I can identify) caught hold of me and assisted by others carried me forcibly out of the room and intimated that if I returned they would break my head. I did not return in order that no breach of the peace should take place.

A month later the sergeant tried again. This time he was allowed to stay but all the Communists departed.[42]

Representations from foreign governments at the activities of political refugees were one of the pressures which led during the 1880s to the founding of Britain's first 'political police'. A German socialist refugee in London, Johann Most, who wrote an article applauding the assassination of Tsar Alexander II by a Russian nihilist in March 1881, was arrested after complaints by the German government, and convicted of incitement to murder. As a result of the Most case, Gladstone's Home Secretary, Sir William Vernon Harcourt, ordered the Met to keep a regular watch henceforth on all 'Communist' meetings. But the main stimulus to the creation of a political police came from the resurgence of Fenian terrorism. A bombing campaign in England during the first six months of 1881 killed a boy of seven outside Salford Barracks but otherwise did little damage and collapsed after the capture of two Fenian bombers and the discovery of an arms cache. Though the CID set up a Fenian Office to liaise with the Royal Irish Constabulary (RIC) and Queen Victoria enquired what was being done to protect Buckingham Palace, Harcourt dismissed the London bombs as 'a Fenian scare of the old clumsy kind'. The government reacted with much greater urgency to the assassination of Lord Frederick Cavendish, chief secretary for Ireland, and Thomas Burke, the permanent under-secretary, as they were walking through Dublin's Phoenix Park in May 1882. An emergency cabinet meeting in London set up a special anti-Fenian detective force in Dublin under the command of the former IB officer, Colonel (later Major-General) Henry Brackenbury, who became 'spymaster general' with the official title of Chief Special Commissioner. Though a firm believer in military intelligence, Brackenbury was dismayed by his Irish appointment and quickly began trying to arrange a transfer. He was succeeded as 'spymaster general' in August by Edward Jenkinson, a former divisional commissioner in India whose experience of the Mutiny was thought to equip him for the struggle against Fenian terror. Early in 1883 that terror entered its most acute phase with the beginning of a 'dynamite war' against British cities. In London alone Fenian bombs exploded at the Local Government Board in Whitehall, the offices of *The Times*, the Houses of Parliament, the Tower of London, several main railway stations, the London underground and Scotland Yard itself – all in the space of under two years. 'The Houses of Parliament', said *The Times* in March 1883, 'are searched as if continually on the eve of a GUY FAWKES plot ...' Harcourt complained in April that the Fenian menace was demanding 'every available moment of my time'. He wrote to Gladstone a month later:

> This is not a temporary emergency requiring a momentary remedy. Fenianism is a permanent conspiracy against English rule which will last far beyond the term of my life and must be met by a permanent organisation to detect and to control it.

The 'permanent organisation' which Harcourt had in mind was centred on the 'Special Irish Branch' which he set up at Scotland Yard in March 1883 under the veteran detective Superintendent 'Dolly' Williamson. At the same time Jenkinson was summoned from Dublin to co-ordinate anti-Fenian operations in the capital. At its peak in the mid-80s these operations involved the Special Irish Branch; 79 policemen drawn from Scotland Yard and the RIC watching the ports; hundreds of uniformed and plain-clothes men (some drafted in from Ireland) protecting London buildings; a network of informers in mainland Britain run by a provincial 'spymaster', Major Nicholas Gosselin, appointed by Jenkinson; Jenkinson's own network in Ireland, the United States and the Continent; and seven Scotland Yard men in continental cities. The anti-Fenian campaign enjoyed the active patronage of the royal family which rightly feared that it was one of the Fenians' targets. Queen Victoria was 'in a great state of fuss about the situation in general', fearful that the royal train might be bombed on its way to Balmoral, and the Prince of Wales personally recommended a secret agent who was taken on by Jenkinson. Harcourt, who had frequently to reassure the Queen, complained to his son in February 1884: 'I have sunk now into a mere Head Detective and go nowhere and see nothing'.[43]

The Special Irish Branch was more vulnerable to Fenian attack than it realised. Its offices were imprudently situated on the first floor of a small building in the centre of Great Scotland Yard, immediately above a public urinal. Though a police constable on duty in front of the building 'observed nothing suspicious in any persons who entered the urinal', the Fenians succeeded in planting a large bomb which demolished the Special Irish Branch offices on the evening of 30 May 1884. Jenkinson was outraged at the laxness of Scotland Yard security:

> If the Constable had been properly posted I do not see how men could have approached and put anything in the urinal unobserved ... Fancy them allowing the public to go there at night, or indeed at any time after the warnings they had received.[44]

A search was quickly mounted for other strategically-placed urinals. A public lavatory near Windsor Castle was closed down, and there was a flurry of alarm when it was discovered that the entire sanitation of the Houses of Parliament was being overhauled by Irish workmen.[45]

In the event the dynamite war in the capital came to an end early in 1885 without further damage either to public urinals or to Scotland Yard. An attempt to arrange a Fenian 'firework display' during Queen Victoria's golden jubilee in 1887 with explosions during the thanksgiving service at Westminster Abbey and in parliament ended in fiasco. Scotland Yard was forewarned of the bomb plot by informers and had the Irish-American bombers under surveillance from the moment they left the United States. Two of the bombers were arrested soon after they reached Britain; a third died before the police arrived. The Fenian dynamite war was at an end.[46]

From late 1885 the anti-Fenian surveillance system was rapidly run down. In 1886 RIC men were withdrawn from London and the ports. In January 1887 Jenkinson, who had long complained of the 'stupidity of some so-called [English] detectives', 'the greatest jealousy of me and my Irish staff', and his own 'anomalous', 'undefined' position as security coordinator, handed in his resignation. Simultaneously the remnants of the anti-Fenian forces – some from the Irish Special Branch, more from the port police – were drawn together into a new body, the Special Branch of the Metropolitan Police, which was given responsibility for all political crime. Its first head was the assistant commissioner in the charge of the CID, James Monroe, who was made accountable for the Special Branch not to the chief commissioner of the Met but to the home secretary direct. A year later, Monroe was succeeded by Robert Anderson, head of the short-lived Secret Service Department of 1867–8.[47]

The early Special Branch was on a smaller scale than the anti-Fenian operations of the mid-80s. During the 1890s it had only about twenty-five men, many – if not most – of Irish origin. Some of its energies were turned against the anarchists whose continental victims at the end of the century included the President of France, the King of Italy, the Queen of Austria–Hungary and the prime minister of Spain. Anarchist terrorism in Britain was feeble by comparison, though a few inexpert bomb-makers were arrested at Walsall in 1892 (one of their bombs is still in the possession of the Walsall police), and the French anarchist Martial Bourdin, who blew himself up while attempting to demolish Greenwich Royal Observatory in 1894, provided Joseph Conrad with the inspiration for his novel *The Secret Agent*. Some of the Special Branch's energies were also expended on vaguer forms of subversion. It began, for example, to suspect a sinister purpose behind the harmless activities of the Legitimation League, founded to remove the stigma of bastardy from illegitimate children. Inspector John Sweeney became convinced that the League was being used by anarchists to subvert the social order by promoting free love. Sweeney purchased a volume of Havelock Ellis's *Psychology of Sex* from the League's secretary, George Bedborough, then promptly arrested him for selling it. Following Bedborough's conviction for obscene libel in 1898 and a police raid on its offices, the League was wound up.[48] At the end of the nineteenth century the twenty-five officers of the Special Branch had little of importance left to do. Not till the German spy scares which preceded the First World War did the Branch return to something like the prominence achieved by the Special Irish Branch during the Fenian bombings of the 1880s.

The best developed intelligence department at the end of the nineteenth century was in the War Office. Even the IB, however, had an uphill struggle for acceptance in the 1880s. Major-General Sir Archibald Alison, who had succeeded MacDougall as director of the IB in 1878, lacked his predecessor's enthusiasm for intelligence work. Though a dashing field commander who had lost an arm during the Indian Mutiny and received the thanks of Parliament for his valiant service in the Ashanti War, Alison was ill at ease sitting at a War Office desk. When Britain intervened in Egypt in 1882 he jumped at the chance to lead the Highland Brigade which stormed Tel-el-Kebir, received the thanks of Parliament once again, and was promoted to lieutenant-general. Alison left behind a severely depleted IB. He took four IB officers with him in 1882; four more were sent to Egypt in 1885 to form an intelligence department for the Suakin expedition. Alison's own post as director remained unfilled until 1886. The acting head of the IB for most of the interregnum was another wounded military hero, Colonel Aylmer Cameron, who had won the Victoria Cross for killing three Sepoy mutineers in quick succession after his own left hand had been cut off. Despite his bravery in the field, Cameron was also unhappy behind a desk and failed to carry conviction as an intelligence chief. Nor did Gladstone's foreign secretary from 1880 to 1885, the Earl of Granville, show any of his predecessor, Lord Salisbury's, enthusiasm for the work of the IB. By 1885 the IB was widely regarded as a 'harmless but rather useless appendage to the War Office'.[49]

Paradoxically, the Mahdi's conquest of the Sudan which culminated in 1885 with General Gordon's death at Khartoum helped to revive War Office intelligence. The British troops withdrawn from the Sudan included a number of former IB officers who now returned to the War Office. Chief amongst them was Major-General Henry Brackenbury, the anti-Fenian 'spymaster general' of 1882, who was appointed on 1 January 1886 to the post of IB director left vacant by Alison four years before. 'Brack' impressed his staff with what one of them called 'his pasty-yellow, black-moustached face and almost uncanny power of getting at the root of a complicated matter in a word or a question or two'. He had been a firm believer in intelligence work ever since witnessing the efficiency of the Prussian general staff while serving in the British Hospital Unit during the Franco-Prussian War, and worried the Duke of Cambridge with his radical ideas. Major-General Lord Edward Gleichen later recalled how as a young IB officer in 1886 he had found himself sitting next to the Duke at a dinner party after the ladies had withdrawn:

> He very kindly asked me what I was doing, but when I had broken to him that I was working in the Intelligence Department he looked grave; and, leaning over and putting his hand on my knee, he said: 'So you are under Brackenbury? A dangerous man, my dear Gleichen, a very dangerous man!' A curious thing to say to a junior subaltern about his Chief.[50]

'Brack' proved, as the Duke had feared, a successful empire-builder. On 1 June 1887, in recognition of his growing influence, he became the first Director of Military Intelligence (DMI), with the right to report directly to the commander-in-chief. Four months later he persuaded the War Office to increase the IB's permanent intelligence strength by seven officers. In January 1888 Brackenbury was promoted to lieutenant-general and the Intelligence Branch raised in status to the Intelligence Division, later the Intelligence Department.[51]

The venerable Duke of Cambridge was far from alone in his suspicions of the new ID. For most late Victorian army officers intelligence assessment remained an unattractive backwater remote from the command posts to which they aspired. Even when they appreciated the value of tactical intelligence in the field they frequently failed to realise the importance of strategic intelligence in the War Office. Horatio Herbert (later Field-Marshal Earl) Kitchener had won a reputation as an enterprising intelligence officer in Egypt and the Sudan during the early 1880s, making deep reconnaissances into the desert disguised in Arab dress. As commander-in-chief of the Egyptian Army a decade later he lent heavily on his own intelligence department but remained deeply suspicious of the ID at the War Office. When Gleichen arrived as ID representative with the Egyptian Army in 1896, he found himself regarded as 'a spy of the War Office'. 'Although Kitchener was personally very civil to me,' Gleichen later recalled, 'he ... never gave me a hint of what he was doing or going to do, whilst my inquiries in that direction were skilfully fenced with'.[52] Like the IB of the 1870s, the ID of the 1890s was more appreciated by the Foreign Office than by the War Office – and in particular by Lord Salisbury, foreign secretary as well as prime minister for most of the decade. Brackenbury wrote (with some exaggeration) to one of his successors as DMI:

> My experience is that Everything in the ID depends upon your having the complete friendship and hearty cooperation of the Foreign Office. So long as you have that, as I had, you can command the use of all their staff at home and abroad, and they will never let you want for money.[53]

On the North-West Frontier the non-alarmist views of the ID prevailed over those of the IBS which had become the mouthpiece of the Indian 'Forward School', retailing alarmist rumours of Russian intentions to justify its own ambitions. In 1891 Brackenbury was replaced as DMI by Major-General Edward Chapman and sent to reform the Indian intelligence system. After the reorganisation of the IBS in 1892 'Brack' was able to assure the War Office that it was 'no longer ... the agent for provoking Russian scares'. The reformed IBS remained in close liaison with the ID in London. So too did the NID, still clearly the junior partner in the service intelligence partnership. Chapman himself was not a success as DMI. Though his staff were 'all very fond of him personally', they found him alarmingly ignorant of world affairs. That the ID survived his five years as DMI (1891–96) with its reputation scarcely diminished was due chiefly to the able team assembled by Brackenbury who continued to influence, notably, Salisbury's decision to advance down the Upper Nile towards successful confrontation with the French.[54]

The ID, however, had relatively little to do with *secret* intelligence. Its officers spent far more time reading the newspapers than studying secret reports. As Gleichen later recalled:

> ... The chief work was keeping information up to date concerning foreign armies and theatres of war, the sources being mainly official military books of the different countries, magazines, maps and periodicals of all sorts and, largely, the foreign daily press. How I used to hate the 'Temps' and the 'Journal des Débats', the 'Stampa', 'Diario do Governo' and all the rest of them! It meant a good deal of work looking through half a dozen foreign newspapers a day, besides many other weekly and monthly ones, with very little result. Items of military interest were few and far between, but when one did run any important ones to ground each had to be carefully indexed – some under perhaps four or five headings – and, if from the

daily press, cut out and stuck into a big cutting-book.... The reputation, however, that I got in my battalion was that I spent my time in cutting out interesting items and pictures from 'La Vie Parisienne' and sticking them on a screen whilst my hard-worked brother officers were doing my duty![55]

The main asset of the ID and the principal source for its numerous reports was its large library. By 1886 the IB already had close on 40,000 volumes, increasing by 5,500 a year, and subscribed to numerous foreign periodicals. It almost certainly possessed more recent information than any other government library. The Treasury told the British Museum five years later that the ID possessed what was 'believed to be the best Military Library in the world'. The up-to-date professionalism of its information retrieval is indicated by the Library's adoption of the Dewey decimal system within a few months of its invention.

One of the greatest assets, and in the end the greatest liability, of the ID during its first decade was its energetic, largely self-taught librarian, W.H. Cromie, who had entered the War Office as a private soldier. In 1883, while still a quartermaster, Cromie had succeeded in publishing articles on foreign military powers in the prestigious *United Services Magazine*, but continued to be handicapped by his humble origins and lowly status. Brackenbury complained in 1890 that not merely was Cromie 'unable to meet other librarians on equal terms', 'in fact they have hitherto refused to grant him an audience'. After years of studying law in the evenings, Cromie gained his LlB in 1890, and his lot improved a little. In 1891 Sir E. Maunde Thompson of the British Museum, after at first refusing to grant Cromie an audience, agreed to see him, reviewed his plans for a subject catalogue, and condescendingly pronounced them 'quite simple and sensible'. But, despite the DMI's support, the War Office refused to advance Cromie beyond the rank of captain, and the Treasury limited his salary to £271 instead of the £600 or more requested by the ID.

After years of humiliation and low pay Cromie seems to have taken a terrible revenge. Despite his poor salary, he was responsible for what the veteran War Office official Denham Robinson called 'the *secret* documents (obtained heaven knows how) concerning foreign armies, etc'. After a secret investigation in 1898, Major-General Sir John Ardagh (DMI 1896–1901) concluded that his librarian had been selling secrets to the French. Cromie, however, successfully evaded several traps set for him and, in the absence of sufficient evidence for a conviction, had to be dismissed simply for 'irregular conduct'.[56]

By comparison with its efficient, up-to-date (if insecure) library, the ID's covert intelligence system remained amateurish. Secret intelligence arrived, as Denham Robinson put it, 'heaven knows how', rather than from any organised agent network. The total ID budget for all 'Secret Service' work before the Boer War was only £600 a year, though that sum was occasionally supplemented by the Foreign Office. ID informants included a riverboat captain in the Belgian Congo, the head of the Persian telegraphs and British railway officials at various points of the globe who either gave their occasional services free of charge or else received only token payment. Most of the War Office 'Secret Service' budget went to finance foreign travel by the ID officers themselves who were expected to visit those parts of the world which they were responsible for monitoring. Gleichen complained that the niggardly expenses paid from 'Secret Service' funds invariably left ID officers out of pocket. His trip to Montenegro in 1899 cost him nearly £80 of his own money. 'On several other occasions,' he wrote later, 'I only received an insignificant proportion of my expenses back'.[57]

Other ID officers were grateful simply to receive part of their travel costs. 'In those days,' Major-General Sir Charles Callwell later recalled, 'one was expected by the financial authorities to be out of pocket when away on public service'. Secret Service funds allowed ID officers to 'have interesting and often very pleasant trips abroad at trifling cost to their own pockets'. 'It was', he believed, 'no small privilege to be enabled to visit at the public expense parts of the world which one otherwise might never have seen.' Callwell remembered with particular affection the ID officer responsible for North American intelligence, Major Wemyss, who was 'blessed with a decidedly fertile brain':

> He actually persuaded his superiors that it was desirable for him to visit the United States and Canada in order to draw up a scheme for the defence of the latter's three-thousand-mile frontier against an invasion by her neighbour. He was absent quite a long time, and enjoyed himself immensely, bless him! He was a real loss to the Army when, not long afterwards, he left it to go into business, in which he has deservedly succeeded.[58]

The intelligence-gathering missions of the ID staff were supplemented by those of other army officers, and, as Aston described them, 'patriotic folk'.[59] The most enthusiastic of the officers was the future founder of the Boy Scout Movement, Robert (later General Lord) Baden-Powell, who developed a taste for intelligence work during a series of 'jolly larks' on the North-West Frontier in the early 1880s. In 1884 Baden-Powell published *Reconnaissance and Scouting* which, he argued, offered the officer who engaged in them a remarkably 'good chance of distinguishing himself' and which he privately considered 'a grand advertisement for me'. Later he relieved the tedium of regimental life in England by attending foreign military manoeuvres and reporting on them to the War Office. Some of his happiest experiences as a spy were spent roaming the Mediterranean engaged in 'glorified detective work' for the ID.[60]

Baden-Powell included in his memoirs an enthusiastic account of his exploits disguised as an eccentric butterfly collector on the Dalmatian coast:

> Carrying [a sketchbook] and a colour box, and a butterfly net in my hand, I was above all suspicion to anyone who met me on the lonely mountain side, even in the neighbourhood of the forts ... They thoroughly sympathised with the mad Englishman who was hunting these insects. They did not look sufficiently closely into my sketches of butterflies to notice that the delicately drawn veins of the wings were exact representations, in plan, of their own fort, and that the spots on the wings denoted the number and positions of guns and their different calibres.

Baden-Powell was a firm believer in the superiority of the gentleman amateur over the career professional. 'The best spies,' he declared, 'are unpaid men who are doing it for the love of the thing'. He insisted too on the great 'sporting value' of amateur espionage.

> For anyone who is tired of life, the thrilling life of a spy should be the very finest recuperation. When one recognises also that it may have valuable results for one's country in time of war, one feels that even though it is a time spent largely in enjoyment, it is not by any means time thrown idly away; and though the 'agent', if caught, may 'go under', unhonoured and unsung, he knows in his heart of hearts that he has done his 'bit' for his country as fully as his comrade who falls in battle.[61]

Before the First World War, however, there was not much danger that British officers would 'go under'. Until less than a decade before the war all the great powers took a remarkably tolerant attitude towards amateur espionage by foreign army officers. R. B. Haldane, the secretary of state for war, told the Commons in 1908: 'That officers of all nations, when abroad, look about for useful information I have no doubt'. 'But that,' he believed (though Baden-Powell disagreed), 'is a different thing from coming as spies'.[62] If a British agent were caught, wrote Baden-Powell's contemporary, Sir George Aston, 'the penalty would probably only be unpopularity'.[63] At worst he had to face brief incarceration in a foreign fortress.

Late Victorian agents sometimes felt a certain camaraderie with their foreign rivals. Major-General Sir Alexander Bruce Tulloch later recalled how as an IB officer in about 1880 he had been engaged in touring the English coastline checking on likely landing sites for a foreign invasion:

> When doing the Yorkshire coast, I heard of a German officer staying at a hotel at Scarborough, which he had made his headquarters while doing work which turned out to be precisely that in which I also was engaged,

and my headquarters were close to – viz., at Bridlington Quay. My regret was that I did not hear about my German colleague until my work was just finished: we might have done it together.

Tulloch found an equally sporting attitude when he visited Egypt on an intelligence-gathering mission soon afterwards. Indeed, he found military intelligence embarrassingly easy to come by:

> On one occasion I thought the [Egyptian] chief of staff was lifting the curtain too high, so I said to him plainly, "You must not tell me too much. You and I may be on opposite platforms before long." He laughed, saying, "When I am abroad, I keep my eyes open, and I guess you do the same."[64]

Tulloch's were probably the most important of the agent reports (though they were scarcely *secret* intelligence) which went into the compendious *Handbook on Egypt* supplied to the British expeditionary force in 1882. Later ID officers in North Africa were also sometimes surprised by the cooperation they received. While surveying fortifications in Morocco as Assistant Director of Military Operations and Intelligence in 1908, Lord Edward Gleichen found that: 'Oddly enough, the natives raised no objection. On the contrary, they took much interest in my doings, and several of them willingly assisted me in "shooting" angles and slopes'.[65] Though frequently helpful, however, the natives were notoriously unreliable. Callwell complained in a book 'recommended to officers' by the War Office:

> The difficulty of dealing with Orientals and savages, whether as informers or spies, is referred to in many textbooks and works of reference on reconnaissance and intelligence duties. The ordinary native found in the theatres of war peopled by coloured races lies simply for the love of the thing and his ideas of time, numbers and distance are of the vaguest, even when he is trying to speak the truth.[66]

Baden-Powell was not alone in finding in the overseas missions of Britain's amateur agents 'that touch of romance and excitement ... which makes spying the fascinating sport it is'.[67] The romance had little to do with women. British espionage was a strictly male affair. 'The employment of women as spies or as secret agents,' wrote Sir George Aston, 'is not favoured in Britain'.[68] The glamour of late Victorian espionage, even when improved by later recollection, had more to do with George Henty than with James Bond. One of the greatest thrills for Baden-Powell and some of his contemporaries was simply dressing up. While accompanying the British expeditionary force in Egypt, Tulloch 'decided to go up the line in disguise': 'In the morning I had been with our politicals in their room in the town in my usual dress: in the afternoon, before starting, I walked into their room again. The first exclamation was, "What on earth does this confounded Gippy want in here?"[69] Baden-Powell had the similar excitement on his first 'spying expedition' in South Africa of going unrecognised by his own commanding officer: 'Quite forgetting my appearance, I greeted him with the customary "Good morning, Major". He turned and looked at me for a moment, and apparently thinking I was a tramp out for money, he growled savagely: "Get out," and went on his way; and I went mine, with the contented feeling that I was not likely to be taken for a British officer.'[70] The fascination with disguise lingered on in the early years of the professional British secret service founded in 1909. Captain Sir Mansfield Cumming, the first head of what later became SIS or MI6, loved dressing up and noted in his journal details of both his own and his agents' disguises.[71] His first two 'master spies' in Bolshevik Russia, Sidney Reilly and Paul Dukes, both prided themselves on their mastery of multifarious disguise.

It would be wrong to judge the late Victorian ID simply by its often amateurish secret service work. The last and ablest Victorian DMI, Sir John Ardagh (1896–1901), concluded that 'it was not often that a secret agent discovered anything of importance, but it did sometimes happen'.[72] Captain (later Brigadier-General) Wallscourt Waters, who served under Ardagh as head of ID's Section D (Russia-in-Europe and Asia), was similarly convinced that 'Underground intelligence really amounts to very little, nothing to worry about in my opinion'.[73] By far the most valuable work of the Victorian ID was its careful collation of the information which reached London from Africa and Asia. The innumerable border disputes and military operations associated with late nineteenth-century imperial scrambles frequently forced both the Foreign Office and the Colonial Office to seek information from the ID.[74]

Ardagh's reputation in the Foreign Office stood so high that he was given a room in it as well as in the Colonial Office.[75] Within the ID he was regarded by his staff with reverent awe. He reminded Gleichen, then head of Section E (Austrian and Turkish Empires), of a marabou stork, 'silent, monocled, skinny-necked':

> He never spoke, and when he sent for us to give him information on certain subjects, there was dead silence on his part whilst we talked. I once gave him a full account of Morocco matters during the space of something like half an hour. He leant back in his chair, never interrupted once nor took a note, and at the end he slowly screwed his eyeglass in and said in a hollow, faded voice, "Thank you". Yet he had absorbed painlessly all that I had told him, and the issue was a masterpiece of writing.[76]

But despite the personal respect in which Ardagh was held by both Lord Lansdowne, the secretary of state for war, and Lord Wolseley, who had succeeded the Duke of Cambridge as commander-in-chief, he failed to exert much influence on the entrenched bureaucracy of the War Office. He told the Royal Commission on the War in South Africa in 1903 that the ID 'has not now, and has not for many years had, the influence on the military policy of the country that it ought to have':

> My position was very subordinate indeed to the influence exercised by the great military officers at the War Office – the Commander-in-Chief, the Adjutant-General, the Quartermaster-General, the Inspector-General of Fortifications; they were as a rule Lieutenant-Generals or higher rank while I was a Major-General, and rank goes for a good deal in confabulations of military people.[77]

Spenser Wilkinson, first Chichele Professor of War at Oxford, compared the War Office use of the ID during the Boer War to a man who 'kept a small brain for occasional use in his waistcoat pocket and ran his head by clockwork'.[78]

The Royal Commission on the War in South Africa predictably concluded that the ID had been 'undermanned for the work of preparation for a great war'. At the outbreak of war in 1899 the whole ID numbered only eighteen officers. Section B, which was responsible for all British colonies, protectorates, spheres of influence and the two Boer Republics, and had to give advice on issues ranging from frontier disputes to cables, was staffed by two officers, a part-time assistant and a military clerk. The Royal Commission reported that, despite its slender resources, the ID had none the less achieved 'a considerable measure of success'.[79] As early as June 1896 Major (later Lieutenant-General) Edward Altham, the head of Section B, had argued that, contrary to prevailing military opinion, 'the two Boer States may make a dash at Natal', which in October 1899 is precisely what they did. Subsequent ID memoranda also pointed correctly to the Boer threat to Cape Colony, and provided accurate estimates of Boer forces, troops and ammunition.[80]

As so frequently before and since, the great intelligence failures of the Boer War were failures of use rather than failures of collection and analysis. Alone among the great powers of Europe, Britain still possessed no general staff for contingency planning, and thus lacked the machinery to make full use of ID intelligence. And though 'special officers' sent by the ID to South Africa in the summer of 1899 laid the foundation for a Field Intelligence Department to provide tactical intelligence, army regulations prohibited the establishment of that Department until after the declaration of war. Some of the most important ID strategic intelligence was simply not believed. The colonial secretary, Joseph Chamberlain, who, like Lansdowne, opposed sending large troop reinforcements to South Africa in the summer of 1899, was convinced that the ID was exaggerating the size of Boer forces. Much other ID intelligence was ignored.[81] When a copy of the ID manual on South Africa was sent to General Sir Redvers Buller (nicknamed 'Blunder' in the ID and elsewhere) on his appointment as commander-in-chief of the expeditionary force, he sent it back on the grounds that he 'knew everything there was to know about South Africa'. Another copy of the ID manual which found its way to Natal was captured by the Boers in their first attack, and promptly published in the American press. The defeat at Colenso, the climax of the disasters of 'Black Week' in December 1899 which cost Buller his command, was due at least in part to his neglect of intelligence on Boer movements.[82]

The diminutive, white-haired Field-Marshal Lord 'Bobs' Roberts VC, who arrived at Cape Town to succeed Buller in January 1900, brought with him a more enlightened attitude towards intelligence. His intelligence chiefs quickly expanded the Field Intelligence Department, distributed new and better maps, and improved reconnaissance. Official military doctrine was still to provide intelligence officers only at divisional level. Under Roberts, however, all brigades and sometimes smaller units had their own intelligence officers. Unhappily, some commanders had little idea what to do with them. George Aston 'found that the new intelligence officer was looked upon as a sort of handyman, expected to undertake odd jobs of every description'. 'Intelligence officers', he complained, 'did so much of other people's work that they had little time for their own....'[83] The Boer move from conventional to guerilla warfare in the autumn of 1899 also multiplied the problems of the Field Intelligence Department. Kitchener, who succeeded Roberts as commander-in-chief in December 1900, responded by greatly increasing the Department's size. His DMI from February 1901, Lieutenant-Colonel David Henderson, devised the most elaborate field intelligence system in British military history. He divided South Africa into four intelligence districts, appointed an intelligence officer for each district, divided the districts into subdistricts, each with its own intelligence officer, arranged for the continuous exchange of information between these officers and those with independent columns, laid down the distinct responsibilities of officers at different levels, and established a common format and timetable for intelligence reporting. By the war's end in May 1902 the Field Intelligence Department numbered 132 officers, 2,321 white civilians, and several thousand natives. The very pace of expansion, however, meant that most intelligence officers were inexperienced. As one of them later recalled:

> ... Frequently the I.O. was ignorant of the district and the ways of the people, and, moreover, unable to understand native languages. And usually he was casual, supremely self-confident, and wedded to week-old telegrams. 'You must be mistaken' was his favourite comment on a scout's report, unless it tallied with his own theories.

Since most of the guerilla war was fought on Boer territory, the Field

Intelligence Department could scarcely hope to match the Boers' tactical intelligence. But without the improved intelligence provided by the Department the long drawn-out British victory against the much smaller Boer forces would have been even longer delayed.[84]

Like its less elaborate predecessors in earlier wars, the Field Intelligence Department failed to survive by long the war for which it had been created. Covert operations continued for a time on a much reduced scale directed against unrepentant Boers and German South-West Africa. The most remarkable of these operations were probably those conducted by Captain Edmund (later Field-Marshal Lord) Ironside of the Royal Field Artillery. Despite his six-feet four-inch frame and fifty-inch chest, Ironside not merely disguised himself as a Boer, but also succeeded in 1903 in enlisting in the German army in South-West Africa. He was later introduced to Hitler at German army manoeuvres in 1937 wearing the German campaign medal he had won against the Herrero tribesmen in 1904.[85] Though the Field Intelligence Department itself ceased to exist after victory in the Boer War, it was to prove an important precedent for the Great War. Kitchener's DMI, Lieutenant-Colonel David Henderson, used his experience in South Africa as the basis of his influential manual, 'Field Intelligence, Its Principles and Practices', which became the basis of the 'Regulations for Intelligence Duties in the Field' published by the War Office in August 1904 and the inspiration for the Intelligence Corps founded ten years later on the outbreak of war.[86]

The Boer War also led to a modest expansion of British secret intelligence. From 1896 the ID had sent a number of officers, including Altham, the head of Section B, and Baden-Powell, on secret service work to South Africa, disguised (probably rather thinly) as civilian travellers, to gather intelligence on topography, communications and Boer strength. By the summer of 1899 ten officers were on 'special' duties in South Africa. Leo Amery of *The Times* (later a prominent cabinet minister) told the Royal Commission on the War in South Africa that they did 'very good work':

> ... But they were fewer than the men I employed myself as *Times* correspondents, and I should have been ashamed to send *Times* correspondents anywhere, or even a commercial traveller, with the sums of money they were given.

The Commission was also told that in the three years before the war the Boer Republic of Transvaal had spent £286,000 on 'Secret Service' at a time when the total ID budget was only £20,000 a year of which about £2,000 was spent on South Africa.[87]

At the outbreak of war Major (later Brigadier-General Sir) James Edmonds was put in charge of a new Section H in the ID with responsibility for 'special duties' which included censorship, counter-intelligence and 'secret service'.

During a War Office reorganisation in 1901 which amalgamated the ID and the Mobilization Division, Section H was superseded by Subdivision I3, which contained a 'temporary' three-man 'Secret Section', I3(A), responsible for 'secret service' work – in particular 'for watching shipments of ammunition and messages from the Continent [to the Boers], and for carrying out enquiries referred from South Africa'. Ardagh's successor, Lieutenant-General Sir William (later Field-Marshal Baron) Nicholson, whose status was upgraded to Director General of Mobilization and Military Intelligence (DGMI), argued at the end of the Boer War that the Secret Section should be made permanent: 'The branch would be fully occupied in peace time as well as during war; it would train Officers for intelligence work in the field, and would appoint and deal with our secret agents'. The head of I3, Colonel (later Major-General Sir) J.K. Trotter, also argued strongly that 'Secret Service required a permanent organisation':

Before the war money had been wasted on persons who made sham offers of information, and in other ways, owing to want of organisation of Secret Service, and of a record of the previous history of all persons offering information or voluntecring to procure it; if the section was made permanent such occurrences would be avoided in future; the Intelligence Division would then be in touch with reliable agents in such parts of the world as from time to time might be necessary.

The Committee of Enquiry chaired by Lord Hardwicke into the Mobilization and Intelligence Division after the Boer War rejected these arguments. It reported in March 1903 that I3(A) was a purely temporary Secret Section made necessary only by the war: 'There appear to be no sufficient grounds for permanently retaining this increase to the establishment of the Subdivision now that the pressure of the South African work has ceased'. The three officers in I3(A) were returned to their regiments.[88]

In November 1903, prompted by public, parliamentary and Royal Commission criticisms of the conduct of the Boer War, the government appointed a three-man committee chaired by the zealous army reformer Lord Esher to propose changes in the War Office. Its recommendations led both to a radical reform of the War Office and the long overdue introduction of a General Staff. Though the General Staff was not finally established until 1906, the reform of the War Office went ahead with unprecedented speed. On 11 February 1904 the DGMI, Lieutenant-General Sir William 'Nick' Nicholson, was in his office discussing the hectic pace of change with Colonel (later Field-Marshal Sir) Henry Wilson 'when in walked [Major-General] Jimmy Grierson and said Esher had ordered him up from Salisbury to take Nick's office'. Wilson considered this 'most scandalous work': 'Nick himself had not been informed, nor had he been told to hand over ...' The abrupt change of command was accompanied by a change of organisation. Grierson took the title Director of Military Operations and Intelligence (DMO & I, often abbreviated to DMO). Due partly to jealousy within the War Office at Ardagh's dealings with other government departments, Intelligence lost its status as a separate division, and was demoted to an advisory subcommittee of Military Operations. One of the few compensations for intelligence officers was that, like the rest of the War Office, they were now allowed female typists for the first time. 'They were', complained Edmonds, 'kept together on the top floor behind iron bars under a matron'.[89]

As Grierson's abrupt replacement of Nicholson suggested, he was a man of independent views – and among the first in the War Office to be convinced of the need to prepare for war with Germany. By the beginning of 1905 he was already organising war games to study the deployment of a British expeditionary force to meet a German attack on France through Belgium, and in March 1905, together with 'Wully' Robertson made a personal tour of inspection along the Franco-Belgian border. He also inaugurated informal staff talks with the French to discuss cooperation against Germany before he was authorised to do so at the end of 1905.[90] He was punished in October 1906 by being replaced as DMO with two years of his appointment still to run by Major-General (later Lieutenant-General Sir) John Ewart.

Secret service work had little place within the reorganised Directorate of Military Operations. When Major James Edmonds became head of the 'Special Section' (renamed MO5) late in 1907, he found that 'its activities had been allowed to die down'. His staff consisted only of another major, preoccupied by 'nursing' the Woolwich constituency of which he became Conservative M.P. in 1910, and a retired police detective.[91] Covert intelligence operations were still conducted on much the same amateur principles as in the heyday of the late Victorian ID. Intelligence officers at the War Office continued to make enthusiastic forays on the Continent, though to less effect than during their earlier adventures at the outposts of empire. In Lord Edward Gleichen's name-dropping narrative of his early years as Assistant Director of Military Operations and Intelligence (1907–11), espionage sometimes appears simply as a part of the author's hectic social round. In the autumn of 1907, for example, Gleichen went on 'another little spying journey' with his old friend Sir George Aston – this time to Holland:

> We wanted to see what sort of resistance the Dutch would be able to put up against the Germans if attacked by them ... We were not very favourably impressed. And then I went, via Copenhagen and the delightful old castle of Aaleholm, belonging to my excellent friends Count and Countess Raben, to Sweden, where to my delight, I was invited by the King to attend some manoeuvres ... After a pleasant two days at the end of the manoeuvres at the castle of Tjolöholm, near Goteborg, belonging to Count Bonde, the

Rodds very kindly put me up at the Legation. Thence we made a most interesting little excursion to the island of Gotland ... Thence back to England, to a staff ride in Wales and to some stalking in Scotland, followed by some good partridge and pheasant shooting in Suffolk and Essex.

Gleichen had many other opportunities to mix intelligence with pleasure. In the spring of 1908 he concluded that his 'knowledge of the Spanish Army was not what it should be' and decided on 'a little trip to Spain, putting in a week in Morocco with the Gerard Lowthers, who very kindly asked me to stay with them at the Legation in Tangier. Thence back to Seville, Granada and Madrid, where the King was good enough to ask me to luncheon.'[92]

The reorganisation of the War Office in the wake of the Boer War had done little either to interfere with Gleichen's social round or to produce a more professional intelligence system. But the Boer War also bequeathed to Edwardian England a sometimes morbid fear of foreign invasion which, when combined with the further fears created by the construction of a great new German battle fleet, were to lead only a year after Gleichen's 'little trip to Spain' to the founding of the Secret Service Bureau, the first step in the emergence of the modern secret intelligence community.

# 2 | SPIES AND SPY SCARES: THE BIRTH OF THE SECRET SERVICE BUREAU

Britain emerged from the Boer War with a new sense of imperial frailty. The great Empire on which the sun never set seemed even to Joseph Chamberlain, one of its greatest enthusiasts, 'a weary Titan staggering under the too vast orb of his own fate'. The public as a whole, still with little idea of the problems involved in winning wars against guerillas, failed to understand how their army could have required three years and 450,000 men to defeat rebellious foreign farmers. In 1900, with the entire regular army out of the country and not a friend in Europe, Britain was swept by an invasion scare. 'The Empire', declared the leading Liberal journalist, W.T. Stead, 'stripped of its armour, has its hands tied behind its back and its bare throat exposed to the keen knife of its bitterest enemies'.[1]

The power chiefly suspected of designs on the 'bare throat' of the Empire was Britain's oldest enemy France, possibly assisted by her Russian ally. In 1900 Colonel F.N. Maude published an imaginary account of a French invasion to awaken both government and public to the 'constantly recurrent probability of a surprise raid on London by the 120,000 men whom [the French] could without difficulty put on board ship, land in England, and march to within a dozen miles of London in less than three days from receipt of the order to move'. Colonel Maude's melodramatic fictional revelations were swiftly followed by others: among them *The Sack of London in the Great French War of 1901*, *The Coming Waterloo*, *A New Trafalgar*, *Starved Into Surrender* and *Seaward for the Foe*.[2]

The most prolific and successful author of Edwardian invasion scares was William Le Queux, allegedly Queen Alexandra's favourite novelist, an author who is to English prose what William McGonagal is to Scottish verse. Le Queux's fictional invasions, like those of some of his rivals, were prepared by espionage. The chief villain of his book, *England's Peril: A Story of the Secret Service*, was the French spymaster Gaston La Touche, scheming England's downfall. La Touche had some better points. He was, for example, 'the first white man to enter Timbuctoo ..., one of the most easy-going, devil-may-care fellows, who seemed to exist at random anywhere and everywhere':

> Today he would be heard of in savage Africa, a week later he would be seen sipping his *mazagran* before the Grand Café in Paris, and a few days afterwards one would read that he had sailed from Havre, Brest or Marseilles to some other quarter of the globe.

As well as 'possessing an iron nerve and muscles which rendered him practically invulnerable in a tussle', La Touche was full of 'droll stories which convulsed his companions with laughter'. Yet as the chief of the French Secret Service, he also had 'no equal in unscrupulousness'. The woman whom he blackmailed to obtain the secrets of Britain's defences from her distinguished uncle's safe, upbraided him for his un-British behaviour:

> "You, Gaston La Touche, have no pity for a woman! You know well enough that by your fiendish cunning and your master-stroke of ingenuity you have succeeded in holding me fettered as your slave, so that you can now use me as your catspaw to attain your own despicable ends!"[3]

La Touche and his fictional French kind were always foiled in the end. Le Queux had a reassuring message for the readers of *England's Peril*:

> The British Secret Service, although never so prominently before the public as those unscrupulous *agents provocateurs* of France and Russia, is nevertheless equally active. It works in silence and secrecy, yet many are its successful counterplots against the machinations of England's enemies.[4]

At the opposite extreme of literary distinction, Rudyard Kipling gave an equally optimistic assessment of the intelligence duel on India's North-West frontier. In *Kim* (surely the finest of all spy novels, though it transcends the world of espionage), unseen but ubiquitous agents of the Raj play 'the Great Game that never ceases day and night throughout India'. And they do so with a subtlety quite beyond Tsarist Russia, 'the dread Power of the North', and its French ally, whose emissaries are 'smitten helpless'.[5] No other invasion novel or spy thriller during the Boer War came close to *Kim* in literary merit. Most had more in common with the novels of William Le Queux.

Despite the fictional absurdities which it produced, both government and service chiefs took the risk of invasion during the Boer War very seriously. In 1900 the Naval Intelligence Department translated an invasion novel by a French naval officer, *La Guerre avec l'Angleterre*, and circulated it 'For the Use of Her Majesty's Officers Only'. Even the prime minister, Lord Salisbury, departed from his usual phlegmatic calm to warn of the 'great wave' of enemies who threatened 'to dash upon our shores'.[6] Many Frenchmen found the idea of dashing upon British shores rather attractive. During 1900 both the French general staff and foreign ministry considered extravagant schemes for an invasion of England, an expedition to turn the British out of Egypt and an attack on Burma timed to coincide with a Russian march on India.[7]

Such French fantasies did not last long. By 1904 Britain and France had settled their differences. With the making and strengthening of the Entente Cordiale, France changed from a potential enemy to a probable wartime ally. Invasion scares, however, continued under new management. France's role as chief invader was now assumed by Germany. Admiral von Tirpitz, state secretary for the German Navy, believed that war with Britain was in the long run unavoidable. Even in peacetime Germany required a powerful navy as 'a political power factor' in her rivalry with Britain. The Kaiser privately declared: 'Only when we can hold out our mailed fist against his face will the British lion draw back ...'. That mailed fist was to be a great new battle fleet, the *Hochseeflotte*. The dramatic revelation of British vulnerability during the Boer War thus coincided with the beginning of a German challenge to Britain's naval supremacy, the traditional cornerstone of national security. The Earl of Selborne, first lord of the Admiralty, told his cabinet colleagues in 1902: 'I am convinced that the great new German navy is being carefully built up from the point of view of a war with us ...'.[8]

Though the real war with Germany was to be delayed until August 1914, it was preceded by over a decade of fictional conflict. The literary war began in earnest in 1903 with Erskine Childers's best-selling novel, *The Riddle of the Sands*. While yachting off the Frisian Coast, the heroes of the novel, Carruthers of the Foreign Office and his companion Davies, gradually uncover a German invasion plan. Finally the truth dawns on Carruthers as he watches the German fleet:

> Yes, I understood at last. I was assisting at an experimental rehearsal of a great scene, to be enacted, perhaps, in the near future – a scene when multitudes of sea-going lighters, carrying full loads of soldiers, not half-loads of coal, should issue simultaneously, in seven ordered fleets, from seven shallow outlets, and, under escort from the Imperial Navy, traverse the North Sea and throw themselves bodily upon English shores.

The sites for the German landing and the disposition of the English fleet had already been reconnoitred by German spies. Though 'all countries, Germany included, have spies in their service, dirty though necessary tools', Herr Dollmann, the German spymaster, 'was no ordinary spy': Carruthers could 'never efface the impression of malignant perfidy and base passion exaggerated to caricature' in his hunnish features. To give the semblance of reality to his fictional narrative Childers purported to be merely 'editing' a text prepared by Carruthers and Davies themselves: a device later borrowed by John Buchan and other adventure novelists to blur the frontier between fact and fiction. Childers's declared aim was to rouse public opinion to demand action from the slumbering statesmen who had failed to react to the German menace. He added in a postscript: 'Is it not becoming patent that the time has come for training all Englishmen systematically either for the sea or for the rifle?'[9]

Lord Selborne was sufficiently impressed by *The Riddle of the Sands* to call for a detailed report on whether its invasion plan was feasible. NID eventually convinced him it was not.[10] After sending 'a couple of experts' to reconnoitre the Frisian coast, MID reached the same conclusion.[11] Childers disagreed. Conversations with sympathetic statesmen and naval officers gave him 'most remarkable confirmation' of his ideas. He told his close friend, Basil Williams: 'Source confidential of course and details too – but I think there is no doubt that my method of invasion – in general principle – had been worked out by the Germans'.[12]

In 1896, unknown to either NID or MID, the German Admiralty had, as Childers claimed, drawn up elaborate plans to land an army on the east coast of England. But the plans were never practicable and by the time *The Riddle of the Sands* appeared had been finally abandoned.[13] The fact that the Germans no longer *had* an invasion plan, however, did nothing to prevent recurrent invasion scares in Edwardian England. An increasingly prominent element in the mythical German invasion plans which exercised both press and public was the subversive work of German spies. The most successful campaigner against both imaginary invaders and imaginary spies was William Le Queux. Even before he began his anti-German crusade Le Queux had already embarked on a Walter Mitty career as Britain's master spy. In *Secrets of the Foreign Office* published in 1903 he had thinly disguised his own identity as Duckworth Drew, 'secret agent in the employ of the Foreign Office, and, next to his Majesty's Secretary of State for Foreign Affairs, one of the most powerful and important pillars of England's supremacy'. Taken all in all, Drew was 'one of the most remarkable of men, possessing shrewdness, tact, cunning and daring that are utterly amazing'. Le Queux's name (pronounced Kew) rhymed with Drew's. Like Drew he had an English mother and a French father. (On visits to France Drew used his real name Dreux.) Drew also conformed exactly to Le Queux's own self-image: 'dark, of medium height, about 40, unobtrusive, of perfect manner and a born gentleman'. Drew, in short, was all that Le Queux wished to be and finally persuaded himself that he was: sought after by the highest in several lands, irresistible to beautiful, well-bred women (also in several lands), at once a noted *bon viveur* and a brilliantly ingenious secret agent. Scarcely had Drew crossed the Channel than the French foreign minister Delanne (a transparent pseudonym for the real minister, Delcassé) 'admitted that he longed to smoke one of my excellent light-coloured Corona Superbos'. But there was more to Drew's cigars than met Delanne's inattentive eye: 'To this day Monsieur le Ministre is in ignorance that that particular Corona had been carefully prepared by me with a solution of *cocculus indicus* ...'. Outwitted by the cunningly prepared Corona, Delanne conveniently revealed the secret Drew had come to collect.[14]

In 1903 the Kaiser and Imperial Germany still seemed greatly preferable to the vulgar, cigar-cadging Delanne and 'the hot-headed government of the [French] Republic with its parliamentary beargarden opposite the Pont de la Concorde'.[15] After the signing of the Anglo-French Entente Cordiale in 1904, however, Le Queux changed his mind. The turning point came, by his own account, in 1905 when he discovered 'a great network of German espionage spread over the United Kingdom':

> I found out the secret through a friend in Berlin, who was at the time under-director of the Kaiser's Spy Bureau, and who had married an Englishwoman who was believed by all, except her husband, to be German. As is usual in Germany, his master did not exactly "play the game" with him, and, therefore in 1905, he told me frankly what was in progress.[16]

Le Queux's story was of course invention. Though there were occasional (usually part-time) German agents hoping to pick up naval intelligence from British dockyards, there was no 'great network' preparing the path for an invading army nor any plan for a German invasion. It is by no means certain, however, that Le Queux's story was entirely his own invention – though he undoubtedly embroidered it. During the spy scares which preceded the First World War even the War Office was on occasion taken in by both frauds and practical jokes.[17] It is possible that in 1905 Le Queux's fraudulence was equalled, or even exceeded, by his gullibility.

Le Queux's dramatic 'discovery' of a vast network of imaginary German spies coincided with, and is doubtless to be explained by, the sudden worsening of Anglo-German relations. By bringing pressure to bear on France in Morocco during 1905 Germany calculated that she could disrupt the Entente Cordiale. In fact she merely strengthened it. The First Moroccan crisis of 1905–6 led directly to Anglo-French staff talks on co-operation in a war with Germany. But Le Queux complained that the British Government and people seemed blind to the spy peril in their midst: 'My voice was, alas! that of one crying in the wilderness'.[18] The failure of the authorities to respond to his patriotic warnings led Le Queux to downgrade drastically his earlier optimistic view of the British Secret Service. Now convinced that the War Office and Admiralty had no more than 'a kind of scratch intelligence service',[19] Le Queux approached the ageing military hero Field-Marshal Earl Roberts of Kandahar:

> "My dear Le Queux," said the white moustached old soldier, holding out his hand in a fatherly manner, "the world thinks me a lunatic also, because,

after my forty years service in India, I have come home and dared to tell England that she is unprepared for war".[20]

Roberts had come to the conclusion that only conscription could make Britain secure against invasion. Having tried and failed to convert the Committee of Imperial Defence (CID) to his views, he resigned from it in November 1905 to become president of the National Service League and campaign for one year's military service by 'every able-bodied white man in the Empire'. Under Roberts's leadership the League grew from 2,000 strong in 1905 to claim 100,000 full members and 120,000 associates by the outbreak of war.[21]

Among Roberts's most influential supporters was Britain's first mass-circulation newspaper, the *Daily Mail*. Alfred Harmsworth, the *Mail*'s proprietor (soon to become Lord Northcliffe and owner of *The Times* as well), was convinced that the average Briton 'liked a good hate'. His editor, Kennedy Jones, operated on the inflexible principle of 'writing for the meanest intelligence'.[22] The German menace fitted admirably the needs of both 'the meanest intelligence' and those requiring 'a good hate'. Germany, indeed, had become one of Harmsworth's own pet 'hates' and was to figure prominently in his final paranoia. Both his last two wills, written shortly before his death in 1922, complain that he had been 'poisoned by the Germans by ice cream': an affliction 'unknown to any doctors in Great Britain'. (He added that he was also suffering from 'Indian jungle fever'.) Harmsworth's interest in invasion scares predated even his suspicion of Germany. In 1893, three years before founding the *Daily Mail*, he had commissioned a magazine serial called 'The Poisoned Bullet', telling how Britain was treacherously attacked 'one evening in 1897' by the combined forces of France and Russia. 'Everywhere the carnage was terrific' – and it continued remorselessly in weekly instalments. The purpose of this fictional bloodshed, in Harmsworth's view, went beyond mere entertainment. 'The Poisoned Bullet', based 'upon the prognostications of the best living authorities on modern warfare', was intended 'to promote public interest in the idea of a larger fleet'. The author of this early work of 'faction' was William Le Queux. Among those who wrote to commend his message was Lord Roberts.[23]

It was thus natural that in 1905 Harmsworth should publicise the equally implausible German invasion plan presented to him by Le Queux and Roberts. He quickly commissioned from Le Queux another invasion serial, 'The Invasion of 1910', this time for publication in the *Daily Mail*. Le Queux spent several months touring south-east England to work out the most likely invasion route, assisted by advice from Roberts and the *Mail*'s naval specialist, H.W. Wilson. Harmsworth found much to criticise in the original route selected for the German army. It included too many villages where the market for the *Daily Mail* was small. So in the interests of circulation the German invasion route was changed to allow the Hun to terrorize every major town in England from Sheffield to Chelmsford. Special maps were published in the national and provincial press to show which district the Germans would be invading next morning in the *Daily Mail*.[24]

Lord Roberts commended 'The Invasion of 1910' 'to the perusal of everyone who has the welfare of the British Empire at heart'. Le Queux, in return, endorsed Lord Roberts' call for conscription: 'Had we adopted his scheme for universal service such dire catastrophes could never have occurred'. But while his main message was the need for measures to resist invasion, Le Queux also laid bare the spy menace. 'Daring German spies' assisted his invasion by destroying railways and telegraph wires:

> Among the thousands of Germans working in London, the hundred or so spies, all trusted soldiers, had passed unnoticed, but, working in unison, each little group of two or three had been allotted its task and had previously thoroughly reconnoitred the position and studied the most rapid or effective means.[25]

Le Queux later complained of the 'many imitators, who obtained much kudos and made much money' out of the kind of story he had 'inaugurated'.[26] Not all, however, were imitators. His most successful rival, E. Phillips Oppenheim, embarked quite independently on his own 'crusade against German militarism' and made enough from it to give up the family leather business and begin a full-time career as one of England's most prolific popular novelists, producing 116 deservedly forgotten novels as well as innumerable and equally forgettable short stories. Like Le Queux, 'Oppy' considered himself 'a humble follower of Lord Roberts on various platforms and in the Press'.[27] But he was less obsessed than Le Queux with the role of patriotic Cassandra and more concerned with financing a life of ostentatious luxury surrounded by obsequious menials and pliant mistresses (the latter entertained, by preference, on a large floating bed). An eyewitness later recalled 'Oppy''s royal progress from the lift into the lobby of the Splendide Hotel:

> He walks a few paces down towards the flower shop, standing with lowered arms stiffly outstretched backwards, chin up and chest thrust forward, without speaking a word. The girl in charge of the flower shop knows what to do. With a swiftness that is almost terrible to see she whips from the vase a dark red carnation, deftly twisting a little greenery with the stem, and slips it into his buttonhole. Without a word the great man walks crab fashion towards the door, which is flung open for him with a haste that is almost indecent. At the kerb in Piccadilly stands a hired Daimler car, like some vast and imposing royal barge, its deep suspension ironing out the creases of the road. The door slams richly, the chauffeur leaps into the driving seat.[28]

Oppy's discovery of the German menace, which laid the financial foundations for this preposterous lifestyle, dated, like Le Queux's, from 1905. In *A Maker of History*, published in that year, Oppy revealed the Kaiser's intention to rule the German Empire from London and suggested that the British public might be 'unpleasantly surprised' by the Germans 'throwing a million men at different points' of the coastline. *The Secret*, published two years later, described the huge spy network silently preparing for 'Der Tag' – the day of the German invasion. Captain X, the German spymaster in London, told a new recruit:

> My young friend, there are in this country today 290,000 young countrymen of yours and mine who have served their time, and who can shoot ... Clerks, waiters and hairdressers, each have their society, each have their work assigned to them. The forts which guard this great city may be impregnable from without, but from within – well, that is another matter. Listen! The exact spot where we shall attack is arranged, and plans of every fort which guard[s] the Thames are in our hands.

'This', the hero bitterly observes, 'is what comes of making London the asylum for all the foreign scum of the earth'. Indeed the German spies in London grow alarmingly as the book proceeds. Captain X's '290,000 young countrymen' become, only sixty pages later, 'half a million and more of scum eating their way into the entrails of this great city of ours'. Britain, Oppy complained, lacked a properly organised intelligence network capable of dealing with the alien menace. Lord Pollock, the fictional prime minister, is 'one of the old school of statesmen [and] hates Secret Service work'.[29]

The young P.G. Wodehouse published his own satirical account of the German invasion scare under the title *The Swoop! Or How Clarence Saved England*. In Wodehouse's version the first warning of the invasion is noticed by an alert boy scout, Clarence Chugwater, buried in the small print of the stop press news:

> Fry not out, 104. Surrey 147 for 8. A German army landed in Essex this afternoon. Loamshire Handicap: Spring Chicken, 1; Salome, 2; Yip-i-addy, 3. Seven ran.

At first only Clarence sees the danger. Even his parents fail to grasp the sinister intentions of the German soldiers calling at their home. Sensing their opportunity, 'eight other hostile armies' follow the Germans' example. As a bemused and inert populace looks on, the Mad Mullah captures Portsmouth, the Swiss Navy bombard the bathing machines at Lyme Regis, a boisterous band of Young Turks seizes Scarborough and the Chinese – having 'at last awakened' – swoop down upon 'that picturesque little Welsh watering-place,

Lllgxtplll'. But Clarence is equal to the danger. 'England looks to us', he tells the scouts, 'and it is for us to see that she does not look in vain'. The invading armies first fall out among themselves and are then swept aside by the scouts. Thanks to Clarence, 'our beloved England no longer writhes beneath the ruthless heel of the alien oppressor'.

The British public was not amused. Wodehouse's book was a flop.[30] Le Queux and Oppenheim, by contrast, were amazingly successful. In book form *The Invasion of 1910* appeared in twenty-seven languages and sold over a million copies – though, to the fury of its author, the German translation ended with a German victory. In London clubs and dinner parties, Le Queux was, by his own account, 'hailed as the man-who-dared-to-tell-the-truth'. Success on so heady a scale launched him further into a fantasy career as secret agent and spy-catcher extraordinary. He became a member of a 'new voluntary Secret Service Department': 'Half-a-dozen patriotic men in secret banded themselves together. Each, paying his own expenses, set to work gathering information in Germany and elsewhere that might be useful to our country in case of need'.[31]

The new 'voluntary Secret Service Department', in so far as it existed outside Le Queux's imagination, had its main home in the Legion of Frontiersmen founded by Roger Pocock at the end of 1904. Pocock inhabited a Walter Mitty world as extravagant as Le Queux's full of *Boy's Own Paper* villains and heroes. He was, he claimed, 'a vagrant adventurer' who had been 'labourer, painter, missionary, mounted policeman, seaman, cowboy, arctic explorer, miner, pedlar, and the like on the fringes of civilisation or beyond them, mostly in the American continent'.[32] Pocock intended his Legion as an 'army of observation, a unit for field intelligence in peace and war, its duties being those of scouting – "to see, run and tell" – in case of any menace to the British Peace'. Pocock appears to have secured the blessing for the Legion of Lord Roberts, Prince Louis of Battenberg (then DNI), Baden-Powell and other celebrities who were unaware of the extent of Pocock's personal eccentricities. He considered the Legion Intelligence Branch, to which Le Queux belonged, 'a little group of irresponsible young ruffians, but for all their blithe contempt of danger ... in deadly earnest'. 'To the credulity of German spies', wrote Pocock later with unconscious irony, 'there was no known limit'. It is doubtful, however, whether any German spy ever equalled Pocock's own credulity. His tales of German women spies ('really wonderful people') are preposterous even by his own impressive standards. One intrepid Legionary, Pocock relates, was invited to dinner by a female spy posing as a lion-tamer with a back-yard menagerie of man-eating pets. After dinner the spy showed her guest around her bizarre back-yard, finally locking him into a cage of leopards, saying as she did so, 'Now you will be my slave'. Happily, the Legionary, anticipating just such a misadventure, had concealed about his person during supper a large pepper pot which he now began to shake about with startling effectiveness. 'The leopards sneezed, the lions, tigers, everybody sneezed', the menagerie was reduced to chaos and the Legionary made a triumphant escape.[33] His epic adventure still appears in the 'History of the Legion of Frontiersmen' circulated by its Canadian branch.[34] By a superb irony, Pocock's eccentric behaviour eventually persuaded both the War Office and some leading Legionaries that he was a German spy himself. In 1909 he was ousted from the Legion he had founded.[35]

Spy mania was not, of course, universal. Most Edwardian radicals and a part of the establishment never took it seriously. Even when taken over by Northcliffe, *The Times* continued to view the scares its new proprietor was promoting in the *Daily Mail* with lofty disdain as not 'worthy of the serious notice of a great nation'[36]. But in the press as a whole more column inches were devoted to documenting, than to doubting, the spy menace. Even the radical *Nation* acknowledged that invasion and spy scares had created by 1909 a public mood bordering on mass hysteria: 'There is in the blood of us all a primitive instinct of alarm which takes fire at the very mention of a spy'.[37] Le Queux was merely the most financially successful of a group of farcical Cassandras who struggled to awake a sleeping nation to a non-existent peril. Leo Maxse, editor and proprietor of the influential *National Review*, had by his own admission 'Germany on the brain'. He warned his readers that 'our eastern counties were studded with spies ... disguised as waiters and hairdressers'.[38] Not to be outdone, the rival *Quarterly Review* declared in July 1908 that the 50,000 German waiters in Britain and the large number of German publicans gave Germany 'such an intelligence system as no other country has ever maintained upon the territory of another'.[39] What *The Nation* called 'a brisk competition in scare-mongering' quickly multiplied the number of German spies. Sir John Barlow M.P. demanded to know whether the secretary of state for war was aware of the 66,000 trained German soldiers in England with 50,000 stands of Mauser rifles and several million rounds of ammunition stored in cellars not a quarter of a mile from Charing Cross. Lord Roberts had even worse news for the House of Lords:

> It is calculated, my Lords, that there are 80,000 Germans in the United Kingdom, almost all of them trained soldiers. They work in many of the hotels at some of the chief railway stations, and if a German force once got into this country it would have the advantage of help and reinforcement such as no other army on foreign soil has ever before enjoyed.

To Captain D.P. Driscoll, DSO, of 'Driscoll's Scouts' even these figures fell far short of the truth: 'Living in our midst, under the protection of the British flag', were, he calculated, 350,000 German soldiers − more than half the peacetime strength of the German army.[40]

Le Queux, however, was too clever for the imaginary German spies. His first major coup as a 'voluntary secret agent' came in July 1908 when he received 'a guarded note' from a German friend, 'Herr N—', asking 'whether I could meet him in Switzerland'. With a perspicacity worthy of Inspector Clouseau, Le Queux 'read between the lines that he wished to see me'. At the Dolder Hotel in Zurich, Herr N handed over the verbatim text of an address by the Kaiser to a secret council of war a month before. Wilhelm's manner had been 'somewhat nervous and unstrung', but what he said was grim news for Britain:

> To find an outlet for the discontent of the nation; to nip the growing republican sentiment in the bud; to fill our treasury; to reduce the burden of taxation; to gain new colonies and markets for our industries across the seas; to accomplish all this and still more, we simply have to invade England ... We shall strike as soon as I have a sufficiently large fleet of Zeppelins at my disposal. ... Do you remember, my Generals, what our never-to-be-forgotten Field Marshal Gebhard Lebrecht von Blücher exclaimed, when looking from the dome of St. Paul's Cathedral upon the vast metropolis at his feet? It was short, and to the point: 'What a splendid city to sack!'
>
> You will desire to know how the outbreak of hostilities will be brought about. I can assure you on this point ... My army of spies scattered over Great Britain and France, as it is over North and South America, as well as all the other parts of the world where German interests may come to clash with a foreign power, will take good care of that.[41]

Not surprisingly, the speech 'created a great sensation' among those shown it in London who included, according to Le Queux, Lord Roberts, Lord Northcliffe, Prince Louis of Battenberg, Rear-Admiral H.W. Wilkin and Admiral Lord Charles Beresford. Others, to Le Queux's disgust, 'pooh poohed it'. Soon afterwards, the speech was 'stolen' from his publisher's office. Le Queux wrote later: 'German secret agents undoubtedly committed the theft ... for I have since learnt that my manuscript is now in the archives of the Secret Service in Berlin!' Le Queux had, however, kept a copy of the speech, though he did not publish it until after the outbreak of war.[42] When he did so his book included in its foreword enthusiastic endorsements from five peers, two M.P.s, the Lord Mayor of London, Sir Arthur Conan Doyle, five national and four provincial newspapers. The *Evening Standard* found Le ꞌ Queux's revelations 'as sensational as any of his romances':

> Indeed it may be questioned whether Mr Le Queux would have gone the length of introducing into a fictional plot so extraordinary a chapter as that in which he reports one of the Kaiser's speeches.[43]

Like Le Queux himself, the Kaiser's speech was, of course, a preposterous

fraud. Yet more remarkable even than Le Queux's fraudulence was his ability
to take in so many otherwise sane and intelligent men. Sir Robert Gower,
M.P., who wrote the foreword to Le Queux's official biography, called him

> ... a *man*, a man in thought and deed, whose interest was directed solely to the
> welfare of his country, who imperturbably risked his life in countless exploits
> for that country's benefit – exploits far exceeding in their daring the most
> colourful adventures of his bravest fictional heroes – it is to his credit that in all
> his Secret Service operations he paid all his expenses out of his own pocket.[44]

At least part of Le Queux's secret lay in his immense clubability. He moved
effortlessly around clubland and society dinners, establishing a reputation as
wit and raconteur. 'In fact', claims his official biographer, 'he was outstandingly
the life and soul of a party': 'His personality seemed to be magnetic'.[45] Most
of those who listened spellbound to Le Queux's stories failed to realise that
they were tall stories. As he travelled around Europe, dropping names as he
went, hinting at confidential missions on which he was engaged, striking up
acquaintances in the underworld of part-time agents, Le Queux gradually
built up a reputation 'to his obvious delight' as a 'man of mystery'.[46] He
persuaded Gustav Steinhauer, the German spymaster, that he 'had more than
a nodding acquaintance with most of the spies of Europe'.[47] But his most
important conquest was Lieutenant-Colonel James Edmonds, who became
responsible for counter-intelligence and 'secret service' at the War Office in
1907. Edmonds had a growing reputation as one of the army's intellectuals,
and was later to become the official historian of the First World War. But he
was also a friend of Le Queux and was utterly deceived by him.[48]

Le Queux was not the only fraud to make a living from the German
menace. Like the Red Scares which followed the Bolshevik Revolution, the
pre-war German invasion and spy scares produced a ready market for bogus
as well as genuine intelligence. One of the main centres of both was Brussels
where freelance agents advertised openly in the press. Owing largely to the
loopholes in Belgian law, Brussels became, in Baden-Powell's words, 'a sort
of international spy exchange'.[49] One of the most active Brussels intelligence
entrepreneurs, R.H. Peterssen (alias Müller, Pieters, Schmidt and Talbot),
who seems to have worked chiefly for the Germans, advertised openly in the
press for secret intelligence.[50] Baden-Powell himself became a regular customer of a Brussels 'spy bureau' run by German Americans, and was well
satisfied with the service he received:

> If the plans of a new fort, or the dimensions of a new ship, or the power
> of a new gun were needed, one merely had to apply and state a price to
> this bureau to receive fairly good information on the subject before much
> time had elapsed.

Most of the intelligence on sale in Brussels was probably low-grade, obtained from technical journals and public sources. But some was forged and Baden-Powell, among others, was hopelessly deceived by it. In 1908 Baden-Powell received from the spy bureau the most amazing document yet: the outline plan for a German invasion of Britain prepared by 'a small army of [German] spies' already in the British Isles. The invasion was to be launched on August Bank Holiday, thus catching the British people entirely off their guard:

> The spies stationed in England were to cut all telephone and telegraph wires, and, where possible, to blow down important bridges and tunnels, and thus to interrupt communications and create confusion.

With the straits of Dover blocked by mines and submarines, 90,000 German troops would land in Yorkshire to 'destroy towns, mines and factories'. England would be cut in half and 'some 14 millions of people [thrown] suddenly into a state of homelessness, starvation and panic'. Even Baden-Powell felt that: 'At first glance, it seem[ed] too fanciful a plan to commend itself to belief'. However, on thinking it over, he concluded that the invasion scheme was absolutely genuine, and prepared a magic lantern lecture on it which he gave to several groups of territorials and other army officers:

> [When] the report of this leaked into the papers I realized how nearly I had "touched the spot". For, apart from the various indignant questions with which the Secretary of State for War was badgered in the House of Commons on my account, I was assailed with letters from Germans of most violent abuse from various quarters, high and low, which showed me that I had gone even nearer the truth than I had suspected.[51]

Baden-Powell was by no means alone in being fooled by bogus Brussels intelligence. Even on the eve of war the first head of the future SIS paid £600 for a forged German codebook.[52]

Le Queux's most widely publicised exploits as spy-catcher extraordinary were his successes in unmasking German spies in Britain itself. His investigations prompted questions in the Commons by Colonel Mark Lockwood, M.P., in July 1908, complaining that German spies had actually organised 'a staff ride through England' to prepare for an invasion.[53] After publishing some examples of his counter-espionage work in the press Le Queux produced a comprehensive record of his investigations in 1909 under the title *Spies of the Kaiser. Plotting the Downfall of England.* For 'obvious' (though unspecified) reasons Le Queux 'refrained from giving actual names and dates' and decided instead 'to present the facts in the form of fiction – fiction which, I trust, will point its own patriotic moral':

I have no desire to create undue alarm. I am an Englishman, and, I hope, a patriot. What I have written in this present volume in the form of fiction is based upon serious facts within my own personal knowledge.... During the last twelve months, aided by a well-known detective officer, I have made personal inquiry into the presence and work of these spies, an inquiry which has entailed a great amount of travelling, much watchfulness, and often considerable discomfort. ...

The menace was extreme. Over 5,000 German spies were at work in England: 'Every six months an "inspection" is held, and monetary rewards made to those whose success has been most exemplary'. What most outraged Le Queux was the spineless attitude of the authorities towards the spy menace:

As I write, I have before me a file of amazing documents, which plainly show the feverish activity with which this advance guard of our enemy is working to secure for their employers the most detailed information. These documents have already been placed before the Minister for War, who returned them without comment!

What was needed was a professional counter-espionage service and changes in the law: 'Under our existing law it seems that a foreign spy is free to go hither and thither, and plot the downfall of England'.[54]

The flavour of Le Queux's investigations is well conveyed by his own account of how he and his companion, Ray Raymond ('a typical athletic young Englishman – clean-shaven and clean-limbed') discover a spy's lair in Beccles. On entering the lair, Le Queux knocked over some glass negatives which fell to the floor 'with a loud crash':

We both stood breathless. There was a quick movement in the room adjoining, and we heard men's voices shouting to each other in German.

"Stay here", Ray said firmly. "We must not show the white feather now".

Almost as the words left his mouth we were confronted by the two men whom we had seen surveying the railway line.

"Well!" cried Ray, gripping his precious bag and facing them boldly, "you see we've discovered your little game, gentlemen! Those notes on the map are particularly interesting".

"By what right, pray, do you enter here?" asked the bearded man, speaking in fairly good English.

"By the right of an Englishman, Herr Stolberg", was Ray's bold reply. "You'll find your clever wife tied up to a tree in the field opposite".

The younger man held a revolver, but from his face I saw that he was a coward.

"What do you mean?" demanded the other.

"I mean that I intend destroying all this excellent espionage work of yours. You've lived here for two years, and have been very busy travelling in your car and gathering information. But", [Ray] said, "you were a little unwise in putting upon your car the new Feldmarck non-skids, the only set, I believe, yet in England. They may be very good tyres, but scarcely adapted for spying purposes."[55]

That such fantasies found an audience far beyond what Winston Churchill called 'the inmates of Bedlam and writers in the *National Review*'[56] was possible only because of the fears produced by the German fleet. Until 1906 the massive size of the Royal Navy had made impossible any short-term threat to British naval supremacy. But with the launching of the new British battleship *Dreadnought* in that year, Anglo-German naval rivalry took a new and dangerous turn. By its size and firepower the *Dreadnought* made all other battleships obsolete. With ten twelve-inch guns, each with a range of over eight miles, it was more than a match for any two of its predecessors. Overnight, the Royal Navy, like every other navy in the world, became out of date. Germany, it seemed, might soon catch up.

Not all British statesmen and service chiefs considered these apprehensions undesirable. Lord Esher, one of the leading defence experts of his time, wrote in October 1907:

A nation that believes itself secure, all history teaches is doomed. Anxiety, not a sense of security, lies at the root of readiness for war. An invasion scare is the will of God which grinds you a Navy of Dreadnoughts and keeps the British people war-like in spirit.[57]

The announcement of an accelerated German naval building programme a month later led to prolonged controversy within the Liberal cabinet, with alternate threats of resignation from both doves and hawks (or 'economists' and 'navalists' as they were termed at the time). By the autumn of 1907 a press campaign led by Leo Maxse, Colonel Repington (military correspondent of *The Times*) and H.W. Wilson (former collaborator of Le Queux and naval 'expert' of the *Daily Mail*), with support from Lord Roberts and some of the Tory leadership, had persuaded the government to appoint a subcommittee of the Committee of Imperial Defence to consider the invasion threat. The membership of the subcommittee bears witness to the importance of its task. The chair was taken by Asquith, then chancellor of the exchequer but soon to become prime minister. With him sat four senior ministers (the lord president, the foreign secretary, the secretary for war, and the first lord of the Admiralty) and an impressive array of service chiefs. They met sixteen times between November 1907 and July 1908, completing their report on 22

October 1908. The result of their deliberations was to demolish most of the arguments of the invasion theorists and show surprise attack to be impossible.[58]

The subcommittee's conclusions predictably failed to carry conviction with most of those whose arguments it had demolished. During summer naval exercises a small force of invaders managed to elude the fleet and scramble ashore in the north of Scotland. With the Admiralty maintaining an embarrassed silence, the alleged numbers of the invaders multiplied alarmingly. Speaking in the Commons in December, Reginald McKenna, the first lord of the Admiralty, was forced to deny a report that 70,000 invaders had landed at Wick. His critics remained sceptical. The *Daily Mail* reported that, despite the use of two charabancs and a steam engine, the Territorials had taken three hours during an invasion exercise to reach the threatened coastline.[59] Though Tory diehards were particularly prone to have 'Germany on the brain', they were not alone in their imaginings. The socialist writer, Robert Blatchford, lay awake at night repeating to himself: 'My God! This horror is marching steadily upon us and our people will not believe it'. According to the writer Wilfrid Meynell, even King Edward VII – influenced perhaps by the Queen's library of Le Queux novels – spoke in August 1908 of the Kaiser's plan to:

> Throw a *corps d'armée* or two into England, making proclamation that he has come, not as an enemy to the King, but as the grandson of Queen Victoria, to deliver him from the Socialistic gang which is ruining the country.[60]

Fear of the invading Hun was further fuelled in the autumn of 1908 by reports that Germany was secretly stepping up her dreadnought building. Though quite inaccurate, the reports were confirmed by the naval attaché in Berlin and the consul in Danzig.[61] The cabinet dispute which ensued began with acrimony and ended in farce. 'In the end', wrote Winston Churchill, 'a curious and characteristic solution was reached. The Admiralty had demanded 6 ships: the economists offered 4: and we finally compromised on 8'. This remarkable decision was the result of outside pressure. The Tory opposition, Tory press, the Navy League and other patriotic pressure groups worked themselves into a frenzy as they denounced government hesitation in the face of the German naval menace. 'We are not yet prepared to turn the face of every portrait of Nelson to the wall', declared the *Daily Telegraph*, 'and to make in time of peace the most shameful surrender recorded in the whole pages of history'. Assailed by the slogan 'We want eight, and we won't wait', the Liberal cabinet surrendered to it.[62]

The assorted naval, invasion and spy scares of late Edwardian England threw into sharp relief the deficiencies of Britain's intelligence system. When Major Edmonds became head of MO5, which ran the 'Special Section' of the War Office, late in 1907, he discovered that 'its records contained only papers referring to the South African War and some scraps about France and Russia – nothing whatever about Germany'.[63] Major-General Ewart, the DMO, acknowledged during meetings of the invasion subcommittee in 1908 that 'the existing machinery for obtaining information from Germany and the Continent generally during peace or war' was highly unsatisfactory. In assessing likely German invasion plans, the general staff was forced to work on 'hypothetical assumptions': 'Facts we have not got – thanks to the total absence of secret agents'. As things stood, Germany might well be able to mobilise in secret:

> If however we had a reliable organisation of secret agents the probabilities are that we should hear of the movement within a few hours. In any case we should in all human probability hear of it within 24 to 30 hours.[64]

NID agreed. When Rear-Admiral (later Sir) Esmond Slade became DNI in October 1907, he was dismayed to discover that naval 'Secret Service' also 'was not organised in any way'.[65] 'The only consolation', the War Office concluded, after reviewing the state of British espionage, 'is that every foreign government implicitly believes that we already have a thoroughly organised and efficient European Secret Service'.[66]

With Ewart's blessing, Edmonds set out to organise an espionage network in Germany at the end of 1907. Though Edmonds spoke fluent German and was well acquainted with the German army, he knew much less about secret agents. His first attempts at recruitment were both fumbling and farcical. Incredibly, he sought to discover potential agents on the German coast and in 'other important areas' by asking friends visiting Germany to enquire at local police stations for the names of British residents on 'the excuse that they must have an English witness to a signature on a document'.[67] Edmonds's first agent, however, was supplied not by enquiries at German police stations but by the managing director of Courage and Company, the London brewers. Early in 1908 Courage put pressure on their Hamburg representative, Mr Rué, to collect 'various information as to naval and military matters in connection with harbour works, number of ships, railway arrangements, movement of troops, etc.' for MO5. Rué was assured this 'would not interfere' with his brewery work, and was paid an additional salary of £250 a year. For the next two years he was never given what he considered a 'specific task' and supplied only reports 'of a general political nature'.[68] The War Office eventually realised that Rué was simply inventing 'whatever he thought would be pleasing to his employers'.[69]

Rear-Admiral Slade was also on the look-out for agents in Germany and anxious to co-operate with Edmonds. In March 1908 he sent an NID officer to Germany to contact a potential agent recommended by Sir William Ward, the consul-general at Hamburg, and wrote optimistically in his diary, 'I don't think there will be any difficulties in starting this thing in a small way'. When Slade retired as DNI a year later, he was able to report:

There are now three or four secret agents in our employ, most of whom work for the War Office and Admiralty jointly. It is impossible to draw the line between the information which would be useful to one Department or the other, so I endeavoured to establish a working agreement between the two Offices, and this procedure was beginning to bear fruit.

Slade believed, however, that a new organisation to run British espionage in peace and war was now required. Ewart too was convinced that British espionage was still 'lamentably behind other nations'. In the winter of 1908–9 he began to lay plans for a Secret Service Bureau to put British intelligence on a professional footing.[70]

The main immediate priority, however, was for an improved counter-espionage system. Major (later Major-General Sir) William Thwaites, head of the German section at the War Office, MO2c, had been convinced since 1907 that there was 'much truth' in newspaper reports that German intelligence officers were at work in every county and that 90,000 German reservists were at large in the British Isles. Ewart too believed that Germany was pouring 'hosts of agents and spies' into Britain.[71] Edmonds agreed. German friends had told him of requests by the German Admiralty to report on the movement of warships, work in dockyards and arsenals, aeroplane development and the building of munitions factories. Edmonds also thought he recognised a former German artillery captain working as head waiter at the Burlington Hotel with what seemed a suspicious addiction to early morning walks.[72] But Edmonds had little experience of counter-espionage work and was 'in a quandary' as to how to begin. Then he had a brainwave. He decided to consult some of the more successful spy novelists, but discovered, to his 'surprise', that most novelists knew no more than he did.[73] 'Two pieces of luck' then came his way. One of his friends, F.T. Jane (the founder of the naval and military annuals which bear his name), who was 'on the lookout for spies', found a suspicious German in Portsmouth, drove him to Woburn and 'deposited him in the Duke of Bedford's animal park'. Immediately following this exploit Jane received a series of letters about other suspected spies which he passed on to the War Office. Edmonds's second stroke of 'luck' was a similar flood of correspondence to William Le Queux from other amateur spywatchers alerted by Le Queux's patriotic fiction, reporting suspicious-looking aliens on 'early morning walks and drives', correcting maps, showing 'curiosity about railway bridges' and making 'enquiries about gas and water supply'. Even in retrospect it seems never to have occurred to Edmonds that Le Queux was a preposterous fraud. In his unpublished reminiscences written many years later, after Le Queux's death, Edmonds refers to him simply as his 'friend'. Of the dimensions of Le Queux's fraudulent fantasy world he seems to have had no idea. During

1908 Edmonds got in touch with 'the most promising' of Le Queux's and Jane's correspondents and made further enquiries into their reports of suspicious aliens. Within a few months he had arrived at a fourfold classification of the German spies in Britain:

(a) those who had taken houses close to important engineering structures (railway bridges, tunnels, magazines);

(b) those who kept apartment houses, to which small parties of Germans came to stay, to motor about the country with maps out;

(c) tradesmen, photographers, bakers, even doctors and eye specialists, permanently established in our dockyard towns and ports, and very inquisitive;

(d) postes restantes, spy centres for receipt of letters to agents.[74]

R.B. Haldane, the secretary of state for war, was at first bemused by the extraordinary evidence of German espionage presented to him by Colonel Edmonds. Unlike Edmonds, Haldane remained anxious to build bridges to Berlin. After the outbreak of war he was to be hounded from office for his alleged pro-German sympathies. His initial reaction, when confronted with Edmonds's evidence, was to believe that the alleged spies were really 'the apparatus of the white slave traffic'.[75] Some of Edmonds's evidence – for example, that concerning the suspicious Germans with photographic equipment in Epping 'occasionally visited by women from London for weekends'[76] – did indeed seem to lend itself to this interpretation. Edmonds, however, 'persisted', though – as he admitted later – 'I was very nearly thrown out of my job for my pains'. Finally, Haldane yielded to Edmonds's persistence and allowed himself to be convinced of the spy menace. 'What turned the scale', in Edmonds's view, 'was a letter from the Mayor of Canterbury, Mr F. Bennett-Goldney, which related that he had found two Germans wandering in his park, had talked to them and invited them in to dinner'. After dinner, the two men had revealed to a stunned Bennett-Goldney the sinister nature of their apparently harmless excursions: 'Their tongues loosened by port, they told him they were reconnoitring the country for an advance on London from the ports of Folkestone, Dover, Ramsgate and Margate'. Even when recounting this remarkable episode many years later Edmonds seemed unaware of its unusual irony. Germans and Britons had reversed their national stereotypes. Two fun-loving German tourists had played a British practical joke on their British host who had reacted with the incomprehension commonly associated with the humourless Hun. Few German practical jokes can have had such remarkable consequences. If Edmonds's account is to be believed, the mischievous German loquacity around the port decanter, by taking in Haldane as well as Bennett-Goldney, was to mark a significant step towards the creation of the modern British secret service.[77]

At a deeper level Haldane's readiness to believe some of Edmonds's and Bennett-Goldney's remarkable tales reflected his enormous respect for the professionalism of the German General Staff. He impressed on Vernon Kell, later head of MI5, 'the excellence and precision of their planning'[78] and undoubtedly considered them well capable of creating a dangerous spy network in Britain. But Haldane also found the invasion and spy scares a useful recruiting aid for the newly founded Territorial Force, his most important innovation as secretary of state for war. In January 1909 *An Englishman's Home*, a dramatised story of invasion by 'The Empire of the North' written by Major Guy du Maurier of the Royal Fusiliers, opened on the London stage. Haldane was amazed at the effect the play had on recruiting in London, hitherto the least successful recruiting area. On 6 February he told his mother: 'In London alone 300 recruits came in yesterday'. The War Office installed a recruiting booth complete with sergeant in the foyer of the theatre. Defending such 'modern methods of recruiting' in the Commons, Haldane said they had produced 30,000 recruits in the first seven weeks of 1909.[79] Major Ostertag, the German military attaché (known to British officers as 'Easteregg'), came to the War Office to complain that Major du Maurier's alien invaders were clearly intended to be Germans. 'Easteregg', whom Edmonds considered 'really a head spy', had an unsympathetic reception from Major Thwaites, head of the German section (and later DMI) at the War Office. 'Thwaites put up his eyeglass, looked at him and said: "Bad conscience, Ostertag! Bad conscience"'.[80]

In March 1909 Haldane set up, with cabinet approval, a subcommittee of the Committee of Imperial Defence to consider 'the nature and extent of the foreign espionage that is at present taking place within this country and the danger to which it may expose us'. The chair was taken by Haldane himself. Its other members were the first lord of the Admiralty, the home secretary, the postmaster-general, Lord Esher, the permanent under-secretaries of the Treasury and the Foreign Office, the commissioner of the Metropolitan Police, the DMO, the DNI, the director of military training and Rear-Admiral Sir C.L. Ottley. Edmonds told the subcommittee of a rapid rise in 'cases of alleged German espionage' reported to the War Office. 'No catalogue of such cases was kept until the end of 1907', he explained, 'as very few were reported; it is only since certain newspapers have directed attention to the subject that many cases have come to notice'. Five cases had been reported in 1907, 47 in 1908 and 24 in the first three months of 1909. Edmonds gave some particulars of thirty of these cases. Following Haldane's advice to 'lay stress on the anarchist (demolitions) motive', Edmonds emphasised the 'aggressive' nature of German espionage, claiming that it aimed not merely at intelligence gathering but also at preparing the destruction of docks, bridges, ammunition stores, railways and telegraph lines 'on or before the outbreak of war'.[81]

There were, of course, some real German spies in Britain. They were, however, concerned almost exclusively with naval espionage. As it grappled with the problems of a war on two fronts against the great armies of France and Russia, the German general staff scarcely considered the problems of operations against the British. Though German military intelligence was hard at work in France and Russia, it had no spy network at all in pre-war Britain, and no plans for wartime sabotage.[82] Sir Eric Holt-Wilson, deputy-head of the interwar MI5, later acknowledged that before the war:

> [Germany] took no interest in our army, and probably still remembered the famous remark, made I think by Bismarck, who upon being asked if he had contemplated the possibility of the British army coming to the aid of France in 1870, replied "Yes I have, and if they do I shall most certainly ring the bell and send for the police".[83]

Gustav Steinhauer, the German naval intelligence officer and former Pinkerton detective responsible for pre-war espionage in Britain, ran only an inefficient network of poorly-paid and clumsy part-time agents. He later blamed the 'meagre pittance' on which he operated for the slender achievements of his agents: 'the sum total of their remuneration was not worth bothering about'.[84] During the final years of peace Steinhauer's espionage network was no match even for the understaffed and inexperienced British counter-espionage office (the future MI5) founded after the meetings of the CID subcommittee in 1909. By the outbreak of war the whole network had been mopped up.[85]

Edmonds, however, completely misunderstood both the nature and extent of German espionage in Britain. He believed that most of it was not naval but military and that it was directed towards preparations for invasion and sabotage:

> Day in, day out, the ceaseless work of getting information and throwing dust in the eyes of others goes on, and the final result of it all, as far as we are concerned, is this: that a German general landing a force in East Anglia would know more about the country than any British General, more about each town than its own British Mayor, and would have his information so methodically arranged that he could, in a few minutes, give you the answer to any question you asked him about any town, village or position in that area.[86]

In the evidence presented by Edmonds to the CID subcommittee in 1909 real German spies were heavily outnumbered by imaginary ones. As Edmonds acknowledged, 'We have ... no regular system or organisation to detect and report suspicious cases, and are entirely dependent on casual information'. Counter-espionage at the Admiralty was in an even sorrier state. Captain R.C. Temple of NID told the subcommittee that his department was unable to carry out any 'investigations into espionage' at all, and therefore passed on any reports that came its way to Colonel Edmonds. In presenting his evidence to the subcommittee Edmonds 'laid great stress on the fact that none of these cases were reported by the police authorities, and that he was indebted for information regarding them to private individuals'.[87] He seems, at the very least, to have been insufficiently surprised by the failure of the police to detect a single suspicious German as well as insufficiently sceptical of the information supplied by 'private individuals'.

Edmonds's evidence now appears remarkably flimsy. His first twelve cases concerned 'alleged reconnaissance work by Germans'. In half these cases the suspicious persons were not even clearly identified as Germans. A report from a Norfolk inn-keeper referred simply to 'two foreigners, stoutish, well-set-up men' who had called at a Norfolk public house; another informant had 'noticed individuals, unmistakably foreigners' who were 'too absorbed and businesslike for ordinary tourists' in the North Walsham area. Nor did any of the reports concern naval or military installations. The 'alleged reconnaissance work by Germans' was confined to other, less probable – sometimes highly *im*probable – targets: stretches of coastline, reservoirs, railways, dykes and rivers. A 'Lincolnshire J.P.' reported that:

> A foreigner, who gave the name of Colonel Gibson and said he was a retired officer, with a German woman and a boy, neither of whom could speak English, stayed at Sutton-on-Sea, Lincolnshire, for several months in the summer of 1908. He took much interest in the coast, and was known locally as "the German spy".

The most farcical 'reconnaissance' report seems to have come, appropriately, from Le Queux himself (though, like other informants, he is not identified by name and is referred to only as a 'well known author'):

> Informant, while motoring last summer in an unfrequented lane between Portsmouth and Chichester, nearly ran over a cyclist who was looking at a map and making notes. The man swore in German, and on informant getting out of his car to apologize, explained in fair English, in the course of conversation, that he was studying at Oxford for the Church, and swore in German to ease his conscience. He was obviously a foreigner. Informant's suspicions being aroused, he returned to the neighbourhood on several subsequent days, and found the cyclist and companions still engaged in exploring tracks and lanes.[88]

Edmonds's second category of evidence consisted of twelve cases of 'Germans whose conduct has been reported as giving rise to suspicion'. The most suspicious was probably Herr Sandmann, said to rent three rooms in

Portland, who had supplied inside photographs of the Portland defences published in the German periodical *Die Woche*. Even if Sandmann was a spy, however, his flair for publicity raises some doubt about his proficiency. Most of Edmonds's other evidence was flimsier still. 'A well-known author' – probably Le Queux again – reported that a German barber in Southsea named Schweiger had been 'discovered by accident to wear a wig over his own thick head of hair', and showed 'much interest in navy gossip'. Some allegedly suspicious Germans showed no reasonable grounds for suspicion at all. 'A journalist', for example, reported that:

> Cobletz, a German, aged 40, who has served in the German army, lives at St. Alma, Wellesley Road, Clacton-on-Sea. He makes a point of being on friendly terms with everyone; does a little shooting, but has no occupation. He receives remittances from abroad. He has lived at various places on the East Coast.

Edmonds's third and final category of evidence consisted of six 'houses reported to be occupied by a succession of Germans which it is desirable to watch'. Once again Le Queux ('a well-known author') seems to have supplied one of the examples: 'A series of Germans come and go at 173, Powerscourt Road, North End, Portsmouth. They receive many registered letters from Germany'. Grounds for suspicion at the other five houses were equally slight.[89]

From such flimsy evidence Edmonds deduced the existence of an 'extensive' German espionage network in Britain directed, he believed, from a special office in Brussels. Furthermore, 'the use of motors has facilitated espionage, as it enables agents to live at a distance from the scene of their operations, where their presence excites no suspicion'.[90] At least one member of the subcommittee, Lord Esher, was less than impressed with Edmonds and unkindly described him in his Journal as 'a silly witness from the WO': 'Spy catchers get espionage on the brain. Rats are everywhere – behind every arras'.[91] Probably to test the limits of Edmonds's credulity, Esher asked him whether he 'felt any apprehensions regarding the large number of German waiters in this country'. Edmonds remained calm. He 'did not think that we need have any apprehensions regarding the majority of these waiters'.[92] Esher's initial scepticism gradually waned as the War Office revealed the extent of its concern. Whatever doubts remained on the subcommittee were successfully dispelled by the chairman. Haldane had a reputation for having not espionage but German culture on the brain. John Morley, the secretary of state for India, complained that he 'wearies his Cabinet colleagues by long harangues on the contribution of Germany to culture'. Leo Maxse simultaneously attacked Haldane as one of the 'Potsdam Party' in the Cabinet, 'an authority on Germany on the strength of his having been annually bamboozled by German professors in his earlier days'.[93] Thus when Haldane, having just returned from a visit to Germany, 'did not think that there was any doubt that a great deal of German espionage was being undertaken in Great Britain', much of it probably to 'enable important demolitions and destruction to be carried out in this country on or before the outbreak of war', his views carried unusual conviction.[94]

Haldane brought before the third and final meeting of the subcommittee on 12 July the most remarkable piece of bogus intelligence it had yet considered. Within the last week, said Haldane, the War Office had received a document from abroad 'which threw some light on what was going on':

> This document had been obtained from a French commercial traveller, who was proceeding from Hamburg to Spa. He travelled in the same compartment as a German whose travelling-bag was similar to his own. The German, on leaving the train, took the wrong bag, and on finding out this the commercial traveller opened the bag left behind, and found that it contained detailed plans connected with a scheme for the invasion of England. He copied out as much of these plans as he was able during the short time that elapsed before he was asked to give up the bag, concerning the loss of which the real owner had telegraphed to the railway authorities where the train next halted.

Haldane had at first rightly regarded the plans as forged, and possibly planted by the French to provide a stimulus for Anglo-French staff talks. Generals Ewart and Murray (Directors, respectively, of Military Operations and Military Training) persuaded him otherwise. The plans, in their view:

> showed great knowledge of the vulnerable points in this country, and revealed the fact that, as we had already suspected, there were certain places in this country where German agents are stationed, whose duty it would be to take certain action on the outbreak of war, or during the time of strained relations preceding that outbreak.[95]

Some years later Edmonds acknowledged that the plans were an obvious forgery, though he concluded that they were probably planted by the Germans rather than the French. An even more farcical piece of evidence which came Edmonds's way was a letter allegedly from a German officer to his English girlfriend in Bournemouth, begging her to flee with him to Germany since England would shortly be invaded. At the time, however, Edmonds took the letter sufficiently seriously to deliver it personally to Sir William Nicholson, the Chief of the Imperial General Staff (CIGS). Nicholson 'laughed and said it seemed to be a matter for the Director of Public Morals', but added that as a precaution Edmonds should send a copy to the Admiralty.[96]

The final meeting of the subcommittee was presented by Edmonds with eleven further 'cases of alleged reconnaissance work by Germans' and details of five more 'houses occupied by Germans in suspicious circumstances'. On this occasion four 'cases of alleged reconnaissance' had been reported by the police, perhaps spurred on by earlier complaints at their inattention to the spy menace. The Norfolk police simply reported 'three Germans reconnoitring at Dersingham and West Newton'. The other three police reports were slightly more substantial. The chief constable of the Yorkshire East Riding reported that two Germans 'of military appearance' had stayed at a Bridlington Hotel where the proprietor had observed in their rooms 'maps with military details added'. Also in Yorkshire, three other Germans had been observed 'reconnoitring the country' in the Whitby area. The main ground for suspicion in their case appeared to be their failure to purchase 'local maps' on the grounds that their own were 'much more detailed'. A further suspicious German of 'military appearance' had enquired 'the depths of certain waterways' from coastguards at Whitby and Sunderland. He had claimed to be a motor-car agent but, according to a garage proprietor, 'knew nothing about motors'.[97] If the Germans listed in these reports were spies engaged in 'reconnaissance work' their training had clearly been seriously deficient. A year earlier Haldane would not have regarded their activities, even if accurately reported, as coming close to espionage. He had told the Commons in July 1908 that foreign officers looking about for 'useful information' were not to be confused with spies.[98] Most of the additional reports from the public were even less alarming than those from the police. None from either police or public made any reference at all to military or naval installations. A 'retired military man' reported that the postmistress at Old Charlton, Kent, had 'married a German named Kerweder, who lives in the post office'. A Chatham lieutenant found it suspicious that the proprietor at the Sun Hotel was a Mr H.A. Klockenbosch. A 'landed proprietor' who had let a house to Germans at Banstead, Surrey, had his suspicions aroused by the ease with which he overcharged them. His tenants had taken the house 'without inspection and at an excessive rent "because of the view"'.[99]

Haldane suggested to the third meeting of the subcommittee that they now possessed sufficient evidence to issue a report. His colleagues agreed:

> The evidence which was produced left no doubt in the minds of the subcommittee that an extensive system of German espionage exists in this country, and that we have no organisation for keeping in touch with that espionage and for accurately determining its extent or objectives.[100]

That naive conclusion, which owed as much to the imaginary spies of William Le Queux as to the real machinations of German intelligence, led directly to the foundation of the modern British Secret Service. The subcommittee's report was responsible for the creation later in 1909 of the Secret Service

Bureau, initially divided into military and naval sections. Within a year these had given way to a home department responsible for counter-espionage (the ancestor of MI5) and a foreign department in charge of espionage (the forerunner of SIS or MI6).[101]

The first head of the military section, later the home department, of the Secret Service Bureau (the future MI5) was Vernon Kell, a thirty-six-year-old army captain. Kell had been born while his mother was on a seaside holiday at Yarmouth and liked to describe himself as a 'Yarmouth Bloater'. His oddly-chosen nickname was misleading. Kell's father was an army officer who had distinguished himself in the Zulu Wars and other conflicts at the outposts of empire, while his mother (later divorced) was the daughter of a Polish count with a string of exiled relatives scattered across Western Europe. Kell had a private education and a cosmopolitan upbringing, travelled widely on the Continent to visit friends and relatives, and – according to his widow – learned five foreign languages in the process. After Sandhurst, he joined his father's regiment, the South Staffordshire, 'determined to strike out on his own and make use of his languages'. Having qualified with ease as an army interpreter in French and German, Kell left in 1898 for Moscow to learn Russian. Two years later he set out for Shanghai with his newly-married wife to learn Chinese.[102] The outbreak of the Boxer rebellion in China gave both a remarkable opportunity to study the corrosive effects of subversion at close quarters. As Kell's widow later recalled, 'We were constantly hearing of how the Boxers were succeeding with alarming swiftness to poison the minds of the villagers and townsmen'.[103] That memory remained with Kell when he later came to combat first German, then Soviet 'subversion'.

On his return to London in 1902, Kell was employed in the analysis of German intelligence at the War Office. No doubt because of the paucity of intelligence coming in, he found the work 'not particularly interesting'.[104] His opportunity to make his mark came soon after the outbreak of the Russia-Japanese War in 1904 when the officer in charge of the Far Eastern Section was found to have confused Kowloon (the city) with Kaoling (Indian corn), and to have made other embarrassing errors. Edmonds was chosen to replace him and selected Kell as his deputy and 'right-hand man'. In 1909 it was Edmonds (now head of MO5) who proposed Kell (now assistant secretary of the CID) as first head of the future MI5.[105]

Kell started work in the newly founded Secret Service Bureau in August 1909 'with just one clerk'. By the outbreak of war he had a total staff of three officers, one barrister and seven clerks. The first officer to join was Captain Frederick Clark (who made comparatively little mark on the new bureau), followed shortly afterwards by Captain Reginald Drake (remembered by Lady Kell as 'a most able man and most successful sleuth – small hope for anyone who fell into his net') and Walter Moresby, the barrister son of Admiral John Moresby, who became legal adviser. The last pre-war officer recruit was

Captain (later Brigadier Sir) Eric Holt-Wilson, an Old Harrovian instructor in military engineering at Woolwich Royal Military Academy, who joined early in 1912. Holt-Wilson was a formidable all-round sportsman, a 'champion revolver shot' (to quote his own description) and later president of the Ski Club of Great Britain. He was also, according to Lady Kell, 'a man of almost genius for intricate organisation' and 'an intensely loyal and devoted friend'. Holt-Wilson became Kell's deputy during the war and remained in that position until sacked with Kell from MI5 in 1940.[106]

Kell also had the assistance of the Special Branch at Scotland Yard. Founded chiefly to keep track of suspicious-looking Irishmen, the Special Branch now concentrated on suspicious-looking Germans instead. Contrary to popular belief, however, the Special Branch took no initiative of its own when investigating espionage but acted on instructions from the Secret Service Bureau's home department. Kell approved of the popular misconception of the Special Branch's role. As Holt-Wilson wrote later: 'We welcome the unshakeable belief of the public that "Scotland Yard" is responsible for dealing with spies. It is a valuable camouflage'.[107] In June 1913 the Criminal Investigation Department and the Special Branch were given a new and dynamic head, Basil Thomson, son of the late archbishop of York. After Eton and Oxford Thomson had begun a remarkable, if sometimes idiosyncratic, career in the Colonial Service. He later recalled:

My first native friends were cannibals, but I learned very quickly that the warrior who had eaten his man as a quasi-religious act was a far more estimable person than the town-bred, mission-educated native.

In the course of a remarkably varied career Thomson had been prime minister of Tonga (at the age of only twenty-eight), private tutor to the Crown Prince of Siam and governor of Dartmoor prison.[108] Once at Scotland Yard he threw himself energetically into counter-espionage work, though his collaboration with Kell was later to be marred by personal rivalry.

As home secretary from 1910 to 1911, Winston Churchill also played an important part in the growth of the home department of the Secret Service Bureau. Kell was given Home Office introductions to all chief constables authorising him to seek their help on 'certain questions regarding undesirable aliens and persons suspected of espionage in this country'. Churchill served as first chairman of the Aliens Subcommittee of the CID, founded in March 1910, and approved the preparation by Kell of a secret register of aliens from probable enemy powers (chiefly Germany) based on information supplied by local police forces. On the 'Return of Aliens' form devised by Kell in October 1910, chief constables were also asked to report on 'Any specific acts of espionage on the part of the persons reported on; or other circumstances of an unusual nature'. In the following year Churchill added a major weapon to

Kell's armoury by greatly simplifying the interception of suspects' correspondence. Hitherto home secretaries had signed individual warrants for every letter opened. Churchill introduced the practice of signing 'general warrants authorising the examination of all the correspondence of particular people upon a list to which additions were continually being made'. By December 1913 the secret 'Register of Aliens' was almost complete except for London (where about half the aliens lived), and Kell wrote to the Home Office 'to express our gratitude to the Chief Constables and their Superintendents for the excellent work they have done for us during the last three years' and to request that their local registers 'be kept under constant current revision'.[109]

The evidence of suspicious aliens compiled by Kell with the assistance of the police served to convince the Home Office and the service ministries that the Germans had 'an extensive and systematic machinery of Secret Service' at work in Britain.[110] In reality it was neither extensive nor very systematic. Kell's first case exemplified the amateurishness of most pre-war espionage in Britain. The case concerned Lieutenant Siegfried Helm of the 21st Nassau Pioneer Battalion, the first foreign spy charged under the 1899 Official Secrets Act. Though described by *The Times* when he appeared in court in September 1910 as 'a young man of soldierly appearance', Helm seems to have stepped straight from the pages of *Punch*. Helm had written from Germany to the friend of a fellow officer, Miss Wodehouse, hoping to make her acquaintance during a forthcoming visit to London. On arriving in London, he discovered that Miss Wodehouse had moved to Fratton and wrote in *Punch*-like prose to express his dismay: 'I did hope to have a jolly time in London. Here in my boarding-house there are living only very old ladies, 45 to 70'. Helm then proposed a visit to Fratton, but asked 'Will Fratton be far from Portsmouth? I will willingly see the harbour and big steamers'. Miss Wodehouse wrote an encouraging reply and booked him lodgings near her own. Upon his arrival, however, Helm quickly aroused her suspicions. According to the prosecution at his committal proceedings:

> The defendant ... produced a local map of Portsmouth on which he showed the route he had taken and on which were marked in pencil the positions of certain fortifications on either side of Portsmouth. Miss Wodehouse rather twitted her guest upon the use of his pencil, and that put him further on his mettle. Saying "You must not tell", he produced a pocket-book and showed her some pencil sketches of forts in the harbour.[111]

Next day Miss Wodehouse reported Helm to the local barracks and on the following day he was apprehended in the act of making further drawings. On arrest Helm said that most of his information was obtained from a map on the South Parade Pier, and that he had made the drawings of the forts by looking through a large public telescope on the parade. He then wrote Miss Wodehouse a pained but determinedly cheerful letter:

> It is a dreadful thing, but they have taken me as a spy! It was all for my own study. The officers here are very kind to me. So comfortable a time I never had![112]

At this point the case was handed over to Kell though, as in subsequent cases, his name went unmentioned in either court or the press.[113] Investigation revealed that Helm had what his defence counsel called 'a mania for writing things in his pocket book' and a Teutonic thoroughness in doing so, noting down exact details of his bedroom furniture and the precise distance between the chest of drawers and his bed.[114] Though found guilty at his trial, Helm was merely bound over and discharged, with a cordial if condescending farewell from Mr Justice Bankes:

> I trust that when you leave this country you will leave it with a feeling that, although we may be vigilant, and perhaps, from your point of view, too vigilant, yet ... we are just and merciful, not only to those who are subjects of this realm, but also to those who, like yourself, seek the hospitality of our shores.[115]

The next spy trial a year later concerned less trivial espionage but an equally incompetent spy. Unlike Helm, Dr Max Schultz, the first doctor of philosophy ever to be jailed for espionage in Britain, had a definite intelligence mission. Schultz, however, did not believe in concealment. He established himself in a houseboat near Plymouth, flew a German flag from the stern and threw a series of parties at which he tried to turn the talk to naval matters. Though he quickly aroused suspicion, he acquired no useful information. His superiors in Germany remonstrated with him for his 'continual failures', complained at the waste of money, and were on the point of ending his mission altogether when Schultz announced that a local solicitor, Mr Duff and his friend Mr Tarran, had agreed to supply him with naval intelligence. Duff and Tarran, however, informed the Plymouth chief constable who in turn informed the Secret Service Bureau. Kell then supplied bogus information for passing on to Schultz who forwarded it to Germany. Rightly or wrongly, Kell suspected Duff of playing a double game. His suspicions were strengthened when on approaching Schultz's houseboat with the special branch, Kell saw Duff arriving from a different direction. Fearing that the solicitor was about to warn the spy to dispose of incriminating documents, Kell – with great presence of mind – diverted a flock of sheep into Duff's path. According to Kell's account, recalled later by his widow, the solicitor tried to wave the sheep away but 'got thoroughly mixed up with them ... careering first one way and then the other'. Kell arrived at the houseboat first to discover Schultz in possession both of coded telegrams from Germany and of a codebook which enabled the messages to be decoded. By the time Duff had extricated himself from the sheep, 'poor Schultz looked very crestfallen and smiled sadly at the baffled solicitor'. At Schultz's trial the whole affair came to an appropriately eccentric conclusion. He was tried in the name of Dr Phil Max Schultz, the authorities failing to realise that 'Phil' on statements signed by Schultz referred not to a Christian name but to his doctorate of philosophy. Lord Chief Justice Alverstone told Schultz before sentencing him to twenty-one months in jail that it was 'a sad thing to think that you, a man of education, should be capable of coming over here posing as a gentleman', attempting to obtain improper information:

> I am thankful to know that the relations between the two countries are most friendly and amicable, and no one would repudiate and condemn the practices of which you have been guilty more strongly than all the leading men in Germany.[116]

While the case against Schultz was proceeding the law was being changed. The 1889 Official Secrets Act had been condemned as inadequate by the 1909 espionage subcommittee, by Kell and by the Committee of Imperial Defence. The Helm case lent further weight to their arguments. The magistrates court had thrown out the charge of felony alleging intention to communicate 'certain sketches and plans ... to a foreign State – to wit the Empire of Germany' and committed Helm for trial only on a lesser charge. Under the 1889 Act it was necessary to prove intent to obtain information illegally. This, claimed Viscount Haldane, at the Lords' second reading of a new Official Secrets Bill in July 1911, created intolerable problems in preventing espionage:

> I will give one or two instances showing what our difficulties have been. Not many months ago we found in the middle of the fortifications at Dover an intelligent stranger, who explained his presence by saying that he was there to hear the singing of the birds. He gave the explanation rather hastily, because it was mid-winter. Then there was another case, in which somebody was found looking at the emplacement of guns in a battery at Lough Foyle, and he declared that he was there for the purpose of paying a call upon somebody.[117]

The new bill making it illegal to obtain or communicate any information useful to an enemy as well as to approach or enter a 'prohibited place' 'for any purpose prejudicial to the safety or interests of the State' placed the onus on the accused to show that his actions were innocently intended. The bill was introduced in the Commons, after passing all its stages in the Lords, on 17 August. Placing the onus of proof on the accused was not entirely without legal precedent; it applied in a roughly similar way to the crime of 'loitering with intent' under the 1871 Prevention of Crimes Act.[118] But the attorney-general, Sir Rufus Isaacs, was stretching a point when he assured the Commons on 18 August that, by comparison with the 1889 Official Secrets Act, 'there is nothing novel in the principle of the Bill which the House is being asked to accept now'. The Liberal M.P., Sir Alpheus Morton, immediately retorted: 'It upsets Magna Carta altogether'. Nonetheless Colonel 'Jack' Seely, the under-secretary for war, was able to exploit the sense of urgency created by the Franco-German Agadir crisis to push the bill through all its Commons stages in the scarcely precedented space of less than an hour.[119] Later attempts to reform the Act were to prove as protracted and as unsuccessful as its initial passage had proved swift and successful.

The first case tried under the 1911 Official Secrets Act was that of Heinrich Grosse, alias Captain Grant, at the Winchester assizes in February 1912. Grosse was a convicted forger who had served ten years hard labour in Singapore before being released in 1908. He was recruited as a German agent by the Brussels intelligence entrepreneur R.H. Peterssen, and sent to Portsmouth where his attempts at espionage showed an incompetence worthy of Helm and Schultz. The main witness at Grosse's trial was William Salter, a naval pensioner who had placed a small advertisement in the press offering his services as an enquiry agent. Grosse was both his first, and apparently his last, customer. He commissioned Salter to discover the extent of Portsmouth coal supplies and the number of men in naval barracks, and told him his next mission would probably be in Southampton. 'Some people', admitted Grosse, 'would call this spying'. But, he added implausibly, he required the information 'for commercial purposes only'. A second witness at Grosse's trial was a newsagent named John Bunn. On only his second visit to Bunn's shop, Grosse had asked:

if he could find out the approximate number of sailors in the naval barracks at that time, explaining that he had a £5 bet on the subject and it was a condition that he was not to ask a soldier or a sailor.

Bunn agreed to try to find out. Grosse's naiveté during a period of spy scares in entrusting enquiries which 'some people would call spying' to complete strangers, while at the same time keeping incriminating evidence in an unlocked room, almost passes belief. Predictably, both Salter and Bunn went to the police. Kell's methods of bringing Grosse to justice were based on the three simple but effective techniques he had already employed against Schultz. Salter and Bunn were provided with bogus intelligence which Grosse passed on to Germany. Grosse's control was sufficiently pleased to forward a more detailed list of enquiries on wireless telegraphy, range-finding, naval guns and coal supplies. Grosse was, however, told that his report about 'a floating conning-tower' (apparently one of Kell's less plausible inventions) was 'surely imaginary'. This, like the remainder of Grosse's correspondence, was duly intercepted. Finally, Kell ordered a police raid on Grosse's lodgings to recover the further incriminating evidence which Grosse kept conveniently to hand. While in prison, Grosse received one further letter (also intercepted), probably from Peterssen, promising him 'a sum of money' which could be used either for his defence or to assist him on his release, with the implication that the latter might be the more prudent course. 'Under no circumstances,' Grosse was told, 'can I do anything more for you'. The judge at Grosse's trial, Mr (later Lord) Justice Darling, who managed to preside over a remarkable number of official secrets trials, found several opportunities amid the bizarre evidence for displays of his celebrated judicial wit, each greeted by sycophantic courtroom laughter. He concluded, when sentencing Grosse to three years penal servitude, on a more sententious note:

> We desire to live on terms of amity with every neighbouring nation and the practice of spying can but tend to inflame hostile feelings ... Spying upon one another gives rise to such ill-feeling that if it could be stamped out it should be.[120]

The next German spy brought to trial, Armgaard Karl Graves, was even more bizarre than his predecessors. Like Grosse, Graves was a criminal adventurer who had drifted into espionage. Unlike Grosse, he was a successful confidence trickster who added both the German and British intelligence services to his list of victims. His bizarre behaviour also suggests a Walter Mitty world worthy of Le Queux. Having returned to Germany after a period in Australia, Graves persuaded the German Admiralty to finance a Scottish intelligence mission to investigate the Rosyth naval base and the Glasgow arms manufacturers, Beardmore & Sons, with which he falsely claimed to have important contacts. Steinhauer, who was responsible for German naval intelligence in Britain, was not consulted before Graves was taken on. He later dismissed him as 'a double-dyed rascal, ... one of those international adventurers who were continually giving the world the impression that Europe was overrun with spies and agents of the German Secret Service'.[121]

Once in Scotland, Graves quickly aroused suspicion. His first move was to apply for a post as locum tenens to a Leith doctor on the basis of bogus Australian medical qualifications. Though the doctor was taken in by the bogus qualifications, he decided that Graves's strong German accent 'would not go' in Leith. Graves then struck up an acquaintance with the assistant manager of the Glasgow Central Hotel who introduced him to his club as 'my friend, the German spy'.[122] According to Graves's own bizarre account, having aroused suspicion he decided to try 'a right royal bluff' by calling at police headquarters and demanding to see the chief constable:

> Presently I was shown into the chief's room, and was received by a typical Scottish gentleman. I opened fire in this way:
> 'Have you any reason to believe that I am a German spy?' I saw that it had knocked him off his pins.
> 'Why, no,' he said, startled, 'I don't know anything about it at all'.
> 'It's not by your orders then that I am followed?'
> 'Certainly not', he replied.[123]

Graves's correspondence was by now being intercepted and Kell moved to Glasgow to take personal charge of the investigations.[124] According to Steinhauer (whose account is at least partially corroborated by evidence given in court), 'most of the letters and telegrams that he sent from Glasgow contained nothing but requests for money, which is always the way with these swindlers'.[125] When finally arrested, Graves had about him a series of maps (including one of the Rosyth naval base), a note-book and pocket-book (including a code for correspondence with Germany), a number of phials filled with 'deadly poisons' together with hypodermic syringe and needles (whose purpose in Graves's fantasy world remains unclear), and notepaper with the forged letter head of Burroughs, Wellcome & Co., the London chemists. On the basis of this motley evidence and the intercepted correspondence, the prosecution tried and failed to prove Graves guilty of espionage at Beardmore & Sons. Instead Graves was found guilty of 'making or obtaining a telegraphic code for the purpose of communicating information relating to the British Navy and land fortifications'. The Scottish solicitor-general successfully persuaded the jury that the code in Graves's possession was 'a very deadly document': 'By this means he would be able to telegraph information of great importance to an enemy in times of emergency and stress'. Graves accepted his eighteen months sentence with an eccentric display of good humour. 'Exit, Armgaard Karl Graves!', he declared: 'Well, it has been a fair trial!'[126]

That was not the end of Graves. While in prison he is said to have asked to see 'the chief of the Secret Service' and to have persuaded Kell of his potential as a double agent if sent to the United States. Graves was secretly released in December 1912 and given a free passage to New York. But once in the United States he failed to adopt the role of double agent, and returned instead to a life of confidence tricks and blackmail, expounding his own fantasy world further in published 'memoirs' of his years as 'the Kaiser's special investigator' and lecture tours in which he claimed access to most of Europe's diplomatic secrets.[127]

The next spy trial, in January 1913, was even more sensational than those which had preceded it, for it was the only pre-war trial which concerned an Englishman, George Charles Parrott, a warrant officer in the Royal Navy. Parrott, as Mr Justice Darling told him at his trial, had been 'entrapped by a woman'. Kell had a generally low opinion of female agents. According to his widow: 'Women were occasionally used by the Germans as agents if they were possessed of a ready wit and adept at using it when in a tight corner. But their usefulness was somewhat limited'.[128] The Parrott case, however, appeared to provide a successful example of the German use of female 'ready wit'. While in charge of the naval rifle range of Sheerness, Parrott had made the acquaintance of Karl Hentschel, a German language teacher, and his English wife. Like Grosse and Graves, Hentschel was a criminal adventurer, though he lacked Graves's well-developed fantasy world. According to Steinhauer, 'Hentschel did something that even the most unscrupulous of spies would hesitate to do' and encouraged a liaison between his wife and Parrott: 'Whether Hentschel indulged in subtle blackmail of some sort, or whether Parrott was in fact a willing victim, there was no doubt that he responded to Hentschel's requests for confidential naval information'. After a time, however, Hentschel and Parrott fell out – according to Steinhauer because Parrott concluded that 'Hentschel was making a fortune out of him' and that he would do better to sell information direct to German naval intelligence. Hentschel, annoyed at being bypassed, betrayed Parrott to the police.[129] From then on Parrott was kept under surveillance and his correspondence intercepted. As in previous cases, Kell's task was made easier by Parrott's lack of even elementary precautions. While travelling to Ostend to pass on information to German naval intelligence, Parrott aroused the suspicions of a port detective (apparently unaware that Parrott was also being tailed by the special branch) and gave a series of contradictory explanations for both the documents in his possession and the purpose of his visit, first denying and then admitting that he was in the Royal Navy. Once in Ostend Parrott was observed making contact with his German control.[130] According to a later MI5 report, 'For £400 [Parrott] gave away our latest torpedo secrets and sat under viva-voce examination before a board of German naval engineers at Ostend.'[131] Mr Justice Darling sentenced him to four years' hard labour but promised to try 'to procure some remission' if Parrott revealed all he knew to 'the authorities'.[132]

Parrott's conviction had a series of bizarre sequels. Hentschel and his wife disappeared to New South Wales, no doubt with Kell's consent. Once there, however, Hentschel wrote to Steinhauer (whom he doubtless hoped was unaware of his treachery) threatening to sell his memoirs unless he continued to receive his old salary. For a time money was sent to keep him quiet.[133] But after a few months Hentschel became, in Steinhauer's view, 'such a nuisance' that payments were stopped. With his marriage also on the rocks,

Hentschel returned to England in October 1913. He immediately presented himself at Chatham police station, announced that he was a German spy and asked to be arrested. The Chatham police declined but on the following day Hentschel tried again at the Old Jewry police station in the City of London. 'I wish to give myself up for being a German spy', Hentschel declared: 'You may think I am mad, but that is not so. I have had trouble with my wife; and have decided in consequence to confess what I have been doing since I have been in England'. This time he was brought before the Westminster Police Court on a charge of conspiracy with ex-Gunner Parrott 'to disclose naval secrets'. Hentschel's protestations of guilt caused Kell some embarrassment. It was acknowledged in court that Kell's organisation (identified only as a department unconnected with the police 'especially charged to deal with matters of that kind') had paid Hentschel for 'confidential information' incriminating Parrott and had promised him immunity from prosecution provided he kept secret what had passed. However, counsel for the Crown suggested disingenuously that, being a foreigner, the defendant might not have understood that 'if he made any communication in an open or public manner avowing his own participation in crime', his immunity from prosecution lapsed. The attorney-general had therefore thought it right to offer no evidence and allow the charges to be withdrawn. But Hentschel was warned in no uncertain manner not to cause Kell any future embarrassment:

> If the defendant should, under any circumstances whatever, henceforth make any open or public repetition of his own complicity in crime the authorities would hold themselves perfectly free to prosecute.[134]

The last two German spies convicted before the war were, in very different ways, as unreliable as their predecessors. The first was Wilhelm Klauer, alias William Clare. Klauer had arrived in England as a kitchen porter in 1902 but after a period as a dentist's assistant set himself up as a dentist in Portsmouth where he supplemented his meagre fees from pulling teeth by living off the immoral earnings of his prostitute wife. Late in 1912 Klauer wrote to the German Admiralty to report that he was willing to supply secret naval intelligence. Steinhauer was sent to visit Klauer and, by his own account, came to the accurate conclusion that he was a fraud who believed, probably from reading Le Queux's novels, that vast sums were to be made from espionage. Against Steinhauer's recommendation, the German Admiralty decided none the less to see if Klauer could obtain a secret report book on torpedo trials. Klauer had so little idea how to lay hands on the books that he sought the help of a friendly German-Jewish hairdresser and chiropodist, Levi Rosenthal. Klauer told Rosenthal that it would be worth £100 to have the report book 'long enough for it to go to Germany and back'. And that, he said, was only the beginning; there were 'hundreds' more pounds where the first hundred came from. But Rosenthal was, for at least two reasons, ill-suited to the quest for secret documents. First, he was illiterate. Secondly, without telling Klauer, he went to the police. From then on he acted the role of *agent provocateur*, eventually introducing Klauer to a dockyard official who provided him with a confidential document, thus giving the signal for his arrest. In March 1913 Klauer was sentenced to five years hard labour amid applause from a crowded courtroom.[135]

The last German spy convicted before the outbreak of war was also by far the most successful. Frederick Adolphus Schroeder alias Gould had been born in Germany of an English mother and after service in the Germany army had settled in England. Following the failure of some business ventures he began dabbling in part-time espionage early in the twentieth century. His most productive period, however, began in 1908 when he became licensee of the Queen Charlotte public house in Rochester, frequented by naval personnel from Chatham. In Steinhauer's professional opinion, Schroeder

> was not a man whom anyone would take for a spy. Had you met him in the street you would have turned round to look at him and said to yourself: "What a fine-looking fellow!" Broad-shouldered, bearded, nature – plus twelve years in the German Army – had given him a big, athletic frame and a pleasant, cheery manner.

Schroeder's sources of information remain largely unknown, though he seems to have been assisted by a cashiered ex-officer, Stewart Stevens, 'who had no particular scruples worth mentioning'. According to Steinhauer, Schroeder provided 'more information on naval matters than all other spies put together'. Among the documents referred to at his trial were 'important matters relating to engines, engine-room and engine arrangements of battleships'. Like his less successful predecessors, however, Schroeder's indiscretions made Steinhauer's 'blood run cold'. When he gave up the Queen Charlotte in December 1913, he left a mass of incriminating documents – including correspondence with Steinhauer – in the attic. By then Kell had probably had Schroeder under surveillance for at least a year, and had discovered from his intercepted correspondence that he was also engaged in free-lance espionage for a Brussels 'spy bureau' which had supplied him with a list of the naval intelligence it required. In April 1914 he was sentenced to six years' hard labour.[136]

Kell considered his greatest success not the conviction of Schroeder and his predecessors but the surveillance for three years before the war of a German spy ring. The discovery of the spy ring, according to Holt-Wilson, was due mainly

> to a conversation overhead in a railway carriage, which was fortunately reported to us at once, and led to the capture of what afterwards proved

to be a complete list of 22 paid German Secret Service agents in this country.[137]

The author of the indiscretion – fully in keeping with the general amateurishness of pre-war German espionage in Britain – was a German 'Admiralty official', probably a naval intelligence officer, on a visit to Britain.[138] Rather than arrest the members of the network, Kell kept them under surveillance and had their correspondence intercepted in order both to trace their contacts and to be in a position to cripple German espionage in Britain at the outbreak of war. During the final days of peace Kell remained in his office twenty-four hours a day, sleeping surrounded by telephones, ready to order the arrest of the spy ring as soon as war was declared.[139] On the evening of 3 August he was given twelve hours' notice of the declaration of war. Immediately secret instructions were issued to the police by pre-arranged coded telegrams. By the time war was declared twenty-one of the twenty-two German agents had been arrested; the twenty-second was later discovered to be in Germany and never returned to Britain. MI5 still remembers these arrests as one of its triumphs. According to Holt-Wilson:

This sudden action had the effect of destroying the complete spy organisation built up by the enemy in peacetime. As a proof of this statement, a German Order came into our hands early in the war which disclosed the fact that as late as the 21st August (i.e. 17 days after war was declared), the German Military Commanders were still ignorant of the despatch or movements of our main Expeditionary Force, although this had been more or less common knowledge to thousands in this country.[140]

Of the twenty-one German agents and other suspicious persons interned on 4 August 1914 only one was brought to trial. The exception was Karl Ernst, a London barber, who appealed successfully against detention under the Aliens Restriction Act on the grounds that, though of German parents, he was an English subject born in Hoxton. It was claimed in court, on Ernst's behalf, that 'He had built up a most successful haircutting business, and some of his most esteemed clients were officers of Pentonville Prison, which was near his shop. One of the officials whose hair he cut was the chaplain'. Ernst's main role had been that of postman, or – as he was more glamorously (though less accurately) described by *The Times* – 'The Master Spy's Postman'.[141] He posted in London letters sent to him from Germany already addressed and stamped with English stamps, and forwarded other letters he received from English addresses to Steinhauer. Among those who used Ernst as a post-box were Parrott, Graves and Schroeder. He was also used for correspondence with disgruntled or hard-up seamen whom Steinhauer had persuaded to supply 'innocent information to real or bogus continental technical newspapers', in the hope of leading them on to provide less innocent information.[142] On occasion Ernst was also used by Steinhauer directly. Some of his intelligence missions were quite remarkably humdrum. He was, for example, asked to supply Steinhauer with English stamps, check addresses, and – on one occasion – to obtain a *Daily Express* article on Steinhauer himself entitled 'German Spy Bureau. Chief Organizer and How He Works. A Man of Mystery. Victims Made to Order'. On one occasion Steinhauer asked Ernst to make enquiries concerning one of his contacts whom he suspected of dealings with Kell. But his instructions to Ernst make clear that he considered him ignorant of even the most basic espionage techniques:

> It is suspected that [the contact] is in connexion with the Intelligence Department, and it is therefore very important to have searching and quick information ... without his noticing anything. Postmen, porters, and such are good sources of information. Do not take it ill if I, as an old criminologist and detective, give a few suggestions. I have always had success if I mention a similar name [to the one I am looking for]. People then think involuntarily of the correct [name], and you can in all safety make your enquiries with the apology that the person concerned has given you or your firm large orders such as furs, automobiles or [a bet] on a horse.[143]

Ernst was, however, remarkably inattentive. According to Steinhauer, one or two of the postmen who delivered letters to him, thinking that he was conducting an illegal betting business, warned him that his letters were being opened. Steinhauer claimed that he discovered that Ernst and his contacts had been compromised but was told by the Chief of the German Admiralty Staff: 'Let them go on thinking we know nothing about it'. So Ernst continued to be sent letters 'often with mysterious contents which must have sorely puzzled the officials who opened and read them'.[144] Though Steinhauer may well have exaggerated the success of his countermeasures once Ernst was compromised, Kell and his department were indeed 'sorely puzzled' by some of the correspondence which they intercepted. According to Lady Kell's later recollection, some of the sequences of German messages were so bizarre that they must have been 'puzzling even to their intended recipients':

> One rather curious one was a telegram which read: 'Father deceased, await instructions', which was turned into 'Father deceased, what action'. Back came a wire: 'Father dead or deceased, please explain'.[145]

Though unobservant, Ernst inevitably became worried by the trial and conviction of some of his correspondents. At his trial he claimed to have broken contact with Steinhauer early in 1914. He had, he added, 'done no harm because all the letters going out have been intercepted, and what came in were of great use to this country'. Mr Justice Coleridge was not impressed:

> You are a mean, mercenary spy, ready to betray your country to the enemy for money, equally ready, I dare say, to betray Germany to us for an increased reward. With such a man I can have no sympathy. You will go to penal servitude for seven years.[146]

Steinhauer claimed later that Ernst and the others arrested at the outbreak of war did not really amount to a spy ring. Most, in his view, were men like Ernst: 'agents, yes', but incapable of functioning as spies in the usual sense: 'To utilise these sort of men for unearthing secrets of the British Navy, why, the idea is too ridiculous for words'.[147] Kell, too, had a generally low opinion of those he arrested. According to his widow, 'Most of the agents employed by the Germans worked only for the money they gained and were regarded with contempt'. They included men 'of low morality, or drunkards of a bad type, down and outs generally'.[148] Those spies Kell considered capable of sending important naval intelligence out of the country had already been brought to trial before the war began. Even they had, in every case, contributed to their own downfall by elementary lapses.

Kell, however, greatly exaggerated the significance of the spy ring he had arrested. Like Edmonds, he mistakenly believed that the purpose of the German agents was not merely to gather information but also to prepare for sabotage. He told chief constables in 1912:

> Several [German agents] have now been brought to trial, and we shall also be in a position to take effective action, in time of strained relations or war, against others whose activities are at present of no great detriment. It may be thought that but little harm can be done by these agents, and little of importance gleaned, but though this may be true of individuals in peace-time it is impossible to over-estimate the harm they can do collectively, both just prior to and in a time of national emergency. Not the least vital part of their duties is, probably, to prepare for the destruction of vital points, and to create panic in this country on or before the outbreak of war.[149]

German agents were also suspected of financing the growing industrial unrest during the three years before the war. Lieutenant-Colonel Adrian Grant Duff, assistant secretary of the CID, wrote in his diary during the railway strike of August 1911: 'It would be very interesting to know whether there is any German money behind these troubles'.[150] Chief constables were warned by Kell a year later:

It is obvious that periods of great industrial unrest provide favourable opportunities to a hostile nation to strike unexpectedly. It is therefore worth endeavouring to find out whether funds are furnished by foreign secret service departments to the trades union organisation concerned.[151]

As well as suspecting the involvement of German agents in a non-existent masterplan for war-time sabotage, Kell also exaggerated their potential as intelligence gatherers. It is highly doubtful whether the twenty-two agents still at large on the eve of war would have proved capable of furnishing any high-grade intelligence on the movements of the British Expeditionary Force even had they remained at liberty. Kell's later claim that their arrest had kept the Germans in ignorance of the despatch of the BEF for over a fortnight was wildly exaggerated. The major failings of German intelligence lay not in Britain but in the battle area. Even those failings, however, were overshadowed by the almost catastrophic French failure to grasp the extent of the German sweep through Belgium. When advance guards of the BEF and invading Prussian Uhlans stumbled into each other near Mons on 22 August both sides were taken equally by surprise. Only after a stunned pause did each side realise it was facing the enemy.[152]

Though Kell exaggerated the scale of his achievements in August 1914, he had none the less totally defeated third-rate opposition. With four assistants, seven clerks, and the assistance of the Special Branch and local police forces, he had tracked down all the real German agents in Britain. But he was far less successful with the imaginary German spies whose numbers grew to record proportions on the outbreak of war. On 9 October 1914 Reginald McKenna, the home secretary, claimed quite accurately that 'little valuable information' had been obtained by pre-war German spies and that the whole spy network in Britain had in all probability been 'crushed at the outbreak of the war'. Like the public at large, *The Times* was 'more than a little incredulous':

It does not square with what we know of the German spy system.... In their eager absorption of the baser side of militarism, the Germans seem to have almost converted themselves into a race of spies.[153]

Britain's pre-war intelligence collection was less successful than her counter-espionage. The first head of what became the foreign section of the Secret Service Bureau (the future SIS or MI6), probably founded in October 1909, was a short, thick-set naval officer, Commander (later Captain Sir) Mansfield George Smith-Cumming (usually abbreviated to 'Cumming').[154] In Cumming's honour the present head of SIS is still known as 'C' (not 'M', as in Ian Fleming's novels) and signs his name in the special green ink used by Cumming. Cumming was born Mansfield George Smith on April Fool's Day

1859. After attending Royal Naval College, Dartmouth, he began his naval career as acting sub-lieutenant in HMS *Bellerophon* in 1878. Over the next six years he served on patrol in the East Indies, took part in operations against Malay pirates, and was decorated for his role in the Egyptian campaign of 1882. His naval record described him as 'a clever officer with great taste for electricity' and 'a knowledge of photography' who 'speaks French' and 'draws well'. Cumming also had a brief spell on board the royal yacht and later told young relatives how he had played needle-threading games with the royal princesses in which none of the players were allowed to lick the thread. But his health during his twenties was poor and he suffered increasingly from severe sea-sickness. In 1885 he was placed on the retired list as 'unfit for service'. In the same year he married a South African wife, Dora Cloete. Four years later, after Dora's death, he married again, this time to a Scottish heiress, Leslie Valiant 'May' Cumming, and as part of the marriage settlement changed his name to Smith-Cumming. Much of the next decade seems to have been spent on May's Morayshire estate.[155]

In November 1898, while still on the retired list, Cumming was posted to Nelson's old flagship *Victory* 'for special service at Southampton'.[156] Later, as head of the Secret Service Bureau foreign section, he sometimes used the title 'Captain of the *Victory*'.[157] It seems probable that Cumming's 'special service' during the decade after 1898 included occasional intelligence forays abroad in the traditions of the late Victorian MID and NID. But his main work during this period was the construction and command of an elaborate system of Southampton boom defences incorporating wooden men of war. He retained command of the boom defences even after moving to the Secret Service Bureau. According to an enthusiastic visitor from MO5, Major (later Major-General Sir) Walter Kirke, who was shown round the defences by Cumming in 1913:

> One has to get out half mile across marshes on a pier built from old ships masts etc., and across creeks where he has miniature booms and boom smashers for testing purposes, and he has a staff of some 50 bluejackets.[158]

Before the war Cumming managed to spend long weekends in his country home at Bursledon, overlooking the river Hamble. He had the cross-trees of an iron-clad warship stuck in the sands at Hamble and used to demonstrate his fitness by climbing up them. Cumming owned a houseboat, a motor launch, a luxurious ten-ton yacht, 'any number' of other yachts, and spent much of his weekends sailing in Southampton Water and messing about in boats.[159] He also had a passion for motorcars and was notorious for driving his Rolls 'at breakneck speed about the streets of London to the terror of police and pedestrians alike'.[160] One of his great-nieces still recalls how 'Uncle Manny' encouraged her to steer his Rolls down Piccadilly at the age of twelve.[161] In his early fifties Cumming took up flying and in 1913 gained both the French Aviators and Royal Aero Club certificates.[162] His fascination with methods of transport extended even to bicycles. Colonel Humphrey Quill, the son of one of Cumming's friends who lived near Hamble, remembers being taught by him at the age of eight or nine to ride a bicycle without his hands on the handlebars while reading a newspaper. Cumming also taught him conjuring tricks and had a fund of schoolboy jokes.[163] To the children who knew him Cumming became a favourite uncle. He enjoyed their company. At Bramshaw in the New Forest, where he acquired another house at about the time of the First World War, he and his wife were remembered by the children at the village school for giving them a 'Christmas treat' at their home and a present each to take away.[164]

Major Kirke of MO5, who saw Cumming almost daily during the two years before the war, considered him 'the cheeriest fellow I've met, full of the most amusing yarns'.[165] Compton Mackenzie, who got to know him during the war, found him 'a pale, clean-shaven man', with a 'Punch-like chin, a small and beautifully fine bow of a mouth, and a pair of very bright eyes', who habitually glared at newcomers through a gold-rimmed monocle.[166] Paul Dukes, one of Cumming's 'master spies' in revolutionary Russia, later wrote of him:

> At first encounter he appeared very severe. His manner of speech was abrupt. Woe betide the unfortunate individual who ever incurred his ire! Yet the stern countenance could melt into the kindliest of smiles, and the softened eyes and lips revealed a heart that was big and generous. Awe-inspired as I was by my first encounter, I soon learned to regard 'the Chief' with feelings of the deepest personal admiration and affection.[167]

There was a tough and ruthless streak in Cumming as well as a 'big and generous' heart. Few intelligence chiefs, however, have inspired so much sentimental affection.

Cumming set up both the Secret Service Bureau foreign department and his own London flat at the top of 2 Whitehall Court in 'a regular maze of passages and steps, and oddly shaped rooms', reached by a private lift. Bernard Shaw and other celebrities who lived on the lower floors seem never to have realised that the headquarters of the secret service were directly above them. Cumming called those who were privy to the secret work of his top-floor offices his 'top-mates'. Within his own office a frequent visitor noted

> A plain work-table, a big safe, some maps and charts on the walls, a vase of flowers, one or two seascapes recalled 'C's' passion for sailing and inevitably, scattered about, various examples of the mechanical gadgets in which he revelled with boyish enthusiasm – a patent compass, a new sort of electric clock.

Cumming once startled his attractive young secretary by telling her he proposed to publish his memoirs after he retired:

> I shall call them 'The Indiscretions of a Secret Service Chief'. It will be a splendid-looking publication bound in red with the title and my name embossed in gold, and consisting of 400 pages – every one of which will be blank![168]

Cumming did, however, regularly enter details of his intelligence work in naval logbooks which are retained in the office of the present head of SIS and sometimes shown to new recruits when they meet C for the first time.[169] The information they contain is still regarded by the Foreign Office (whose attitude to ancient secrets sometimes shows an unconscious absurdity worthy of a Le Queux novel) as too vital to national security ever to be revealed. It is known, however, that as well as directing the work of British agents abroad, Cumming also went on spying expeditions himself armed with a swordstick and in a variety of disguises.[170] He kept in his office a photograph of 'a heavily-built German-looking individual in most unmistakably German clothes', and was delighted when visitors failed to recognise it as himself. During the First World War, he once asked a young relative, unaware of the identity of the German in the photograph, what she would do if she met him in London. The little girl suggested shooting him. 'Well, my dear', replied Cumming, 'in that case you'd have killed your uncle!'[171] During the war he looked back nostalgically to the fun he had had on pre-war intelligence expeditions. 'That', he told Compton Mackenzie, 'is when this business was really amusing. After the War is over, we'll do some amusing secret service work together. It's capital sport!'[172]

Cumming's expeditions to Germany, despite his disguises, were handicapped by the fact that he spoke little or no German. During his early years at Whitehall Court, however, he developed a close connection with the German-Jewish educationalist, Kurt Hahn. While Hahn was at Oxford University before the First World War, he formed an intimate friendship with Cumming's only son, Alastair, and through him became a friend of the family, spending long periods at their homes in Bursledon and Morayshire. Hahn said later that he 'left Oxford in 1914 with one idea: to found a public school in Germany':

> Among the best reared in the public schools I had again and again met with certain qualities which seemed characteristic: confidence in effort; modesty in success; grace in defeat; fairness in anger; clear judgement even in the bitterness of wounded pride; readiness for service at all times.

There is no evidence that when he left England in 1914 Hahn had yet even visited a public school. His image of the public school ideal was based instead on the ex-public schoolboys whose qualities he most admired, among them his friend Alastair Cumming.[173] Hahn's friendship with the Cumming family was so deep that it survived both Alastair's death in October 1914 and the First World War. Before Mansfield Cumming died in 1923, he probably visited Hahn's school at Salem near Lake Constance. After her husband's death, Lady May Cumming continued to be a regular visitor. When Hahn was forced to flee from Germany after the Nazi takeover in 1933, she accompanied him to England, provided some of the money with which he founded his new school at Gordonstoun, and became the school's first hostess. In honour of the Cumming family Hahn established a Cumming House which still endures. Cumming's great-nephew Norman Pares (also a friend of Hahn's) became housemaster to Gordonstoun's two most famous pupils, Prince Philip, Duke of Edinburgh, and Charles, Prince of Wales.[174] By the time he fled to England in 1933, Hahn had become a 'source' for SIS.[175] Before the First World War, however, he may well have had no inkling of Mansfield Cumming's intelligence activities, and it is unlikely that he played any direct part in them. But he probably did provide Cumming with a series of introductions in Germany which eased his travels round a country whose language he barely understood.

From 1910 until the outbreak of war the foreign section of the Secret Service Bureau was responsible to the Admiralty, its principal customer, though it also continued to supply intelligence to MO5 at the War Office.[176] Its slender resources meant that, in the words of a secret post-war report, 'its restricted energies were almost entirely directed against Germany'.[177] The main purpose originally envisaged for Cumming's secret espionage agency was to collect evidence of German planning for a sudden 'bolt from the blue' against England. Since no such planning existed, there was no evidence for Cumming to collect. But since evidence of invasion plans was expected of it, the Secret Service Bureau seems to have reported rumours from time to time which suggested that surprise attack remained a possibility. Even at the outbreak of war when the Germans were preoccupied by the attempt to win a lightning victory on the Western Front, Winston Churchill (first lord of the Admiralty from 1911 to 1915) was convinced that they were also making preparations for an invasion of England, and anxiously sought ways 'to get early intelligence of the sailing of the expedition'.[178]

Continued concern over the imaginary menace of a German invasion merely served to distract attention from the real threat of the secret 'Schlieffen Plan' for a German sweep through Belgium to catch the French armies off their guard. The failure to foresee the Schlieffen Plan was by far the costliest error of judgement made by Anglo-French forces on the eve of the First World War. But it was a French rather than a British failure, and a failure of the high command rather than of its intelligence services. The Deuxième Bureau provided sufficient intelligence to indicate at least the possibility of a German sweep through Belgium. Joffre, the French commander-in-chief, confident both of a German attack through Alsace-Lorraine and of a quick French victory, ignored the warning and came perilously close to losing the war in the first six weeks.[179]

Cumming's priorities before the First World War were naval rather than military. As a post-war report acknowledged, however, he lacked the resources to employ full-time agents:

> With the funds then available attempt could only be made to unravel a few technical problems, and for this purpose use had to be made of casual agents whose employment as a class has by war experience been clearly demonstrated to be undesirable.[180]

The best of the 'casual agents' were a handful of men in the shipping or arms industries who were either based in Germany or regularly travelled round it and used their business cover to engage in part-time intelligence work. But, as one of the part-time agents later recalled, much of their work did not really amount to espionage:

> A great deal of information, and that not the least valuable, was collected by perfectly legitimate means. The newspapers published at Kiel, Wilhelmshaven, and Danzig, to say nothing of the Berlin journals, often contained, in spite of careful censorship, Service news which contained useful facts to the trained reader. Again, a trip round Kiel harbour, or along the waterfront of Hamburg or Bremen, where the great shipyards are situated, rarely failed to bring to light some new development of importance. Occasionally, however, it was necessary to resort to less overt measures.[181]

The most successful of Cumming's German networks detected by the Germans was run by Max Schultz, a naturalised Southampton ship-dealer (not to be confused with the German spy Dr 'Phil' Max Schultz). During travels in Germany in 1910–11 Schultz recruited four informants of whom the most important was an engineer named Hipsich in the Weser shipyards at Bremen who was given an advance of £20 and paid £2 a week. According to the findings of the German Supreme Court in December 1911:

> In his official capacity [Hipsich] had an opportunity to learn about plans for battleships and to obtain knowledge of many secret matters. He had made a large collection of drawings and other important materials, and he handed over the whole of it to the English Intelligence office. The great value of this material is best proved by the surprise and unconcealed

pleasure expressed by the Englishmen at the fact that it was at all possible to supply such material.

Hipsich may well have been one of Cumming's most valuable sources. His twelve-year sentence (one of the heaviest at a pre-war espionage trial) reflected the court's belief in the 'great value' of the intelligence he supplied. Schultz was treated more leniently on the grounds both that he was 'to be regarded as a foreigner' who had not shown Hipsich's disregard of patriotism, and that he had confessed the extent of his espionage though not all he knew about the Secret Service Bureau. He was sentenced to seven years in jail. The other three members of his spy-ring received sentences of two or three years.[182]

It is unlikely that Schultz, like Cumming, found espionage 'capital sport'. His trial inevitably strengthened the apprehensions of Cumming's other agents, most of whom found their part-time intelligence work a nerve-wracking experience. One of them said later:

It is safe to say that none of the survivors [of the pre-war secret agents] would ever dream of taking up Intelligence work again, under any consideration whatever. The romantic associations of Secret Service exist largely in the imagination of writers who have had no experience of the real thing ... Every British member of the Intelligence Service abroad with whom I was acquainted took up the work, not in the hope of pecuniary reward, but from motives of patriotism, and in most cases only after repeated and urgent appeals by the I[ntelligence] D[epartment] chiefs in London.[183]

Cumming's German network helped to provide a wealth of technical intelligence on the German navy on subjects from fire-control to range-finders, all of it carefully logged in NID by the head of the German section, Fleet Paymaster C.J.E. Rotter.[184] The majority of reports in Rotter's logbooks came from published sources, but a substantial proportion even of these sources would have passed unnoticed by NID but for Cumming's agents. It is clear that, though far less numerous than published sources, agent reports were of importance in keeping NID informed of the construction programmes of both the *Hochseeflotte* and the U-boats. Agent reports were sometimes the only ones to record the final stages of battleship construction or to give details of U-boat speed and endurance trials.[185]

Cumming also seems to have turned his attention to Zeppelins after a report by the CID technical subcommittee in the summer of 1912 which found it 'difficult to exaggerate the value' (though that is precisely what it did) of airships to Germany both for bombing raids and high-altitude reconnaissance.[186] The probability is that by 1913 Cumming had an agent in Germany reporting on Zeppelin construction. His name was John Herbert-Spottiswoode (often abbreviated to Spottiswoode). Born John Herbert in 1882, he had changed his surname after inheriting the Scottish estate of his great-aunt, Lady Montagu-Douglas-Scott-Spottiswoode in 1900. Like Cumming, Spottiswoode had a passion for both cars and aeroplanes. He worked for a time at Rolls Royce, enjoyed motoring round the Continent, was a good linguist speaking fluent German, and had a number of dealings with the Mercedes-Benz factory. He also became an Avro test pilot and probably got to know Cumming in about 1912 when both were members of the Royal Aero Club. The previous two years had been traumatic ones for Spottiswoode. Thirty-four aviators (some known to him personally), whose names are recorded in Spottiswoode's few remaining papers, were killed in flying accidents in 1910 and 1911. During the same period he ran £10,000 into debt through an unsuccessful flying venture, his marriage began to break up, and he had to sell part of his Scottish estate. Anxious to escape the collapse of both his business and his marriage, Spottiswoode seems to have responded to Cumming's suggestion that he pose as an Irish-American and use his fluent German and aeronautical skill to investigate Zeppelin construction. Spottiswoode later claimed to have actually worked in a Zeppelin factory and to have sent some blueprints of Zeppelin engines back to London. Unlike most of Cumming's 'casual agents', Spottiswoode's pose as an American citizen enabled him to stay on in Germany after the outbreak of war. Before long he was arrested and interned but clung successfully to his claim of American citizenship and was allowed to leave Germany after an operation for acute appendicitis. Like Cumming's other prewar 'casual agents' Spottiswoode would never have considered 'taking up Intelligence work again, under any consideration' whatever. He quarrelled with Cumming after his return and claimed he had 'told the old bastard to clear off back to the *Victory* where he belonged'. His family recall that many years later Spottiswoode still had nightmares about his experiences in Germany.[187]

Cumming failed to gain a complete monopoly of British espionage until after the First World War. Before the war both the Admiralty and the War Office continued on occasion the earlier traditions of the patriotic amateur, usually to the intense annoyance of the Secret Service Bureau. One of Cumming's agents in Germany claimed that among the experiences they 'most dreaded' was 'a visit from some enthusiastic British officer on leave, who had persuaded the authorities at home to put him in touch with the man on the spot' before spending his leave engaged in espionage.[188]

Two such enthusiastic officers on leave were Lieutenant Brandon of the Admiralty Hydrographic Department and Captain Trench of the Royal Marines, who went to reconnoitre German North Sea coastal defences in August 1910. Both men showed their inexperience not merely by the large amount of incriminating documents captured from them but also by their behaviour during cross-examination. Counsel for the prosecution acknowledged that it was only as a result of Trench's evidence at the trial that they knew he had entered the Borkum fortifications at all. In reply to further questions about incriminating correspondence with one 'Reggie', Brandon replied: '"Reggie" is a personal friend of mine. "Sunburnt London" is his private telegraphic address'. Under cross-examination he admitted that '"Reggie" is not the person's name', but when pressed further, replied: 'I decline to give any further information about "Reggie"'.[189] Trench was slightly more forthcoming. '"Reggie"', he admitted, 'is connected with the Intelligence Bureau of the Admiralty'. When asked what the connection was, he refused to say. There were other moments of light relief in the trial. When asked if he knew *The Riddle of the Sands* (which was set on the coastline at the centre of the espionage mission), Brandon replied, amid laughter in court: 'Yes, I have read it three times'. Trench said simply that he knew the book. Both men were sentenced to four years' imprisonment. The trial ended, however, in a remarkably amicable atmosphere, which reflected the gentlemanly traditions of espionage by serving officers and respect for their patriotic motives. According to *The Times* correspondent: 'When it was all over, [Brandon and Trench] remained for some minutes chatting with counsel and others and shaking hands with acquaintances such as the Juge d'Instruction who conducted the preliminary hearing ... They were very gay and perfectly satisfied with the result of the trial'. Their place of imprisonment was to be a fortress where they would be 'allowed to provide their own comforts and to enjoy the society of the officers, students and others, all men of education and good social position, who share the Governor's hospitality in the fortress'. 'There are no irksome regulations', concluded *The Times* report, 'and it will not be difficult for them to obtain leave to make excursions in the town'.[190]

While in the fortress Trench secretly put on paper what he could remember of his espionage mission and smuggled it back to the Admiralty with the help of a visiting priest. He and Brandon were released seventeen months early in May 1913 to mark the German state visit by King George V. Once back at the Admiralty, Trench was dismayed to be told that the information he had smuggled out of the fortress was 'no use'. 'We had', he was told, 'two more following on behind you'. [191] Though Trench was to spend most of his remaining career in naval intelligence, he seems never to have known who the 'two more' were. They were in fact the British vice-consul at Emden and his wife who memorised what the Admiralty considered 'valuable information about the coastal defences'. He put nothing on paper but brought fresh information each time he visited England.[192] Trench learned from his own inexperience under cross-examination. During the Second World War he became one of the ablest naval interrogators, particularly adept at planting 'stool pigeons' among German POWs.[193]

*The Times* expressed indignation at claims in the German press during 1911 that youthful members of the English upper orders were led by their 'sporting instincts' to spy in Germany.[194] 'Sporting instincts' certainly played a part, however, in the brief career of Bertrand Stewart as a secret agent. Stewart was an Old Etonian lawyer with a private income, a member of seven London clubs and a territorial officer. During the Agadir crisis of 1911, when war with Germany seemed in sight, he decided, according to Kell's assistant Captain Drake, that he 'wanted to do something spectacular in the way of discovering German preparations for war', and presented himself at the War Office. From the War Office he was sent to call on Cumming who found him 'without the faintest knowledge of S[ecret] S[ervice] work' and ideas about espionage 'much in the manner of William Le Queux'. But despite his protests, Cumming received orders from the War Office to let Stewart 'have a "run" and act according to his own ideas'.[195]

Stewart's first idea seems to have been to try to discover the whereabouts of *Hochseeflotte* after the Admiralty lost track of it during the Agadir crisis, by doing the rounds of the German ports. 'The whole thing is like a Pantomime', complained the DMO, Brigadier-General (later Field-Marshal) Sir Henry Wilson. By the time Stewart left, however, the *Hochseeflotte* had turned up again, and Stewart decided instead to pose as 'a traitor ready to betray his country' in order to 'worm his way into the confidence of the German Intelligence and so glean information of the utmost value'. Cumming told him 'he was running his head into a noose'. Stewart swiftly did so. Crossing into Holland he made contact with the longest-serving 'casual agent' Rué, who was now a double agent working for the Germans and lured Stewart over the frontier with promises of secret documents. Stewart was handed allegedly secret papers in Bremen, suddenly realised he had been trapped, and made for the nearest public lavatory where he tried unsuccessfully to dispose of the documents. He was arrested before he had time to do so. His father told *The Times* that his son's adventures demonstrated only that 'young men will be young men', and that the conduct of international relations required more experienced men with 'steady heads' and 'discreet tongues'. The War Office was sufficiently embarrassed by the whole affair to announce publicly that it had ordered all officers travelling in Germany in future to 'inform the local authorities of their presence'. *The Times* considered this order 'opportune and likely to create a good impression'.[196]

As well as sending agents to Germany itself, Cumming also had agents collecting German intelligence in Rotterdam, Brussels and St Petersburg. There were problems in all three cities. The head of Cumming's operations in Rotterdam was a retired naval lieutenant (later captain), Richard Tinsley (codenamed T), who had built up a successful shipping business which he used as a cover for intelligence work. But the young diplomat Ivone Kirkpatrick (later permanent undersecretary at the Foreign Office) found T 'a liar and a first-class intriguer with few scruples'. During the war he became involved in blackmail.[197] Cumming's Belgian network was larger but even shadier than the Dutch. His head of operations in Brussels from 1910 until the outbreak of war was an engineer called Henry Dale Long (codenamed L) who by 1914 had at least three other agents working with him and a fourth at Dinant.[198] But Cumming's Brussels network became involved with the free-lance Brussels spy bureaux who peddled sometimes doubtful intelligence to the highest bidder and had already deceived Baden-Powell and others with bogus German invasion plans. Cumming was persuaded to part with £600 to purchase in Brussels an alleged German codebook which a wartime cryptanalyst was later to expose as 'a pup of the poorest class'.[199] Rear-Admiral Sir Henry Oliver, DNI from 1913 until three months after the outbreak of war, later concluded that the 'head agent' in Brussels, Captain James Cuffe of the Royal Marines, had 'double-crossed us'. 'In this underground business', he concluded, 'there is always the danger of being double-crossed'.[200]

Cumming's most remarkable, though not his most reliable, agent was Sidney Reilly in St Petersburg, the dominating figure in the mythology of modern British espionage. Reilly, it has been claimed, 'wielded more power, authority and influence than any other spy', was an expert assassin 'by poisoning, stabbing, shooting and throttling', and possessed 'eleven passports and a wife to go with each'.[201] The reality, though far less sensational, is still remarkable. Reilly was born Sigmund Georgievich Rosenblum in 1874, the only son of a rich Jewish landowner and contractor in Russian Poland. Some time in the 1890s he left home, broke off all contact with his family, and emigrated to London. At the turn of the century, having changed his name to Reilly, he moved to Port Arthur, the base of the Russian Far Eastern Fleet, where he worked first as partner in a firm of timber merchants, then as manager of the Danish Compagnie Est-Asiatique. By the time Reilly returned to London on the eve of the Russo-Japanese War in 1904, he had become a self-confident international adventurer, fluent in several languages, already weaving around his cosmopolitan career a web of fantasy which has since ensnared most of those who write about him. 'He had', writes his most recent biographer, 'passed his test with the SIS with flying colours, and they decided that they had a most promising recruit on their hands, who merited very special training'.[202] Not the least problem with this romantic view of Reilly's intelligence initiation is that SIS did not yet exist. It is quite possible, though there is no proof, that Reilly did provide NID with intelligence on the Russian Far Eastern Fleet during his years in Port Arthur. But it is scarcely possible that his unusual experience of higher education over the next few years was specially devised as a training programme by NID.[203] In 1904–5 he successfully completed a year's course in electrical engineering in the Royal School of Mines. In October 1905 he went up to Trinity College, Cambridge, as an 'advanced student' but left two or three years later without taking any degree. To gain admission to both the Royal School of Mines and Trinity College, Reilly used a bogus certificate from Roorkee University in India and claimed, also falsely, to have been born in Calcutta and worked as an engineer on

Indian railways. After leaving Cambridge, Reilly invented a different but fictitious postgraduate career, and enjoyed boasting that he had a doctorate from Heidelberg.[204] Reilly's extraordinary range of personal fantasies, some of which seem to have deceived himself as well as others, went far beyond the practical needs of providing intelligence 'cover'. According to one of his secretaries, Eleanor Toye, 'Reilly used to suffer from severe mental crises amounting to delusion. Once he thought he was Jesus Christ'.[205]

But Reilly also had a remarkable personal charisma and flair for intelligence work which was to win the admiration of both Cumming and Winston Churchill. Robert Bruce Lockhart, the first British diplomat to arrive in Bolshevik Russia, who had a generally low opinion of Cumming's agents, made an exception in the case of Reilly. Though Lockhart had 'not a very high opinion of his intelligence' and thought his range of knowledge superficial, he found his courage and indifference to danger 'superb' and his personality a mixture of 'the artistic temperament of the Jew with the devil-may-care daring of the Irishman'. Probably soon after Cumming took over the foreign section of the Secret Service Bureau, Reilly established himself in St Petersburg as a successful commission agent for a variety of businesses and the Russian agent for the Hamburg shipbuilders Blohm and Voss.[206] According to a recent biographer, relying presumably on Reilly's own immodest account of his exploits, this position allowed him to make the most astonishing intelligence coup:

> For three vital years before the outbreak of the First World War, the British Admiralty were kept up to date with every new design or modification in the German fleet – tonnage, speeds, armament, crew and every detail even down to cooking equipment.[207]

Such claims are impossible to reconcile either with the later official admission that Cumming's pre-war agents had collectively succeeded only in unravelling 'a few technical problems' or with the surviving files of NID.[208] But Reilly clearly did enough to persuade Cumming to take him on again half-way through the First World War. Characteristically, Reilly combined both business and part-time espionage in pre-war St Petersburg with a variety of expensive pleasures and a bigamous marriage to a beautiful Russian divorcee.[209]

Given the bizarre circumstances of the Secret Service Bureau's birth, prompted by the imaginary menace of a German invasion, the exiguous funds devoted to it, and the general ignorance of modern intelligence gathering and counter-espionage within Whitehall, neither Kell nor Cumming could reasonably be expected to have accomplished much more than they had achieved by the outbreak of war. Of the two, Kell was the better prepared for war, both because the problem of German wartime espionage was to prove relatively limited, and because the cooperation of the Metropolitan Special

Branch and other police forces enabled him to stretch his own limited resources. Cumming's small network of part-time agents, however, could not possibly cope with the vastly increased demands of wartime intelligence gathering.

As well as being chronically undermanned and underfinanced, Britain's foreign intelligence network on the eve of the First World War also contained one crucial gap. Until the emergence of spy satellites in the 1960s the most important category of twentieth-century intelligence was signals intelligence or sigint. The great powers learned more of their rivals' secrets by intercepting and decrypting their diplomatic and military communications than by the use of secret agents. By 1914 several continental powers already had secret *cabinets noirs* or 'black chambers' specialising in sigint. Both France and Russia had broken, at least intermittently, British diplomatic codes. A century before, the Foreign Office had had its own codebreaking department, the Decyphering Branch, but by the early twentieth century the British government had put such practices far behind it. Indeed the Foreign Office was now such a byword for diplomatic probity that the Cambon brothers, French ambassadors in London and Berlin, fearing to entrust their private correspondence either to the French post office or to the French foreign ministry (both of whom opened interesting letters), regularly corresponded via the British Diplomatic Bag instead.[210] Until the British government was prepared to adopt the less gentlemanly practices of its continental rivals it could not hope to develop a modern intelligence system. The event which persuaded it to do so was the First World War. Under the pressure of war, and after a break of seventy years, the British government began once again to intercept other governments' communications. It has never stopped since.

# 3 | ROOM 40:
THE REBIRTH OF BRITISH
CODEBREAKING

On 4 August 1914, the day that Britain went to war, Rear-Admiral (later Admiral of the Fleet Sir) Henry 'Dummy' Oliver, the taciturn Director of Naval Intelligence (DNI or DID), received a series of coded signals believed to be of enemy origin from an Admiralty wireless station. Other intercepts landed on his desk over the next few days from the Marconi Company and the Post Office. At first Oliver had little idea what to do with them. Then while walking to the United Services Club one day in mid-August to lunch with the Director of Naval Education, Sir Alfred Ewing, it suddenly struck Oliver that Ewing was 'the very man I wanted'. Ewing was a short, softly-spoken Scot with piercing blue eyes and, in Oliver's view, 'very great brainpower, in fact a man who stood out among clever men'. In the course of a career as Professor of Engineering at Tokyo, Dundee and Cambridge Universities, he had acquired 'an expert knowledge of radio-telegraphy' and briefly dabbled in codes and ciphers. Ewing's work as Director of Naval Education was disrupted by the decision to mobilise naval cadets at the outbreak of war. Oliver, as usual, did not waste words. He told Ewing bluntly that since 'education would probably be considered of little importance for the next few months', he would do better to apply himself to the intercepted enemy signals. Ewing agreed.[1]

The Admiralty had as yet no inkling of the revolution in naval intelligence which Ewing would inaugurate. For centuries past, frigates and look-out vessels had patrolled off foreign harbours in time of war to bring back warning as soon as the enemy fleet put to sea. By 1914 the minefield and the submarine had made such ancient methods of intelligence-gathering suicidal folly. 'The risk to such ships', instructed the first lord of the Admiralty, Winston Churchill, on 18 September, 'is not justified by any services they can render'. Four days later, before his instructions had been acted on, three cruisers on slow patrol near the Dogger bank were sunk by a single submarine with the loss of 1,400 lives.[2]

While one form of naval intelligence came to an abrupt and tragic end in the North Sea, another was slowly emerging in Ewing's office. On 5 August the British cable ship *Telconia* began cutting Germany's overseas telegraph cables, forcing her to resort either to wireless messages or to foreign cables which could be tapped by her enemies. As a result a stream of German intercepts poured daily into the Admiralty. Early in September a barrister friend of Ewing, Russell Clarke, called on him with the news that he and another radio ham, the Somerset squire Colonel Hippisley, had been listening to German signals on their receiving sets. With better facilities, both claimed, they could intercept messages on lower wave-lengths than the Admiralty. Ewing quickly obtained permission for Clarke and Hippisley to set up an interception post in Hunstanton Coastguard Station: the first of fourteen wartime listening posts manned by GPO operators in the British Isles, all with direct land lines to the Admiralty. Hippisley was also to set up three interception stations overseas in Otranto, Malta and Ancona. During the early weeks of the war, however, Ewing could make little sense of the increasing flow of intercepts. He spent some days delving, with little success, into all the codebooks he could find at Lloyds, the British Museum and the GPO. The bogus German codebook purchased by Cumming earlier in the year merely added to his problems until it was exposed as 'a pup of the poorest class'. As Director of Naval Education, Ewing sought assistance first in the naval colleges of Dartmouth and Osborne which sent four language teachers to the Admiralty to help him during their summer vacation. The ablest of these volunteers, A.G. 'Alastair' Denniston, like Ewing a diminutive Scot though also a considerable athlete, later became operational head of interwar signals intelligence (sigint) and the first head of Bletchley Park in the Second World War. The teachers were joined by Lord Herschell, Lord in Waiting to King George V, on the strength of his – rather dubious – reputation as a German linguist. Apart from their knowledge of German, Ewing's recruits had no qualification for codebreaking save 'a reputation for discretion'. Not one knew anything about cryptography. Denniston wrote later: 'Cryptographers did not exist, so far as we knew'.[3]

While Ewing was recruiting his first apprentice cryptographers, the War Office was simultaneously establishing a codebreaking unit of its own under Brigadier F.J. Anderson who had had some experience of communications intelligence in the field during the Boer War. Ewing sent Denniston and another Osborne linguist, W.H. Anstie, to liaise with the War Office unit, soon to be known as MI1b. At the same time he strengthened his own team by recruiting two naval instructors (Parish and Curtis) with some grasp of mathematics. In the early stages of the war, with no great naval battle yet in prospect and the Germans threatening to win a lightning victory in France, military signals seemed clearly more important than their naval counterparts. As the Germans swept through Belgium to threaten Paris Denniston dis-covered that 'their movements could be dimly observed' even from *en clair* (uncoded) wireless traffic. For almost two months the War Office, like the Admiralty, made little progress with cipher traffic apart from identifying the call signs of a series of German stations. According to Denniston, Brigadier Anderson's staff proceeded 'with the utmost enthusiasm and entire lack of discretion'. On 1 October cryptanalysts at the French war ministry at last cracked the main German military code in use on the Western Front and passed on the solution to the British. The work of decrypting German military traffic was then briefly shared between Anderson's and Ewing's staffs. But, as Denniston noted, 'signs of jealousy' were apparent from the start and by mid-October all cooperation had ceased. Denniston believed that 'a climax was reached' when Churchill told Kitchener, his opposite number in the War Office, the contents of a military intercept '*before* his own section had managed to get the information through to him'. The breach between the codebreakers of the War Office and the Admiralty remained total until the spring of 1917 when limited cooperation (consisting chiefly of an exchange of decrypts) was resumed. During the two and a half years of non-cooperation the codebreakers of the Admiralty were to establish a decisive lead over their rivals at the War Office. As the early war of movement gave way to the relative immobility of trench warfare the volume and significance of German military radio messages rapidly declined. And, despite some successes, British military cryptanalysts were overshadowed by the more experienced and more successful French. None the less the Admiralty as well as the War Office suffered from the breach between them. Denniston wrote later:

> Looking back over the work of those years, the loss of efficiency to both departments caused originally by mere official jealousy is the most regrettable fact in the development of intelligence based on cryptography.[4]

At the time of the breach with the War Office, Ewing had a total staff of six cryptanalysts: Naval Instructors Parish and Curtis, Professor J.B. Henderson from the Greenwich Naval College, Denniston, Lord Herschell and R.D. Norton from the Foreign Office.[5] The first three knew mathematics but little German, the others German but little mathematics. 'All six', wrote Denniston, 'were singularly ignorant of cryptography ...' The apprentice cryptographers were cramped as well as inexperienced. Since all six could not squeeze simultaneously into Ewing's office, they worked a shift system, but the room was scarcely big enough even for three. When Ewing received visitors, the cryptographers had to gather up their papers and disappear into the adjoining boxroom used by Ewing's secretary Mountstephen. After the decision to reopen the naval colleges in October, Ewing himself had to divide his time between cryptography and naval education.[6]

While still groping awkwardly in the dark the cryptographers received three remarkable windfalls from three quite different sources: the Royal Australian

Navy, the Imperial Russian Navy and a British trawler captain. By early December these windfalls had given Ewing's team all three of the main German naval codes. The first to be captured was the *Handelsverkehrsbuch* (HVB) used chiefly by the German Admiralty and warships to communicate with merchantmen but also employed within the High Sea Fleet itself. It was seized near Melbourne on 11 August by an Australian boarding party from a German-Australian steamship still unaware that war had been declared. Failing to realise the importance of the HVB, the Australian Naval Board omitted to inform London of its capture for another month. It did not reach the Admiralty until the end of October. German signal security was so poor that it continued in use by German outpost vessels and airships until March 1916.[7]

By the time the HVB arrived in the Admiralty, Ewing had received a much more important windfall from the Russians: the *Signalbuch der Kaiserlichen Marine* (SKM). On 6 September Churchill was brought news by the Russian naval attaché that the German light cruiser *Magdeburg* had been wrecked in the Baltic:

> The body of a drowned German under-officer was picked up by the Russians a few hours later, and clasped in his bosom by arms rigid in death were the cypher and signal books of the German Navy ...

After some delay HMS *Theseus* set sail from Scapa Flow to bring a copy of the SKM back to Britain. On 13 October Churchill and the First Sea Lord, Prince Louis of Battenberg, 'received from our loyal allies these sea-stained priceless documents'. Churchill's enthusiastic account of the Russian gift is probably romanticised. The copy of the SKM (declassified only in 1980) in the Public Record Office shows no sign of sea-staining, and was probably recovered from the *Magdeburg* more prosaically than Churchill was led to believe. Though it was indeed a 'priceless' gift, it did not immediately provide the key to high-grade German naval signals. Only weather reports were coded simply in the SKM; all other signals were coded and then reciphered.[8] Probably disappointed by the slow progress of his apprentice cryptographers, Ewing failed at first to take them into his confidence. In mid-October there were frequent visits from the Russian naval attaché during which they were banished to the boxroom. There followed several days when Ewing was away from the Admiralty and an unidentified naval officer worked long hours in the boxroom. The cryptographers were 'almost rudely discouraged' from entering, but were asked to retrieve from Ewing's cupboards the coded intercepts which had so far defeated them. The mysterious officer in the boxroom entrusted by Ewing with the HVB and the intercepts was Fleet Paymaster (later Captain) Charles J.E. Rotter, the principal German expert in NID. Ewing seems not to have grasped the principles of re-encipherment and initially instructed Rotter to decode all German intercepts strictly according to the *Magdeburg* codebook in the mistaken hope that the incomprehensible results might somehow yield a meaning. Years later another naval codebreaker, William F. ('Nobby') Clarke, while looking through Rotter's papers, came across 'sheet after sheet of paper filled with incomprehensible symbols, a testimony to the incompetent direction of Sir Alfred and the uncomplaining efforts of Rotter doing a job at the direction of his chief which he must have realised quite early were entirely misdirected'. But in the evenings Rotter applied himself to what he recognised as the underlying problem of re-encipherment and eventually discovered that the key consisted of a comparatively simple substitution table (a=r, b=h, etc).[9]

At the beginning of November Ewing at last introduced Rotter to his curious staff and told them the story of the capture of the HVB. Though the Germans soon changed the key to their cipher, the new key, which remained in use for three months, was solved by Rotter more quickly than the first.[10] Within a month the cryptographers had received a further remarkable stroke of luck which they christened 'The Miraculous Draught of Fishes'. On 30 November a British trawler fishing off the Texel found in its nets a lead-lined chest from a sunken German destroyer. Among the papers recovered from the chest was a copy of the *Verkehrsbuch* (VB), the last of the three German naval codes. By 3 December it was in the hands of the Admiralty.[11]

The *Magdeburg* codebook and Rotter's success together fired Winston Churchill with an enthusiasm for signals intelligence which was to last for the rest of his life. On 8 November he composed a memorandum for which he devised the unique formula 'Exclusively Secret', initialled by himself and by Battenberg's successor as First Sea Lord, Jackie Fisher:

> An officer of the War Staff, preferably from the I[ntelligence] D[ivision], should be selected to study all the decoded intercepts, not only current but past, and to compare them continually with what actually took place in order to penetrate the German mind and movements and make reports. All these intercepts are to be written in a locked book with their decodes and all other copies are to be collected and burnt. All new messages are to be entered in the book and the book is only to be handled under instructions from C[hief] O[f the Admiralty War] S[taff].
>
> The officer selected is for the present to do no other work. I shall be obliged if Sir Alfred Ewing will associate himself continuously with this work.[12]

Churchill was the first British minister to grasp the potential importance of sigint. But his belief that a single officer was capable of studying all the intercepts 'not only current but past' and comparing them 'continually with what took place' shows that in November 1914 even he had no idea of the sheer scale sigint was soon to acquire. Churchill's proposal to enter all the intercepts in a single 'locked book' to be made available only on the orders of the COS was also quite impracticable, and he was persuaded to allow additional copies of the intercepts to be forwarded in sealed envelopes to the COS and DID. 'The log', one of the cryptographers later recalled, 'became an object of hatred':

> ... In the days when a watchkeeper averaged 12 messages it could be written up, though even then it was the fashion to let the messages accumulate and allow the new watch to write up the log and thus appreciate the situation! But it was beyond a joke when naval actions were pending or Zepp[elin]s fluttering and the watchkeeper had 12 or 20 pages of the book to write up.[13]

Even more important to naval codebreaking than the blessing of Winston Churchill was the appointment following 'Dummy' Oliver's promotion to COS early in November 1914 of a new Director of the Intelligence Division, forty-four year old Captain (later Admiral Sir) William Reginald 'Blinker' Hall, son of the first DNI, Captain William Henry Hall. 'Blinker' Hall had been an able captain of the battle cruiser *Queen Mary* until uncertain health forced him to give up his command when the war was only three months old. He was a Punch-like figure, prematurely bald with a large hook-nose. The wartime secret agent Compton Mackenzie found him very like his own chief Mansfield Cumming: 'His nose was beakier; his chin had a more pronounced cutwater. Nevertheless, when I looked at the two men I could have fancied that each was a caricature of the other'. Unlike Cumming, however, Hall had a pronounced facial twitch and a habit of high-speed blinking which gave him his nickname. When not blinking, he also possessed a piercing gaze of quite unusual intensity. Compton Mackenzie felt 'like a nut about to be cracked by a toucan' when Hall fixed him with 'a horn-rimmed horny eye'.[14] Dr Walter Page, the American ambassador in London was, quite literally, spellbound in Hall's presence:

> Neither in fiction nor in fact can you find any such man to match him ... The man is a genius – a clear case of genius. All other secret service men are amateurs by comparison ... I shall never meet another man like him; that were too much to expect.
>
> For Hall can look through you and see the very muscular movements of your immortal soul while he is talking to you. Such eyes as the man has! My Lord![15]

Hall quickly performed two important services for the naval cryptographers. First, he found them less cramped accommodation in Room 40 in the Admiralty Old Building. As their numbers grew, the cryptographers spilled over into a series of adjoining rooms but continued to be known collectively as 'Room 40 O.B.', a name sufficiently innocuous to give no hint of its significance. When Lord Balfour succeeded Churchill as First Lord of the Admiralty in May 1915, he sometimes referred to the cryptographers by the alternative pseudonym 'the Japanese', because of their allegedly Oriental inscrutability.[16]

Hall's second great service to Room 40, in November 1914, was to appoint Commander (later Admiral) Herbert W.W. Hope to analyse the German intercepts and provide the professional naval expertise which the cryptographers lacked – or, as Hall put it, 'to sift the messages and extract the juice'. Hope was put at first in a small room in the NID some way from Room 40 where he received at most half a dozen intercepts a day which he found 'not, in themselves, of much importance and, in some cases, not very intelligible'. The comments he added were, he later confessed, 'very amateurish'. 'Dummy' Oliver, now COS, took a dim view both of the comments and of Hope himself. 'I realised', wrote Hope, 'that if I was to make anything out of these messages it was absolutely necessary that I should be in close touch with the producers and that I must have access to the Holy of Holies where these messages were produced'. After some initial opposition (probably from Ewing) Hope gained admittance to Room 40 on 16 November and 'was introduced to the Mystery'. He knew almost no German and no cryptography at all. But 'Nobby' Clarke, who worked under him and was usually a hard judge, felt none the less that his consummate seamanship and ability to read the enemy's mind made his election 'a stroke of genius': 'If one took him a version of a German signal, which one had carefully prepared, he would often say: "I do not like that, can it not be ——?" and he was practically always right'.[17]

By the time Hope joined Room 40 the number of intercepts decrypted each day was steadily increasing.[18] The cryptographers were helped not merely by the captured codebooks and their own increasing skill but also by the lax security of the Germans. The German naval high command was well aware of the danger that the *Magdeburg* codebook had been captured by the enemy but evidently considered it sufficient simply to change the key.[19] Each night every German squadron and unit was ordered to report its position by radio, thus allowing Hope to work out 'their complete organisation'. Submarine commanders in particular showed little grasp of wireless security:

> It was very amusing (altho' rather sad) to note the pride and haste with which the C.O. of a homeward bound submarine would signal his report of tonnage of ships sunk as soon as he got into the North Sea; we used to note that the figures given by the C.O. always required to be cut down by about 50 per cent.

Even when the German navy introduced frequent key changes, it still continued to send out large numbers of routine signals which Room 40 was able to anticipate and found of great assistance in solving the new keys.[20]

At the end of 1914 Ewing had five permanent staff in Room 40. Hope was responsible for analysing the decrypts, Rotter for the codebreaking proper. Each worked from nine in the morning to seven at night. In addition Herschell, Denniston and Norton worked as 'watchkeepers', decoding, translating and logging intercepts as they came in. Naval instructors Parish and Curtis and Professor Henderson worked as part-time watchkeepers when not required for naval education. 'A never-ending stream of postmen' arrived in Room 40 from the telegraph office in the Admiralty basement bearing bundles of intercepts sent in by the growing network of wireless stations. During the spring of 1915 the postmen were replaced by a pneumatic tube from the basement which discharged metal cylinders containing intercepts into a wire basket with a whoosh and thump which 'shook the nerve of any unwitting visitor and very much disturbed the slumbers of a night-watchman taking his time off'. For a time all intelligible messages were entered by the watchmen in the logbook and copies prepared for Hope, Hall and Oliver. Unintelligible messages and fragments were logged but not circulated and put in a tin which bore the large, black letters 'N.S.L.' ('Not Sent, Logged'). Later unintelligible intercepts were often not logged at all and 'N.S.L.' came to mean 'Neither Sent nor Logged'.[21]

The very success of Room 40 led to a dispute for control of it between Ewing and Hall. Ewing wished to retain personal command of the cryptographers; Hall wanted to incorporate them into the Intelligence Division. In the summer of 1915 Oliver, as COS, was forced to arbitrate between them. Oliver retained a high respect for what he considered Ewing's mixture of 'very great brainpower' and common sense. He therefore laid down a rather confused compromise which more or less confirmed the status quo. Ewing retained control of Room 40; Hall retained the right of direct access to it.[22] In practice Hope effectively replaced Ewing as the operational head of Room 40 and looked for guidance to Hall rather than to Ewing. Ewing's influence waned steadily. Even his son later acknowledged that 'in the discovery of the enemy cipher Ewing took little direct part, except during the first year', and that his staff included men 'whose faculty for that kind of inspired guessing and quick inference was far greater than his own'.[23] Some of his staff took a much dimmer view of Ewing's role. According to 'Nobby' Clarke, 'he never really understood the problems and wasted more valuable time of his subordinates than can be imagined'.[24] On 1 October 1916 Ewing resigned as Director of Naval Education to become vice-chancellor of Edinburgh University. He was pained to hear the university tailor remark, as he tried on the vice-chancellor's gown: 'Yes, we'll hae to shorten it … We'll hae to tak a couple of the frogs off it and pit them awa'. Maybe we'll get a langer Vice-Chancellor next time.'[25] For a time Ewing continued to commute to Room 40 once a week but in May 1917 he left the Admiralty altogether. Room 40 was then formally incorporated into the NID as section 25 of the department – ID25. [26]

Despite his limitations as a cryptographer, Ewing performed one service for Room 40 which was of great importance during the First World War and served as a vital precedent in the Second. He recruited to Room 40 what Denniston was to call in the early days of Bletchley Park 'men of the professor type': civilian intellectuals whom most Admirals would never have dreamed of involving in naval affairs. The single most valuable source of 'professor types' was Ewing's former Cambridge college, King's, with which he retained close links notably through his son-in-law who was a Fellow. Early in 1915 King's provided Room 40 with its 'most brilliant member', Alfred Dillwyn Knox. 'Dilly' Knox was the second of four remarkable sons of the bishop of Manchester. Edmund, the eldest, later became editor of *Punch*; Wilfred was an Anglo-Catholic theologian, later Canon of Ely Cathedral and Fellow of Pembroke College, Cambridge; Ronald, the youngest, who also worked for a time in Room 40, was winning a reputation as 'the wittiest young man in England' and the most influential Roman Catholic convert of his generation. Dilly himself was an Old Etonian classicist, briefly tutor to Harold Macmillan, who had quickly established himself as a leading King's eccentric and a prominent supporter of his friend Maynard Keynes's campaign against the Bursar. In successive issues of the King's journal *Basileon*, Dilly called on the Bursar to inspect the rats in Fellows' rooms, then to protect the rats from attack by water-rats attracted by the rising damp, and finally to have a care for the water-rats whose 'nasty cough' was disturbing younger Fellows' repose. Dilly was also pursued for a time by the predatory homosexual Lytton Strachey who complained that: 'His method is, you see, to lure you on with his beauty, until at last, just as you step forward to seize a kiss, or whatever else you may want to seize, he lets down a veil, and you simply fall back disgusted. Isn't it a horrid trick?' Dilly did some of his best work for Room 40 lying in a bath in Room 53, claiming that codes were most easily cracked in an atmosphere of soap and steam.[27] His belief in the creative powers of bathtime lasted into the Second World War. One of his colleagues at Bletchley Park was to write of him:

> At his billet [Dilly] once stayed so long in the bathroom that his fellow-lodgers at last forced the door. They found him standing by the bath, a faint smile on his face, his gaze fixed on abstractions, both taps full on and the plug out. What then was passing in his mind could possibly have solved a problem that was to win a battle.[28]

Somewhat improbably, one of Room 40's few romances blossomed in the bathroom. Miss Olive Roddam, sent to Room 53 as Dilly's secretary, married him soon after the end of the war.[29]

Two other Fellows of King's were among the leading figures of Room 40 during the Hope (or Ewing) era. The ancient historian, Frank Adcock (later knighted and Professor of Ancient History at Cambridge), who had studied in Berlin and Munich, arrived at about the same time as Dilly. In 1916 Knox and Adcock were joined by the King's historian Frank Birch, who had arrived as an undergraduate from Eton in 1909, a year before Dilly became a Fellow. Birch was a brilliant conversationalist and comic actor, later becoming the first Fellow of King's to appear as the Widow Twankey in pantomime at the London Palladium. One of the best-known items in his undergraduate repertoire was a macabre impersonation of the Classics don J.E. Dixon who lacked a hand and an eye and, in Birch's sketch, entirely dismantled himself in his room each night. Even as an undergraduate Birch had a deep influence on Knox, liberating within him, it has been claimed, a 'vein of wild fantasy'.[30] Knox in turn provided Birch with some of the inspiration for his classified comic history of Room 40, *Alice in I.D.25*:[31]

> The sailor in Room 53
> Has never, it's true, been to sea
> But though not in a boat
> He has yet served afloat –
> In a bath at the Admiralty.

Knox also appears in Birch's history as 'Dilly the Dodo', working in a bathing machine: '"My idea", smiled the Dodo self-consciously; "you see, with an ordinary bathing-machine, you have to leave it to bathe. But in this one you can bathe without leaving it".' The Dodo also suffers from Dilly's angular frame and absent-minded untidiness:

> Alice thought he was the queerest bird she had ever seen. He was so long and lean, and he had outgrown his clothes, and his face was like a pang of hunger...
>
> 'Perhaps you would like to see some of my work', [he asked] and he handed her a sheet of very dirty paper on which a spider with inky feet appeared to have been crawling.

The spruce and slightly fussy Frank Adcock was a quite different figure. Birch portrays him as the White Rabbit:

> ... obviously very important and in a great hurry. He was dressed in his Sunday best – spats, spectacles, and a little black coat, and he kept doing up and undoing its buttons with nervousness.
>
> 'Dear me, dear me,' Alice heard him say as he passed her, 'it's past ten. I shall be late for the DIND ["Blinker" Hall], I *must* be there when he comes round. I *always* am,' and with that he bustled out of earshot.

The King's classicists were joined in 1916 by a theologian from Westminster College, Cambridge, the Reverend William Montgomery, a tall grey-haired authority on St Augustine and the early church fathers as well as a noted translator of German theology. Other classicists to arrive in Room 40 later in the war included John Beazley from Oxford, the foremost authority on Greek vases, and Ernest Harrison, Tutor of Trinity College, Oxford. There was also a succession of modern languages dons beginning with two young German lecturers, Edward Bullough from Cambridge and Leonard Willoughby from Oxford, later followed by E.C. Quiggin and two of his pupils (C.W. Hardisty and W.H. Bruford) from Cambridge, Neville Forbes from Oxford, Gilbert Waterhouse from Dublin, Douglas Savoy from Belfast, C.E. Gough from Leeds and F.E. Sandbach from Birmingham.[32]

Curiously, despite Ewing's background in engineering, none of the university dons were mathematicians. Room 40 seems to have shared something of the arts graduate's traditional suspicion that, whatever their dexterity with numbers, able mathematicians tend to have withdrawn, uncommunicative and unimaginative personalities which make them unsuitable for the collaborative solution of practical problems. When the first American codebreaking unit, the Black Chamber, later sought advice from its British allies on the right kind of recruit, it was told to beware of mathematicians. What was needed was 'an active, well trained and scholarly mind, not mathematical but classical.'[33]

Like Ewing, 'Blinker' Hall was actively involved in recruiting for Room 40 from the moment he became DID. In December 1914 he made one of Room 40's earliest recruits, the Old Etonian Lord Herschell, his personal assistant. Hall seems to have had a weakness for Old Etonians. Convinced that he required 'men of wider experience of the world' than the Admiralty or Whitehall could provide, he took on as a second personal assistant the Old Etonian stockbroker Claud Serocold who struck Frank Birch as 'a slim well-groomed creature with a black moustache' (later removed). Between them, Hall's two assistants had an impressive range of acquaintances within the establishment. It was probably through Serocold and Herschell that Hall recruited for Room 40 two Old Etonian peers, Lords Lytton and Monk Bretton, and other well-connected German speakers from a wide variety of professions: among them Ben Faudel-Phillips, Lionel Fraser and Frank Tiarks from the City, W.F. Clarke (the son of Oscar Wilde's counsel) from the law, Nigel de Grey from publishing, the dress-designer Edward Molyneux, the art expert H.W. Lawrence and his actor brother Gerald, the critic Desmond McCarthy, the cartoonist G.P. Mackeson, and the authors H.A. Morrah and G.C. Rawson.[34] Nigel de Grey, depicted by Birch as 'the Dormouse' ('very quiet and apparently asleep'), became, after his fellow Old Etonian Dilly Knox, the ablest codebreaker in Room 40. He was not, however, the most convivial:

The animals were pushing and dragging the dormouse into the passage ...
'What's the matter?' asked Alice, who felt sorry for the poor creature.
Whereupon they all screamed: 'He does his own work and minds his own
business. We don't want *that* sort of thing here', and pushed him out of
the room.[35]

As Room 40 expanded, it acquired a female secretarial staff under the
formidable, cigar-smoking Lady Hambro, wife of a city banker. Birch called
her 'Big Ben' 'because she's so striking'. Alice found her 'a huge creature
conducting an orchestra of typewriters with the much-bitten end of a pencil'
until 'she shouted "Tea" in an authoritative voice, whereupon the typewriting
creatures all ran out of the room and an entirely different lot of animals took
their places.'[36]

Room 40 contained probably the oddest collection of people ever to work in
the Admiralty. Together they provided better intelligence than ever before in
British history. Their greatest achievement was to make surprise attack
impossible. Until Room 40 got into its stride, the Grand Fleet, based
inconveniently far north at Scapa Flow in the Orkneys, was forced to spend
much of its time sweeping the North Sea for an enemy it failed to find,
continually fearful of being caught off its guard. But from December 1914
until the war was over no major movement by the German *Hochseeflotte* –
save, briefly, in 1918 – escaped the notice of the cryptanalysts. The first
warning provided by Room 40 of a major German sortie came on 14 December
when Admiral Friedrich von Ingenohl, commander-in-chief of the *Hochseeflotte*,
ordered a raid by his battle cruisers under Admiral Franz von Hipper on
British east coast towns, combined with a minelaying expedition off the
Yorkshire coast. On the same evening Jellicoe was warned that the German
battle cruisers would be setting out next day. Oliver, however, wrongly deduced
from incomplete intelligence – as usual without consulting Room 40 – that
the German battleships were 'very unlikely to come out'. Unaware that the
German battle fleet *had* been ordered to support Hipper's raid from a position
in the middle of the North Sea, the Admiralty therefore ordered only part of
the Grand Fleet to come south from Scapa Flow to lay a trap for the German
battle cruisers.[37]
    At 8.30 a.m. on 16 December while Churchill lay soaking in his
bath, the door burst open and an officer hurried in with a naval signal
which the First Lord of the Admiralty 'grasped with dripping hand'.
The now damp signal reported 'German battle-cruisers bombarding
Hartlepool'. Jumping out of the bath 'with exclamations', Churchill pulled
on his clothes over a still moist body, raced downstairs to the War
Room, conferred excitedly with Fisher and Oliver, and ordered the trap to
be sprung.[38]

What happened in the remainder of that day later appeared to both sides as a tragically wasted opportunity to win a major victory. The first contact between the opposing fleets took place between Vice-Admiral Sir George Warrender's Second Battle Squadron and the light forces screening the *Hochseeflotte*. Wrongly believing he was facing the whole of Jellicoe's forces, Ingenohl broke away and thus missed an opportunity which would never recur to engage a detachment of the Grand Fleet with superior German forces. 'On 16 December', wrote the father of the *Hochseeflotte*, Admiral von Tirpitz, a few weeks later, 'Ingenohl had the fate of Germany in the palm of his hand. I boil with inward emotion whenever I think of it.'[39]

By 11 a.m., his mission completed but denied the protection of the *Hochseeflotte*, Hipper was heading without realising it for a trap laid by the battle cruisers of Admiral Beatty and the six battleships of Warrender. At 11.25 the two sides' light cruisers made contact. Beatty wrote later with the same sense of exasperation as Tirpitz: 'We were within an ace of bringing about the complete destruction of the Enemy Cruiser Force – and failed.'[40] Scarcely had the British light cruisers made contact with the enemy than a signalling error by Beatty's Flag-Lieutenant, Lieutenant-Commander Ralph Seymour, led them to break it off. Thereafter Hipper was saved by bad weather which reduced visibility to 2–3,000 yards and by an intercept from Room 40 at 1.50 a.m. which at last alerted the Admiralty to the presence of the *Hochseeflotte* in the North Sea. Unaware that the enemy battleships had been there all the time, the Admiralty wrongly assumed that Ingenohl was advancing rather than retreating, feared a surprise encounter in the mist, and instructed the British squadrons: 'High Sea Fleet is out ... so do not go too far to Eastward.' The last chance of catching Hipper disappeared because of the Admiralty's delay in responding to another German intercept ten minutes later. At about 1 p.m. Room 40 provided Hipper's position, course and speed at 12.45. But that information was not passed to the British squadrons until nearly two hours later. By then it was too late to catch the German battle cruisers before nightfall. At 3.45 p.m. the chase was abandoned.[41]

'All concerned', wrote Fisher furiously, 'made a hash of it'. The enemy had escaped from '*the very jaws of death!*' Jellicoe too was '*intensely* unhappy'. 'We had', he said, 'the opportunity of our lives'.[42] And yet, for all the intense frustration which followed Hipper's escape, the German raid was also reassuring. So long as Room 40 could decrypt the German signals, the Admiralty would always be forewarned of any major German move into the North Sea. As the naval staff later summarised the position at the end of 1914:

The result was that it was no longer necessary for the Grand Fleet either to carry on the continual sweeps of the North Sea, as prescribed in the

War Plans, or to be constantly in a state of complete readiness. It was now possible for rest and training to be looked upon as matters of essential routine. On the whole, the Grand Fleet was less harassed, more secure, and stronger than when war broke out.[43]

The public mood after the German raid, however, was one of outrage rather than reassurance. In the German bombardment of Scarborough, Hartlepool and Whitby 122 civilians had been killed and 443 wounded. The Hague Convention forbade 'the bombardment by naval forces of undefended ports' and though Hartlepool was a defended port, Scarborough and Whitby were not. 'Where was the Navy?' asked the coroner at the Scarborough inquest. His question was many times repeated by press and public but the Navy, to Churchill's regret, could give no convincing reply:

> We had to bear in silence the censures of our countrymen. We could never admit for fear of compromising our secret information where our squadrons were, or how near the German raiding cruisers had been to their destruction. One comfort we had. The indications upon which we had acted had been confirmed by events. The sources of information upon which we relied were evidently trustworthy. Next time we might at least have average visibility. But would there be a next time?[44]

The 'next time' was little more than a month in coming. On 23 January 1915 Admiral Sir Arthur Wilson, a 'glow' still in his eye from reading Room 40's latest decrypts, marched unannounced into Churchill's room in the Admiralty, followed by Oliver bearing maps and compasses. 'First Lord', he announced, 'these fellows are coming out again'. 'When?' demanded Churchill. 'Tonight. We have just got time to get Beatty there'. At 5.45 p.m. Admiral Hipper set out from the Jade estuary unaware that his plans were known and his movements followed by the enemy. That evening Churchill attended a dinner at the French embassy, struggling to contain his mounting excitement:

> ... Only one thought could reign – battle at dawn! Battle for the first time in history between mighty super-Dreadnought ships! And there was added a thrilling sense of a Beast of Prey moving stealthily hour by hour towards the trap.

Churchill was up before dawn on the 24th, waiting impatiently with Fisher, Wilson and Oliver in the Admiralty War Room. At last, just after 8 a.m. came the news that the enemy had been sighted off the Dogger Bank. In a long life crowded with dramatic incident Churchill underwent 'few purely mental experiences more charged with cold excitement' than the silent hours which he spent in the War Room following the course of the battle. Out in the

North Sea the day ended with one of Hipper's four battle cruisers, *Blücher*, sunk, Beatty's flagship *Lion* put out of action, 951 German and 10 British sailors killed.

But in Whitehall only the clock ticks, and quiet men enter with quick steps laying slips of pencilled paper before other men equally silent who draw lines and scribble calculations, and point with the finger or make brief subdued comments. Telegram succeeds telegram at a few minutes' interval as they are picked up and decoded, often in the wrong sequence, frequently of dubious import; and out of these a picture always flickering and changing rises in the mind, and imagination strikes out around it at every stage flashes of hope and fear.[45]

At 10.47 Beatty signalled to his ships: 'Close the enemy as rapidly as possible consistent with keeping all guns bearing'. By now the *Blücher*, though fighting bravely to the last, was doomed, and Beatty's main objective was to sink Hipper's three remaining, outnumbered battle cruisers. But at 10.54, submarines were reported on the starboard bow, Beatty himself thought he saw a periscope and immediately ordered a 90 degree turn to port, placing his ships astern of their enemy. There were in fact no submarines at hand and the 'periscope' seen by Beatty was probably a destroyer's torpedo surfacing at the end of its run.[46] The Admiralty knew from German signals decrypted by Room 40 that the nearest submarines were hours away but had failed to tell Beatty and thus left him fearful of a non-existent danger.[47] Beatty's turn to port began a chain of events which allowed the German battle-cruisers *Derfflinger*, *Seydlitz* and *Moltke* to escape. By failing to explain that the order to turn to port was made to avoid submarines, Beatty at first gave the misleading impression that he was breaking off the action. Then, with the damaged *Lion* falling behind, he ordered the signal raised 'Attack the rear of the enemy'. Unhappily his Flag-Lieutenant, Ralph Seymour (whom Beatty later accused of losing him two battles) left the previous signal 'Course N.E.' still flying and together the two signals seemed to order an attack on the already doomed *Blücher* (whose bearing was N.E.) rather than on its three companions. By the time Beatty had hoisted his own flag in the *Princess Royal* at 12.20 and ordered the chase to be resumed, Hipper's three remaining battle cruisers were out of reach. Half an hour later, sick at heart, Beatty abandoned the chase. He wrote to a friend a few days later:

The disappointment of that day is more than I can bear to think of. Everybody thinks it was a great success when in reality it was a terrible failure. I had made up my mind that we were going to get four, the lot, and *four* we ought to have got.[48]

The experience of the December raid and the January engagement off the Dogger Bank led to a series of additions to the signal book designed at least in part to avoid the signalling confusion which had twice assisted Hipper's escape.[49] But the much larger problems of the use of signals intelligence were not examined with similar care. The most basic issue posed by sigint was whether it was best handled at the centre by the Admiralty or handed over with its source disguised to commanders at sea with freedom to use it as they saw fit. With the gift of hindsight Captain Stephen Roskill, a former deputy DNI as well as a distinguished naval historian, later concluded, after examining the experience of Room 40, in favour of a delegated system particularly in the North Sea where rapidly changing weather conditions are always likely to interfere with calculations made in Whitehall. In estimating Beatty's speed of advance to the Dogger Bank in January 1915, for example, the Admiralty had neglected to allow for the delays caused by sudden fog and Beatty cut unnecessarily across waters believed to be mined in order to arrive in time.[50] Much worse, however, was the Admiralty's failure to pass on signals intelligence to commanders at sea in time to be acted on, and in some cases its failure to pass it on at all. Hipper's escape had been assisted in December by the Admiralty's delay in sending Beatty his intercepted signals, and in January by the failure to report to Beatty the whereabouts of German submarines (likewise based on their intercepted signals). Similar failures at Jutland in May 1916 were to prove even more disastrous.

The Admiralty's failings in dealing with sigint were due in part to Oliver's overwork and reluctance to delegate as COS. He slept in the War Room, hardly ever left it by day and invariably insisted on drafting signals based on sigint himself. Beatty complained that Room 40 gave Oliver 'priceless information ... which he sits on until it is too late for the Sea Forces to take action ... What it amounts to is the War Staff has developed into a One Man Show. The man is not born yet who can run it by himself'.[51] But the underlying problem for Room 40 was the weight – often the dead weight – of naval tradition. An Admiralty which had long resisted the creation of the Naval Staff (forced on it by Churchill only in 1912) was unlikely to adjust itself overnight to the even greater novelty of Room 40. Traditionally minded naval officers were bound to look askance at civilian meddling in naval matters. Initially at least, their prejudices were reinforced by the inexperience of the new cryptographers. What Denniston wrote of one batch of recruits to Room 40 was true of most:

They knew ordinary literary German fluently and they could be relied on. But of cryptography, of naval German, of the habits of war vessels of any nationality they knew not a jot. Their training was of the shortest before they were told off in watches of 2 men each and given the responsibility of looking after the German Fleet. Worse than that, they had to learn the intricacies of office routine. They had probably had more than their fair share of log-writing, they had to sort and circulate. They had to turn the German squared chart into latitude and longitude of which they had not heard since the geography class of their schooldays. It is to be imagined that Hope had an anxious time when he arrived each morning, fearing to find that the German mineseekers had found a mine apparently off New Zealand which on closer examination proved to be off Heligoland and then a hurried correction "in our no. XYZ for SO & SO please read thus & thus" would be circulated in triplicate.[52]

The un-naval language of the civilian cryptographers was also liable to raise naval hackles. Even Denniston, despite his years at Osborne, was capable in the early days of translating a decrypt to read 'The Fleet will proceed into harbour athwartwise'. One of his colleagues produced an even more bizarre translation: 'Fishermen have reported that a destroyer with a bulwark over the sternpost rammed and sank a submarine'. Hope gradually taught Room 40 correct naval terminology, with the result that naval susceptibilities were decreasingly disturbed by non-naval language.[53]

Two early mistakes by the cryptographers in the autumn of 1914 had, however, left a lingering distrust in Operations Division. Owing to a garbled interception, further confused by the ignorance of the cryptographers, an intercepted signal was circulated reporting that the *Ariadne* (which had in fact been sunk) was proceeding to the Jade river. Worse still, intercepts circulated on two or three successive evenings reported that German destroyers had been ordered to patrol the Inner Gabbard. English destroyers were sent to meet them but without success. The German destroyers had in reality been sent to Heligoland (wrongly identified by a geographically ignorant watchkeeper).[54]

An enlightened Director of Operations would have regarded such errors as the teething problems in a new organisation of enormous potential. But Rear-Admiral Thomas Jackson was not an enlightened man. The unnaval bearing of the cryptographers continued to antagonise him. Lionel Fraser later recalled 'many odd incidents' when the professor types of Room 40 'plonked into the uniform of an officer in the RNVR' forgot to salute senior officers or mislaid parts of their uniform: 'Once one particularly absent-minded professor set off from home without his cap! And another wore it back to front'.[55] As stories leaked out of Dilly Knox's bathtime brainwaves and the practical jokes played on and by Frank Birch, Admiral Jackson's suspicions must surely have deepened and darkened. William Clarke later wrote of him:

Admiral Thomas Jackson ... displayed supreme contempt for the work of Room 40. He never came into the room during the writer's time there except on two or three occasions, on one of which he came to complain that one of the locked boxes in which the information was sent him had cut his hand, and on another to say, at a time when the Germans had introduced a new code book, "Thank God, I shan't have any more of that damned stuff!"[56]

Not merely was Room 40 not allowed to send intelligence direct to commanders at sea. It was denied the information it required to interpret fully the signals it decrypted. For a few weeks late in 1914 the white form submitted daily to the COS and Flag Officers afloat giving the latest positions of the German ships was also sent to Room 40 which was asked to add any information it could. Early in 1915 the practice was discontinued, allegedly for fear that cryptographers might 'blow the gaff'. Not until Room 40 was incorporated into the NID as ID25 in 1917 was it allowed the flagged charts on which enemy naval movements were plotted. Captain Hope found the Admiralty's failure to exploit Room 40's expertise tragically absurd:

In a very few months we obtained a very good working knowledge of the organisation, operations and internal economy of the German Fleet. Had we been called upon by the [naval] staff to do so, we could have furnished valuable information as to movements of submarines, minefields, etc.

But Room 40 was not so called upon. The Naval Staff proposed to use it defensively but not offensively: to give advance warning of enemy attack but not to assist in operational planning.[57]

For almost two years the war at sea defied all men's expectations. For sixteen years the Germans had been building a High Seas Fleet with which to challenge British supremacy at sea. But when war came, the *Hochseeflotte* – with only eighteen modern battleships to Britain's thirty-one – dared not make the challenge. For fifteen months after the Dogger Bank engagement, wrote Churchill (with some exaggeration), 'halcyon calm reigned over the North Sea and throughout Home Waters'.[58] Though the submarine menace to merchant shipping continued to grow, conflict between the rival battle fleets had sunk to the most minor skirmishing. Cooped up in their northern bases at Scapa Flow and Rosyth, enduring the boredom of long, dark, winters and the discomfort of stormy seas, the officers and men of the Grand Fleet waited with growing impatience for a naval Armageddon.

In the spring of 1916 Admiral von Scheer, the new commander-in-chief of the *Hochseeflotte*, gave the Grand Fleet its opportunity at last. Scheer's plan was to lure part of the Grand Fleet into battle, then suddenly confront it with the whole of the *Hochseeflotte*. On the morning of 30 May 1916 Room 40 decrypted signals revealing Scheer's intention to put to sea early next day.

Admiral Sir John (later Admiral of the Fleet Earl) Jellicoe, the commander-in-chief of the Grand Fleet at Scapa Flow, and Vice-Admiral Sir David (later Admiral of the Fleet Earl) Beatty, commander of the battle cruiser squadron at Rosyth, were warned at noon. That evening Jellicoe ordered the Grand Fleet to raise steam for full speed. The effect on his frustrated sailors was electric. In the battleship *Revenge* officers and men jumped to their feet, cheered and hugged each other. The waiting was at an end.[59]

In the early hours of the morning of 31 May a decoy force of battle cruisers set sail from the Jade, followed at a distance by Scheer himself. Scheer should perhaps have been alerted by British signals intercepted at daybreak by German Intelligence and by U-boat reports showing that ships of the Grand Fleet had put to sea. 'These reports', admitted Scheer, 'could suggest that the enemy has received intelligence of our sailing'. But, determined to go ahead with his plan, he convinced himself that 'it is unlikely that there is any connection with our operation'. Having set out to trap the enemy, Scheer was himself – thanks to Room 40 – sailing into a trap.

But the British trap failed to operate correctly. The complex reasons for its failure have been endlessly debated since. At least one of the reasons, however, was the Admiralty's inability to make full use of the priceless intelligence it received. The Admiralty's handling of sigint early in the battle also served to undermine both Jellicoe's and Beatty's confidence in Room 40. On the morning of 31 May Admiral Thomas Jackson made one of his rare visits to Room 40 to ask the meaning of the German call-sign DK. He gave no explanation for his question and was told that it was the call-sign of Admiral von Scheer. Had he enquired further or explained his question he would have been told that when Scheer went to sea he used a different call-sign and transferred DK to the Wilhelmshaven wireless station in an attempt to conceal his movements. But Jackson left Room 40 without this information and so misread an intercepted signal from Wilhelmshaven bearing the call-sign DK to mean that Scheer had yet to put to sea. Soon after midday the Admiralty sent Jellicoe and Beatty the disastrously erroneous signal: 'At 12 noon our directional stations place the German fleet flagship [at its base] in the Jade. Consider it probable that lack of air reconnaissance may have delayed their start'. That news deprived Jellicoe of any sense of urgency as he steamed south from Scapa Flow to rendezvous with Beatty and he stopped en route to inspect neutral ships to make sure they were not enemy scouts. When Beatty made contact with the German fleet at 2.20 p.m. Jellicoe was still almost seventy miles away. Beatty, however, was confident of victory. He believed himself faced only with Hipper's battle cruisers and that Scheer had still to put to sea. This time he was determined to 'bag the lot' and redeem the failure at the Dogger Bank. Like Churchill during the Dogger Bank engagement, his successor as First Lord, the usually urbane and unflappable Arthur Balfour, waited with mounting tension in the eerie calm of the

Admiralty for news of the battle. Beatty began badly. In little more than half an hour two of his six battle cruisers, their magazines unprotected against flash, had been sunk and his flagship badly damaged. As Beatty himself laconically remarked, 'There seems to be something wrong with our bloody ships today'. Then the battleships of the *Hochseeflotte* appeared on the horizon and the nature of the battle changed. Turning north, apparently in flight, Beatty succeeded in luring Scheer towards the whole of the Grand Fleet. Suddenly, Scheer found himself outnumbered and the Royal Navy seemed within sight of a decisive victory.

Jellicoe, however, was acutely conscious that he was, in Churchill's words, 'the only man on either side who could lose the war in an afternoon'. He was doubtful whether even a decisive victory would do much to improve Britain's existing naval supremacy. Starting from such premises, Jellicoe was unlikely to take risks. He was deeply concerned, too, by the possibility of serious damage to the Grand Fleet from enemy torpedoes. Ever since the beginning of the war he had been convinced that a pursuit of the German battle fleet would be a hazardous undertaking. In October 1914 he had written in a memorandum to the Admiralty: 'If ... the enemy battle fleet were to turn away from our advancing fleet, I should assume that the intention was to lead us over mines and submarines and decline to be so drawn'. Twice during the battle of Jutland the hail of fire from the Grand Fleet forced Scheer to break off the engagement and turn his fleet away. On both occasions a determined pursuit might have led to a decisive British victory. On both occasions Jellicoe refused a pursuit because of the danger of torpedo attack.

When night fell on 31 May, Jellicoe still lay between the German fleet and its home base, and hoped for victory on the following day. Scheer, however, had two alternative routes back to base. Tragically, Jellicoe chose to cover the wrong one. Part of the blame for this critical decision lies with Jellicoe himself. Even with the information he possessed, he might have deduced that Scheer was heading for home, under cover of darkness, by the Horn Reef passage off the coast of Denmark. A very much greater share of the blame, however, belongs to the Admiralty. Room 40 produced a series of decrypts identifying Scheer's escape route, but most of this crucial intelligence was either not passed on to Jellicoe at all or – in one instance – passed on with insufficient clarity and emphasis. The one intercept pointing to the Horn Reef passage passed on to Jellicoe (at 10.41 p.m.) failed to impress him partly because a slightly earlier signal from the Admiralty (at 9.58 p.m.) had given a position which he knew to be mistaken, but even more because his confidence in Admiralty intelligence had been badly undermined by the disastrously mistaken signal earlier in the day that Scheer was still in port. As Beatty later rhetorically demanded: 'What am I to think ... when I get that telegram and in three hours time meet the whole German Fleet well out at sea?' Jellicoe also claimed, with reason, that the failure to send him all the signals intelligence on Scheer's escape route – sufficiently convincing to have overcome the suspicions left by the Admiralty's earlier errors – was 'absolutely fatal':

> It is impossible to understand this extraordinary omission on the part of the Admiralty Staff, but there can be no doubt whatever that the escape of the High Sea Fleet from being engaged at daylight off the Horn Reef was due to this neglect.[60]

There were perhaps two underlying reasons for the Admiralty's failure to make proper use at Jutland of the excellent intelligence it possessed. The first was Oliver's extreme reluctance to delegate. So far as possible he insisted on drafting all 'Out signals' to the Fleet based on decrypts himself. Despite his phenomenal capacity for intolerable workloads, he could not possibly find the time during a great naval battle to interpret personally all the decrypts from Room 40. Nor had he ensured that, when forced to rest, he would always have a trained deputy to hand experienced in dealing with sigint. On the evening of 31 May, with no prospect of a resumption of the battle till the following morning, Oliver retired to snatch a few hours of badly-needed sleep, his first since the Grand Fleet had put to sea. While Oliver slept, Captain A.F. Everett, the naval secretary to the First Lord, stood in for him. Everett had a reputation as a competent, level-headed officer but little if any experience of either sigint or German naval procedures. His inexperience must surely have contributed to the fateful decision simply to put on file the decrypts which would have enabled Jellicoe to bar Scheer's path at Horn Reef.[61]

A second underlying reason for that and other errors by the Admiralty was what Captain Roskill has called 'the excessive dominance of the executive or "line" officer over the specialist and the scientist'.[62] Many of the weaknesses revealed at Jutland – inadequate armour-plating, faults in ammunition, lack of training in nightfighting, communications failures, as well as inadequate use of sigint – had their origin in the inferior status of the technical officer, epitomised in Admiral Thomas Jackson's arrogant disregard for Room 40. When Commander (later Admiral Sir) William 'Bubbles' James replaced Captain Hope in Room 40 in May 1917, he found the cryptographers 'still simmering with resentment' at their treatment by Operations during Jutland. 'Blinker' Hall was convinced that the disastrous error at Jutland could never have happened had Room 40 been allowed to submit full intelligence reports, based on their accumulated experience of German signals, instead of simply transmitting decrypts whose significance Operations sometimes failed to grasp. Oliver, predictably, was not easily convinced. But Hall's hand was enormously strengthened in the spring of 1917 by his success in bringing off the most sensational intelligence coup of the entire war.[63]

That coup was not naval but diplomatic. In the summer of 1915 Hall had founded, without consulting Sir Alfred Ewing, a diplomatic annex to Room

40 which came directly under his own authority. Its first head was Sir George Young, an Old Etonian baronet and widely travelled diplomat, assisted initially by two other Old Etonians, Faudel-Phillips (who later succeeded Young as head) and Nigel de Grey, and by the Reverend William Montgomery.[64] The new department was set up to exploit the capture of a German diplomatic codebook.

The first major attempt to obtain the German codebook was through an Austrian wireless engineer, Alexander Szek, employed by the Germans to repair the Brussels wireless transmitting station after they had overrun Belgium. Unknown to the Germans, Szek had been born and educated in Britain and was persuaded by an unidentified British agent to copy a series of columns from a German diplomatic codebook to which he gained access early in 1915.[65] In August 1915 Szek at last succeeded in crossing the Dutch border and delivering extracts from the codebook to the British military attaché in The Hague, Major Laurie Oppenheim, who forwarded them to Hall.[66] Szek was killed not long afterwards, possibly by the Germans but more probably on the orders of Hall who feared that Szek was becoming a security risk who would alert the Germans to the insecurity of their codes with disastrous consequences for Room 40. Oliver later claimed he had provided £1,000 for a contract killing. He repeated several times to Captain Roskill in his declining years, 'I paid £1,000 to have that man shot'.[67]

Szek's information on German codes was probably made obsolete by a remarkable windfall from Persia. One day in the spring or summer of 1915 Hall was told by a naval officer invalided from the Persian Gulf the remarkable tale of how Wassmuss, a German vice-consul and Arabian adventurer, had been forced to flee on horseback in his pyjamas, leaving his baggage behind. Hall quickly enquired where the baggage was, only to discover it in the cellars of the India Office. After a search by a member of Hall's staff, a German diplomatic codebook was found intact.[68]

Intercepting Germany's diplomatic traffic was less straightforward than intercepting her naval signals. Some German diplomatic traffic was transmitted by radio, but messages to America usually went by transatlantic cable. After the Germans' own transatlantic line was cut, they used two alternative routes to America. The first became known in the Admiralty as the 'Swedish roundabout'. From early in the war the neutral but pro-German Swedes allowed the Germans to use their own cable to North America. When Britain protested in the summer of 1915, Sweden agreed to stop. Instead, the same German messages – now disguised by re-encipherment in Swedish ciphers – were sent by cable from Stockholm to Buenos Aires and thence to Washington. But that cable route also touched England and, by the spring of 1916, the Swedish ruse had been detected. This time, however, Britain made no protest. The 'Swedish roundabout' was too valuable an intelligence source to be sacrificed to diplomatic propriety.[69]

At the end of 1916 the Germans acquired a second and more direct route to North America. Having persuaded President Woodrow Wilson that his peace initiatives would be facilitated by speedier communications, Bernstorff, the German ambassador, was given access to the American transatlantic cable. That cable too went via Britain and Room 40 was 'highly entertained' to detect German codes in American diplomatic traffic.[70] It was doubtless also entertained by the simplicity of American codes and ciphers. The State Department had yet to emerge from a state of cryptographic innocence, and placed its faith in what one of the first American codebreakers later described as 'schoolboy codes and ciphers'. President Wilson was even more naive than the State Department. Anxious to ensure the absolute secrecy of his own personal communications, Wilson spent 'many hours of many nights', sometimes assisted by his wife, laboriously encoding and decoding telegrams to and from Colonel House, his confidential agent to the capitals of Europe. In his own secret code, the code word he employed for 'secretary of war' was 'Mars'.[71] The reader may test his own skill as a codebreaker by attempting to deduce Wilson's code word for 'secretary of the navy'.[72] Room 40 must surely have found the few hours required to decrypt Wilson's most secret communications unusually diverting.[73] The great champion of open diplomacy was splendidly unaware of the degree to which he was practising it himself.

Hall kept most of the diplomatic intercepts to himself. 'He had', in the opinion of 'Bubbles' James, 'unbounded confidence in his ability to decide how much of the information in the messages should be passed on to other Government departments'.[74] Hall usually decided that other government departments could be trusted with very little – and even the little was usually disguised. Maurice Hankey, the cabinet secretary, discovered in February 1916 that Hall had failed to pass on 'priceless' intelligence from the secret telegrams between President Wilson and Colonel House even to his own First Lord, Arthur Balfour.[75]

Early in 1917, however, Hall for once required the assistance of his political masters to make use of German intercepts. On the morning of 17 January Nigel de Grey, who had been on night duty with the Reverend William Montgomery, called on Hall in Serocold's room in the Admiralty. 'Do you want to bring America into the war?' enquired de Grey. 'Yes, my boy', said Hall. 'Why?' 'I think I've got something here for you', replied de Grey, handing him an incomplete translation of an intercepted telegram from Zimmermann, the German foreign minister:[76]

BERLIN TO WASHINGTON. W 158. 16 January 1917.

Most secret for Your Excellency's personal information and to be handed on to the Imperial Minister in (?) Mexico with ... by a safe route.

We propose to begin on the 1st February unrestricted submarine warfare.

In doing this however we shall endeavour to keep America neutral ... (?)
If we should not (? succeed in doing so) we propose to (? Mexico) an
alliance upon the following basis:

    (joint) conduct of war

    (joint) conclusion of peace ...

    ... Your Excellency should for the present inform the President secretly (?
that we expect) war with the U.S.A. (possibly) (... Japan) and at the same
time to negotiate between us and Japan ...

    ... Please tell the President that ... our submarines ... will compel
England to peace within a few months. Acknowledge receipt.

ZIMMERMANN.[77]

Because of its importance the Zimmermann telegram (as it has since become
known) was transmitted not merely by the Swedish roundabout but also via
the American transatlantic cable. By a supreme diplomatic impertinence the
United States was thus made to provide the channel by which Germany hoped
to persuade Mexico to join the war against her. But the Zimmermann telegram
was sent in a variant of the diplomatic code captured in 1915: a variant which
was still only partially solved in January 1917.[78] When Hall was shown the
partial solution on 17 January he found it 'shadowy' and questioned de Grey
closely on his prospects of solving the missing groups. It was already clear,
however, that Hall had in his hands a diplomatic bombshell. All that remained
was to discover a safe method of exploding it. After de Grey and Serocold
had made suggestions, Hall said he must think things over by himself.[79]

Hall, almost certainly, saw three main problems in using even a fully
decrypted version of the Zimmermann telegram. First, how could he disclose
the telegram without Germany guessing that her codes were broken and
depriving Britain of her most valuable wartime source of both naval and
diplomatic intelligence? Second, how could he avoid revealing that Britain
had been intercepting at least the Swedish roundabout? And if the Americans
knew that Hall had been intercepting the diplomatic traffic of one neutral
power, might they not also correctly deduce that he had been intercepting
their own as well?[80]

Hall hoped initially to find a way of informing the Americans of the German
approach to Mexico without revealing his source. The first solution he
suggested to de Grey was for Arthur Balfour, who had become foreign
secretary in the Lloyd George government formed in December 1916, to
warn the United States. Balfour, said Hall, was 'the only man in this country
whom the Americans might believe without real proof'. De Grey agreed. But,
on further reflection, Hall concluded that he must none the less devise some
cover story to conceal the skill of his codebreakers. According to de Grey's
later recollection, the first stratagem suggested by Hall was to steal a copy of
the telegram in Buenos Aires, the main staging post in the Swedish roundabout.

But in that case there would be 'no proof that the telegram had ever reached Mexico', and this – in Hall's view – was essential.[81]

For over a fortnight Hall kept the secret to himself and Room 40. There was, after all, the prospect that the United States might enter the war without prompting by Room 40. On 1 February Germany began unrestricted U-boat warfare. On the 3rd Wilson broke off diplomatic relations with the Germans, but declared his hope that war could still be avoided. On the 5th Hall at last presented himself at the Foreign Office and showed the Zimmermann telegram to Lord Hardinge, the permanent undersecretary. Some of the gaps in the original intercept had since been filled in by de Grey and Montgomery. Others still remained. Hall announced that he was asking Thurston, the British minister in Mexico, to obtain the version of the Zimmermann telegram which had arrived in Mexico City. The German legation in Mexico, he believed, did not possess the variant of the diplomatic code employed for messages to the Washington embassy. The version of the telegram forwarded to it by the Washington embassy would thus probably prove easier for Room 40 to decrypt in its entirety. And so it proved. On 10 February Hall learned that Thurston had gained a coded copy of the Zimmermann telegram from the Mexico City telegraph office. The code in which it was sent was essentially that retrieved from Wassmuss's baggage in the cellars of the India Office in the summer of 1915. By 19 February Hall had in his hands the transcript of the Zimmermann telegram which was to appear in the American press on 1 March:[82]

19.1.17

We intend to begin on the first of February unrestricted submarine warfare. We shall endeavour in spite of this to keep the U.S.A. neutral. In the event of this not succeeding we make Mexico a proposal of alliance on the following terms:—

Make war together.

Make peace together.

Generous financial support and an undertaking on our part that Mexico is to reconquer the lost territory in Texas, New Mexico and Arizona. The settlement in detail is left to you.

You will inform the [Mexican] President of the above most secretly as soon as the outbreak of war with U.S.A. is certain, and add the suggestion that he should on his own initiative invite Japan to immediate adherence and at the same time mediate between Japan and ourselves.

Please call the President's attention to the fact that the ruthless employment of our submarines now offers the prospect of compelling England in a few months to make peace.

ZIMMERMANN.[83]

The Mexican origins of this version of the Zimmermann telegram made it possible to show it to the United States without revealing that American cables had been tapped. A few hours after receiving it, Hall rang Eddie Bell, the American diplomat in London responsible for liaison with British intelligence departments. Within half an hour Bell was in Hall's room at the Admiralty, reading – off the record – the Zimmermann telegram. Hall said later that he had rarely seen anyone 'blow off steam in so forthright a manner': 'Mexico to "reconquer the lost territory"! Texas and Arizona? Why not Illinois and New York while they were about it?' But, added Bell, might the telegram be a hoax? Was it to be given officially to the United States? That, said Hall, had still to be decided by the Foreign Office. He failed to tell Bell that Hardinge was still reluctant to do anything which suggested that the British government engaged in codebreaking.[84]

Next day, 20 February, Hall called on Hardinge's private secretary, Ronald Campbell, and argued once again that the Zimmermann telegram be used to secure 'America's entry into the war'. He made two suggestions as to how to do it. The first was that he be authorised to continue as he had secretly begun and 'give the substance to Mr Bell of the United States Embassy who after informing the Ambassador would see that it reached the President':

Or, if it be desired to give the matter more publicity and consequently to produce more effect on the American people, for whose unanimity President Wilson is waiting, Captain Hall could arrange for it to come out in the American press without any indication that H.M. Government or any British official, was at the bottom of the exposure. Whichever plan is adopted, Captain Hall is confident that he can arrange things so as to prevent any risk of the source of his information being compromised.

Despite Hall's assurance to the contrary, Hardinge remained anxious that the source would be compromised. He inclined, without enthusiasm, for the second alternative. Balfour, who had gained great confidence in Hall as first lord of the Admiralty, had no such inhibitions: 'I think Captain Hall may be left to clinch this problem. He knows the ropes better than anyone'. Hall had, at last, been officially given the free hand he had already begun to use.[85]

'Prolonged discussions' followed at the American embassy between Hall, Eddie Bell and the ambassador, Dr Walter Page. The effect on President Wilson, Page insisted, would be greatly heightened if a copy of the telegram were formally handed to the embassy by Balfour himself. Balfour readily agreed. He had a reputation for what a French friend once called 'seraphic equanimity': a patrician calm and graceful bearing which were rarely ruffled. But when Balfour received the American ambassador at the Foreign Office on Friday 23 February he found it difficult to conceal his excitement. The moment when he handed Page the decoded Zimmermann telegram was, he later recalled, 'the most dramatic in all my life'.[86] For Page too it was an unforgettable moment. He spent most of the night in his office at the embassy drafting a lengthy telegram to the State Department. When Room 40's diplomatic section decrypted Page's telegram (probably with little delay) Hall must surely have been delighted at what he read. Unaware that Hall had known the gist of Zimmermann's message for the past month, Page reported quite inaccurately:

> The receipt of his information has so greatly exercised the British Government that they have lost no time in communicating it to me to transmit to you, in order that our Government may be able without delay to make such disposition as may be necessary in view of the threatened invasion of our territory.

What doubtless gave Hall the greatest pleasure was Page's repetition of his ingeniously mendacious account of how he had come by the Zimmermann telegram in the first place:

> Early in the war, the British Government obtained possession of a copy of the German cipher code used in the above message and have made it their business to obtain copies of Bernstorff's cipher telegrams to Mexico, amongst others, which are sent back to London and deciphered here. This accounts for their being able to decipher this telegram from the German Government to their representative in Mexico and also for the delay from January 19 until now in their receiving the information ... The copies of this and other telegrams were not obtained in Washington but were bought in Mexico.[87]

The Zimmermann telegram was probably less decisive than Hall believed in Wilson's decision to make war. Wilson had secretly made that decision before Page's telegram arrived in Washington on the evening of 24 February. But by cutting the ground from beneath the anti-interventionist lobby, Room 40 enormously smoothed America's passage into the war. Wilson himself was shocked and angry at the German government's perfidy in plotting war with Mexico while still discussing peace moves with the United States and, by its abuse of American cables, 'having made us the innocent agents to advance a conspiracy against this country'.[88]

The Zimmermann telegram was published in the United States on 1 March, causing the greatest sensation of the war so far.[89] But there remained an influential minority – not limited to German Americans – who denounced the telegram as a forgery. Accordingly, on the evening of 1 March, the State Department telegraphed Page in London that in order to disprove these charges:

... it would be of the greatest service if the British Government would permit you or someone in the Embassy to personally decode the original message which we secured from the telegraph office in Washington ... and make it possible for the Department to state that it had secured the Zimmermann note from our own people.

Hall was delighted to oblige. On 2 March Page telegraphed Washington: 'Bell took the cipher text of the German messages ... to the Admiralty and there, himself, deciphered it from the German code which is in the Admiralty's possession'.[90] In fact Bell merely watched while de Grey deciphered most of the message for him. De Grey later recalled that by mistake he brought with him a 'copy of the decoding book which was a month out of date; but by this time he knew the telegram's contents more or less by heart and bluffed the thing out'.[91] Room 40 also supplied decrypts of three other coded German telegrams sent by the State Department. But Page reported that Hall was unwilling to release a copy of the German codebook itself.

I am told actual code would be of no use to us as it was never used straight, but with a great number of variations which are known to only one or two experts here. They cannot be spared to go to America.

The State Department, which had as yet no Room 40 and shared Page's cryptographic innocence, appears to have been satisfied by this misleading information. Hall did, however, offer to decrypt promptly any German telegrams the State Department cared to send him.[92]

The steps taken to demonstrate the authenticity of the Zimmermann telegram turned out to be unnecessary. On 3 March Zimmermann himself, to the surprise of both Washington and Whitehall, admitted he had sent it. But Hall's attempts to cover his tracks worked like a dream. Berlin jumped to the conclusion that a decoded copy of the telegram had been stolen and cabled Eckhardt, the German minister in Mexico City:

Various indications suggest that the treachery was committed in Mexico. The greatest caution is indicated. Burn all compromising material.

Incredibly, that telegram was sent by the 13040 code captured by the British two years before. Eckhardt's indignant reply – in the same code – was greeted with hilarity in Room 40:

Greater caution than is always exercised here would be impossible. The text of the telegrams which have arrived is read to me at night in my dwelling house by Magnus [the embassy secretary] in a low voice. My servant who does not understand German, sleeps in an annexe. Apart from this, the text is never anywhere but in Magnus's hand or in the steel safe, the method of opening which is known only to him and myself.[93]

Eckhardt then tried to shift the blame to Bernstorff. In the Washington embassy, he reported, 'even secret telegrams were known to the whole Chancery'.[94] As Hall had intended, credit for the Allied intelligence coup was generally given to the American Secret Service (with which its British counterpart was unfavourably compared). To Hall's delight, the American press published improbable stories of heroic backwoodsmen from Arizona who had broken through the lines in France to steal German codes in Brussels, of a German submarine captain robbed of secret documents on Broadway, and of a disaffected German secret agent who had burgled Bernstorff's safe. Hall also had 'no little fun' with American journalists in London. Much of his 'fun' concerned a trunk of Swedish diplomatic papers seized by the British from the ship bringing Bernstorff back to Germany under safe conduct after the breach of German-American diplomatic relations in February. Rumours spread, carefully fostered by Hall, that the Swedish trunk also contained some of Bernstorff's secret papers. Hall wrote gleefully on 22 March to the naval attaché in Washington:

> [The journalists] are quite convinced that the American Secret Service abstracted the Zimmermann telegram from the trunk ... They tackled me yesterday about it, and I had to admit that all the evidence pointed to the seals having been broken before we took the chest. It is a very safe line and I think we will stick to it.

A fortnight later, on 6 April 1917, the United States formally declared war on Germany. That night Hall and de Grey celebrated with champagne.[95]

Though Hall's years as DNI are now remembered chiefly for his association with the codebreakers of Room 40, he also showed throughout the war a less productive fascination for cloaks and daggers. His first major 'secret service' exploit of the war was an eccentric scheme in the autumn of 1914 to investigate unfounded rumours of German submarine 'beds' off the west coast of Ireland and better-founded reports of plans by the Irish Nationalist exile, Sir Roger Casement, to land in Ireland with German arms to stir up a rebellion. In cooperation with Basil Thomson, the head of the Special Branch, he chartered the 581 ton steam yacht *Sayonara* from an American millionaire, and sent it to cruise round the west coast of Ireland with a fifty-man crew posing as Americans. The captain was Lieutenant F.M. Simon of the Royal Naval Reserve who had learned to mimic United States passengers during service with the Cunard line and gave his men a crash course on 'Yankee traits'. The 'owner' was a cosmopolitan soldier of fortune, Major Wilfred Howell DSO, who had been educated in Austria and posed as Colonel McBride of

Los Angeles, advertising pro-German sympathies by an up-turned moustache, Homburg hat and strong Teutonic accent. The comic-opera cruise of the *Sayonara* failed to find any U-boat lairs in the west of Ireland for the simple reason that there were none to find. It is also unlikely that the crew's attempts to speak in American accents won the confidence of Sinn Fein. The *Sayonara* did, however, cause growing consternation among both Irish Loyalists and the Royal Navy. After one attempt to fraternise with Sinn Feiners, the crew were stoned by Loyalists and had to be rescued by the police. Finally in Westport harbour the *Sayonara* was put under arrest by Captain F. le Mesurier of HMS *Cornwallis* who concluded that 'McBride' was 'an obvious Hun'. When the yacht was released on Hall's orders, the Marquess of Sligo left Westport House for the Admiralty to protest in person. He arrived in Hall's office in a mood of patriotic outrage, insisting that he had seen the yacht planting mines in Westport Harbour. 'These fellows may be Yankees', he told Hall, 'but they're in the pay of the Germans, and I'm not going to sit still and watch them planting mines under my very nose ... There's been enough dilly-dallying, and I don't return to Ireland until I know that something has been done'. To prevent Lord Sligo raising the whole affair in the House of Lords Hall was forced to reveal, after first swearing him to secrecy, that the *Sayonara*'s crew was British. He had, he later recalled, 'rarely seen anybody quite so astonished'. Curiously, Hall remained quite proud of the whole farcical episode. He later claimed, without much justification, that intelligence obtained by the *Sayonara* had proved very valuable during the Irish Easter Rising of 1916. For the remainder of the war Hall tended to confuse good Irish intelligence from Room 40 (which included intercepts dealing with the movements of Sir Roger Casement) with far less reliable agent reports on sometimes mythical German intrigues.[96]

The main focus of Hall's covert action, however, was Spain. Because of the importance of monitoring U-boat movements around the Spanish coast Mansfield Cumming agreed early in the war to leave control of secret service there to NID.[97] Hall repeated the experiment of the *Sayonara* cruise, with somewhat less farcical disguises, in Spanish waters. In 1915 he sent the improbably named Irish baronet Sir Hercules Langrishe by yacht to Spain, ostensibly on a pleasure cruise. Though Langrishe's main mission was to reconnoitre U-boat refuelling points, he was also liberally supplied with champagne to win the sympathies of influential Spaniards.[98] But the most indefatigable Spanish yachtsman was the middle-aged novelist A.E.W. Mason whose enthusiasm for cloaks and daggers exceeded even Hall's. Mason spent much of 1915 and 1916 happily cruising around Spain and the Western Mediterranean in a steam yacht. According to his enthusiastic biographer:

> He appeared to have no connection with the War; he was just one of these
> mad Englishmen – *locos ingleses* – enjoying himself in his yacht, at the risk

of running across a German mine, or being torpedoed from a German submarine if the Germans cared to waste ammunition on this crazy millionaire in his beautiful yacht.

Mason sometimes persuaded his friends to join in. Late in 1916 he sailed round the Spanish coast in Lord Abinger's yacht with a large, mixed 'house party' whose 'careless sightseeing' – according to his biographer – 'formed an excellent cover under which he made a careful search for German submarine bases'. Such agreeable adventures provided Mason with rich source material for his short stories and novels, some of which were published while he was still working for Hall. The first short story based on his Spanish adventures, 'One of Them', published in March 1916, describes how Mason, thinly disguised as 'Anthony Strange', discovers that a load of barrels in a Spanish port, allegedly filled with bicarbonate of soda, actually contain much needed fuel for a German U-boat which is sunk when it calls to collect it.[99]

Within Spain itself Hall's personal assistant Lord Herschell ran a substantial agent network based at Gibraltar and headed by Major (from 1916 Lieutenant-Colonel) Charles Thoroton of the Royal Marines, usually known as 'Charles the Bold'. Thoroton's most important source was Juan March, reputedly the chief smuggler in southern Spain with an income of £10,000 a year and a huge network of informants, some of them corrupt officials, whom he enlisted as submarine watchers. The Germans made a number of attempts to persuade March to change sides. After offers of money and decorations had been rejected, they tried seduction. Basil Thomson, who was kept informed by Hall and Thoroton, took a prurient interest in what followed and wrote chauvinistically in his diary in June 1916:

> [The Germans] tried a lady from Hamburg, who first would and then would not, though he offered her 30,000 pesetas. This infuriated him. Thoroton had him told that she was a spy. He said he did not care what she was. He meant to have her. Thoroton became nervous, but early this month he (the smuggler) returned triumphant from Madrid with a scratch across his nose inflicted by the lady, who resented having received only 1,000 pesetas. Now the smuggler is in harness again.[100]

March eventually became a millionaire and offered his services again to NID in the next war. Associated with Thoroton, but also reporting directly to NID, was another agent network in northern Spain run by Commander Maurice Mitchell from Bilbao.[101]

Thoroton's organisation claimed in January 1917 to have three striking achievements to its credit. The first was the 'frustration of German shipping policy'. Intelligence on U-boat movements was said, 'on several occasions', to have saved steamers from destruction:

Thus, two English steamers and one Italian, about to sail from the port of Barcelona during this month, January 1917, were prevented because we had precise and definite information that submarines had instructions to sink these particular boats and were waiting for them.

Thoroton also claimed to have prevented substantial quantities of 'supplies and information' reaching U-boats and – more dubiously – to have defeated attempted German sabotage of Spanish factories, mines and communications supplying the Allied war effort.[102]

Hall's Spanish operations had a high reputation outside as well as inside the Admiralty. Military intelligence considered them 'a good show'.[103] Eddie Bell of the American embassy in London later sent an extraordinary tribute to Hall's wartime organisation to the American delegation at the Paris peace conference in May 1919:

> In Spain it became immensely powerful and used frequently to give information to the Spanish Government of disaffection and proposed strikes in Spain itself, and when a few months ago Admiral Hall started to cut down his organisation after the armistice the Spanish Government actually requested him not to do so on the ground that his organisation was to them a far more reliable source of information of what was going on in the country than their own police and civil authorities.[104]

Bell's eulogy probably owed as much to Hall's considerable gifts as a story-teller as to the achievements of his Spanish network. Hall made a habit of telling tall secret service stories to the Americans both because he enjoyed telling them and because they served to conceal how much he learned from codebreaking. As Undersecretary of the Navy in 1917, Franklin D. Roosevelt was enthralled during a visit to London by Hall's long and fictitious descriptions of how British spies crossed the German-Danish border every night, went by boat to Sylt and thence by flying boat to Harwich. Hall's successor as DNI during the Second World War, Admiral John Godfrey, was disconcerted to be greeted by Roosevelt, now President of the United States, in the oval office at the White House in 1941 with the words, 'Of course, Hall had a wonderful intelligence service but I don't suppose it's much good now'. The President then launched into a long description of how spies had crossed the German-Danish border. Godfrey wrote later:

> Blinker Hall must have deployed some fantastic cover story, and the young Under Secretary of the Navy not only swallowed and believed it but remembered to recount it to Hall's fifth generation successor twenty-four years later.[105]

In reality cloaks and daggers contributed less to the wartime work of NID than Hall and his sometimes credulous American admirers believed. In a secret postwar history of Naval Intelligence Frank Birch and Nobby Clarke of Room 40 dismissed the 'shilling-shocker element in Secret Service work' as not worth the risks:

> Agents supplied little more than back-stairs gossip, and, for the rest, activities of the kind subsided into petty chicanery and propaganda.... There was a tendency 'to bring off a coup', to disregard the results of patient observation in favour of flashy windfalls, to neglect the main sources of information and to seize upon and brandish individual documents or scraps of intelligence of a superficially thrilling nature, without regard for their ultimate value.[106]

'Blinker' Hall found it difficult to resist the temptation 'to bring off a coup'. Over the Zimmermann telegram he succeeded brilliantly. Other coups which depended more heavily on secret agents were usually less successful. His most carefully planned covert operation in Spain originated in the autumn of 1917 as an attempt to prevent the Germans smuggling badly-needed wolfram (the ore producing tungsten) out of Spain. During October Room 40 provided evidence from intercepts of a plan to ship wolfram back to Germany by submarine. Commander Mitchell and his agents found the warehouse where the wolfram was stored, and kept it under surveillance. Further intercepts revealed that it was to be loaded on board the Spanish ship *Erro Berro* which would transfer its cargo to two U-boats. Hall laid an elaborate trap. Soon after it put to sea the *Erro Berro* was intercepted and boarded on 1 January 1918 by a prize crew from the *Duke of Clarence*. Sadly the vessel sank before it could be towed back to Devonport. Worse still, a plan to ambush the U-boats misfired. Three torpedoes were fired at one of the U-boats; two missed and the third failed to explode. Few episodes in the war caused Hall more personal irritation. It was probably after receiving news of the failed ambush that he stormed home, found his wife entertaining some friends to tea, kicked over one of the tea tables and slammed the door.[107]

Hall's Spanish operations also suffered from a vein of fantasy. The vein was probably richest in A.E.W. Mason whom Hall considered his 'star turn'. Mason held his friends in the Garrick and Beefsteak Clubs spellbound at the end of the war as he related his wartime adventures. Even some of his fellow novelists were impressed. 'He was very good as a *raconteur*', wrote Arnold Bennett in his journal, 'and evidently has a great gift for secret service, though he said he began as an amateur. Mason said that practically all the German spies and many of the Zeppelin men carried a packet of obscene photographs on their persons'. Using his adventures as material for short stories which he began publishing during the war itself, Mason found it increasingly difficult to distinguish fact and fantasy in his own career. In one of his stories he describes how the fearless yachting secret agent Martin Hillyard, seeking to defeat any attempt 'to force him to speak' if the Germans captured him, 'carried hidden in a matchbox a little phial, which never left him, to put the sure impediment between himself and a forced confession of his aims and knowledge'. For many years after the war Mason too kept a little phial in a secret desk drawer. He was fond of bringing it out to show his friends, telling them that it contained high explosive and, if broken, would instantly destroy them and the entire room.[108]

Mason undoubtedly had some considerable achievements to his credit. In Barcelona, for example, he won the confidence of Señor Carbonell, the head of the criminal police, and so harassed the rival German intelligence organisation that it allegedly decamped to Valencia. Among well-to-do Spaniards Mason's affable manner won him the same easy popularity as in London clubland. That popularity was fortified by Mason's repeated hints of English decorations for his Spanish helpers. By the autumn of 1916, as one of his reports shows, he had become uneasy at the level of expectations he had aroused:

> The question of a British decoration is one which is becoming an urgent matter. A very great deal of work, in the hope of this particular reward, is being done for us by Spanish officials such as Heads of Police, Captains of Carabineers, who are in a position to put a great number of men at our disposal ... I cannot afford to say to any of them 'The likelihood of your getting a British decoration is a small one', for I should strike the heart out of all their assistance. But, nevertheless, I cannot help feeling that I am getting their assistance now under something very like false pretences.[109]

Mason may thus have been relieved to be moved by Hall to Mexico in 1917. In Mexico as in Spain it is sometimes difficult to draw a clear distinction between fact and fantasy in Mason's adventures. While hunting for German wireless stations he adopted Baden-Powell's disguise as an eccentric British butterfly collector, though he confessed that he knew nothing about butterflies and detested moths. He succeeded in putting out of action the wireless station at Ixtapalapa. Though Germans in Mexico may have used the station at night to receive radio messages from Germany, it is doubtful whether, as Mason claimed, they were also able to transmit.[110] Perhaps the most difficult of all Mason's activities to assess are his efforts to foil German germ warfare. On one occasion the German embassy in Madrid asked Berlin for two phials of cholera bacilli with which to poison Portuguese rivers at source and thus 'close the Spanish-Portuguese frontier and make communications difficult between Portugal and the Allies'. Berlin refused and Room 40 successfully decrypted the exchange of telegrams between Berlin and the Madrid embassy.

German plans to poison Allied livestock progressed somewhat further, but it seems likely that some of the germ warfare schemes believed in by Mason (and perhaps by Hall) were mythical. It seems improbable for example that, as Mason believed, the Germans were planning to cause an anthrax epidemic on the Western Front, and possibly in England too, by spreading infected shaving brushes, or that anthrax was being injected by German agents into mules exported from Latin America to France.[111]

The vein of fantasy in Hall's cloak and dagger operations went undetected in Whitehall. His reputation as the most important of Britain's wartime intelligence chiefs, however, rested first and foremost on the achievements of Room 40. The Zimmermann telegram won Hall a knighthood. More important, it also won him for the first time direct control of the naval as well as the diplomatic section of Room 40. In May 1917 Room 40 was formally incorporated into the Naval Intelligence Division as section 25 (ID25 for short) under Commander William 'Bubbles' James.[112] The new head of ID 25 owed his un-nautical nickname to a portrait by his grandfather, Sir John Millais, which showed him as a child with golden curls, dressed in a green velvet suit watching seraphically as the soap bubbles he had blown floated into the air. For many years an advertising campaign by Pear's Soap, who had purchased the portrait, plastered the childhood portrait of the new head of ID25 over billboards up and down the country.[113]

Room 40's transformation into ID25 came at a critical moment in the naval war. In the spring of 1917 Britain seemed to have no answer to the unrestricted submarine warfare begun in February. In April alone German U-boats sank 835,000 tons of Allied shipping. Jellicoe, now First Sea Lord, told Admiral Sims of the U.S. Navy: '[The Germans] will win the war unless we can stop these losses – and stop them quickly'. Sims asked if there was no solution. 'Absolutely none that we can see now', Jellicoe replied. The solution Jellicoe failed to see was the convoy. 'One of the most extraordinary aberrations of maritime strategists of the late nineteenth and early twentieth centuries', Commander Waters has written, 'was the irrational conviction that the greater the number of ships in convoy the greater was the risk to ships in convoy'. When Germany began her all-out submarine offensive opinion in both the Royal and the Merchant Navies was still overwhelmingly against the convoy system. Beaverbrook's famous description of Lloyd George descending on the Admiralty on 30 April, seating himself in the First Lord's chair and introducing the convoy system is doubtless overwritten. But the war cabinet, urged on by Hankey, the cabinet secretary, saw sense before the admirals. Convoys did not defeat the U-boat menace overnight but they reduced it to manageable proportions. In the eighteen months that remained of the war less than one per cent of ships in convoy were lost from any cause.[114]

Ocean convoy had a number of auxiliary aids. One was air escort and support up to a hundred miles from shore by airships, flying boats and aeroplanes – though, unlike the U-boat killers of the Second World War, their First World War predecessors could do no more than force submarines to submerge. A second important auxiliary to the convoy system – again even more important in the Second World War – was cryptography. In June 1917 the Admiralty established a Convoy Section to provide escorts and organise 'evasive routing' to steer convoyed ships away from enemy U-boats. The Convoy Section maintained close liaison with NID and obtained from it much of the intelligence on which evasive routing was based. It was, however, only the transformation of Room 40 which enabled NID to cooperate effectively with the Convoy Section. Before May 1917 Room 40 had worked in almost total isolation from both NID's German Section (ID 14), which collated intelligence on the German Navy, and from the Enemy Submarines Section (E1), which kept track of the U-boats. As a post-war 'Naval Staff Appreciation' concluded, 'Room 40 could have supplied the German Section with priceless information' but was not allowed to do so:

> The case of E1 Section was precisely similar ... All reports [from British and neutral sources] of ships attacked and reports of sighting and attacking German submarines came to E1, and were duly plotted and recorded there. Room 40, on the other hand, obtained its information from German sources, and knew nothing of British reports. It took in the submarines' signals and knew their identity and time of departure. E1 followed their track across the ocean so far as British reports could give it, but the two sections were not allowed to work in conjunction.

From its foundation in June 1917, however, the Convoy Section had available to it the latest intelligence from ID25:

> For the first time one could see the latest information as to enemy submarines side by side with the track of a convoy, and as the Commodore's ship was always equipped with wireless, it was possible to at once divert a convoy from a dangerous area.

By the autumn of 1917 the Enemy Submarine Section had been incorporated into ID25. Its head, Fleet Paymaster E.W.C. Thring, had what one of his assistants called 'an uncanny "feel" for what the enemy was doing':

> From a chart of plotted sinkings he would say 'That ... and that ... are the work of Submarine U- : she will have so and so many torpedoes and so and so much fuel left'. The various Captains acquired recognized characteristics in his mind ... and his forecasts were of uncanny accuracy.[115]

The creation of ID25 immediately increased both the quantity and quality of intelligence sent by the Admiralty to naval commanders at sea. The flow of 'special telegrams' based on or concerning enemy codes and intercepts, which had averaged 27 a month during 1915–16 and 39 a month during the first four months of 1917 (before the creation of ID25) jumped to 66 a month for the remainder of 1917 and to 172 a month during 1918.[116] The most important intelligence provided by ID25 concerned the position of enemy U-boats. 'The submarines talked a lot when they were at sea', wrote James later, 'and the interesting thing is that it was we who made them talk'. By repeatedly mining the 'swept channels' which led to Wilhelmshaven and Brunsbüttel, the Royal Navy forced submarine commanders to arrange the details of their return to base by radio. But many radio messages from the submarines were unprovoked. The frequent signalling by U-boats as they concerted their plans of attack on Atlantic shipping often allowed the forty wireless stations around the British Isles to fix their bearings even when changes in their ciphers caused delay in decrypting.[117]

It is difficult – if not impossible – to estimate with precision the contribution made by NID to the success of the convoy system. Though that contribution is unlikely to have been crucial, the Admiralty undoubtedly considered it highly significant. In October 1917 after 'several valuable convoys' had successfully evaded U-boats in the North Atlantic, both 'Bubbles' James and Commander (later Admiral Sir) Reginald Henderson, who worked on submarine tracking in ID25, were promoted Captain. 'This immediate promotion of two Commanders', wrote James later, 'was I think a unique occurrence'. As convoy losses fell, U-boat losses rose. In each of the first two quarters of 1917 ten U-boats were sunk; in the third and fourth quarters sinkings jumped to 22 and 21. Hall himself felt personally involved in the attack on every enemy submarine. Whenever news of a U-boat sinking arrived in NID, he would turn to one of his assistants, the Oxford German don, Leonard Willoughby, and announce, blinking furiously: 'Willoughby, go and fetch the rum!'[118]

But though ID25 continued to be pleasantly surprised by the 'extreme garrulity' of U-boat commanders, it faced increasingly complex cryptographic problems as the result of the introduction of new German codes and more frequent changes of keys and call signs.[119] The new codes caused problems even for the Germans. Soon after Jutland the German naval staff recommended the use of a new 4-figure code – the FVB – to replace the old 3-figure HVB, but was met with howls of protest from signals officers who found the new system too difficult to use. As a result work began in the autumn of 1916 on a new but simpler 3-figure naval code – the FFB – and on a modified version of the FVB – the AVB – for general wireless use.[120] ID25 had advance knowledge of the introduction of the new codes in the early summer of 1916 from intercepts in the old codes. It prepared for the period when it would be temporarily – as it was hoped – without the new codes, by an ingenious exercise in what was later known as 'traffic analysis'. A group of cryptographers headed by 'Nobby' Clarke were put in a room by themselves, given coded German signals as they came in, and told to deduce what they could of German fleet activity without breaking the code, simply by studying the patterns of transmission and call-signs:

> Then at the end of the day they were shown the decodes and could see how well or badly they had guessed. The results after a period of training were remarkable and when the new [codes] came into use we were able to give a very good idea of what was happening.[121]

The breaking of the new codes, like the old, was assisted by documents captured from the enemy. In September 1916 the charred but valuable remains of what seems to have been the FVB codebook were recovered from a Zeppelin shot down near Billericay.[122] Hall also had standing arrangements for any accessible sunken U-boat to be searched by divers who were instructed 'to open torpedo-hatch, open five water-tight doors, turn sharp to right and retrieve top drawer in which were all papers'.[123] Shipwright E.C. Miller, a diver who explored twenty-five sunken U-boats, found it a grisly business. Even when he had overcome his revulsion at moving among corpses, he found other 'pretty weird scenes inside the boats':

> The dogfish are always about and will eat anything. In the mating season they naturally resent any intruder, and on lots of occasions when they chased one I offered them my boot, and they never failed to snap at it ... I found scores of conger eels, some of them seven to eight feet long and five inches or so thick, all busily feeding. They gave one a bit of a shock.[124]

From documents found in UC61, sunk off Dover, Hall discovered in August 1917 that the Germans had broken the British code used to report mine-sweeping.[125] Instead of changing the code immediately he used that discovery to lure another U-boat, UC44, to its destruction. Following a bogus wireless message in the broken code reporting that a German minefield off the southern Irish coast had been cleared, UC44 arrived to lay a new minefield and was blown up by the old one. Among the documents retrieved from UC44 seems to have been Miller's most valuable find of all – a copy of the new FFB signalbook.[126]

Though extensive, ID25's mastery of German codes and of the numerous keys, call-signs and other variations employed with them was never complete. Even in the final days of the war some important U-boat signals could not be decrypted.[127] And while U-boat commanders remained talkative, the *Hochseeflotte* had learned some of the advantages of radio silence. As a result, its last major sortie of the war – on 23 April 1918, to attack Scandinavian convoys – almost went undetected. A British submarine on patrol incredibly mistook ships of the *Hochseeflotte* for the Royal Navy. Fortunately for the Admiralty, the battle cruiser *Moltke* broke down with her engine room flooded just over twenty-four hours afterwards and ended radio silence to tell Scheer – and, inadvertently, the Admiralty – of her predicament. Alerted by ID25, the Grand Fleet put to sea in what Beatty boasted was 'the shortest time on record', but not in time to head off the enemy. Even the *Moltke*, though torpedoed by a British submarine, struggled back to base. An informal court of enquiry held soon afterwards exonerated ID25. Two intercepted signals might have given earlier warning of the German sortie. But the first, from a submarine depot ship, could not be decrypted in time, and the second, a report on German aircraft movements, was inconclusive.[128]

The Germans, as ID25 was well aware, were making progress not merely in making their own movements more difficult to detect but also in decrypting Royal Navy signals and capturing British documents. But the German high command made the mistake of allowing intelligence from intercepts to appear in coded radio messages, some of which were decoded by ID25. Hall was determined to allow no similar indiscretion by the Admiralty. All messages based on German decrypts were marked 'Notbywit' ('not by wireless telegraph') and sent either by cable or messenger to avoid interception by the enemy. Hall found it more difficult, however, to impose similar standards of discretion on his allies. His decision to send one of his most successful cryptographers, Nigel de Grey, to liaise with Italian codebreakers in the summer of 1917 was surely taken with the intention not merely of increasing the flow of Mediterranean intelligence but also of making the Italians more discreet.[129] In this second task de Grey was only partially successful. But Hall's most persistent anxieties concerned the French whose pre-war revelations of their cryptographic coups had reached farcical proportions.[130] Less serious French indiscretions continued during the war. On more than one occasion Hall tried without success to persuade the French to leave the decrypting of German naval messages entirely to the British. Soon after founding ID25, at the height of the U-boat offensive, afraid that further French indiscretions might do irreparable harm, Hall decided on his most dramatic initiative yet. Colonel Cartier, head of the cryptographic unit at the French war ministry, was summoned urgently to London. Instead of meeting Hall as on his previous visits, he was driven by two non-French-speaking naval officers to a house on the outskirts of Brighton. Here he was given a glacial reception by Captain James and his wife, neither attempting even a forced smile. Cartier found the dinner – boiled meat, jacket potatoes, cheese, cakes and champagne – almost as disconcerting as his welcome. He refused to drink champagne with boiled meat and was given soda water instead. As Cartier ate alone, Captain James discussed with him the general progress of the war while Mrs James and the naval officers drank whisky in a corner. After dinner James and Cartier retired alone into a side room with coffee, brandy and cigars. James immediately began to complain in a low voice of the damage done by France's lack of security in handling German intercepts. Cartier admitted that 'one or two' of his subordinates had been indiscreet but insisted that most indiscretions came from those to whom the decrypts were circulated. James retorted that he had personal control over the circulation of ID25 intercepts and his cryptographers knew that he 'would have them hung' if they gave away the secret. He put two blunt questions to Cartier:

> First, will you hand over responsibility to us for decoding naval radio messages? Second, what guarantee could you give us that you would not continue to intercept and circulate them?

Cartier replied that he could give neither assurance. Although his department had formerly been responsible for naval as well as military codebreaking, the naval ministry now had a cryptographic unit of its own with which Cartier collaborated. Rattled by James's menacing manner, Cartier added that if 'for any reason' he disappeared, he had ensured that his work would continue. James said that had he known Cartier no longer controlled all naval codebreaking he would never have summoned him to a secret meeting. As Cartier took his leave of James and his wife after midnight he found their expressions less frosty than on his arrival and their farewells 'almost friendly'. But he later recalled that as he was driven back to London

> Thinking over what had been said to me on the fate of indiscreet colleagues, I congratulated myself – whether rightly or wrongly I don't know – on having made it clear that I was not the only one able to decrypt naval wireless telegrams.[131]

The great efforts to conceal the work of ID25 foreshadowed the even greater efforts in the Second World War to guard Ultra: the greatest secret in the history of warfare.

For the officers and men of the Grand Fleet the abrupt end of the First World War in November 1918 came as an anti-climax. The great naval battle for which Admiral Beatty had been waiting ever since taking command of the Grand Fleet never came. 'The Fleet, my Fleet, is broken-hearted', he wrote mournfully to his mistress, 'but are still wonderful, the most wonderful thing in Creation....'[132] Beatty, however, almost had his wish. On the evening of 29 October the High Seas Fleet began preparations for a final, desperate sortie on the following day. The duty officer in ID25 that night was the musician and journalist Francis Toye who had served there for less than a year. As evidence from intercepts pointing to a sortie began to multiply, Toye became increasingly agitated. At about 2 a.m. on the morning of the 30th he visited Operations Division to report 'the various signs and portents'. But 'signs and portents' were not enough. Operations demanded to know definitely whether or not the German Fleet was leaving harbour. Toye was appalled by the responsibility suddenly thrust upon his shoulders:

> It was just before four, I think, that I made up my mind. Over I went again to Operations to tell them that it was my opinion that the German fleet was moving and that they must act as they thought fit. So in the space of an hour or two England spent some half a million pounds; the DNI and, in all probability, the First Lord of the Admiralty, not to mention the sea lords and a whole bevy of admirals and captains, were roused from their beds by the insistent ringing of the telephone. How I sweated! The cold, clammy sweat of sheer funk! Presently Admiral Hall and Captain James arrived, but by that time it had become clear that something was up, that the German fleet was indeed in motion. I seem to remember – or maybe it is a remembrance born of wishful thinking – that DNI clapped me on the back. Then we waited. About eight o'clock a German signal was intercepted that I shall never forget: "All officers on board the flagship." After that, silence. Nobody could make head or tail of the situation. Eventually I went home to bed.[133]

The 8 o'clock signal gave the first hint of a major mutiny in the German navy. Scheer believed it 'a question of honour' for his fleet to go down fighting:

> ... An honourable battle by the fleet – even if it should be a fight to the death – will sow the seed of a new German fleet of the future. There can be no future for a fleet fettered by a dishonourable peace.

Most of his sailors were not attracted by the prospect of a glorious, futile death. Mutiny in various forms and varying intensity forced the German high command to cancel the sortie by its High Seas Fleet. By 4 November the red flag of revolution flew at all the naval bases.[134] During the first week in November the Admiralty cryptographers read with mounting excitement the flow of intercepts which revealed the High Seas Fleet, unbeaten in battle, collapsing as a fighting force in its home ports.[135] For Beatty, grieving for the great naval victory he had failed to win, the war finished in anti-climax. But for the men of ID25 it ended in a thrilling climax.

# 4 | SECRET INTELLIGENCE ON THE WESTERN FRONT

Plans for an Intelligence Corps responsible for field intelligence had been developing since 1904. But when Britain went to war on 4 August 1914 the Corps had still not been created. Major T.G.J. Torrie of the Lucknow Cavalry brigade was then on home leave from India and determined not to miss Britain's first war in Europe for over half a century. His wish was granted by a relative in the War Office, Colonel (later Lieutenant-General Sir) G.M.W. Macdonogh, the able and austere head of MO5, to whose bizarre mixture of pre-war duties (ranging from 'policy regarding submarine cables and wireless telegraphy' to the General Staff Library) was now added the organisation of field intelligence.[1] On 5 August, without previous warning or any training in intelligence, Torrie was told by Macdonogh that he had been appointed commandant of a newly established Intelligence Corps to accompany the British Expeditionary Force to France. In the corridors of the War Office Torrie bumped into another unsuspecting Indian Army officer on home leave, Captain (later Lieutenant-Colonel Sir) John Dunnington-Jefferson, enquired briefly as to his knowledge of French and German, and made him his adjutant. About a dozen other regular officers, whose names had been earmarked by Macdonogh in advance or who were simply recruited on the spur of the moment, found themselves suddenly seconded to the Intelligence Corps. Among them was Cumming's only son, a lieutenant in the Seaforth Highlanders. Most of the new recruits, however, were civilian volunteers. According to an Intelligence Corps historian, they included 'university lecturers, masters of public schools, artists, actors, musicians, men from industry and commerce, and professional adventurers of all kinds', chosen chiefly for their knowledge of the Continent and foreign languages. To most, if not all, these volunteers, the offer of commissions in a corps of which they had never heard came as a complete surprise.[2]

One of the many young volunteers who answered the call to arms was Roger West, a Cambridge engineering graduate, convinced that 'old England was on her beam ends and needed every man she could get'. As soon as war was declared he left his job in Birmingham and rode his motorcycle to the local recruiting office only to be told that there were no more vacancies for motorcyclists and to try Battersea instead. But Battersea too was packed with men on a great variety of motorcycles ranging 'from big "Bat Japs" and "Indians" to home-made contraptions; one was painted bright blue with a crude red cow on its tank and the legend "1 cow power"'. West fought his way through the throng only to be told that since he came from Birmingham he had better try there again. Birmingham, however, was still full up, so West rode off to try his luck at Cambridge, pausing only to repair an ageing clutch en route. At Cambridge he encountered an old college friend and both were given 'fine testimonials' by their college to take to the Royal Engineers barracks in Chatham. But his motorbike broke down near Baldock and his friend drove off overnight to Chatham alone, leaving West to follow on by train next day:

> "Extraordinary thing", he said before he left, and for a moment I glimpsed the serious thoughts behind his humorous blarney. "Extraordinary thing to think that we are going out to a *real* proper war!" That was the keynote of all my thoughts during that time, wondering what *real* war was like, real fighting, real lead slung at one, real courage, real fear, and how they differed from what one had read!

By the time West reached Chatham, the Royal Engineers were 'full up', but told him there was still a vacancy at the War Office. The vacancy turned out to be a commission as second lieutenant in the Motor Cyclist section of the Intelligence Corps 'for six months, or the duration of the war' which was confidently expected to be briefer still. West explained his qualifications to the captain who interviewed him: he spoke German and French, could repair motorcycles, had travelled over a thousand miles trying to enlist – 'and he had got to give me something'. West got the commission and began a hectic search for kit. Officers' tunics were by now almost unobtainable, but West found one secondhand at Moss Bros in Covent Garden 'and became the complete officer for thirty shillings'. On 12 August he stood in his second-hand uniform on Southampton quay, a new army-issue Premier motorcycle by his side, waiting to embark for France with some of the first units of the BEF:

> There we waited with the bright August sunshine flashing on our polished new machines; all talking about trivial matters, and laughing loudly at anything resembling a joke. Yet, over all lay a shadow not exactly of fear, but an anxiety as when runners in a race are lined up for the starting gun.[3]

Sigismund Payne Best joined the Intelligence Corps by a route as eccentric as West's. He spent the evening of 4 August with a friend at the Café Royal

drinking endless cups of coffee as they waited on tenterhooks for the news –
eventually brought by a newspaper seller at midnight – that war had been
declared. From that moment his 'one desire' was to get into the army. Best
came from an unusually cosmopolitan background. His paternal grandmother
was the Anglo-Indian daughter of a Maharajah, though this 'black and
shameful cloud' was never mentioned by his mother's family. His father, a
well-to-do Cheltenham doctor, had been reading a history of the Holy Roman
Empire at the time of his birth in 1885 and quixotically named his son in
honour of the medieval Holy Roman Emperor Sigismund. With a private
income of £800 a year inherited from his father, Sigismund went to Munich
in 1908 to study first at the School of Music, then at the University. By the
time he left Munich at Christmas 1913 he had little doubt that war with
Germany was on the way. Despite his cosmopolitan early life he remained
intensely patriotic. In retirement over half a century later he recalled his pre-
war conviction that 'I was superior simply through the fact that I was English':
'On the continent every Englishman who was respectable and had money,
well he was "Milord", he was the salt of the earth. We were all superior
people'.

Even before war broke out Best had written to the War Office volunteering
for war service and listing his qualifications: perfect French and German, a
working knowledge of Flemish, and extensive travel by motorcycle and car all
over Europe. On 5 August he joined the crowds queueing at the recruiting
office in Scotland Yard, only to be rejected when it was discovered he needed
to wear a monocle. Much the same thing happened at other recruiting offices.
Even at the Army Service Corps where Best hoped his experience with cars
would count in his favour, he was turned away because of his poor eyesight.

Then in mid-August Best received out of the blue a telegram telling him
to report to the War Office. He did so at once and was conducted by a boy
scout upstairs and along passages to a little group of men standing outside a
door:

Apparently, men were being ushered in, one by one to this room. Some
of them came out very promptly, others stayed there some time, and
gradually it was rumoured that it was intelligence. They were recruiting
men for intelligence work in France. A lot of talk then went on about
Intelligence service. Spying. You get shot if you got caught spying in
France. Well I noticed that a few people seemed to vanish and eventually
I was called in and a very pleasant man in ordinary civilian clothes who
said he was Major So and So. He had a talk with me and he said: "Well,
if your languages are all right and you can ride a motorcycle, you'll get a
commission as Second Lieutenant and we shall give you an allowance of
£50 to buy your uniform and equipment".

Well, I had to go outside and wait with the other men who were out there. I should think there were about twenty or twenty-five men left. They were a pretty rough lot, most of them. When the last man had been interviewed, we were told to follow a sergeant and he led us out and we marched, or rather we straggled, behind the sergeant to Burlington House. Well, the Sergeant walked in front. I think if he'd walked at the back, perhaps more of us would have reached Burlington House, for I certainly noticed that quite a number of people seemed to disappear. In fact by the time we reached Burlington House I don't think there were more than ten of us left. I think the others had got cold feet. They'd got the idea that we were to spy and that spying was a dangerous job.

At Burlington House the ten who had survived the march from the War Office were taken to be interviewed by army interpreters in French and German, then sent to ride a motorcycle up and down the Broadwalk in Kensington Gardens. Having passed these tests with flying colours, Best was ordered back to the War Office, given a warrant to buy his uniform and equipment, commissioned as second lieutenant in the Intelligence Corps, and told to get his hair cut. His usual barber having failed to remove sufficient of his long black curls, a second was needed in order to complete a regulation short back and sides. A few days later he was ordered to Euston station with about twenty others to collect their motorcycles. At Euston he set to work with a crowbar on a large packing case, extracted from it a Rudge motorcycle (a model of which he disapproved), filled it with petrol and oil from a tanker, tested it and sent it on ahead by train to await him at Southampton. On 23 August Best sailed for France. During the few days before he left, he wondered for the first time, like Richard West, whether he would be equal to what lay ahead:

I was so afraid of being afraid ... I had not the slightest idea of military life. I did not know what ranks there were, I did not know what the conventions were, I didn't know whom you had to salute, I didn't know how to salute – I just knew damn all. I was also frightened. I was scared that if I came under fire I might get up and run. It was a horrible feeling.[4]

The British Expeditionary Force which sailed for France in August 1914 was, in the opinion of Colonel James Edmonds, who later became its official historian, 'incomparably the best trained, best organised and best equipped British army which ever went forth for war', though the war of movement for which it was trained and equipped was very different from the trench warfare in which it became bogged down a few months later. Lieutenant (later Major-General Sir) Edward Spears, the liaison officer with the French *Deuxième Bureau*, marvelled at the 'utmost smoothness and despatch' with which the BEF crossed to France.[5]

The sheer speed with which the Intelligence Corps had been improvised and the inexperience of most of its officers meant that its early months were bound to be chaotic. Colonel Macdonogh, who moved to France to become the head of intelligence at British GHQ, had originally intended that the Intelligence Corps should comprise, in addition to its headquarters section, a Mounted Section (using horses requisitioned from the Grafton Hunt), a Motor Cyclist Section and a Dismounted Section. In France, however, it was quickly decided that all Intelligence Corps officers required motorcycles and that GHQ needed a car pool as well. The bravado of the new intelligence officers combined with their lack of driving experience proved a dangerous, and sometimes deadly, mixture. Lieutenant (later General Sir) James Marshall-Cornwall had expected to ride a chestnut gelding named 'Sunbeam' from the Grafton Hunt when he landed at Le Havre. Instead he was given a motorcycle which he had no idea how to ride. He therefore asked an extrovert Irish recruit, Lieutenant W.L. Blennerhasset, to let him ride pillion. The two lieutenants careered out of control fifty yards down the road before coming to grief in a ditch. 'Blenner' then admitted he knew no more about motorbikes than Marshall-Cornwall. Another inexperienced motorcyclist, Lieutenant C. Fairbairn, caught his rifle in his front wheel and was thrown off.[6]

The enthusiastic officers of the new Intelligence Corps had for several months hardly any 'other ranks' to command. During that period they were at their most deadly behind the wheel and came close to killing the heads of both the Intelligence Corps and the Secret Service. On 7 September an Intelligence Corps car containing Colonel Macdonogh, his deputy Major Walter Kirke, and Major Torrie, failed to negotiate a right-angle corner at speed, hit a tree, careered into a ditch and threw its occupants out. Macdonogh broke his collarbone, Torrie was knocked unconscious and the driver 'put his knee out', but Kirke was able to borrow a peasant's cycle and ride off to seek help. Kirke continued to be apprehensive of being driven by what he called 'the IC sportsmen'. He wrote to his wife on 19 September: 'Had a bit of shrapnel the other day – only a very little, but it was a rest cure to some of the motor drives I have had. Torrie is going off to command a squadron of the 9th Lancers and is very pleased about it'.[7] A fortnight later there was an even more serious crash. Lieutenant Alastair Cumming was driving his father in a Rolls-Royce on the road to Paris when he ran into a tree near Meaux and was fatally injured. 'C' himself lost a foot in the crash and was critically injured. Best helped to organise a military funeral in which the coffin of C's son was driven on a gun carriage 'through pretty well every road in Meaux'.[8] C made a remarkable recovery. Only a week after the accident Kirke reported to his wife: 'Captain Cummin[g] is out of danger now, I am glad to say, though minus a foot, but the life and soul of the hospital – wonderful fellow!'[9] Cumming's accident quickly passed into the mythology of the Secret Service.

While on intelligence work in Greece in 1916 Compton Mackenzie was given as genuine a lurid account by the naval attaché:

> The car, going at full speed, had crashed into a tree and overturned, pinning C by the leg and flinging his son out on his head. The boy was fatally injured, and his father, hearing him moan something about the cold, tried to extricate himself from the wreck of the car to put a coat over him; but struggle as he might he could not free his smashed leg. Thereupon he had taken out a penknife and hacked away at his smashed leg until he had cut it off, after which he had crawled over to his son and spread a coat over him, being found later lying unconscious by the dead body. That's the sort of old chap C is.[10]

During his convalescence C was fitted with a wooden leg. Soon afterwards he bought a child's scooter. Placing his wooden leg upon it he learned to propel himself at speed along the War Office corridors.[11] Despite the accident, C's driving remained as hair-raising as his son's. Paul Dukes, one of his favourite post-war agents, later described with affectionate pride how C's Rolls-Royce continued to terrorise both pedestrians and police.[12]

The rapid, sometimes inspired, sometimes eccentric, improvisation of the Intelligence Corps in the early months of the war paralleled the experience of Room 40. So too did the suspicion of Operations for Intelligence. Spears found the French and British armies much alike:

> Operations said – 'What can be the use of Intelligence knowing our plans? Their sole duty is to watch the enemy and report his movements and numbers'. 'That's all very well', Intelligence would argue, 'but we have to divine the enemy's intentions. These are based largely on what he can guess of ours. He forms his conclusions on what he can see or hear of the movements of our troops, and how can we enter into his mind and read his thoughts if we know nothing of our own Army?' The Intelligence officers were right, but for a long time they had to work in the dark.

Neither high command in the early months of war paid adequate heed to its intelligence officers. The French commander-in-chief, General Joffre, and his Operations Division could not bring themselves to credit early intelligence reports of the great German sweep through Belgium whose possibility they had earlier denied. Until 23 August Joffre continued to underestimate the German troops advancing through Belgium by the staggering figure of almost 300,000 men. Spears was thinking especially of Joffre when he complained 'how difficult it is to eradicate a preconceived idea from the military mind'. But the British commander-in-chief, Sir John French, and his Operations section had their own preconceived ideas.[13]

French had made his reputation as the ablest cavalry officer of his generation. Though he saw the cavalry essentially as shock troops, he was a firm believer also in their traditional use for scouting and reconnaissance. On the Western Front, however, the cavalry found few of the opportunities which French had expected to cut down the enemy with the sword or to impale him with the lance. Nor was it much use for reconnaissance. The most valuable intelligence during the early war of movement came for the first time from the air. In August the newly founded Royal Flying Corps assembled four squadrons with 68 aeroplanes, 105 officers and 755 other ranks at Maubeuge aerodrome. Sir John French visited the Corps on 15 August, and was, he wrote, 'much impressed with the general efficiency of the aircraft force. I saw the squadron commanders and told them so'.[14] Airpower remained none the less in its infancy. At the outbreak of war Britain lacked even an aero-engine industry and remained for six months totally dependent on France for its engine supply. During these six months, however, the magnificent men in their flying machines had the freedom of the skies. Aircraft armed with Lewis or Vickers guns were a rarity until the Germans introduced the Fokker monoplane in May 1915. In the early phases of the war, air battles consisted of little more than airborne observers discharging rifles and carbines at each other.[15] Sometimes, as Kirke later recalled, opposing pilots 'could only shake their fists at each other'.[16]

The RFC flew its first reconnaissance sorties on 19 August but saw no large bodies of enemy troops. Next day, however, it observed a column of troops passing through Louvain, 'stretching as far as the eye could see'. The morning of the 21st was too foggy for planes to take off, but the weather cleared in time for reconnaissance sorties in the afternoon to report a large body of cavalry with infantry and guns south-east of Nivelles. The RFC report was confirmed by an Intelligence Corps officer actually in Nivelles when the German cavalry arrived, who managed to escape by car. Largely on the basis of these reports Macdonogh correctly deduced that a column of all German arms was rapidly advancing on Mons from Brussels. Operations loftily dismissed his intelligence appreciation as 'somewhat exaggerated'.[17]

Within Operations the dominant figure was the deputy chief of the general staff, General (later Field-Marshal Sir) Henry Wilson whose influence exceeded that of the CGS himself, General Sir Archibald Murray. Wilson was a tall, rugged Ulster extrovert who as pre-war Director of Military Operations had been the driving force behind the staff talks with the French which had prepared the way for the BEF. He had, Kirke later recalled, 'one peculiarity, one fixed idea, which doubtless derived from his Ulster heritage, an intense dislike and distrust for what he called "Papists". From this followed an almost fanatical determination that Protestant Ulster should never come under their heel'.[18] During the 'Curragh crisis' in the spring of 1914 he had led the campaign within the War Office to threaten the Liberal government with mass resignations if it sought to coerce Ulster into Home Rule. Macdonogh took a much sterner view of the officer's duty to obey distasteful orders. He was, in addition, an Irish Catholic and – worse still, in Wilson's eyes – a convert from Methodism.

During the early weeks of the war Wilson thus had, not surprisingly, much greater confidence in Joffre's unfounded optimism than in Macdonogh's level-headed caution, and instilled the same attitude in Sir John French. On 22 August the BEF exchanged its first shots near Mons with the advance guard of the German 1st Army sweeping south-west through Belgium to encircle the French. Despite Macdonogh's warning of the previous day, and despite further air reconnaissance reports on the 22nd, French still clung to the belief that the enemy forces facing him amounted to 'very little ... except cavalry supported by small bodies of infantry', and continued preparations for an advance on the following day. Later on the 22nd, however, Brigadier-General (later Lieutenant-General) Sir David Henderson, the commander of the RFC, arrived at GHQ bringing a further reconnaissance report which reported a German army corps apparently engaged in an enveloping manoeuvre around the BEF. On the same evening Spears too arrived at GHQ, handed Macdonogh half a bottle of champagne, and reported that the BEF was now nine miles ahead of the Fifth French Army on its flank and dangerously exposed to encirclement by superior German forces. Together the two men called on French. While the commander-in-chief listened in silence, Spears presented his evidence and Macdonogh weighed in with Henderson's latest air reconnaissance reports. Twenty minutes later French called off the advance he had planned for the following day.[19]

French still believed it possible, however, to stand his ground and relieve the pressure on his allies. Next day, 23 August, the two divisions of the BEF were engaged by six of the enemy at the battle of Mons. Wilson spent the afternoon preparing a 'careful calculation' of enemy strength designed to refute Macdonogh's estimate and show that the Germans had only one corps and a cavalry division, or possibly two corps. Once again French preferred Wilson's estimate to Macdonogh's and ordered an attack on the following day. At 7 p.m., however, a warning arrived from Joffre that the BEF was threatened by three German corps and the advance was cancelled. According to wartime legend, the outnumbered British forces, for the only time in the war, were assisted by the heavenly hosts. With some help from the 'Angels of Mons', whose numbers were variously estimated at from two to a platoon, the enemy was beaten off.[20]

At midnight on the night of the battle Spears arrived with the news that the French Fifth Army had been ordered to withdraw, thus exposing the BEF to certain destruction if the battle continued. French now had no option but to order a retreat. At Le Cateau on 26 August, General Smith-Dorrien, commanding II Corps, fought a 'brisk stopping action', hoping to halt the German pursuit. He suffered 7,812 casualties for which French never forgave him, but thereafter the BEF's retreat continued undisturbed, its forced march taking it 200 miles in 13 days, often stopping for only four hours' sleep a night.[21]

Two days before the battle of Mons some Intelligence Corps officers had been assigned 'special duties' in ciphers, interrogation, the issue of passes and photography. But in the chaotic weeks of the German sweep through Belgium and Northern France, finally brought to a halt by the battle of the Marne (5–12 September), many of the new intelligence officers were given little idea what was expected of them. 'There was nothing for any of us to do', Best later complained: 'They seemed to have no use for us'. The first duties assigned to both Best and West consisted largely of dispatch riding on their motorcycles. Marshall-Cornwall, though an intelligence officer, was put in command of a cavalry squadron of the 15th Hussars decimated at the battle of Le Cateau. All three lieutenants, however, found opportunities to distinguish themselves. During the retreat from Mons, West won the DSO – the Intelligence Corps's first decoration – for blowing up the bridge at Pontoise on 30 August just as the enemy was advancing on it. After the 'miracle of the Marne' a fortnight later, Marshall-Cornwall led the British advanced guard in pursuit of the retreating Germans. From captured documents and the interrogation of prisoners he was able to reconstruct the entire battle order of the German rearguard.[22]

Early in October Best was sent to Antwerp by motorcycle to liaise with the ill-equipped naval brigade sent by Churchill to stiffen Belgian resistance. He set out with a captain but, at a Reims restaurant where they stopped en route, the captain took off his Sam Browne belt, accidentally discharged his pistol and shot himself in the foot. Best went on alone. When he arrived in Antwerp, resistance was already crumbling. He tried to direct the retreating British marines to the ferry across the Scheldt which would have enabled them to help resistance to the German advance in Flanders, but 'got properly told off' for presuming to interfere with troop movements. Most of the marines headed instead for the Dutch frontier and were interned in Holland for the remainder of the war. Best himself had a narrow escape. He took the ferry across the Scheldt and then drove west. At Bruges he climbed the thirteenth-century belfry just in time to see the first German troops arriving on the outskirts of the town. Realising that the telephone lines might not yet be cut, he just had time to ring Major Kirke at GHQ from the Bruges GPO and warn him of the German advance. Best then headed west along the coast road towards France. At Ostend he ran into a German cavalry unit but, thanks to his unrecognisably filthy uniform, lack of headgear and bilingual German, was able to bluff his way through. At the Ypres canal Best ditched his motorcycle and plunged into the water. Scrambling out on the other bank of the canal wearing only his identity disc on a cord around his neck, he eventually convinced the local inhabitants that he was a British officer, and rang Major Kirke who drove over to bring him his uniform and take him back to GHQ. A few days later Best was taken to receive the congratulations of Sir John French.[23]

Intelligence officers, as one of them later complained, continued nonetheless to be unpopular for some time:

> The green tabbed official of the Intelligence Corps was at first regarded with the utmost suspicion. His reserve was very marked and he had an insatiable curiosity, a combination of characteristics which the average Britisher resents, and this rather led the soldier to imagine that his efforts were not so much directed towards gleaning information about the enemy as about the state of the unit that he visited, and he was consequently looked upon at first as suspect.[24]

By December 1914 the Western Front had solidified into an almost immovable line of trenches. 'All the wars of the world', wrote Winston Churchill later, 'could show nothing to compare with the continuous front which had now been established. Ramparts more than 350 miles long, ceaselessly guarded by millions of men, sustained by thousands of cannons, stretched from the Swiss frontier to the North Sea'.[25] The main troop movements behind the German lines now took place by rail and were far less easy to follow from the air than the earlier movements by road through Belgium and northern France. 'Aeroplanes', wrote Kirke on 8 December, 'have ceased to be any use for intelligence'. Six weeks later he slightly revised that judgment. 'Aerial reconnaissance', he concluded, was now 'of little use'. It could detect 'abnormal collections of rolling stock, but it could not say whether troops were entraining or detraining, nor say in which direction the trains were moving full – still less give any idea of the units in them'.[26]

Aerial reconnaissance on the Western Front gradually increased in value as photography improved. But in January 1915 aerial photography was still in its infancy. Lieutenant (later Wing Commander) W.S. Douglas was appointed air photographer in number 2 Squadron simply because he had had a box camera as a child. He cut a hole in the bottom of his cockpit and thrust a folding bellows camera through it to photograph the ground below. Each photographic plate had to be changed by hand and he 'spoilt many plates by clumsy handling with frozen fingers'. In March a slight advance was made with the introduction of a Thornton-Pickard camera which the photographer held over the side of the plane. Over half a century after flying as an observer with the RFC in 1915, Marshall-Cornwall still had 'vivid recollections of leaning out of the cockpit with a hand-held camera at a height of 800 feet being peppered by German machine guns'.[27] By the summer of 1915 a method had been devised of fixing the camera to the plane together with a semi-automatic plate-changing mechanism. But aerial reconnaissance became even more dangerous in the autumn of 1915 when the Fokker monoplane fitted with a light machine gun capable of firing through the orbit of the propeller, established its supremacy over the Western Front. On 14 January 1916, after a series of losses, RFC headquarters issued the following order:

> Until the Royal Flying Corps are in possession of a machine as good or better than the German Fokker, it seems that a change in the tactics employed becomes necessary ... It must be laid down as a hard and fast rule that a machine proceeding on reconnaissance must be escorted by at least three other fighting machines. These machines must fly in close formation and a reconnaissance should not be continued if any of the machines become detached.

During the spring of 1916, however, Fokker supremacy in the air was disputed by both Farman Experimental 2Bs and De Havilland Scouts. In the course of the year the RFC completed a photographic map of 'Hun-land', the territory immediately behind the enemy lines in the British sector of the Western Front. During British offensives 'contact patrols' by low-flying aircraft reported the positions of advancing forces and helped to lessen the losses caused by British guns firing on their own troops. Aerial reconnaissance was also used to locate enemy batteries. But Sir Henry Rawlinson, the commander of the Fourth Army, complained in October 1916 that only a minority of the observers involved in battery location possessed the necessary skill: 'Aeroplane observation for artillery purposes is skilled work of a very high order. With an unskilled observer the best-trained and best-equipped battery is useless'. The long drawn-out battle of the Somme in the second half of 1916 also showed the difficulty of analysing and using much of the diffuse and disparate intelligence provided by aerial reconnaissance. As a result each RFC squadron at the end of the year was provided with an intelligence section consisting of an Intelligence Corps officer, two draughtsmen with duplicators, one clerk with a typewriter, and an orderly.[28] Improved RFC observation of enemy batteries greatly assisted the better performance of British artillery during 1917. But despite the sometimes valuable intelligence provided by aerial reconnaissance on the German front line, it remained of very limited value in tracing enemy troop movements behind it. For that reason Kirke believed his most valuable intelligence during the years of trench warfare were agent reports on troop trains from occupied France and Belgium. Only when trench warfare began to give way to a war of movement in the spring of 1918 did aerial reconnaissance become once again, as in the opening phase of the war, more valuable than agent reports.[29]

In the war at sea signals intelligence was clearly more important than agent intelligence. In the war on land the reverse was true, at least until the final months. With interior lines of communication the German land forces made limited use of wireless during the period of trench warfare. Even within the British army the official historian of the Signal Service later described the adoption of wireless as 'a long uphill struggle': 'It was not until 1918 that forward wireless really came into its own, though both in 1916 and 1917 individual cases occurred when wireless proved the only survival of a shattered inter-communication system'.

Signals intelligence in the trenches consisted chiefly of attempts to overhear enemy telephone messages. But not until the introduction of French listening sets in February 1916 was much progress made. Even then the results were modest. Kirke noted in September 1916 that only four of the fifteen sets in use were intercepting German messages, and these were 'with a few exceptions not of very much use'. The Germans had far more success in intercepting British messages. According to the historian of the Signal Service: 'Officers could not be made to understand that half their own worries and a considerable proportion of the casualties suffered by their units were due to their own indiscreet use of the forward telephones'. In the autumn of 1916 after the capture of the village of Ovillers-la-Boisselle on the Somme, British troops discovered a complete copy of a previous British operation order taken down by German intelligence from an intercepted telephone conversation:

> Hundreds of brave men perished, hundreds more were maimed for life as a result of this one act of incredible foolishness, persisted in in the face of informed opposition ... It was not until this tale and many others had gone the rounds that officers commenced to realise that discretion was not only desirable but a duty second in importance to no other.[30]

After the breach of diplomatic relations with the Admiralty in the autumn of 1914, the military codebreaking unit MI1b was much slower to develop than Room 40. In December 1915 it still remained only a four-man section. In that month, however, MI1b came under the command of Major Malcolm Hay, a Gordon Highlander seriously wounded at the battle of Mons, captured by the Germans and repatriated in March 1915 as unfit for military service. Following Ewing's example at the Admiralty, Hay quickly began to scour the universities for bright young men, most of them linguists. Under his leadership the staff of MI1b was to increase to eighty-four by the end of the war. By September 1916 Kirke noted that the GHQ Cipher Section under another linguist, Captain Oswald Hitchings, was also 'going well'. When 'Blinker' Hall took charge of ID25 the long and damaging cryptographic breach between naval and military intelligence was ended. Sigint none the less remained of secondary importance in British operations on the Western Front. MI1b's greatest success during the last two years of the war was in decrypting coded messages transmitted by the German station at Nauen near Berlin to German forces and agents outside Europe. When the German use of radio on the

Western Front began to increase after the beginning of their March offensive in 1918, the greatest cryptographic successes were to be achieved by the French.[31]

Neither aerial reconnaissance nor sigint was as important as human intelligence gathering in the history of the Western Front. On the outbreak of war Cumming's priorities became military rather than naval. The espionage agency run from his top-floor office in Whitehall Court (renamed MI1c in January 1916) was brought under War Office instead of Admiralty control, though by an administrative anomaly it drew its budget from the Foreign Office Secret Vote.[32] But the unprecedented rigidity of the Western Front quickly disturbed the delicate relationship between Cumming, who was charged in principle with gathering strategic intelligence from all parts of the world, and GHQ at St-Omer in France, which was responsible for collecting tactical intelligence affecting only its own front. Once the solid line of trenches from the Swiss border to the English Channel barred most intelligence gathering directly across the front line, GHQ concluded that the only solution was to 'get round the end of the wall' either through neutral Holland in the north or through neutral Switzerland in the south. Holland initially seemed the better bet: it was far more accessible from Britain and lay immediately behind the German armies in Belgium and Northern France which confronted British troops along the northern sector of the Western Front. But in both Holland and Switzerland the tactical intelligence network run by GHQ collided with the strategic intelligence network run by Cumming. The problems caused by that collision were never completely solved at any stage in the war.

The thousands of Belgian refugees who had flooded into Northern France ahead of the advancing German armies provided Kirke, who was responsible for secret service work at GHQ, with an ample supply of prospective agents. Selection was more difficult. There was no time for lengthy training, frequently no means of checking volunteers' credentials, and interviews had usually to be conducted through interpreters. The agents selected returned to Belgium by a roundabout route: first across the Channel to England, then to Holland by the Folkestone-Flushing ferry, and finally over the Dutch-Belgian border if they succeeded in dodging the German patrols. Agents' reports had to follow the same circuitous route in the reverse direction. An allied conference on 22 November therefore decided to found a joint bureau at Folkestone to sift the agents' reports and telegraph digests of them to the allied GHQs. The bureau was in practice to be composed of three separate offices – British, French and Belgian – each running a distinct intelligence service and liaising with its colleagues.[33]

The head of the British section, quickly installed in a house on the Folkestone seafront, was a former gunnery officer, Captain (later Major) Cecil Aylmer Cameron of the Camerons of Lochiel, son of an acting head of the Victorian Intelligence Branch, and nephew of a general. He struck Best as having 'a sort of foxy look about him', though his wife seemed 'very charming'. Cameron's impeccable military pedigree and his wife's unusual charm, on which all her visitors agreed, concealed a criminal record. Mrs Cameron had claimed in 1910 that a pearl necklace given her by an elderly admirer and insured for £6,500 had been snatched from her in the street while her husband was in a chemist's shop purchasing a hypodermic needle. At her trial in May and June 1911 on a charge of insurance fraud, however, it emerged that both the necklace and the elderly admirer were figments of her imagination. Mrs Cameron and her husband, who was found guilty of conspiring with her, were both sentenced to three years penal servitude. At a subsequent examination a condescending medical expert, Sir Thomas Clouston, found that Mrs Cameron, 'whilst not being beautiful ... was undeniably very pretty, vivacious and attractive'. But she inhabited 'a world of romance and unreality', and after being injected with morphine during illness in India had become addicted to it. Following Clouston's report, Mrs Cameron was released early from prison on condition that she lived under the supervision of her parents. Her husband served his full term. Most of his fellow officers believed that, in spite of damning evidence at his trial, Captain Cameron was innocent and had gone to jail simply for standing loyally by his wife. When he was released in 1914 they persuaded the usually level-headed Macdonogh and Kirke of Cameron's innocence and of his suitability for an intelligence posting. Once in Folkestone Cameron also won the support of Sir Herbert Raphael M.P. and, at the third attempt, he was given a free pardon. Not all intelligence officers were convinced of Cameron's innocence. Best believed that Cameron owed his job at least partly to the widespread 'idea that anybody who indulged in espionage was necessarily a scoundrel'. Heavily in debt, probably through his wife's extravagance, Cameron was to commit suicide ten years later.[34]

While serving with the Intelligence Corps in France, Best became anxious to organise an intelligence service of his own in occupied Belgium. He got his chance to do so when invalided back to London at Christmas 1914. While still on sick leave early in the new year, Best began to interrogate Belgian refugees arriving at Tilbury on the Rotterdam ferry. He quickly ran into difficulty. The local police suspected him of being an enemy agent and locked him in a cell from which he was only released after appealing to the War Office. Best realised that as a second lieutenant acting on his own initiative, he would get nowhere. 'I must', he told Kirke, 'have some kind of organisation'. Kirke responded in April 1915 by establishing an office in Basil Street, Knightsbridge, under Major Ernest Wallinger, a gunnery officer who had lost a foot at the battle of Le Cateau. Best, who became his second-in-command, found him 'a great big man, very good-looking and extremely pleasant'. Wallinger had married into money and lived in some style attended by a housekeeper and a batman in a flat above the Basil Street office. With Wallinger comfortably installed in Knightsbridge, Best quickly settled into a daily routine, going each afternoon to Tilbury to meet passengers from the four o'clock Rotterdam ferry run by the Batavia Line. French and Belgian passengers from the ferry were shepherded into a waiting room for interrogation. At first Best found his Flemish inadequate for military matters but recruited a Belgian refugee, Joseph Ide (who took the alias 'Monsieur Emil' to protect his relatives in occupied Belgium) to help him. Each evening Best and Ide returned to London, had dinner, and cabled anything urgent from their interrogation notes to GHQ in France. Best spent the rest of the evening, and sometimes the early hours of the next morning, drafting reports on the interrogations which a secretary then had to type in twelve copies for various departments in the War Office and GHQ. Gradually he began to recruit agents from the refugees as well. One of the first and most useful was a disabled miner who, since losing a leg in a mining accident, had worked on a barge travelling between Holland and Belgium and possessed a pass enabling him to cross the Dutch-Belgian border. He was not an easy agent to deal with: Best later recalled that he had 'never met a man with such an overpowering smell'. But despite his body odour he proved brave and resourceful, returning to Belgium to found a network of agents (codenamed 'service Pegoud') in the area between Courtrai and Ghent, and smuggle intelligence reports by barge across the border into Holland.[35]

By the spring of 1915 GHQ at St Omer, 40 kilometres from Calais, thus had two separate networks bringing intelligence from behind German lines in Belgium (and, to a limited degree, in northern France), run by Cameron in Folkestone (CF) and Wallinger in London (WL). Their first priority throughout the war was to monitor German troop movements by rail. In all at least 2,000 Belgians worked for the CF and WL networks at some stage during the war, the majority as train-watchers. Many of the agents refused to regard themselves as spies, whom they associated with cloaks, daggers and doubtful morals, and regarded their intelligence-gathering as quite distinct from espionage. During the early days of train-watching there was a high degree of improvisation. Some of Best's train-watchers were housewives in houses overlooking railway lines who recorded troop movements not on paper but in their knitting – plain stitches for coaches carrying men, purl for wagons containing horses. Gradually reporting became more systematic. Best devised tiny questionnaires printed on very thin rice paper, small enough to be placed in a bicycle valve or carried in the mouth and swallowed in an emergency.[36]

During 1915 the difficulties of getting the train-watchers' reports across the Belgian-Dutch border were multiplied by the German erection of first one, then two, electrified fences along the full length of the frontier. Methods were eventually devised for passing messages and, less frequently, agents through or over the fences, but the elaborate business of collecting and transmitting intelligence reports by a difficult and circuitous route from occupied Belgium to GHQ in France usually took ten days or more. The intelligence staff at GHQ under Colonel Macdonogh and his deputy, Major Kirke, in charge of secret service work, thus continued with attempts to obtain more rapid intelligence directly across the German line. The most successful method they employed was carrier pigeons. On 11 September 1914 fifteen homing pigeons were presented to the Intelligence Corps by the French. From these humble beginnings pigeon recruitment grew apace. Kirke was doubtful at first whether pigeons were really suitable for secret service work but eventually decided to try an experiment. On 2 November a consignment of French homing pigeons was despatched to Holland via England and the Folkestone-Flushing ferry, doped to ensure their silence, then smuggled across the Belgian frontier. The results of the pigeon trial exceeded all Kirke's expectations. By 20 December 21 of the 28 birds released by agents in Belgium had returned safely to GHQ with secret messages tied to their legs. Pigeon morale too remained remarkably high. 'The birds', claimed the official historian of the Signal Service, 'had no great objection to shell fire; they were much less susceptible to the effects of poison gas than human beings'.[37]

But as the difficulties of smuggling even comatose pigeons across the Dutch-Belgian border multiplied, Kirke was forced to devise other methods of delivering them to his agents behind the German lines. On 27 November 1914 he began discussions with the Royal Flying Corps on methods of delivering pigeons by air. The RFC was not enthusiastic. Kirke, however, pressed ahead and with the assistance of Sergeant Lynon, an experienced pigeon fancier, organised a demonstration of pigeon-dropping by parachute on 27 May 1915. During the first flight the parachute become entangled with the plane which was forced to land dragging the pigeon baskets behind. Though Sergeant Lynon was reduced almost to tears as he watched his pigeons bumping along the ground in their baskets, Kirke noted that the birds themselves bore their ordeal with remarkable sangfroid. At the second attempt, the parachute opened correctly, descended normally and 'the birds flew off gaily home none the worse'.[38]

Two problems remained. The first was the attitude of the RFC which felt its dignity threatened by the role of pigeon transporter and understandably disliked the idea of being caught in aerial dogfights with the German Fokkers whilst encumbered with pigeons. Though it reluctantly accepted the role forced on it by GHQ, the RFC successfully insisted on remaining sole judge of the timing of its missions. A more serious problem was the growing nervousness of British agents, alarmed by German threats to shoot all unauthorised civilians caught in possession of carrier pigeons. Happily, in the summer of 1915 Kirke recruited possibly his most successful agent, a French soldier and pre-war smuggler named Victor Marie, with a house near the German-Belgian border with hiding places and a secret passage equally suitable for both contraband and espionage, and overlooking the main Namur-Cologne railway line which carried most German troops on their way to the

Belgian front. Marie made so powerful an impression on Kirke as a good-natured villain that he made him the hero of a post-war novel under the pseudonym Jean Bart:

> A determined cheery-looking fellow, ... in private life he was a "fraudeur" in a big way of business apparently, and thoroughly proud of the fact. Did he not possess a fast lorry and a motor-car? And had he not, on one of his last trips, got across the frontier with 20,000 francs' worth of tobacco, and only one man wounded? ... His cheery face shone as he recounted the various exploits which the familiar landmarks recalled. "*Ma foi!* but this life in the trenches, like a rat in a sewer, at the beck and call of fat-headed *sous-officiers*, was *très ennuyant*. No scope for a man of brains and intelligence", said he, twirling his moustache. "Only put me over there in my own country amongst my friends, and I will give the '*sales Boches*' something to think about."

Victor Marie's career in smuggling gave him training in espionage techniques which most other British agents lacked. He quickly established himself as the spymaster in a crucial area of Belgium, lying low by day and moving around under cover of darkness to recruit agents and collect reports on troop movements. Marie overcame the problem of timing the pigeon drops by a simple device probably derived from his pre-war life of crime. When conditions were suitable he hung out his washing; when they were not he took his washing in. Kirke's diary for the winter of 1915–16 contains regular references to 'Victor Marie's washing'.[39]

Kirke, however, foresaw the day when the pigeons employed for intelligence work would be rendered obsolete by portable radio. Early in 1915 he embarked on a scheme to establish a radio station behind enemy lines. The agent he selected after a meeting on 12 February was Mademoiselle de Bressignics, codenamed 'Ramble', the daughter of a well-to-do refugee family with both country estates and a town house in Lille, then perhaps the main railway centre in occupied France. Thinly disguised as Adrienne de X, Ramble became the heroine of Kirke's post-war novel: a vision of loveliness with a 'charming smile', 'quick brain', 'shapely ankles', 'hot French blood', 'well-cut blue serge knickers', 'incredible boldness' and 'astonishing coolness'. The admiration felt for Adrienne by Lieutenant Archer of the RFC, the English hero of Kirke's novel, probably reflects the feelings stirred by Ramble herself in some British intelligence officers. Archer, with both the moral fibre and 'frank cheery face of the public schoolboy', felt it 'dishonourable to take advantage' of Adrienne. At their last meeting, before meeting a hero's death, Archer 'after a silent but eloquent interval' merely raised her hand to his lips and 'dropped it quickly':

In thinking over their last interview, as she did many times in the succeeding months, Adrienne came to the very definite conclusion that the circumstances would have justified him in proceeding to a stage beyond merely kissing her hand, but the fact remains that he did not do so, and whilst secretly regretting the fact, she honoured him for it.

Like Adrienne, Mademoiselle de Bressignies disguised herself as a nun in a Lille convent. The bulky radio equipment was smuggled to her piece by piece by Cameron's agents via the Folkestone-Flushing ferry. As soon as the reassembled equipment began operating on 1 September, however, the generator required to power the transmitter proved so noisy that Ramble was forced to use the radio only as a receiver, sending messages back to Kirke by pigeon post. She none the less provided Kirke with an efficient channel for sending urgent instructions to his agents. 'If anything happened to her', wrote Kirke in his diary on 27 September 1915, 'it would be nothing less than a calamity'. Five weeks later the calamity occurred. Early in November, just as Kirke had agreed with her mother that she should be recalled for a rest, news reached him that she had been arrested but had managed to eat the report she was carrying. In Kirke's novel, Adrienne survives cruel interrogation, 'mock condemnation and sentence to death' to take her vows as a nun after Archer's death:

> Who knows but that, as the years roll by, Adrienne may not acquire something of the glamour of the Maid of Orleans, and by her example inspire future generations with the spirit of her own burning patriotism?

In real life, Ramble was less fortunate. She was sentenced to life imprisonment and died in prison two months before the armistice. But even before her capture she had acquired the reputation that came to Adrienne only years afterwards. To Sir John French, the British commander-in-chief, she seemed 'a regular modern Joan of Arc'.[40]

The greatest achievement of the GHQ intelligence staff during the first year of the war was to reconstruct with considerable accuracy the enemy order of battle. That, wrote Kirke after the war, was 'the bedrock of all intelligence work'. Macdonogh had a three-man staff (including Major Edgar Cox, who was to become head of intelligence at GHQ in 1918) continuously engaged in keeping the German battle order up to date. He himself carried most of it in his head. According to Kirke, 'he could remember the exact location of any German formation as it had been fixed months before. The appearance of any new unit caught his attention at once, without having to look up any records'.[41] In January 1916 Marshall-Cornwall, now a major, became responsible for keeping the battle order up to date, exchanging the latest intelligence on German troop movements with his opposite number in the

French *Deuxième Bureau* every evening by telephone. He began compiling an 'Index to the German Forces in the Field', popularly known as the 'Brown Book', which was issued to every intelligence officer and went through five revisions by October 1917.[42]

GHQ was, however, faced with increasing problems as the result of the rivalry of the CF and WL networks in the Low Countries both with each other and with Cumming's organisation. Kirke noted in his diary on 1 April 1915: 'Wallinger and [Cameron] seem to be running the same show only separately. This was not the original idea'.[43] As a post-war report acknowledged:

> They were, in fact, not only in actual if unconscious competition with each other, but also with parallel systems controlled by [Cumming] and our French and Belgian Allies ... In spite of the excellent results produced, there is little doubt that denunciations, buying up other services' agents, duplication of reports, and collaboration between agents of the various Allied systems were not uncommon, so that the information arrived at the various Headquarters in a manner which was not only confusing but sometimes unreliable and apt to be dangerous. This was due to the fact that there was an apparent confirmation of news really originating from the same source, owing to its being received at Allied Headquarters from what appeared to be different and independent places of origin.[44]

Cumming took a dim view of the competition to his own secret service in Holland organised by Cameron and Wallinger. But after his car accident in October 1914 he was out of action for several months and his operations had temporarily to be run for him by MO5 at the War Office. Cumming's station chief in the Netherlands was the Old Harrovian consul-general in Rotterdam, Ernest Maxse, who in fact resided at The Hague. With a dyed blacked moustache waxed into points at either end, a monocle dangling on a black silk ribbon, and 'fiery eyes set in a sallow, hollow-cheeked face', Maxse looked the part of a fictional spy or stage villain. In real life he was something of both.[45] As consul-general, however, he was forbidden direct contact with the spies he employed. His head of operations, responsible for the day-to-day running of the Dutch network, was R.B. Tinsley (codenamed 'T'), Cumming's pre-war agent in Rotterdam. Tinsley was short, tough, and broad-shouldered, with piercing eyes and a ruddy complexion, described by one of his staff as a 'combination of sea captain and prize fighter'. Kirke instinctively distrusted him. T might be 'a smart fellow', but no 'really high-class agent' would work for him: 'With him it is a matter of business and I doubt his imparting patriotic enthusiasm to agents'. T also spoke little Dutch and no French or German, and was thus ill equipped to run a train-watching service behind enemy lines. But he viewed the rival CF and WL networks with an evil eye.[46]

The intelligence collected by Tinsley was analysed by the military attaché at The Hague, Major Laurie Oppenheim, and then sent on to Cumming at the War Office. 'Oppy' was almost the opposite of 'T' in both manner and appearance: 'fairly tall and somewhat frail, scholarly in appearance, highly strung, and retiring in disposition'. One of T's deputies wrote later that he seemed to have little idea of the life of an agent in the field:

> He was, however, a brilliant staff officer, as I found out afterwards from his masterly analyses of the reports I sent him. He got every scrap of information there was to glean from them, and in the examination of train-watching reports, he was an expert in gauging the exact volume of each troop movement.[47]

Oppy's judgement of men was to prove less sound.

Macdonogh had no objection in principle to the existence of several independent agent networks gathering intelligence through Holland from behind the German lines. Parallel systems seemed useful partly as an insurance policy in case the Dutch government tried to close one network down, partly because each network provided some check on the accuracy of intelligence provided by its rivals. During 1915, however, Macdonogh took the view that 'no secret service work should be done in Belgium except under his orders' as head of intelligence at GHQ. The War Office disagreed. Lieutenant-Colonel C.N. French of MO6 (which became responsible for liaison with Cumming in an administrative reshuffle of April 1915) objected that 'C' was the servant of the Admiralty and the Foreign Office as well as of the War Office and had to collect information which was not necessarily of value to the Army in France. In November 1915 he proposed giving Cumming overall control of all Dutch operations: 'T should act as Head Agent for all secret service organisations in Holland, communicating directly to "C" and through him to the other parties concerned'. A compromise worked out in a meeting between French, Kirke and Cumming at the end of November gave Cumming the area to the east of Brussels and Cameron the area to the west. Wallinger (now more successful than Cameron) remained 'free to work all over Belgium' provided he did not interfere with the rival networks. Though Cumming 'did not see why he should not do what he liked in Belgium', the compromise survived until the summer of 1916.[49]

Similar tensions between C and GHQ showed themselves at the southern end of the Western Front. Early in the war Cumming established an agent network in Switzerland run by Lieutenant L.G. Campbell from the French frontier town of Annemasse, near Geneva. But Kirke considered 'C's Swiss system not as extensive as it might be', lacking 'men with local connections', and could see 'no objections to our trying to start an independent [system]'.

In fact Kirke started two independent systems. The first was organised by Lieutenant (later Colonel) George Pollitt, a tall, sandy-haired industrial chemist with a close-cropped moustache, later to become one of the founding directors of ICI, and variously described by those who knew him either as having 'a natural talent for leadership' or as being 'bluff, tactless [and] masterful'. At the outbreak of war Pollitt had dropped his career as one of Brunner Mond's leading scientists, bought a motorcycle, spent a day learning to ride it, and enlisted as a motor despatch rider. After the retreat from Mons his fluent French and German, acquired during a Continental childhood, won him a commission in the Intelligence Corps. Pollitt seemed ideally qualified for the Swiss assignment. He had a doctorate from Basle University, knew Switzerland well, and his expertise as an industrial chemist made it possible to arrange cover for him as British representative on an international analine dyes commission. Pollitt was instructed to establish an intelligence network based on the British consuls in Switzerland, some of whom had extensive pre-war German contacts. Though the consuls were forbidden direct involvement in secret service work, they were allowed to recommend the names of likely agents and forward messages delivered to the consulates. Arthur Abbott, vice-consul at Zurich, had been acting consul at Munich for three years before the outbreak of war and seems to have provided Pollitt with his first agent, codenamed Frey, who crossed into Germany on 12 March. Kirke was pleased with the results. A long report from Frey forwarded by Pollitt on 3 April was, he noted in his diary, 'good stuff'. 'Pollitt', he wrote a week later, 'appears to have started several good systems'. The most promising was based on an informant named Romulus, described by Kirke as 'an idealistic socialist, Russian-German Jew':

> He thinks the success of Germany will put back the socialistic clock so he wants to down them. He is helped by one Schmidt who runs a socialist paper, and who is doing all he can to bring off a socialist stop-the-war coup.
> He is in correspondence with socialists all over Germany who send him military information which they hope will enable him to judge his opportunity for the coup. They have no idea that they are helping the enemy, or doing anything like spying.

In late March Kirke persuaded Brunner Mond to send another of their employees, E.B. Harran, on a mission to Switzerland which would provide cover for espionage. Harran took over the Romulus/Schmidt network from Pollitt and by early June was receiving regular reports from Mannheim, Nuremberg, Stuttgart, Bremen and Frankfurt.[50]

As well as sending Pollitt to Zurich in March 1915, Wallinger also gained Kirke's approval to 'try and work Geneva'. Wallinger handed over the Genevan 'show' and general control of his Swiss operations to his elder brother Captain (later Major Sir) John Wallinger of the Indian police. The elder Wallinger was already in France on the look-out for signs of disloyalty among Indian troops and was able to use his new post to report to the India Office on Indian nationalists who had sought refuge in Switzerland.[51] He is said to have been an avid reader of detective stories and spy thrillers, and to have derived from them 'a great belief in waiters' who could, he believed, 'so easily get into places where information was lying about to be picked up'. To at least one of his agents, however, Wallinger seemed rather in awe of waiters in the more expensive restaurants:

> ... he could never face the business of tipping a waiter without an embarrassment that was obvious in his demeanour. He was tortured by the fear of making a fool of himself by giving too much or of exciting the waiter's icy scorn by giving too little.

Wallinger found at least one waiter who seemed likely to live up to expectations, a Swiss-German with the codename 'Bernard' and – allegedly – 'a bullet-shaped head, close-cropped, fair, with shifty blue eyes and a sallow skin' who, for a consideration, agreed to cross the border regularly into Germany.[52] Kirke was initially impressed. '*Bernard*'s first report', he noted in March 1915, '... is very promising. Man is undoubtedly careful to put down nothing of which he is not sure'. In June Kirke noted that two other agents sent by John Wallinger to Germany, codenamed Chillon and Rémond, were also sending 'good reports' and that a further agent, 'Lefebvre', had been established at Coblenz. To provide a channel of communication and payment for his network Wallinger established two further agents, one curiously named Dr Condom on the Swiss shore of Lake Geneva, the other Baron Brault (codenamed Baudin) at Evian on the French shore.[53]

By the autumn of 1915, however, the whole Swiss intelligence network was in disarray. George Pollitt, despite Kirke's high hopes in the spring, became disillusioned with his agents and obtained a transfer in July to the newly-established 'Special Brigade' for gas warfare.[54] His first agent, Frey, had proved to be a fraud, though he was kept on till the end of the year for fear, wrote Kirke, 'that he might give us away if dismissed'.[55] Harran, Pollitt's former colleague at Brunner Mond, became confused by the complexities of intelligence work and wrongly addressed some of his reports which ended up at the Berlitz School in Paris. By October, Kirke had concluded that Harran was 'not getting anything of value to us now'. Kirke was also increasingly anxious about the assistance provided by the British consuls. As early as 22 February he had denounced John Milligan, the vice-consul in Zurich, as a man of 'apparently no guts and very little brains' who had telegraphed intelligence reports *en clair*. By the summer he suspected both Richard de Candolle and Sander Gutman, respectively consul and pro-consul at Geneva, of pro-German sympathies. Despite the rules forbidding direct contact between consuls and agents, the Foreign Office was becoming increasingly uneasy over their involvement in intelligence work. In August Sir Henry Angst, the British consul general in Zurich, was accused by the Swiss police of involvement in espionage, and forced to retire soon afterwards.[56]

Switzerland proved much less hospitable to British agents than the Netherlands. Fearful that spies and revolutionaries from the warring powers who encircled them might undermine their precarious neutrality, the Swiss authorities kept watch on both. By late August John Wallinger's Swiss operations were close to collapse. One of his chief recruiters, Mayol, who treated his work – according to Kirke – as 'an easy way of making money', was denounced to the Swiss police by a man he tried to recruit, and then betrayed Chillon and Lefebvre in turn. Having been tipped off by Mayol, the Swiss police also tried unsuccessfully to lure Baron Brault across the frontier in order to arrest him. Brault was forced to leave Evian, change his name and hand his remaining agents over to Condom. But the Swiss were on the trail of Condom too and he was forced to flee by motor boat to the French shore of Lake Geneva.[57]

Kirke believed that Cumming's Swiss network was also doing 'no good at all'. C's agents, in his view, took unnecessary risks – 'or say they do' – by frequently crossing the Swiss border into and out of Germany. In June Cumming sought the help of scientists at London University in discovering secret inks to enable his agents to communicate at less risk to themselves. His researches had a remarkable outcome. C reported to Kirke in October that 'the best *invisible ink* is *semen*', on the grounds that it failed to react to iodine vapour, charring, 'or any test so far devised'. Kirke asked Cumming what semen did react to. He seems to have received no answer.[58]

To revive his crumbling organisation John Wallinger recruited the 41-year-old author Somerset Maugham. Maugham later wrote patronisingly that Wallinger appeared:

A very ordinary man on the fringe, I would have said, of the upper middle class ... I perceived that he was excessively flattered to be the lover of a handsome woman whom, in his simple-minded innocence of social conditions, he took for a great lady.

Wallinger's 'handsome woman' was a close friend of Maugham's own mistress, Mrs Syrie Wellcome, and the two couples dined several times together. Maugham was 'at a loose end' after an earlier spell with an ambulance unit on the Western Front, and jumped at the offer of intelligence work in Switzerland. He owed his recruitment as a secret agent partly, he believed, to his fluent French and adequate German, and partly to Wallinger's desire to please his mistress and her desire in turn to be agreeable to Syrie Wellcome.

The pretext for Maugham's sojourn in Switzerland – 'to write a play in the peace and quiet of a neutral country' – appeared moderately plausible. Within a few weeks he had written *Caroline*, a comedy loosely based on his affair with Syrie, which opened in London to packed houses and critical acclaim on 8 February 1916. His few months in Switzerland also gave him material for the first of his semi-autobiographical short stories about the secret agent Ashenden. Maugham's first Swiss mission, a visit to Lucerne to investigate an English expatriate with a German wife, served as the basis for 'The Traitor' in which Ashenden lures an Englishman with a German wife working in Lucerne for the German secret service over the border to a firing squad in France. Though Maugham made Ashenden's adventures 'coherent, dramatic and probable' instead of 'scrappy and pointless', like his own, the background detail of his life in Geneva, where he established himself after the Lucerne assignment, was remarkably accurate. The *Ashenden* stories were, said Maugham, 'on the whole a very truthful account of my experiences'. Some, indeed, were too truthful. He burned the manuscripts of fourteen of the stories after his friend Winston Churchill complained that they broke the Official Secrets Act, and he did not publish the remainder until 1928 because of the alleged security risks involved.[59]

Maugham took John Wallinger as the model for Ashenden's boss 'R'. When 'R' innocently enquires whether Ashenden likes macaroni, the scornful reply betrays the cosmopolitan Maugham's own disdain for his uncultivated chief:

> "What do you mean by macaroni?" answered Ashenden. "It is like asking me if I like poetry. I like Keats and Wordsworth and Verlaine and Goethe. When you say macaroni, do you mean *spaghetti, tagliatelli, vermicelli, fettuccini, tufali, farfalli,* or just macaroni?"
>
> "Macaroni", replied R, a man of few words.

Maugham's routine work in Geneva, like his relations with his boss, differed little from Ashenden's:

> He saw his spies at stated intervals and paid them their wages; when he could get hold of a new one he engaged him, gave him his instructions and sent him off to Germany; he waited for the information that came through and despatched it; he went into France once a week to confer with his colleague over the frontier and to receive his orders from London; he visited the market-place on market-day to get any message the old butter-woman had brought him from the other side of the lake; he kept his eyes and ears open; and he wrote long reports which he was convinced no-one read, till having inadvertently slipped a jest into one of them he

received a sharp reproof for his levity. The work he was doing was evidently necessary, but it could not be called anything but monotonous.

The 'old butter-woman' from French Savoy who crossed into Switzerland to sell butter, eggs and vegetables in the Geneva market-place figured prominently in Maugham's as well as Ashenden's career as a secret agent:

> Indeed this old lady looked so bland and innocent, with her corpulence, her fat red face, and her swirling good-natured mouth, it would have been a very astute detective who could imagine that if he took the trouble to put his hand deep down between those voluminous breasts of hers, he would find a piece of paper that would land in a dock an honest old woman (who kept her son out of the trenches by taking this risk) and an English writer approaching middle age.[60]

The old lady seems to have carried notes in both directions, giving and receiving them when Maugham bought vegetables from her. Kirke and Wallinger discussed alternatives to the old lady but decided that 'there would be nothing gained' by finding a substitute.[61]

Kirke had by now, however, grave doubts about the future of all intelligence operations in Switzerland. The Foreign Office had become uneasy about Romulus, the 'enthusiastic anti-Boche socialist' who had been reporting to the consul in Geneva, but was afraid that if it ended contact with him, 'he might turn nasty and accuse [the] consulate of espionage'. It was also, in Kirke's view, becoming 'very reactionary' over any involvement by consuls or embassy staff in intelligence work, despite Kirke's assurance that 'so far as complications with neutrals were concerned we were just as anxious to avoid them as [the Foreign Office] was, and no more injudicious than C's people and more careful than the French and Belgians'. Kirke suspected that Cumming's 'jealousy of our operations in Switzerland' was partly to blame for the Foreign Office's attitude. Since, however, he had no great hopes for the future of the Swiss operations, he declared that GHQ was 'ready to hand over the Swiss show entirely to C'. His offer was not taken up. Privately Kirke believed that Cumming himself had 'done no good down there at all'. On 30 November he saw Lieutenant L.G. Campbell, Cumming's station chief in Annemasse, who claimed to have given full details of the transfer of eleven divisions from the Eastern to the Western Front but complained that 'as he knows nothing of the Order of Battle or situation he never knows when he is being done down by his agents'. Kirke arranged for Campbell and an assistant to be fully briefed at GHQ. Six weeks later, however, Kirke heard that many of Cumming's agents in Switzerland had been arrested. Campbell himself had escaped: the 'Swiss apparently arrested the wrong Campbell and so gave our man warning'.[62]

Maugham, too, achieved very little. His main function had been to relay messages to and from a network of agents based on Frankfurt, Koblenz, Trier and Mainz. Some at least were fraudulent or non-existent. In February 1916 Cumming warned Kirke that one of Maugham's agents, 'Bernard', who had aroused high hopes a year earlier, 'has been doing us down'. Kirke had suspected as much for several months and after going though his reports thought it 'doubtful if he ever went to Germany – recently in any case'.[63] In one of Maugham's short stories 'Bernard' threatens Ashenden with a gun in a vain attempt to get more money out of him. Another agent, 'Gustav', also proves to be a fraud who had never been to Germany but concocted his reports by reading German newspapers and keeping his ears open in restaurants and beer-cellars frequented by German travellers.[64] Maugham's period in Switzerland, though of little significance in the history of espionage, marked a turning point in the development of the spy novel. His best-selling but ill-informed predecessors, William Le Queux and E. Phillips Oppenheim, had made their reputations and their fortunes by combining breathless excitement with unquestioning patriotism and daring coups which changed the course of history. Maugham emphasised instead the monotonous routine of much intelligence work and the detached boredom which it induced in him. Ashenden was the first in a line of cynical middle-aged heroes later continued by Eric Ambler and Graham Greene. Alec Leamas, the disillusioned British agent in *The Spy Who Came in from the Cold*, is cast in the same mould. John Le Carré, like Maugham a former British agent, was to acknowledge Maugham's influence on him as 'the first person to write about espionage in a mood of disenchantment and almost prosaic reality'.[65]

The monotony of Maugham's career as a secret agent was in striking contrast to the exotic complexity of his private life. He had, as Kirke noted in his diary in early February, 'got into the Divorce Court'. Though Mrs Wellcome had a number of lovers, Maugham alone was cited as co-respondent because, he complained, he was both 'unmarried and well-to-do'. On 14 February, a week after his new play opened on the London stage, Mr Wellcome was granted a decree nisi in an undefended suit on the grounds of his wife's adultery. Maugham wrote to his brother a month later: 'The future cannot have in store any worse harassment than I have undergone in the last eight months'. On 7 December, while Syrie's divorce proceedings were pending, Gerald Haxton, Maugham's homosexual American lover, was indicted at the Old Bailey on six counts of gross indecency. Though Haxton was acquitted, he left England under a cloud shortly afterwards. When he returned three years later he was deported as a security risk, apparently suspected not merely of unnatural vice but also of working for a foreign intelligence service.[66]

Captain Wallinger accepted Maugham's resignation in February 1916. But Syrie was anxious to get away from lurid London gossip about her well-publicised divorce and returned with Maugham to Geneva where he agreed to continue work as a free-lance, unpaid agent. The arrangement was not a success. Maugham later complained, self-pityingly, that 'left much to herself, Syrie was irritable and made many tiresome scenes' until she decided to return to England. With both Gerald Haxton and a disintegrating intelligence network on his mind, Maugham was not in the best of tempers himself. Of his intelligence work Maugham later said simply: 'After some time in Switzerland I found that there was nothing much more that I could usefully do there and I asked [Wallinger] to release me'.[67] By the time the American-born playwright Edward Knoblock replaced Maugham at the end of May 1916, Captain Wallinger's Swiss operation was on its last legs. 'JAW's Swiss show', wrote Kirke in July, 'so far as we are concerned is a waste of money...'. Captain Wallinger had attempted to remedy his lack of success in Switzerland by developing contacts with Germany through Denmark and Holland. But his Danish venture was a total failure and his Dutch operations were 'merely poaching' on his younger brother's territory. 'Therefore', concluded Kirke savagely, 'his organisation is useless, and has as a matter of fact not produced one report of any real value'. On 28 July he recorded in his diary the 'parting of the ways' with Captain Wallinger.[68]

Cumming was barely more successful in Switzerland than the elder Wallinger. He decided in April to give the operation run by Lieutenant L.G. Campbell from Annemasse a final two months in which to produce results. The trial failed. For the remainder of the year GHQ and Cumming's secret service (now known as MI1c) tried vainly, in a new spirit of cooperation, to salvage something from their Swiss operations. At the end of the year Cumming decided to cut his losses and sacked Lieutenant Campbell. Kirke concluded that GHQ should concentrate its secret service work in Holland which offered the best prospects not merely for intelligence from behind the German lines in Belgium and occupied France but also from Germany itself. 'Had we started to work Germany from Holland earlier instead of from Switzerland', he wrote in August 1916, 'we should have done much better'. 'Our only real professionals at the game' were, in his opinion, the younger Wallinger, Cameron, and their two most capable subordinates, Captains Best and W.L. McEwen.[69]

Within the Netherlands, however, the fragile compromise between the rival British networks worked out in November 1915 broke down in the summer of 1916. In May 1916 Tinsley's cover was blown in the Dutch press, and the Germans demanded his expulsion. A month later some of the reports from Tinsley's agents, forwarded by Oppenheim to Cumming, were captured when the Germans seized the British steamer *Brussels* on the North Sea. There followed the virtual collapse of Cumming's organisation of over forty train-watching posts in occupied France and Belgium. Frankignoul, the agent appointed by Tinsley to run the network from Maastricht, had over-centralised his system and the capture of some of his Belgian train-watchers – identified from the captured reports – led to the breakdown of the network as a whole. Kirke noted on 17 August that the network was producing 'no information' and showed 'no signs of resuscitating'. Oppenheim, the military attaché, probably at Tinsley's instigation, tried to blame Cameron's organisation for the Cumming network's downfall. Kirke dismissed the allegation as absurd, and believed that Tinsley was trying to steal Cameron's agents. Cameron retaliated by extending his own train-watching network into what had formerly been Cumming's territory.[70]

In November 1916 both the Cameron and Wallinger networks suffered a temporary setback when the Folkestone-Flushing ferry (their usual method of communication between Britain and the Netherlands) was intercepted by a German destroyer force from Zeebrugge. Remembering the fate of the *Brussels*, agents and couriers from several nations rushed to the side and began heaving their bags overboard while the Germans lowered boats and struggled to retrieve the sinking secrets with boat hooks and fishing tackle. At least one British bag floated long enough to be recovered. This bizarre episode led to the suspension of the cross-channel commercial ferry services for the remainder of the war, though there was later an irregular government-sponsored ferry from Harwich to the Hook of Holland which had usually to be provided with a naval escort.[71]

Both Wallinger in London (WL) and Cameron in Folkestone (CF) now proposed that their own officers direct Dutch operations on the spot. In the early days of WL and CF, it had been feared that the neutral Dutch would find British officers engaged on undercover work an intolerable provocation. But by the end of 1916 'experience had showed that the Dutch authorities did not intend to take a strong line against espionage'. Cumming's representatives in the Netherlands, Maxse and Tinsley, however, were determined to protect their own intelligence empire and protested strongly, with Oppenheim's support, against any proposal to send GHQ officers to Holland.[72]

Further complications were caused by the change of intelligence staff at GHQ which followed the appointment of Sir Douglas (later Earl) Haig to succeed Sir John French as commander-in-chief in December 1915. Macdonogh was recalled to the War Office as DMI together with Edgar Cox who became head of MI3, responsible for battle order intelligence. Though French had recommended Kirke as Macdonogh's successor at GHQ, Haig installed his own man, Brigadier John Charteris, with Kirke as his deputy. Charteris was a determined optimist and his intelligence analyses were soon in conflict with the more realistic estimates produced by Macdonogh in the War Office. Though Kirke's sympathies were with Macdonogh, Haig sided with Charteris and sharply criticised Macdonogh whose views, he claimed, caused 'many in authority to take a pessimistic outlook, when a contrary view, based on equally good information, would go far to help the nation on to victory'.[73]

In the quarrel between Tinsley and the GHQ networks, Charteris sided firmly with Cameron and Wallinger, claiming that during the second half of 1916 Cumming's intelligence from occupied Belgium contained 'no information of value'. Cox jumped to C's defence with a 'comparative table' designed to prove that his reports had been 'invaluable': 'in addition to a certain amount of information received only through "C", Major Cameron's train-watching reports would not have been complete without the corroboration of "C"'. After two months' quarrelling, a fragile compromise was reached in mid-February 1917. Tinsley was to establish a 'clearing house' for all intelligence reports from the CF and WL networks. Colonel Oppenheim would 'edit' these reports and telegraph any 'important information' to both the War Office and GHQ. That compromise, however, did little to reconcile either Maxse or Tinsley to the arrival a month later of Captains Best and Verdon to run, respectively, the WL and CF networks.[74]

By the time Best and Verdon arrived, Maxse had fallen victim to a German intelligence coup. He had, by his own melodramatic account, already survived several such coups. On one occasion he claimed to have recognised his taxi driver as a German agent just in time to jump out before the taxi smashed against a lamp post. This time he found himself hoist by his own anti-Semitism. On 18 February 1917 Francis Oppenheimer, the commercial attaché at The Hague legation responsible for monitoring the blockade of Germany (and not to be confused with Oppenheim, the military attaché), found photocopies of two of Maxse's letters among his morning post. The originals had been extracted by German intelligence from a diplomatic bag thrown overboard the previous November from the Flushing ferry. Oppenheimer found a description of himself in the letters as 'a typical Boche Jew' who was playing the enemy's game, as well as various suggestions for wrecking his career. When confronted with the letters, Maxse at first claimed that they were 'privileged' and refused to recant but, under threat of legal action, finally made an abject written apology on 26 February. Though he kept his job, he was officially informed that his name would under no circumstances ever appear in a war honours list.[75]

Tinsley's behaviour was even more villainous than Maxse's. Before Best left for the Netherlands, Cumming phoned to say Tinsley had been ordered to give him as much help as possible. 'But', he added, 'I must tell you that he's an absolute scoundrel'. At the Rotterdam quay Best was met by one of Tinsley's men, Peter Peterson, who drove him to his hotel. Best was suspicious:

I didn't like the hotel, I didn't like Peterson, so I put a hair round the lock of my suitcase and went and had a bath. When I came back to my room it was quite obvious that my suitcase had been opened and probably searched through. Of course I had nothing in it that was secret because in

those days I had a good memory. I never bothered to take notes of anything ...

Next morning Best called at Tinsley's office and found him fairly affable but
'a very rough looking customer, rather like the cartoon pictures of convicts'.
He was given an upstairs office which he shared with a naval intelligence
officer working for 'Blinker' Hall, 'a very nice young fellow' named English.
'Be careful', said English. 'Anything you say on the phone is listened to below
and you can be quite sure that all your letters will be gone through ... I've
been told to try to keep a watch and listen in if you have any people to see
you'.[76]

Soon after his arrival Best was waylaid by a man with a cosh who tried
and failed to lay him out. English told him that his assailant had been sent
by Tinsley. With Best's less robust deputy, Lieutenant Bennett, who had a
withered left arm, Tinsley tried more direct intimidation. Meeting him on the
stairs leading to Best's office, Tinsley threw him out. Best left, rented a house,
set up an office 'completely independent of Tinsley', and the 'clearing house'
compromise collapsed.[77]

There followed what Best called 'a furious correspondence with London'
which confirmed his independence from Tinsley. Gradually Best came to the
conclusion that Tinsley was involved in blackmail. A subsidiary part of
Tinsley's work was to put pressure on Dutch businessmen not to trade with
Germany and thus weaken the Allied blockade. The British legation in The
Hague kept a 'Black Book' of Dutch firms dealing with the Germans who
were debarred from all dealings with the Allies. Best believed that Tinsley
was demanding protection money from firms who wished to keep off the
British black list. He once called on a Dutch shipowner and found Peterson
apparently demanding money on Tinsley's behalf. Best blamed Tinsley,
probably correctly, for his recall in November 1917. His successor as head
of Wallinger's Dutch operations, Ivone Kirkpatrick (later permanent undersecretary at the Foreign Office), denounced Tinsley to the War Office as 'a liar
and a first-class intriguer with few scruples'. A War Office investigation found
no evidence that Tinsley had been involved in embezzlement or blackmail
but concluded, with some understatement, that he was 'difficult to get on
with'.[78]

Despite the feud with Tinsley, during the spring and summer of 1917,
Best – as Kirkpatrick noted – quickly 'bucked things up in Holland'.[79]
Wallinger's most successful Belgian network — the Lux service — was already
underway when he arrived. Towards the end of 1916 Van Tichelen, Wallinger's
chief Belgian agent, had approached the Abbé Buelens, a priest close to
Cardinal Mercier, the primate of Belgium, and asked him to organise a train-
watching service from Antwerp. The Abbé agreed, chose the codename Lux,
recruited his brother the Abbé René Buelens to organise a branch service

based on Malines and found other agents to watch the Mons and Brussels regions.

The weekly reports of the Lux service rolled towards the Dutch border, as one of Wallinger's staff put it, 'like a snowball'. Each Monday the agent at Mons received reports from Peruwelz and Boussu. On Tuesday he completed his own report and sent the three to Nivelles, where the agent added his and sent the four to Brussels. By now the Brussels agent had also received reports from Lessines and Peruwelz via Ath and from Waterloo farther south. Each Wednesday he forwarded the seven reports to the Abbé Buelens at Antwerp and the Abbé's brother sent him four more from Mélines, Neckerspoel, Muysen and Hombeek. Copies of all eleven reports were then sent to Holland by two separate routes. The slower but safer route was by barge. The quicker but riskier method was to use *passeurs* or professional smugglers to cross the electrified fence. Each *passeur* required three assistants, a hundred yards of string, rubber boots and gloves and a specially devised and insulated climbing frame. As the *passeur* crawled towards the wire he was followed by an assistant attached by string to two look-outs fifty yards away on either side. Each look-out tugged the string as soon as the sentry patrolling on his side of the *passeur* was out of sight. But it sometimes took more than one night in the cold and wet before both ends of the strings were pulled together and the *passeur* could use his climbing frame to cross the wire.[80]

The success of the Lux service owed much to Lux himself, the Abbé Buelens, a man of enormous energy and attention to detail. On one occasion he walked fifty-five miles from Antwerp to Mons to make changes in the railway watching system. On another he wrote to Wallinger in slightly halting English to express his determination to improve his network further:

Notwithstanding I already several times said to my [agent] 106 that he had to give us more complete information especially for military trains, I see that his report remains all ways as insufficient as before. So you would oblige me very much by indicating me any wants of details or information, even of trains perhaps not noticed... By that way I could give to my 106 the proof that his observation is not sufficient and that he has to give us better work.

Buelens paid great attention also to the security of his network. By the use of dead letterboxes such as church collection boxes he tried to prevent couriers meeting agents so that one arrest would not imperil the whole system. Buelens fell victim, however, to the inferior security of one of Cameron's networks, the Biscops service. When the Biscops courier service broke down after the treachery of one of its members in September 1917, Buelens offered to send the Biscops reports to Holland with his own. By tracking down first the Biscops couriers, then the Biscops agents, the Germans were able to track down Lux himself. Soon after Best was recalled from Holland in November 1917, the Abbé Buelens was arrested by the Germans.[81]

The intelligence lost after the disintegration of the Biscops and much of the Lux networks was more than compensated for by the dramatic revival of Cumming's Dutch and Belgian operations after their virtual collapse a year before. The recovery was due chiefly to Captain Henry Landau, the South African son of Anglo-Dutch parents who had lived through the Boer War on the Boer side. At Durban High School he was 'changed into an Englishman': 'I was taught to play the game; I excelled in athletics, and I was turned out a scholar'. In 1913 he graduated with first-class honours in natural sciences at Gonville and Caius College, Cambridge, where he spent 'the happiest days in my life'. After volunteering for military service he rose to the rank of captain in the Royal Field Artillery, and in 1916 was summoned to Cumming's office at the top of Whitehall Court. Cumming swung his swivel chair round to face him, and came brusquely to the point:

> I know all about your past history. You are just the man we want. You are to join T in Rotterdam, leaving tonight via Harwich and the Hook. Our trainwatching service has broken down completely in Belgium and in north-eastern France – we are getting absolutely nothing through. It is up to you to reorganize the service. I can't tell you how it is to be done – that is your job. You have *carte blanche*.

Unlike Tinsley, who knew little Dutch and no French or German, Landau was fluent in all three. One of his first contacts was a retired senior executive of the Belgian railways living in Holland named Moreau, who put him in touch with other Belgian railwaymen working in both Holland and Belgium who formed the basis of a new train-watching service.[82] Landau's greatest intelligence coup, however, came in July 1917 when he succeeded in taking over from Cameron what was to become the most important Belgian network of the war, *La Dame Blanche*, named after the legendary White Lady of the Hohenzollerns whose appearance was supposed to herald the downfall of the dynasty. The leaders of *La Dame Blanche*, Walthère Dewé and Herman Chauvin, both electrical engineers from Liège, who had grown increasingly irritated by the 'utterly contradictory instructions' they received from Cameron's agent Liévin, lost confidence in him altogether after one of his couriers betrayed some of the network to the Germans.[83]

Both Captain Landau and his assistant, Lieutenant (later Major) Hugh R. Dalton, who took control of Cameron's former network on Cumming's behalf, later proved to be rather doubtful characters themselves and ended up in the rogues' gallery of the interwar SIS (successor to the wartime MI1c). Landau, 'ever a gambler' by his own admission, left SIS soon after the war and spent the early twenties 'now frantically engaged in putting over some financial project in order to make the much-needed money, now dashing back to Brussels in the Opera season' to dally with the mistress of 'one of the most powerful men in Belgium'. His subsequent business ventures included smuggling Tsarist diamonds out of Soviet Russia and publishing a volume of secret service memoirs in the United States which outraged SIS and was banned in Britain.[84] Dalton remained in SIS between the wars, despite a report by Best that he had been involved in Tinsley's 'Black Book' blackmail, and became station chief in the Netherlands. In 1936 he committed suicide after embezzling several thousand pounds of SIS funds.[85]

During the First World War, however, Landau and Dalton were probably Cumming's two most successful agents. Walthère Dewé, a devout Catholic with a strict, almost puritanical sense of duty, later paid tribute to the 'remarkable judgement' shown by both Landau and Dalton in giving 'firm leadership' to *La Dame Blanche* without wounding its deep sense of national pride. 'British Intelligence', wrote Dewé, 'played a decisive role in ensuring the success of our organisation'. He also gave Landau and Dalton full credit for solving the difficult problem of communicating across the Dutch-Belgian border.[86] Their solution was relatively simple. Local peasants who owned fields bordering the electrified frontier threw tightly rolled bundles of messages over at three prearranged points. According to Landau:

> We were handicapped by the fact that at the frontier of Belgium we were forced to use Belgian peasants of a mental capacity far inferior to our agents in the interior; the Germans would have been suspicious of any other type, and besides, the peasants in tilling their soil, had an excuse to approach the wire.[87]

Little more than a month after Landau took control of *La Dame Blanche*, he achieved a major breakthrough. Dewé and Chauvin sent to see him a novice priest, Edmond Amiable, who came from Hirson, a town at a strategically vital point in the railway system of occupied France. For two years no Allied intelligence service had succeeded in organising regular surveillance in this crucial area. Amiable (codenamed A91) agreed to organise as part of *La Dame Blanche*'s network a tram-watching service on the Hirson-Mézières line which ran parallel to the German battlefront. The basis of the new system were two new observation posts (numbers 200 and 201) at Hirson and the neighbouring village of Fourmies, both operational by the end of September. Landau wrote to the leaders of *La Dame Blanche* to send them the congratulations of GHQ:

> Together with your existing organisation at Liège and Namur, you will have a complete check on all traffic coming from the East to the Western Front between Verdun and the sea. You will also be able to observe all lateral movements along this front ...

The Fourmies post was operated by a childhood friend of Amiable, Felix Latouche (codenamed 'Dominique'), his wife and two teenage sisters, who lived in a cottage overlooking the railway line. Together the family worked shifts twenty-four hours a day, watching the railway track through a narrow slit in heavily-curtained windows and using foodstuffs to count the contents of passing trains: beans for soldiers, chicory for horses, coffee for guns, and so on. Their reports were kept rolled up inside the hollow handle of a broom left in a corner of the kitchen for the courier to collect. Landau believed that from the moment the Fourmies post started work on 23 September not a single German troop train passed unobserved.[88]

Simultaneously, Landau had to deal with the difficult problems caused by the demand of *La Dame Blanche* that its members secretly enlist in the British army. Landau groaned inwardly at the problems of making British soldiers out of Belgian subjects, some of them women and most of them unknown to the War Office. He was, however, determined not to discourage the network and suggested that *La Dame Blanche* nominate a number of captains and lieutenants 'on a provisional basis' while the Army Council was considering the request. In February 1918, probably after vigorous lobbying by Cumming, *La Dame Blanche* was told that its '*militarisation*' had been approved by the Army Council. This vague formula was to produce problems after the Armistice. *La Dame Blanche* was officially recognised in 1919 as a 'Volunteer Service attached to the British Army in France', Dewé and Chauvin were given the CBE, and its other members received the war medal and a citation in a special order of the day. But no ranks were specified and the network was not recognised as an integral part of the British army. Despite post-war problems, *militarisation* gave a powerful boost to wartime recruitment and morale. As Chauvin put it:

> Enlistment as a soldier gave the new recruit certain proof of the value of the work asked of him. It offered the prospect of official recognition after the war of the services he had rendered ... and of being seen as a brother in arms by the valiant soldiers at the Front to whom all thoughts were turned.

The sense of being under military discipline also encouraged accuracy of reporting which became increasingly systematic and comprehensive. Late in 1917 the leadership of *La Dame Blanche* distributed to its members lead identity disks giving name, date, place of birth and network number, together with orders to bury each disk until the war was over. *La Dame Blanche* was now established as the most successful intelligence network in the history of the Western Front.[89]

Efforts also continued during 1917 to improve the flow of intelligence from behind the German lines direct to GHQ (which had moved to Montreuil in

March 1916), where Major Reginald Drake (formerly of MI5) had now succeeded Kirke as head of secret service work. The main drawback even with the reports from railway watchers supplied by *La Dame Blanche* was that, by the time they had followed the difficult and circuitous route from Belgium or Northern France to The Hague to London to Montreuil, they were ten days old or more. Intelligence reports from agents or local inhabitants brought by carrier pigeon from behind enemy lines direct to GHQ were neither as important nor remotely as comprehensive as those from *La Dame Blanche* but they had the advantage of being sometimes only a few hours old when they arrived at Montreuil. During 1917, however, the RFC refused to land either agents or pigeons more than fifteen miles behind the German front line and restricted its flights to nights when it considered both the phase of the moon and the weather were suitable. As Drake concluded in his bureaucratic prose: 'It therefore became essential to think out some other means of conveying agents to the desired localities'.[90] The discovery of that 'other means' derived from one of Best's brainwaves in the autumn of 1916. Why not, he suddenly asked, use balloons? Off he went to the Naval Ballooning School at Hurlingham run by Commander 'Pink Tights' Pollock, an elderly prewar solicitor and amateur balloonist who had earned his curious nickname during an embarrassing incident when he became entangled in the mooring ropes of a balloon, lost his trousers and revealed a pair of pink combinations. Pollock quickly agreed to train two of Wallinger's lieutenants, Ivone Kirkpatrick and a wounded officer called Saxton, in the art of ballooning so that they could then pass on their expertise to Wallinger's agents.[91]

The first attempt to send agents by balloon took place early in 1917, supervised by Commander Pollock in a field nine miles from the front line. The two French agents selected for the first flight, Lefebvre and Faux, intended to land as close as possible to their home village near Valenciennes, organise an espionage network and communicate with Wallinger through Holland. Kirkpatrick later recalled the scene as the agents were provided with baskets and carrier pigeons, and climbed into the balloon at 1 o'clock in the morning:

> I seemed to be seeing two men off for execution. We shook hands with them and wished them bon voyage. Pollock tested the "lift" of the balloon and in a quiet voice said "Go". The balloon rose slowly, Lefebvre said "Vive la France" and in a few seconds they were gone and completely lost from view. We tramped silently through the mud back to our cars.

The next day a third agent, Jules Bar, was despatched by the same method. This time, however, a gramophone was introduced which played the *Marseillaise* as Bar rose into the heavens. For future flights the gramophone was retained but the record changed to the *Brabançonne* when Belgian agents were employed.[92]

So far as agents were concerned the 'balloon stunt' was an ingenious idea with disappointing results. Faux and Lefebvre sent only one carrier pigeon and then went to ground for the remainder of the war. GHQ believed they had lost their nerve. Jules Bar descended too quickly, broke a leg, was captured by the Germans and shot by a firing squad. Partly because of the difficulty of guiding the balloon to the desired landing site, only seven further agents were sent by balloon behind enemy lines during the remainder of the war. Only one – a Belgian army officer sent to Luxemburg – sent back information of much value.[93] He and his less successful colleagues were the forerunners of the thousands of agents parachuted into occupied Europe by SOE in the Second World War.

The balloons turned out to be better suited to pigeons than to people. Pollock, Best, Kirke and others developed an ingenious Heath Robinson apparatus consisting of an eight-foot balloon fitted with an alarm clock and cross frame from which were suspended four carrier pigeons, each in a wicker basket with its own parachute and covered in wire netting to protect it from ground attack by rats and ferrets. Fully assembled, the whole apparatus stood about twenty feet high. Ivone Kirkpatrick had to tour London pawnshops looking for the right kind of alarm clock. Only the American Waterbury make would do. It alone had a handle which revolved when the alarm went off and could be used to release the pigeon baskets from the balloon. Not surprisingly, Colonel Drake demanded a demonstration before allowing such a fantastical apparatus to be used on the Western Front. At a secret trial in London a Waterbury alarm was fixed to the ceiling, with four captured German army boots taking the place of the pigeon baskets. As soon as the alarm went off, the boots thudded to the ground. Drake's doubts vanished and he immediately authorised the purchase of a hundred balloons with all necessary alarm clocks, baskets, hydrogen gas and other equipment. By calculating wind speed and direction it was possible to drop the pigeons in approximately the right area by setting the alarm to go off at the right time. When the supply of imported Waterbury clocks ran out, yellow cotton fuse of variable length was used instead. With the pigeons went questionnaires printed in French and Flemish, with instructions for fixing the completed questionnaires to the pigeons' legs by a special clip, and an appeal to the patriotism of the finder:

> The resistance of the Boche is being exhausted by the Allied attacks, which have already freed a part of French soil. In order to maintain the advance, it is necessary that the Allies should be well informed regarding the position of the enemy and his intentions. It is your duty as good patriots who are in the midst of the enemy troops to render this service to the Allies. The means of doing so are here at hand. You may risk your life, but think of the Allied soldiers who give theirs so gallantly to set you free. By sending information you will be doing your country an incalculable service and you

will hasten the end of the war. We shall know how to reward you when peace comes and you will always have the satisfaction of knowing that you acted as a good patriot.[94]

There were inevitably some mishaps. Some of the pigeon parachutes failed to open. Others landed many miles off target. One group of pigeons landed on a hungry section of the Canadian Corps who ate all but one which was sent back to base with a ribald message of thanks. By and large, however, the 'pigeon stunt' was a success. After the first pigeon drops by balloon behind the lines at the end of February 1917, wrote Kirkpatrick later, 'GHQ ... changed their tune from polite scepticism to enthusiasm'. Wallinger and Pollock who had supervised the first launches returned triumphant to London, leaving Kirkpatrick and a tough South African former mining engineer, Captain R.G. Pearson, in charge. The results exceeded Drake's wildest expectations. He had expected five per cent at most of the pigeons to fly back with messages. In fact, he calculated at the end of the war that at least forty per cent had returned:

The information in most cases was of a very high order and had the advantage of being fresh and rapidly transmitted ... The balloons were usually despatched about 11 o'clock at night and many of the messages were received at 9 o'clock the next morning.[95]

Remarkable myths grew up behind the German lines about the secret service work of British pigeons. One German admirer wrote after the war:

With the practical genius of their nation, the English, after long preparation, accomplished a piece of espionage unexampled in the history of the prewar secret service. The British secret service agents had noted that their carrier pigeons followed, in the one case the course of the Rhine, and in the other the railway between Amsterdam and Thorn. They now had tiny cameras made, so light that they could be fastened to the birds' tails. These appliances were fitted with clockwork, which at set times would expose portions of a film, and since a whole flight of pigeons was always released simultaneously, and their cameras could be set to make exposures at different times, it would be possible to obtain a fairly continuous series of photographs.[96]

Equally remarkable myths grew up behind the British lines. Best mischievously informed one curious general that he had just succeeded in crossing pigeons with parrots, thus producing super-pigeons capable of reporting by word of mouth. The general not merely failed to see the joke but allegedly reported Best to GHQ for 'having divulged most secret information'.[97]

Though the success of the intelligence missions flown by allied pigeons surpassed all expectations, two problems remained. The first was the growing difficulty of recruiting enough trained pigeons. By 1918 the pigeon wing of the Signal Service required 20,000 birds in addition to those needed for intelligence work.[98] Then there were the risks run by patriots in occupied France and Belgium. Pigeons frequently refused to remain silent while secret information was being attached to their legs and could not be hidden in private dwellings because they were, as Kirkpatrick complained, 'liable to coo'. Those who wrote intelligence reports for the pigeons thus usually did so in a hurry. 'The problem', it seemed to Kirkpatrick, 'was to substitute a mechanical device for a live pigeon'. After considerable thought, he and other members of the Wallinger organisation devised an ingenious pigeon-substitute, code-named the 'tin-pot stunt':

a system by which small balloons for use by the inhabitants in lieu of pigeons, together with small tin canisters containing the necessary chemicals for the production of hydrogen or similar gas, were despatched by our pigeon balloons to the inhabitants with the necessary instructions.

The tins were cleverly designed. Each had two spouts on top, one with a balloon on the end, the other open. Once the tin was placed in a bucket of water, water entered through the open spout, activated the chemical and inflated the balloon. The apparatus and instructions were accompanied by a patriotic appeal printed in French and Flemish:

Attention!
Are you a good patriot? Will you help the Allies to beat back the enemy? Yes.
Then open this packet; take it unobserved to your home; open it in the evening when you are alone and act according to the instructions which you will find in it.

A hundred-balloon trial ordered by Drake failed, however, to live up to expectations. Ingenious though it was, the 'tin-pot stunt' was no real substitute for pigeons. Only one hydrogen balloon bearing secret information was observed approaching the Western Front and by sheer bad luck it burst just over the German front line, impaling its message on enemy barbed wire. Fortunately for the sender, who had given her name and address, the message – after fluttering for a few days on the wire – was captured in a raid on German trenches. Drake discontinued the experiment. 'The system', he unkindly concluded, 'was perhaps too complicated for the intelligence of the average peasant'. Kirkpatrick too was inclined to blame the peasants. 'From my experience', he wrote, 'I doubt if all of them would recognise an Easterly wind when they saw it'.[99]

'Tin-pot stunt' was abandoned after the failure of the hundred-balloon trial. It proved in any case to be unnecessary since the pigeon shortage feared by Drake never occurred and pigeon recruitment continued at an adequate level until the end of the war. The regular flow of train-watchers' reports despatched to GHQ through Holland and the intelligence brought direct by carrier pigeon from behind enemy lines were supplemented by a more irregular supply of intelligence from prisoners of war and the occasional deserter. As an intelligence officer with the British Second Army during 1915 Marshall-Cornwall had three German-speaking officers under him specialising in interrogation or – as it was then called – 'the examination of prisoners':

> Whenever a prisoner was captured at any point on our Corps front, or a German aircraft was shot down, I sent one of my officers on a motor cycle to carry out an immediate examination. We found that prisoners-of-war were much more inclined to be communicative immediately after capture, if treated with kindness and given a cigarette, than later on when incarcerated in the Corps POW cage.

Gradually the Intelligence Corps developed what it euphemistically termed 'special examination' by stool pigeons. The best results were obtained from carefully coached 'pigeons' in casualty clearing stations during battle.[100]

As so often in the history of intelligence, the main problem on the Western Front was the use made of it. Good intelligence was, all too frequently, badly used. Haig was not disposed to credit intelligence reports which clashed with strong inner convictions derived, he believed, from providence as well as his own intuition. He wrote to his wife from GHQ soon after becoming commander-in-chief: 'All seem to expect success as a result of my arrival and somehow give me the idea that they think I am "meant to win" by some SUPERIOR POWER'. As soon as sufficient shells were available, Haig told *The Times* correspondent, 'we could walk through the line at several places'. Just as Haig dreamt of a dramatic breakthrough to end the deadlock on the Western Front, so Brigadier John Charteris, his head of intelligence at GHQ from December 1915 to December 1917, yearned for some spectacular intelligence coup which would make unnecessary the tedious business of plotting the enemy's order of battle and troop movements from thousands of agent reports. He instructed Major Kirke in 1916 that his main objective should be to get agents directly through the enemy front line. As the year wore on, relations between Kirke and Charteris steadily deteriorated. Kirke noted in frustration: 'He has no clear idea how [the agents] are to get through, what they are going to do when they get through or how they are to communicate but he pictures us pushing men over by the tens, all with means of com[municatio]n.' Kirke argued strongly that GHQ should continue to concentrate its efforts on obtaining intelligence through Holland, and not 'waste our experts' time in visionary schemes'. Charteris paid no attention and Kirke became increasingly despondent as he watched his men 'taken away from their regular work for any new hare'. The time wasted by Charteris's various hares was, in Kirke's view, 'appalling'. Charteris, in turn, implied that Kirke did not know his job, and gradually made his position impossible:

> His constant intervention in matters of detail makes it almost impossible to do anything – as unless he is asked first in every detail his inclination is to reverse anything one has done.

Kirke's posting to the 4th Infantry Division in January 1917 was, he told his wife, 'a blessed relief from intrigue and political scheming'.[101]

Kirke's successor, Major Drake, had greater sympathy with Charteris's schemes for getting agents across the enemy front lines. So, apparently, did Drake's deputy, Major (later Major-General Sir) Stewart Menzies, who was to become head of SIS in the Second World War. During 1917 a group of agents was assembled, irreverently known as the 'Suicide Club', in order to take advantage of the breaches in the enemy line which Charteris, like Haig, confidently expected to result from allied attacks. All were trained in fieldcraft, communications, riding, map reading and the use of the compass. They led a miserable life, usually resented or ignored by the cavalry officers from whose breaches in the line they were supposed to profit, poorly provided with food and blankets, and suffering a variety of other hardships 'in addition to incurring the risk of being taken for enemy agents and shot'. Not until trench warfare began to give way to open fighting in the final months of the war did some members of the 'Suicide Club' finally get across the German line. Even then, as Drake acknowledged, the intelligence they gathered was 'of a useful though not perhaps highly important nature'.[102]

In a staff lecture at GHQ in February 1916 Charteris listed 'the desire to please' as first among the 'great pitfalls that every Intelligence Officer must avoid'. He failed to heed his own advice. Marshall-Cornwall, who served under him, was alarmed by his 'breezy optimism'. His intelligence summaries 'seemed intended to bolster up our own morale rather than to paint a true picture of the enemy's strength and fighting qualities'. Macdonogh, the DMI at the War Office, and Edgar Cox, head of MI3, who were, in Marshall-Cornwall's view, 'the finest intelligence brains at the disposal of the country', produced much more cautious estimates of the enemy's strength, but it was Charteris who had Haig's ear. During April 1916, with Charteris on sick leave in the south of France, Marshall-Cornwall was told to brief Haig in his stead. He was appalled by Haig's low opinion of the German troops: 'He seemed to think that they were on the verge of collapse, and that only one more push was wanted to create a gap for the cavalry to break through'. In that firm conviction, which Marshall-Cornwall could not shake, Haig began on 1 July 1916 the disastrous offensive on the Somme. The British troops, weighed down by sixty-six pound packs, advanced at walking pace in even lines towards the enemy trenches, presenting German machine-gunners with their best target of the war. As one line of troops was cut down, so others came on, regularly spaced at intervals of a hundred yards. At the end of the first day's fighting the British had lost almost 60,000 killed and wounded: more than on any other day in the history of the British army, greater too than the losses suffered by any other army on any day of the First World War. Haig failed utterly to grasp the nature of the catastrophe which had befallen him. He wrote in his diary on the following day: 'The enemy has undoubtedly been severely shaken. Our correct course, therefore, is to press him hard with the least possible delay'. When the battle ended five months later in a wilderness of mud, although the front line had here and there advanced about five miles, some of Haig's objectives for the first day's fighting had still not been achieved. Comforting himself with inflated intelligence estimates of enemy casualties, he still persuaded himself that the Somme had been a successful battle of attrition. 'The results of the Somme', he wrote, 'fully justify confidence in our ability to master the enemy's power of resistance'.[103]

Charteris's intelligence reports throughout the five-month battle were designed to maintain Haig's morale. Though one of the intelligence officer's duties may be to help maintain his commander's morale, Charteris crossed the frontier between optimism and delusion. After tanks were used for the first time – without any great success – in September 1916, Charteris confidently announced: 'It is possible that the Germans may collapse before the end of the year'. On one occasion Charteris also arranged for Haig to visit a prisoner of war camp from which all the healthiest Germans had been removed so that the commander-in-chief might be encouraged by the poor condition of those who remained. Haig's diary strongly suggests that during 1916 and 1917 he was fed with a highly selective intelligence diet which left him with a misleading impression that riots and pestilence were spreading through the Fatherland at an encouraging rate. He was confidently forecasting in the summer of 1917 that in six months' time, with fighting at the present rate, Germany would have reached the end of her manpower reserves. In reality the disintegration of the Russian war effort before and after the October Revolution allowed the Germans to shift many fresh divisions to the Western Front.[104]

Major Desmond Morton (later Churchill's intelligence aide during the

Second World War) served as one of Haig's ADCs from September 1917 to April 1919 and for two months as his private secretary also. His verdict on Haig, though harsh, reflects the dismay of those who did not share Charteris's optimism:

> He hated being told any new information, however irrefutable, which militated against his preconceived ideas or beliefs. Hence his support for the desperate John Charteris, incredibly bad as [head of GHQ intelligence], who always concealed bad news, or put it in an agreeable light.[105]

Charteris's nemesis came in November 1917 at Cambrai, the first real tank battle of the war. Over a week before the British offensive began, Marshall-Cornwall discovered from captured documents and prisoners of war that three German divisions from the Russian front had arrived to strengthen the Cambrai sector. Almost identical intelligence arrived from Holland. Charteris refused to believe either. He told Marshall-Cornwall:

> This is just a bluff put up by the Germans to deceive us. I am sure the units are still on the Russian front; they are not to be shown on our order of battle map. If the commander in chief were to think that the Germans had reinforced this sector, it might shake his confidence in our success.

On 20 November, 381 British tanks broke through the German lines before Cambrai to win what seemed a famous victory. For the first and only time in the war the church bells of London were rung in celebration. But the celebrations were shortlived. Ten days later the German forces, strengthened by the reserves in which Charteris had disbelieved, had retaken all the lost ground and more at the cost of heavy British casualties. Both Marshall-Cornwall and Best found it difficult to forgive Charteris's error of judgment. Even before the offensive began Marshall-Cornwall had told Haig's Director of Military Operations that, faced with Charteris's suppression of information 'to suit his own ideas', he could no longer serve under him. In January 1918 he was transferred to the War Office as head of MI3. By that time, however, the war cabinet – furious at the failure of intelligence at Cambrai – had already forced Haig, against his wishes, to move Charteris to another job. 'He seems', wrote Haig later, 'almost a sort of Dreyfus in the eyes of our War Office authorities'. To Macdonogh's delight, Charteris was succeeded after a brief interval by the former head of MI3, Brigadier Edgar Cox.[106]

The intelligence available to Haig and Cox was better in 1918 than ever before. Over the final year of the war as a whole their most valuable source was probably *La Dame Blanche*, whose agents increased from 129 when Landau assumed control of the network in July 1917 to 408 by January 1918 and 919 by the Armistice, reporting from ninety observation posts. About eighty per cent of their reports concerned military movements by rail, but the network also contained *agents promeneurs* who reported on movement by road and activities at military bases. The Fourmies post provided particularly valuable intelligence on preparations for the German March offensive. Landau wrote to the leaders of *La Dame Blanche* in January 1918:

> There is no doubt that at this critical moment you represent by far the most abundant Allied intelligence source and that the results you are achieving are of inestimable value.

Cumming himself wrote to congratulate *La Dame Blanche* six months later:

> The work of your organisation accounts for 70 per cent of the intelligence obtained by all the Allied armies not merely through the Netherlands but through other neutral states as well ... It is on you alone that the Allies depend to obtain intelligence on enemy movements in areas near the Front ... The intelligence obtained by you is worth thousands of lives to the Allied armies.

Landau's own estimate was that the network was providing seventy-five per cent of all Allied intelligence received through neutral states. Both his estimate and that of Cumming were probably exaggerated but it is unlikely that any other British source provided such regular, detailed and dependable intelligence on German troop movements.[107]

The Wallinger organisation in the Netherlands, headed after Best's recall late in 1917 by Ivone Kirkpatrick, who also took over the few remaining remnants of Cameron's organisation, ran eleven much smaller Belgian networks during the last year of the war (codenamed Alice, Caligula, Faust, Felix, Hadrian, Le Poilu, Lux, M.S., Moïsé, Negro, Venus). Three (Faust, Felix, Negro) were run by double agents: Belgians or Dutchmen who also worked for German Intelligence. The Felix network was based on Belgian prostitutes who passed on information gathered from German soldiers and were paid in either cash or drugs which Kirkpatrick had to obtain from England. Most of Kirkpatrick's networks, however, were mainly concerned, like *La Dame Blanche*, with train-watching, though none compared with it in size or significance. The largest, Lux, reconstructed by one of the Abbé Buelens's friends, never exceeded fifty agents.[108] Some consisted of only a handful of people. In all about three thousand Belgians worked for one of Cumming's networks at some time during the war, and about two thousand for the two GHQ organisations (WL and CF). The much smaller networks run by Belgian and French Intelligence contained about seven hundred members each. Kirkpatrick considered them 'insignificant' and claimed they 'did little more than interrogate German deserters and retail gossip picked up on the frontier'.[109]

Though Kirkpatrick regarded Tinsley with extreme distrust, he found Landau 'exceptionally efficient'.[110] Landau's priorities were unusually far-sighted. Unlike Charteris and Menzies, he was resolutely opposed to any dramatic coup which risked disrupting the humdrum, but ultimately more important, flow of train-watchers' reports. At the end of February 1918 *La Dame Blanche* announced that the German supreme commander, Field-Marshal Hindenburg, was due to visit German headquarters at the Belgian town of Spa in mid-March and asked if it should organise an assassination attempt. Landau replied that the risk to the whole network was too great. He gave the same reply to a suggestion by *La Dame Blanche* in July 1918 that it engage in what it called '*espionage proprement dit*'. 'The information obtained', wrote Landau, 'does not justify the risks involved'.[111]

Haig later claimed that even before opening his morning post he went through the 150 pages of *La Dame Blanche*'s weekly reports and made 'constant use of them' when planning operations. His diary for 1918 tells a different story. He refers quite frequently to documents captured from the enemy, to information from POWs, to aerial reconnaissance, to articles in the German press. But he refers only once to the work of the train-watchers which depended on the patient accumulation of information and was almost devoid of the more exciting nuggets obtained by other usually less important sources.[112]

During the early months of 1918 Brigadier Cox at GHQ received a stream of good intelligence from a variety of sources on preparations for the last great German offensive in March 1918. At the turn of the year *La Dame Blanche* and other train-watchers revealed the transfer of forty German divisions from Russia and Rumania to the Western Front. The Belgian networks also reported that artillery camps to practise offensive tactics had been established at Antwerp and Liège, and the Fourmies post of *La Dame Blanche* disclosed that a new body of shock-troops, 'Force D', was training nearby. Cox knew that when these formations left for the Front, the offensive would be imminent. During January aerial reconnaissance and photographic interpretation revealed new trench-mortar emplacements and piles of shells near the German front-line. During February the train-watchers reported large numbers of enemy troops pouring into the triangle Valenciennes-Hirson-Douai, and aerial reconnaissance revealed almost daily extensions to the German light railway network. On 16 February Brigadier Cox told a conference of British army commanders presided over by Haig that they must 'be prepared to meet a very severe attack at any moment now'. According to Haig, 'All felt confident on being able to hold their front'. Then, in early March, came the news that the artillery units from Antwerp and Liège and 'Force D' from Fourmies were on the move. Cox was now convinced that the offensive would begin within the month. Though Haig accepted Cox's forecast, he remained as usual over-optimistic about the outcome, 'only afraid that the enemy would find our front so strong that he will hesitate to commit his Army to the attack with the almost certainty of losing very heavily'.[113]

A German pilot shot down on 18 March revealed that the attack would come on the 20th or 21st. His information was confirmed on the following day by a captured German artillery NCO, by a group of infantry prisoners and Alsatian deserters from a trench-mortar battery on the British Fifth Army front, and by a prisoner and a Polish deserter on the Third Army front. General Sir Hubert Gough, the commander of the Fifth Army, recorded in his diary that on the night of 20 March 'all of us felt perfectly certain that we would be wakened before morning by the roar of battle. And so we were'. The attack began on the morning of the 21st at almost precisely the point predicted by Cox.[114] The Germans, however, still had one surprise in store. On the evening of the following day, 22 March, the clerk to Colonel Oppenheim, the military attaché in The Hague, tiptoed into his room and whispered to him to look through the keyhole into his typist's room. To his horror Oppenheim saw the typist putting copies of secret telegrams into his pocket. A search of the typist's rooms revealed that for three months past he had been selling to the Germans copies of Oppenheim's intelligence reports.[115] Happily, they failed to compromise the train-watching networks.

Haig's optimistic assessment of British defences was confounded by the stupefying violence of the opening German offensive: bombardment by nearly 6,000 guns, followed by attack under cover of fog by sixty-two infantry divisions (fifty of them identified by Cox on the first day of the battle). No previous advance since the Western Front had solidified at the end of 1914 had much exceeded ten miles. In the offensive begun on 21 March 1918 the Germans advanced forty miles in a few days. A second offensive opening in Artois on 9 April carried the Germans ten miles in three days. Pétain, the French commander-in-chief, began speaking as if the war was almost lost. 'The Germans', he told Clemenceau, the French prime minister, 'will beat the English in the open field, after which they will beat us too'. It was Haig's alarm at Pétain's apparent 'funk' which led the British to take the initiative in the appointment on 14 April of Marshal Foch as the first 'Commander-in-Chief of the Allied armes in France'. Even Foch at first seemed less than optimistic. When congratulated by Clemenceau on his appointment, he replied, 'A fine gift! You give me a lost battle and tell me to win it.' To Haig also it seemed that the supreme crisis of the war had come. He told his men in an order of the day on 11 April: 'Every position must be held to the last man: there must be no retirement. With our backs to the wall, and believing in the justice of our cause, each one of us must fight on to the end.'[116]

Military intelligence was equal to the great demands made on it by the German offensive. The Cumming and Wallinger networks provided daily reports on 'all the rail moves of Hun troops' in occupied France and Belgium, air reconnaissance came once again into its own as the trenches gave way to a war of movement, and a further flow of intelligence came from POWs and captured documents. Though Haig had underestimated the impact of the offensive on 21 March, Cox had forecast its strength and timing with great precision. 'You were right', Gough told Cox's deputy, 'right to the tick, and thanks'.[117] Haig too phoned his congratulations. Before the second wave of the German offensive on 9 April Haig made a different error of judgment. He remained convinced that the enemy would attack the Vimy ridge – the objective that, in their place, he would have chosen himself — and discounted aerial reconnaissance reports which correctly pointed to an attack further south. Before the third and final wave of the German offensive on 27 May GHQ intelligence itself at first misread the enemy's intention. As late as 24 May Cox still expected the attack to come in the Albert-Arras sector. But on the 26th he reported the movement south from Belgium of four enemy divisions and heavy artillery towards Laon, on the German side of the Chemin des Dames sector of the Front. He also produced a captured letter from a German soldier correctly reporting the coming attack on the Chemin des Dames. Haig thought such an attack quite likely, but Foch did not and on 27 May was taken by surprise.[118]

With Macdonogh as DMI at the War Office and Cox as head of intelligence at GHQ the tension evident earlier in the war between War Office and GHQ disappeared. Neither, however, had the ear of Haig. Cox was tragically drowned off Le Touquet at the end of August. A few days earlier Marshall-Cornwall had found him 'disheartened by the fact that Douglas Haig appeared to ignore his advice on intelligence matters and still placed his confidence in the wishful thinking of Charteris'.[119]

But Haig, on this occasion, was right. His invincible optimism, which had hitherto been something of a liability, now became a valuable asset to the Allied cause. With the gift of hindsight it is possible to see the three waves of the German offensive not as a strategy which stood a serious chance of success but as a desperate gamble on short-term victory as the only means to stave off long-term defeat: a defeat made inevitable by the five million Americans who would be fighting on the Western Front in 1919 and by the growing success of the Allied naval blockade. The Germans lacked the resources to extend, or even to sustain, their early successes.

The most telling evidence of the turning tide came from French rather than British intelligence. The greater German use of radio to communicate with their forward positions offered increasing scope to French military cryptographers. On 3 June the greatest of the French codebreakers, Georges Painvin, decrypted a German signal later christened 'le radiotélégramme de la victoire' which revealed plans for the German assault on the French lines between Montdidier and Compiègne which opened at midnight on 9 June.[120] Forewarned, the French resisted the German onslaught. For the first time since the opening of his offensive on 21 March, Ludendorff was forced to suspend an operation before it had reached its target. Though the French had to parry further German thrusts during June, the tide of battle swung thereafter in favour of the Allies. Yet it was Haig rather than the French who drew the correct conclusions from intelligence on the crumbling of the German offensive. Even after the great British victory on 8 August at Amiens, which Ludendorff later called 'the black day for the German army in the history of the war', Foch did not foresee a decisive breakthrough until April 1919. Haig was convinced that, on the contrary, the war could and must be won in the autumn of 1918 before the enemy had a chance to recover. It was the armies of the British Empire which bore the main brunt of the fighting in the final stages of the war. In the three months between the battle of Amiens and the armistice of 11 November the British army under Haig captured 188,700 prisoners of war and, 2,840 guns. 'Never at any time in its history', said Foch, 'has the British army achieved greater results in attack than in this unbroken offensive'. On Armistice Day GHQ intelligence produced the last of a series of weekly 'Order of Battle' summaries showing the location of the 186 enemy divisions. Only two were shown in the wrong position.[121]

# 5 | COUNTER-ESPIONAGE AND COUNTER-SUBVERSION: MI5 AND THE SPECIAL BRANCH

British counter-espionage was better prepared for war than British espionage or sigint. Before the Intelligence Corps had been organised or Room 40 even thought of, Vernon Kell's secret counter-espionage department, assisted by the Special Branch, had mopped up the only enemy espionage network in Britain – though it was uncertain at the time whether further German spies remained at large.[1] Before the war Kell had been assisted by only three army officers, one barrister and a few clerks. In August 1914 his department was formally reconstituted as sub-section MO5g of the War Office, and its establishment increased to 9 officers, 3 civilian assistants, 4 female clerks and 3 policemen. In the War Office reorganisation of January 1916 MO5g acquired its modern name MI5. By the armistice in November 1918 the original wartime staff of 19 had grown to 844.[2]

The rapid expansion of MI5's wartime work took its toll on Kell's health. His worsening asthma eventually forced the Kell family to abandon their cherished country home at Weybridge in Surrey, which Kell had adorned with four hundred rose trees, a grass tennis court and a well-equipped billiard room, for a house at Campden Hill in London. The move, on a snowy day early in 1917, did not go well. The last furniture van, which also contained the maids and what the Kells called the 'livestock' – 'our beloved Scottie dog, the cat and the parrot' – skidded off the road into a shop window and 'slung the parrot cage through it, the screeching bird adding to the confusion'.[3]

Office life in MI5 was more humdrum. Most of it revolved around a rapidly growing card index of suspicious persons in its Central Registry. Its basis was Kell's pre-war register of aliens compiled from information provided by local police forces. In all about seventy thousand enemy aliens over the age of fourteen were resident in Britain in 1914. MO5g claimed at the outbreak of war to have all those outside London (about half the total) on its files.[4] Its wartime index was expanded to include suspicious British subjects and other nationals, some reported by Allied intelligence services. By the spring of 1917 MI5's Central Registry contained 250,000 cards and 27,000 personal files on its chief suspects kept up to date by 130 women clerks. Lieutenant-Colonel Claude Dansey, then responsible for liaison with the United States, told American military intelligence that the Registry's filing system was 'our great standby and cornerstone': 'We have brought it to a point where every department in the government comes to us for information'. So did security services in the Empire and Allied countries.[5]

The Central Registry quickly developed standardised classifications for its suspects. First on each card in its index came the 'civil classification': B.S., A.S., N.S., or E.S. (British, Allied, Neutral or Enemy Subject). Then followed the 'general military (special intelligence) classification' along a mildly comic scale running from AA to BB:

AA : 'Absolutely Anglicised' or 'Absolutely Allied' – undoubtedly friendly.
A : 'Anglicised' or 'Allied' – friendly.
AB : 'Anglo-Boche' – doubtful, but probably friendly.
BA : 'Boche-Anglo' – doubtful, but probably hostile.
B : 'Boche' – hostile.
BB : 'Bad Boche' – undoubtedly hostile.

Finally came a series of 'Special Intelligence Black List (SI/BL) subclassifications':

A. 'Antecedents' in a civil, police, or judicial sense so bad that patriotism may not be the dominant factor, and sympathies not incorruptible.
B. 'Banished' during the war from, or forbidden to enter one or more of the Allied States.
C. 'Courier', letter carrier, intermediary or auxiliary to enemy agents.
D. 'Detained', interned or prevented from leaving an Allied State for S.I. reasons.
E. 'Espion.' Enemy spy or agent engaged in active mischief (not necessarily confined to espionage).
F. 'False' or irregular papers of identity or credential.
G. 'Guarded', suspected, under special surveillance and not yet otherwise classified.
H. 'Hawker', hostile by reason of trade or commerce with or for the enemy.
I. 'Instigator' of hostile, pacifist, seditious or dangerous propaganda.
J. 'Junction' wanted. The person, or information concerning him, wanted urgently by S.I. or an Allied S.I. Service.
K. 'Kaiser's' man. Enemy officer or official or ex-officer or official.

The secret MI5 classification handbook added:

It will be appreciated that an actively hostile person may fall under several of the above special classifications. Such cases are designated thus: e.g. Class: SI/BL. BEFHKJ France.

To a Special Intelligence Officer who has memorized the standard classifications this abbreviation conveys the following information:

> "Is considered an enemy (prefixed BL [Black List]); already expelled from allied territory during the war (B); considered an active enemy agent (E); who has been known to carry false papers, (F); is suspected of trading with the enemy (H); was formerly a German official (K); and French S.I. is anxious to hear of his present whereabouts and actions (J)."[6]

MI5 continued to depend on police reports and surveillance of suspects. But its most important source of wartime intelligence was probably cable and postal censorship. Prompted by the experience of the Boer War, MO5 had drawn up detailed plans for cable censorship before the war began and earmarked officers and clerks for war service under the chief cable censor, Colonel A.G. Churchill, whose department became MO5d (later MI8) at the outbreak of war. No such preparations had been made for postal censorship. A pre-war sub-committee of the Committee of Imperial Defence had concluded, on GPO advice, that large-scale postal censorship was unworkable. As a result the War Office contained at the outbreak of war only a single censor responsible for removing indiscretions from soldiers' letters. Neither the War Office nor the Admiralty had yet grasped the potential importance of postal censorship as an intelligence source. Both the Home and Foreign Offices remained opposed to mass censorship of civilian mail. The Home Office still insisted that civilian post could be opened only on the home secretary's warrant, and the Foreign Office was anxious not to alienate neutral countries by interfering with their mail.[7]

In September 1914 MO5 began to realise the importance of correspondence to Sweden and other neutral countries as a way of keeping track of German espionage. But the handful of MO5 staff sent to the Mount Pleasant sorting offices found the sheer volume of mail too much for them. When Colonel G.K. Cockerill visited Mount Pleasant shortly after taking over as head of MO5 in October, he discovered piles of opened letters awaiting further examination, cheques scattered around the room, and heaps of mail bags which had still to be opened. In November 1914 an M.P. called on 'Blinker' Hall at the Admiralty with exaggerated reports from a Mount Pleasant sorting clerk that messages to the enemy were getting through the censorship 'in some abundance'. Hall took the allegations at face value, hurried round to MO5 and insisted 'that *all* foreign mails are opened and that no secret message gets through'. Cockerill replied that the Cabinet was unhappy even with the existing level of censorship but agreed to allow censors chosen by

Hall to make their own inspection of the mails for a two-month trial period on condition that Hall reported 'any weak spots' he discovered in the War Office censorship. Hall persuaded Churchill to provide £1,600 to fund his new 'show' but was 'purposely vague' about what the money was for. His friend Lieutenant-Colonel Freddie Browning (later of MI1c) agreed to run Hall's 'little private censorship' and found him volunteers from the National Service League to act as censors. For three weeks all went well. Then Browning rang Hall to report that a censorship form had been accidentally left in a letter addressed to an M.P. whom he was keeping under surveillance and considered the 'ruddiest of rascals'. The outraged M.P. protested to the home secretary, Reginald McKenna, who summoned Hall and Cockerill to the Home Office. Hall found McKenna standing sternly in front of the fireplace, flanked by his permanent secretary. Was it true, demanded McKenna, that Hall had dared without his authority to tamper with the royal mail? 'Quite true, Mr Home Secretary', replied Hall. The penalty for that, said the home secretary, was two years in jail. McKenna then dismissed his permanent secretary and his mood softened as Cockerill argued that, in a national emergency, he had felt entitled to use what temporary help he could. Hall then urged on McKenna the importance of the intelligence obtained by censorship in organising the economic blockade of Germany. Within twenty-four hours he had been summoned by Asquith to repeat his argument, and – by his own account – persuaded the prime minister to found the War Trade Intelligence Department (later subsumed by the Ministry of Blockade) whose first head was Freddie Browning.[8] In April 1915 the postal censors were formally reconstituted as a new department in the War Office, MO9 (later MI9) under a retired diplomat, G.S.H. Pearson. Their numbers grew steadily from the original single censor in August 1914 to 170 at the end of the year and 4,861 (of whom three-quarters were women) by the Armistice.[9]

The First World War confronted Kell with three main security problems: a vast increase in imaginary espionage, a much more limited outbreak of genuine German espionage, and the gradual growth of what appeared to be subversion. The first problem, though the least serious, was also the most intractable.

The outbreak of war provoked an unprecedented wave of spy mania. Though the twenty-one real German spies were arrested immediately, many thousands of imaginary agents remained at liberty plotting imaginary acts of sabotage and communicating with the enemy. During the first day of the war Basil Thomson, assistant commissioner at Scotland Yard and head of the 114 man Special Branch, was solemnly informed that a culvert near Aldershot and a railway bridge in Kent had been blown up by saboteurs. Next day both were found to be intact.[10] Soon afterwards *The Times* denounced 'a particularly mischievous rumour' which had 'caused serious loss to boarding-house keepers and others at some holiday resorts on the East Coast':

> The report was that the pier at Walton-on-the-Naze had been blown up
> by the Germans, and though the statement is absolutely untrue, a large
> number of holiday-makers have either left the town or abandoned their
> proposed visit. It is hoped that the public will realise the hardship thus
> quite unnecessarily caused to many hard-working people, and where holiday
> arrangements have been made endeavour to carry them through.[11]

Spy mania, noted Thomson, 'assumed a virulent epidemic form accompanied
by delusions which defied treatment': 'It attacked all classes indiscriminately
and seemed even to find its most fruitful soil in sober, stolid, and otherwise
truthful people'.[12]

One of the earliest casualties of the spy mania was the pigeon population
of the capital which was suspected of bearing messages to the enemy:

> In September 1914, when this phase [of the mania] was at its height, it
> was positively dangerous to be seen in conversation with a pigeon; it was
> not always safe to be seen in its vicinity. A foreigner walking in one of the
> parks was actually arrested and sentenced to imprisonment because a
> pigeon was seen to fly from the place where he was standing and it was
> supposed that he had liberated it.

The popular press suggested that suspect homing pigeons should be shot on
sight. After several prosecutions by the National Homing Union, pigeon
mortality declined.[13]

There were many reports also of illicit wireless transmissions – despite the
fact that Marconi transmitters then required 4-horse-power engines which
were ill-suited to concealment:

> On one occasion the authorities dispatched to the Eastern Counties a car
> equipped with a Marconi apparatus and two skilled operators to intercept
> any illicit messages that might be passing over the North Sea. They left
> London at noon; at 3 they were under lock and key in Essex. After an
> exchange of telegrams they were set free, but at 7 p.m. they telegraphed
> from the police cells in another part of the country, imploring help. When
> again liberated they refused to move without the escort of a Territorial
> officer in uniform, but on the following morning the police of another
> county had got hold of them and telegraphed, 'Three German spies arrested
> with car and complete wireless installation, one in uniform of British
> officer'.[14]

The most frequently reported form of communication used by the imaginary spies was night-signalling, often to guide Zeppelins or U-boats to their prey. During the Lords debate on the King's speech in November 1914 the Earl of Crawford drew attention to the problem in Scotland:

> ... Night signalling from our shores ... is continuous. I can if you like give you the names of 6 places within a very few miles of my own home where this lamp signalling has been in regular progress.[15]

Thomson was sent similar reports from the heart of London:

> Morse-signalling from a window in Bayswater, which could be seen only from a window on the opposite side of the street, was believed in some way to be conveyed to the commanders of German submarines in the North Sea.

Thomson encountered 'many thousand' such cases. Not one proved genuine.[16]

The dramatic revival of imaginary espionage gave Le Queux a new lease of life. He was, he declared, 'not affected by that disease known as spy mania' and he was full of praise for the 'unremitting efforts' of 'a certain nameless department, known only by a code number'. Since the founding of the Home Department of the Secret Service Bureau under Vernon Kell in 1909, Le Queux claimed to have been 'intimate with its workings':

> I know its splendid staff, its untiring and painstaking efforts, its thoroughness, its patriotism, and the astuteness of its head director, who is one of the finest Englishmen of my acquaintance.

But he now considered the scale of the spy menace altogether beyond the capacity of Kell's 'nameless department':

> The serious truth is that German espionage and treasonable propaganda have, during past years, been allowed by a slothful military administration to take root so deeply that the authorities today find themselves powerless to eradicate its pernicious growth.

The authorities in general and the home secretary, Reginald McKenna, in particular, were engaged in a massive cover-up 'to hide the true state of affairs from the public, and even to lull them into a false sense of security'. Le Queux had found the Metropolitan Police quite 'hopeless' but was so outraged by 'the still greater discourtesy and amazing chaos' in the Home Office that he was driven to ask himself 'whether it is of any use whatever *to trouble, or even exert oneself further in the matter*'. German spies were to be found everywhere and in all classes, from hall-porters in the leading hotels and the hundreds of 'clever and capable' German prostitutes around Piccadilly Circus at one end of the social scale to '"naturalised" foreign baronets, financiers, merchants, ship-owners, and persons of both sexes of high social standing':

> No such system has ever been seen in the world; I hope it is safe to say that no such system will ever be seen again.[17]

Even more remarkable than the scale of Le Queux's own fabrications and delusions was the readiness with which others believed them. His book *German Spies in England: An Exposure*, first published in February 1915, went through six editions in three weeks and contained endorsements from the lord mayor of London, Sir Arthur Conan Doyle and seven other 'great men' (as well as a full page advertisement for a proprietary medicine claiming to 'cut short attacks of spasms, hysteria, palpitation'). It was well reviewed also in a sizeable section of the press. 'It is', said the *Daily Mail*, 'a book which should be carefully studied from cover to cover'. The proprietor, Lord Northcliffe, joined Le Queux in denouncing the German moles active in Whitehall. 'It is beyond question', he believed, 'that, for some reason, the Government are protecting spies – and spies in high places'. He hinted mysteriously at financial corruption as the cause: 'There are persons who speak of recent contributions to the Liberal exchequer, but I do not like to think of anything of the sort'.[18]

Milder forms of spy fever were common even among those who escaped the wilder fantasies of Le Queux and Northcliffe. They were strengthened by the sinking of three British cruisers by U-boats in the North Sea on 22 September. Admiral Lord Charles Beresford, M.P. for Portsmouth and former commander-in-chief of the Channel Fleet, told a recruiting drive in Aberdeen on 2 October:

> Three cruisers were lost by information given from this country to the German Admiralty. The British people should insist that the Home Office prevent the British Army and Navy being stabbed in the back by assassins in the shape of spies. All alien enemies should be locked up!

Soon afterwards he claimed in a letter to the press: 'Numbers of men have been caught red-handed signalling etc. and have been discharged through not enough evidence'. Requests to the admiral for evidence as to precise cases from the office of the Director of Public Prosecutions brought only confused and choleric replies. But the attorney-general, Sir John Simon, was inclined to believe Beresford's explanation of the sinking of the cruisers. He wrote privately on 26 October:

> Experience has shown that the German Navy is extraordinarily well

informed of our movements, and though I have the greatest detestation of spy mania, I do not think it is open to doubt that there are a number of unidentified persons in this country, who have been making treacherous communications, and who were not known to us at the beginning of the war.[19]

The chief scapegoats of spy mania were inevitably enemy aliens. The commissioner of the Metropolitan Police, Sir Edward Henry, a more credulous man than Basil Thomson, told the Home Office in November:

... The operations of the German Secret Service have been on such a large scale that it is necessary in the interests of public safety, that the Police should be almost unreasonably circumspect in dealing even with [aliens] against whom nothing specific may be known.

To deal with the alien menace the government, the police force and MI5 had a formidable array of legislation. The Aliens Restriction Act, drafted in readiness for war and rushed through parliament on 5 August 1914, gave the government carte blanche 'to impose restrictions on aliens and make such provisions as appear necessary or expedient for carrying such restrictions into effect'. The Defence of the Realm Act (DORA), passed three days later, gave the government powers close to martial law

  i    to prevent persons communicating with the enemy or obtaining information for that purpose or any purpose calculated to jeopardise the success of the operations of any of His Majesty's Forces or to assist the enemy; and
  ii   to secure the safety of any means of communications, or of railways, docks or harbours.

Enemy aliens were required to register with the police and forbidden to live in a large number of 'prohibited areas' without permits from the police. The government claimed early in 1915 that 'Every single alien enemy in this country is known and is at this present moment under constant police surveillance'. But for the popular press and probably for most of the public, surveillance was not enough. Spy mania and indignation at [mostly mythical] war crimes by the German army fuelled protests against government reluctance to intern more than a small minority of enemy aliens. In May 1915, somewhat against his better judgment, Asquith gave way to public pressure. McKenna reluctantly concluded that anti-alien feeling ran so high that male enemy aliens might well be safer if interned. Henceforth the government adopted (though it did not always enforce) the principle that all enemy aliens should be interned unless they could prove themselves to be harmless. Ultimately at least 32,000 (mostly men of military age) were interned, at least 20,000 (mostly women, children and non-combatant men) repatriated, and the remainder subjected to numerous restrictions.[20]

Though there is no evidence that Kell suffered from spy mania, he took a hard line on internment. MI5 calculated in the autumn of 1917 that there was, on average, one 'vulnerable point' to every seven square miles of Britain. As a result each enemy alien confined to a radius of only five miles (an area of 78 square miles) had access to about eleven 'vulnerable points'. The need, it argued, was for more surveillance and more internment. The Home Office suspected, probably rightly, that MI5's hard line derived not merely from a realistic concern for national security but also from sensitivity to criticism of War Office 'inertia' by victims of spy mania. When the Home Office asked for evidence of suspicious aliens living near 'vulnerable points', the War Office could only reply vaguely that

... the credentials of a large number of such persons are at all times under inquiry and examination by the competent military authorities and officers engaged in intelligence duties with a view to arranging for such legitimate precautionary action and safeguards as may be appropriate in time of war to each individual case.

The Home Office was not impressed. J.F. Moylan of the Aliens Division minuted:

Not a single instance of an alien enemy having improperly gained access to a vulnerable point is adduced nor apparently can be adduced and it is well known to MI5 that it is not amongst alien enemies now at large that the real danger from enemy agents exists but amongst alien friends and British subjects without any German blood, whether whole or half. But enemy agents are elusive and hard to find in the mass of British subjects and alien friends, while the alien enemy presents a known and easy target at which MI5 owing to the difficulty and scarceness of the other quarry, keep firing away in their natural anxiety to appear always on the *qui vive*.[21]

In one important respect, Moylan's minute was unfair. So far from finding the real German agents in Britain 'elusive and hard to find', MI5 tracked them down with great efficiency. Kell had the advantage, however, of dealing with weak opposition. The wartime operations of Gustav Steinhauer, the organiser of German espionage in Britain, were scarcely more extensive or professional than those of his pre-war network arrested on the outbreak of war. His first wartime agent in Britain was Karl Lody, a German naval reserve officer, who spoke excellent English with an American accent and had some experience of intelligence work in the United States. Steinhauer later claimed that he had warned the German naval intelligence staff that Lody 'was everything in the world that was likeable – brave, good-tempered, generous, but no detective, which every spy must be':

> But as he had specially volunteered for the task – and I must admit there were very few people in Berlin just then anxious to accompany him – they allowed him to go.[22]

Lody was supplied with a stolen American passport in the name of Charles Inglis, but left Berlin before being given training in either codes or secret inks. He made first for Edinburgh to discover how much of the Grand Fleet was stationed in the Firth of Forth. From the North British Station Hotel he despatched a telegram to a German agent in Stockholm which immediately attracted the suspicions of the wartime censors. Henceforth Lody was under constant surveillance. He spent a fortnight cycling around the Rosyth Harbour area 'asking too many questions for the ordinary sightseer' and then moved to London where he showed a similar curiosity about the capital's anti-aircraft defences. After a further visit to Edinburgh, he travelled to Liverpool where ocean liners were being fitted out as auxiliary cruisers, and thence to Ireland. From the Gresham Hotel in Dublin Lody wrote to tell his contact in Stockholm that the questioning to which he had been subjected on arrival in Ireland had left him rather apprehensive. But he seems never to have suspected that this letter, like all its predecessors, would be intercepted. 'His information', wrote Basil Thomson later, 'would have been of comparatively little value even if it had reached the Germans, which it did not'. The only report from Lody which Kell allowed to reach Stockholm was one based on the absurd wartime rumour that Russian soldiers, with snow on their boots, were passing through England on their way to the Western Front.

On 2 October 1914 Lody was arrested while on his way to the Irish naval base at Queenstown. He was tried by court-martial at the end of the month in Westminster Guildhall. His counsel pleaded in mitigation only that Lody had done his patriotic duty and stood before his judges in the spirit of his grandfather who had held a fortress against Napoleon. Though Steinhauer and German naval intelligence had not expected Lody to be executed, he was sentenced to death by firing squad at the Tower of London. 'There was', wrote Thomson later, 'some difference of opinion as to whether it was sound policy to execute spies and to begin with a patriotic spy like Lody'. Kell regarded Lody as a 'really fine man'. According to his wife, he 'felt it deeply that so brave a man should have to pay the death penalty'. The bravery with which Lody met his end strengthened Kell's feelings of remorse. Lody wrote to his family on the eve of his execution:

MY DEAR ONES, — I have trusted in God and He has decided. My hour has come, and I must start on the journey through the Dark Valley like so many of my comrades in this terrible War of Nations. May my life be offered as a humble offering on the altar of the Fatherland.

Lody wrote to the officer commanding Wellington Barracks:

SIR, — I feel it my duty as a German Officer to express my sincere thanks and appreciation towards the staff of Officers and men who were in charge of my person during my confinement.

Their kind and considered treatment has called my highest esteem and admiration as regards good-fellowship even towards the Enemy, and if I may be permitted I would thank you for make this known to them. – I am, sir, with profound respect.

CARL HANS LODY, Senior Lieutenant, Imperial German Naval Res. II.D.

On the morning of his execution, Lody said to the Assistant Provost Marshal, 'I suppose you will not shake hands with a spy?' The officer replied: 'No, but I will shake hands with a brave man'. Thomson shared Kell's admiration for Lody's patriotism:

He never flinched, he never cringed, but he died as one would wish all Englishmen to die – quietly and undramatically, supported in his courage by the proud consciousness of having done his duty.[23]

Baden-Powell agreed and used Lody to support his general maxim that 'The best spies are unpaid men who are doing it for the love of the thing.' In reality Lody was as inept as he was brave. 'One must confess', wrote Steinhauer, 'that his capabilities for such important work were practically nil'.[24]

The next spy caught by Kell, a German NCO named Anton Küpferle, was as brave as Lody, slightly better trained, and even more inept. Küpferle had spent a brief period as a wool merchant in Brooklyn and posed unconvincingly as an American commercial traveller of Dutch extraction. Thomson found it incomprehensible that German intelligence 'could have sent a man so obviously German, so ignorant of the English language and the American accent, into an enemy country'. By the time he arrived at Liverpool on a transatlantic steamer, he had already aroused suspicion. From Liverpool he wrote an innocuous letter to a forwarding address in Holland but added, in secret ink (which he was the first German spy in Britain to use), information about warships he had observed during the Atlantic crossing. Küpferle's correspondence was intercepted and the secret ink detected. He was followed from Liverpool to Dublin and from Dublin to London, then arrested with the secret ink still in his possession. Küpferle failed to arouse anything approaching the sympathy extended to Lody, striking his interrogators as 'a typical German non-commissioned officer, stiff, abrupt, and uncouth'. In the middle of his trial at the Old Bailey he was found hanging by a silk handkerchief from the ventilator in his cell. By his body was a message written on a slate:

I can say that I have had a fair trial in the U. Kingdom, but I am unable to stand the strain any longer and take the law in my own hand. I fought many battles and death is only a saviour for me ... What I done I have done for my country. I shall express my thanks, and may the Lord bless you all.

An intercepted letter written by Küpferle to another German agent showed less charity towards his captors. In it he welcomed the use of poison gas against English soldiers and the 'stupefying death' it would cause. This letter, Thomson believed, showed that Küpferle, unlike Lody, was a typical Hun with 'the true Prussian mentality'.[25]

Most of Küpferle's successors aroused even less sympathy. Kell believed they 'worked only for the money' and viewed them with contempt. Thomson dismissed them as 'hireling spies'.[26] The most successful was probably Karl Müller, detected like his predecessors by the postal censors. Unlike Lody and Küpferle, however, he failed to simplify Kell's job by including his name and address in his correspondence. He first attracted the censors' attention by writing to a suspicious address in Rotterdam. When the censorship flat-iron was heated and run over his letter it revealed information on army training at Aldershot, ship-building on the Clyde, and civilian morale. The writer signed himself L. Cohen and gave his address as 22 High Street, Deptford, but enquiries at that address revealed no trace of either Cohen or any likely author of the letter. Several further letters followed over the next month, none revealing the writer's identity. Then came an important clue. The censor's flat-iron revealed a postscript in invisible ink on a letter in a different hand also postmarked Deptford and sent to the suspicious address in Rotterdam: 'C has gone to Newcastle, so I am writing this from 201 instead'. 'C' was assumed to be the mysterious 'Cohen', and 201 the number of a street. A phone call to the Deptford police station quickly revealed that only the High Street contained over two hundred addresses and that the occupant of number 201 was one Peter Hahn, a baker and confectioner of German extraction. Though Hahn denied all knowledge of 'C', the Special Branch discovered secret inks in his back room and his neighbours reported regular visits from 'a tall Russian gentleman' called Müller with a London address somewhere in Russell Square. A search of Bloomsbury boarding-houses soon revealed a landlady with a Russian boarder called Müller. 'But he is not here just now', she said, 'he has gone to Newcastle to see some friends'.

On arrest in Newcastle Müller at first stuck to his claim that he was

Russian. In fact he was a German, fluent in Russian, English and several other languages, who had settled in England before the war and drifted through a variety of professions. According to an officially inspired account of his arrest, he had also 'gone through the usual routine of spies, the love-making to impressionable young women, the fulsome promises of wealth to come and talk of many friends in high places'. His assistant Hahn had gone bankrupt in 1913 and was suspected of joining Müller for mercenary motives. He was sentenced to seven years' penal servitude while Müller was shot in the Tower on 23 June 1915.

Even after Müller's execution, money and requests for further information continued to arrive from the forwarding address in Rotterdam. Kell decided to reply to them by sending bogus information in handwriting resembling Müller's. He thus anticipated the Double Cross system successfully employed during the Second World War. But the deception lacked two of the essential elements of the Double Cross system. The bogus intelligence was not devised with the same elaborate care and Müller was no longer available to add credibility to it. Before long the German intelligence station in Rotterdam broke off contact.[27]

In the summer of 1915 Kell had a second opportunity to start a Double Cross system. Early in May the postal censors discovered in a mailbag from Denmark a letter addressed to Berlin which had been wrongly included in the London post. The letter was from one Robert Rosenthal in Copenhagen to an intelligence office in Berlin reporting that he was about to leave for England disguised as a travelling salesman of cigar lighters. On his arrival at Newcastle Rosenthal at first protested his innocence. But when confronted with his letter to Berlin, he jumped to his feet, clicked his heels, and declared: 'I confess everything. I am a German soldier'. But Rosenthal was not a German soldier. He was a twenty-three-year-old convicted forger and cocaine addict who had spent several years in Texas and volunteered for intelligence work early in the war.[28] After his confession he quickly offered to become a double agent and, as evidence of his changed convictions, gave detailed information on secret inks, secret codes and the methods of passport forgery employed by German intelligence.[29] But Rosenthal's offer to change sides, which MI5 would doubtless have accepted in the next war, seems in 1915 merely to have inspired contempt at his capacity for treachery. He went to the scaffold on 15 July pleading for his life and, it was said, 'gave unutterable disgust to the authorities by his lack of common courage'. The commandant of Wandsworth military prison, where he was executed, dismissed him as a 'cur'.[30]

During interrogation Rosenthal had warned MO5g that, instead of using German spies, German intelligence intended to make increasing use of agents from neutral countries disguised, like himself, as commercial travellers. The first to be detected, shortly after Rosenthal's arrest, were two Dutchmen,

Haicke Janssen and Willem Roos, posing as cigar merchants. Both attracted the attention of the cable censors by telegraphing improbably large orders of cigars from British ports to a suspicious address in Rotterdam. Both were using a simple code in which, for example, an order for 10,000 Cabanas, 4,000 Rothschilds and 3,000 Coronas from Portsmouth reported the presence in the harbour of ten destroyers, four cruisers and three battleships.[31] On 15 June Colonel Cartier, the head of French military cryptography, handed to Kirke at British GHQ in France a series of decrypted German naval wireless messages which revealed the location of German agents then in British ports. One of the messages clearly identified Janssen, then already under arrest, and Kirke noted with satisfaction that 'it should ensure his being shot'. The decrypts were immediately passed on to Kell, whom Cartier arranged to meet soon afterwards in London.[32] It was probably these signals which enabled Kell during June to round up seven German spies in little more than a fortnight – a record unsurpassed in the remainder of the war.[33]

Janssen and Roos, like Rosenthal, were ready to change sides. Janssen claimed after his conviction that his sympathies had really been with Britain all the time and provided intelligence on the German espionage network in Holland which he hoped would save his life and which helped in the discovery of subsequent German agents. Roos feigned madness also in an attempt to avoid execution. Both were shot in the Tower of London on 30 July. Kell seems never to have contemplated using either as a double agent. His wife's judgment probably reflected his: 'It was all done for money and therefore Janssen and Roos were despicable men ready to do any dirty work merely for gain'.[34]

After the arrest of seven German agents in June 1915, Germany made no further wartime attempt to establish a resident spying in Britain. She relied instead largely on brief visits by bogus commercial travellers from neutral countries who carried as much information as possible in their heads rather than on paper. They had little success. MI5 concluded that most had neither the aptitude nor training required for successful espionage. One, Adolfo Guerrero, arrested in February 1916, spoke not a word of English. The flow of German spies gradually dried up. The last to be executed was Ludovico Hurwitz-y-Zender, a Peruvian of Scandinavian descent who aroused the suspicions of the censors by sending bogus orders for large quantities of Norwegian sardines at the wrong season, and was shot in the Tower – nine months after his arrest – on 11 April 1916.[35]

The increasing number of agents from neutral countries encouraged exaggerated fears in MI5 that neutral embassies in London were assisting German espionage. Reginald Drake, the head of counter-espionage in MI5, claimed in May 1916 that the Germans were 'making great use of Danes, and probably sending most of their stuff by Danish or other neutral diplomatic bags – a very hard thing to stop'. The Danish under-secretary for foreign affairs was, he declared, 'a strong pro-Bosche, and helps them in every way he can'.[36] During 1916 MI5 continued to exhort chief constables to ensure that 'all commercial travellers of alien origin arriving in your jurisdiction' were 'severely interrogated'. It also warned them in July 1916 that it had 'reason to believe that the German Government is endeavouring to recruit circus-riders, music-hall performers, and persons on the regular stage for purposes of espionage in this country'.[37] In reality, German espionage in Britain had come close to collapse. After the death sentence (later commuted) passed on the youthful Norwegian spy, Alfred Hagn, in August 1917, there were no further espionage trials for the remainder of the war.[38]

The decline of German espionage by no means ended the menace of the imaginary spy. Perhaps the most ludicrous of all the wartime spy sensations occurred less than six months before the armistice. The principal author of the sensation was the Independent M.P. for mid-Hertfordshire, Noel Pemberton Billing, a figure as preposterous as Le Queux himself, noted for his skill as an aviator, his habit of wearing long pointed collars without a tie, and his campaigns against those in high places whom he claimed were undermining the war effort. In an article in his weekly newspaper, the *Imperialist*, Pemberton Billing revealed the existence of a Black Book 'compiled by the [German] Secret Service from the reports of German agents who have infested this country for the past twenty years'. The Black Book allegedly began with 'general instructions regarding the propagation of evils which all decent men thought had perished in Sodom and Lesbos', and went on to list the names of 47,000 British sexual perverts, mostly in high places, being blackmailed by the German Secret Service:

> It is a most catholic miscellany. The names of Privy Councillors, youths of the chorus, wives of Cabinet Ministers, dancing girls, even Cabinet Ministers themselves, while diplomats, poets, bankers, editors, newspaper proprietors, members of His Majesty's Household follow each other with no order of precedence ... The thought that 47,000 English men and women are held in enemy bondage through fear calls all clean spirits to mortal combat. There are 3,000,000 men in France whose lives are in jeopardy, and whose bravery is of no avail, because of the lack of moral courage in 47,000 of their countrymen, numbering in their ranks, as they do, men and women in whose hands the destiny of this Empire rests ... The story of the contents of this book has opened my eyes, and the matter must not rest.

Nor did Pemberton Billing allow it to rest. Soon afterwards, in an article entitled 'The Cult of The Clitoris', he previewed a private production of *Salome* in which the classical dancer Maud Allan took the title part and the proceeds went to charity:

To be a member of Maud Allan's private performances of Oscar Wilde's *Salome* one has to apply to 9, Duke Street, Adelphi, W.C. If Scotland Yard were to seize the list of these members, I have no doubt they would secure the names of several thousand of the first 47,000.

Miss Allan and her producer, Mr J.T. Grein, took offence and brought an action for criminal libel. The case opened on 29 May 1918 at the Old Bailey before Acting Lord Chief Justice Darling, whose own suspicions of Germany bordered on paranoia. The prosecution was led by Mr (later Sir Ellis) Hume-Williams K.C., assisted by Mr (later Mr Justice) Travers Humphreys and Mr Valetta. Pemberton Billing conducted his own defence alone, but had the support of enthusiastic crowds outside the court, a crowded gallery, and a remarkable series of witnesses who spoke with feeling on either sexual perversion or German espionage or both. His first witness was Mrs Eileen Villiers Stuart, an attractive young woman who, a few months later, was to be sent to prison in the same court for bigamy. Mrs Villiers Stuart explained that she had been shown the Black Book of the German Secret Service by two politicians since killed in action. Though evidence is not normally allowed in court about the contents of documents which cannot be produced, exceptions may be made in the case of documents withheld by foreign enemies. Mrs Villiers Stuart explained that the Black Book was just such an exception. Her life, she added, had recently been threatened in connection with the case. When Mr Justice Darling intervened at this point to reprove the defendant for his line of questioning, Pemberton Billing moved quickly and dramatically to the counter-attack.

'Is Mr Justice Darling's name in that book?' he asked the witness.

'It is,' replied Mrs Villiers Stuart, 'and that book can be produced.'

Darling was understandably bemused. 'It can be produced?' he queried.

'It can be produced', declared the witness. 'It will have to be produced from Germany, it can be and it shall be. Mr Justice Darling, we have got to win this war, and while you sit there we will never win it. My men are fighting, other people's men are fighting.'

The dramatic quality of Pemberton Billing's cross-examination was well sustained. 'Is Mrs Asquith's name in the book?' he asked the witness.

'It is in the book.'

'Is Mr Asquith's name in the book?'

'It is.'

'Is Lord Haldane's name in the book?'

'It is in the book.'

Darling had had enough. 'Leave the box,' he told the witness.

'You daren't hear me!' shouted Mrs Villiers Stuart.

To his later regret Darling relented and allowed Pemberton Billing to continue his bizarre cross-examination. Before long, however, he found himself assailed by both defendant and witness and brought the cross-examination to a close.

The next witness was a Captain Spencer who claimed to have been shown the Black Book by a German prince and gave some further details of its contents. During cross-examination Mr Hume-Williams K.C. enquired as to his mental stability. Captain Spencer retaliated by asking whether Mr Hume-Williams was working for the Germans. He was followed into the witness box by a doctor, a surgeon, a literary critic and a cleric who testified to the depravity of *Salome*. Then came Pemberton Billing's star witness, Oscar Wilde's disaffected former lover, Lord Alfred Douglas, who complained of being 'bullied and brow-beaten' by both Darling and Hume-Williams.

The final witness was Mrs Villiers Stuart, whose second appearance was as sensational as her first. 'Did you take any steps', asked Pemberton Billing, 'to put this knowledge [of the German Black Book] before any public person in this country?'

'I did.'

'Was he a prominent public man?'

'You may ask his name,' Darling told Pemberton Billing.

'Mr Hume-Williams!' replied Mrs Villiers Stuart, pointing dramatically at the leading counsel for the prosecution. After cross-examination by Hume-Williams' colleague, Travers Humphreys, Pemberton Billing began a re-examination. Uproar followed. Hume-Williams called Pemberton Billing a liar. Pemberton Billing threatened to thrash Hume-Williams.

In his final address Pemberton Billing won the hearts of the jury by denouncing the 'mysterious influence which seems to prevent a Britisher getting a square deal'. Hume-Williams made a less successful defence of Darling's reputation. 'It has recently pleased the King', he reminded the jury, 'to make him a member of the Privy Council.' 'I wish you would not allude to that', said Darling, 'because privy counsellors are particularly mentioned among the 47,000.'

In the course of his summing-up Darling lost most of what control he still exercised over the proceedings. Lord Alfred Douglas intervened to call him 'a damned liar', stormed out of the court, and then returned to ask if he might collect his hat. A series of spectators were ejected and Darling finished his address amid scenes of chaotic farce. The jury returned after an hour and a half to find Pemberton Billing not guilty. Tumultuous cheering filled the court and was echoed by the enormous throng outside. Pemberton Billing emerged to a hero's welcome. The case remains mercifully unique in the history of the British courts.[39] Thomson, no doubt like Kell, was appalled by the whole affair. 'Every-one concerned', he wrote in his diary, 'appeared to have been either insane or to have behaved as if he were'.[40]

Sidney Felstead, the semi-official historian of German espionage in Britain, who was given access to MI5 reports, acknowledged the existence of 'quite a healthy rivalry' between MI5 and the Special Branch 'as to who could claim most credit for the capture and conviction of the many spies who came to this country':

> Scotland Yard always smiled in a superior fashion when the subject came up for discussion, asking where would the Counter-Espionage section [MI5] be without them, whilst the officials of that department, with great complacency, would merely reply: 'Well, of course, you know Scotland Yard ...'[41]

In reality the rivalry was a good deal less healthy and more fraught than Felstead suggested. MI5 was solely responsible for the detection of spies. 'Scotland Yard', wrote Felstead, 'does not advance any claim in that direction'. The Special Branch did not become involved until surveillance began. Since MI5, then as now, possessed no power of arrest, the Special Branch also carried out arrests, but Kell seems to have resented the way Basil Thomson sought to monopolise the interrogation of spies once taken into custody at Scotland Yard.[42] As a secret organisation MI5 could not publicly claim credit for its part in the capture of German spies. The more flamboyant Thomson, already well used to publicising his achievements, could and did. In the process he earned the collective emnity of most of MI5. Reginald Drake, head of counter-espionage in MI5 for much of the war, wrote later to 'Blinker' Hall:

> As you know B.T. did not know of the existence, name or activity of any convicted spy until I told him; but being the dirty dog he was he twisted the facts to claim that he alone did it.[43]

There was, inevitably, some overlap in the activities of MI5 and the Special Branch which added further to the rivalry between them. Eddie Bell, who was responsible for intelligence liaison at the American embassy, wrote after the war that when the embassy wished to make enquiries about people claiming American citizenship arrested on suspicion of being German spies 'it became almost a question of flipping a coin to decide whether application for information should be made to Scotland Yard, the Home Office or MI5'. 'Blinker' Hall had much greater sympathy for the flamboyant Thomson than the retiring Kell. Bell reported 'considerable jealousy between the Intelligence Department of the War Office and the Admiralty, the latter affecting to despise the former, particularly MI5, whom they always described as shortsighted and timorous ...'[44] Thomson, like Hall, enjoyed the limelight. Kell shunned it. His only known publication is a newspaper letter describing the behaviour of the lapwing.[45]

The area of greatest overlap and eventual rivalry between Kell and Thomson concerned the monitoring of subversion. MI5 had as yet no concern with purely civil threats to law and order. But after the passage of DORA the wartime dividing line between civil disturbance and threats to the war effort was vague and confused. Each year MI5 considered hundreds of articles, pamphlets and reports of speeches critical of the war. Under DORA the decision whether to initiate prosecution lay with the 'Competent Military Authority' but the surviving records suggest that these authorities were usually content to defer to MI5. There were frequent 'consultations' also between MI5 officers, the Director of Public Prosecutions, and the Home Office.[46] In the case of names on the MI5 blacklist Kell was quite willing to prosecute merely technical breaches of DORA. He informed the Home Office in May 1918 when assembling the case against the anti-war campaigner ex-Lieutenant Goulding:

It is possible that an offence of a minor character has been committed under DRR 41 as I am informed that Goulding wears two wound stripes and a red and two blue chevrons. It appears that his service abroad only entitles him to wear one blue chevron and (probably) one wound stripe.[47]

During the final stages of the war MI5 was more concerned by the menace of domestic subversion than by German espionage. Until 1916, however, the threat posed by pacifism and labour unrest seemed slight. In August 1914 the TUC announced an industrial truce for the duration of the war and Labour leaders joined their social superiors on recruiting platforms. Kell and his wife remembered with particular pleasure a public meeting in 1915 at which the veteran strike-leader Ben Tillett joined forces with the Duke of Rutland to appeal for warm clothing for the troops. 'Never shall I forget', wrote Lady Kell, 'the picture of Ben Tillett, very short of stature, and the Duke, very long indeed, standing together side by side, one with an amused expression, the other looking down benevolently ...'. 'Can you picture those men', Tillett asked his audience, 'with nothing but their bare bodies to oppose to the guns of the enemy?' Lady Kell found that 'a telling phrase'.[48]

Though six of the forty Labour M.P.s (including the future prime minister, Ramsay Macdonald) opposed the war, Arthur Henderson, the wartime leader of the parliamentary party, joined the coalition government formed by Asquith in May 1915. Early opposition to the war centred on the small Independent Labour Party (ILP). Initially neither Thomson nor Kell seemed greatly concerned by it. When the chief constable of Norwich sought advice in March 1915 on a forthcoming ILP conference in Norwich, he was advised by the Home Office – probably in consultation with Thomson – to take 'as little notice as possible' of it:

The meeting itself is not likely to do any great harm in this country but if it acquires a fictitious importance owing to attempts to suppress it, or otherwise, the result may be to encourage the enemy.[49]

When one of the most militant ILP leaders, C.H. Norman, founded the 'Stop-the-War-Committee' soon afterwards, Kell ordered a 'check' on its correspondence. The results were reassuring. According to a report prepared for Kell in July 1915, letters to the Committee were few and declining in number:

No letter has been seen which would appear to indicate that the writer has anti-British sentiments or that the Committee is in any way inspired or assisted from enemy sources ... It appears therefore that the members of the Committee are obtaining very small results from their propaganda and the harm they are causing at the present time is practically negligable [*sic*].[50]

Kell was also encouraged by popular hostility to anti-war speakers. In July 1915 an open-air ILP meeting on Hampstead Heath was disrupted by outraged patriots who tried to throw the speakers into the Whitestone Pond. After another ILP meeting at Marple had been broken up later the same month, the local police reported with relish to the Home Office that the speakers' 'little entertainment from the crowd' would 'teach them and their Independent Labour Party to remain in Derbyshire with their adverse speeches'.[51]

As the assistant commissioner in charge of the Special Branch, Basil Thomson dealt briskly with publications which he judged subversive. When *The Globe* alleged that Kitchener had resigned as secretary of state for war, Thomson simply removed a vital piece of machinery from the printing press 'until such time as the directors of the newspaper had come to an agreement with the Government'.[52] Though the attorney-general concluded in September 1915 that there was 'no legal method' of preventing the publication of an American work entitled *The Socialists and the War*, Thomson successfully put pressure on its London publisher, Constable, to withdraw it.[53] He was less successful in his attempts to confiscate anti-war literature from the offices of the ILP and its newspaper, *The Labour Leader*. After a police raid in August 1915, a magistrate ordered the literature to be returned and *The Labour Leader* suffered no further police raids.[54]

'It was not until 1916', wrote Thomson later, 'that the Pacifist became active'.[55] The immediate cause of the pacifist revival was the introduction of conscription, first for unmarried men between 18 and 41 in February 1916, then for married men in the same age group two months later. *The Herald* attacked conscription as 'an act of tyranny as open and shameless as the

German invasion of Belgium', a Labour Party conference denounced it by an overwhelming majority, and massive strikes were threatened on Clydeside and in the South Wales mines.[56] But little came of the first wave of protest. The three Labour ministers remained in the government and the strikes were stillborn. Thomson noted with satisfaction that conscientious objectors were generally unpopular:

> Public feeling ran strongly against them, and even in Princetown, Dartmoor, where the population had been accustomed to see the worst class of felon, murmurs were heard that it was time to send back the old convicts who knew how to behave themselves instead of the dreadful people with long hair and curious clothing ...[57]

In June 1916 Thomson ordered a Special Branch raid on the offices of the No-Conscription Fellowship, and removed its membership list, accounts and publications. He also approved and may well have encouraged unofficial action against 'Peace Cranks'.[58] In November a peace conference at Cardiff organised by the National Council for Civil Liberties was broken up by a mob which smashed its way into the hall, overpowered the stewards, set about the delegates, and passed a resolution 'pledging the meeting to assist the government to wage war to the bitter end'.[59] About 7,000 conscientious objectors agreed to non-combatant service, usually with field ambulances; another 3,000 were sent to labour camps run by the Home Office; 1,500 'absolutists' who refused all compulsory service were called up and then imprisoned for refusing to obey orders. 'While they gave great trouble to government officials, from the tribunals down to the prison warders', the objectors – in Thomson's view – were 'really of very little importance'.[60]

From 1916 onwards Thomson was more concerned with industrial unrest than with opposition to the war or to conscription. At the beginning of the year his main anxieties, probably like Kell's, centred on 'Red Clydeside', which was beginning to acquire a largely mythical reputation as the home of a powerful revolutionary movement.[61] On Christmas Day 1915, while on a visit to Glasgow intended to calm labour unrest, Lloyd George, then minister of munitions, was shouted down by angry munitions workers in St Andrew's Hall. The socialist newspaper *Forward*, which reported his speech and its hostile reception, was promptly suppressed.

Labour unrest reached its peak with a strike wave at munitions factories in the early spring of 1916 which led to the deportation of strike leaders from the Clyde under the Defence of the Realm Act. As industrial unrest grew at the beginning of the year, Lloyd George's parliamentary undersecretary Christopher Addison (who later became minister of munitions himself) began to suspect 'a systematic and sinister plan' to sabotage 'production of the most important munitions of war in the Clyde district' and thus frustrate the great

offensive planned for 1916 on the Western Front. His suspicions were fuelled
by alarmist reports of German machinations from a small Clydeside intelligence
service secretly organised by Sir Lynden Macassey K.C., Chairman of the
Clyde Dilution Commissioners (who dealt with the 'dilution' of skilled by
unskilled labour). Addison wrote in his diary after receiving Macassey's
reports:

> He has traced direct payments from Germany to three workers and also
> discovered that ... the man who is financing the Clyde workers ... has a
> daughter married in Germany, a son married to a German and his chief
> business is in Germany. He is evidently on the track of a very successful
> revelation.[62]

Macassey's reports prompted the Ministry of Munitions to found an intelligence service of its own. Kell provided a 'nucleus' of MI5 officers under
Colonel Labouchère who set up a secret intelligence department (later known
as PMS 2) within the ministry on 19 February 1916 to monitor aliens and
labour unrest.[63] To Macassey's extreme annoyance, his own intelligence
service, of which he was inordinately proud, was taken over by Labouchère.[64]

Thomson viewed PMS 2 with a predictably jaundiced eye, dismissing it as
an expensive 'amateur service' based on 'a host of private agents who produce
little that cannot be found in the local press'.[65] Addison himself rapidly lost
faith in the reports of German machinations on the Clyde which had led to
the foundation of PMS 2. By the time he became minister of munitions in
July 1916 he had probably concluded that, as he later wrote in his memoirs,
'There never was any evidence' of German involvement in the labour
troubles.[66] The most celebrated case investigated by PMS 2 was an alleged
plot to assassinate Lloyd George. The alleged conspirators were a Derby
second-hand clothes dealer of 'extreme anarchical opinions', Mrs Alice
Wheeldon, her daughters Harriet and Winnie, and Winnie's husband Alfred
Mason, a chemist who had 'made a special study of poisons'. According to
PMS 2, the farcical plot finally devised by Mrs Wheeldon to murder Lloyd
George was to fire a poisoned dart from an air rifle while he was playing golf
on Walton Heath. The plotters were arrested in January 1917 and given jail
sentences two months later. Mrs Wheeldon was not helped by an eccentric
counsel who asked the judge to order trial by ordeal:

> 'That the ladies should walk over hot ploughshares or something of that
> kind – is that it?'
> 'I do suggest that, my Lord, in order that they may prove their innocence'.

In retrospect much of the evidence produced appears flimsy as well as farcical.
It emerged in the course of the trial that the PMS 2 case officer, Major

William Melville Lee (the brother of Lloyd George's military secretary), had employed two rather dubious agents provocateurs to investigate the Wheeldons. His brother complained that Major Lee 'received no recognition or even thanks' for his investigation.[67]

Major Lee, by nature more alarmist than Thomson, appears to have criticised Special Branch intelligence on labour unrest as insufficiently alarming. Thomson retorted that 'it was very dangerous to have soldiers spying on workmen. They would raise a cry of military dictatorship and provoke strikes'.[68] Thomson's view prevailed. By December 1916 the Ministry of Munitions had grown dissatisfied with the performance of PMS 2 and asked Thomson to found a new 'intelligence service on labour matters for the whole country on behalf of the Ministry'. Thomson agreed, drafted twelve sergeants from the CID into the ministry, and was given an annual budget of £8,000 a year to run the new intelligence system. In April 1917, soon after the Wheeldons' trial, the out-of-favour PMS 2 was formally 'reabsorbed' by MI5.[69]

Though Thomson had scored a significant victory over Kell and had clearly established himself as the leading intelligence expert on industrial unrest, he had yet to win a monopoly of it. The proliferation of wartime labour departments produced a corresponding proliferation of labour intelligence agencies. The new Ministries of Labour and National Service (set up by Lloyd George when he became prime minister in December 1916), the Board of Trade, the Admiralty Shipyard Labour Department, the Army Contracts Department, the GHQ Home Forces all concerned themselves with various forms of labour intelligence. In April 1917 Lloyd George's five-man war cabinet took steps to collate this bewildering variety of information. All government departments receiving 'labour intelligence' were told to pass it on to the Ministry of Labour, which was instructed to prepare for the war cabinet a weekly 'statement as to stoppages, disputes and settlements and labour propaganda brought to their notice during the week, together with a general appreciation of the labour situation'.[70]

The compiler of these weekly reports was Sir David Shackleton, a former Labour M.P. and president of the TUC who had become the first permanent undersecretary of the new Ministry of Labour. His first report in May 1917 coincided with the peak of a new strike wave which, he warned, was not only causing serious damage to munitions production but also showed 'a deep-seated unrest in the minds of a section of the civil population which, unless removed, may make it difficult to prosecute the War at all'.[71] On 9 May the war cabinet asked Thomson for his views. Thomson proposed the arrest of the shop stewards who were leading the strikes in opposition to their own union leaders.[72] Though his proposal was accepted, the strike wave was finally ended without arrests by conciliation. At the meeting between Addison, the minister of munitions, and the shop stewards on 19 May, it was agreed that the eight strike leaders so far arrested would be released on bail, that the shop stewards would recommend a return to work, and that there would be no victimisation.[73] The process of conciliation continued when Winston Churchill succeeded Addison as minister of munitions in July. On 7 August he interviewed David Kirkwood, the leader of the munitions workers deported from the Clyde in the spring of 1916. Kirkwood wrote later:

> I expected arrogance, military precision, abruptness. When he appeared, I knew I was wrong. He came in, his fresh face all smiles, and greeted me simply, without a trace of side or trappings, I felt I had found a friend ...
>
> Then he rang a bell, saying: 'Let's have a cup of tea and a bit of cake together'.
>
> What a difference so small a thing can make! Here was the man, supposed never to think of trifles, suggesting tea and cake – a sort of bread and salt of friendship.
>
> It was magnificent. We debated over the teacups.

Three days after taking tea and cake with Churchill, Kirkwood was offered a job as a manager at one of the Beardmore shell factories from which he had been expelled over a year before. Six weeks later, thanks to a bonus scheme introduced by Kirkwood, shell production at the factories was the highest in Britain.[74]

There were few in Whitehall so skilled in the application of tea and sympathy to labour disputes. The shock waves from the Russian revolution which overthrew the Tsar in March left lingering fears that revolutionary agitators were out to undermine the war effort through industrial action. These fears were strengthened when the M.P.s and the National Council of the ILP acclaimed 'the magnificent achievement of the Russian people' as a step towards 'the coming of peace, based not on the dominance of militarists and diplomats, but on democracy and justice'.[75] At a Home Office conference on 5 April Thomson found 'a good deal of ignorant alarmism, especially among the generals present', and was instructed to prepare intelligence reports on 'the growth of anarchist and socialist movements and their influence on the strike'. Thomson had a healthy respect for what a determined minority of revolutionaries could achieve. 'A single fox', he believed, 'will clear out a hen-roost while it is cackling its indignation to the skies'.[76] Shackleton reported that:

> The extremist section among Shop-Stewards have received considerable encouragement from the recent events in Russia ... The purely revolutionary element, though probably negligible in itself, thrives on the general uncertainty of opinion ...[77]

But both Thomson and Shackleton were convinced that the basic causes of the strike wave had little to do with revolutionary politics. They put the emphasis instead on war-weariness and industrial grievances – notably the 'dilution' of skilled workmen by unskilled labour in the munitions factories. Most strikers, Thomson argued, had little interest in politics: 'So far from collecting at street corners and listening to Pacifist haranguers, the Lancashire men took advantage of the fine weather at Blackpool, or were found quietly working in their allotments'.[78]

The reports of the regional Commissioners on Industrial Unrest appointed after the spring strikes were equally reassuring. Forwarding them to Lloyd George in July, the Labour representative in the war cabinet, George Barnes (temporarily replacing Arthur Henderson), reported 'a strong feeling of patriotism on the part of employers and employed throughout the country'. 'Feelings of a revolutionary character', he added, 'are not entertained by the bulk of the men'. In hindsight the war years now appear as a period of relative industrial peace. The yearly average of four million working days lost through wartime strikes was only a quarter of the pre-war average for the period 1910–14 and less than a tenth of that for the three years following victory.[79]

Faced with the unending carnage of the Western Front and the threat of Russian collapse in the East, few ministers found it possible to take so detached a view. Lord Milner, next to Lloyd George the most influential voice in the war cabinet, wrote to the prime minister on 1 June 1917: 'I fear the time is very near at hand when we shall have to take some strong steps to stop the "rot" in this country, unless we wish to "follow Russia" into impotence and dissolution'. But the 'rot' continued. Two days later the ILP and the smaller Marxist British Socialist Party (BSP) convened a conference at Leeds to honour the Russian Revolution. Among the 1150 delegates were 580 from trade unions and trade councils. The conference endorsed the demand by the Russian provisional government for 'peace without annexations or indemnities', told the British government to demand the same, and called for British workers and soldiers' councils on the Soviet model.[80] The British Soviets, however, were to be still born. Many hall owners were persuaded to cancel meetings organised by prospective Soviets. Where meetings were held, Thomson was glad to connive at counter-demonstrations by outraged patriots. The organisers of the London Soviet, he wrote gleefully in his diary on 27 July, were in for 'a rude awakening': 'I have arranged with the *Daily Express* to publish the place of their meeting and a strong opposition may be expected'.[81] Leaflets were also distributed in the East End announcing that a pro-German meeting was taking place and urging East Enders: 'Remember the last air-raid and turn up'. The conference was broken up by a mob of 8,000 including soldiers who stormed the platform. Soviets in other cities met similar fates. The BSP journal *The Call* declared in September 1917:

The interference with the right of public meeting has now reached a critical stage. It is now practically impossible to obtain a hall if the object is in any way opposed to the war.[82]

In August 1917 a pretext was found for the arrest of E.D. Morel, the secretary and – in the eyes of the authorities – the evil genius of the Union of Democratic Control (UDC) which had opposed the war from the outset. The Home Office had long wanted Morel 'safely lodged in jail' but took some time to overcome the fears of the director of public prosecutions that a trial would offer him 'a larger publicity for his mischievous propaganda'. On 31 August Morel was charged with violating the Defence of the Realm Act 'by inciting' a Miss Ethel Sidgwick to transmit 'otherwise than by post' two of his anti-war pamphlets to the French pacifist Romain Rolland, then living in Switzerland. The charge was trivial. Morel was legally entitled to send the pamphlets to Rolland in France, and only the accident of Rolland's temporary residence in Switzerland made Morel liable to prosecution. Though found guilty on a technicality, Morel was sentenced to six months in goal. Without him, Thomson believed, the UDC was clearly less effective.[83]

The government remained anxious. George Roberts, the minister of labour, believed the ILP was making 'great strides' and 'rapidly becoming a numerically powerful organisation, ... acquiring large funds from its membership'. Even the less alarmist Lloyd George believed that both the membership and 'agitation' of the ILP was on the increase. In reality, ILP membership in England, though not on Clydeside, actually declined between 1915 and 1917. The war cabinet was also concerned by growing 'pacifism' within the Labour Party. In August a special Labour Party conference decided to send delegates to a Stockholm conference to meet socialists from enemy as well as allied and neutral states. Though the seamen refused to allow the delegates on board, the issue led to Arthur Henderson's resignation from the war cabinet.[84]

The leader of the Ulster Unionists, Sir Edward Carson, who joined the war cabinet in July, warned Lloyd George in August that Unionists were 'everywhere very disgruntled' at the rapid strides made by pacifism on the left.[85] In a cabinet memorandum of 3 October Carson declared that neither the ministry of labour intelligence summaries nor the reports of the Commissioners on Industrial Unrest went deep enough. The Ministry of Labour based its reports on its contacts with 'the properly accredited trade union officials' and was out of touch with 'the various more recent labour organisations which appear to be the principal field of operations for pacifist propaganda'. Carson declared it a 'fact' that German money had been 'promoting industrial trouble' in Russia, France, Italy, Spain, the United States, Argentina, Chile – 'in fact wherever conditions were suitable for their interference'. The war cabinet therefore required 'reports from the various Secret Services to show whether there is any evidence at all that the enemy are supplying funds, either directly or indirectly, for the pacifist propaganda'.[86]

Carson's alarmism was taken quite seriously by his colleagues. At the war cabinet on 4 October:

> It was pointed out ... that the only really efficient system of propaganda at present existing in this country was that organised by the pacifists, who had large sums of money at their disposal and who were conducting their campaign with great vigour.

The cabinet minutes record no challenge to this preposterous allegation.[87]

The home secretary, Sir George Cave, who shared many of Carson's fears, was further alarmed by a series of articles in *The Times* entitled 'The Ferment of Revolution'. On 10 October he summoned Thomson and called for a report.[88] As Cave subsequently told his colleagues, Thomson's reassuring report failed to satisfy him. The war cabinet discussed the question of German finance for pacifist propaganda again at its meeting on 19 October. The minutes reveal, once again, extravagant conspiracy theories:

> ... A case had recently been brought to light in which the pacifists had been refused the use of a hall in Bradford for the purpose of holding meetings, and, on receipt of the refusal, had bought the hall for the sum of £18,000. It was suspected that anti-war propaganda was being financed by wealthy men, who were looking forward to making money by opening up trade with Germany after the war, and it was rumoured that certain financiers were already entering into *post*-war contracts with a view to making profits out of German trade.

The war cabinet agreed that, despite the arrangements made in April for the ministry of labour to collate intelligence from other departments, its weekly reports 'by no means covered the whole of pacifist activities in this country'. In particular, they failed to take account of 'a great deal of information' collected by Kell and the War Office (who probably showed less *sangfroid* than Thomson or Shackleton).[89] It was therefore decided that the Home Office (in other words Thomson) should 'undertake the coordination and control of the investigation of all pacifist propaganda and of the wider subjects connected therewith', and report to the war cabinet.[90] Thomson groaned inwardly at the news. While he considered Cave and the war cabinet too alarmist, he was conscious that failure to give their alarms due – or rather, undue – weight might be interpreted as complacency in the face of subversion. He wrote in his diary on 22 October:

> ... The War Cabinet ... are not disposed to take soothing syrup in these matters. Being persuaded that German money is supporting [pacifist and revolutionary] societies they want to be assured that the police are doing

something. I feel certain that there is no German money, their expenditure being covered by the subscriptions they receive from cranks.[91]

In a revised verson of the report which had dissatisfied Cave, Thomson contrived to show a prudent awareness of the dangers of German-financed subversion which worried the war cabinet, while none the less arriving at a reassuring conclusion. Germany's role in financing various sorts of pre-war subversion (though in reality non-existent) was, he reported, 'well known'. He also alleged that German finance probably lay behind the two best-known anti-war publicists, Norman Angell and E.D. Morel. Angell's celebrated pre-war work, *The Great Illusion*, was – he claimed – 'said to have been financed' by the heir to an Austrian banker. Thomson damned Morel by equally crude innuendo:

> There is no proof that he received money from German sources, but this has been stated publicly on several occasions, and he has never thought fit to vindicate himself. The probabilities are certainly strong that Mr Morel did not work out of pure altruism ... As his activities have certainly been in the German interest, as well as those of his friend, Sir Roger Casement, in his latter years, the public cannot be blamed for believing that Mr Morel has been financed by Germany in the past and may possibly be expecting financial reward for his peace activities in the future.

Having thus conceded that the war cabinet's fears had some foundation, Thomson went on to argue that there was no cause for alarm. German money had been neither widely nor effectively deployed. Except for the ILP, pacifist organisations had been 'financially in low water for some time'; the UDC was 'not a revolutionary body' and had little appeal outside 'the intellectual classes'; the British Soviets were 'moribund'; the BSP, though 'very noisy', did not 'carry very much weight' and had to be bailed out by the ILP; the shop stewards were 'generally ... in favour of continuing the war'. Boredom, concluded Thomson, did more than Germany to encourage pacifist propaganda. The working classes (particularly young, unmarried men with money in their pockets) missed 'the relaxations to which they were accustomed before the war, owing to the curtailment of horseracing, football and other amusements, and to the reduction of hours when public houses are kept open':

> ... In so far as it is practicable, everything should be done to cater for the reasonable demand of the working classes for relaxation and amusement, so as to relieve their lives of the burden of melancholy dulness [sic] which impels so many to take up agitation as a pastime.[92]

In his monthly intelligence report for the Ministry of Munitions in November 1917, Thomson repeated the same message. It was, he argued, remarkable, 'considering the amount of inflammable material available', that 'so little disturbance', had resulted. The food supply, not the political situation, caused 'the strongest feeling of resentment'.[93] But the war cabinet was not easily reassured. Shortly before ministers read Thomson's soothing memorandum, they received news of the Bolshevik Revolution. In the wake of the triumph of subversion in Russia their fears of subversion in Britain were to reach new heights.

# 6 'ADVENTURE AND ROMANCE IN THE SECRET INTELLIGENCE SERVICE IN RED RUSSIA': THE FAILURE OF COVERT ACTION

British wartime intelligence organisation in pre-revolutionary Russia was almost as confused as the Tsarist régime. At the outbreak of war the military attaché in Petrograd, Colonel (later General Sir) Alfred Knox, a blunt but shrewd Ulsterman, was outraged to discover his own responsibility for military liaison threatened by interlopers on what he denounced as pointless 'joy rides'. The most senior interloper was General Sir John Hanbury-Williams, posted as head of a wartime military mission to the Russian GHQ on the grounds that Knox's rank and social standing were insufficient to impress the Russian commander-in-chief, Grand Duke Nicholas.[1]

Knox was 'not even civil' to Hanbury-Williams. He reserved his greatest ire, however, for Major Archibald Campbell, a tactless Scot who arrived in Petrograd as Cumming's station chief in September 1914. Unusually for one of C's agents, Campbell wore military uniform, probably to please the Russians, and had offices in the headquarters of the Russian general staff overlooking the Winter Palace. Despite what the War Office considered these 'somewhat exceptional facilities', Campbell's mission was to end in failure. His attempt to improve signals intelligence on the Eastern Front by a network of British wireless operators foundered on Russian unwillingness to allow foreign involvement in such a sensitive part of their own operations, and his efforts to build up a network of Russian informants yielded – in his own words – 'no results'.[2]

Campbell's mission was thus reduced to liaison work with Russian military intelligence, in particular on the enemy's battle order and troop movements. Knox inevitably complained that Campbell was encroaching on his own territory, and was supported by the ambassador, Sir George Buchanan. Campbell was further accused of causing 'constant offence' by his lack of tact and discretion, and of 'assuming unwarrantable authority'. After a number of preliminary skirmishes, the conflict between Knox and Campbell reached a head in the spring of 1915. On 23 March both Knox and the naval attaché, Captain Cromie, telegraphed London demanding either their own recall or

Campbell's. The situation, declared Buchanan, was 'intolerable'. In April Campbell was recalled.

Knox argued strongly that Cumming should have no independent station chief in Petrograd: 'The secret service presumably would not be directed against Russia, and therefore there seemed no valid argument against its control by the Military Attaché.' Liaison work with Russian intelligence would also, Knox claimed, be better conducted by his own office. In any case, the intelligence the Russians were willing to hand over was of 'very small value' by comparison with what 'a man who knows the army and people' – meaning Knox – could 'ascertain in spite of them'. Knox had a good case. After the war the former Russian chargé d'affaires in London wrote that he 'was better informed than the Russian General Staff themselves'.[3] Robert Bruce Lockhart, perhaps the ablest British diplomat in wartime Russia, likewise concluded that 'Up to the revolution no man took a saner view of the military situation on the Eastern Front and no foreign observer supplied his Government with more reliable information'.[4]

Cumming, predictably, was not prepared to abandon his Petrograd station. Since the Foreign Office accepted that embassies and the service attachés who worked in them should 'steer clear of secret service', he argued that secret service could only be run by himself. He also convinced the Foreign Office that 'the chief Russian military authorities will not communicate very secret military intelligence if they think it is going to be known to their own F.O. or to Embassies at Petrograd'. Cumming won most of his case. In May 1915 another of his officers, Major (later Colonel) C.J.M. Thornhill, arrived in Petrograd to replace Campbell. Unlike Campbell, Thornhill got on well with Knox. In February 1916 the War Office formally approved an arrangement which made Thornhill subordinate to Knox 'as regards military discipline', but left him free to report direct to Cumming. Lieutenant-Colonel C.N. French of the War Office military intelligence secretariat noted that Knox had been given only 'a shadow authority' over the MI1c station and that 'existing arrangements' remained unchanged. Cumming, however, was not happy. In the process of falling in with Knox, Thornhill had fallen out with Cumming.

At this point the Conservative M.P. and future foreign secretary, Sir Samuel Hoare, arrived on the scene. Hoare had been commissioned in the Norfolk Yeomanry but after a serious illness at the end of 1914 was declared unfit for active service. Growing restive during 1915 in his job running a recruiting office in Norwich cattle market, Hoare learned Russian in the hope of finding a job on one of the military missions in Russia. In February 1916 a friend in the War Office told him of a possible 'billet in Petrograd'. Hoare hurried to London 'without an hour's delay' and found that the job was in MI1c. Most of Cumming's agents were somewhat overawed by their first meeting with him in his roof-top office in Whitehall Court. Possibly because of his previous experience of public life, Hoare was not. He found Cumming 'jovial and very human, bluff and plain speaking, outwardly at least, a very simple man': 'In all respects, physical and mental, he was the very antithesis of the spy king of popular fiction'. The Chief used none of the theatrical devices he sometimes employed to test the mettle of new agents. Hoare had expected a thorough examination on his knowledge of the Russian language, army and politics. Instead, after 'a few conventional words in a very conventional room', Cumming told Hoare that the job he was offering was 'not much of a job' but that he could have it if he wanted it. Hoare jumped at the chance.[5]

The job turned out to be twofold: to examine the working of the British intelligence mission in Petrograd and the effectiveness of the Russian blockade on trade with the enemy. Before leaving London, Hoare underwent a short but intensive course on wartime intelligence: 'One day, it would be espionage or contre-espionage, another coding and cyphering, another war trade and contraband, a fourth, postal and telegraphic censorship'. His main guide during this hectic induction was his old friend, Cumming's extrovert, games-playing deputy, Lieutenant-Colonel Freddie Browning, 'famous upon every cricket ground and in every racquets court, the friend of more people in the world than almost anyone I knew'.[6]

Hoare's first impressions of Petrograd were mixed. He reported 'somewhat slightingly' on Thornhill's work, which he considered too preoccupied with tracing enemy troop movements on the Eastern Front (whose importance, in the War Office view, he had failed to grasp) and too little concerned with the economic blockade and other aspects of the war.[7] On the other hand he saw in the personal cooperation between Thornhill and Knox the basis of a working relationship between the MI1c mission and the embassy. Whilst preparing his report, Hoare was horrified to receive a letter on 25 May telling him he was to replace Thornhill as MI1c station chief. He wrote to his wife:

Apart from my personal view that Thornhill is *much* the best man for the job, a sudden change will make hay of the whole mission. You cannot imagine the complications between the various military authorities here, and I was just on the point of getting everybody smoothed down when the news of Thornhill's recall arrived. The announcement of it would have simply fuelled the fire with oil. I have therefore got them to agree to keep the whole thing quiet pending further communications ...[8]

During a fortnight's visit to London in June Hoare arranged a complicated compromise. Instead of being recalled to London, Thornhill was transferred to the embassy as second assistant military attaché with special responsibility for battle order intelligence which was, however, still to be forwarded to London by the MI1c station. Hoare himself succeeded Thornhill as station chief with the rank of acting lieutenant-colonel. Captain Scale, then on active service in France, was transferred to Petrograd to advise Hoare on battle order intelligence and take responsibility for it during Thornhill's frequent visits to the Eastern Front.[9]

This complex compromise produced growing friction between Knox and Hoare, and growing exasperation in the War Office. Macdonogh, the DMI, considered 'the crux of the problem' the personalities of Knox and Hoare, and asked General Sir Henry Wilson to find a solution while on an Allied delegation to Russia early in 1917. Wilson telegraphed the War Office on 6 February that 'the existing distribution of duties' was 'quite impracticable'. But his proposed solution led to further dissension. By now the triangular tension between Knox, Hoare and Hanbury-Williams had been further complicated by the appointment of General Frederick Poole as technical adviser to the Grand Duke Serge with responsibility for all ammunition, artillery and aviation supplies from Britain.[10]

The confusion of the British intelligence system in Russia was further complicated by the even greater bureaucratic chaos of Tsarist intelligence. The General Staff, every army group HQ and the Ministry of Marine had its own secret service, its own agents and – it seemed to Hoare – such a jealousy of each others' operations that 'they would almost rather catch each other out than catch a German spy'. Hoare was also convinced that the Russian government was less interested in military and naval intelligence than in the totally distinct secret services run by the Court, the Ministry of the Interior and the Holy Synod:

> How could I create an effective liaison, when there was an almost complete want of system, and when many of the most important officials were uninterested in our attempts at war espionage and contre-espionage?[11]

Like other British intelligence officers, Hoare found himself constantly approached by the rival sections of Russian intelligence with 'bright ideas for finishing the war': 'Now it might be a scheme for substituting British for German capital in Russia, now a plan for sabotage in Germany, now an offer of a complete system of espionage for the enemy countries'. Hoare was driven still closer to distraction by being regularly pestered about matters which had nothing to do with intelligence. On one occasion, in response to desperate appeals from the Holy Synod, he had to arrange for a large supply of wax for church candles to be shipped from England to Archangel.[12]

By the time General Sir Henry Wilson arrived in Russia in February 1917, Hoare could stand it no longer. He accompanied Wilson back to England to take sick leave and did not return to Petrograd. Much to his relief, he was transferred by Cumming to Rome in May. Hoare was succeeded in Petrograd by his former deputy, Major Stephen Alley, who had been born and brought up in Russia.[13]

British intelligence reporting from pre-revolutionary Russia was rather better than its chaotic organisation might suggest. While Knox provided a series of shrewd assessments of the Russian army, Thornhill – to judge from the incomplete evidence available – seems to have given the War Office an accurate picture of German troop movements on the Eastern Front.[14] Despite his troubled term in Petrograd, Hoare greatly improved Anglo-Russian cooperation in the economic blockade of Germany and built up a wide range of contacts among Russian politicians, especially in the Kadet party, the pro-Western constitutional democrats. Like Lenin and the revolutionaries themselves, Hoare failed to foresee the February Revolution which overthrew the Tsar. But he did predict the disintegration of the Russian war effort. He reported at the end of 1916:

> The conditions of life have become so intolerable, the Russian casualties have been so heavy, the ages and classes subject to military service have been so widely extended, the disorganisation of the administration and the untrustworthiness of the Government have become so notorious that it is not a matter of surprise if the majority of ordinary people reach at any peace straw. Personally, I am convinced that Russia will never fight through another winter.[15]

Inevitably, Hoare got some things wrong. 'Anyone, Russian or foreign, who lived in Petrograd in 1916', he wrote later, 'was certain to be constantly talking about Rasputin', the charismatic but dissolute monk who had the confidence of the German-born Tsarina. Like many of his Kadet friends, Hoare had an exaggerated belief in the responsibility of pro-German 'Dark Forces' orchestrated by Rasputin for the régime's administrative and military failings. On New Year's Eve 1916 he sent Cumming an urgent telegram, encoded by his wife, which contained the first news to reach the West of Rasputin's assassination on the night of 29 December. So good were Hoare's sources and so detailed his information about the grisly details of the murder that he came under suspicion at the Imperial Court of complicity in it. Sir George Buchanan had solemnly to certify Hoare's innocence at his next audience with the Tsar. In the immediate aftermath of Rasputin's death, Hoare, as he later admitted, optimistically 'imagined that the murder would destroy the "Dark Forces", and enable Russia to continue her war with a singleness of purpose that had hitherto been impossible'.[16] That illusion did not last long. By the time he left Russia in February 1917 his earlier pessimism had returned, though he still believed 'that matters were more likely to drift from bad to worse than to take any sudden or revolutionary turn'.[17]

Hoare arrived back in England at the beginning of March. During his sick-leave over the next fortnight the Tsarist regime was swept away by the 'February Revolution' ('February' because of the thirteen-day time-lag in the

Russian calendar) which he, like Lenin, had failed to predict. Hoare responded with a renewed surge of optimism:

> ... The Allies may now rest assured that Russia will not make a separate peace. For months past I was convinced that internal demoralisation made it impossible for Russia to continue the War over the winter of 1917. I now believe that the unity of national action which has been made possible by the Revolution will enable Russia to continue fighting until Germany is definitely defeated.[18]

In March 1917 Hoare's belief that the Revolution would rejuvenate rather than disrupt the Russian war effort was widely shared in Allied capitals. Such hopes were quickly dashed. Even before the socialist Kerensky succeeded Prince Lvov as head of the provisional government in May, Buchanan saw only an 'almost forlorn hope of saving the military situation' on the Eastern Front.[19] By the time the last great Russian offensive collapsed in July, Cumming had begun to consider covert action as a way of keeping Russia in the war. So too had Hanbury-Williams's successor, General Sir Charles Barter.[20] The British embassy pinned most of its remaining hopes on General Lavr Kornilov who became commander-in-chief on 31 July after the collapse of the offensive. But while Buchanan hoped for cooperation between Kornilov and Kerensky, Barter seems to have given covert support to an abortive military coup. On 9 September Kornilov ordered the troops under his command to march on the capital. One of the few units which answered the commander-in-chief's call was a British armoured-car squadron under Commander Oliver Locker-Lampson (later a Tory M.P.), who would have been unlikely to join the attempted coup without at least tacit consent from Barter or Knox. Kerensky later accused Knox of both subsidising and distributing pro-Kornilov propaganda. In the event the coup was a fiasco, and collapsed without a shot being fired. By enabling the Bolsheviks to pose as the saviours of the capital from counter-revolution, Kornilov merely brought closer Lenin's conquest of power.[21]

While Barter and possibly Knox seem to have been conniving at Kerensky's overthrow, MI1c was seeking ways to preserve him. The main agent it eventually selected to assist in his salvation was the novelist Somerset Maugham. Not long after Maugham's ill-fated marriage to Syrie Wellcome in Jersey City in May 1917, he received a telephone call from an old family friend now in MI1c, Sir William Wiseman.[22] At the age of thirty-two Wiseman still appeared, despite his moustache, 'the merest boy' to his American friends. He was, however, a former Cambridge boxing blue, held a baronetcy dating back to 1628, and came from an old and distinguished naval family; his father had annexed the Pacific island of Tongareva in 1888. After an unsuccessful career as a journalist and an even more unsuccessful career as a playwright whose plays were never performed, Wiseman had come to seek his fortune in America in ventures ranging from Canadian property development to Mexican meat-packing. At the outbreak of war he had volunteered for service on the Western Front but after being gassed in Flanders in 1915 was recommended to Cumming by one of his father's former shipmates. Wiseman was just the sort of adventurous, resourceful, clubbable maverick who appealed to C. Early in 1916 he became Cumming's station chief in the USA with an office in New York from which he reported regularly on pro-German activities and attempts to sabotage the flow of munitions to the Western Front.[23]

Maugham was 'staggered' by the proposition Wiseman put to him in June 1917. 'The long and the short of it', he wrote later, 'was that I should go to Russia and keep the Russians in the War'. After forty-eight hours' thought Maugham accepted. Remembering his Swiss experience, however, when he had worked for nothing and found himself regarded 'not as patriotic or generous but merely as damned foolish', he asked for both salary and expenses. Thanks partly to his friendship with President Woodrow Wilson's confidential agent, Colonel House, Wiseman was able to supply both. By telling the Foreign Office that the Americans supported his plan for a Russian mission and telling Colonel House that he had Foreign Office support, Wiseman obtained $75,000 from each side. Maugham thus became charged with, in effect, a joint Anglo-American mission. In August he arrived in Petrograd via the Trans-Siberian railway well supplied with funds by Wiseman and with instructions to support Kerensky's government against the Bolsheviks and pacifist propaganda (both of which, in Wiseman's view, owed much to German inspiration). With him went a group of four Czechoslovak refugees headed by Emmanuel Voska, Director of the Slav Press Bureau in New York, with instructions to 'organise the Czechs and Slovaks of the Empire to keep Russia in the war'.

In Petrograd Maugham's first meeting with the British ambassador 'could not have been more frigid'. Maugham was nervous and stammered badly; Buchanan took it as 'a grave affront' that his embassy was expected to involve itself in secret service work by cabling Maugham's messages to Wiseman in a code it could not read. Maugham's relations with Buchanan improved after he had helped heal a breach between him and Mr Francis, the American ambassador ('something of a roughneck' in Maugham's view) who claimed 'Sir George had high-hatted him'. According to Maugham's own account, he persuaded Francis that Buchanan was 'no stuffed shirt' but 'a regular guy'. Maugham's most important contacts in Petrograd, however, were outside the embassies. Voska introduced him to the future Czech president, Professor Thomas Masaryk, who impressed Maugham deeply by his 'good sense and determination' and helped set up a Slav press bureau to disseminate anti-German propaganda. Maugham's greatest stroke of luck was to meet again in Petrograd one of his former mistresses, Alexandra ('Sasha') Kropotkin, daughter of the former anarchist exile in London, Prince Kropotkin, and now 'very much in with the Kerensky government'.[24]

Much of Maugham's life in Petrograd later reappeared in his Ashenden short stories. Ashenden uses Maugham's own codename 'Somerville' and gives Maugham's London address in Chesterfield Street, Mayfair. Buchanan reappears as Sir Herbert Witherspoon, who receives Ashenden 'with a frigidity that would have sent a little shiver down the spine of a polar bear'. Witherspoon thaws somewhat after Ashenden helps improve his relations with the American ambassador, Wilbur Schäfer, whose mobile face 'looked as though it were made out of the red india-rubber from which they make hot-water bottles'. Masaryk becomes Professor X, with whom Ashenden drinks a cup of chocolate each day at the Europe hotel and discusses 'how best to make use of his devoted Czechs'. Sasha Kropotkin reappears in the Ashenden stories as Anastasia Alexandrovna:

> Anastasia Alexandrovna had fine eyes and a good, though for these days too voluptuous, figure, high cheek-bones and a snub nose (this was very Tartar), a wide mouth full of large square teeth, and a pale skin. She dressed somewhat flamboyantly. In her dark melancholy eyes Ashenden saw the boundless steppes of Russia, and the Kremlin with its pealing bells, and the solemn ceremonies of Easter at St Isaac's, and forests of silver birches, and the Nevsky Prospekt...[25]

As well as captivating Maugham with her dark, melancholy eyes, Sasha Kropotkin introduced him to most of the provisional government. With Sasha acting as his hostess and interpreter, Maugham entertained Kerensky or his ministers once a week at the Medvied, the best restaurant in Petrograd, paying for the finest vodka and caviar from the ample funds supplied by Wiseman. 'I think Kerensky must have supposed that I was more important than I really was', wrote Maugham later, 'for he came to Sasha's apartment on several occasions and, walking up and down the room, harangued me as though I were at a public meeting for two hours at a time'. Maugham became uncomfortably aware that he was treading on the toes of other British intelligence officers in Petrograd who must surely have resented both his interference and his unusually generous expense account. Late in September he proposed to Wiseman that he work in collaboration with the official MI1c station chief in Petrograd, Major Alley, 'thereby benefiting both and avoiding confusion'. By now, however, Maugham doubted whether Kerensky could survive. On 16 October he telegraphed to Wiseman recommending a programme of propaganda and covert action whose cost he estimated at 500,000 dollars a year. The Slav Press Bureau being founded by Voska and Masaryk could, he argued, both conduct 'legitimate propaganda' and act as a cover for 'other activities' in support of the Mensheviks and against the Bolsheviks. In addition, he proposed to set up 'special secret organisations' recruited from Poles, Czechs and Cossacks with the main aim of 'unmasking ... German plots and propaganda in Russia'. Wiseman was attracted by the scheme and approached Colonel House for funds.[26]

Maugham was by now in fatalistic mood. He wrote to his fellow playwright, Edward Knoblock, then on an intelligence mission in Greece with Compton Mackenzie:

> It seems incredible that one of these days we shall all settle down again to normal existence and read the fat, peaceful *Times* every morning and eat porridge for breakfast and marmalade. But, my dear, we shall be broken relics of a dead era, on the shelf all dusty and musty.[27]

On the evening of 31 October Maugham was summoned by Kerensky and asked to take an urgent secret message to Lloyd George appealing for guns and ammunition. Without that help, said Kerensky, 'I don't see how we can go on. Of course, I don't say that to the people. I always say that we shall continue whatever happens, but unless I have something to tell my army it's impossible'. Kerensky was critical of the official Allied representatives in Petrograd. The ambassador, though 'a perfectly honest man', was 'identified with the old regime' and needed replacing; Knox and the military advisers understood 'nothing of the political situation'. Maugham left the same evening for Oslo to board a British destroyer which, after a stormy passage across the North Sea, landed him in the north of Scotland. Next morning he saw Lloyd George at 10 Downing Street. The prime minister gave him a cordial welcome, said how much he enjoyed his plays but conveyed the strong impression that he already knew what Maugham had to tell him. Afraid that his stammer, which often appeared at moments of tension, might spoil his delivery, Maugham handed Lloyd George a note summarising Kerensky's message. The prime minister read it quickly and handed it back.

> 'I can't do that', he said.
> 'What shall I tell Kerensky?' asked Maugham.
> 'Just that I can't do that. I'm afraid I must bring this conversation to an end. I have a cabinet meeting I must go to'.[28]

The prime minister shook hands and bade Maugham a cordial farewell. On 7 November Kerensky was overthrown by the Bolshevik Revolution. Sir Eric Drummond, private secretary to the foreign secretary, noted on Maugham's document, 'I fear this [is] of only historical interest now'.[29] Wiseman, then on a visit to London, offered Maugham a new intelligence assignment in Rumania. But Maugham was suffering from tuberculosis and went instead to a Scottish sanatorium to recover. 'Perhaps if I had been sent to Russia six months sooner', Maugham speculated later, 'I might have been able to do something ...' That retrospective judgment was as naive as Wiseman's belief in the summer of 1917 that an agent well supplied with funds but with no previous experience of Russia could somehow 'guide the storm' of the revolutionary upheaval. Both betrayed a basic misunderstanding of the limitations of covert (or semi-covert) action.[30]

By the time Maugham retired to his Scottish sanatorium Lloyd George and the war cabinet already had their eye on a shrewder and more experienced – but equally unconventional – agent in revolutionary Russia. Robert Bruce Lockhart had been posted to Moscow in 1912 as vice-consul and later became acting consul-general. He rapidly acquired a reputation as the unofficial British ambassador in Moscow and impressed Hoare as the ablest member of the consular service he had ever met.[31] Sir George Buchanan also had a high opinion of Lockhart's ability but a low opinion of his morals. Possibly reacting against a severe Scottish Calvinist upbringing, Lockhart had already had one promising career in Malaya cut short after the 'resounding scandal' caused by his love affair with the ward of a local Sultan. Six weeks before the Bolshevik Revolution he was ordered back to London, ostensibly on sick leave, in reality to avert another public scandal. Buchanan was sympathetic but insisted that duty came before 'self-indulgence'. Lockhart 'slunk out of Moscow', expecting never to return. His fortunes, however, were unexpectedly revived by the Bolshevik Revolution. For several weeks he went the rounds in London of 'scores of politicians and experts', urging on them the need to establish contact with the Bolsheviks. On the morning of 21 December he was summoned to 10 Downing Street. 'From the wisdom of your reports', the prime minister told him, 'I expected to see an elderly gentleman with a grey beard'. A fortnight later Lockhart was appointed 'head of a special mission to establish unofficial relations with the Bolsheviks' after the recall of Buchanan and Knox. His instructions, as he later complained, were 'of the vaguest': 'I was to have the responsibility of establishing relations. I was to have no authority'.[32] Lieutenant (later Commander) Ernest Boyce, who succeeded Alley as MI1c station chief in Petrograd, made little attempt to conceal his 'disgust' at Lockhart's appointment.[33]

Lockhart achieved little. The main aim of his mission – to encourage the Bolsheviks to continue the war against Germany with promises of Allied assistance – stood no chance of success. By the time that Soviet Russia made peace with Germany at Brest-Litovsk on 3 March 1918 London was already considering intervention against the Bolsheviks. 'Your Lloyd George', Trotsky told Lockhart scornfully, 'is like a man playing roulette and scattering chips on every number'.[34] But Lockhart did not yet lose hope. He cabled London after Brest-Litovsk that there were 'still considerable possibilities of organising resistance to Germany'.[35] Trotsky and Chicherin, the Soviet foreign commissar, both anxious to keep open channels of communication with Allied capitals, flattered Lockhart and encouraged him to believe that Brest-Litovsk would not last long. Lockhart, however, had lost the ear of his government. 'Although Mr Lockhart's advice may be bad', commented one Foreign Office official acidly, 'we cannot be accused of having followed it'.[36]

During the spring of 1918 Lockhart himself rejected his own earlier advice and changed from diplomat to conspirator. By mid-May he was already in contact with agents of the anti-Bolshevik underground organised by Boris Savinkov. Somerset Maugham had been much taken by Savinkov, and considered him the most remarkable of the men introduced to him by Sasha Kropotkin in 1917. As well as being 'a genial, likeable fellow' according to Maugham, Savinkov was 'by way of being a terrorist' and before the Revolution had organised several assassinations – including those of Plehve, minister of the interior, in 1904, and the Grand Duke Serge in 1905.[37] In 1917 Savinkov served as Kerensky's deputy minister of war before plotting against him also. In his memoirs Lockhart later denied giving Savinkov any encouragement. His telegrams to London tell a different story. On 23 May 1918 he forwarded without comment to the Foreign Office details supplied by one of Savinkov's agents of a plan 'to murder all Bolshevik leaders on night of Allies landing and to form a Government which will be in reality a military dictatorship'. Lockhart now became an ardent advocate of allied intervention. On 4 June he told the Foreign Office: 'If you do not intervene within the next few days or weeks if possible we shall have lost a golden opportunity'. Balfour, the acting foreign secretary, replied acidly:

> You have at different times advised against Allied intervention in any form; against it by the Japanese alone; against it with Japanese assistance; against it at Vladivostock; in favour of it at Murmansk; in favour of it with an invitation; in favour of it without an invitation since it was really desired by the Bolsheviks; in favour of it without invitation whether the Bolsheviks desired it or not.[38]

Though Lockhart became increasingly involved in covert action, he himself was not responsible for intelligence operations in Bolshevik Russia. In addition to the MI1c station chief Lieutenant Boyce, who remained nominally in charge of secret service work in Russia, Cumming sent out several other agents to try their luck in the early months of 1918. Lockhart formed 'a very poor opinion' of their work. 'However brave and however gifted as linguists', they were, in his opinion, 'frequently incapable of forming a reliable political judgement'. 'With very few exceptions', Lockhart cabled Balfour on 18 March, 'your agents here have only one policy – to prove that Bolsheviks are pro-German'. They were deceived both by forged documents alleging that the Bolshevik leaders were in German pay and by false reports that 'Siberia was teeming with German regiments composed of war prisoners, who had been armed by the Bolsheviks'. For all their swashbuckling adventures, Cumming's agents served no useful purpose. Their reports had no significant influence on British policy to Bolshevik Russia.[39]

Despite Lockhart's low opinion of MI1c agents, the sheer audacity of Cumming's 'master spy', Sidney Reilly, took his breath away.[40] Reilly had spent most of the first two and a half years of the war in the United States purchasing war supplies for the Tsarist government, remaining in contact during that time with both Sir William Wiseman, Cumming's station chief in New York, and Wiseman's assistant, Major (later Lieutenant-Colonel) Norman Thwaites. Though Reilly's business prospered, Thwaites noted that he 'never could keep his money. He was a gambler by nature, whether in hazardous occupations or in games of chance'. His appearance struck Thwaites as 'remarkable':

> Complexion swarthy, a long straight nose, piercing eyes, black hair brushed back from a forehead suggesting keen intelligence, a large mouth, figure slight, of medium height, always clothed immaculately, he was a man that impressed one with a sense of power.

After the fall of the Tsar in the February Revolution of 1917, Reilly decided to enter the RFC and, on Thwaites's recommendation, was given a commission. He then changed his mind and asked Thwaites to find him a job in MI1c. Convinced that Reilly was 'wasted' in the RFC, Thwaites sent him to London to see Cumming who immediately assigned him to 'special duties in the Baltic and East Prussia'.[41] The next year in Reilly's life is so overlaid by myth (some of it constructed by Reilly himself) that it has become impossible to disentangle the truth about it. Reilly claimed, for example, to have attended a meeting of the German high command chaired by the Kaiser himself. Cumming probably believed too many of Reilly's tales. He had mixed feelings about him none the less. Reilly was, he believed, 'a man of indomitable courage, a genius as an agent but a sinister man who I could never bring myself wholly to trust'. In April 1918 Cumming, probably hoodwinked by Reilly's fantastic tale of his meeting with the Kaiser, decided to send him to Russia with the codename S.T.1 to see what he could make of Lenin.[42] Reilly announced his arrival in Moscow on 7 May by marching up to the Kremlin gates, telling the sentries he was an emissary from Lloyd George, and insisting on seeing Lenin personally. Remarkably, Reilly managed to get as far as one of Lenin's leading aides, Bonch-Brouevich, who telephoned Lockhart. Lockhart dressed Reilly down 'like a schoolmaster' and threatened to send him straight home, but found him 'so ingenious in his excuses that in the end he made me laugh'.[43] Reilly then acquired a new identity as a Greek from the Levant, added further to an already impressive string of mistresses, and began plotting Lenin's overthrow in earnest.

The most celebrated of Reilly's colleagues in MI1c's Russian operations during 1918, Captain (later Brigadier) G.A. Hill, code-named I.K.8, also cultivated a larger than life reputation. 'Jolly George Hill', as Philby later described him,[44] considered his days as a British spy in Russia 'a joyful adventure in the pages of my life'. Hill was the son of 'an English pioneer merchant of the best type' whose business interests had stretched from Siberia to Persia, and his boyhood travels had given him what he considered a better preparation for espionage than any amount of professional training. Following a varied wartime career in the Intelligence Corps and the RFC, Hill was sent to join an RFC mission to Russia two months before the Bolshevik Revolution. After the Revolution Hill engaged in a number of free-lance skirmishes with German secret agents and army units and other adventures aimed at keeping the Bolsheviks in the war.[45]

Following the Russo-German peace treaty at Brest-Litovsk on 3 March 1918, Hill told the War Office there was still 'valuable work' for him in Russia and was given 'a fairly free hand' to do it. His first priority was to identify German units and report on their movements in occupied Russia. In April he began cooperating with Cumming's station chief, Lieutenant Boyce, and by July was working chiefly for MI1c. To begin with, he also cooperated with the Bolsheviks in the hope their peace treaty with Germany would break down.[46] Hill's memoirs of his years in Russia, grandly entitled *Go Spy The Land*, are engagingly free from modesty about his intelligence mission. By his own immodest account, he won the confidence of Trotsky and played an important part in the early development of both the Cheka (the forerunner of the KGB) and Soviet military intelligence (now the GRU):

> Lectures to Trotsky, theatre and supper parties did not interfere with the work I had planned. First of all I helped the Bolshevik military headquarters to organize an Intelligence Section for the purpose of identifying German units on the Russian front and for keeping the troop movements under close observation ... Identifications came to me every day, and a copy of them was telegraphed to the War Office in London. Time and again I was able to warn London that a German division had left the Russian for the Western Front.
>
> Secondly, I organized a Bolshevik counter-espionage section to spy on the German secret service and Missions in Petrograd and Moscow. Our interception organization worked well. We deciphered German codes, opened their letters and read most of their correspondence without even being suspected.[47]

Hill's contemporary reports to Cumming and the War Office tell a less sensational, though still impressive, tale. He 'got the Moscow District Military Commander to organise a Bolshevik identifications section, and promised them every assistance from England'. But there is no evidence that, as Hill claimed in his memoirs, he personally helped to found the section. Nor is there any contemporary reference to his establishment of a 'Bolshevik counter-espionage section' which read 'most' German correspondence. But there is evidence that for several months Hill obtained an impressive amount of intelligence, especially on German troops in occupied Russia, which he telegraphed to London 'every few days' (not 'every day' as he later claimed).[48]

By the summer of 1918, Hill had despaired of cooperation with the Bolsheviks:

> I organized a secret organization of my own which was divided into three sections; the first, for the identification of German and Austrian units, acted as a check on the information I obtained from the Bolshevik Military Section and the Social Revolutionaries; the second, a courier service, made me independent of the post and telegraph office ... The third was a special section of patriotic Russian officers operating within the German lines, arming peasants, derailing troop and supply trains on their way to Germany and generally harrying the Germans by every means in their power; this required money, passes and, most of all, direction, with all of which I supplied them.[49]

Contemporary reports tell, once again, a less sensational story. The two couriers sent to Archangel in July took, respectively, twelve and twenty days to make the hazardous round trip from Moscow, and suffered, not surprisingly, great 'nervous strain'. During August, 'as results were so poor', Hill 'decided to discontinue the direct messenger service and attempt to organise a large chain service'. Preparations for sabotage were also on a smaller scale than Hill later suggested. By the beginning of August only 'a small destruction gang' had been organised.[50] Since April Hill had none the less acquired a considerable reputation in MI1c which still endured at the beginning of the Second World War. 'He was', wrote Kim Philby, 'one of the few living Englishmen who had actually put sand in axle-boxes'.[51]

By July 1918 Lockhart was himself deeply involved in covert action. Together with Grenard, the French consul-general in Moscow, he handed over ten million rubles to the counter-revolutionary National Centre group in Moscow, loosely linked to Savinkov in the north-east and the White Army of the Tsarist General Alekseev in Kuban. Lockhart, however, was no more successful than the MI1c agents of whose work he formed such a low opinion. It is probable that the Bolsheviks possessed his code and were able to intercept at least some of his reports to London on his dealings with the National Centre.[52] Felix Dzerzhinsky, the head of the Cheka, also used *agents provocateurs* to penetrate Lockhart's operations. Two Lettish Cheka agents, Jan Buikis and Ian Sprogis, gained the confidence of the British naval attaché,

Captain Cromie, who sent them on to Lockhart. On 14 August Buikis and Colonel Eduard Berzin, commander of a Lettish battalion in the Kremlin guard, called on Lockhart with false reports of serious disaffection among the Lettish troops. Reilly was then brought into the conspiracy by Lockhart and supplied Berzin with 1,200,000 rubles to finance an anti-Bolshevik coup, which Berzin handed over to the Bolsheviks instead.[53]

Preparations for an anti-Bolshevik coup in Moscow coincided with the beginning of British military intervention against the Bolsheviks in northern Russia. The first company of marines commanded by Major-General Frederick Poole had landed at the Arctic port of Murmansk on 6 March, only three days after the treaty of Brest-Litovsk. But the marines had not been sent to overthrow the Bolsheviks. Their landing was intended instead to prevent the Germans seizing the vast quantities of Allied war materials shipped to Murmansk which had never reached the Eastern Front. Allied intervention changed in character, however, when Poole made a second landing at Archangel on 2 August with a detachment of Royal Marines, a French battalion and fifty American sailors. The ostensible purpose of the Archangel landing was, once again, to prevent war supplies falling into German hands, but it was timed to coincide with an anti-Bolshevik coup. On 3 July Poole had warned the War Office that both the success of the landing and his move inland would require the extensive use of secret agents. Two groups of Allied agents landed secretly about a fortnight before the landing were caught and imprisoned by the Bolsheviks. But a successful coup was engineered in Archangel itself on the night of 1 August. Its author was a Russian naval officer formerly attached to the Royal Navy, Captain Georgi Chaplin, almost certainly acting in concert with his close friend Colonel Thornhill, formerly of MI1c and now Poole's intelligence chief. By the morning of 2 August the Bolshevik administration in Archangel had been ousted by a government of anti-Bolshevik socialists under the veteran Populist N.V. Chaikovsky which styled itself the 'Supreme Administration of the Northern Region', appointed Chaplin 'Commander-in-Chief of Russian Forces', and invited Poole's troops to land. Chaikovsky's government was little more than a façade. Poole became a virtual viceroy, ruling by decree. Almost certainly with Thornhill's connivance once again, Chaplin deposed the Chaikovsky government on 6 September. After protests by the remaining Allied diplomats in Russia, who had sought refuge in Archangel, the deposed government was reinstated.[54] Major-General Edmund Ironside, who replaced Poole in October, complained that Thornhill and his intelligence staff were wasting their time in intrigues rather than collecting the intelligence needed for military operations.[55]

Curiously, the landing of Allied troops at Archangel on 2 August did not immediately cause an open breach between Britain and the Bolsheviks. Balfour cabled Lockhart on the 8th: 'You should, as far as possible, maintain existing relations with Bolshevik Government. Rupture, or declaration of war, should come, if come it must, from Bolsheviks not from the Allies'.[56] For the moment the Cheka preferred to bide its time and give the Allied conspirators in Moscow enough rope to hang themselves. This leisurely game of cat and mouse was cut short on 30 August when Uritsky, the head of the Petrograd Cheka, was assassinated by a military cadet, and Lenin himself was shot and gravely wounded by the Socialist Revolutionary Dora Kaplan. These two unconnected incidents unleashed a Bolshevik reign of terror. In Petrograd alone over five hundred political prisoners were executed in two days. The Cheka stormed the British embassy, shooting the naval attaché, Captain Cromie, when he offered resistance. Lockhart was arrested on 31 August, released the following day and rearrested on 4 September.

The Soviet press published wild allegations that Uritsky had been killed because he was unravelling 'the threads of an English conspiracy in Petrograd'. Behind these insubstantial allegations lay more substantial charges on two other counts: first, the 'Lockhart case', based on Lockhart's and Reilly's dealings with the Lettish *agents provocateurs*; second, the 'envoys' plot', involving alleged plans for Reilly and other Allied secret agents to destabilise and sabotage the Bolshevik régime after the remaining Western diplomats had left.[57] There was a good deal of substance to the second as well as the first charge, though allegations of a British assassination squad were largely (but not entirely) Soviet fabrications. On about 22 August Berzin had tried to persuade Reilly to organise a plot, which the Bolsheviks could then have publicised, to assassinate both Lenin and Trotsky. Berzin argued that it would be dangerous simply to arrest the Bolshevik leaders after the planned coup since 'their marvellous oratorical powers' might win over the men sent to arrest them. Furthermore, 'the assassination of two of the leaders would create a panic so that there would be no resistance' after the coup. Reilly refused even to consider assassination, telling Berzin that his aim was 'not to make martyrs of the leaders but to hold them up to ridicule before the world'.[58] The particular form of ridicule Reilly had in mind was to debag Lenin and Trotsky, then to parade them trouserless through the streets of Moscow.[59] Boyce, the less imaginative MI1c station chief, was less hostile to the idea of an assassination plot. He seems to have enquired, probably speculatively, of one of his Russian agents, 'if he was prepared to do away with one or two prominent members of the Soviet government'. When the agent threatened blackmail on 6 September and demanded money not to reveal Boyce's enquiry, it was thought 'advisable to pay up rather than have anything fresh brought up against us'.[60]

By the time of the attempted blackmail MI1c operations in Soviet Russia had virtually collapsed. Boyce was thrown into a hideously overcrowded jail and survived the ordeal thanks largely to the ministrations of the American Red Cross. The Cheka arrested several of Reilly's mistresses and came close to capturing Reilly himself, who borrowed a forged passport from Hill and paid 60,000 rubles to be smuggled out of Russia on board a Dutch freighter. After eighteen of Hill's couriers and agents had been caught and executed, he too concluded that he would have to seek new instructions and more funds in London, and 'start afresh with new personnel and new headquarters'. In October 1918 Lockhart, Boyce and Hill were allowed to return home with other Allied personnel in exchange for the release of Maxim Litvinov and Soviet officials in London. On reaching Finland, Hill was ordered by Cumming to return to Russia for a few weeks on a sabotage mission. Lockhart and Reilly continued to London. In December both were sentenced to death *in absentia* by the Moscow Supreme Revolutionary Tribunal. On Cumming's recommendation, Hill was awarded the DSO and Reilly the MC for their Russian exploits.[61]

'With the defeat of Germany', wrote Lockhart on the eve of the Armistice, 'it is clear that our intervention in Russia has now entered upon a most dangerous phase ... Our victories over Germany have removed our original pretext for intervention, and have at the same time strengthened the position of the Bolsheviks'. Britain and her allies, he argued, now had three options: to abandon intervention altogether and come to 'a working arrangement with the Bolsheviks'; to abandon intervention but support the Bolsheviks' opponents with arms and money; or 'to intervene immediately on a proper scale' and overthrow the Bolshevik régime. But the Allies chose none of these options.[62] They neither abandoned intervention nor intervened 'on a proper scale'. In none of the Allied countries was public opinion prepared to tolerate intervention on more than a token scale. Those troops which were sent served mainly to discredit the Bolsheviks' opponents. They were too few to affect the outcome of the Civil War but sufficient to allow the Bolsheviks to brand the White armies as the tools of Western imperialism.

MI1c operations during the Civil War had little long-term significance (save to Bolshevik propagandists) but led in the short term to some spectacular adventures. The most remarkable were those of Paul Dukes who, like Lockhart and Hill, had passed part of his childhood in Tsarist Russia. After studying at the St Petersburg conservatoire Dukes had embarked on a musical career, working for a time in the Imperial Marinsky Opera. In 1916 he left the Marinsky Theatre to work first for the Anglo-Russian Commission, studying the Russian press, and then for the Foreign Office with a 'roving commission' to report on conditions in post-revolutionary Russia. For the first six months of 1918 he 'roamed all over Russia' and found 'a state of indescribable confusion'. In the summer of 1918 Dukes was summoned back to London to be interviewed by Cumming in his roof-top office in Whitehall Court. While waiting to see 'the Chief', Dukes idly pulled down a copy of Thackeray's *Henry Esmond* from a bookshelf in the waiting room, only to discover that it was a dummy volume apparently containing secret documents from the German War Ministry. Dukes had just replaced the volume when one of

Cumming's assistants entered to tell him that the Chief was out and to ask him to return the following day. Next day Dukes returned to the waiting room, was asked if he would like to see 'the fine edition of Thackeray' on the bookshelf and handed a copy of *Henry Esmond* which on this occasion turned out to be entirely genuine. Dukes was understandably bewildered. 'Feeling as foolish as a cricketer who has got stumped for a "duck" because he didn't know the wicket-keeper had the ball', Dukes was ushered in to meet the Chief. Cumming's welcome was abrupt and severe. Dukes was almost overcome by an 'overpowering atmosphere of strangeness and mystery', and felt momentarily unable to offer 'a sane opinion on any subject under the sun'.[63] Cumming was disappointed with Dukes's bewildered response to his initiation tests. Towards the end of the interview, however, Dukes recovered sufficiently to show an interest in the impressive array of firearms which the Chief kept in his office. 'But for Paul's interest in my firearms', said Cumming later, 'I might never have taken on one of my very best agents!'[64] After a brief course of instruction in ciphers and secret inks in C's laboratories, Dukes was told to work out both his own route back to Russia and what to do when he arrived. Despite his bizarre introduction to MI1c, Dukes rapidly acquired a great affection for Cumming:

> 'The Chief' was a British officer and English gentleman of the very finest stamp, fearless, gifted with limitless resources of subtle ingenuity, and I counted it one of the great privileges of my life to have been brought within the circle of his acquaintance.[65]

Having been helped over the Russian frontier by Finnish smugglers and made his way to Petrograd, Dukes – like Lockhart in the previous year – made contact with the National Centre, whose prospects of organising a successful conspiracy against the Bolshevik régime improved as the White armies prepared to advance: Admiral Kolchak from the east, General Denikin from the south, General Yudenich from the north-west. The National Centre supplied the White armies with valuable intelligence on the movements and battle order of the Red Army, and began preparing insurrections in Moscow and Petrograd. As Yudenich advanced on Petrograd in May 1919, Lenin and Dzerzhinsky issued a strident proclamation demanding 'Death to spies!': 'The Whites possess an extensive organisation for espionage, treason, blowing up of bridges, insurrection in the rear, killing of Communists and of prominent members of workers organisations'. Dukes helped to finance the National Centre's preparations for insurrection in Moscow and Petrograd despite being sent on one occasion a large consignment of obviously forged Russian currency from Cumming. He also smuggled intelligence to MI1c in Finland which enabled another of Cumming's agents, Lieutenant Augustus Agar R.N. (ST 34), to lead motor torpedo raids which sank a Soviet cruiser on 17 June and two Soviet battleships on 17 August.[66]

Dukes prided himself on becoming a master of disguise during his Russian mission. In the space of ten months he used at least twenty different Christian names and twelve different surnames. At different times he posed as a member of the Cheka with the aid of forged papers, enlisted in the Red Army, and joined the Communist Party. But in other ways, as Dukes himself realised, he was an unprofessional as well as an unconventional agent. Significantly, he subtitled his memoirs 'Adventure and Romance in the Secret Intelligence Service in Red Russia'. Dukes spent much of his time as a Scarlet Pimpernel smuggling endangered White Russians across the Finnish frontier out of the clutches of the Cheka. He was much too preoccupied with the individual fates of his White Russian friends to concentrate single-mindedly on the overthrow of the Bolshevik régime. Dukes's essentially romantic view of intelligence work pervades the pages of his memoirs:

> I lay full length, my head at the open end of the tomb, recalling the events of the day. I was happy. Klachonka was safe – that she would get off I never doubted. Peter, brave Peter, was at that very moment hidden in the reeds waiting in his skiff, munching the sandwiches Klachonka had prepared, and pulling at his little whisky flask. Sonia, poor Sonia, was still in prison, but with faith – and ingenuity – surely a way to free her would be found? And who, I ask you, could have been gifted with greater ingenuity than my dear friends, who were far more to me than mere collaborators or conspirators? I pondered and wondered much, while the long light hours of the evening faded imperceptibly into a sweet and gentle dusk. I thought no more of the gruesome bones of Michael Semashko outstretched a foot or two beneath me.[67]

By September 1919 both Dukes and the National Centre had been outwitted by the Cheka. Following the capture of one of his couriers, the chairman of the National Centre, N.N. Shchepkin, was arrested on the night of 28–29 August together with a courier from Admiral Kolchak. During September one thousand National Centre conspirators were rounded up by the Cheka in a single night in Moscow alone, and sixty-seven of the Centre's leaders (including Shchepkin) were executed.[68] After Lieutenant Agar had tried in vain to rescue Dukes from the Russian coastline of the Finnish gulf by running the gauntlet of the Kronstadt forts, Dukes managed to cross Lake Luban and escape into Latvia. Soon afterwards a sensational account of Dukes's adventures (which he had incautiously revealed to White Russians in Reval) appeared in the Latvian press. 'The fat was in the fire,' wrote Dukes later. 'The Finnish and Swedish papers promptly quoted the story, and long before I reached London I realised that Red Russia was closed to me, perhaps for ever'.[69]

Dukes and Agar returned by separate routes to a discreet but heroes' welcome in London. They met for the first time on the top floor of Whitehall Court. As Dukes was leaving the Chief's office he met a young naval officer on the threshold, 'very handsome, with wavy hair, and a frank and most engaging smile'. For a moment neither spoke.

'Hello,' said the naval officer finally, 'are you Dukes?'

'Yes. Agar?'

'Yes.'

Cumming, who enjoyed arranging dramatic encounters, leant on his stick and smiled.[70] Both Dukes and Agar were summoned to Buckingham Palace to tell their stories in person to King George V, who had developed a deep personal interest in the adventures of his secret service. The King told Dukes that he thought the spy the greatest of all soldiers; the enemy detested him so much only because he feared him above all others.[71] He regretted that, as a civilian, Dukes was not eligible for the Victoria Cross but said that he had another reward in mind. Dukes was knighted in the 1920 New Year Honours List. Agar was at first overawed when ushered into the presence of his monarch, but soon sensed the same 'kindly atmosphere' he felt in his meetings with Cumming: 'an atmosphere which forces one to be quite natural and not self-conscious'. The King insisted on hearing 'every detail' of Agar's adventures, then presented him with the Victoria Cross, looking carefully at the back of the medal to make sure all the details were correct. To Agar's surprise, he was given the D.S.O. as well. He left Buckingham Palace convinced that he had been 'conversing with a wonderfully kind and wise man'. That night Cumming and his 'top-mates' (as he described his inner circle on the top floor of Whitehall Court) gave a private dinner party for Dukes and Agar at the Savoy Hotel of which Cumming's deputy, Lieutenant-Colonel Freddie Browning, was a director. After dinner and presentations to Dukes and Agar (each inscribed 'From his top-mates'), the party retired to watch the dancing in the public rooms. Cumming selected the prettiest girl on the dance floor and insisted that she dance with Agar. To Agar's delight she agreed. The Chief, wrote Agar proudly, 'always managed to get his own way'.[72]

The heroism and tactical success of some of MI1c's Soviet operations blinded Cumming and his 'top-mates' to their strategic failure. The less than half-hearted commitment of the government to intervention in the Russian Civil War deprived Cumming's covert action of any long-term significance. The cabinet decided to withdraw forces from North Russia and Transcaucasia in March 1919 at a time when the Bolsheviks' survival still seemed in doubt and the threat from the White armies was still growing. In his Guildhall speech of 8 November 1919, less than three weeks after White troops had reached the outskirts of Petrograd, Lloyd George publicly announced the virtual end of British intervention. Given the cabinet's reluctance to sanction military intervention on more than a token scale, the limited range of covert operations organised by Cumming and by military intelligence stood no realistic chance of influencing the outcome of the Civil War. Even with more substantial Allied intervention, it seems unlikely that they could have been decisive.

The greatest weakness of British intelligence during the Civil War was simply its failure to perform its primary function – to collect intelligence. From the departure of Lockhart in September 1918 to the signature of the Anglo-Russian trade agreement in March 1921 Britain possessed no official representative in Bolshevik-controlled Russia to report on conditions. Secret intelligence failed notably to fill the gap. A cabinet memorandum prepared by the Political Intelligence Department of the Foreign Office concluded in October 1919: 'No authoritative statement has ever been made about conditions in Soviet Russia and there is no question upon which people differ more widely'.[73] 'Adventure and Romance in Red Russia' were no substitute for intelligence.

# 7 | THE RED MENACE AT HOME

Though the government paid little attention to British intelligence operations in revolutionary Russia, it showed grave – if intermittent – anxiety at the Red Menace in Britain and the Empire. Counter-espionage and counter-subversion at home thus had a higher priority than intelligence gathering and covert action in Russia. The Foreign Office reported on 12 November 1917, five days after the Bolshevik seizure of power, that Bolshevism had been 'fastened on and poisoned by the Germans for their own purposes' to undermine the Russian war effort: 'It is not yet possible to say which of the Bolshevik leaders have taken German money; some undoubtedly have, while others are honest fanatics.'[1] Some ministers inevitably feared that German-financed subversion was making headway in Britain too. Sir Edward Carson, who coordinated government propaganda, told the Commons on 13 November:

> The amount of subterranean influence of a pernicious and pestilential character that has developed, particularly within the last few months, goes far beyond anything that has been described in this House ...[2]

Kell shared at least some of Carson's fears. The MI5 New Year card for 1918, personally designed by Kell's deputy, Major Holt-Wilson, and drawn in the pre-Raphaelite manner by the well-known illustrator Byam Shaw, shows the loathsome figure of Subversion, smoke billowing from its nostrils, crawling on all fours towards a British fighting man, clad in the garb of a gladiator and oblivious of the danger to his rear, his eyes fixed firmly on the vision on the horizon of 'Dieu et Mon Droit' and victory in 1918. Just in time MI5, depicted as the masked figure of Britannia, impales Subversion with a trident marked with her secret monogram before it can stab the British warrior in the back.[3]

The home secretary, Sir George Cave, suspected that German-financed subversion had been more widespread than Thomson had suggested before the Bolshevik Revolution. On 13 November 1917 he told the war cabinet he was ordering 'further investigations' by a joint committee of MI5 and the Special Branch who were examining the records of pacifist and revolutionary societies seized in police raids to trace the source of their income.[4] Thomson tackled the task with greater reluctance than Kell. 'It is', he wrote gloomily, 'an enormous quest. The investigations into hundreds of people's banking accounts must be expensive, and the result must necessarily be negative, but the public will not be satisfied with less'.[5] As Thomson had predicted, no evidence of German money was discovered. His dismissive comments on the No-Conscription Fellowship, circulated to the war cabinet on 13 December, were typical of his contemptuous attitude to pacifists in general:

> The documents disclose no evidence of Enemy influence or financial support. The Fellowship is conducted in an unbusinesslike way by cranks, and its influence outside the circle of Conscientious Objectors seems to be small.[6]

The immediate impact of the Bolshevik Revolution on the British labour movement appears, in retrospect, surprisingly small. It aroused much smaller support than the overthrow of the Tsar eight months before. While the small British Socialist Party (BSP) supported the Bolsheviks, most Independent Labour Party (ILP) leaders did not. N.H. Brailsford in *The Herald* denounced the Revolution as 'reckless and uncalculating folly'.[7] Thomson was more concerned by the growth of war-weariness in the winter which followed. He reported 'a decided increase' in the number of intercepted letters whose writers wanted 'an immediate peace'.[8] Although the food supply was actually better at the end of 1917 than in the previous spring, a wave of panic-buying forced the Ministry of Food to introduce rationing early in 1918. In December 1917 the Labour Party and the TUC issued a joint statement of war aims little different from those of the Union of Democratic Control (UDC), denounced secret diplomacy and called for reconciliation with Germany. Lloyd George responded to the challenge with a speech on 5 January 1918 looking forward to a peace founded on moral principle and a new world order in which a League of Nations would find 'an alternative to war as a means of settling international disputes'. Significantly, the prime minister made his speech – the fullest statement of British war aims before the armistice – not to parliament but to a trade union congress.[9]

On 22 January 1918 Thomson reported to the war cabinet 'a rather sudden growth of pacifism' over the previous fortnight, caused by government plans for a further 'comb-out' of the labour force to meet the manpower crisis on the Western Front.[10] The age for military service was raised to fifty and some of those in previously protected jobs found themselves liable to conscription. Strikes and protests against the 'comb-out' were accompanied on Clydeside and in the Welsh mining valleys by a revival of revolutionary rhetoric. The

Clyde Workers Committee called for 'action to enforce the declaration of an immediate armistice'.[11] Thomson was confident, however, that the 'strong bias towards a revolutionary movement' among strike leaders had little support among the rank and file. He quoted an intercepted letter from one of the strike leaders complaining that the purpose of the protest movement was simply 'to save our skins' rather than 'strike for a People's Peace'. 'If it were possible to apply such a test', Thomson concluded, 'an announcement that the comb-out had been abandoned would prove immediately that the strikers were not pacifists at all'.[12] Sir David Shackleton, the permanent undersecretary at the Ministry of Labour, was less optimistic:

A good deal of treason is being talked, and the idea of "peace by negotiation" is making headway, induced largely by the mental apathy resulting from war-weariness. Some of the leaders are talking very high and appear prepared to go to extreme lengths, and in the general atmosphere of sentimentality and unreason which is prevalent at the moment, the Russian Revolution has awakened much wider echoes than would have been the case at a time when men's minds were not unbalanced by the strain of the prolonged war conditions, and were more capable of seeing the facts in their true light. It would be rash to venture any prophecy as to what will happen. The Government has to a large extent lost its authority in the eyes of the workers, and there is a general impression that it is bound to obey their demands.[13]

Once again, Thomson's assessment proved more accurate. The Man-Power bill extending the call-up became law in February 1918 without serious resistance.

Paradoxically, both the peace of Best-Litovsk and the beginning of the last great German offensive on the Western Front in March undermined opposition to the war. Brest-Litovsk seemed evidence of the Bolsheviks' German sympathies, and Haig's 'Back to the Wall' message to his troops on the Western Front was widely supported on the Home Front. Thomson declared himself taken aback by the strength of the popular reaction against pacifism due chiefly – according to all his local informants – to 'the critical position of the relations of the working class who are fighting in Flanders':[14]

There has been an almost entire cessation of public meetings to advocate immediate peace ... I hear that the Union of Democratic Control have instructed their members not to agitate for Peace in public just now, and the Independent Labour Party and the British Socialist Party are abstaining from Public Meetings, because they believe they would be broken up.[15]

That belief, as Thomson knew, was well founded. Soon after the Bolshevik

Revolution, Cave had approved a proposal to enlist the aid of the patriotic National War Aims Committee to combat pacifism. The Committee was provided with ample funds for propaganda which enabled it to spend more in a few months than the Union of Democratic Control in the entire war. On 22 November 1917 Thomson had promised the Committee's secretary, Thomas Cox, advance notice of all pacifist activities which came to his notice. In return Cox agreed to 'try and arrange out-door or indoor meetings as a counterblast'.[16]

Thomson noted with satisfaction in May 1918 that pacifists all over Britain had been 'driven to underhand activities' conducted with a 'disregard of common honesty'.[17] He himself, however, also employed a wide range of simple but effective 'underhand activities'. One of his favourite weapons against pacifists, strikers and all varieties of labour militant was carefully cultivated rumour. In one report to the cabinet Thomson related with obvious relish how he dealt with strikes at Coventry and Birmingham in July:

> ... A stranger appeared in Coventry, and in conversation with some of the strikers in a saloon bar, adopted the one certain method of spreading news, and told them in the strictest confidence that he had come from the Ministry of National Service to arrange for the issue of calling-up notices. The news flew all over the town in a very few hours. He went on to Birmingham, and there strikers approached him asking advice as to how they could avoid being called up. He gave them, as the only method, to go straight back to work. I may quote, as an illustration, the fact that at one works, where the daily average of absentees on Monday morning is about 30, only 6 men failed to turn up on the day the strikers returned to work, and 4 of these sent telegrams to say that they had missed their trains and were coming on.[18]

The unidentified 'stranger' about whom Thomson was so well informed must surely have been one of his agents.

Thomson's view of the working class and left-wing politics was a blend of the shrewd and the simplistic. He continually emphasised 'how generally sound in their judgment ... the great silent mass of working men are'. The soundness Thomson had in mind was an odd mixture of common decency and animal appetites: concern for their own self-interest, general indifference to politics, and intellectual horizons which rarely rose above beer and football. Bolshevism Thomson saw less as a political ideology than as a species of mental disorder:

> An exact definition of the term 'Bolshevik' is, I am told, 'out-and-outer', but people who live under the Bolshevik regime describe it as a sort of infectious disease, spreading rapidly, but insidiously, until like a cancer it

eats away the fabric of society, and the patient ceases even to wish for his own recovery. A nation attacked by it may, if we may judge from the state of Russia, be reduced to a political and social morass, which may last perhaps for a generation or more, with no hope of reaction; whilst civilisation crumbles away and the country returns to its original barbarism.[19]

The civil unrest which most concerned both Thomson and the government during the last summer of the war was a strike by the London police. On 30 August 10,000 of the 19,000 Metropolitan Police failed to report for duty, demanding both the recognition of their union and an immediate rise in pay. Even Lloyd George was so shaken that he later claimed that Britain 'was nearer to Bolshevism that day than at any other time since'. Thomson took a less alarmist view. 'No strike would have taken place', he believed, if the pay rise promised as soon as the strike began had been announced beforehand.

It was waiting only for actuarial calculations to be worked out, and the Commissioner, Sir Edward Henry, declined to be hurried over this essential.

The pay rise was sufficient to persuade the police to return to work without their union being recognised. Sir Edward Henry was sacked and replaced as commissioner of the Met by Sir Nevil Macready, then adjutant-general in the War Office.[20]

Though the strike, in Thomson's view, was both unnecessary and quickly settled, it left him with a lingering unease about the willingness of the police to deal with Bolshevik-inspired unrest. In the short term, however, the turning of the tide in favour of the Allies on the Western Front removed the last fears of serious wartime subversion. As victory came in sight pacifism disappeared from view. Working class morale all over the country, wrote Thomson on 21 October, was 'probably at its highest point':

In Liverpool ... what is most interesting is that many who were formerly advocates of a round table conference are now not only determined to beat the Germans, but also to make them bear the cost of the War, 'even if it takes a thousand years to do it' ... A woman who is in close touch with the directors of the Women's Peace Crusade says that they have come to the conclusion that house to house visiting in the cause of Peace is useless, for the visitors are often subjected to abuse, and the doors are shut in their faces.

But Thomson warned that victory and demobilisation would cause new problems. A 'well-informed' agent in the engineering industry described the labour force as 'sick of Parliament and officialism': 'As soon as the restraining influence of the war is removed he thinks that there will be a revolt everywhere'.

The leaders of the Electrical Trades Union were, said Thomson, 'openly revolutionary' and preparing a major strike.[21] The minister of labour reported to the war cabinet that Thomson and GHQ Home Forces were jointly making arrangements for 'an immediate supply of auxiliary labour'.[22] Thomson believed that 'nations with the genius for practical organisation' like England would be spared the full horrors of Bolshevism. But 'it would not take very much in the midst of serious labour disturbances, carried on with the sympathy of the Police, to do enormous damage to the credit of the country'. And the police in the big cities, Thomson warned, could not be depended on to deal with 'serious labour disturbances'.[23]

The Armistice on 11 November 1918 strengthened Thomson's apprehensions. The pacifists, he reported, were 'busy tearing off their disguise, and reappearing in their proper garb as revolutionaries'.[24] Even moderate Labour leaders felt their hands freed by peace. Hitherto most trade-unionists and Labour politicians had been reluctant publicly to oppose intervention in Russia for fear of undermining the war effort of which it was still alleged to be a part. With the armistice their inhibitions disappeared. By the spring of 1919 Thomson reported that 'every section' of the Labour movement had come out in opposition to Russian intervention: 'Even mild trade unionists are said to be strongly moved over the matter'.[25]

During the final months of the war Thomson had been canvassing support for a post-war intelligence organisation headed by himself to monitor subversion. Schemes for a new peacetime intelligence agency had been developing in Thomson's mind since early in 1917 when he received from the chief constable of Sheffield, Major Hall-Dalwood, a 'Suggested Scheme for the Formation of a National Intelligence Service'. Hall-Dalwood acknowledged the problem of reconciling domestic intelligence-gathering with 'the spirit and genius of the British Race' and its concern with the liberties of the subject, but argued that the war had proved the need for a centralised intelligence network covering the whole country:

> The present need of a highly organised system to deal scientifically and swiftly with undermining movements, whether affecting naval, military, or industrial activities, is apparent to all close observers, and more particularly to those in executive authority.
>
> For example, immediately following the cessation of the War, certain disintegrating elements – internal hostility, foreign enemy agency, or both, or a combination of both – will probably assert themselves. Whichever country possesses the machinery to effectually counter the moves of these maleficent agencies will be the one to most quickly recover from the effects of the War and to gain commercial stability and national supremacy.

'There is', Thomson noted on 10 January 1917, 'a sound kernel to this rather ambitious scheme ...' He wrote to Sir Edward Troup, permanent under-secretary at the Home Office, on 4 April 1917: 'I think that some sort of Unrest Intelligence for the whole country may be necessary after the war, but not of course on the scale set out in [Hall-Dalwood's] pamphlet'.[26] By the final months of the war, however, Thomson was thinking on an even more ambitious scale than Hall-Dalwood.

He was encouraged in his ambitions by the Naval Intelligence Division. Both 'Blinker' Hall and his assistant, Claud Serocold, were on friendly terms with Thomson but disliked Kell as 'short-sighted and timorous'. Impressed with Thomson's growing authority as Whitehall's leading authority on subversion, both saw him as the head of a peacetime intelligence system which would have domestic subversion as its main target.[27] Thomson also enjoyed more powerful support than Kell within the government. His most committed supporter was Walter Long, secretary of state for the colonies from 1916 to 1919. As 'Liaison Minister in connection with Ireland' in 1917, Long had been 'horror struck' at the lack of coordination between the various intelligence services – echoing views already expressed by Thomson in a secret report on Irish intelligence in September 1916.[28] On 14 October 1918 Long sent Thomson 'unofficially and as a friend' an alarmist memorandum 'on the question of our Secret Service'. 'There is in this country', wrote Long, 'a very strong Bolshevik Agency which succeeds, owing to the want of efficient Secret Service and prompt action, in causing great domestic trouble'. Long admitted that he might be 'unduly suspicious' but argued strongly that the strikes in the police, on the railway and on the Clyde, as well as 'minor incidents like the Pemberton Billing case', were all due to 'German intrigue and German money'. During the police strike, wrote Long, 'I have undoubted information that we escaped really by the skin of our teeth from a disaster of terrible dimensions in London'. British intelligence was 'in a wholly unsatisfactory condition' to deal with the menace of subversion. 'A good many' intelligence officers were not up to their jobs. But the main problem was lack of coordination and 'actual jealousy' between the various branches of the intelligence community. Long recognised the need for the War Office and the Admiralty to continue 'to make their own arrangements' for military and naval intelligence. But the only way to counter domestic subversion and espionage was to establish a unified 'Civil Secret Service ... with a competent man at the head, who would have the power to deal promptly with any suspicious characters':

> I believe an efficient Secret Service is the only way in which to cope with the Bolshevik, Syndicalist, and the German spy. I am satisfied that these three are still actively pursuing their infernal practices.[29]

Privately Thomson did not take seriously Long's fears of a vast German-financed subversive conspiracy embracing everything from the police strike to the Pemberton Billing case. But he was anxious not to undermine either Long's advocacy of a unified 'Civil Secret Service' or his own prospects of heading it. He therefore agreed with Long on the existence of 'a strong Bolshevik agency in this country, which is growing' – but added reassuringly that he knew 'the principal persons concerned in it and to some extent the source of their funds'. Similarly Thomson accepted the gravity of the police strike, but, unlike Long, stressed its potential danger for the future rather than suggesting that it had brought Britain within a hair's breadth of catastrophe:

> Without going too far into details it may be said that the promoters of the strike used the demand for extra pay only as a means to induce the orderly men to join them; their real object was to obtain recognition of the union in the interests of revolution in the future.

Thomson went on to endorse enthusiastically Long's call for a coordinated domestic intelligence system. He predicted that the main opposition would come from MI5 which wished to preserve a peacetime monopoly of counter-espionage – in Thomson's view 'a very essential part of Home Intelligence, the experience of the War having shown that Contra-Espionage goes far beyond the business of detecting foreign spies, since their enemy intrigue ramifies in every direction'. Thomson's proposals for intelligence coordination, however, went even further than Long's. With 'Blinker' Hall's and Serocold's support he put the case for a civilian head of the entire intelligence community with, beneath him, directors of naval, military, foreign and 'home (labour unrest)' intelligence:

> The Director of Home Intelligence would work closely in touch with the Police, and deal specially with questions:-
> (a) of Labour Unrest
> (b) of Revolutionary matters
> (c) of Aliens
> (d) of Contre-espionage.

Thomson also adopted Hall's and Serocold's scheme to help finance peacetime intelligence through a secret War Loan investment of about a million pounds managed by trustees: 'It is very doubtful whether parliament will continue to vote an adequate sum for Secret Services after the War, more especially if a Labour Government comes into power'. Thomson emphasised the urgency of an intelligence reorganisation. His whole existing organisation outside London, he told Long, was financed by the Ministry of Munitions, and he feared 'that the money will stop as soon as Peace comes'.[30]

Long accepted Thomson's scheme in preference to his own and sent it to the prime minister.[31] Over the next few months he bombarded Lloyd George with messages about the secret service. 'Unless prompt steps are taken', he wrote on 18 November, 'I am informed we shall find the Secret Service seriously crippled just when we shall need it most'.[32] On 9 January 1919 Long forwarded a report from an un-named secret agent phrased in apocalyptic terms:

> I now find myself convinced that in England Bolschevism [*sic*] must be faced and grappled with, the efforts of the International Jews of Russia combated and their agents eliminated from the United Kingdom. Unless some serious consideration is given to the matter, I believe that there will be some sort of Revolution in this country and that before 12 months are past ... At the present time the Secret Service receives reports from Switzerland, Holland, Scandinavia and Russia on Bolschevik activites, of agents being sent to France or England, of agitators and their schemes ... Many will scoff at these ideas, yet how many 'extreme' British Bolscheviks are there, say 5,000! A bigger percentage in proportion to the population than Russia started with!

Long added in a covering note to the prime minister: 'I beg your attention to enclosed. I am confident the danger is real.'[33]

Soon afterwards the cabinet set up a Secret Service Committee under Lord Curzon, who was in charge of the Foreign Office while Balfour was at the Paris peace conference and was to become foreign secretary in June. As viceroy of India at the beginning of the century Curzon had become involved in the Great Game on the North-Western frontier. He viewed Bolshevik designs on India with even greater suspicion than those of their Tsarist forebears. Like Long, who also served on the Secret Service Committee, he attached great importance to intelligence reports on the advance of the Red Menace and regarded Thomson as 'an invaluable sleuth hound'. The Secret Service Committee under Curzon's chairmanship met intermittently for two years, overseeing the reorganisation on a peacetime footing of the greatly expanded intelligence services which emerged from the First World War. The committee rejected Thomson's ambitious proposal for a single civilian head of the whole intelligence community. But it did approve Long's proposal for a 'Civil Secret Service' to monitor subversion. Its first report in February recommended Thomson's appointment as head of a new Directorate of Intelligence under the Home Office.[34] Thomson's new office, which he assumed on May Day 1919, formally confirmed him as the chief watchdog of subversion and left him in control of the Special Branch. Since the armistice he had been providing the cabinet with fortnightly reports on the progress of 'revolutionary organisations'. From May 1919 his reports became weekly.[35]

Though MI5 retained control of counter-espionage, its budget of almost £100,000 in the 1918–19 financial year was cut back to £35,000 in the next. Kell, who like Cumming and Thomson was knighted in the 1919 New Year's honours list, sought to persuade ministers that MI5's work was now more complex than ever before:

> ... Counter-espionage is no longer merely a question of steaming open a letter and reading the contents. The vast improvement in methods of collecting and transmitting information (e.g. development of wireless telegraphy, aircraft, abstruse secret inks, photography, etc), has added very greatly to the difficulty of detecting espionage, and, *inter alia*, it has been found necessary to add to the staff of MI5 a chemical section
>
> To sum up, MI5 must in future be prepared to cope with the agents of not one Power but several Powers, using agents writing in different languages, on different subjects, and using methods which can only be detected by expert officers having at their disposal a staff of linguists and chemists specially trained for this class of work.

MI5 claimed, inaccurately, that Germany remained 'very active in matters of espionage'. It also had 'under observation' the 'agents' of two other powers – Japan (though, as MI5 acknowledged, Japanese espionage was chiefly directed against India) and Soviet Russia.[36]

Kell, however, was far less successful than Thomson in gaining the ear of government. What most concerned ministers in the aftermath of victory was not foreign espionage but domestic subversion. The months which preceded Thomson's arrival at Scotland House, opposite Scotland Yard, as Director of Intelligence, were among the most dramatic in British labour history. 'During the first three months of 1919', wrote Thomson later, 'unrest touched its high watermark. I do not think that at any time since the Bristol Riots [of 1831] we have been so near revolution'. As during the war, the main revolutionary centre was – or appeared to be – Red Clydeside. In January 1919 a general strike was called in Glasgow to gain the forty-hour week and the red flag raised over the city hall. The secretary of state for Scotland told the war cabinet (which formally became a peacetime cabinet only in November 1919) 'that it was a misnomer to call the situation in Glasgow a strike – it was a Bolshevist rising'. Glasgow, said the *Glasgow Herald*, was witnessing 'the first step towards that squalid terrorism which the world now describes as Bolshevism'. Both troops and tanks were called out, though in the event the police restored order without them. The Glasgow general strike was not a serious attempt to launch a revolution.[37] Thomson, however, believed that it was. He reported to the cabinet:

> The plan of the revolutionary minority was to use the Clyde as the touchstone for a general strike and, if it proved to be successful, to bring out the engineers and the railways all over the country, to seize the food and achieve a revolution.[38]

Most ministers seem to have accepted Thomson's interpretation. So did the king, whom Bonar Law, the chancellor of the exchequer, found 'in a funk ... talking about the ... danger of a revolution'.[39]

At the beginning of February the government was faced with a bus and underground strike in the capital itself as well as the threat of an electricians' stoppage. The cabinet responded by setting up an Industrial Unrest Committee (IUC) under the home secretary, Edward Shortt, 'to make the necessary arrangements for dealing with any situation that might arise from industrial unrest both at the present moment and in the future'. At its first meetings the IUC earmarked 40,000 lorries and 100,000 cars for use in a transport strike and drew up plans to run power stations with volunteers and naval stokers. Although the London transport strike quickly collapsed and the electricians' strike failed to materialise, the government also had to face during February the more menacing prospect of a revival of the pre-war Triple Alliance of miners, railwaymen and transport workers. On the eve of war the Triple Alliance had been preparing something like a general strike. Ministers feared that the Alliance's demands in February 1919 for higher wages and shorter hours threatened a new and massive strike wave. These fears recurred at intervals for the next two years until the Triple Alliance collapsed in April 1921. Lloyd George, though less alarmist than most of his cabinet, told the Alliance leaders in 1919:

> Gentlemen, you have fashioned, in the Triple Alliance of the unions represented by you, a most powerful instrument. I feel bound to tell you that in our opinion we are at your mercy. The Army is disaffected and cannot be relied upon. Trouble has occurred already in a number of camps. We have just emerged from a great war and the people are eager for the reward of their sacrifices, and we are in no position to satisfy them. In these circumstances, if you carry out your threat and strike, then you will defeat us.[40]

The problems of demobilising by far the largest army in British history made the threat from the Triple Alliance all the more menacing. The failure at the outset to adopt the simple principle 'First in, first out' bred a sense of injustice which erupted in mutinies at army camps in Calais and Folkestone. MI5 reports linking some of the troubles with pro-Soviet agitators led the War Office to circulate in February a 'secret and urgent' questionnaire to the commanding officers of all British military installations asking for information 'without fail' each week on the political sentiments of their forces 'with a view to the establishment of an efficient intelligence service whereby the Army Council can keep its finger on the pulse of the troops'. COs were asked, *inter alia*, whether any 'soldiers' councils' on the Russian model had been formed; whether troops would 'respond to orders for assistance to preserve the public peace' and 'assist in strike breaking'; and whether they would 'parade for draft to overseas, especially to Russia'. The questionnaire, however, backfired. A copy was published in the *Daily Herald* and produced, according to Thomson, 'great resentment against the Government'.[41]

Hall's successor as DNI, Captain (later Admiral Sir) Hugh 'Quex' Sinclair (who was to succeed Cumming as head of the Secret Intelligence Service in 1923), was also concerned about subversion in the navy. What worried him most was the continuation of wartime licensing laws and restrictions on beer production. He wrote to the first lord of the Admiralty:

> ... Certain extremists are using this question of the restrictions on beer as a lever to produce unrest in the Navy. I do not know if the Cabinet realise what a deep-seated feeling of resentment is being produced throughout the country ...[42]

Thomson and Kell reported that both the Germans and the Bolsheviks were hatching schemes to exploit labour and military unrest. According to Thomson:

> The personnel of the old [German] Secret Service is still intact and amply supplied with funds, which are being devoted almost entirely to Bolshevik propaganda in Allied countries. There are no doubt two motives, first to break up the Allies before an indemnity is imposed on Germany, and secondly (though this is conjectural), to produce such a revulsion of feeling among the bourgeoisie that a restoration of the [German] monarchy might become possible.[43]

There is little doubt that in reaching this alarmist conclusion Thomson had been taken in by forged documents. The forgeries probably included an alleged German document submitted to the cabinet on 10 February which revealed plans 'to subdue our deadly enemies, England and France, by spreading [Bolshevism] among the ranks of their armies with the hope that the German lion may reawaken'.[44] Thomson seems later to have realised that he had been taken in. Significantly, at the end of the year when he came to compile a lengthy 'Survey of Revolutionary Feeling in the Year 1919' based on his weekly or fortnightly reports, he omitted all mention of the hidden hand of Germany.[45]

The hand of Soviet Russia, though its influence was often exaggerated, was real enough. After the October Revolution about forty Bolshevik émigrés remained in London. The leading figure among them, Maxim Litvinov, was allowed diplomatic immunity from January to September 1918 as the semi-official representative of the Soviet government, and provided the main channel of communication between the Bolsheviks and their British sympathisers. After Litvinov's deportation, another Russian émigré, Theodore Rothstein, both a Bolshevik and a long-standing member of the BSP, became, in Thomson's words, the chief 'intermediary for subsidies to the revolutionary organisations'. Among the pro-Bolshevik groups and splinter-groups to whom Rothstein distributed Russian funds over the next two years were the British Socialist Party, the Socialist Labour Party, the Communist Unity Group, the Hands Off Russia Movement, the People's Russian Information Bureau and the Workers Socialist Federation. During the prolonged debate within the BSP over whether to join the Communist Third International (Comintern) founded in March 1919, Rothstein was the leading advocate of membership and a key influence on the final decision to join.[46]

There was also a stream of other Russian and Comintern couriers bringing funds, propaganda and exhortation to Bolshevik sympathisers in Britain. The amateurishness of many of them made it relatively easy for Thomson and Kell to follow their movements. Chief Inspector Herbert Fitch of the Special Branch, who, after what he termed 'four strenuous years of spy-catching', turned to counter-subversion at the end of the war, considered that his 'public school education', 'good physique' and 'fluent knowledge of several languages' gave him a distinct advantage over most Bolsheviks. In February 1919, for example, he had to deal with 'a big, bearded, sallow-faced Russian named Myer Hyman':

> I went along to his lodgings one evening, sent up a note indicating that I was a Swedish agitator of some repute known to him by name but not by sight, and finally went in and discussed with him his plans for sowing disaffection among the lower ranks in the Army. Having obtained enough information, I finally arrested him.

During the conversation which preceded his arrest, Hyman unwittingly betrayed two other Bolshevik agents: Max Segal, who had brought £4,000 from Moscow, and Jules Soermus, 'outwardly a respectable member of a cinema orchestra' who carried seditious documents in his violin case. Hyman, Segal and Soermus were tried together, then deported together, 'Hyman apparently rather depressed by his friends' black looks in his direction'.[47]

Fitch found that 'it is very often the dreamer who proves to be the really troublesome man, while the black-bearded dark-eyed anarchist frequently proves to be nothing but a windbag after all'. One of the most dangerous dreamers, in Fitch's view, was Axel Zachiaressen, a Norwegian student who adopted a transparent disguise as a Russian journalist and in the early summer of 1920 brought further Comintern funds to Britain in response to what *The Times* later called 'an urgent appeal for funds from revolutionary quarters in this country'. When Zachiaressen was arrested at a Camberwell lodging house, he at first 'volubly protested his innocence'. Fitch was not deceived:

I noticed, however, that a quick glance went towards a very heavy pair of boots lying in the corner of the room. I had a look at them, and, as I more or less expected, the uppers were lined with waterproof pouches in which some of the money and bonds had doubtless come over from Russia. The man's waistcoat was also false-lined, and from one of the papers I found in it I obtained the principal facts that were used against him in his trial.[48]

Thomson's most important capture during 1919 was the Russian American Communist Jacob Nosivitsky. On arrival at Liverpool in June 1919 Nosivitsky was arrested, questioned by the Special Branch, then taken to Scotland House. Here Thomson persuaded him to become a double agent with the mission of tracking down the chief Bolshevik agent in Britain. Having successfully identified Rothstein as that agent, Nosivitsky then acted as courier between him and Martens, the Soviet representative in the United States. As well as enabling Thomson to intercept the correspondence between Rothstein and Martens, Nosivitsky also provided intelligence from meetings of the Comintern and its bureau established in Amsterdam in November 1919.[49]

The Russian subsidies distributed by Comintern to their British sympathisers seem to have been surprisingly generous. Whether Comintern got value for money is more doubtful. The Bolsheviks undoubtedly purchased influence in the exiguous splinter-groups of the revolutionary left and played an important – perhaps crucial – part in the foundation of the Communist Party of Great Britain (CPGB) in the summer of 1920. But they did little or nothing to advance the prospect of a British revolution.

Early in 1919 GHQ Great Britain, which had been set up early in the war to direct military organisation at home, was drawn into the secret struggle against revolutionary subversion. The commander-in-chief was ordered by the cabinet to prepare to assist the civil power 'in the event of a national strike of a revolutionary character'. From March onwards GHQ Great Britain was also instructed to help gather intelligence on labour disputes and to liaise with chief constables, the Home Office, Kell and Thomson. Haig, who succeeded Robertson as commander-in-chief in April, regarded domestic intelligence gathering as 'hateful'. He told Thomson bluntly that he 'would not authorise any men being used as spies'. 'Officers', he insisted, 'must act straightforwardly and as Englishmen' – and Thomson's Directorate of Intelligence must work 'independently of the Army and its leaders'. But GHQ's intelligence-gathering activities probably did infringe the principle that 'no form of Military espionage should be carried on in any civilian matters'. The former DMI, Sir George Macdonogh, now adjutant-general, wrote in October 1919: 'It seems to me that we have been attempting to perform duties which appertain to the civil power, and that in so doing we have not merely greatly strained the military machine but the British Constitution as well'. When GHQ Great Britain was abolished in February 1920 its domestic intelligence responsibilities went with it.[50]

By the spring of 1919 cabinet anxiety at the rise of the Red Menace had somewhat abated. In a graph later prepared by Thomson showing the fluctuations of 'revolutionary feeling' during 1919, the peak came at the end of January and beginning of February. Thomson's graph touched bottom on May Day when a threatened twenty-four hour strike failed to materialise. It quickly rose again thereafter and reached its summer peak with the strike of the Yorkshire miners in July and of the police at the beginning of August. Thomson reported evidence that 'revolutionary leaders in England, France and America were in touch with one another and with Moscow'. The police strike, he argued, 'was not industrial but revolutionary'. It was, however, poorly supported, and Thomson believed that its collapse within a week was a severe blow to those 'extremists' who had counted on it as the springboard for revolution. Part of Thomson's explanation for the rise and fall of 'revolutionary feeling' was seasonal. In early summer 'revolutionary propaganda was fostered by the fine weather for open air meetings' but it was 'always noticeable that the approach of the summer holidays is a palliative to discontent'. By the end of August and early September Thomson's graph had descended almost to its May Day low. Thereafter it began to rise again.[51]

A railway strike on 26 September revived the prospect of a general strike organised by the Triple Alliance. The IUC was replaced by a stronger 'Strike Committee' under the cabinet's trouble-shooter Sir Eric Geddes which met daily throughout the strike. It ordered the army to secure 'all the important Railways, Power Stations, etc.' against 'destruction and violence', and, following a proposal by Thomson, concluded that the threat of a general strike made it 'essential to set up at once a new organisation, to be entitled "The Citizen Guard", to meet all contingencies and to relieve the military forces as far as possible'. On 5 October, however, the strike was settled on the railwaymen's terms and plans for the Citizen Guard were shelved. The cabinet was reassured by the success of the Strike Committee and the anti-strike precautions. 'The Government's organisation', wrote the cabinet secretary, Sir Maurice Hankey, had 'fairly knocked the strikers endways'. The flow of industrial intelligence had also proved highly satisfactory. On 14 October the war cabinet (which continued in being for a year after the armistice) established the innocuously named 'Supply and Transport Committee' (STC) with Sir Eric Geddes in the chair to supersede the Strike Committee and perfect the machinery for coping with industrial emergencies.[52]

Thomson ended the year on a note of cautious optimism. Though he had never doubted the fundamental respect for law and order and distaste for revolutionary agitation among most of the working class, he had been worried at the beginning of the year by the fact that 'the revolutionary minority ... are organised and the steady-going people are not'.[53] By December Thomson's faith in the power of inertia possessed by the 'steady-going' to thwart the designs of the extremists had reasserted itself:

> ... A dwindling minority of extremists still believe that a violent revolution can be achieved by means of a general strike; but every strike which fails has tended to discredit them, and the experience of the past year has shown that, while working class opinion is tending slowly but surely to the left, the belief in the possibility of violent revolution has waned ... There has been nothing more satisfactory than the admission of Communists in other countries that the British public is too far sunk in apathy and in acquiescence with its condition of slavery to Capitalism to make it worth while to spend energy or funds in attempting to convert it to the gospel of Revolution ... It may confidently be said that in the violent dislocation of the social machinery, caused by the war, England is readjusting herself more smoothly than any other country in the world.

'Revolutionary feeling', in Thomson's view, was promoted less by revolutionary agitation than by a deep sense of injustice among the have-nots: 'Every act of foolish ostentation on the part of the well-to-do is fuel to this smouldering fire'. The three main 'causes which contribute to revolutionary feeling' were in order of importance:

1. Profiteering and high prices.
2. Insufficient and bad housing accommodation.
3. Class hatred, aggravated by the foolish and dangerous ostentation of the rich, the publication of large dividends, and distrust of 'a Government of profiteers'.

At the top of Thomson's list of 'steadying influences' came the popularity of the royal family and sport among the lower orders. Royalty, he believed, would always be more popular than revolutionaries and the resumption of league football in 1919 would interest the working class more than politics.[54]

It was accepted in Whitehall that the intelligence struggle against subversion could not be confined to Britain. The basis of the counter-subversion system set up outside Britain during 1919 was the wartime network of Military Control Officers established by MI5 as 'the first line of defence against enemy agents and other undesirable aliens'. In Paris a *Bureau de Contrôle* jointly directed by MI5 and the Home Office had supervised the issue of visas required by all visitors to wartime Britain. In other Allied states Military Control Officers were attached to British military missions and in neutral countries to British consulates to advise on visas, and were kept 'fully supplied with information as regards suspects by letter and wire' from MI5. A secret 'system of signal on the passport' was devised to enable Military Control Officers to alert MI5 Port Control Officers to suspicious visitors on their arrival in Britain.[55]

The transformation of the wartime Military Control network into a peacetime Passport Control system was supervised by the Passport Control Subcommittee founded in February 1919, and initially composed of representatives from the Home Office, Foreign Office, Admiralty, MI5, MI1c, Special Branch, Board of Trade, Department of Overseas Trade and the Ministry of Labour. 'The unsettled political conditions which were likely to prevail for some time in Eastern and Central Europe' persuaded the subcommittee of the need for a peacetime passport control system whose principal aim would be 'to exclude Bolshevik agents from the United Kingdom' and gather intelligence on Bolshevik subversion. Doubtless to Kell's dismay, he lost control of the new system. In August 1919 the war cabinet approved the creation of a Passport Control Department at the Foreign Office and the attachment of Passport Control Officers (PCOs) to most continental and some overseas embassies and legations. Although the Foreign Office took formal responsibility for the new department, however, it did not run it and disclaimed all concern 'with any of its ultimate objects'. Instead the PCO system was supervised by a subcommittee comprising Thomson and representatives of the Home Office Aliens Branch, MI5 and MI1c.[56]

Operational control of the PCO system was given to Cumming. The nominal head of the new Passport Control Department, responsible for the administration of the system, was Major Herbert Spencer, formerly Chief Port Control Officer in MI5, who moved into MI1c headquarters at 2 Whitehall Court.[57] The PCO network came to provide cover for Cumming's station chiefs abroad, but it was not fully integrated into MI1c (by then usually known as the Secret Intelligence Service or SIS) for another two years. Initially PCOs were 'debarred from having any dealings with Secret Service agents', and their work was limited to 'enquiries of an anti-Bolshevik and Counter-Espionage nature'. The secret budgets submitted by Cumming for the immediate post-war period took no account of the PCO network which he saw primarily as 'a useful liaison with continental police and counter-espionage services'.[58]

Thomson was an enthusiastic advocate of the PCOs. He wrote two years after his appointment as Director of Intelligence:

> Passport Control serves a double purpose. On the one hand it is a fine-meshed sieve through which the stream of alien visitors to this country is filtered; on the other, it provides an all important intelligence service on the movements of international revolutionaries. The Passport Control Officer is in close and friendly touch with the local Police Authorities and acts as a *liaison* officer between Scotland House [Thomson's headquarters] and the Continental Police ... As long as there remains in Europe a Government whose avowed object is to provoke a world revolution, equipped with funds of gold which it is prepared to lavish on this object, to abolish the Passport Control system would be an act of suicide.

The PCO network also had the great advantage that, because of visa fees (£155,000 in 1920), it was self-financing. 'Indeed', claimed Thomson, 'some profit accrues from it'.[59] The Foreign Office agreed. 'The visa system', it concluded, 'is in the main really effective in keeping out Bolshevist agents ... It pays for itself and for certain other essential [intelligence] services abroad'.[60]

Though MI5 lost control of the passport control system, its Registry remained essential to the running of it. By the end of the war, the 'Defence Black List' compiled by the Registry included 13,500 names. Retitled the 'Precautionary Index', it grew to 25,250 names by 1925, and provided 'a central register of persons potentially dangerous to National Defence' in the form of a card catalogue. The index was divided into twelve categories ranging from 'persons connected with foreign secret service' to 'persons of foreign blood or connection in British Government civil service'. Within each category names were also 'grouped by races'. According to Kell's deputy, Holt-Wilson:

> ... It is not the nationality by place of birth, or by law, but nationality by blood, by racial interests, and by sympathy and friendship that is taken as the deciding factor in all classifications of possible enemy agents and dangerous persons.

Kell believed that the British people regarded 'with pity and contempt a decent British subject who wilfully becomes naturalised as the subject of a foreign State, and are equally sorry for any of our women folk who marry a foreigner'. He was also suspicious of British subjects who had one foreign parent: 'We had enough trouble in the late war with half-hearted hybrids who asked not to be sent to the front to kill their relatives ...'[61]

Kell claimed in 1920 that one of his officers and nine clerks in the MI5 Registry were employed full-time in answering 'numerous queries' from PCOs and the Home Office 'respecting the characters of applicants for permission to enter or leave the United Kingdom'.[62] A Home Office circular singled out from 'a great many examples' the case of 'a middle-aged Russian lady who appeared to all intents and purposes highly respectable and of good character and antecedents' who applied in Paris for a visa to learn English at a convent near London:

> ... Her dossier at MI5 showed that she was quite notorious, having been charged with incitement to murder in a political crime many years previously in Russia and having subsequently served a long term of imprisonment in Italy for being an accessory to a well known Lake murder. When told by the Passport Control Officer that she could not be granted a visa she gave vent to a string of oaths in, needless to say, the most fluent English![63]

Though Kell had lost control of the PCO network, he remained in charge of a similar 'chain of Imperial Special Intelligence' in the British Empire. With the support of the Colonial Office he had established 'personal liaison' with colonial administrations in August 1915. 'Special Intelligence liaisons' with the dominions took longer to establish. The Union of South Africa did not authorise its Provost Marshal to cooperate with Kell until June 1917. But by the end of the war Kell reported that all dominions were 'eager to cooperate' with MI5 in counter-espionage and 'the prevention of Bolshevik activities'.[64]

Counter-espionage had become both more complex and more tedious since the Armistice. Kell told chief constables, with whom he remained in close touch:

> ... Before the Great War, as far as we were aware, there was only one power engaged in this business, viz. Germany, but since the Great War most of the big Powers have been bitten with the virus, and it has become what I call a 'great international game' – a competitive game as to who can find out most about each other.

The crude methods used by prewar and wartime German agents had been replaced by 'more subtle ones'. 'Technically trained men', often using commercial cover, now sent back their reports not through the post but by diplomatic bags:

> The detection therefore of offenders has become such a difficult task that most of our energies and ingenuity must be concentrated on the preventive side and on the protection of those naval, military and Air Force secrets that *really* matter ...

'Preventive work' was much more humdrum than either the prewar spy hunts when Kell had spent the night hiding in doorways with Special Branch detectives or the wartime espionage trials which had sometimes led enemy agents to the scaffold. MI5's most time-consuming peacetime work, apart from updating its card index, was keeping 'a complete current record of all the information which is being sought concerning our defence matters by each foreign power', based chiefly on usually legitimate enquiries made by foreign service attachés. Just as Kell believed he had the best 'Precautionary Index' in the world, so he thought his record of sought-after defence secrets 'more precise and scientific than that of other countries'. MI5 was thus able to give detailed guidance to 'all the custodians of such secret information'. Kell regularly exhorted chief constables not to relax their vigilance. He urged them to keep watch on accommodation addresses; to make 'regular periodical examination of hotel registers', especially those near naval bases and army garrisons; to keep their aliens registers up to date; and to 'keep a look-out for any photos or picture postcards exhibited on sale which are likely to infringe the Official Secrets Acts', particularly those of defence establishments taken from the air.[65]

For Kell, as for Thomson, the main enemy was Bolshevism. But he was obliged to tell chief constables that MI5 was 'only concerned with Communism as it affects the Armed Forces of the Crown'. 'Civil' subversion was Thomson's responsibility.[66] Kell followed its development none the less with deep concern. From the beginning of 1920 both Kell and Thomson laid renewed emphasis on foreign support for domestic subversion. Kell's New Year card for 1920 showed the attractive figure of 'Liberty and Security' dressed in diaphanous gown, holding aloft the torch of freedom, standing on a pedestal erected by the heroic efforts of British fighting and working men (stage right). But 'Liberty and Security' was menaced by an assortment of subversives (stage left): a defeated Hun in pumpernickel helmet (by now a reminder of past dangers rather than a present menace), the rebel Irish (a much smaller threat on the mainland than in Ireland), and Bolshevik revolutionaries of probably intentionally Jewish appearance. The main threat came, predictably, from the Bolsheviks who are shown attempting to undermine the foundations of 'Liberty and Security'. Kell draws an appropriate moral from the initials MIV: 'Malevolence Imposes Vigilance'. Lying full-length at the bottom of Kell's New Year card is the reassuring figure of a note-taking Special Branch policeman, keeping careful watch on the subversives' every movement.[67]

Both Kell and Thomson were concerned lest Allied governments prove less vigilant than themselves. On 16 January 1920 the Allied Supreme Council formally declared the blockade of Soviet Russia at an end, and proposed a new policy of peaceful 'exchange of goods'. 'Commerce', Lloyd George believed, 'has a sobering influence ...' 'The moment trade was established with Russia', he optimistically explained to his Allies, 'Communism would go'.[68] Thomson believed that, on the contrary, trade simply offered the Bolsheviks new opportunities for subversion. Throughout 1920 he reported to the cabinet that 'revolutionary agitation was proved ... to depend almost entirely on the supply of funds from abroad'. The year, in Thomson's view, 'opened inauspiciously':

> Talk of revolution was on every tongue and the efforts of the revolutionaries were concentrated upon welding political activity and industrial unrest into a weapon strong enough to overthrow the Government.

Thomson reported in January that 'the revolutionaries were opening up regular communications with the Soviet Government'. A delegation of four had gone to 'a secret meeting of Bolsheviks' in Holland which founded the Western European Bureau of Comintern. Thomson reported with satisfaction that though the British delegates had expected to 'come back with full pockets', Dutch police had broken up the meeting and forced them to flee before they had obtained the funds on which they were counting. 'If it had not been for the failure of the stream of Russian money', Thomson believed, 'the situation would have gone from bad to worse'. Before long the flow resumed. On 19 March George Lansbury, the editor of the socialist *Daily Herald*, returned from Russia, having – according to Thomson – 'concluded an agreement with the Soviet Government by which he was to receive from Frederick Ström, the Bolshevik agent in Sweden, 500 tons of paper, then valued at £25,000, free of charge'. The *Daily Herald* was also 'to receive material for publication from the Soviet Government'.[69]

In April Thomson reported substantial Soviet finance for the pro-Bolshevik BSP: 'Practically all the extremist societies were in debt, and were only saved from bankruptcy by Russian money'. Russian money also allegedly found its way to the miners of the Rhondda Valley.[70] But while Thomson was monitoring Soviet finance for British subversion, Lloyd George was simultaneously gaining the support of his colleagues on the Allied Supreme Council for a further initiative towards the resumption of trade with Soviet Russia. On 26 April, meeting at San Remo, the Council authorised negotiations in London with the Russian Trade Delegation 'at the earliest date convenient to them'.

May was a disturbing month for Kell and Thomson for at least two reasons. The first was the revival of the 'Hands off Soviet Russia' movement. During 1919 there had been much talk of 'direct action'. In May 1920 direct action finally occurred. Outraged by the Polish invasion of the Ukraine, the *Daily Herald* declared: 'The marionettes are in Warsaw, but the strings are pulled from London and from Paris'. On 11 May stevedores on the East India Docks refused to load arms for Poland on the S.S. *Jolly George* which was forced to sail without them. A week later the dockers met for their triennial conference and passed a resolution congratulating the London stevedores for 'refusing to have their labour prostituted' by the capitalist campaign against Soviet Russia, and calling on the entire labour movement to follow their lead.[71] At that very moment the advance guard of the Russian Trade Delegation was arriving in London to set up their headquarters in the First Avenue Hotel in High Holborn. On 27 May, the commissar for foreign trade, Leonid Krasin, arrived to head the delegation. Krasin gave a verbal promise, and the rest of his staff written undertakings, not to 'interfere in any way in the politics or internal affairs of the country'. Thomson regarded the urbane and elegant Krasin as – relatively speaking – a good Bolshevik whose personal preference would have been 'to deal Bolshevism into the ways of normal democracy'. But Thomson had few illusions that the delegation would respect its undertakings of non-interference in British affairs. He reported that Krasin's principal assistant, N.K. Klishko, had made contact with 'Communist elements' as soon as he arrived in London.

Krasin paid his first call at 10 Downing Street on the afternoon of 31 May. It was a historic moment – the first official reception of a Soviet emissary by the head of a major government. Churchill stayed away rather than 'shake hands with the hairy baboon'. *The Times* warned Bonar Law and Curzon – the two leading Conservatives in the coalition government – of the consequences of shaking hands with the 'representative of a blood-stained despot, for whom they have consistently professed their horror and contempt'. After Lloyd George had welcomed Krasin, however, Bonar Law was the first minister to shake his hand. Curzon was the last. When Krasin held out his hand, Curzon at first remained motionless, his hands clasped firmly behind him. 'Curzon!' Lloyd George exclaimed, 'Be a gentleman!' Curzon took Krasin's still outstretched hand. The enemy was within the gates.[72]

# 8 | THE IRISH DÉBÂCLE

Intelligence in Ireland during the final years of British rule suffered from even greater lack of coordination than in Britain. Before the war political intelligence in the capital had been in the hands of the detective unit (G division) of the Dublin Metropolitan Police (DMP). Outside the capital it was controlled by the Special Crimes Branch of the Royal Irish Constabulary (RIC). As the Inspector General of the RIC, Brigadier-General J.A. Byrne, complained in 1916, it made little sense 'to have Dublin under the supervision of one secret service special crimes system and the remainder of the country under another'.[1] The war made the confusion worse. On the outbreak of hostilities the chief of the RIC Special Crimes Branch, Inspector Ivon Price, was made head of a military Special Intelligence Branch in the army's Irish Command with the rank of major. As well as 'working under the direction of the Commander-in-Chief', Price reported regularly to Vernon Kell in London. There was also a small Admiralty Intelligence section under W.V. Harrell, a former assistant commissioner sacked by the DMP, who reported to the admiral commanding the main naval base at Queenstown and was virtually independent of 'Blinker' Hall and NID. In addition to the Irish-based intelligence networks, Hall, Thomson and Kell all added to the confusion by taking independent initiatives of their own in Irish affairs from time to time. There was also 'much overlapping' in intelligence surveillance of Irish nationalists in the United States.[2]

After investigating the chaotic structure of Irish intelligence in the autumn of 1916, Basil Thomson concluded: 'There is certainly a danger that from lack of coordination the Irish Government may be the last Department to receive information of grave moment to the peace of Ireland'.[3] Though Thomson failed to mention it, the Irish government had already been denied intelligence 'of grave moment' on the eve of the Easter Rising a few months before. The chief culprit was 'Blinker' Hall. Until the United States entered the war, the decrypted telegrams exchanged between the German foreign ministry and its Washington embassy gave Hall access to some of the most important Irish intelligence, enabling him to follow in particular attempts by the Irish nationalist Sir Roger Casement to obtain German assistance for an Irish rising. Through the intercepts Hall gained advance knowledge that German arms were to be landed in Tralee Bay in the spring of 1916 and that Casement was following by U-boat. The steamer *Aud*, carrying German munitions, was duly intercepted by HMS *Bluebell* on 21 April 1916, ordered to proceed to Queenstown and scuttled by its German crew just as it arrived. Next day, Good Friday, Casement was captured within hours of landing in Tralee Bay.[4]

Hall, probably fearful of compromising Room 40, failed to give advance information to the Irish government in Dublin Castle. Its only warning came on 17 April in a letter to the army commander, General Friend, from General Stafford in Cork who had heard the news 'casually' from Admiral Bayly at Queenstown. The commission of enquiry into the Easter Rising later described this failure of communication as 'very extraordinary' but offered no explanation for it. Even when Casement arrived in London on Easter Sunday to be jointly questioned by Hall and Thomson, Dublin Castle was not properly informed about his interrogation. Casement asked for an appeal by him to call off the planned rising to be made known in Ireland, better still that he be allowed to make it himself in Ireland and 'stop useless bloodshed'. Hall refused, possibly in the hope that the rising would go ahead and force the government to respond with the repression he thought necessary. Casement alleged that he was told by Hall: 'It is better that a cankering sore like this should be cut out'. An appeal by Casement would not in any case have deterred the seven-man military council of the Irish Republican Brotherhood from going ahead with their Dublin rising on Easter Monday. Dublin Castle can scarcely be blamed for being caught unawares. Even Eoin MacNeill, chief of staff of the Irish Volunteers (the forerunner of the IRA), who had tried to call the rising off when he heard of Casement's arrest, was taken by surprise when it went ahead.[5]

Hall continued to allow himself an outrageous freedom of action during the preparations for Casement's trial. To undermine sympathy for Casement, particularly in the United States, and prejudice his prospects of a reprieve, he secretly circulated to the American embassy and around London clubs lurid extracts from Casement's diaries containing records of numerous payments for homosexual services, enthusiastic descriptions of '*huge*', '*enormous*' genitalia, and details of exhausting sexual marathons with 'awful thrusts', 'much groaning and struggle and moans'. Dr Page, the American ambassador, read half a page and declared himself unable to continue without becoming ill. Hall also offered Ben Allen of the Associated Press extracts from the diaries for exclusive publication, but Allen turned them down. 'Bubbles' James, who was shortly to become Hall's deputy, later acknowledged that his action might be thought 'not entirely to his credit', but 'he would not stand aside when a traitor might escape his just fate through the emotional appeals of people who did not know the gravity of the offences'. Though prey to what even a sympathetic biographer has called 'almost pitiable' sexual obsessions, Casement was an idealistic convert to Irish nationalism of proven courage who went to the scaffold on 3 August with, in the words of the priest who walked with him, 'the dignity of a prince'. Ellis, his executioner, called him 'the bravest man it ever fell to my unhappy lot to execute'.[6]

To the Irish administration, as to the intelligence services concerned with Ireland, the outcome of the Easter Rising seemed as reassuring as Casement's execution. The self-styled provisional government of the Irish Republic, proclaimed on Easter Monday 'in the name of God and of the dead generations', won little support from the living, and surrendered after six days of street fighting. In the short term it achieved only the destruction of much of central Dublin. In the longer term, however, the 450 lives lost during the rising and the sixteen executions which followed ('few but corroding', as Churchill called them) shocked most Irishmen outside Ulster into supporting the nationalist demand for complete independence. But in the aftermath of the Rising there was no visible sign that the Union was doomed. The military intelligence officer for the Irish Midlands wrote confidently in October 1916:

> The presence of the military and the rapid dispersal of all armed bodies in the past rebellion have put an end to all hope of success by armed opposition in the future and the extremists recognise this.

By the end of 1917, after a series of nationalist bye-election victories by Sinn Fein candidates, the same intelligence officer was less optimistic. The Sinn Fein movement was, he reported, 'peculiarly well disciplined', and intelligence reports of its meetings 'very hard to obtain'. He noted with particular surprise that drunkenness was 'almost unknown' among Sinn Fein militants and 'apparently severely dealt with'.[7]

Until the end of the First World War British Intelligence in Ireland was aimed at the wrong target. It concentrated overwhelmingly on tracking down minor German intrigues rather than on following the much more important development of Irish nationalism. GHQ Ireland was later to regret that 'the opportunity was not taken to create an intelligence branch of trained brains working together to examine the military possibilities of the Sinn Fein movement'.[8] Though the potential challenge from Sinn Fein was underestimated, the German menace in Ireland was greatly – and sometimes wildly – exaggerated. In February 1917 the breaking of diplomatic relations between the United States and Germany, and the consequent cessation of diplomatic traffic between Berlin and Washington, removed the only reliable source of monitoring German assistance to Irish nationalists. The break in the flow of intercepts came at a tantalising moment, immediately following revelations that the Irish-American Clan na Gael was seeking German arms and troops to support another rising. Deprived of intelligence from intercepts, Hall turned instead to much less reliable sources of information. A White Paper later claimed that by the autumn of 1917 Germany was communicating with Sinn Fein 'by means of U-boats off the West Coast of Ireland and German propaganda leaflets and pamphlets were thus disseminated in Ireland'. By 1918, according to the same White Paper, arms and ammunition were being landed from submarines and Sinn Feiners were exchanging coded messages with off-shore U-boats. The flimsy evidence for these extraordinary assertions consisted chiefly of rumour and gossip. One of the rumour-mongers, credited by both Hall and Thomson, peddled an improbable anti-Catholic conspiracy theory according to which 'communications between the Sinn Feiners and Germany are kept up largely through Maynooth [seminary] and the Vatican'. Within Ireland itself neither military, naval nor police intelligence found evidence of significant German assistance to Sinn Fein either by submarine landings or by covert operations. Hall and Thomson, however, preferred their own more sensational and less reliable reports.[9]

Fears of a German plot reached a climax after the announcement on 9 April 1918, in response to the desperate situation on the Western Front, that conscription was to be extended to Ireland. Even the Roman Catholic hierarchy, hitherto aloof from politics, denounced conscription as 'an oppressive and inhuman law which the Irish have a right to resist by every means that are consonant with the laws of God'. Sinn Fein under Eamonn De Valera, the sole survivor of the leaders of the Easter Rising, led a campaign of resistance. On 12 April, acting on a tip-off from naval intelligence, the RIC in County Clare arrested Corporal Joseph Dowling, a former POW in Germany who had joined Casement's Irish brigade. Under interrogation in London, Dowling gave a highly coloured account of his mission as a German envoy to Sinn Fein sent to arrange the landing of 'arms, artillery, machine guns and German troops'. He is alleged to have claimed that a U-boat, summoned by waving a handkerchief from the shore, would take him back to Germany to prepare for the invasion. Four days after Dowling's arrest, two men were arrested while sailing in Dublin Bay on suspicion that they were trying to make contact with an enemy submarine. At almost the same moment Hall received a report from Copenhagen that two German submarines were being loaded with arms for Ireland. Both Hall and Thomson treated these improbable reports with utmost seriousness.[10]

Walter Long, the former leader of the Irish Unionists, now colonial secretary, complained that the government had not 'properly realised the dangerous state of things in Ireland – especially the prevalence of German intrigue'. The war cabinet responded in early May 1918 by appointing Field-Marshal Viscount French Lord Lieutenant of Ireland with the mission of '*restoring order* and combating German intrigues', and by making Long responsible for liaison between London and Dublin. Acting on the advice of Hall and Thomson, Long and French agreed on a plan to arrest Sinn Fein leaders on the night of 17–18 May and then announce the discovery of a Sinn Fein-German conspiracy. Though the cabinet gave its approval, the cooler heads within it were rightly concerned at the 'danger of discrediting the government if they made a great deal of pro-German activities in Ireland, and then found out that the evidence was not very considerable or convincing'.[11]

The mass arrests proceeded with remarkable smoothness. Of the main Sinn Fein leadership only Cathal Brugha and Michael Collins escaped. Unlike the founders of Sinn Fein, who had preached non-violent resistance to British rule, both were ardent advocates of force and the imprisonment of their moderate rivals increased their influence. The evidence of a German-Irish plot produced to justify the arrests was, as Lloyd George complained, 'of the most flimsy and ancient description'. 'So the Government are put in a hole, as I expected they would be', noted Hankey. Both French and Long suffered from two major misconceptions. First, they enormously exaggerated the extent of German intrigues with Sinn Fein. Dissatisfied with the paucity of intelligence on the largely imaginary Irish-German connection, French 'roused up the Detective Dept. with a view to getting at more of these intrigues'. 'I know there *are* more', he insisted. Long saw the 'hand of Germany' behind both labour unrest in Britain and nationalist unrest in Ireland. 'All this', he wrote, 'is due to German intrigue and German money'.[12] As well as overestimating German influence, both French and Long gravely underestimated Sinn Fein's growing support among the Irish people. 'If they could only be got to realise the true character of such leaders as De Valera', wrote French, '... I feel sure the Irish would cast them out like the swine they are'.[13]

The new and tougher Irish policy inaugurated in the spring of 1918 quickly backfired. Plans to introduce conscription had finally to be abandoned in the face of mass opposition, having served only to rally Irish opinion behind a Sinn Fein increasingly dominated by Brugha and Collins. The arrests of most other Sinn Fein leaders led to no prosecutions and were widely interpreted as British revenge for Irish opposition to conscription. The post-war elections of December 1918 produced a landslide victory for Sinn Fein, whose seventy-three M.P.s boycotted Westminster, denounced the Union with Britain, and set up the Dail as an independent parliament of the Irish Republic. Though one of French's informants at the early meetings of the Dail told him that it represented 'the general feeling in the country', French continued to misread the situation. 'These seventy-three devils', he told Long, 'will soon go bag and baggage over to Westminster'. Long agreed that the lure of Westminster salaries would prove too great for the impoverished Sinn Feiners to resist.[14]

Brigadier-General Byrne, Inspector General of the RIC, was more realistic. The time had come, he argued, to negotiate with Sinn Fein and try to separate the moderate politicians from the Irish Volunteers (now also known as the IRA), who were committed to armed struggle.[15] French dismissed Byrne's views as a sign of weakness rather than realism. At the end of 1919 he sent Byrne on leave, ostensibly for health reasons, and did not allow him to return to office.[16]

The decline and fall of British rule during the three years after the Armistice was accompanied, and perhaps accelerated, by the partial collapse of British Intelligence in Ireland. In January 1919 Major Ivon Price, the wartime coordinator of intelligence in Ireland, returned to Britain and was not replaced. Naval intelligence in Ireland was wound up, military intelligence was cut back, and French had no confidence in the intelligence assessments of the head of the RIC.[17] He wrote despairingly to Churchill, then secretary for war, on 10 April 1919: 'We are suffering terribly in Ireland for the want of a proper Criminal Investigation Department'. He therefore urgently requested the loan of Vernon Kell (whom he misnamed 'Kells') 'to advise on those subjects'.[18] Whatever advice Kell provided was, however, ineffective.

During all previous Irish 'Troubles', the British administration in Dublin Castle had its informers in the rebel camp. 'These creatures of the dark', wrote David Neligan, an early member of the IRA, 'had ever been the Castle's last line of defence. In every age an Irish Judas was hidden in the undergrowth'.[19] But in 1919 the IRA under its director of intelligence, Michael Collins, turned the tables on the Castle. Neligan was one of four IRA agents infiltrated into the headquarters of the RIC and DMP. The Castle, however, found it more difficult to recruit informers than ever before. As military intelligence later acknowledged, 'the bulk of the people were our enemies and were therefore far more incorruptible than has been the case in former Irish movements'.[20]

Only in Protestant Ulster did the flow of intelligence remain undiminished. But, as military intelligence quickly discovered, its prejudiced alarmism often made it useless: 'Almost every Protestant saw a Sinn Feiner and potential murderer in every Roman Catholic'. In the South the most useful informers were women, though, in the prim view of military intelligence, 'their employment sometimes involved relations that were more than friendly. This was occasionally inconvenient':

> Other classes which could be tapped were the clergy (who are generally safe in Ireland whatever their religion), bank managers, shop owners and employees, military contractors, farmers and civilians employed by the military or police.

But IRA action against informers became increasingly brutal, and was 'effective because of its sheer brutality'.[21]

In all the long line of Irish rebels Michael Collins was the first effective revolutionary. His strategy was twofold: to reduce Ireland to 'a general state of disorder', and to 'put out the eyes of the British', thus making them helpless to counter the disorder. In his own words:

> Without her spies England was helpless. It was only by means of their accumulated knowledge that the British machine could operate. Without their police throughout the country, how could they find the man they wanted? Without their criminal agents in the capital how could they carry out that 'removal' of the leaders that they considered essential for their victory?[22]

Unlike Dublin Castle, the IRA had no shortage of willing informers. In the view of military intelligence:

> There were spies everywhere, and a very large percentage of the population were ready to act as extra eyes and ears for Sinn Fein and for the IRA even if they were not prepared to fight for them. It was necessary to employ civilian labour in various capacities and it was comparatively easy for the IRA to have their agents working among the Crown Forces and even to enlist them in the RIC and DMP.[23]

By far the most valuable of the IRA agents were four DMP and RIC detectives in Dublin Castle itself. One of them, Eamonn 'Ned' Broy, had been secretly sending reports to Sinn Fein since March 1917. In January 1919 Broy met Collins for the first time. 'Immediately I met him', Broy said later, 'I knew he was the man who could beat the British and I decided to work for him from then on'. On the evening of 7 April Broy smuggled Collins into the Brunswick Street Police Offices and left him to spend the night going through his own and other intelligence files. Scarcely had Collins left at 7 o'clock the following morning than, to Broy's horror, he returned to the file room to collect documents he had left behind, allegedly saying a cheerful 'Good morning' to the policeman on the door.[24]

Collins's four moles within the Castle and six other informers in the uniformed branch of the DMP supplied his hand-picked 'Squad' of gunmen, formed in September 1919, with the names of British agents and informers who then became their targets. As one member of the Squad later recalled:

> [Collins] gave us a short talk, the gist of which was that any of us who had read Irish history would know that no organisation in the past had an intelligence system through which spies and informers could be dealt with effectively. That position would be rectified by the Squad which would take orders directly from himself.[25]

The Squad operated at first from the Antient Concert Room in Brunswick Street, where James Joyce and John McCormack had once sung, later from a painter's and decorator's offices in Abbey Street. According to Bill Stapleton, one of the gunmen:

> Two or three of us would go out with an [IRA] Intelligence Officer walking in front of us, maybe about ten or fifteen yards. His job was to identify the man we were to shoot ... The Intelligence Officer would then signal to us in the following way. He would take off his hat and greet the marked man. Of course, he didn't know him. As soon as he did this we would shoot. We had to accept the GHQ knew the right men to shoot.[26]

By the end of 1919 five of the ten DMP detectives working on political intelligence had been killed or wounded, one of the survivors had left for a safer job in England, and French himself had narrowly escaped assassination in an IRA ambush near Phoenix Park.[27] French was reduced almost to despair at the collapse of his intelligence network and the infiltration of Dublin Castle by the IRA:

> Our Secret Service is simply non-existent. What masquerades for such a Service is nothing but a delusion and a snare. The D.M.P. are absolutely demoralised, and the R.I.C. will be in the same case very soon if we do not quickly set our house in order.[28]

French and his advisers decided that in future secret service work in Ireland should be directed from Scotland House in London by Sir Basil Thomson in the belief that 'agents could be collected in England and sent to Ireland more easily and safely than if the head office were in Ireland':

> The military authorities in Ireland agreed that with the exception of any agents already employed by the Intelligence Branch at GHQ, all agents should be controlled from Scotland House, and an officer from Scotland House was attached to GHQ for liaison duties.

The result of this civil-military compromise, GHQ complained, 'was a sort of hermaphroditic intelligence service'. 'Parallel systems', it concluded, 'are invariably vicious'. The rivalry between Thomson and military intelligence in Ireland reproduced many of the failings of the competing wartime British espionage networks in the Netherlands: 'duplication, jealousy, expense and leakage of information'. Both networks also lacked the support of a well-organised counter-espionage system. 'Yet', as GHQ later acknowledged, 'never was an efficient system of contre-espionage more needed than in Ireland'.[29]

Dublin Castle's main hopes of reviving the DMP were pinned on an able Belfast police inspector, W.C.F. Redmond, who was made assistant commissioner of the DMP at the end of 1919, and told to 'take care of political crime'.[30] Redmond struck Neligan as 'a neatly-built man of about forty, nattily dressed and wearing a bowler', who 'looked more like a stockbroker than a policeman'. Soon after his arrival in Dublin Redmond summoned the 'G-men' of the DMP, including Neligan, for a 'pep talk' in which he announced proudly that an agent sent from England (probably by Thomson) had managed to meet Michael Collins. The agent was the son of an RIC district inspector named Burns who had previously served with the Special Branch in London. In Dublin Burns assumed the alias of 'Jameson' and passed himself off to Collins as a delegate of the Soldiers', Sailors' and Airmen's Union which he claimed had supported the police strike. Neligan considered him 'a star secret-service operator, with that blend of audacity, eloquence, and three o'clock in the morning courage required in this service'. Redmond, however, unwittingly blew his cover. He also made the fatal error of making another of Collins's moles, James McNamara, his confidential secretary.[31]

On 21 January 1920 Redmond was shot by the Squad at close range on the way to his hotel. Half a century later one of his killers, Joe Dolan, told the story with what his interviewer called 'an almost schoolboy giggle'. 'We knew he had a bullet-proof waistcoat', said Dolan. 'So we shot him in the head'.[32] Military intelligence drily observed that, after Redmond's death, G division 'ceased to affect the situation'.[33] Redmond's successor, wrote Neligan, 'did not go looking for trouble and was not interfered with'. In February the Squad killed Burns.[34] In March Alan Bell, a magistrate who seems to have been the local coordinator of Thomson's secret service network, was taken from a Dublin tram and shot in the street.[35]

The exploits of the Squad in Dublin were part of a general escalation of the Troubles. During the first six months of 1920, 16 occupied RIC barracks were destroyed and 29 damaged in IRA attacks. Another 424 abandoned barracks were destroyed, the majority to mark the fourth anniversary of the Easter Rising.[36] The British government responded by bringing in aggressive reinforcements for the RIC from England: the 'Black and Tans' (so called after a pack of hounds in Tipperary) and the Auxiliary force (or 'Auxis') of ex-officers. As the year went on, the Troubles became dominated by increasingly vicious guerilla warfare between the IRA and the combined forces of 'Black and Tans' and 'Auxis' (often collectively known as the 'Tans').

In April 1920 the cabinet decided on a radical reform of the Irish Executive. A tough Canadian, Sir Hamar Greenwood (aptly described as 'a man of one idea at a time'), succeeded Macpherson as chief secretary, and Lord French quickly found his position as lord lieutenant reduced to little more than figurehead. General Sir Nevil Macready, commissioner of the London Metropolitan Police, was appointed GOC Ireland – having been offered and refused joint command of both the army and the police. Macready regarded the Irish police as 'hopelessly out of date' and 'disorganised', and believed their reorganisation would leave him no time for the army.[37] But his refusal to accept joint command helped to perpetuate the damaging division between military and police intelligence.

Macready was aware, however, of the damage done by that division. On 11 May 1920 the cabinet approved his proposal that all Irish intelligence be placed under a single Director of Intelligence. The officer chosen was the forty-five-year-old Brigadier Ormonde de l'Epée Winter, codenamed 'O'. With his monocle, black greased hair and cigarette dangling from his lips, Winter looked as if he had stepped straight from the pages of a spy thriller. Mark Sturgis, the assistant under-secretary at Dublin Castle, thought him 'a most amazing original': 'He looks like a wicked little white snake, is clever as paint, probably entirely non-moral, a first-class horseman, a card genius, knows several languages'.[38] Unhappily, Winter had no previous experience of full-time intelligence work. He concentrated his attention on Dublin rather than on coordinating intelligence for Ireland as a whole and preferred the excitement of covert action to the patient collation and analysis of all information on the IRA. As a result, in the army's view, 'the double system of police and military intelligence continued to involve loss of efficiency, duplication of work and complications in almost every way'.[39] 'Winter', concluded Macready, 'has not got the right method, and we here doubt very much whether he will ever get it. He is, I fancy, a "born sleuth", but I doubt his organising power, and that, so far as I can see, is what is holding up the machine'.[40]

Despite his lack of 'the right method', 'O' threw himself enthusiastically into his job. Because of the difficulty of recruiting agents in Ireland, he set up a secret recruiting office in London and – probably unwisely – selected as its head his friend, Major C.A. Cameron, formerly head of the wartime CF network in the Low Countries. Cameron sent sixty agents to Ireland in the space of eight or nine months, but – as Winter complained – 'many proved unsatisfactory and had to be discarded'.[41] Probably Winter's most effective unit was the Dublin District Special Intelligence Branch built up by ex-officers whom military intelligence considered 'enthusiastic amateurs'.[42] With the assistance of MI5,[43] a 'school of instruction' for these agents was started in London Once trained, they were given 'suitable cover' in Dublin 'such as shop assistants, garage hands, and similar occupations'. In Winter's view they achieved 'admirable results' but 'their losses were heavy'.[44]

The greatest single British intelligence loss came in Dublin on 21 November 1920, the first 'Bloody Sunday' in twentieth-century Ireland. Picked gunmen from Collins's Squad, some having just attended Mass, entered seven Dublin houses and the Gresham Hotel, and killed twelve officers, all of whom were believed to be (and most of whom were) British secret agents. 'It's to be done exactly at nine', Collins had insisted, 'neither before nor after. These "hoors", the British, have got to learn that Irishmen can turn up on time'. In one house which the gunmen entered early, they waited on the landing studying their watches until the hour struck. Not all the killings, however, were as finely timed as Collins had intended. Some of the British officers were shot in bed, some against walls, others while trying to escape. 'For myself', wrote Collins later, 'my conscience is clear. There is no crime in detecting and destroying in war-time the spy and the informer. I have destroyed without trial. I have paid them back in their own coin.'[45] Even Winter could not 'withhold a certain respect for the bravery' and 'intense patriotism' of the IRA leaders and especially of Collins, whom he saw as a mixture of Robin Hood and 'an elusive Pimpernel'.[46]

'Bloody Sunday', as military intelligence acknowledged, 'temporarily paralysed the Special Branch':

> Several of its most efficient members were murdered and the majority of the others resident in the city were brought into the Castle and the Central Hotel for safety. This centralisation in the most inconvenient places possible greatly decreased the opportunities for obtaining information and for re-establishing anything in the nature of secret service.[47]

But the intelligence war was not entirely one-sided. Seven of the IRA gunmen involved in Bloody Sunday were later hanged; an eighth was convicted but escaped from prison. The regular IRA killings of suspected informers were evidence of Collins's continuing fear of British intelligence penetration.[48] In October 1920 Winter organised a Central Raid Bureau in Dublin Castle which by the Truce of July 1921 claimed to have made 6,311 raids and searches in the Dublin area.[49] Military intelligence summarised the results as follows:

> In 1921 nearly all the officers of the Dublin Brigade, I.R.A., were known, and a good percentage of them had been arrested, including the I.R.A. Director of Intelligence, the head of their secret service and four battalion I[ntelligence] O[fficer]s. There were trained agents on most of the boats coming to Dublin and Kingstown. Eight of the principal departments of Dail Eireann and the I.R.A. had been raided successfully and three [arms] dumps had been taken. Twice was the G.H.Q. of the I.R.A. raided, on one occasion the Chief of Staff's personal office and plans being captured, and only three days before the Truce the office of the I.R.A. police was taken.[50]

The most valuable British intelligence source – both a cause and a consequence of many of the raids – was captured documents. 'It was fortunate', wrote Winter, 'that the Irish had an irresistible habit of keeping documents'. To file and correlate the documents seized in raids, the Central Raid Bureau brought over staff from England, all 'of English extraction, whose antecedents and activities were carefully screened by Scotland Yard'.[51]

But the handling of captured documents was deficient in two major ways. A military order of 7 March 1921 gives a graphic, if barely comprehensible, illustration of the way in which captured documents fell prey to the administrative confusion of the intelligence system:

(a) All documents captured by the troops are forwarded to the Brigade Headquarters. All documents captured by the police are forwarded to the local centre at the Divisional Commissioner's office.

(b) The military intelligence service is responsible for dealing with all documents relating to the operations, armament, training and organisation (including the order of battle and the names of commanders and officers) of the I.R.A. After duplication of such documents they are passed in original to the police intelligence service as signatures, handwriting, typing of such papers may often be important links in a chain of evidence.

The military intelligence service transfer to the 'Local Centre' of police intelligence all documents referred to in (c) below.

(c) The police intelligence service is responsible for passing through to the military intelligence service all documents referred to in (b) above and for dealing with all documents relating to individuals, addresses, Sinn Fein police, Sinn Fein courts, Sinn Fein organisation in Great Britain and abroad, propaganda, etc., etc., and for working up the police cases against individuals.

(d) In cases where documents form the evidence against an individual or individuals charged with possession of seditious documents, the documents are forwarded by the local C[ompetent] M[ilitary] A[uthority] through the usual military channels to G.H.Q., except in the martial law area where they are dealt with by the Military Governor.[52]

Even more serious than administrative confusion was what military intelligence condemned as '*the almost universal ignorance of all ranks*' among British forces in Ireland '*as to what intelligence might be. It was generally regarded as secret service and nothing else . . .*' Some army officers scarcely bothered to read the lengthy intelligence 'summaries' circulated by the Central Raid Bureau which were often over a hundred, and sometimes over two hundred, foolscap pages long. Other officers went further and 'stated that intelligence summaries were a waste of time and labour, and a source of leakage of information'.[53]

The IRA had no prospect of a military victory. It never had more than 5,000 men – and usually only 3,000 – on active service at one time. Its greatest show of strength, the burning of the beautiful eighteenth-century Customs House in Dublin in May 1921, ended in disaster. Several IRA men were killed and most of the remainder, over a hundred, surrendered. But while it was clear that the British army would not be beaten, it was increasingly plain also that it could not win. At the May 1921 elections for the two Home Rule Irish parliaments established by the Government of Ireland Act in the previous year, a six-county Ulster returned a large Unionist majority to Belfast. But the twenty-six counties of the rest of Ireland (save for Trinity College, Dublin) returned Sinn Fein candidates who once again boycotted the parliament to which they were elected and set themselves up as the Second Dail.

The British cabinet still oscillated between coercion and conciliation. During June 1921 the South African prime minister, Jan Christian Smuts, in England for an imperial conference, and King George V, who opened the Belfast parliament with an appeal for 'forbearance and reconciliation', helped to tilt the balance in favour of conciliation. Though no formal truce was signed, fighting ended on 11 July. After months of bargaining the terms of a twenty-six-county Irish Free State, excluding Ulster, were agreed in the early hours of 6 December. In Britain the treaty was greeted with jubilation. Lloyd George, euphoric at being rid of the Irish problem, called it 'the greatest day in the history of the British Empire'. In Ireland the treaty was to lead to a new and more terrible phase of the Troubles. Michael Collins said soon after adding his signature to it: 'I have signed my death warrant'. Though the Dail approved the Anglo-Irish treaty by a seven-vote majority, much of the IRA denounced it and began a civil war which lasted for sixteen months. In August 1922 Collins, first chairman of the Irish provisional government, was killed as he had predicted in an ambush by his former comrades-in-arms.[54] Some British ministers found it difficult to conceal a sense of *Schadenfreude* at the sight of Irish nationalists tearing each other to pieces. The lord chancellor, the Earl of Birkenhead, told the Lords:

I, for one, rejoice, as I have said before in this House, that this task [the suppression of the republican rebellion], painful, costly, bloody as it must ultimately prove, is being undertaken by those to whom it properly falls.

Former members of the fragmented British intelligence community in Ireland must have been tempted to agree.

# 9 GC & CS, SIS, AND ANGLO-SOVIET RELATIONS 1920–1924

By the time that Anglo-Soviet trade negotiations began in May 1920 Britain's most valuable source of Soviet intelligence was provided by codebreakers. For the next seven years, until the codebreakers were compromised by the cabinet in May 1927, sigint (signals intelligence) remained more important than humint (human intelligence). Some of the Soviet communications intercepted by British intelligence were letters and despatches – a source sometimes muddied by forged documents. But the most numerous and the most valuable intercepts were the coded telegrams and wireless messages of the Soviet government.

Early in 1919 the war cabinet decided, on the recommendation of Curzon's Secret Service Committee, to establish a peacetime cryptographic unit. Captain (later Admiral Sir) Hugh 'Quex' Sinclair ('Blinker' Hall's successor as DNI) was given the task of assembling a team of codebreakers and cryptographers under Admiralty control from the 'remnants of Room 40 and MI1b'. After lengthy negotiations between Admiralty, War Office, Foreign Office and Treasury, the new unit was eventually installed in Watergate House, Adelphi. There was a long argument over the name of the new unit. 'Nobby' Clarke, one of the veterans of Room 40, suggested 'Public Benefactors' on hearing that his basic salary would be only £500 a year. Eventually the title 'Government Code and Cypher School' (GC & CS), suggested by Courtenay Forbes of the Foreign Office Communications Department, was accepted. The publicly announced function of GC & CS was 'to advise as to the security of codes and cyphers used by all Government departments and to assist in their provision'. But it was also given a secret directive 'to study the methods of cypher communications used by foreign powers', and told to send all decrypted telegrams to the foreign secretary who would decide which were worth distributing to other members of the cabinet. According to 'Nobby' Clarke, despite the sensational revelation of the intercepted Zimmermann telegram in 1917, Lord Curzon at first expected GC & CS to produce little of diplomatic interest. He quickly changed his mind. By the summer of 1920 he was studying Soviet intercepts with almost obsessional interest. The Foreign Office was eventually embarrassed into taking over direct responsibility for GC & CS from the Admiralty in April 1922 after its codebreakers had decrypted a telegram from the French ambassador in London reporting that Curzon had secretly criticised cabinet policy.[1]

The head of GC & CS from 1919 to 1942 was Alastair Denniston, known to his staff as 'the little man', one of Ewing's earliest recruits to Room 40. He had, in the opinion of one of those who later served under him, 'little liking for questions of administration' and 'even less for the ways of bureaucracy and the demands of hierarchy'. But until the vast wartime expansion of GC & CS at Bletchley Park these qualities were considerable assets. For almost twenty years Denniston succeeded in running on a shoestring a new and highly secret government department. When his resources were increased, on the eve of war, he began the expansion which made possible the remarkable achievements of Bletchley Park.[2] Many of his best cryptanalysts would not have taken kindly either to civil service hierarchies or to a chief devoted to bureaucratic routine. Denniston's personal experience of cryptography, informal manner, lack of pomposity and willingness both to trust and delegate to his sometimes unorthodox subordinates smoothed many of the difficulties involved in creating a single unit from the rival remnants of Room 40 and MI1b.

Beneath him Denniston had initially 6 senior assistants (increased to 10 in 1925) who were paid the salaries of civil service principals. They included probably the best cryptanalysts of, respectively, Room 40 and MI1b, Dilly Knox and Oliver Strachey. There were also 18 junior assistants (increased to 20 in 1925) paid on the assistant principal scale, and a clerical staff of 28.[3]

Unlike the French *cabinet noir*, GC & CS had little success with post-war German codes even before the Germans introduced the highly complex 'Enigma' machine cipher in the later 1920s. 'Germany', wrote Denniston later, 'knew well we had read her diplomatic traffic for the last three years (e.g. Zimmermann Letter) and no one prevented Germany from replacing her compromised codes by the safest methods she could devise'. GC & CS had far more success with the codes of wartime allies. The new American diplomatic code, reciphered quarterly, was broken in time to provide intelligence on American policy during the Washington Naval Conference of 1921–2. GC & CS also began 'a concentrated attack on French diplomatic cyphers, which had received no attention during the war'. It was gratified to discover that French code and cipher systems tended to be 'conservative' and 'presented little difficulty'. According to Denniston, 'Only about 1935 did the French introduce any system which defied solution'. The proximity of London and Paris meant, however, that many more French than American diplomatic communications went by diplomatic bag and were thus normally out of the reach of GC & CS.[4] French and American codebreakers were simultaneously able to decrypt significant amounts of British diplomatic traffic.[5] By enabling each major foreign ministry to read at least some of its rivals' communications, the *cabinets noirs* thus introduced, in a rather curious and incomplete way, the open diplomacy advocated by enthusiasts of the League of Nations. Historians of international relations have scarcely begun to consider the consequences of that mutual eavesdropping on the diplomacy of the world between the wars.

Throughout the 1920s GC & CS also had little difficulty with Japanese codes and ciphers. To translate the Japanese messages Denniston recruited Ernest Hobart-Hampden, a retired diplomat who had spent twenty years in Japan and 'soon acquired an uncanny skill in never missing the important':

> ... Throughout the period down to 1931 no big conference was held in Washington, London or Geneva in which he did not contribute all the views of the Japanese Government and of their too verbose representatives.

In 1926 Hobart-Hampden was joined by another retired Japanese-speaking diplomat, Sir Harold Parlett, who had in Denniston's view 'an equal sense of the essential'. The two men combined their work for GC & CS with the preparation of an *English-Japanese Dictionary of the Spoken Word*.[6]

Much the most valuable intelligence provided by GC & CS until 1927, however, was the decrypted diplomatic traffic of the Soviet government. The Bolsheviks suffered during their first decade in power from two serious cryptographic handicaps. The first was their fear of relying on the relatively sophisticated codes and ciphers which they inherited from the Tsarist régime, and their consequent introduction of less secure systems based at first on simple forms of letter transposition.[7] The second was the dispersion of the Tsarist codebreakers who had given pre-revolutionary Russia probably the world lead in cryptanalysis. Worse still, from the Bolshevik point of view, some of the best defected to the opposition.

The head of the Russian section at GC & CS between the wars, E.C. Fetterlein, had been one of the leading cryptanalysts in Tsarist Russia. He was a small, bespectacled, rather solitary man of grisled appearance whose social contact with most other members of GC & CS went little beyond saying 'Good morning' in a thick Russian accent. Conscious of his loneliness, Denniston several times invited him and his silent wife, who spoke little English, to Christmas dinner.[8] The great American cryptographer, Walter Friedman, who met Fetterlein at the end of the war, was struck by the fact that 'he wore with great pride on the index finger of his right hand a ring in which was mounted a large ruby':

When I showed interest in this unusual gem, he told me that the ring had been presented him as a token of recognition and thanks for his cryptanalytic successes while in the service of Czar Nicholas, the last of the line.

Ironically, those 'successes' had included decrypting British diplomatic traffic.[9]

During the ten months of Anglo-Soviet trade negotiations which followed Krasin's arrival in London at the end of May 1920, the single most important intelligence source available to the British government was the Soviet diplomatic traffic decrypted by Fetterlein and his assistants at GC & CS. Lloyd George, who took personal charge of the negotiations, spelled out from the start three main conditions for the resumption of normal trade: an end to all hostile activities and propaganda in and on the borders of the British Empire; the prompt exchange of all remaining British and Russian prisoners; and Soviet recognition 'in principle' of pre-revolutionary Russian debts to the Allies. Krasin's initial approach was conciliatory. There were, he told Lloyd George at a private meeting, 'extremists on both sides'. Those in Russia 'preferred world revolution to world peace', but were outnumbered by the doves; 'the Allied extremists preferred war with Russia to peace with the Soviet Government'. On receiving Krasin's reports of his first two meetings with Lloyd George, however, Chicherin, the Soviet commissar for foreign affairs, instructed him to take a much tougher line:

You must in no wise yield to British blackmailing. The situation that has been created in the East is a difficult one for England. In Persia they are almost helpless in the face of the revolution. Disloyalty is increasing amongst the Indian troops ... By a policy of capitulation we shall attain nothing ...

Lenin's advice was blunter still:

That swine Lloyd George has no scruples or shame in the way he deceives. Don't believe a word he says and gull him three times as much.

Both messages were decrypted by GC & CS and passed to Lloyd George and his senior ministers. The prime minister cannot therefore have been greatly surprised when Krasin arrived at 10 Downing Street on 29 June in an unyielding mood, and read the text of a long note which Lloyd George considered 'more in the nature of a lecture than of a business reply'. On the following day Lloyd George sent Krasin a formal memorandum setting out Britain's conditions for a trade agreement and asking for 'categorical replies, yes or no' from the Soviet government. On 1 July Krasin set sail for Russia on a British destroyer to seek fresh instructions.[10]

Thomson reported that while negotiating with Lloyd George the Trade Delegation had simultaneously been financing subversion. During June 'the "Hands off Russia" Committee, which was in touch with and received money from the Russian Trading Delegation, entered on a period of intense activity'. Krasin seems initially to have been nervous of direct involvement with the socialist *Daily Herald*. The *Herald*'s youngest director, the twenty-nine-year-old Francis Meynell, therefore went to Maxim Litvinov, the Soviet deputy commissar for foreign affairs then in Copenhagen, to plead the case for financial help. According to Thomson, 'the subsidy was apparently obtained by a threat on the part of Lansbury [the editor] that otherwise the paper would have to turn "Right"'.[11] There is some evidence for this assertion in the decrypted telegrams of Litvinov who cabled Chicherin in mid-June: 'If we do not support the "Daily Herald" which is now passing through a fresh crisis paper will have to turn [to] "Right" trade union'. Unlike other decrypted Soviet telegrams in 1920, however, this intercept came not from GC & CS but from Lord Kilmarnock, the British minister in Berlin, who obtained it from 'an absolutely sure source' which he was 'not at liberty to reveal'.[12] As well as seeking funds for the *Daily Herald*, Meynell became by his own later admission 'a willing carrier' from Litvinov to both the Trade Delegation and Theodore Rothstein, a pre-war Russian émigré who was the chief Comintern representative in Britain until he left in August 1920 and was refused readmission. At Litvinov's request, Meynell brought jewels 'sometimes from Denmark, sometimes from Sweden, once from Finland' which were sold in London to subsidise various pro-Bolshevik causes. Conscious that Thomson's 'sleuths' were on his track, Meynell used a variety of stratagems to smuggle the jewels back to England. On one occasion he brought two strings of pearls from Copenhagen buried in a jar of Danish butter. On another occasion he posted a large box of expensive chocolate creams, each containing a pearl or diamond, to a friend in London, the philosopher (and later star of the BBC radio Brains Trust) Cyril Joad. Once back in London he was taken to Scotland Yard and searched in vain. Two days later Meynell and his wife recovered the chocolate creams from Joad ('a greedy eater' in Meynell's view) and 'spent a sickly hour sucking the chocolates and so retrieving the jewels'. On his return from another 'jewel-trip' Meynell was stopped and his baggage searched. Nothing was found. 'The sleuths were helpful', Meynell later recalled, 'but I found it difficult to thank them and at the same time prevent three large diamonds in my mouth from rattling'. Once placed on the London market, however, the diamonds in Meynell's mouth, like most other jewels smuggled in by other Soviet couriers, were quickly identified. Neither Meynell nor the Russians realised that Russian diamonds were cut in a distinctive style which made it easy for both London jewellers and the Special Branch to identify them.[13]

Early in August 1920 Krasin returned to England to resume negotiations with Lloyd George. This time he was accompanied by Lev Kamenev, president of the Moscow Soviet and head of the Moscow Communist party, who now became head of the trade mission. Together, Kamenev and Krasin smuggled in a large consignment of precious stones, mostly diamonds, and platinum. The trade delegation's speedy sale of most of its treasure chest was closely watched by Thomson. 'Rumour of these large disposals', he reported, 'has brought Jew dealers from all parts of Europe to London'. He obtained a photograph of 'two of the largest gems' and carefully noted the banknote numbers of much of the proceeds. Within a few weeks the *Herald* was supplied with £75,000. Smaller sums were given to other left-wing periodicals and to the Communist Party of Great Britain (CPGB) on its foundation in August.[14] The Trade Delegation subsequently discovered that most, if not all, of these subsidies, were monitored by Thomson. Krasin reported to Litvinov on 10 September in a telegram decrypted by GC & CS: 'All our payments in banknotes are controlled by Scotland Yard'.[15]

The Second Congress of Comintern, which met in the summer of 1920, adopted 'twenty-one conditions', mostly drafted by Lenin, imposing what amounted to military discipline on the infant CPGB as on all its other members. Labour leaders had good reason to describe the CPGB as 'intellectual slaves of Moscow'. But the servitude was freely, even joyously, entered into. One of the more critical British delegates wrote after his return from the Comintern Congress: 'It is fairly evident that to many Communists Russia is not a country to learn from, but a sacrosanct Holy of Holies to grovel before as a pious Mohammedan faces the Mecca in his prayers'.[16] The 'twenty-one conditions' required total and unconditional support of Soviet Russia by legal as well as illegal means, including subversion in the armed forces:

> It is necessary to have systematic propaganda and agitation in the armed forces and the organisation of Communist cells in every military unit. This work by Communists will for the most part have to be conducted illegally.

The Soviet-dominated executive committee of Comintern, headed by Gregori Zinoviev, took care at regular intervals to spell out to member parties what was expected of them.

MI5 viewed Comintern's commitment to military subversion with peculiar horror and almost continuous concern. For most of the interwar period Kell had an exaggerated fear of the long-term impact of Communist propaganda in the armed services. During the war DORA regulation number forty-two had made 'any act calculated or likely to cause mutiny, sedition or disaffection among any of His Majesty's forces' punishable by life imprisonment (or death if the act was intended to assist an enemy). To Kell's dismay the Commons rejected an attempt to embody this draconian regulation in the 1919 Army Act on the sensible grounds that it would tend to stifle legitimate criticism of the peacetime army. He denounced the lack of legislation specifically directed against civilian attempts to stir up 'disaffection' in the services as a 'serious gap in the national armour'. For the next fifteen years MI5 campaigned within Whitehall for new legislation. In 1934 its long campaign succeeded at last.[17]

In the summer of 1920, however, the government was far more concerned by subversion in the labour movement than in the armed forces. 'Labour opposition to the Government', wrote Thomson in a retrospective survey of 'revolutionary movements' during 1920, 'reached its zenith during August'. 'Even moderate trade unionists', he reported, were in 'a surprising state of excitement.'[18] The chief cause of the excitement was a dramatic turning of the tide in the Russo-Polish war in favour of the Bolsheviks. By the time Kamenev and Krasin had their first joint meeting with Lloyd George on 4 August, the prime minister feared the war would end in total Polish defeat. *The Times* and the *Daily Herald* for once agreed both with each other and with Lloyd George that the situation was 'the most dangerous one that had arisen since 1914'.

The labour movement inevitably feared that Allied intervention against the Bolsheviks was once again imminent. The Poles indeed were already being assisted by a French military mission of 600 officers. On 4 August Arthur Henderson, as secretary of the Labour Party, telegraphed local branches urging them to organise mass demonstrations against intervention. The popular response during the following weekend (7–8 August) made a deep impression on Thomson who usually relied on the summer holidays to defuse labour unrest. He told the cabinet:

> There were remarkable demonstrations against war in practically every part of the country and in spite of the holiday season audiences which generally number a hundred or so grew to thousands ... Some fifty reports received on this subject may be summed up in the words of my Lancashire correspondent, who writes: 'Never have we known such excitement and antagonism to be aroused against any project as has been aroused amongst the workers by the possibility of war with Russia'.

On 9 August the Parliamentary Labour Party, the Labour Party Executive and the Parliamentary Committee of the T.U.C. met at the Commons and formed a Council of Action to oppose intervention by extra-parliamentary means. Across the country 350 local councils quickly sprang up. Four days later delegates representing the entire labour movement met to support the Council of Action and resolved to resist intervention by 'any and every form of withdrawal of labour which circumstances may require'. For the first time the whole labour movement had resolved to use industrial action for political ends. 'It means', said the Labour M.P. and trade-union leader J.H. Thomas, 'a challenge to the whole Constitution of the country'.

The challenge, however, never materialised. Lloyd George had no intention of being drawn into intervention and accused the Council of Action of 'swinging

... a sledge hammer against an open door ... merely for purposes of display'. With another turn in the tide of war, the case for intervention virtually collapsed. On 16 August at the gates of Warsaw the Polish forces won an unexpected victory and the rapid Soviet advance turned into precipitate retreat. But the Soviet intercepts decrypted by GC & CS disclosed that Kamenev had deliberately misled Lloyd George over the terms of peace the Bolsheviks had intended to impose on a defeated Poland. In particular he had concealed the Russian aim to set up a 'civic militia' of armed Polish workers, more powerful than the weakened Polish army, to bring about a Communist coup. Even Chicherin was alarmed that when the real peace terms were discovered there would be 'an impression of perfidy'. And so there was.[19]

Thomson saw two reasons for the unprecedented support for politically motivated strikes during the normally quiescent holiday season. The first was 'genuine fear of conscription' due to the Polish crisis. But the second was 'artificial agitation directly controlled from Moscow by means of the Russian Trading Delegation':

> ... The 'Daily Herald', having the advantage of close association with the Delegation and the opportunity of increasing its funds from Russia by faithful service to the Soviet Government, was able by skilful perversion and suppression of news to work even moderate trade unionists into a surprising state of excitement.[20]

Despite the Polish victory at the battle of Warsaw, the fears aroused by the founding of the Council of Action and the subversive intrigues of the Trade Delegation did not quickly subside. Service and intelligence chiefs feared a general strike leading on to attempted revolution. On 17 and 18 August the Chief of the Imperial General Staff, Field-Marshal Sir Henry Wilson, met both his own staff and the chiefs of staff of all home commands to prepare for 'a possible war with the "Council of Action"'. MI5 put the number of ex-servicemen among the 'revolutionaries' at about 100,000 and emphasised that the extremists among them 'meant business'.[21] Wilson could scarcely contain his sense of outrage that the Trade Delegation was being allowed to stay in England while revolution was in the air. On 18 August he composed an indignant memorandum which he believed might force his resignation, summarising the evidence of the intercepts:

> These telegrams establish beyond all possibility of dispute three amazing and disturbing facts:-
>
> 1. That Kameneff and Krassin while enjoying the hospitality of England are engaged, with the Soviet Government, in a plot to create red revolution and ruin in this country.

2. That Kameneff and the Soviet Government are engaged in a plot to split the Alliance and the Friendship between England and France.
3. That the 'Council of Action' is in the closest touch and collaboration with the Russian Soviet for the downfall and ruin of England.

In view of the dispersion of our Forces, in view of the dangerous weakness to which we are reduced in every theatre but more particularly in Great Britain, and in view of the insidious and disloyal propaganda to which all of His Majesty's Forces are being subjected it is a military necessity to expose the whole of this traitorous combination, to explain to the troops what it is they may be called upon to fight and to make clear to them by drastic action against both the "Council of Action" and the Russian delegates in England what attitude His Majesty's Government is going to adopt in this matter. Without such action I cannot say what may happen in the event of a Revolutionary attempt by the "Council of Action" in Great Britain and by affiliated societies in Ireland, Egypt, Mesopotamia, India and other theatres.

I await the decision of the Government.[22]

For some time the suspicion had been growing in Wilson's increasingly agitated mind that the prime minister was a secret Bolshevik '*deliberately shepherding England into chaos and destruction*'. 'Is L.G. a traitor?', he wrote on 23 July; 'I have often put this query in my Diary'. The intercepts, he told his diary on 17 August, were 'a most terrifying set of telegrams and the most terrifying part of it all is the fact that L.G. and his Cabinet read all of this and *are afraid* to fling Kameneff & Krassin out of England'.[23]

Lloyd George treated the intercepts with a coolness and objectivity beyond the capacity, and sometimes the comprehension, both of his service and intelligence chiefs and of most of his ministers. He freely acknowledged that 'The Soviet delegates have been guilty of a flagrant breach of the conditions under which they were permitted to enter England'. But there was, he argued:

An undoubted advantage in our being able to tap these messages as it gives us real insight into Bolshevist interests and policy. That is an undoubted gain. If these delegates were expelled that source of information would be cut off.

The two crucial issues, in Lloyd George's view, were whether the 'propaganda engaged in by the delegates' was dangerous, and whether their expulsion would help to stop it. To both questions he replied in the negative. Bolshevik propaganda was so crude that it did 'more to discredit Bolshevism than any amount of general abuse directed against it'. Subsidising the *Daily Herald* and similar acts of subversion could in any case be done just as effectively from abroad.[24] Most of the cabinet, like most of the intelligence and service chiefs, disagreed. Men who would subsidise the *Daily Herald* were, in their view, men who would stop at nothing.

But for Lloyd George, the evidence of the intercepts would almost certainly have persuaded the cabinet to expel the Russian delegation and bring the trade negotiations to an end. As the price of continuing negotiations, however, the prime minister had to agree to the public disclosure of at least some of the evidence of Soviet subversion. Although Sir Henry Wilson did not know it when he composed his furious demand for government action on 18 August, the cabinet had already decided to publish a selection of the intercepts. On the same day, eight intercepted messages concerning Soviet subsidies to the *Daily Herald* were given to all national newspapers (except the *Herald*) for publication on the following day. All were wireless messages in the 'Marta' cipher. It was doubtless hoped that the Russians might not realise that their cable telegrams in other ciphers were also being intercepted and decrypted. In a further attempt to limit the intelligence damage, the press was asked to say that the messages had been obtained from 'a neutral country'; it was thus hoped to mislead the Russians into believing that there had been a leak from the entourage of Maxim Litvinov in Copenhagen. Most newspapers played the game. *The Times* did not. To Lloyd George's fury, it began its story with the words: 'The following wireless messages have been intercepted by the British Government'. The Russians paid little attention.[25] Either they did not read their *Times* attentively, or they carelessly concluded that, save for the Marta cipher, their ciphers were still secure.

Pressure rapidly built up in Whitehall for further public revelations of Soviet subversion. The threat of a new strike wave inevitably added to anxieties about the machinations of the Trade Delegation. On 30 August a miners' ballot produced a large majority in favour of strike action. A meeting of the Triple Alliance on the following day called for the miners' wage demands to be 'conceded forthwith'. On 1 September Wilson, Thomson and 'Quex' Sinclair, the DNI, sent Churchill a joint memorandum which concluded:

> The presence of the Russian Trading Delegation has become in our opinion the gravest danger which this country has had to face since the Armistice.
>
> This being so, we think that the publication of the de-cyphered cables has become so imperative that we must face the risks that will be entailed.

As prime minister in the Second World War Churchill would have been horrified by any proposal which might compromise the work of GC & CS. But in 1920 he was 'convinced that the danger to the state which has been wrought by the intrigues of these revolutionaries and the disastrous effect which will be produced on their plans by the exposure of their methods outweighs all other considerations'. Sinclair, who as DNI was responsible for GC & CS, admitted that the codebreakers were 'very concerned' by the likely effect of further revelations on their work, but he overrode their objections:

> ... I am most strongly of opinion that publication of the telegrams offers such an opportunity of dealing a death blow to the revolutionary movement in this country as may never occur again. I will go so far as to say that *even if the publication of the telegrams was to result in not another message being decoded, then the present situation would fully justify it.*[26]

Curzon, the foreign secretary, was later to be responsible for publishing a further set of Soviet intercepts. But in September 1920 he was far less concerned with the merits (or otherwise) of publication than with the urgent necessity to expel the Trade Delegation. Thomson's weekly reports demonstrated, he believed, that 'the revolutionary virus is spreading with dangerous rapidity among the classes with whose leaders these men are in daily contact'. The intercepts also revealed that the Russian delegates were 'constantly in the company of notorious agitators ... behind much of the trouble in India'. As a former viceroy Curzon read with a deep sense of personal outrage the evidence of a Soviet plot to undermine the Raj from both within and without. The Russians, he declared, had been 'pressing upon the Amir of Afghanistan a treaty aimed directly at our Indian Empire' and had already 'plunged Northern Persia into peril and anarchy'.[27]

Though determined not to sacrifice the prospect of a trade agreement, Lloyd George felt it prudent to respond to the sense of outrage which united most of his ministers, service and intelligence chiefs. He therefore decided on a showdown with the chief villain, Kamenev, while allowing the rest of the Soviet delegation to remain in London. At a meeting with the delegation on 10 September the prime minister declared that he had 'very disagreeable' things to say about Kamenev. Krasin had, so far as he knew, remained 'faithful to the honourable pledge which he gave'. But Kamenev had been guilty of a 'gross breach of faith'. He had secretly subsidised the *Daily Herald* and intrigued with the Council of Action. For these reasons, said Lloyd George, Kamenev would have been expelled had he not in any case been leaving for Russia on the following day. He would not be allowed to return. Lloyd George went on to accuse Kamenev of deliberate deception over the peace terms which the Bolsheviks had intended to impose on the Poles. 'I can', he added, 'make no more serious charge against any public person than that'. Kamenev denied it all. Lloyd George insisted, however, that he had 'irrefutable evidence'. While he was willing to continue discussions with Krasin, Kamenev's 'startling' denials were further proof of the impossibility of negotiating with him.[28]

The expulsion of Kamenev did little to mollify the main opponents of the trade delegation. Curzon, Churchill and Walter Long all wrote cabinet memoranda designed to demonstrate that Krasin, even if marginally less villainous, also deserved to be sent packing. Immediately after Kamenev's departure, GC & CS decrypted what Wilson considered 'a scandalous wire' from Chicherin to Krasin 'advocating the most barefaced "red" action over here'.[29] For some of those who shared Wilson's sense of outrage, the publication on 14 September of a letter from Kamenev to several M.P.s protesting his innocence was the last straw. On the same day the two leading anti-Bolshevik newspapers, the *Daily Mail* and the *Morning Post*, were given 'detailed accounts of the financial transactions between the Russian Trade Delegation and the *Daily Herald*', obtained from intercepted telegrams. Of the possible sources of this leak of secret information, an outraged intelligence officer is the most probable. The leakage of extracts from Russian intercepts to the *Daily Mail* provides a significant precedent for the leakage of the 'Zinoviev letter' to the same newspaper four years later.

The cabinet considered the disclosures on 15 September:

> The revelations in the 'Morning Post' and the 'Daily Mail' appeared to be based on official information and the premature issue of this, at the very moment when the government were considering the expediency of issuing a statement of this definite question, was generally deplored.[30]

Despite the urging of the intelligence and service chiefs, powerfully supported by Churchill, the cabinet decided to publish no further intercepts. Hankey, the cabinet secretary, believed that the decision was due mainly to his warnings of the danger of compromising GC & CS and to his argument that 'a very good case could be made' without publishing the intercepts. H.A.L. Fisher, the minister of education, drafted what Hankey considered 'an admirable communiqué' referring to 'evidence which flatly contradicts' Kamenev's statements but declining to identify the source.[31]

By the time the communiqué was issued cabinet indignation at the perfidy of the trade mission was overlaid by anxiety that a threatened miners' strike supported by the Triple Alliance would lead to a general strike. On 15 September even Lloyd George, though calmer than most of his ministers, enquired of Sir Henry Wilson whether the army was 'sound'. Wilson assured him that it was. Infantry battalions were being brought back from the Rhine and the Middle East to strengthen home forces. Civil preparations for a strike were stepped up by the cabinet's Supply and Transport Committee (STC) which had replaced the Industrial Unrest Committee in October 1919. Regional 'Civil Commissioners', chosen from junior members of the government, were briefed on their duties 'in the event of all communication with the Central Government breaking down'.[32]

The miners' strike, which eventually began on 18 October, showed up the

Lieutenant-Colonel
Thomas Best Jervis, the
founder and first
superintendent (1855–57)
of the Topographical and
Statistical Department of
the War Office.
(© *British Library*)

General Sir Patrick
MacDougall, the first head of
the Intelligence Branch at the
War Office (1873 78).
(*Courtesy of the Commandant,
British Army Staff College,
Camberley*)

General Sir Henry Brackenbury, the first director of Military Intelligence (1886–91). (*Courtesy of the National Army Museum, London*)

Brigadier-General Sir James Edmonds, Royal Engineers, head of MO5 (1907–10). (*Courtesy of the National Army Museum, London*)

Captain Sir Mansfield Cumming, R.N.: "C"
(1909–23), shortly after the First World War.
(*Courtesy of Mrs Pippa Temple*)

The official portrait of Cumming
which hangs today in the office of
his successor.
(*Courtesy of Mrs Pippa Temple*)

The roof line of Whitehall Court,
Sir Mansfield Cumming's first
HQ, as it appears today.
(© *Jed Corbett, 1985*)

MI5's New Year card for 1918 was personally designed by its deputy head, Major (later Brigadier Sir) Eric Holt-Wilson, and the artist was Byam Shaw. It shows Subversion crawling towards a British fighting man, whose eyes are fixed firmly on the vision of Dieu et mon Droit and the coming victory. Just in time MI5, in the guise of a masked Britannia, impales Subversion with a trident bearing her monogram.
(© *Imperial War Museum*)

In the New Year card for 1920, the initials MIV are used once again to form an appropriate motto. An assortment of malevolents (Bolshevik revolutionaries, defeated Huns and Irish rebels) appear stage left, out to undermine Liberty and Security on her pedestal erected by the fighting and working men (stage right). But the subversives' every move is being noted by the attentive Special Branch policeman.
(*Courtesy India Office Library and Records*, © *British Library*)

The New Year card for 1921 was probably designed by MI5's first legal adviser, Walter Moresby. MI5 appears as a knight in shining armour amidst the "Troubles" and other perils preceding Irish independence. (*Courtesy India Office Library and Records,* © *British Library*)

With best wishes for 1922
from "The Old Firm"

MI5's greeting verse for 1922 is based on the lines of Heinrich Heine:

> *I don't know what it means*
> *That I am so sad.*
> *An eye that keeps me always in its gaze*
> *Follows me wherever I go.*

The metaphor becomes somewhat mixed. As well as being an ever-present eye, MI5 also remains a hidden hand (identified by an MI5 cuff-link). (*Courtesy of India Office Library and Records,* © *British Library*)

Ich weiss nicht was soll es bedeuten
Dass ich so traurig bin
Ein Aug' das stets auf mich aufpasst
Folgt mir wo auch immer ich bin.

Admiral Sir W. Reginald "Blinker" Hall,
director of Naval Intelligence (1914–18).
(*Courtesy of BBC Hulton Picture Library*)

Sir Alfred Ewing, director of Naval
Education (1902–17) and first head of Room
40, painted in 1929 by Henry Lintott RSA
in the robes of principal and vice-chancellor
of the University of Edinburgh.
(*Courtesy of the University of Edinburgh*)

Sir Basil Thomson, assistant commissioner
Metropolitan Police and head of the Special
Branch (1913–21), director of Intelligence
(1919–21).
(*Courtesy of BBC Hulton Picture Library*)

hollowness of the Triple Alliance. 'In spite of much verbal protestations of solidarity', wrote Thomson, 'there was throughout the crisis little fear that railwaymen or transport workers would strike in large numbers'.[33] Lloyd George settled the strike by agreeing an interim pay rise with the miners, leaving a more permanent settlement to be made when the mines (taken under state control during the war) were handed back to private ownership in 1921. But he also used the strike to push through the Commons in less than a week the Emergency Powers Act which received the Royal Assent on 29 October 1920. That Act made permanent the almost dictatorial wartime powers which the government had possessed under the Defence of the Realm Acts, and still remains the legal basis for government strike-breaking today. It was, A. J. P. Taylor has claimed, 'as big a blow against the traditional constitution as any ever levelled'.[34]

The hard-liners in the cabinet were also heartened by the imprisonment of several prominent pro-Bolsheviks. Thomson noted with satisfaction that the arrests 'damped the ardour of the agitators who seemed to have a strong aversion to prison'. The most prominent of those arrested, Sylvia Pankhurst of the famous suffragette family, now a dissident Communist, was sentenced to six months' imprisonment on 28 October for publishing seditious articles. But the arrest which gave Thomson most pleasure was probably that of a Comintern courier named Erkki Veltheim, detained on 25 October as he was leaving the home of the Communist M.P. Colonel L.'Estrange Malone. Veltheim was found in possession of a series of documents (one in a code cracked by GC & CS) which he was taking to Russia. These, in Thomson's view, 'threw considerable light on the British communist movement'. Chief among them was a training manual entitled 'The Red Officers' Course' intended for recruits to a British Red Army, which the outraged Detective-Inspector Fitch of the Special Branch called 'the most damnable stuff I have ever seen during my whole career'. Veltheim was sentenced to six months' hard labour followed by deportation. Malone was arrested in November after an Albert Hall meeting to celebrate the third anniversary of the Bolshevik Revolution (attended, according to Thomson, chiefly by 'aliens, Jews, Sinn Feiners and degenerates') at which he had spoken in favour of hanging 'a few Churchills or a few Curzons on lamp-posts'. Like Veltheim, he was sentenced to six months in jail.[35]

As evidence of Soviet-supported subversion mounted, Kell's resentment of Thomson's exclusive responsibility for monitoring all forms of civil subversion, labour unrest and revolutionary activity steadily increased. In October 1920 the American military attaché reported 'considerable antagonism' between Thomson and the more alarmist Kell:

Sir Basil has on several occasions urged the admission of certain people who were objectionable to MI5 or to the police authorities, and has used them as agents in the United Kingdom ... It is reasonable to suppose that some of the men have been acting in double capacity, taking pay from the British Secret Service while retaining their connection with Moscow. The result of recent controversies between Sir Vernon Kell and Sir Basil Thomson has been that disputed questions concerning individuals have been referred to Mr W. Haldane Porter, the head of the [Home Office] Aliens Service for final decision, and many of these references have placed him in a rather embarrassing situation as his decision was bound to incur the disapproval of one or other of these British officials.

By October Kell had persuaded the War Office that the Soviet threat to national security was now so serious that MI5 must investigate directly 'the activities of all Russians' and 'their sympathisers' in Britain. The American military attaché reported, not surprisingly, 'considerable irritation on the part of Sir Basil Thomson'.[36] His deputy added that there were now fears in Whitehall that the government would be accused of 'using the Military arm for espionage upon labor':

The work of British MI5 is now carried on under the plea that revolutionary agents are attempting to create trouble in the British Army and to discourage recruiting. If this matter is raised through questions in Parliament, the answer will be that this work is done for the defense and security of the country against foreign agitators. Officially the British MI5 is only concerned with civilian activities as they affect the army, but in reality and especially recently, they have concerned themselves in general with revolutionary and bolshevik agents, using the Suspect List, built up during the war and since added to, as a basis for operations.[37]

During the autumn of 1920 the Anglo-Soviet trade talks hung fire. In addition to the setback caused by recriminations over the trade delegation's interference in British affairs, the Anglo-Soviet exchange of prisoners, which Lloyd George had made a condition of negotiations, took several months to arrange. On 30 September and again on 12 October the cabinet postponed the resumption of talks. Only on 18 November, following the release of the last British prisoners from Soviet jails, did the cabinet agree to restart negotiations. Though foreign secretary, Curzon washed his hands of the whole affair. 'I desire to have nothing to do with the agreement myself,' he told his permanent undersecretary, Sir Eyre Crowe, in December 1920. The initiative for the resumption of talks came once again from the prime minister. Lloyd George's most persuasive argument with his colleagues was the prospect that Anglo-Soviet trade would create new jobs. With the end of the brief post-war boom unemployment rose rapidly from 318,000 in August 1920 to 2,078,000 in the following May – about twenty per cent of the industrial labour force. Sir Basil Thomson warned the cabinet in December 1920:

> Unemployment hangs like a dark shadow over the community. It is far from having touched the bottom, and if we may judge by the present temper of the men, serious disturbances are only a matter of time ...

'If the negotiations are broken off by the pompous obstinacy of Lord Curzon', declared the *Daily Herald*, 'it is the British workers, already scourged by unemployment, who will be the chief sufferers'.[38]

With the resumption of negotiations, GC & CS was able once again to provide a valuable insight into the Soviet bargaining position. It was clear from decrypted telegrams that Krasin was allowed real flexibility by the Politburo only on conditions of trade. On the cessation of hostile activities and propaganda against the British Empire and on the settlement of pre-revolutionary debts he was under strict instructions to make 'merely a statement of principles'.[39] Early in January 1921 Krasin left for Moscow bearing a draft agreement. By the time he did so, however, Britain had lost her main intelligence source on Soviet policy.

The Russians had failed to deduce the extent of British penetration of their code and cipher systems from the newspaper revelations of the previous summer. They were finally alerted on 19 December not by the indiscretions of the British but by a report from Mikhail Frunze, the commander of the Soviet forces fighting the White general, Baron Wrangel:

> It emerges from the report furnished to me today by Jamchenko, former head of the Wrangel radio station at Sevastopol, that absolutely all our ciphers are being deciphered by the enemy in consequence of their simplicity ... The overall conclusion is that all our enemies, particularly England, have all this time been entirely in the know about our internal work, military-operational and diplomatic.

A week later the Trade Delegation in London received instructions to conduct as much as possible of its correspondence by courier 'until the establishment of new cypher systems'. Those new systems, when introduced, at first defeated GC & CS. Sinclair reported to the cabinet on 22 March 1921 that 'although a large number of such telegrams are received daily, it is not possible at present to decypher them'.[40] Unaware of Frunze's warning of 19 December, Sinclair thought there was 'no doubt' that newspaper revelations of Soviet intercepts during the previous summer were to blame. Conveniently forgetting his own earlier insistence that 'even if the publication of the telegrams was to result in not another message being decoded, then the present situation would fully justify it', Sinclair concluded sanctimoniously in a secret memorandum to the cabinet secretary:

This state of affairs was forecasted by the Director of Naval Intelligence when the publication of the telegrams referred to was under consideration in August 1920.

Rear-Admiral Sinclair begs to again point out that if this form of intelligence is employed for the purposes of publicity, there appears to be a very grave danger that the fighting Services and the Government may lose it altogether.[41]

By the time Krasin returned to London to resume trade negotiations on 4 March the Soviet régime was in the midst of a major crisis. During February the Cheka had reported 118 risings by peasants and workers against the privations and repression of Bolshevik rule. On 1 March the sailors at the Baltic Fleet base on the island of Kronstadt, previously acclaimed by Trotsky as the 'beauty and pride' of the October Revolution, rose in revolt together with soldiers from the fortress garrison. On 8 March the Red Army, with Cheka machine-gunners in the rear to discourage deserters, tried and failed to storm the island base. On the 10th an 'experienced' SIS agent reached Kronstadt across the ice from Finland and reported back to Cumming's Helsinki station next day that the mood of the rebels was 'very confident, but anti-White', 'non-party but probably Soviet'. That assessment was almost certainly correct. Lenin himself acknowledged that 'They do not want the White guards and they do not want our power either'. Cumming's agent reported that though the rebels had at least six months' stock of ammunition, their food supplies would last only for another ten days. On 17 March 50,000 Red Army troops, camouflaged in white uniforms, stormed Kronstadt in a dawn attack across the ice, and after losing 10,000 men killed and wounded, finally crushed the mutiny around midnight.[42]

The Kronstadt rebellion hastened, though it did not cause, the announcement by Lenin of a major change in Bolshevik policy. Under 'War Communism' the Soviet economy had come close to collapse. Industrial production in 1921 sank to less than a third, and grain production to about two fifths, of the pre-war level. In the course of the year millions were to die of famine. At the Tenth Party Congress which met during the Kronstadt rebellion, Lenin abruptly announced that 'War Communism' was to be abandoned for the 'New Economic Policy' (NEP). Food requisitioning was stopped, private trading and small-scale private enterprise were restored.

The shift in economic policy made the Soviet régime all the more anxious for a trade agreement with Britain. Intent on a swift settlement, Krasin brought back to London only minor modifications to the draft accord he had taken to Moscow two months before. Talks resumed on 11 March, concluded on the 14th, and the Anglo-Soviet trade agreement was signed on the 16th. The Russian trade mission in London now became a permanent presence; a British trade mission in Moscow opened in August. Though diplomatic relations did not follow for another three years, Soviet Russia had taken the first crucial step to acceptance by the international community. Within little more than a year of the accord with Britain, trade agreements followed with Germany, Italy, Sweden, Norway, Austria and Czechoslovakia.[43]

So far from producing a calmer period in Anglo-Soviet relations, however, the trade agreement led to further long and acrimonious disputes. The agreement was subject to one major condition, set out in a preamble: 'that each party refrains from hostile action or undertakings against the other and from conducting outside of its own borders any official propaganda direct or indirect against the institutions of the British Empire or the Russian Soviet Republic respectively'. Arguments over the interpretation of that preamble were to embitter Anglo-Soviet relations for the remainder of the decade. Curzon, Churchill and Montagu (the secretary of state for India) had gained the formal agreement of their colleagues 'That, in the case of the Agreement being concluded, it should be understood that the Russian Government would not be allowed to escape responsibility for hostile propaganda by sheltering itself behind the activities of the "Third International"'.[44] The Soviet government sought to do just that, implausibly insisting that Comintern was an international organisation over which it had no control.

On 1 April 1921 the Foreign Office opened a new file entitled 'Violations of the Russian Trade Agreement'. 'I hope it may remain a slender one,' wrote a Foreign Office official. 'It will not,' replied Lord Curzon grimly.[45] For the moment GC & CS was unable to break the new Russian code and cipher systems introduced at the beginning of the year. But there was no shortage of evidence for the new file from other intelligence services.

On 8 April Thomson forwarded to the Foreign Office the copy of an intercepted letter sent from Moscow on 28 March by H. Watkyn, a British delegate to the Bolshevik-dominated Red International of Labour Unions (RILU or Profintern), to a comrade in Manchester, announcing RILU's despatch of £4,000 to its British supporters and its decision that 'India should be tackled at once'. The letter was, said Thomson, 'fairly definite evidence that the Russians do not intend to adhere to the stipulations of the Trade Agreement'. By the time his letter arrived, Watkyn expected Britain to be 'in the throes of another industrial upheaval of gigantic proportions, which should certainly move a step forward towards the world revolution'. He was particularly cheered by the news of 'revolutionary work among the miners' and signs of their 'speedy conversion from Yellow to Red'.[46] During the first quarter of 1921 intense competition from the revived French and German coal industries almost halved the price per ton of British coal exports. Faced with increasing losses in the mines the government decided to hand them back to their pre-war owners five months earlier than planned, on 31 March. The owners demanded wage cuts. The miners refused. On 1 April the owners began a lock-out and the miners appealed to the Triple Alliance to strike in sympathy.

The Supply and Transport Committee (STC) ordered a series of emergency measures including the suspension of horse racing 'both in order to save coal and petrol and in order to bring home to the public the seriousness of the situation'. The CIGS, Sir Henry Wilson, believed 'we should prepare for & consider the worst' and was summoned to address the cabinet on 4 April where he enjoyed himself 'frightening the Frocks'. He was authorised to summon infantry units back from Ireland, Malta and the Rhine, to concentrate tanks and armoured cars at London, Glasgow, York and Worcester, and to establish a special camp for cavalry and infantry in Kensington Gardens.[47]

All this excitement ended in anti-climax. The transport and rail leaders announced a strike in sympathy with the miners from 10 p.m. on Friday 15 April. A few hours before the deadline they called it off. 'Black Friday', as the Labour movement was to remember it, destroyed the Triple Alliance. *The Communist* weekly published a double-page drawing of the Last Supper depicting J.H. Thomas, the general secretary of the NUR, as Judas. In an unsuccessful last-minute attempt to prevent a libel suit, a bag containing thirty pieces of silver was erased from Thomas's hands. The trial before Lord Justice Darling contained a few moments of farce almost worthy of the Pemberton Billing case three years before. At one point Darling ordered Arthur McManus, chairman of the Communist Party, to stand up. McManus did not move. 'Stand up, I say!' repeated the judge. 'Did you hear me? Stand up!' McManus was a shorter man than Darling realised. 'I *am* standing up, my Lord', he replied. Thomas was awarded £2,000 damages.[48]

'Black Friday' left the STC, according to Hankey's assistant, Tom Jones, feeling 'very sick':

> They had been waiting for two years to press the button. They had pressed it ... But Jim Thomas upset it all and despoiled Sir Hindenburg Geddes [chairman of the STC] of the fruits of victory ...[49]

Sir Basil Thomson was quick to emphasise, however, how close the country had come to anarchy and how much the credit for its fortunate escape belonged to Scotland House and the PCOs abroad:

> During the past few weeks Communism has made great strudes [*sic*] in the United Kingdom, but if there had been no Passport Control system it is believed that the present Labour crisis would have been accompanied by scenes of violence amounting to an attempted revolution, which would have greatly damaged the national credit abroad and even the stability of the civilised world.[50]

At the beginning of July the miners were forced to settle on the owners' terms. Horse racing resumed and Thomson told the cabinet to relax: 'The general aspect of labour is more peaceful now than it has been for several years'. With unemployment at over two million, labour militancy was at a low ebb.[51]

By the summer of 1921 Soviet subversion in India and on India's borders seemed – at least to the Foreign Office – a more serious menace than in Britain itself. Curzon denounced the Soviet threat to India in apocalyptic terms. 'The Russian menace in the East', he told the cabinet, 'is incomparably greater than anything else that has happened in any time to the British Empire'. The secretary of state for India, Lord Montagu, also believed that India was 'the main objective of Bolshevik foreign policy', and rashly concluded that much of the unrest attributed to Gandhi and the non-cooperation movement was 'really due to undiscovered ramifications of international revolutionaries'.[52]

Montagu assured the Commons in March 1921 that Bolshevik activities in India were being countered with 'every step necessary to checkmate them'.[53] At the centre of the anti-Bolshevik campaign was the intelligence bureau of the Indian government's Home Department, better known as the Delhi Intelligence Bureau (DIB), headed from 1919 to 1924 by Colonel (later Sir) Cecil Kaye. In addition to intercepting the correspondence of suspected subversives and running a substantial network of informers,[54] Kaye also exchanged intelligence with the metropolitan intelligence services through his London liaison office, Indian Political Intelligence (IPI). According to DIB, 'definite and continuing relations between Moscow and Indian revolutionaries' began in October 1920. Chattopadhyaya, regarded by the Raj as 'the doyen of Indian revolutionaries living abroad', was promised help by Lenin 'if he could produce a mandate signed by leading Indian revolutionaries and Communists'. During the early months of 1921, carefully monitored by Cumming's agents, Chattopadhyaya assembled a group of Indian 'revolutionaries' in Berlin, whence they proceeded to Moscow in May. They were, however, preceded by M.N. Roy, founder of a rival group of Indian Communists, who persuaded Lenin that the Chattopadhyaya group was nationalist rather than Communist. Kaye's successor as head of DIB, Sir David Petrie, wrote seven years later:

> Roy's group was unconditionally recognised as the one with which the Communist International would work, and it was agreed to start 'intensified propaganda in India', for which the Soviet Government undertook to provide ample funds. From that time onwards Roy has managed to retain the ascendancy he then acquired, and though his position has at times appeared to be shaky, he has managed somehow or other to cling to it.[55]

In February 1921 Cumming's espionage agency, now usually known within Whitehall as the Secret Intelligence Service (SIS), claimed to have discovered a major new intelligence source. At a time when GC & CS was unable to break the new Soviet codes, Cumming believed he had found an alternative method of intercepting Soviet communications. The SIS station chief in the Esthonian capital Reval (now Tallinn), Colonel Ronald Meiklejohn, reported that 'an agent whose reliability has been proved on many occasions', codenamed B.P.11, had successfully penetrated the Reval office of Maxim Litvinov, Soviet deputy commissar for foreign affairs, and gained access to its code department. During the next few months B.P.11 (probably a Volga German named Gregory) provided more than two hundred 'summaries and paraphrases' of telegrams exchanged between Litvinov in Reval, Russian leaders in Moscow, and the Trade Delegation in London. The most sensational of these intercepts were those which described Soviet aid (mostly channelled via the London Trade Delegation) to two Sinn Fein 'germ cells' in Ireland. The term 'germ cell', according to SIS, was 'used by the Bolsheviks to denote the small Communist groups which they insinuate into unions and movements of any character suitable to their purpose'. According to B.P.11, a telegram from Zinoviev to Litvinov of 19 March contained 'instructions to notify "germ cell" no. 31 in Dublin to act as pre-arranged by 27 April'. Cumming reported that SIS had issued 'instructions with regard to the proposed action in Dublin on [*sic*] 27th April'; what those instructions were remains unclear. A further telegram to Litvinov of 23 March told him 'to ascertain whether Krasin, in accordance with instructions given him, was in contact with "germ cell" no. 31'. On 29 March Zinoviev sent two more telegrams to Litvinov. The summary of the first provided by B.P.11 instructed: 'Find out how many arms at disposal of "germ cells" in Dublin'. The second added: 'Must subsidise "germ cells" in Dublin with £50,000 through Krasin'.[56]

Curzon was greatly excited by B.P.11's evidence of Bolshevik intrigues in Ireland. He minuted on 13 April: 'Please keep a particular eye on the Irish question. This would bring home to the Cabinet the character of this conspiracy more quickly than anything else.' More dramatic Irish intelligence quickly followed. B.P.11 reported that Litvinov had sent two telegrams to Bukharin on 13 April:

From Vienna five agitators sent to "germ cell" no. 30 in Ireland. April 21st, expect result activities "germ cell" no. 30 in Ireland as per instructions given to Krassin.

Bukharin was said to have replied with two telegrams on 23 April:

Inform Krassin to instruct "germ cell" no. 30 to act quickly and carefully, and that £195,000 sterling is assigned for the month of May for this.

Warn Krassin that "germ cell" no. 31 is acting too indiscreetly and that greater caution must be exercised.

Some of Curzon's officials were by now less impressed than their minister by B.P.11's sensational reports. Esmond Ovey of the Northern Department minuted on 18 May: 'Sir R. Nathan [of SIS] tells me they have been unable to discover anything more about these two germ cells'. Curzon replied on the same day:

> But surely the evidence is damning and sufficient although the file is quite imperfect. Please put up to me the entire case.[57]

By now, however, the 'the entire case' had begun to crumble. B.P.11 had still failed to provide more than 'summaries and paraphrases' of the Reval telegrams: 'Through fear of compromising his agents and owing to the close watch maintained over this organisation our representative has not yet felt justified in attempting to secure the originals of these telegrams'. According to a 'Secret Report' of 20 May:

> Sir Basil Thomson is not convinced that the telegrams are authentic because no evidence can be traced of the money having been drawn by Krassin in London or transmitted to Ireland, the Sinn Fein are in serious financial difficulties and no reply from Krassin to Reval has been intercepted.

SIS still considered it 'hardly possible that the long series of telegrams could be a forgery'. The confidence of the Foreign Office in B.P.11 had, however, been severely shaken. On a secret report of 21 June summarising thirty-six further 'decoded telegrams' from Reval, R.C. Lindsay (assistant undersecretary) minuted simply: 'But the Reval source of information is a little doubtful'. Curzon initialled the minute and added no comment of his own. Thereafter B.P.11 seems to have been discredited. There is no further reference to the Reval intercepts in the Foreign Office files, and the interdepartmental committee on Bolshevism, which reported on 1 July, ignored them altogether.[58]

Two other forms of secret intelligence on Bolshevik policy were, however, now available. By the end of April GC & CS was once again able to decrypt, at least in part, the telegrams exchanged between Moscow and Soviet representatives in London and the Middle East. Indeed, the real intercepts decrypted by GC & CS had helped to discredit the bogus intercepts from Reval. The intelligence chiefs, chastened by the loss of the Russian codes earlier in the year, were now far more anxious than before to conceal the success of their codebreakers. Lindsay minuted after the meeting of the interdepartmental committee on Bolshevism on 1 July:

I was struck by the extreme anxiety of the experts present to do nothing which would make the Bolsheviks suspect we are still reading their telegrams. This, of course, makes it difficult to cite facts in support of our charges against the Moscow Government. Sir B. Thomson said he did not at all like the prospect of having to face even three weeks without intercepts.[59]

An alternative intelligence source was, however, available, from which 'to cite facts in support of our charges against the Moscow Government'. SIS also provided the interdepartmental committee on Bolshevism (whose 'vigilance committee' began fortnightly meetings in July) with a series of documents which it claimed to have secretly obtained from the office of Kopp, the Soviet representative in Berlin. By September 1921 Curzon believed that sufficient evidence had been obtained to indict the Soviet government of breaching the undertaking in the trade agreement without compromising GC & CS. Most of this evidence concerned Soviet subversion in India and on India's borders, much of it obtained by SIS in Berlin. On 7 September he dispatched a protest note to Hodgson, the British representative in Moscow, for delivery to Chicherin. The note was, he told Hodgson, 'based on evidence which has been most carefully examined by an interdepartmental committee, and which must be regarded as irrefutable'.[60]

The presentation of the note did not, according to Hodgson, produce 'the paralysing effect which might have been expected'. The Soviet reply was somewhat disconcerting:

A cursory glance over the document on its delivery was sufficient to enable the People's Commissary for Foreign Affairs to state to Mr Hodgson that the charges contained therein are either unfounded or based on false information and forgeries ... In an attempt to follow up these forgeries to their sources, the Russian Government came across a document published in Germany under the title 'Ostinformation', published by an anonymous group of detectives and supplied mostly to counter-revolutionary papers and to secret agents of various Governments anxious to obtain secret documents on Soviet Russia ... It is surely no mere coincidence that the majority of the apocryphal reports and speeches of Stalin, Eliava, Nuorteva, Karakhan, and Lenin are to be found in the bulletin of the German detectives practically in the same wording as they are cited in the British note ...

It was, indeed, 'no mere coincidence'. After seeing copies of *Ostinformation*, Hodgson reported home: 'Everything points to our having been unfortunate in the selection of some of the data advanced in support of our allegations.'[61] Despite assurances to the contrary from SIS, J.D. Gregory, the head of the

Northern Department, could not 'help half-wondering whether there is not some foundation for the Bolshevik assertions':

> Berlin is certainly full of White Russians, all probably ready to make money by selling forgeries, and it is precisely through these White Russians that our documents are obtained, i.e. it is they who are the actual instruments in obtaining them from Kopp.

However, after an SIS investigation, Gregory thought it 'fairly safe to assume ... that, if any forgeries have crept in, they are very few'. 'I hope so', commented Curzon. 'But I do not quite like it'. He liked it even less a week later after his officials had been through the evidence. On being told that 'the bulk of our information did come from, or is at any rate in suspicious identity with, tainted sources (the German paper)' and that 'we can only substantiate 2 or possibly 3 of our charges', Curzon exploded with rage: 'I am positively appalled ... at the entire history of this case'. He vented his wrath on both his own advisers and SIS. He had relied upon the interdepartmental committee to investigate the evidence and draw up charges, and had 'never interfered' with its investigations. It had then handed him a document which he should never have signed. As for SIS, 'I infer from the whole case that ... S.I.S. does rely, or has relied, on the German sources of information. If so I regard the position with dismay'.[62]

The British reply to the Soviet reply was one of the most curious compositions produced by the Foreign Office in modern times. Curzon felt unable to ignore (and thus 'imply acceptance of') the charge of forgery. But in order to deny it he was forced into terminological inexactitude. His denial that any part of his protest had been drawn from *Ostinformation* was true – if at all – only in the sense that documents published by *Ostinformation* had probably been purchased by SIS before publication. At other points in his reply Curzon's confusion was such that he contradicted himself. In his protest note of 7 September he had quoted reports to the Third International by, among others, Stalin, 'president of the Eastern Section of the Third International', and Nuorteva, 'Director of the Department of Propaganda under the Third International' (who turned out to be in prison). In his further note of 12 November Curzon countered the Soviet claim that neither Stalin nor Nuorteva nor others named in his protest were members of the Comintern by the risible falsehood that: 'of none of these was it said that they belonged to the Third International – though the point is immaterial'.[63]

The inevitable consequence of the intelligence débâcles of 1921 was a tightening of security procedures. All information contained in intelligence reports had henceforth to be 'submitted to careful consideration, both as regards reliability and value'. The reports were given one of three gradings:

A.1. Those whose subject matter suggests their being regarded as of primary importance, and which are based on:

Original documents actually in the possession of S.I.S. or to which a representative of S.I.S. has had access.

Statements by agents of exceptional reliability in which the S.I.S. repose especial confidence for peculiar reasons.

A.2. Those which, for various reasons, cannot be classified as A.1, but which are of significance, both as regards subject matter and reliability.

B. Those of less importance, but the interest and reliability of which are such as to justify their being issued.

Intelligence consumers were also reminded that SIS reports 'should, of course, be considered in conjunction with reports from official sources'.[64]

Shortly after the fiasco of Curzon's protest notes, a committee of senior civil servants (Hankey, the cabinet secretary, Sir Warren Fisher and Sir Eyre Crowe, permanent undersecretaries at the Treasury and the Foreign Office) appointed by the cabinet in March 'to examine the Secret Service expenditure' issued their report.[65] Hankey and his colleagues directed most of their fire at Thomson's Directorate of Intelligence which they criticised both for overspending and for overlapping with the work of other intelligence services. In 1920, for example, Thomson had dispatched a fifteen-man troupe to Poland under a well known producer, according to the Foreign Office 'merely to photograph one or two streets and a few villages with peasants, etc.' for 'a Russian anti-Bolshevik propaganda film'.[66]

General Horwood, the commissioner of the Metropolitan police, seized the opportunity to add his own criticisms of Thomson. Doubtless to Kell's satisfaction, he sent the prime minister a lengthy memorandum denouncing 'the independence of the Special Branch' as 'a standing menace to the good discipline of the force'. He claimed that the Directorate of Intelligence was expensive, wasteful and inefficient, that Thomson failed to obey instructions to keep him informed, and that in 'no instance' had intelligence from Thomson led to successful police action against political crime:

... As to its information regarding Labour matters at home, I have recently called the attention of the Secretary of State to misleading and inaccurate reports by the Directorate of Intelligence to the Cabinet in regard to meetings of the unemployed in London itself ...

Sir Basil Thomson's organisation has achieved, probably undeservedly, a reputation for espionage on Labour which causes resentment among a proportion of the working classes ... English public opinion ... is most suspicious and resentful of anything approaching the Continental system of domestic espionage.[67]

Horwood insisted on a reorganisation which would place Thomson and the Special Branch firmly under his control. Thomson refused and was, in his own words, 'kicked out by the P.M.'[68] The cabinet, as a whole, was not consulted. There was a brief flurry of protest from some of the leading anti-Bolsheviks. Curzon was outraged to discover Thomson's 'enforced resignation' from the press:

> ... As chairman of the Committee that created his office and as For[eig]n Sec[retar]y, I am bound to say that I regard the loss of his services with consternation. He struck me as a very able and indefatigable public servant and – to us in the Foreign Office – as an invaluable sleuth hound ...[69]

Walter Long (now Viscount Long of Wraxhall), who had left the government earlier in the year, was 'amazed and distressed beyond measure' to hear of Thomson's removal: 'Of course this is not a question which can be discussed in Parliament, but I am quite confident that there is already a rising feeling of indignation and dismay'.[70] The question was, however, raised in parliament by none other than 'Blinker' Hall, now M.P. for a Liverpool constituency. Moving a motion for the adjournment on 3 November, he declared: 'There is no man who has been a better friend of England than Sir Basil Thomson'. His downfall was due not merely to his 'open enemies, the Bolsheviks, the Russians, the extremists', but to a secret plot. Amid what he described as 'the cheers and laughter of the extremists', Hall went on to suggest that the Labour Party had promised the government its support in return for Thomson's removal. Hall almost lost control of his own rhetoric as he denounced the 'unctuous tones' of Arthur Henderson, the Labour chief whip, and had to withdraw comments made, as he acknowledged, 'in the heat of my speech'. None the less he went on to force a division and forty-one Tory die-hards went into the lobbies with him to vote against the coalition government dominated by their own party.[71]

Thomson himself quickly elaborated a conspiracy theory similar to Hall's to explain his dismissal. His 'anti-Bolshevik and Communistic intelligence work' had, he declared, been 'interfering' with Lloyd George's plans to give diplomatic recognition to the Soviet government.[72] Thomson's subsequent career contained a strong element of black comedy. He took to writing volumes of reminiscences and detective stories with titles such as *Mr Pepper, Investigator*. In December 1925 Thomson and a Miss Thelma de Lava were arrested in Hyde Park on a charge of committing an act in violation of public decency. Despite character evidence for the defence by 'Blinker' Hall and the former home secretary, Reginald McKenna, Sir Basil was found guilty and fined five pounds. His supporters hinted darkly that he had been framed either by his enemies in the Met or by subversives.[73]

With Thomson's dismissal the Directorate of Intelligence disappeared, though the Special Branch remained. The outcry raised by Thomson's friends prevented Sir Joseph Byrne, the man originally chosen to succeed him, from taking over as assistant commissioner responsible for the Special Branch. Byrne was a Catholic and former head of the RIC, and many Tory die-hards felt, like Long, that 'it is most dangerous to put a *devout* Roman Catholic in charge of the Secret Service'.[74] Thomson's successor was instead Sir Wyndham Childs, whose deep respect for higher authority earned him the nickname 'Fido' in the Home Office.[75] Though Kell continued to chafe at his lack of authority to monitor 'civil' subversion, he undoubtedly found the pliable Childs a great improvement on the flamboyant, empire-building Thomson. Cumming also gained from Thomson's dismissal. In what had become known as Thomson's 'world work' – defined by the home secretary as 'getting information about sedition, seditious movements, dangerous movements all over the world, the attacks upon the British Empire, and so on' – Thomson had been able to collect foreign intelligence without reference to Cumming and to deal direct with PCOs on counter-subversion matters.[76] With Thomson's dismissal Cumming at last secured a monopoly of espionage and counter-intelligence work outside the United Kingdom and the British Empire, supplying foreign intelligence to the service ministries, to the Foreign Office (which had overall responsibility for SIS), and – in smaller quantities – to the India, Colonial and Home Offices.[77] The Foreign Office had originally seen the PCO system as only temporary. 'With the gradual return to peace conditions in Europe generally', it had concluded in July 1920, 'it may be possible to dispense with the passport control system altogether'. Cumming persuaded the Foreign Office to take a broader view. The PCO network became the main cover for secret service work in general rather than, as originally intended, simply a defence against Bolshevik subversion. It was, said Sir Eyre Crowe in 1923, 'extremely helpful to our Secret Service abroad, which, using it as a cover, could be run vastly more safely and economically than without it'. Since visa and other fees paid for the covert as well as the public side of passport control, 'if this cover were [to be] abolished, the Secret Service vote would have to be increased'.[78]

Twenty-three of the twenty-eight passport control offices in 1921 were in Europe. Of the extra-European offices two were in the Far East: at Vladivostock (not yet under Soviet control) and at Yokohama (moved to Tokyo in 1922). There were also two Middle Eastern offices at Constantinople and Beirut. The only station in the Americas was at New York, though a second was opened at Buenos Aires in 1922.[79] Cumming's main extra-European priority seems to have been to obtain intelligence on American preparations for chemical warfare on which the general staff were 'particularly anxious to have information'. SIS energies were, however, overwhelmingly concentrated in Europe. Cumming claimed to be obtaining 'valuable information and original documents bearing on the armed forces and internal conditions of

Germany' through the Netherlands, Switzerland and Czechoslovakia.[80] But by far the chief target of SIS until the early 1930s remained Soviet Russia. Ironically, Moscow was one of the few European capitals without a passport control office. Even when Anglo-Soviet diplomatic relations were established in 1924, Moscow remained too hostile an environment for a secure SIS station. SIS Soviet operations were conducted instead from states on Russia's borders, especially from Finland and the Baltic states. The general principle was established, but not fully followed, that passport control offices did not conduct operations against the states in which they were situated.[81]

The organisation of the small SIS headquarters was rudimentary, informal and largely determined by Cumming himself who had no great liking for bureaucratic routine. The main postwar innovation was the introduction of 'liaison officers' from MID and NID, Major Stewart Menzies and Commander (later Captain) 'Barmy' Russel, in 1919, followed by a Foreign Office representative, Major Malcolm 'Woolly' Woollcombe, in 1921. These three liaison officers headed what became known as 'circulating sections', assessing intelligence reports as they came in, passing what they judged of interest to the departments they represented, and advising on priorities for intelligence collection. Operations were run by Cumming and one or two assistants who acquired the name 'G officers'. Major Herbert Spencer administered the passport control organisation and Commander P. Stanley 'Pay' Sykes, a naval paymaster and old friend of Cumming, ran SIS finances.[82]

After the flurry caused by the exchange of notes in the autumn of 1921 a calmer period ensued in Anglo-Soviet relations. On the British side, Curzon was not inclined to draft further protests with the humiliation of September still fresh in his mind. The initiative in Britain's Russian policy passed once again to Lloyd George, who looked forward to the Genoa conference of spring 1922 as an opportunity to reintroduce Russia to the international trading community. Russia, meanwhile, was in the grip of a major famine. The grain harvest in 1920 had been only fifty-four per cent of the pre-war average. In 1921 it sank to forty-three per cent. Millions died of hunger and disease, millions more roamed the countryside looking for food. In the summer of 1921 an emergency famine relief committee was formed, including several prominent non-Communists, to appeal for foreign aid 'from whatever source'. For a time the appalling problems of the famine left Soviet leaders with little energy for spreading the revolution abroad. According to a secret Foreign Office memorandum:

On the 4th June [1921], at a secret meeting of the leaders of the Communist Party, it was determined that until such time as the food supply of Russia was assured nothing in the way of active propaganda was to be carried on by the revolutionary parties outside Russia, and that the propaganda school at Tashkent was to be closed down. The Sinn Fein envoy, Macdonald, was informed at the same time that material help would not, for the moment, be forthcoming. Towards the end of the month the Indian revolutionaries were told that they would not receive the funds sanctioned in 1920. On the 28th August the agents of the Third International outside Russia were informed that direct action must cease until the Soviet Government had overcome its difficulties.[83]

This information, which does not appear to have been available to Curzon in September 1921, must, in retrospect, have made his protest note appear all the more ill-timed.

To Sidney Reilly, however, the problems of the Soviet economy suggested a further opportunity to bring down the Bolshevik régime. Ever since his Moscow adventures in 1918, Reilly had regarded the 'salvation of Russia' as 'a most sacred duty'. 'I also venture to think', he told Cumming at the end of the war, 'that the state should not lose my services. I would devote the rest of my wicked life to this kind of work.' Cumming promised to consult the Foreign Office about his future. The upshot of these consultations was that Reilly, whose erratic talents inspired even greater caution in the Foreign Office than in Cumming, was not taken on to Cumming's full-time staff but retained a looser association with SIS.[84]

For several years Reilly combined a variety of business ventures with the construction of sometimes fantastic schemes to bring about the downfall of the Bolsheviks. The main confederate in his schemes was Boris Savinkov, the veteran terrorist who had impressed both Maugham and Lockhart. Winston Churchill, who also met Savinkov in 1919, was captivated by him:

> I had never seen a Russian Nihilist except on the stage, and my first impression was that he was singularly well cast for the part. Small in stature; moving as little as possible, and that noiselessly and with deliberation; remarkably grey-green eyes in a face of almost deathly pallor; speaking in a calm, low, even voice, almost a monotone; innumerable cigarettes ... Boris Savinkov's whole life had been spent in conspiracy.

More romantically still, Churchill persuaded himself that Savinkov was a good terrorist, indeed 'a Terrorist for moderate aims'. During the Russo-Polish War of 1920 Savinkov established himself in Warsaw as head of a 'Russian Political Committee'. Churchill found his achievements 'little short of miraculous':

> Without funds, staff or equipment, with only his old friend General Pilsudski as protector, with an authority among the anti-Bolshevik Russians always doubtful and disputed, he nevertheless had by September, 1920,

collected 30,000 officers and men, and formed them into two organised corps.

These Savinkov proposed to 'push forward into Soviet territory collecting a huge snowball of Anti-Bolshies'.[85] The Foreign Office had a less romantic view than Churchill of Savinkov as a trustworthy 'Terrorist for moderate aims'. Sir Eyre Crowe considered him 'most unreliable and crooked'. With Polish independence secured at the gates of Warsaw in August 1920, Savinkov was told two months later by the British minister in Warsaw that his and other anti-Bolshevik forces could expect no further British support. 'It is a shame we are putting a spoke in his wheel', Churchill wrote to Lloyd George, 'I never thought you would allow it'.[86] Reilly was determined not to allow it. According to the Soviet records of his interrogation five years later, he confessed:

At the end of 1920, having become a rather close intimate of Savinkov's, I went to Warsaw, where Savinkov was then organising a foray into Byelorussia. I personally took part in the operation and was inside Soviet Russia. Ordered to return, I went back to London.[87]

The order, though Reilly's interrogation does not mention it, probably came from Cumming.

Early in 1921 Reilly began a new stage in his chequered business career. His main associate was the former military intelligence officer, Brigadier (later Major-General Sir) Edward Spears, who resigned as head of the British Military Mission in Paris in 1920 to enter business. Spears told his friend Winston Churchill that he had received an attractive offer from 'a big financial group interested in opening up Poland, the Ukraine and Rumania and in securing trade privileges in those countries for Great Britain'. Though out to make his 'fortune', Spears, like Churchill, was a supporter both of Savinkov and of further Allied intervention against the Bolsheviks. 'It is suggested', he told Churchill, 'I s[houl]d go on working with Savinkoff and Pilsudski, and I w[oul]d hope to continue giving you useful information'. Savinkov held out extravagant prospects of the vast economic resources waiting to be developed into areas of Russia liberated from Bolshevik control, praised Spears for his 'exceptional understanding of Russian affairs', and suggested him as a possible Allied High Commissioner in South Russia.[88]

Spears was also offered the opportunity to handle Czech radium exports and set up the Radium Company to do so. Reilly, with his wide experience of Eastern Europe, helped the still inexperienced Spears exploit his profitable connections with the Czechs. 'Reilly', said Spears later, 'accompanied me in the capacity of an able businessman which I certainly was not myself at the time'.[89] To begin with, Spears found Reilly 'rather seedy but really quite nice' and 'quite interesting'. Reilly's extrovert business style, however, proved disconcerting. Spears's brief diary entries for 1921 contain tantalising glimpses of Reilly 'playing the goat over phosphates' and taking Spears for a night out in Prague which ended with grateful Russian émigrés singing 'Gipsy songs to us overcome by R's generosity'. Some of Spears's British associates were 'not at all keen on Reilly' and Spears himself sometimes found him exasperating. 'I won't stand cheek,' he wrote in his diary after one 'rude' telegram from the master spy. But Spears also found Reilly's cosmopolitan experience indispensable, admired his endless ability to concoct new (if sometimes fantastic) business schemes, and tried to 'calm him' when he threatened to resign.[90]

Spears, like Reilly, remained in touch with Cumming. On 26 May he spent the 'whole morning' with him, probably to discuss possible Russian business ventures, and found him 'v. nice' and helpful. Spears also found Savinkov 'v. interesting' in interpreting Russian affairs and was attracted by his highly optimistic assessments of business opportunities in Russia. But Spears became concerned that Reilly was spending too much time plotting with Savinkov, who had organised an intelligence network based in Poland to carry out a variety of covert operations in Soviet Russia. When Spears remonstrated with Reilly on 'the danger of dealing with shady people & mixing politics with business' he doubtless had some of Savinkov's covert operations in mind.[91] According to a Soviet historian, 'nearly all Savinkov's agents were simul-taneously on Poland's payroll, with the Polish police helping to put them across the border'.[92] Savinkov was also secretly assisted by Cumming's station chief in Warsaw, Commander Andrew Maclaren, a friend of Reilly, probably on Spears's list of 'shady people', with gold earrings and 'the look of a pirate'. In his correspondence with Reilly, Maclaren repeatedly emphasised that, despite some French, Polish and Czech subsidies, Savinkov's main problem was money. He wrote in June 1921:

> The position is becoming desperate. The balance in hand today amounts to 700,000 Polish Marks, not even sufficient to pay [Savinkov's] staff their salaries for the month of July.

Reilly seems to have contributed personally to Savinkov's funds from the proceeds of his numerous business ventures.[93] His business associates certainly accused him during 1921 of claiming extravagant expenses and milking company funds. Spears was outraged to arrive at his office one morning to find the phone cut off 'owing to Reilly not having paid'.[94]

By the spring of 1921 Reilly believed the Bolshevik régime to be in far more serious straits than Savinkov. The British Mission in Moscow reported at the end of May that since the introduction of the NEP there had been a 'complete change in the Soviet internal economic situation'. The Soviet government was now 'consciously encouraging the growth of capitalism'.[95] The invitations to foreign capitalists to apply for concessions to develop oil, mines, timber and other industries held out the prospect (never realised) of a large enclave of foreign capitalism within Soviet Russia. As the famine spread during the summer the Russians seemed increasingly desperate for foreign aid. Reilly convinced himself, and on 5 August sought to convince Winston Churchill also, that there was now a 'unique opportunity' for removing the Bolshevik régime. Churchill urged him to put his views to Lloyd George. Reilly did so in a long and visionary memorandum which, he grandly claimed, was 'based on facts acquired from continuous personal contact with the leaders of democratic anti-Bolshevik activities in Russia, and may be said generally to be representative of the united views and suggested policy of the leaders of all sections of Russian constructive opinion'. The famine and domestic disaffection (including 'the certainty of an attempt at a General Peasant Rising') made it impossible for the Bolshevik régime to survive. The West, Reilly extravagantly argued, was therefore in a position to impose four conditions for providing the economic aid which alone could save Russia from anarchy. The Cheka was to be abolished; the Soviet government reorganised to exclude 'the present more extreme Bolshevik leaders, such as Lenin, Trotsky, Zinoviev, Radek, Kamenev, Litvinov, etc., etc.'; all Soviet currency and precious metal reserves placed in an 'inviolable Trust Fund abroad'; and 'unrestricted freedom and the utmost assistance' given to all 'Economic Commissions which may be sent to Russia'. 'These International Commissions', concluded Reilly, 'will naturally fall into the position of practically administering Russia and would, of course be supported by the new moderate Government...' Though he did not record his views, Lloyd George can scarcely have been impressed.[96]

Even to cooler heads than Reilly's, however, there seemed increasing evidence that the Soviet régime was willing to make important concessions. At the end of October Chicherin announced Soviet readiness in principle to accept responsibility for the Tsarist government's pre-war debts. In return the Soviet government would expect international recognition, substantial economic aid and foreign investment, an international conference to settle 'reciprocal financial claims', and 'a final peace treaty' between Russia and other powers. Before long, preparations were underway for a conference to meet at Genoa in the spring of 1922 to re-establish ties between Russia and the West, and promote the economic reconstruction of Europe. Lenin, declared the *New Statesman* in November 1921, was 'driving the Russian State furiously back on the road to capitalism ... All in Russia acknowledge this save a handful of desperate doctrinaires'. The Soviet leaders themselves, concluded the *Economist*, had recognised that the 'attempt to force Communism on the nation had failed'; there were 'undoubtedly big possibilities' for Western businessmen.[97]

Savinkov, however, found it increasingly difficult to find a secure base from which to mastermind the transformation of Bolshevik Russia. In the autumn of 1921, after Soviet protests to the Poles, he was forced to leave Warsaw for Prague, only to discover that he had become an embarrassment to the Czechs as well. Spears noted in November, 'R[eilly] has I fear compromised his position in Prague by identifying himself too much with Savinkoff who is now out of favour there'.[98] Reilly determined to revive Savinkov's cause by bringing him to London. The Foreign Office, which believed Savinkov to be actively engaged in stirring up a rising in Soviet Karelia, refused to admit him. Reilly then went to Cumming and tried to persuade him to ignore the Foreign Office and order the Paris Passport Control Office to give Savinkov a visa. When Cumming also refused, Reilly returned to Paris and persuaded the PCO, Major T.M. Langton, or more probably his deputy, Reilly's friend, Major W. 'Robbie' Field-Robinson, to provide the missing visa.[99]

Once in London, Savinkov began, with Reilly's help, an extraordinary round of visits. First, he excited Spears with visions of the limitless business opportunities in Russia as soon as the Bolshevik régime had been 'transformed on acceptable lines'.[100] Then he called on Krasin at the Trade Delegation and tried to persuade him of the economic necessity of such a transformation. By Savinkov's own unreliable account, Krasin was so impressed that he suggested Savinkov should join the Soviet government.[101] Shortly before the Christmas holidays Churchill motored down to Chequers with Savinkov to see the prime minister. They found Lloyd George surrounded by Free Church ministers and a Welsh choir who for several hours 'sang Welsh hymns in the most beautiful manner'. When the hymns were finished Savinkov tried and failed to win Lloyd George over to his visionary schemes. The prime minister argued that the Soviet leaders would either gradually learn sense or suffer the fate of Robespierre and St Just and be replaced by more moderate men. Savinkov predicted that, if left to their own devices, the Bolsheviks would preside instead over a new Dark Age.[102] By the time of the Chequers meeting Lloyd George had probably already seen a report by Cumming that, so far from finding Krasin in favour of inviting him to join the Soviet government, Savinkov had in reality 'met with a far from favourable reception'. Sir Eyre Crowe wrote after reading Cumming's report: 'I am much afraid that Savinkoff is misinforming us, and basing bad advice on wrong information'.[103] Even Churchill, though he retained some admiration for Savinkov, began to realise his unreliability. Soon after the Chequers meeting he received from an unknown source Savinkov's own version of the meeting. In this account the hymn singing by the Welsh choir became largely transformed into singing by Lloyd George and his family of 'God Save the Tsar' and other songs designed to please Savinkov. On leaving Chequers, Churchill was alleged to have told Savinkov: 'Do not put too much trust in Lloyd George, he is first a nationalist, but one also meets in him a desire for personal gain, and the elections play a part in this'. Churchill sent on to Lloyd George Savinkov's version of their conversation. 'This will amuse you', he wrote.[104] By the spring of 1922 Savinkov, now based in Paris, was peddling a less benevolent view of Lloyd George. He wrote to *The Times* to accuse the prime minister of using the Germans and the Bolsheviks to pillage Russia's wealth.[105] Savinkov was now an embarrassment to most of his former supporters in the West. His mother appealed vainly to Reilly to persuade Savinkov to give up plotting against the Bolsheviks: 'It is impossible, sitting in Paris and without a great deal of financial backing, to plan any armed resistance or strike against the present authorities in Russia'.[106] Unknown to Savinkov, the Cheka (now renamed the GPU) began in the summer of 1922 a long and finally successful plot to lure him back to a show trial in Moscow.[107]

Savinkov's discredit inevitably reflected on Reilly as well. He had disobeyed both Cumming and the Foreign Office and brought to Britain a veteran terrorist who had lied shamelessly once he arrived. During 1922 Reilly's business career, like his life as a secret agent, began to falter. Spears, who no longer found Reilly indispensable, moved steadily to what he called a 'Dust-up' with him. A number of business ventures in which Reilly was involved, including a Czech loan and 'a big Moravian scheme' went 'fut', and Spears became increasingly uneasy of his unscrupulous business methods. On 2 August Spears wrote in his diary:

> V. important day. B[runströ]m [Spears's business associate] and I broke our connection with Reilly at lunch – v. pleasantly.[108]

By 1923 Reilly was broke and borrowed £200 from Major Field-Robinson to pay for passages for himself and his latest wife to the United States where he hoped vainly to collect commission owing from some of his wartime purchases for the Tsarist government and to make his fortune in new business ventures. Spears was persuaded to write references to two Chicago businessmen announcing that Reilly had lately formed the Modern Medicine Company Ltd which appeared to have 'a brilliant future before it', and was seeking to sell the American rights of a new preparation known as 'Humagsolan'.[109]

In the spring of 1922 the Soviet government and Comintern resumed their support for foreign revolutionary movements. In the Foreign Office view, this was probably due to their 'increased sense of their own importance' as a result of the Genoa conference, during which they concluded the Rapallo treaty with Germany, and to their 'more optimistic outlook as regards the famine'. An intelligence report 'from an entirely reliable source' reported that immediately after the Genoa conference Chicherin 'received Indian revolutionaries and promised them full support'. According to a Foreign

Office review of Soviet policy during 1922, 'it is from June onwards that the stream of evidence [from intelligence sources] is observed to swell'. The Special Branch furnished 'irrefutable evidence' that 'money is sent each week from the Russian Trade Delegation to the Communist headquarters in King Street'. What most concerned Curzon, however, was once again Soviet subversion in India and on India's borders. He had available to him three main intelligence sources: reports from SIS and IPI, and – probably most important – intercepted telegrams exchanged between Moscow and its representatives in Persia and Afghanistan. These sources disclosed that Russian agents were distributing large amounts of money and propaganda to anti-British nationalist movements. Raskolnikov, the Soviet envoy in Kabul, was also supplying arms and ammunition.[110]

On 25 April 1923 Curzon obtained cabinet authority to prepare a further protest note, appropriately known to posterity as 'the Curzon ultimatum', which threatened to cancel the trade agreement unless the Soviet Union promised to mend its ways. This time Curzon was determined to avoid all risk of a humiliation such as had overtaken him eighteen months before. He therefore decided to base his new charges of subversion on the absolutely reliable evidence of the intercepts from GC & CS. The cabinet considered the text of the Curzon ultimatum on 3 May. After a prolonged discussion (which is not recorded in the minutes) it was agreed:

(a) That the advantages of basing the published British case on actual extracts from the despatches [in fact mostly telegrams] which had passed between the Soviet Government and its agents outweighed the disadvantages of the possible disclosure of the secret source [GC & CS] from which these despatches had been obtained, more especially as this was actually known to the Russian Soviet Government.

(b) That the actual source of this information should not be disclosed in Parliament.[111]

The final draft of the 'Curzon ultimatum' rehearsed all outstanding British grievances against Russia. Its main charge, however, was subversion and anti-British propaganda in India and India's neighbours. The phrasing of the protest was intended to deny the Soviet government the opportunity to reply with 'allegations as to false information and spurious documents'. 'His Majesty's Government ... are', said Curzon, 'content to rely exclusively upon communications which have passed in the last few months between the Russian Government and its agents, and which are in their possession, and upon the recorded acts of members of the Soviet Government itself'. Indeed, not content with quoting from Russian intercepts, Curzon repeatedly – and undiplomatically – taunted the Soviet government with the successful interception of their communications:

The Russian Commissariat for Foreign Affairs will no doubt recognise the following communication dated 21st February, 1923, which they received from M. Raskolnikov ... The Commissariat for Foreign Affairs will also doubtless recognise a communication received by them from Kabul, dated the 8th November, 1922 ... Nor will they have forgotten a communication, dated the 16th March, 1923, from M. Karakhan, the Assistant Commissary for Foreign Affairs, to M. Raskolnikov ...[112]

The Soviet reply described some of Curzon's charges as 'invention', others as based on 'decyphered parts of telegrams tendentiously manipulated and arbitrarily extended'. It thus implicitly admitted that its telegrams had been successfully intercepted. The Soviet government reproved the British government for stooping to such methods and virtuously declared its own refusal 'to base its protests upon reports of informers and intercepted documents'. In the last resort, however, Russia was determined to preserve the trade agreement. She therefore turned the other cheek and promised 'not to support with funds or in any other form persons or bodies or agencies or institutions whose aim is to spread discontent or to foment rebellion in any part of the British Empire'.[113] The Soviet government also recalled Raskolnikov, its envoy in Kabul, whom Curzon viewed with particular disfavour.

The drafting of the Curzon ultimatum coincided with, and perhaps helped to precipitate, a protest by the services at the Foreign Office monopoly of GC & CS. In January 1923 the Directors of Naval Intelligence (DNI), of Military Operations and Intelligence (DMO & I) and of Air Operations and Intelligence (DAO & I) jointly founded an Inter-Service Directorate Committee to consider the question of cryptography. The Committee reported in April that in the next war, as in the last, cryptography was certain to become for the services 'a most important – and, to the navy, a primary – source of intelligence':

After most careful consideration, the Committee unanimously have arrived at the conclusion that the sole control of the Government Code and Cypher School by [the Foreign Office] has inevitably affected the Fighting Services as follows:-

(a) They only receive a small proportion of the messages translated.
(b) They have no voice in the distribution of messages.
(c) They have no means of ensuring that all messages which they may consider of interest to them are received by them.
(d) They have no voice in what cyphers are to be attacked, or what special 'Subjects' are to receive attention.
(e) No provision is made for attacking or even systematically watching purely naval and military cyphers, nor for scrutinising cyphers of

local interest to various departments. Although information gained from them would be of little value at the time, a knowledge of the methods and systems as well as the vocabularies would be invaluable on the outbreak of war even though the actual cyphers were changed.

(f) In certain cases in the past, cyphers, which have been broken by the Government Code and Cypher School, have been arbitrarily withheld from military organisations to whom they would have been of considerable value, on the grounds that the Foreign Office were not satisfied with the security of these organisations.[114]

A testy correspondence followed between the Foreign Office and the service ministries. The interservice report, according to a patronising Foreign Office memorandum, was evidently produced by persons 'ill-acquainted with cryptographic work'. Curzon loftily confessed himself 'a little surprised' that the service ministries should have thought fit to hold an enquiry into a department under another ministry's control. The Foreign Office none the less conceded the essence of the service case:

There can be no doubt that it is essential to be able to read naval and military messages in times of emergency and this can only be effected by continuous research in peace.[115]

Cumming's death in June 1923 offered the possibility of a compromise arrangement between the Foreign Office and the service ministries. By the beginning of 1923 Cumming had developed heart trouble, was in failing health and had decided to retire. To C's pleasure, the former DNI, Rear-Admiral Hugh 'Quex' Sinclair, was chosen to succeed him later in the year when he finished a tour of duty as head of the submarine service. Cumming regarded Sinclair as 'in every way qualified and suitable' to take over SIS, and told his former station chief in St Petersburg and Rome, Sir Samuel Hoare: 'I feel sure that in his capable hands this organisation will grow to be very useful – it is not too much to say essential – to the Govt. Departments we serve'.[116] On the afternoon of 14 June, shortly before the date fixed for his departure, Cumming's friend, the writer Valentine Williams, called to wish him well in his retirement. After chatting over old times, he said good-bye at about 6 p.m., leaving Cumming comfortably installed in the corner of a sofa. When Cumming's secretary entered his office soon afterwards, she found him dead. Williams believed that 'He had died in harness, as he would have wished'.[117]

Sinclair succeeded Cumming with the official, though secret, title 'Head of the Secret Service'. In addition to taking over SIS, he was also appointed Director of GC & CS, though Denniston remained its operational head.

Though the Foreign Office retained control of both SIS and GC & CS, Sinclair's appointment as Director of GC & CS (for which he had been responsible as DNI from 1919 to 1921) went some way to meet previous complaints that the services' cryptographic interests were being neglected. He also improved the coordination of signals intelligence by assuming direct control for the first time of the distribution of intercepts from the military listening stations in Palestine, Baghdad and India.[118] A small naval section under Admiralty control was added to GC & CS in 1924.[119] For the next decade decrypted naval messages were usually of little significance (as was to be expected in peacetime) and were therefore rarely circulated to the Admiralty. The naval section considered its primary task 'the cryptographic training of the staff' for a future conflict.[120]

'Quex' Sinclair's service record before the First World War repeatedly describes him as a 'most zealous' officer, 'specially recommended' for promotion. He was praised for his 'excellent tact and temper', 'great judgement', 'marvellous eyesight', and 'exceptional powers of administration and handling of officers and men'. 'Quex' also had a reputation as a *bon vivant*. A large crocodile-skin case containing a hundred cigars was usually near at hand. Even during the First World War he prided himself on serving his guests with delicacies such as Californian peach-fed ham. He derived his nickname from Sir Arthur Pinero's play, *The Gay Lord Quex*, first performed in 1900. Like his namesake, playfully described as 'the wickedest man in London', Sinclair had a stormy private life. While he was serving as captain of HMS *Renown* from 1916 to 1917, news of the violent rows in the captain's cabin during visits from his wife spread throughout the ship. In 1920, embarrassingly soon after becoming naval aide to the king, Sinclair was divorced.[121]

As head of the Secret Service, 'Quex' quickly became highly secretive in most of his habits, but he remained a conspicuous figure to London taxi-drivers, driving round the capital in an enormous, ancient open Lancia. Diplomats always knew that Sinclair was visiting the Foreign Office when they saw the Lancia parked outside the ambassadors' entrance off the Horse Guards.[122] Unlike Cumming, the new 'C' ceased to wear naval uniform when he became head of SIS. Instead he found a bowler hat a size too small for him and, in the words of an admirer, rammed it 'as firmly as possible on his head'.[123]

Sinclair took office as head of SIS and director of GC & CS with a reputation as 'a terrific anti-Bolshevik'.[124] His first year in office, however, coincided both with a lull in Anglo-Soviet controversies and with economies which reduced the passport control network to eighteen stations in Europe and two outside.[125] Until December 1923, despite the remarkable indiscretions of the 'Curzon ultimatum' in May, GC & CS continued to decrypt a substantial number of Russian telegrams which offered Curzon a means of monitoring Soviet compliance with his ultimatum. The Foreign Office was generally pleased with what it read. Gregory, the head of the Northern Department, singled out three intercepts as particularly significant:

(a) On May 16th or 17th Shumiatski, Soviet representative in Tehran, informed his consular officers that by orders from Moscow they were temporarily to cease political activities and to suspend temporarily all work with secret agents.

(b) On October 12th Chicherin sent cipher telegrams to all important Soviet representatives in the East stating that 'the moment demands the greatest care in regard to British interests at all points of contact'.

(c) On October 24th Chicherin sent telegraphic instructions to the Soviet representatives in Kabul 'to refuse to have anything to do with revolutionary or nationalist elements on the spot' . . .

Towards the end of the year, however, the Soviet Union introduced new codes and ciphers which GC & CS was unable to decrypt. For the moment the flow of intercepts dried up.[126]

Curzon had begun his five-year term as foreign secretary convinced that the diplomacy of Soviet Russia was uniquely perfidious. Gradually, however, he came to sympathise with Lloyd George's argument during cabinet discussions of Soviet intercepts in 1920 that 'the trickery of the Russians [was] not worse than that of the French'.[127] Curzon had long been convinced that the French were not the kind of people 'to go tiger-shooting with', but intercepted French telegrams raised his suspicions to new heights. Both Curzon and the War Office were outraged by the evidence of secret dealings between their French allies and defeated Turkish nationalists. French intercepts, wrote the DMI, Major-General Sir William Thwaites, in July 1920, were 'a nice savoury disclosure'. Lieutenant-General Sir 'Tim' Harington. the British commander-in-chief in Constantinople, was also shocked. There was, he wrote a year later, still 'plenty of dirty work going on, as our intercepts show'.[128] The intercepts persuaded Curzon that, particularly over the Middle East, Raymond Poincaré (French premier and foreign minister, 1922–4) 'lied shamelessly'.[129] The evidence of what Curzon considered Poincaré's ill-faith during the Chanak crisis in September 1922 helped to reduce him to a state of nervous collapse. One of the diplomats present at a meeting during the crisis between the two foreign ministers wrote later: 'Curzon's wide white hands upon the green baize cloth trembled violently. He could stand it no longer'. His permanent under secretary, Lord Hardinge, helped him to another room 'where he collapsed upon a scarlet settee. He grasped Lord Hardinge by the arm. "Charley", he panted, "I can't bear that horrid little man. I can't bear him". He wept.'[130]

During his final months in office Curzon became almost obsessed by the belief that the French were plotting against him. In October 1923 he discovered from French intercepts what he described as an 'intrigue between M. Poincaré, Comte de St-Aulaire (French ambassador), H.A. Gwynne (Editor of *Morning Post*) to supplant me at [the] FO'.[131] According to intercepted telegrams exchanged between Poincaré and Saint-Aulaire, the French hoped through the intermediary of Gwynne to persuade Baldwin to replace Curzon by a more Francophile foreign secretary. Curzon could no longer bring himself even to meet the French ambassador whom he henceforth 'declined to see ... on one excuse or another': 'This is the worst thing that I have come across in my public life ... I had not realised that diplomacy was such a dirty game'. Baldwin too, though secretly anxious to replace Curzon, confessed himself 'unaware that such dirty things were done in diplomacy'.[132] When Baldwin's government fell from power in January 1924, Anglo-Soviet relations were thus apparently less troubled than at any other time since the Bolshevik revolution. Curzon had been reassured by the Russian intercepts that the trade agreement was being more or less observed, and the French intercepts had provided an alternative foreign focus for his highly developed sense of personal outrage.

# 10 | ZINOVIEV LETTERS AND THE BREACH WITH RUSSIA

On 22 January 1924 James Ramsay MacDonald, illegitimate son of a Highland ploughman and a Lossiemouth mother, was sworn of the privy council and then kissed the monarch's hands on taking office as Britain's first Labour prime minister at the head of a minority government dependent on Liberal support. George V wrote in his diary: 'Today 23 years ago dear Grandmama died. I wonder what she would have thought of a Labour Government!' Though determined to give the new government 'a fair chance', he told MacDonald he hoped he would not have to meet any ambassador from Russia and asked if the Labour Party would now give up singing the 'Red Flag'.[1] The king's apprehensions were shared by many of the Whitehall officials responsible for foreign and defence policy. Hankey was afraid that the new prime minister would 'cut the throat' of the Committee of Imperial Defence. Crowe had similar fears for the future of the intelligence services. Sir Herbert Creedy, permanent under-secretary at the War Office, wrote to all home GOCinCs requesting them to update their lists both of officers and civilians available for army intelligence work in an emergency.[2]

The intelligence services had particular reason to be nervous of a government some of whose leading members had at various times been under surveillance. During the war MI5 had considered whether to recommend Ramsay MacDonald's prosecution for seditious speeches.[3] Probably no Labour minister in January 1924 even knew of the existence of the codebreakers of GC & CS. Hankey had acknowledged in 1920 that if their existence were known, 'public opinion may experience a shock'.[4] Some Labour ministers would have been very shocked indeed. An example of what intelligence officers must have feared occurred in 1929 when the new American secretary of state, Henry Stimson, was outraged to discover the existence of the Black Chamber (Washington's GC & CS) and ordered its abolition. 'Gentlemen', he insisted, 'do not read each other's mail'.[5] Had Labour ministers been told of the existence of the British 'Black Chamber', some at least would have been as horrified as Stimson. But most of them were not told. Ramsay MacDonald may indeed have been the only member of his cabinet informed of the activities of GC & CS, and at first even he was less than fully informed. When Winston Churchill returned to power in November 1924, eager to catch up on the backlog of intercepts, he discovered that: 'In MacDonald's time he was himself long kept in ignorance of them [the intercepts] by the Foreign Office'.[6] Arthur Ponsonby, MacDonald's undersecretary at the Foreign Office, was refused all access to intercepts and SIS reports, despite the fact that he came to bear the main day-to-day responsibility for the Labour government's Russian policy, on the dubious ground of his 'subordinate position'. Ponsonby regarded all intelligence work as a 'dirty' business, though probably 'you have to do it'. By his own admission he was not sorry to be kept in ignorance of it:

> It is part of the etiquette of the Secret Service that Under-Secretaries are never told about it ... When I mentioned the Secret Service, the officials, the most genial of them, used to become rigid. I was not allowed to know, and even when we got to the verge of that awful mud-bath which surrounded the Zinoviev letter, I was never allowed to come in, and I am glad it was so.[7]

The most frequent intelligence summaries received by MacDonald as prime minister were the now traditional weekly reports on British revolutionary movements sent to the cabinet office by Sir Wyndham Childs, head of the Special Branch. Ever since Childs had succeeded Sir Basil Thomson in 1921 he had considered the battle against Bolshevism 'the most important part of my work'. He could not understand why the governments of Lloyd George, Bonar Law, and Baldwin 'always refused to strike one overwhelming and final blow against the Communist organisation'.[8] His doubts about Ramsay MacDonald's resolve against the Red Peril must have been confirmed by the prime minister's response to his first intelligence report, submitted on 24 January. Ramsay MacDonald was not impressed by Child's report: 'Little of the news contained in it was likely to be unfamiliar ... to anyone who reads the "Workers' Weekly" and similar papers'. The prime minister was also struck by the report's political bias. He suggested facetiously to Childs:

> that it might be made at once attractive and indeed entertaining if its survey were extended to cover not only communistic activities but also other political activities of an extreme tendency. For instance a little knowledge in regard to the Fascist movement in this country ... or possibly some information as to the source of the 'Morning Post' funds might give an exhilarating flavour to the document and by enlarging its scope convert it into a complete and finished work of art.[9]

Childs was not amused. He was not pleased either by the prime minister's request to see his own Special Branch file. MacDonald's request was refused and he did not insist,[10] but he declined to circulate Childs's weekly reports to the cabinet. Sinclair, Kell and Childs must have been further disturbed when, on 2 February, the Labour government became the first to grant the Soviet régime *de jure* recognition.

MacDonald's government turned out, however, to be much less radical than Whitehall had feared. The prime minister, wrote Hankey, 'affects to regard me as a reactionary, and I retaliate by treating him as a visionary, but this is all more or less banter. I continue as Secretary of the Cabinet as of yore.' The revolutionary left was virtually omitted from MacDonald's cabinet; even its most socialist member, the Clydeside businessman John Wheatley, was a conspicuous success as minister of health. The CIGS, Lord Cavan, concluded patronisingly after meeting the new secretary of state for war, Stephen Walsh, a former miners' agent, that 'a more loyal and straightforward little man never existed'. MacDonald's main anxiety as prime minister was to appear 'statesmanlike'. He offered parliament the platitudinous but reassuring maxim: 'Security and confidence based on goodwill'.[11]

Among the most reassuring ministers to the Whitehall machine was the home secretary, 'Uncle' Arthur Henderson, who had served in the war cabinet from 1916 to 1917. Childs found it much easier to gain Henderson's than MacDonald's ear, and the home secretary stoutly defended the Special Branch against attacks by his own back benchers.[12] The government as a whole began to take a much more friendly view both of the Special Branch and of domestic intelligence gathering after its early experience in grappling with the problems of labour unrest. MacDonald's very first cabinet meeting on 23 January had to discuss how to safeguard food, milk and coal supplies during a train drivers' strike. Over the next two months strikes, first of the dockers, then of London tramwaymen, led to government plans to use the Emergency Powers Act, violently denounced by Labour when it had been introduced by Lloyd George.[13] On 15 April the cabinet appointed a five-man Committee on Industrial Unrest to enquire into the recent strike wave 'with a view to ascertaining whether any appreciable percentage of the unfortunate aspects of these strikes was due to Communist activity'. The chairman of the new committee was the Lord Privy Seal, J.R. Clynes, himself a former president of the National Union of General and Municipal Workers. The other members were Henderson, Wheatley, Sidney Webb (president of the Board of Trade) and Thomas Shaw (minister of labour).[14]

Much of the evidence considered by the committee came from intelligence supplied by the Special Branch, SIS and MI5. It included intercepted letters from British Communists, from Zinoviev and Comintern, and from the Red International of Labour Unions (RILU), minutes of the CPGB's Politburo and other party committees, and reports from informers within the Communist

Party and the trade unions. The Committee concluded that the CPGB regularly received both finance and instructions from Comintern and that Communists within the union movement similarly received finance and instructions from the RILU. There was also evidence of Communist involvement (with Comintern and RILU encouragement) in the recent strike wave. According to an intercepted 'secret circular' of 18 February from Harry Pollitt of the CPGB's Central Industrial Committee (and later general secretary of the party) to district party committees:

> The dock strike makes another call upon our party which we must endeavour to fulfil as successfully as we did the recent Railway strike. We have many evidences from all over the country of the valuable work the Party did in that strike. Please note that anything coming to you from the British Bureau of the R.I.L.U. is to be acted upon in the same way as a Party communication.

Willie Gallacher was also said to have written to his wife on 30 January: 'Yesterday I was the whole day preparing reports on the Railway, Dockers and Miners Troubles for the Centre [Comintern]'. An intercepted letter from Sturrock, the Communist provisional secretary of the London Transport Workers Solidarity Committee, declared baldly: 'We must be prepared to sabotage'.

The Industrial Unrest Committee remained fairly optimistic. It concluded that while the Communists had done their best to aggravate the recent strikes, they had played only a minor part in starting them. Despite 'substantial assistance' from Comintern, the CPGB was 'constantly in great financial difficulties'. Though 'extremely active', party membership had probably been only four or five thousand two years before, and there was evidence that it had fallen since. The committee was, however, 'impressed with the evidence' of 'systematic instructions and plans ... issued by the Communist Party' aimed at penetrating and taking over the unions. It believed that 'responsible Trade Union leaders' should be shown this secret evidence 'informally and confidentially'.[15]

The report of the Industrial Unrest Committee, approved by the cabinet on 15 May, marked a turning point in Labour's relationship with the intelligence services. The Labour government in effect sanctioned the interception of Communist and Comintern communications, accepted the authenticity of the intercepted correspondence, and decided 'in favour of some form of publicity' for the intelligence based on it.[16] It was ironic that within six months the government should itself have fallen victim to the publicity given to the interception of a Comintern communication.

The furore which surrounded the publication of the 'Zinoviev letter' later in the year and its supposed part in bringing down the Labour government inevitably raised the issue of the letter's authenticity. But when the Labour cabinet was first confronted with intercepted Comintern communications in the spring of 1924, none were denounced as forgeries. There is no field of modern history in which the historian needs to tread more warily than in deciding the authenticity of secret documents. An impressive list of dis-' tinguished historians, including the leading British authority on Soviet Russia, E.H. Carr, have made notable errors of judgment in these matters. When, as with the Comintern intercepts, most of the originals either do not survive or are unavailable, it is rarely possible to pronounce with certainty in any individual case. The probability is, however, that most of the intercepts were genuine. Significantly, Indian Communists now use DIB reports which make extensive use of intercepted Comintern and other correspondence as a source for their own history.[17] In the case of the wireless and telegraphic intercepts decrypted by GC & CS, and most of the correspondence intercepted in the British post, there can be little doubt about their authenticity. But it is quite possible that the intercepts obtained outside the United Kingdom did contain some forgeries. After the débâcle of 1921, however, both the Foreign Office and the intelligence services were on their guard against bogus documents.[18] The forgeries most likely to slip through a probably imperfect net were those containing intelligence for which there seemed to be some corroboration from other sources.

The 'Zinoviev letter' whose publication was to cause a political sensation on the eve of the October 1924 elections was only one of several considered for publication during the life of the first Labour government. The first was a letter of 7 April allegedly sent by Zinoviev, the president of Comintern, to the CPGB instructing it to mobilize the 'wide working masses' in support of the Soviet delegation recently arrived in London to negotiate a settlement of Anglo-Soviet differences, and indicating that the delegation had brought funds to finance the mobilization. SIS sent a copy of the letter to the Foreign Office towards the end of April just as the Special Branch was reporting 'a distinct recrudescence of activity on the part of the CPGB' and evidence of 'a further subsidy from the Communist International'. Arthur Henderson emphasised the need for 'adequate evidence of the authenticity' of the Zinoviev letter of 7 April, and the importance of safeguarding the source which supplied it. But, subject to these two provisos, he told the prime minister, probably with Childs's support, that Rakovsky, the Soviet chargé d'affaires, 'should be asked for an explanation'.[19] That request clearly carried with it the risk, if not the probability, that Zinoviev's letter would be made public. It was chiefly for that reason that the Foreign Office opposed the idea of a protest to Rakovsky. H.F.B. Maxse of the Northern Department minuted on the Home Office request: 'Apart from the question of betraying our sources of information such action is bound to put the Soviet propagandists on their guard and drive them further underground'. The prime minister, when

Major-General Sir Vernon Kell, director general of MI5 from 1909 to 1940. (© *Times Newspapers*)

Commander Alastair Denniston, RNVR, head of GC&CS (1919–42), leaving Buckingham Palace after being invested with the insignia of the C.B.E., 1933. (*Courtesy of Mr Robin Denniston*)

Admiral Sir Hugh "Quex" Sinclair, "C" from 1923 to 1939, as captain of H.M.S. *Renown* in 1917, followed by a disrespectful sailor. (*Courtesy of Mr P. W. Avery*)

21 Queen Anne's Gate, headquarters of the Passport Control Office and the London residence of "C". The rear of the premises was connected to Broadway Buildings (54 Broadway).
(© *Nigel West and courtesy of Weidenfeld & Nicolson Archives*)

Broadway Buildings today: the office block which housed both the pre-war SIS and GC&CS.
(© *Jed Corbett, 1985*)

Major-General Sir Stewart Menzies, "C" (1939–51).
(*Courtesy of Mr H. Montgomery Hyde*)

Colonel Sir Claude Dansey, founder of the Z organisation and subsequently assistant chief of SIS.
(*Copyright private collection and courtesy of Weidenfeld & Nicolson Archives*)

Major-General Laurence Grand, head of Section D in SIS (1938–40).
(*Courtesy of Mrs M. Ponsonby*)

Sir Frank Nelson, K.C.M.G., K.B., first
head of SOE (1940–42)
(*Courtesy of Lady Nelson*)

Sir David Petrie, director general of MI5
(1940–46).
(*Courtesy of Nigel West and Weidenfeld &
Nicolson Archives*)

Captain Guy Liddell, MC, wartime head of
MI5 Section B (Counter-Espionage)
(© *Daily Express and courtesy of Weidenfeld
& Nicolson Archives*)

Lieutenant-Colonel Valentine Vivian, deputy chief of SIS in World War Two and previously head of Section V. The photograph was taken in India at a much earlier stage of his career. (*Courtesy of India Office Library and Records*, © *British Library*)

Major Maxwell Knight, MI5's most successful "agent-runner" between the wars and head of B5b. (*BBC Copyright*)

Dillwyn Knox, probably Room 40's ablest codebreaker, sketched in 1933 by Gilbert Spencer.
(*Courtesy of Mrs Mavis Batey*)

Alan Turing, probably Bletchley's ablest codebreaker. This photograph was taken to mark his election to the Fellowship of the Royal Society.
(*Courtesy of the Provost and Fellows of King's College, Cambridge*)

Bletchley Park today. (© *Brian Johnson*)

consulted, declared himself unwilling to make an official protest unless the Soviet delegation could be shown to have actually engaged in subversion. If the Special Branch could 'produce unquestionable evidence of definite acts in this country by Mr Tomski or other members of the Soviet Delegation, Mr Ramsay MacDonald will be glad to consider such evidence with a view to taking the matter up with Mr Rakovsky'. Such evidence, however, did not materialise.[20]

Five months later, both the Foreign Office and the prime minister took a different view. In October, unlike May, they considered an intercepted letter from Zinoviev sufficient basis for a protest to the Soviet government. The reasons for their change of heart were closely bound up with the consequences of the Anglo-Soviet negotiations. The negotiations began on 14 April with MacDonald in the chair. Thereafter, however, the prime minister handed over the conduct of the talks to his undersecretary. Unlike MacDonald, Ponsonby remained in close touch with the Union of Democratic Control throughout his term of office and shared the UDC's suspicion of the Foreign Office and of secret diplomacy. During the final stages of the Anglo-Russian negotiations Ponsonby 'made up [his] mind to use the M.P.s and not the [Foreign Office] officials' as his intermediaries. And the M.P. on whom Ponsonby most relied was E.D. Morel, secretary of the UDC and traditional scourge of the Foreign Office. Two Anglo-Russian treaties were signed on 8 August 1924. The first was a further commercial treaty. The second was scarcely a treaty at all in the normal sense; rather it provided for further talks to be followed by a further treaty settling pre-revolutionary Russian debts in return for a loan guaranteed by the British government.[21]

The prospect of 'Money for Murderers' struck an immediate, if irrational, right-wing chord. According to the *Evening News*: 'What Mr MacDonald, Mr Ponsonby and their fellow dreamers about Russia are doing is to pledge the British taxpayer to lend money to the conspirators who want that money to hasten the collapse of the British Empire'. At almost the same moment the Campbell case provided believers in the Red Menace with convincing confirmation of Labour's subservience to Communist pressure. On 5 August John Campbell, a Communist journalist, was charged under the Incitement to Mutiny Act with preaching sedition to the armed forces: an activity always regarded with peculiar horror by MI5. On 13 August charges were suddenly withdrawn. The Communist Party was quick to claim that the government had given way to 'severe pressure' from the Labour left, and Conservatives were quick to believe the Communist claim. As Baldwin said later: 'It was widely felt that the same influence which had been at work in the matter of the Campbell case had also been at work in the matter of the Russian Treaty'.[22]

The Russian treaties and the Campbell case together cost Ramsay MacDonald the Liberal support on which his minority government depended. On 8 October the government lost a vote of confidence, and on the following day parliament was dissolved. The election campaign centred from the first on the issue of the Red Menace. The most difficult charge which Labour had to counter was that of being soft on Bolshevism. MacDonald's sensitivity to that charge and his desire to rebut it provide the key to his handling of the 'Zinoviev letter' which arrived in the Foreign Office from SIS on 10 October. This sinister document, dated 15 September, instructed the British Communist Party to put pressure on their sympathisers in the Labour Party, to 'strain every nerve' for the ratification of the recent treaty with the Soviet Union, to intensify 'agitation-propaganda work in the armed forces', and generally to prepare for the coming of the British revolution.[23]

Crowe's private secretary, Nevile Bland, informed the king that the Zinoviev letter 'was obtained from an absolutely trustworthy agent in Russia'.[24] No more is known about the agent save that SIS believed him to have been executed soon afterwards. Baldwin told the Commons in 1928:

> Not very long after the Zinoviev letter appeared in England, a Russian in Moscow was apprehended by the Soviet Government. They had every reason, I understand, to believe that he was connected with the giving away of the copy of that letter, and he was shot on that account.[25]

It is unlikely that the agent who obtained the letter was, as has been claimed, Sidney Reilly. Bland, probably echoing the Foreign Office view, considered Reilly a 'rather double edged tool' inclined to 'exaggerate his own importance'.[26] It is, however, likely that Reilly played an active part in ensuring that the letter was publicised. A copy of the Russian version of the letter has been discovered in what appears to be Reilly's handwriting,[27] and there can scarcely have been another past or present SIS agent with so few scruples about exploiting it in the anti-Bolshevik cause.

The interception of the Zinoviev letter cannot have caused great surprise in the Foreign Office. Ample warning had already been received from intelligence sources of a new propaganda offensive by Comintern against the British Empire. The main target of that offensive was India. Early in 1924 secret documents, probably obtained by SIS, had revealed a Soviet decision to play down 'the Communist note in propaganda, where it was likely to offend the native populations', and to concentrate instead on exploiting Indian nationalism 'as an unconscious means of furthering Communist aims'. The threat to the north-western frontier revived at almost the same moment. According to intelligence reports, the Politburo decided on 14 January 1924 to instruct the Soviet representative in Kabul to work for 'the establishment of a united Empire of Muslim-India and Afghanistan ... which should liberate millions of Indians from under the foreign yoke'. Late in March 1924 an intercepted letter sent from Moscow by the Indian Communist, M.N. Roy, reported Comintern's intention to devote 'almost unlimited funds' to India.

In order not to prejudice the Anglo-Soviet negotiations Comintern decided to postpone its campaign until the negotiations had been successfully concluded:

> However, on the 8th August 1924, the day [of] the signing of the Anglo-Russian Treaty, the Third International decided that the coast was clear, threw off all restraint and embarked upon a full programme. On that date the Executive Committee decided that it was 'indispensable to review and increase the work of the Comintern in the East', and instructed the President [Zinoviev] ... to take measures to carry out this decision.[28]

Zinoviev was anxious to extend the Comintern campaign to Britain itself. At the fifth congress of the International in June and July 1924 he showed himself 'wildly optimistic' about the prospects for a British revolution. The British Communist Party, he declared, was now 'the most important section of the Communist International' and must launch a new and vigorous offensive. Ramsay MacDonald was quickly provided with intelligence reports of the Comintern congress and Zinoviev's speeches.[29]

Both the prime minister and the Foreign Office must therefore have been expecting subversive correspondence from Zinoviev. The account in Ramsay MacDonald's diary of the Zinoviev letter confirms that this was so. Even before the letter was received, the prime minister 'was on the lookout for such documents and meant to deal firmly with them'.[30] And 'deal firmly' was precisely what MacDonald did. When shown the Zinoviev letter on 16 October, he added the minute:

> We must be sure that the document is authentic.
> I favour the publication of such things, and the way to do it is to address a despatch to M. Rakovsky. Prepare such and see how it looks. It must be so well-founded and important that it carries conviction and guilt. If not, it will do harm.

A draft protest, 'after much elaboration and revision', was dispatched to the prime minister on 21 October, together with a note from Crowe that 'it can be published as soon as it has reached M. Rakovsky's hands'. Because of MacDonald's campaign travels, that draft did not reach him till the 23rd. Despite the pressures of the campaign, the prime minister found time on the following morning to produce a 'practically rewritten' draft.[31] The effect of the rewriting was to make the protest even stronger than before.[32]

At this point a misunderstanding occurred between MacDonald and the Foreign Office, a misunderstanding for which MacDonald's 'state of near exhaustion'[33] is the most likely explanation. The prime minister had expected to see the draft protest again before it was delivered to Rakovsky. Instead he was 'dumbfounded' to discover from a reporter on the evening of 25 October that the protest had already been delivered and would appear in the press on the following day. MacDonald based his expectation that the protest would not be delivered until he had seen it again solely on the fact that he had 'refrained from initialling it'. For the misunderstanding which followed MacDonald was to blame:

> It is true that the draft which he had practically rewritten did not actually bear the Prime Minister's initials at the foot. This is, however, a not infrequent omission, the Secretary of State's manuscript corrections on drafts submitted to him being ordinarily regarded as indicating his definite approval of the document so revised. A number of recent cases of the kind have since been brought to Mr MacDonald's notice. It was accordingly only following the routine of departmental work that action should have been taken so soon as the revised draft note to M. Rakovsky was returned by the Prime Minister. There was the less reason to suppose that the Department were not carrying out his wishes precisely, inasmuch as every aspect of the action to be taken had been exhaustively discussed in minutes. The Prime Minister had explicitly approved publication and had intimated that the appropriate procedure was a note to be addressed to M. Rakovsky. This he had made dependent on two conditions: (1) That the document was authentic; (2) that he should see the draft. Both conditions had, in the view of the Department, been fulfilled.[34]

'Still', MacDonald remarked in his diary, 'nothing untoward would have happened had not the *Daily Mail* and other agencies including Conservative leaders had the letter and were [*sic*] preparing a political bomb from it'.[35] Crowe's discovery that the *Daily Mail* was about to publish the Zinoviev letter was the main reason for his decision to deliver MacDonald's revised protest note without delay. His motive was to protect both the government and the Foreign Office from the charge of suppressing 'information vitally concerning the security of the Empire'.[36] Despite Crowe's prompt action, the charge was made. Baldwin, Curzon, and other Tory leaders claimed, on no evidence, that MacDonald had tried to hush the letter up. The Zinoviev letter was used as dramatic evidence that the Labour government was soft on Bolshevism. And the bewildered inconsistency with which Labour ministers responded to the publication of a letter whose existence they had not suspected gave further substance to the charge.

The 'political bomb' which thus exploded beneath MacDonald's unwary feet was detonated by the *Daily Mail*. But the bomb was planted by others. Thomas Marlowe, the editor of the *Mail*, first heard of the letter's existence on the morning of 23 October from a telephone message left the previous evening by 'an old and trusted friend'. The 'old and trusted friend', was, almost certainly, 'Blinker' Hall.[37] Hall's action was entirely consistent with his earlier career. As DNI during the Dardanelles campaign in 1915, on his own authority and without the knowledge of the cabinet he had sent secret emissaries to Constantinople with authority to offer up to £4 million to secure the passage of the British fleet. Hall left the following account of the interview with the first lord of the Admiralty which ensued:

> [Churchill] was frowning. 'Who authorised this?' he demanded.
> 'I did, First Lord'.
> 'But – the Cabinet surely knows nothing about it?'
> 'No, it does not ...'
> It was one of those moments when dropped pins are supposed to be heard. Then Mr Churchill turned to Lord Fisher [First Sea Lord] ... 'D'you hear what this man has done? He's sent out people with four millions to buy a peaceful passage! On his own!'[38]

Hall had also shown his willingness to reveal secret information when he believed it in the national interest. During the war he had distributed lurid extracts from Casement's diary to ensure that Casement did not 'escape his just fate'.[39]

Nor was Hall prepared to stand aside in 1924. The depth of his suspicion of, and contempt for, Labour leaders was unusual even by the standards of the Tory 'diehards' whose ranks he had joined in the Commons. In 1921 he had publicly alleged the existence of a successful Labour plot to secure the dismissal of the head of the Special Branch, Sir Basil Thomson, 'the one man our enemies had cause to fear', in return for supporting Lloyd George's Irish policy.[40] Hall doubtless felt, when the Zinoviev letter was published, that the Labour government, like Casement, had met its 'just fate'. This time, however, he was acting in the interests of the Tory party as well as of the intelligence services. In 1923 he had been principal agent at Conservative Central Office, and was closely acquainted with both Jackson, the party chairman, and Younger, the ex-chairman. Hall probably acted in concert with Central Office in plotting the publication of the Zinoviev letter.[41]

Hall was by no means the only member of the intelligence community, active and retired, to seek to publicise the letter. By the morning of 24 October Marlowe had received copies of the Zinoviev letter from two separate sources and had discussed it with at least one more (all identified only as 'gentlemen to whom I could not offer money, and who would have been gravely affronted if I had done so').[42] Evidence survives to show that one of these sources was, very probably, Lieutenant-Colonel Freddie Browning, Cumming's former deputy and a friend of both Hall and Marlowe.[43] Among the smaller fry involved in the affair was Donald im Thurn, a former officer of MI5, probably urged on by Sidney Reilly. Though not one of Marlowe's contacts, he was probably the first to alert Conservative Central Office to the existence of the Zinoviev letter.[44] Retired intelligence officers, however, could scarcely have gained access to the letter without the assistance of serving officers.[45]

It is not the habit of the British intelligence services either to commit more than necessary to paper or to preserve compromising evidence for future historians. For that reason neither the identity of all those involved in publicising the Zinoviev letter nor their precise roles will ever be established with certainty. There seems little doubt, however, that the 'political bomb' which exploded in the last days of the Labour government was planted by the intelligence community. The motives of the secret service are not hard to find. In 1920 intelligence chiefs had considered it vital to publish the evidence of subversion from intercepted Soviet telegrams even if, in consequence, no further telegrams could be decrypted. To the indignation of the cabinet, the contents of some of those telegrams had been leaked to the *Daily Mail* and *Morning Post*. The situation, in secret service eyes, was far more serious in 1924 than in 1920. Like Hall, many intelligence officers were Tory diehards with greatly exaggerated fears of the Labour government's susceptibility to Bolshevik pressure. They also had a far more rational fear for the future of the intelligence services following a Labour election victory. In 1925 the Labour Party advisory committee on international questions was actually to propose the suspension of the secret service and the revelation of its activities.[46]

In 1924, as in 1920, the fears of the intelligence services had led to a press leak of intercepted Soviet documents. This time, however, the leak had a much clearer political motive. The Zinoviev letter was intended to bring down the Labour government. Though the letter was not the main cause of the Tory election landslide on 29 October, many politicians on both Left and Right believed that it was. Beaverbrook congratulated Rothermere on winning the election for the Conservatives by his 'Red Letter' campaign in the *Daily Mail*. Rothermere modestly agreed that he had won a hundred seats.[47] Labour leaders were inclined to agree. They felt they had been tricked out of office. And their suspicions seemed confirmed when they discovered the part played by Conservative Central Office in the publication of the letter.

The Soviet Union has always publicly maintained that the letter was forged. The internal evidence is inconclusive. Despite some minor oddities for which there are mostly parallels in other Comintern documents, the letter was largely concerned with applying the resolutions of the fifth Comintern congress to the British situation.[48] The Zinoviev letter placed greater emphasis on Communist propaganda and cell building in the armed forces, but there is other evidence that Comintern did send such instructions to the CPGB.[49] If the Zinoviev letter was not genuine, its contents at least reflected genuine Comintern policy. William Peters, the British envoy in Moscow, reported after the publication of the letter: 'The general view [of the diplomatic corps] is that, whether this particular letter is or is not genuine, other letters of similar tenor are constantly being despatched by the Communist International to various countries'. Peters mentioned the 'somewhat similar case' of a letter from the Soviet Communist Party intercepted by the Finns in 1922 which the Russians had first denounced as a forgery:

> When it was established, by means of examination of the typewriting, that it was the work of the same machine as that on which various undoubtedly genuine circulars had been typed, the Soviet authorities took the fresh line that it was the work of a female typist, Miss Eva Korhonen, and that the committee of the party had nothing to do with it. The matter was dropped, as so many of these matters are.[50]

The strongest evidence in support of the Soviet charge of forgery derives from the existence of known groups of forgers in Berlin, Reval, Warsaw and elsewhere trying to make or supplement their living from bogus documents and, in some cases, work as double agents. The forgers quickly disputed among themselves the doubtful honour of having produced the Zinoviev letter. In 1928 Stanley Baldwin gave the Commons the names of five forgers – Druzhelovsky, Zhemchuzhnikov, Paciórkowsky, Bernstein (alias Henry Lawrence, alias Lorenzo) and Schreck – each of whom had 'provided a most circumstantial story as to how he forged the letter'. Allegations were also made during the 1920s by the Soviet authorities and others against at least four other forgers: Gumansky, H. Siewert, V. Orlov and Alexis Bellegarde (or Belgardt).[51] The claims by Bellegarde and several of his colleagues to have forged the Zinoviev letter were revived in 1966 by Bellegarde's widow and published in *The Sunday Times*.[52] Mrs Bellegarde's memory of events forty years before is, however, very difficult to reconcile with the evidence. If, for example, her clear recollection that her husband and his friends fabricated the Zinoviev letter on a single side of Comintern notepaper stolen from the Soviet embassy in Berlin is correct, then their forgery cannot have been the longer document obtained by SIS. There is little doubt that a number of forged Comintern documents were in circulation during the summer of 1924, as at most other times during the 1920s. But it remains to be shown that any of them was the document which memorably disturbed the last days of the first Labour government.

Perhaps the greatest weakness of the various forgery hypotheses is that they take no account of the large number of genuine Soviet and Comintern documents successfully intercepted by the British and Indian intelligence services. Significantly neither *The Sunday Times* investigation nor the most recent biography of Sidney Reilly, which takes a similar line on the forgery issue, even mentions the existence of GC & CS. In 1924 the intelligence services obtained a substantial number of genuine Soviet and Comintern documents, and were also offered a number of forgeries. The Foreign Office and the intelligence services had by now some experience in distinguishing the two. Austen Chamberlain, foreign secretary in the incoming Conservative government, told the Commons in December:

> It is suggested that the Foreign Office was hoaxed by some vulgar imposture such as have been fabricated in various parts of the world. The Foreign Office and our Secret Service have probably a closer knowledge of these manufactories and manufacturers of forgeries than even hon. Members opposite. We know them, and the fact that we know them is a guarantee that we are not taken in.[53]

The Foreign Office did indeed possess a considerable knowledge of anti-Soviet forgeries and of anti-Soviet forgers. What Chamberlain omitted to mention, however, was the painful way in which much of that knowledge had been acquired. In 1921 the Foreign Office had been deceived by a substantial number of anti-Soviet forgeries.[54] Its misjudgment then makes it impossible to discount the possibility that it was deceived again in 1924. But the traumatic experience of 1921 undoubtedly left it determined to avoid similar errors in future. That experience helps to explain why Crowe refused to forward the Zinoviev letter to the prime minister in October 1924 (despite 'the most convincing assurances of the genuine character of the letter') 'until corroborative proofs were forthcoming of its having reached this country'.[55] The Special Branch was also not easily fooled. Unlike SIS, Sir Basil Thomson had not been deceived by the Reval 'intercepts' in 1921. His successor, Sir Wyndham Childs, 'when dealing with Communism', was also 'constantly coming across the crudest forgeries'. The forgers, some of whom he had under surveillance, were in his view 'an intolerable nuisance', for they 'gave the Russians an opportunity to shout "forgery" when a genuine document was being dealt with'. The experience of Sir David Petrie, the head of DIB (and later of MI5), was very similar.[56]

The forgery hypotheses also fail to take adequate account of the 'corroborative proofs' which convinced Whitehall that the Zinoviev letter was genuine. Only fragments of these 'proofs' now survive. According to spokesmen for Stanley Baldwin's incoming Conservative government, however, the evidence came 'not from one source, but from four different and independent sources, every one of which was a source which had previously been tested and found to be absolutely reliable'. The original source of the letter supplied evidence which allowed the government to follow 'its whole course from its origin until it reached our hands'. Evidence of the letter's authenticity was then supplied by three further 'wholly independent ... and wholly unconnected sources'.[57]

The first of these three independent sources (and the only one to report before the fall of the Labour government) was described by Crowe as 'a trusted agent in the Communist party' who had shown himself to be 'absolutely reliable' and provided MI5 on 11 October with evidence, forwarded to the Foreign Office on the 13th, that 'the Russian letter was received and discussed at a recent meeting of the Central Committee of the Communist Party of Great Britain'.[58] The precise evidence provided either does not survive or remains hidden in MI5 archives. But there seems no doubt that MI5 already had at least one 'trusted agent in the Communist Party' who regularly provided extracts from secret minutes and other documents.[59]

Though responsibility for monitoring civil subversion rested with the Special Branch, MI5 had used the threat of Communist involvement in military subversion as an argument to justify the placing of penetration agents (later known as 'moles') in the CPGB.[60] MI5 headquarters did not deal directly with its agents within the Party. Instead it employed 'agent-runners' who met their agents at neutral locations well away from MI5 offices in Cromwell Road.[61] In the process the agent-runners must sometimes have trespassed into Special Branch territory, but 'Fido' Childs was much less likely to protest than Kell's former rival, Sir Basil Thomson.[62] The call in the Zinoviev letter of 15 September for the CPGB to engage in 'agitation-propaganda work in the armed forces' in any case placed the whole affair squarely within MI5's sphere of action.

Before the Zinoviev letter disrupted its final weeks in office, the Labour cabinet had already accepted as genuine both earlier intercepted Comintern and CPGB correspondence, and informers' reports. After an election defeat which ministers blamed largely on the Red Letter campaign in the Conservative press, they were understandably more cautious. A committee of the outgoing cabinet, set up on 31 October to consider the letter's authenticity, found it impossible to arrive at a conclusion 'in the short time available' before the government's resignation on 4 November. A committee of the incoming Baldwin cabinet found 'not a shade of a shadow of a doubt as to the authenticity of the document'.[63] It had two further corroborative proofs available to it as well as a greater readiness to believe them.

The first of these 'proofs' was the report of a discussion by the Soviet Council of Commissars (Sovnarkom) on 25 October, forwarded by 'Quex' Sinclair to the Foreign Office on 6 November, too late to be considered by MacDonald's committee. Since the report reached SIS from Reval, a source of anti-Soviet forgeries as well as Soviet intelligence, it has to be treated with considerable caution. There is, however, some similarity between the SIS report and the later, independent recollections of Aino Kuusinen, the wife and assistant of Comintern's Finnish secretary-general. According to the SIS report, Chicherin admitted to Sovnarkom that the published version of the Zinoviev letter was correct in substance but claimed that 'the text had been mutilated'.[64] According to Aino Kuusinen, Zinoviev had sent a letter, 'parts of it had leaked', and a new letter had been 'concocted' from these leaks for publication in the British press. When commenting on Chicherin's alleged statement to Sovnarkom, Sinclair told Crowe: 'The reference to mutilation evidently refers to the discrepancy between our translation of the Russian original and that received by the British Communists'.[65]

The expurgated files now available in the Public Record Office do not identify the final 'corroborative proof' provided by the intelligence services. But the official claim that it was entirely independent of both the MI5 informer and the SIS agent points in the direction of either the Special Branch or GC & CS. The Special Branch, according to both Childs and Ramsay MacDonald, provided no corroboration – though it did furnish background information on Comintern activities as well as contradicting some Russian evidence of forgery.[66] The third 'corroborative proof' is thus more likely to have come from GC & CS. The new Russian codes and ciphers introduced late in 1923 had, almost certainly, been broken in time for British codebreakers to give an insight into Soviet reactions to the publication of the Zinoviev letter.[67] In 1921 Soviet decrypts had helped to expose the bogus intercepts obtained in Reval. Three years later they may have helped to reinforce belief in the Zinoviev letter.

Whatever the failings of the Baldwin cabinet's investigation of the Zinoviev letter, they were certainly fewer than those of the enquiry organised by the TUC. On 9 November a TUC delegation arrived in Moscow in a naive attempt to establish the truth about the letter's authenticity. Aino Kuusinen later described the 'three days and nights of feverish activity' which were necessary to remove secret instructions to British Communists and other 'compromising documents' from Comintern archives to make them fit for TUC inspection. The delegation arrived to a hero's welcome and was easily convinced. It quickly announced conclusive proof that the Zinoviev letter was a forgery. 'After the delegation had left', Aino Kuusinen later recalled, 'there was general relief and everyone had a good laugh over the fact that they had been able to pull the wool so easily over the Englishmen's eyes'.[68]

The disreputable use of the Zinoviev letter to try to bring down the first Labour government has, inevitably, made it an emotive issue in the history of the labour movement. Anxious to discredit the document as well as the use made of it, supporters of the forgery hypothesis have (like the TUC delegation) frequently argued their case with greater conviction than the fragmentary evidence can justify. Certainty about the authenticity of the letter will be impossible until, perhaps beyond, the far distant date when both the Soviet government and British intelligence open their archives. For the present the historian can safely do no more than weigh the balance of probabilities. In the case of the letter itself, considered in isolation, the issues seem finely balanced. The disappearance of the original document makes the problem of distinguishing a good forgery from the genuine article even more difficult than usual. But it is hard to dismiss as forgeries both the letter and all three independent 'corroborative proofs' – particularly that from the agent within the Communist party who seems to have supplied so much other secret information. If the Zinoviev letter was forged, it must surely have been sufficiently close to a genuine Comintern communication for the MI5 agent at party headquarters to confuse the two, and for Comintern's secretary-general to conclude that information from a genuine letter had been used to 'concoct' a spurious one.[69]

Sidney Reilly did not long survive his own involvement in publicising the Zinoviev letter. Since 1922 the GPU had been plotting the downfall of both Reilly and Savinkov by operating a bogus anti-Bolshevik Front, the Monarchist Union of Central Russia (MUCR), better known as the Trust, designed to ensnare the remaining plotters against Bolshevik rule. The Trust had its origins in the summer of 1922 when Savinkov's aide, L.D. Sheshenya, a former Tsarist officer, was captured by Soviet border guards as he crossed into Russia from Poland. He and one of his agents in Russia, M.D. Zekunov, were then turned round by the GPU and used as the basis of an elaborate deception plan. A GPU officer, A.P. Fyodorov, posing as one of the leaders of the Trust, paid a number of visits to Warsaw, using the alias A.P. Mukhin, in order to win the confidence of Savinkov's Polish supporters. In July 1923 Fyodorov travelled to Paris and made a first attempt to lure Savinkov himself back to Russia by claiming that only he could heal divisions which had developed within the Moscow Trust. Initially Savinkov was wary of returning and sent one of his deputies, Colonel Pavlovsky, who was arrested by the OGPU (the successor of the GPU), turned round and persuaded to join in the deception of his chief. Early in July Savinkov fell for the bait, decided to return to Russia and telegraphed to Reilly to come over from New York to help plan his secret mission to his homeland. On 15 August, after three weeks' discussion with Reilly, Savinkov crossed into Russia with some of his supporters and was promptly arrested. Under interrogation by the OGPU his resistance collapsed almost immediately. At a show trial on 27 August Savinkov made a full confession:

> I unconditionally recognise Soviet power and none other. To every Russian who loves his country I, who have traversed the entire road of this bloody, heavy struggle against you, I who refuted you as none other did, I tell him that if you are a Russian, if you love your people, you will bend down to worker-peasant power and recognise it without any reservations.

In return for his recantation Savinkov escaped the death sentence and was given ten years in a relatively comfortable prison. Reilly initially refused to believe Savinkov's confession and, in a letter to *The Morning Post* published on 8 September, denounced the whole affair as a 'colossal libel' devised by the Bolsheviks 'to discredit Savinkov's good name'. A week later Reilly changed his mind and told the *Morning Post* that Savinkov's treachery was now established 'beyond all possibility of doubt'. Savinkov tried desperately to persuade Felix Dzerzhinsky, the head of the OGPU, to let him out of prison to start a new life in the Soviet service. When he failed he threw himself to his death from his prison window – or so it is claimed – in May 1925.[70]

Within five months Reilly too had fallen victim to the Trust. His downfall was unwittingly assisted by his old friend Commander Boyce, formerly station chief in Petrograd in 1918, now PCO in Helsinki, the main base for SIS's Soviet operations. Boyce was convinced that, despite Savinkov's capture, the Trust was growing in strength and included even members of the Soviet government. In January 1925 Boyce wrote to Reilly in New York asking him to meet representatives of the Trust in Paris. The cryptic nature of Boyce's coded letter suggests that he was acting without 'Quex' Sinclair's approval. 'The only thing I ask', he wrote, 'is that you keep our connection with this business from the knowledge of my department ... I am not supposed to be connected with any such enterprise'. Reilly's business ventures were collapsing around him, his law suit to try to obtain commission he believed owing to him was failing, and he felt unable to leave immediately for Paris – though he told Boyce he was 'kicking' himself not doing so. But with his gambler's instincts and tendency to self-dramatisation, Reilly could not resist the lure of another attempt to stir up counter-revolution. He wrote to Boyce in March 1925:

> Much as I am concerned about my own personal affairs which, as you know, are in a hellish state, I am, at any moment, if I see the right people and prospects of real action, prepared to chuck everything else and devote myself entirely to the Syndicate's interests.
>
> I was fifty-one yesterday and I want to do something worthwhile, while I can.

Reilly was sent an invitation to meet the leaders of the Trust in Moscow and was easily persuaded that his own involvement was crucial to their success. He wrote self-importantly, if cryptically, to Boyce:

> I think I am not exaggerating in presuming that a successful inspection of the factory [the Trust] by me and the presentation of a fully substantiated technical report would produce a considerable impression in the interested quarters and generally facilitate to realization of the scheme.[71]

According to a Soviet historian, Reilly told the Trust that its success required the use of 'Terror directed from a centre, but carried out by small independent groups and persons against prominent individual statesmen':

The purpose is of prime importance, to stir up the swamp, to end lethargy, to shatter the myth of the authorities' invulnerability, to light a spark ... I am sure that a major act of terror would produce an astonishing impression and stir up worldwide hopes of the imminent fall of the Bolsheviks, and at the same time an active interest in Russian affairs.[72]

After a number of delays caused chiefly by Reilly's 'hellish', debt-ridden business dealings, he arrived in Paris on 3 September where he was met by Boyce and some of Savinkov's former supporters. Persuaded that there was 'really something entirely new, powerful and worthwhile going on in Russia', he crossed the Finnish border on 25 September accompanied by GPU men masquerading as members of the Trust. At a dacha outside Moscow two days later Reilly met the supposed 'political council' of the Trust, was encouraged to reveal his plan of action, and suggested financing the Trust's activities by pillaging Russian museums and selling their art treasures in the West. He was then arrested. After interrogation Reilly was told that the death sentence passed on him *in absentia* after his 1918 escapades would be carried out. In a vain attempt to save himself, according to the Soviet account of his interrogation, he sent a personal appeal to Dzerzhinsky:

After prolonged deliberation, I express willingness to give you complete and open acknowledgement and information on matters of interest to the OGPU concerning the organization and personnel of the British Intelligence Service and, so far as I know it, similar information on American Intelligence and likewise about Russian émigrés with whom I have had business.

Reilly's appeal failed. He was shot early in November 1925. Inevitably, the myths which he had created about his remarkable, though ultimately ineffective, career multiplied after his death. Some believed that he was not dead at all but working for, or possibly against, the OGPU.[73]

One of the consequences of the Zinoviev letter furore within Whitehall was a drastic tightening of security procedures by the incoming Conservative administration. Neither intercepts nor regular Special Branch reports were circulated to Baldwin's second cabinet after it took office in November 1924. Winston Churchill, now chancellor of the exchequer, returned to power eager to catch up on the backlog of Soviet intercepts and was outraged to be denied access to them. He protested to Austen Chamberlain, the new foreign secretary, against 'such serious changes in the system which was in vogue when we were last colleagues':

... I have studied this information [the intercepts] over a longer period

and more attentively than probably any other minister has done. All the years
I have been in office since it began [in Room 40] in the autumn of 1914 I
have read every one of these flimsies and I attach more importance to them
as a means of forming a true judgement of public policy in these spheres
than to any other source of knowledge at the disposal of the State.[74]

Churchill's protests were to no avail. Henceforth a complete set of intercepts
was circulated only to the Foreign Office. The service ministries and the India,
Colonial and Home Offices saw only intercepts which directly concerned them.

Early in 1925 SIS and GC & CS moved from their hitherto separate
headquarters (which for the last few years had been located in, respectively,
Melbury Road and Queen's Gate) to adjacent offices in Broadway Buildings,
54 Broadway, opposite St James's Park tube station, Westminster. Initially,
SIS and GC & CS occupied the third and fourth of the eight floors but
gradually spread upwards.[75] Below them, for a time, were the offices of a
missionary society. One cryptographer retained a possibly fanciful memory of
how 'they used to sing hymns when they were dispatching missionaries to the
lions'.[76]

'C' (Admiral 'Quex' Sinclair) had his offices in the centre of Broadway
Buildings on the fourth floor. His visitors had first to knock on a hatch on
his outer office which was opened by one of his secretaries. If admitted, they
then observed a green light bulb (reminiscent of the green ink reserved to C
alone) over the door of Sinclair's inner office which indicated when he was
engaged. Quex had a flat (where his sister Evelyn kept house) in Queen
Anne's Gate which backed conveniently onto Broadway Buildings and allowed
him direct access between home and office. C sought to preserve the utmost
secrecy about his new address. But, as secret addresses often are, it was
discovered by London taxi drivers, doubtless aided by his open Lancia which
was sometimes parked outside. One morning Quex was shocked to discover
a large arrow painted on the pavement with the words: 'To the British Secret
Service Office'.[77]

Though the circulation of secret intelligence was severely restricted as a
result of the Zinoviev letter, the affair seems to have had little effect on its
supply whether from the intercepted communications of the Soviet government
and Comintern or from informants within the CPGB. Austen Chamberlain,
however, appears to have found all forms of Soviet intelligence something of
an embarrassment. In March 1925 the cabinet authorised him to begin the
negotiations which were to end seven months later in the Locarno non-
aggression pact between France, Germany and Belgium, guaranteed by Britain
and Italy, and usher in (so it was believed) a new era of European peace.
Chamberlain was anxious that no new dispute with Russia should stand in
the way. While still opposing a 'rupture' with Russia, however, he wrote to
Baldwin in July:

A great mass of information has accumulated in this office proving the continuous hostile activities of Soviet Agencies against the British Empire, more particularly in the East. Nearly all this information is of the most highly secret character, which I do not circulate to Ministers lest any carelessness in the handling of the papers should endanger our sources of information ... The provocation offered as shown by this secret information is such as I suppose we have never tolerated from any government and it becomes increasingly difficult to maintain the attitude [of preserving diplomatic relations] which I have thought it right to recommend to the Cabinet.

At Chamberlain's request, a small cabinet committee chaired by himself was appointed to consider the evidence. It unanimously approved a continuation of 'our present policy' and rejected the alternative of 'a publication of the documents and a rupture of relations at the present time'.[78]

For the next eighteen months Chamberlain's policy towards Russia remained remarkably consistent. On the one hand, he continued to believe that 'we should be justified on the facts as now known to us in breaking off [diplomatic relations], if we thought it expedient to do so'. On the other hand, he continued to believe it was not expedient to do so. A new quarrel with Russia would interfere with the more general pacification of Europe on which he had set his heart. As J.D. Gregory, the head of the Foreign Office's Northern Department, explained to Baldwin: 'Peace is the paramount international need and a definitely outlawed Russia would be bound to seek an increased means of disturbing it'.[79]

The evidence from intelligence sources of Russian 'subversion' had lost much of the capacity it once possessed to shock, at least in the Foreign Office. British diplomats had, quite simply, grown accustomed to it. There was a consensus among Chamberlain and his officials that subversion had to be expected and, within limits, to be lived with:

No other government in the world would have received or expected the patience we have shown the Soviet Government, but we have found it best not to take them or their offences against international comity too seriously.[80]

At Locarno in October 1925 Chamberlain 'lived such days ... as it is given to no man to experience twice'.[81] For a time thereafter his view of the whole international system was suffused with optimism. Even the Bolsheviks, Chamberlain believed, though they would not change their spots, were at least likely to calm down:

Up to this point, our policy of aloofness has succeeded very well. Russia is finding out, as I anticipated that it would, that it has more need of us and Europe than we have of it.[82]

Most of Baldwin's ministers viewed the evidence of Soviet subversion with less sangfroid than Austen Chamberlain. The minister with least sangfroid was the home secretary, Sir William Joynson-Hicks, a Tory diehard who insisted on the complete redecoration of his room in the Home Office overlooking the Foreign Office quadrangle and the introduction of a new desk to symbolise, according to his admiring biographer, 'the arrival of the new broom that would impart cleanliness to some neglected corners'. In 'Jix' both Kell and Childs found at last a home secretary after their own heart, anxious to strike 'one overwhelming and final blow against the Communist organisation'.[83]

Behind the resurgence of labour militancy during 1925 Jix predictably detected the barely hidden hand of Moscow. He was not alone in over-reacting to the Red Menace. Though the CPGB had only 6,000 members by the time of the general strike, the Communist-led (and Soviet-financed) National Minority Movement (NMM) within the unions seemed to be making rapid progress. Zinoviev optimistically told the Comintern executive in March 1925 that the NMM already represented 600,000 workers and formed the basis for a mass Communist Party which would make Britain 'the centre of gravity for the further development of world revolution'. In April 1925 an Anglo-Russian Trade Union Conference held in the hope of producing a reconciliation between the Soviet-dominated RILU and the International Federation of Trade Unions (IFTU), to which the TUC was affiliated, ended in an atmosphere of mutual congratulation and a decision to set up an Anglo-Russian Joint Advisory Council. As the Russian trade unionists left Victoria Station bearing bouquets of red roses presented by their British comrades, *The Times* declared that 'The Bolshevization of the British trade union movement has begun'. Zinoviev agreed. The Anglo-Russian Council was, he said, a step towards 'the revolutionization of England and its labour movement'. On 'Red Friday', 31 July 1925, the miners won a victory which was widely interpreted as a spectacular revenge for 'Black Friday' four years before and as further evidence that, as the CPGB claimed, the unions were accepting 'the Class-War policy of the Communist Party'. Faced with the threat of a prolonged coal strike, Baldwin's government conceded a subsidy it had hitherto refused to keep miners' wages at their present level. The miners' leader, A.J. Cook, a Communist fellow-traveller and, in his own words, 'a humble disciple of Lenin', boasted: 'We have beaten not only the employers but the strongest Government of modern times'. The Marquess of Salisbury, Lord Privy Seal, told the prime minister: 'I shall be glad if my confidence can be restored, but the moral basis of the Government seems to have dropped out'. Jix immediately embarked on a series of public speeches in which he asked 'Who rules? The Government or the trade unions?' Zinoviev, he declared, was using Communist infiltration of the unions 'to destroy and ruin us'. At the TUC Congress in September Beatrice Webb concluded that 'communistic T.U. leaders' had taken over the General Council and were 'plunging head over ears into grandiose schemes of immediate and revolutionary change'.[84]

The existing STO (Supply and Transport Organization) machinery prepared to meet a major strike wave was, Jix told the cabinet, 'only a skeleton' which would require many volunteers to run it. However 'various unofficial organisations', such as the Fascisti and the chambers of commerce, were ready to assist 'in case of emergency'. The cabinet cautiously concluded that the use of such organisations 'was one of large policy requiring careful consideration'.[85] Jix's vision of the STO organisation as he built it up was that in an emergency he would become 'dictator of administration, the commander-in-chief of the whole of the operations' with a chief commissioner in London and eleven regional commissioners under him.[86] By the time of the General Strike in May 1926 both Jix and the STO, with some assistance from MI5, were well prepared.[87]

The signs of growing Communist influence within the unions during 1925 were accompanied by intelligence reports of attempted subversion in the armed forces. A letter of 22 May 1925 from Zinoviev to Harry Pollitt, probably intercepted in Britain, urged the CPGB to continue propaganda in the armed forces 'at all costs, heedless of difficulties and obstacles'. Two months later SIS obtained a copy of a letter of 20 July to the CPGB instructing it to send its 'most efficient agitator-propagandists' to open the eyes of the armed forces 'to the nature of the class struggle', and to make urgent preparations for a campaign against militarism. MI5's moles within the CPGB quickly reported on the Party's response to Comintern instructions. On 29 July Kell received details from an MI5 informant of the CPGB's preparations for an 'Anti-War Week' to begin on 2 August and a new propaganda campaign directed at the services. On 13 August the Special Branch reported that 'virtually every direction' in the Comintern letter of 20 July had been faithfully carried out by the CPGB. Party workers were instructed that:

The whole Working Class Movement must be organisationally and ideologically prepared to fight war by the transformation of the Imperialist War when declared into the Civil War and Seizure of Power by the Working Class.

Soldiers and sailors were told to be ready to 'turn their guns on the masters as the workers of Russia had done' when the moment came. On 1 September

Kell also reported a number of attempts by CPGB members to enlist in the forces with the aim of encouraging the growth of Communist cells. Kell believed that the main purpose of the campaign was to 'make the Government apprehensive of employing troops in aid of the Civil power in case of necessity'. While MI5 believed Communist propaganda had so far had very little influence on the armed forces, it remained apprehensive about its long-term effect.[88]

Kell was anxious to use the evidence of subversion in the armed forces to bring the CPGB leadership to trial and thus strike a major blow at Communist influence in the labour movement also. The government agreed. On 13 October the attorney general, Sir Douglas Hogg, informed the cabinet that there was enough evidence 'to justify the arrest and prosecution of nine of the leading British Communists on a charge of sedition, and that in his opinion a prosecution was likely to result in convictions'. The cabinet was asked whether there were 'any factors in the national or industrial situation which rendered a prosecution undesirable' but said that it had 'no objection'. So important was the prosecution considered that Hankey, the cabinet secretary, was instructed 'not to circulate the Minute in regard to this decision until after the arrests had been made'.[89] In the end twelve leading party members, including the main office holders, were charged with sedition under the Incitement to Mutiny Act of 1797 and a large quantity of documents was seized in Special Branch raids on Communist premises.

When the trial opened at the Old Bailey on 16 November the attorney general presented evidence that the defendants were 'preaching and advocating the forcible overthrow of government and, as a necessary preliminary, the seduction of the King's Army and Navy from their allegiance and loyalty towards obedience to orders', that the Communist Party had received money and instructions from Comintern, and that Comintern had ordered 'persistent and systematic propaganda' in the armed forces. Concluding his summing-up after an eight-day trial, Mr Justice Swift told the jury that 'it would indeed be a bad day for the country if, when sedition had been proved to have occurred, there was the slightest faltering either on the part of the jury or the Judge in putting down the offence'. The jury did not falter. They found all twelve defendants guilty after only twenty minutes' deliberation. The judge sent the five defendants with previous convictions to prison for a year, and sentenced the others to six months after an absurd offer to let them off with a caution if they agreed to renounce their political opinions. 'This', writes A.J.P. Taylor, 'was one of the few occasions in recent English history when men were punished for their opinions, not for acts of practical significance'.[90]

In the months which followed the trial of the CPGB leaders the attempt to found Communist cells within the armed forces ended in failure. Kell reported confidently in April 1926 that all the cells had been discovered and 'the ringleaders disposed of'.[91] Communist influence in the unions, however, seemed greater than a year before. Jix claimed, largely on the basis of intelligence reports, that since September 1925, thanks to the founding of the Anglo-Russian Joint Advisory Council, there had been 'intimate and uninterrupted' contact between Moscow and British unions. Probably on the basis of GC & CS decrypts, Jix reported that the Soviet embassy in London had 'even acted as a channel for the transmission of messages' between the two.[92]

With the gift of hindsight it is clear that Jix enormously exaggerated the significance of Anglo-Soviet trade union contacts which in the end were to achieve very little. But many on the Left made the same mistake. Walter Citrine, shortly to begin a twenty-year term as general secretary of the TUC, declared during a visit to Moscow in the autumn of 1925 that British unions were working for a new 'International of trade unions' which 'would be capable of building on the foundations laid by your October revolution' to bring about 'the abolition of Capitalism'. During the winter and early spring of 1926 Comintern continued to lavish praise on the Anglo-Soviet Committee and intermittently indulged in ill-considered fantasies about the prospects for an early British revolution. Zinoviev prophesied that when the miners' wage agreement ran out, 'gigantic struggles' would follow between British workers and their oppressors.[93]

His prophecy was to prove remarkably accurate. At the end of April 1926 the miners refused to accept a pay-cut recommended by a royal commission and on 1 May they were locked out. A special trade union conference then approved plans for a general strike which began at midnight on the 3rd. On the union side detailed preparations for the strike had begun only a week before. Comintern, the RILU and the CPGB were also taken by surprise. Despite earlier intoxication with British revolutionary prospects, all three had lost faith in the readiness of the 'reactionaries' on the TUC General Council to support the miners' cause. Once the general strike began they quickly changed their tune. The strike, declared Comintern, was 'of historic importance'.[94]

Jix was emotionally incapable of seeing the general strike as anything other than a deep-laid plot. Earlier Soviet optimism about forthcoming 'gigantic struggles' in the British labour movement and the attempt by the Soviet-financed National Minority Movement to take control of the unions persuaded him that the plot had been hatched in Moscow. In a secret intelligence summary prepared by Jix for the cabinet he underlined two reports in particular. The first was a report of a meeting in Berlin at the end of August 1925 attended by A. Lozovsky, secretary of the RILU, and A.J. Cook, the miners' leader. Lozovsky was said to have outlined the prospects for strike action in both Britain and the continent early in 1926, involving miners, metalworkers, transport workers and others:

It was anticipated, he said, that the strike would be of several months' duration and would be primarily of an economic nature. As it progressed, however, political demands would be advanced. Mr Cook was present at this Berlin meeting and expressed considerable fear lest anything should be done to provoke repressive measures by His Majesty's Government.

The second intelligence report underlined by Jix was a letter from Comintern to the CPGB of 3 February 1926:

> ... Upon the success of the revolutionary movement in England now depends the whole course of the international socialist revolution. Only a well organised mass strike movement can prepare the way for active revolutionary struggle.[95]

It is impossible to be certain of the authenticity of these and other reports which outraged Jix both because the originals are unavailable and because Jix was more prepared than most intelligence consumers to credit alarmist anti-Bolshevik intelligence. But it seems clear from Comintern and RILU reports which are available that both Lozovsky and Zinoviev did indulge in fantasies about the prospects for British strikes and revolution as remarkable as those quoted by Jix. Out of such fantasies Jix constructed a vast conspiracy theory.

Jix was far better prepared for the General Strike than Communists in either Britain or the Soviet Union. The Supply and Transport Committee (STC) chaired by Jix and strengthened by the inclusion of his fellow die-hards, Churchill and Birkenhead, met at least once a day during the strike. As they had anticipated, road transport filled the gap caused by the striking railwaymen. Emergency communications and intelligence schemes also worked well. MI5 lent London District headquarters in Horse Guards twelve of its officers who were officially described as 'of the greatest assistance during the emergency'. Troops were not needed to preserve order save in the traditionally violent London Docks. Arguably the main problem encountered by the government was the sheer volume of volunteer strike-breakers. By 11 May 114,000 volunteers had registered in the London and Home Counties, of whom only 9,500 had actually been found jobs; 226,000 men were enrolled as special constables in England and Wales – again far more than were needed.[96]

Even when the General Strike was called off unconditionally on 12 May, Jix continued with his attempts to prove to his colleagues that it had been a Soviet plot. On 11 June he triumphantly concluded from MI5 and Special Branch investigations of the almost simultaneous payment of large sums by Arcos (the All-Russian Cooperative Society) to the Cooperative Wholesale Society and the withdrawal of large sums from the latter Society by several unions that the Soviet Union 'was without doubt providing money on the first day of the General Strike for the financing of the strike'. Four days later, while defending his previous statement as 'a natural inference', Jix admitted that he had jumped to false conclusions and that there was, after all, 'no reason to connect the two transactions'. On 11 June Jix had also alleged preparations going back to January to transfer RILU funds to the Strike Committee of the TUC General Council. That allegation too was false, though he failed to withdraw it.[97] Jix was, however, able to save face and conceal his error from all but his cabinet colleagues by publishing a Blue Book containing some of the documents seized in Special Branch raids on Communist headquarters in October 1925. Though the documents had no direct bearing on the General Strike, they were sufficient to establish that both Comintern and RILU regularly subsidised their British supporters. Among the documents he quoted was one from the CPGB secretariat to Comintern asking for greater discretion in its communications, and to avoid 'unnecessary references' so such matters as 'transmitting money by the secret channel'. The Blue Book was subsequently quoted in a Labour Party circular on Comintern strategy for winning control of the British labour movement.[98]

In reality, the TUC General Council was so sensitive to the charge of being financed by 'Red Gold' that when it received a cheque from the RILU and Soviet unions during the General Strike it sent it back on the grounds that it would be 'wilfully misrepresented and acceptance would be misunderstood'.[99] Predictably Comintern decided to send funds by covert means to some of its British supporters, but met with at least one spectacular failure. Allan Wallenius, the English-speaking Comintern librarian, was given £30,000 to deliver to Communist leaders of the London dockers. He set out for Stockholm with a forged Swedish passport, boarded a British ship bound for England and made friends with a stoker who explained that he was not merely a good Communist but actually knew the Communist to whom the money was to be delivered. On his return, Wallenius explained to Otto Kuusinen, Comintern's secretary, that the stoker had agreed to deliver the money himself. Kuusinen's wife later recalled the sequel:

'What was the stoker's name?' asked Otto drily.
'He told me his name, but I've forgotten it'.
Speechless with fury, Otto pointed to the door.
Needless to say, the money never got to its destination.[100]

The miners' strike, which continued after the General Strike collapsed until August, was, however, openly financed by the Russians. The miners raised about £450,000 in the United Kingdom and received £1,233,788 from the Soviet Union, some of it contributed by Soviet miners whose wages were smaller than the strike pay received by their British comrades.[101]

Besides Jix and Churchill, the main anti-Bolshevik crusader within the cabinet was the Earl of Birkenhead, the secretary of state for India. As in the case of Jix, his indignation was regularly fuelled by intelligence reports. Communist subversion in India was monitored not merely by DIB under Sir David Petrie (a future head of MI5) in India itself but also by the Interdepartmental Committee on Eastern Unrest founded in London in February 1922, consisting of members from MI5, the Special Branch, the Indian, Colonial, Foreign and War Offices, and usually attended by representatives of SIS and IPI (the DIB London liaison office). Comintern decreed in 1924 that the task of directing the Communist movement in India and the British Empire should be entrusted not to the imperial peoples themselves but to the CPGB – a decision which as M.N. Roy, the leading Indian Communist in exile, complained, 'smacks of imperialism'. Under instructions from Comintern, the CPGB formed a Colonial Department and despatched a series of agents to organise the Indian party. Comintern also sought on occasion to make 'direct contact' with Indian Communists. Despite keeping two lines of communications open, however, Moscow was frequently less well informed about its Indian supporters than Sir David Petrie and the Interdepartmental Committee on Eastern Unrest. The lengthy Indian intelligence reports (frequently quoting intercepted Comintern and CPGB communications) have since become a major source for both Marxist and non-Marxist historians of Indian Communism.[102]

The first CPGB emissary was Percy Glading (later jailed for spying in Britain for the Soviet Union) who arrived in India in February 1925 using the alias R. Cochrane, ostensibly as representative of the Amalgamated Union of Engineers, in reality with an introduction from Roy and – according to Petrie – secret instructions 'to study Indian labour conditions at first hand, to encourage Bolshevism, and, if possible, to form a Labour Party with certain well-known Indian agitators as office bearers'. Glading returned after two months with a pessimistic report, declaring that he had failed to find a single 'convinced' Indian Communist. Roy, who had been presenting a much rosier picture to Comintern of the situation in India, retorted that Glading's visit had been too short to allow him to contact genuine Indian Communists.[103]

Glading was followed, after a year's interval, by George Allison (also later jailed for espionage in Britain) who landed at Bombay in April 1926 to work in the Indian trade union movement, using the alias Donald Campbell. An intercepted letter from Roy revealed that 'His main task is to develop the left wing inside the Trade Union Congress. He has been advised to keep out of party politics except in an advisory capacity if necessary'. Like Glading, Allison achieved little. He was arrested in January 1927 on a charge of using a forged passport, and sentenced to eighteen months in goal.[104]

The third and ablest of the secret emissaries despatched by the CPGB, Philip Spratt, was Comintern's first Cambridge recruit, the forerunner of the now celebrated moles of the 1930s. Spratt was the withdrawn son of a Deptford elementary schoolteacher who won a scholarship to Downing College in 1921 to read mathematics. At Cambridge he felt socially out of his depth, though he later felt in retrospect that 'The snobbish social hierarchy which made me feel an outcast was to a considerable extent an image of my own creation'. The Communist Party rescued Spratt from his sense of isolation:

> Oppressed by my fear of social and intellectual failure, I grasped what was presented to me as the master-key to all knowledge ... The convert to Marx felt that he was in the vanguard of intellectual progress ... Henceforth I should concern myself with something more important than earning a living, more important than physics, or anthropology, or art: I had devoted myself to the salvation of humanity.
>
> Neither I nor any of my party friends would have indulged in such grandiloquence, but that is what we thought.

As Spratt's passion for Communism deepened, his interest in his work declined. He gained second class honours in Part I of the Mathematical Tripos, but failed to reach honours standard in Part II and graduated in 1924 with an ordinary degree. From Cambridge he went to work in the Labour Research Department, which he discovered 'had been infiltrated by Communists'. He was selected by Comintern for his mission to India in the mistaken belief that he was 'unknown to the police'.[105] In reality he was already under surveillance by 1925. Spratt travelled to India late in 1926 ostensibly on behalf of a firm of London booksellers but with a secret mission, according to Petrie, 'to open a Labour Publishing House in India through which Soviet money could be received and distributed to different centres'.[106] He found Communist prospects scarcely brighter than Glading almost two years earlier. Though there was now a Communist Party of India (CPI), its membership – limited to Bombay and Calcutta – was tiny. According to an intelligence report, attendance at the CPI congress at Bombay in May 1927 did not exceed a dozen.[107] In addition to the covert missions of Glading, Allison and Spratt, Britain's only Communist MP, Shapurji Saklatvala, a Bombay Parsee who represented Battersea North, toured India in the winter of 1926–7 and made what Petrie considered 'a number of objectionable speeches'. Petrie concluded, however, that Saklatvala's visit was in the end probably counter-productive. He treated Indian Communists 'somewhat cavalierly' by telling them 'they were an unrepresentative body infested by spies and *agents provocateurs*', and made himself more generally unpopular by 'contemptuous references to "Mahatma" Gandhi':

> Saklatvala arrived in India with a flourish of trumpets, but his departure some months later passed almost unnoticed. Even the strongly nationalist Corporation of Bombay declined to vote him a farewell address.[108]

Comintern had slightly greater initial success in establishing links with the Indian National Congress than in establishing an Indian Communist Party. Jawaharlal Nehru, who became secretary of the All India Congress Committee in 1925 (and later first prime minister of independent India) maintained a regular (intercepted) correspondence with V.N. Chattopadhyaya, secretary of the League Against Imperialism, which, as M.N. Roy admitted in another intercepted letter, was a cover for Comintern. Nehru left for Europe in 1926, made contact with a number of Indian revolutionaries in exile, represented the Indian National Congress at the Brussels meeting of the League Against Imperialism in February 1927, and was elected to the executive committee. Petrie was gratified to note that, though Nehru sent lengthy reports from Europe to Congress, 'he expressed regret at the apathy of Indian leaders towards the work of the League'.[109]

By the time Anglo-Soviet relations reached breaking point in May 1927, Communist subversion, closely monitored in both Delhi and London, had yet to emerge as a credible threat to the Raj. For the moment both Birkenhead, the secretary of state for India, and the Indian administration were more concerned by the revival, under Bolshevik management, of the traditional Tsarist threat to the north-western frontier. Birkenhead believed that Soviet policy aimed at 'hemming India in with a circle of Bolshevik states' and that 'Afghanistan is destined to be the next region to be drawn into the orbit of the USSR'.[110] Petrie reported that:

Between February and October 1925 it was observed that Afghanistan was being insidiously penetrated, under cover of the new Turkestan Republics, which were being used to create movements in favour of the incorporation in the Soviet Union of the racially allied elements across the border, a process which clearly aimed at Soviet territorial expansion in the direction of India, and at the elimination of Afghanistan.[111]

The India Office was further agitated by the opening of the Kagan-Termez branch of the Trans-Caspian railway. A note by the Political Department concluded in December 1925: 'Intelligence reports ... show that the common opinion is that the railway is a military work and that its completion portends an attack on Afghanistan'.[112] Petrie reported that Comintern decided in August 1926 that 'Revolutionary and Party work in the ordinary sense' were 'out of place' in Afghanistan and that the main aim must be to replace British by Soviet influence. He believed, however, that Russia's 'mixed gang of secret service agents' in Kabul were making limited headway. Though the Russians had 'spared no pains to launch ambitious plans in Afghanistan', their achievements had been 'comparatively small'. He endorsed the conclusions of *The Statesman* of Calcutta in October 1926:

That the Bolsheviks have spent a great deal of money on propaganda in the East, and incidentally wasted a large part of it on worthless and corrupt agents, is of course true ... That there are a great many Russians in the Legation at Kabul is true. So there are in Teheran, and the reason is the same, viz. that life is so much pleasanter even in Kabul than in Moscow that everyone who can gets himself attached to a foreign mission. Let us remember the main point, which is that Russia is on the wrong side of the Hindu Kush, and that Kabul is much nearer to Peshawar than it is to Russia.[113]

But neither Birkenhead nor the general staff nor the Indian high command was prepared to accept Petrie's reassuring realism. With the consolidation of Bolshevik rule the ancient spectre of the Russian steamroller and limitless hordes of Russian troops revived. 'Russia', said the War Office, 'can call upon practically unlimited manpower'. The general staff calculated that the Russians could 'place some 80 divisions on a war footing' in Central Asia – vastly more than those available to the Raj. In addition there was the new menace of airpower. Chamier, the R.A.F. commander in India, concluded pessimistically as early as August 1925:

I really believe (without being an alarmist) that the Russian-on-the-frontier-of-India bogey is due for revival and that the threat is largely in the air, in view of the vast moral effect a small effort can make ... We must look forward therefore to a gradual encirclement of India and a consequent air threat from Quetta to Chitral.

The Foreign Office disagreed. Hodgson, the British chargé d'affaires in Moscow, rightly insisted that the Red Army was in no fit state for a great offensive on the north-west frontier.[114] The Inter-departmental Committee on Eastern Unrest took a more alarmist view. It concluded in July 1926 that India had now become the chief target for Soviet ambitions:

The failure of the Soviet plans to establish a Red government in Peking has recently led Russia to alter her policy. As with the Tsar's Government at the end of the nineteenth century that is now directly aimed at the security of the Indian Empire.[115]

Birkenhead deduced that the Soviet aim in India was 'external attack synchronising with, or consequent upon, internal disruption': almost a mirror image of the equally irrational Soviet fear of British attack. In March 1927 he persuaded the cabinet to found the Defence of India Subcommittee of the CID under his chairmanship.[116]

During the year which followed the General Strike Chamberlain and the

Foreign Office fought and finally lost a rearguard action to preserve diplomatic relations with the Soviet Union against heavy pressure from Churchill, Jix and Birkenhead within the cabinet and a growing anti-Soviet campaign outside. In December 1926 Godfrey Locker-Lampson, the undersecretary of state for foreign affairs, declared that pressure for the breaking of Anglo-Soviet relations was 'becoming well nigh irresistible'. The belief that the Russians were behind anti-Western agitation in China added to resentments caused by Soviet support for British strikers. Sir William Tyrrell, the permanent undersecretary at the Foreign Office, told Baldwin that 'Russian interference in our coal strike and Russian proceedings in China might justify us in assuming that we are virtually at war'. Some of the strongest pressure on Baldwin came from his own backbenchers. According to the *Daily Mail*, 'Ministers will secure no peace from a large mass of their followers so long as they persist in their present passivity'. J.C.C. Davidson, the Party chairman, privately warned Baldwin that it would 'go very hard with the Government' unless it denounced the Russian trade agreement. This alone 'would save the Government's face to some extent'.[117]

Though still unwilling to yield to the anti-Bolshevik crusade, Austen Chamberlain felt obliged to make some effort to placate it. On 17 January 1927 he informed the cabinet that, on his instructions, the Foreign Office was drafting 'a new protest to Soviet Russia based exclusively on published utterances of the Soviet authorities'.[118] Birkenhead and other ministers denounced the Foreign Office draft as too feeble to be worth sending, and the cabinet turned it down. At its meeting on 18 February:

> The view generally accepted by the Cabinet, after considerable discussion, was that, given the state of public opinion in this country, if the present policy of the Russian Soviet Government was continued, a breach of relations within the next few months was almost inevitable.

Chamberlain managed, however, to win a breathing space by persuading his colleagues that 'the present moment was not opportune for a rupture of relations'. A sudden 'rupture' would have 'a very disturbing effect on Germany and throughout Eastern Europe', as well as on international relations generally: 'Moreover, no especially significant event had occurred, comparable to the publication of the Zinovieff letter or the intervention of the Russian Soviet in the General Strike, to justify a sudden rupture'. For the moment it was agreed that Chamberlain should simply prepare a stiffer version of his original note of protest, warning the Russians to mend their ways, which was duly delivered on 23 February.[119]

It was not long, however, before an 'especially significant event', of the kind whose absence had been regretted on 18 February, was brought to the attention of the cabinet. On 3 March Chamberlain informed his colleagues of new and 'highly secret information received by him on the previous evening in regard to the activities of the Soviet Union in this country'. It was decided 'that before the Cabinet could take this information into consideration, the evidence for its authenticity must be examined' by the attorney general, Sir Douglas Hogg. The discussion of this episode was considered so secret that it was not included in the cabinet minutes circulated to ministers. Instead, a single manuscript record was made by Hankey, the cabinet secretary, initialled by the prime minister, and placed in a sealed envelope marked 'Not to be opened except by the Secretary or Acting Secretary [of the cabinet]'.[120]

A fortnight later Sir Douglas Hogg announced to the cabinet that 'the information was genuine'. His report was treated with extraordinary secrecy. Once again, a single manuscript record was made by Hankey, initialled by Baldwin, and placed in a sealed envelope. Even the interior of the envelope, however, was considered insufficiently secure for details of the secret evidence considered by Hogg. The attorney general 'thought it inexpedient to put anything in writing'. But it is clear from Hankey's cryptic minute that the evidence included another and more sinister version of the Zinoviev letter of 1924 (though Zinoviev himself had since been succeeded by Bukharin as president of Comintern). According to Hogg's statement to the cabinet:

> It was known from another source that a communication had been addressed by the Third International to the British Communist Party on the date of the information under consideration. Action had been taken by the British Communist Party at about the date at which the communication would have arrived in this country – action which corresponded to that prescribed in the letter. And the source of the information had in the past proved trustworthy.[121]

The secret record prepared by Hankey does not specify the exact nature of the 'interference by Soviet Russia in the affairs of this country'. But the cryptic nature of Hankey's minute, the extraordinary secrecy with which it was treated, and the subsequent actions of the British government leave little doubt that espionage was involved.

At the end of March the government received further evidence of Soviet espionage. The improbable source of this convincing evidence was a maverick Lloyds underwriter resident in Mayfair named George Monkland who, after a wartime commission in the Black Watch, had tried unsuccessfully to make a career on the stage, and now combined underwriting with a predilection for chemin-de-fer. Early in March Monkland was approached by an even more bizarre acquaintance named Wilfred Macartney who was engaged in espionage for the Soviet Union. After an unusually cosmopolitan childhood Macartney had gained a commission in the Royal Scots in 1915 at the age of only sixteen, and engaged for a time on intelligence work in the Aegean under Compton Mackenzie. He emerged from the war, as he later acknowledged, 'devoid of any money sense'. By 1925 he had squandered a substantial family fortune, was almost bankrupt and a convert to Communism. During 1926 he served nine months in Wormwood Scrubs after a farcically inept attempt to rob a jeweller's shop. According to his own account, in which he described himself in the third person:

> Macartney came from jail fully determined to follow what his vision supposed to be the solitary clear light burning in a corrupt society, but unable to shake off the habit of overcharging his sanguine self with alcohol ... In fact apart from his sincere belief in Communism he was a wild and rather reckless young man of the possessing classes.[122]

He was also a notably inept spy. In the early months of 1927 he was fined twice for being drunk and disorderly and once for an assault on the police. During March Macartney asked Monkland for any information which had come his way as a Lloyds underwriter on arms shipments to countries bordering the USSR. Monkland supplied what he afterwards claimed was 'inaccurate information' which was, however, well received by both Macartney and his employers. At a second meeting a few days later Macartney for the first time identified himself as a Soviet spy, asked for further information, and left a questionnaire in Monkland's possession – an action which Macartney himself later described as showing 'cretin-like stupidity'. Monkland asked for, and was promised, £50 a month for his services. If he discovered any information of particular urgency he was told to call on the Russian military attaché and say that he was 'one of the firm'. Instead, on 29 March, Monkland went to see the former Director of Naval Intelligence, 'Blinker' Hall, who immediately got in touch with Kell. From then on Monkland became a double agent, controlled by MI5, feeding Macartney with obsolete misleading information. Macartney himself was kept under surveillance until he was arrested with his Soviet control, a German named Georg Hansen (alias Johnson), in November 1927.[123]

The evidence of Soviet espionage made Jix, like some of his colleagues, anxious to bring matters to a head. There remained, however, the problem of the evidence required to justify a breach with Moscow. The evidence of espionage supplied by Monkland did not point with sufficient clarity to the Soviet legation, and MI5 was naturally reluctant to arrest Macartney until it could lay hands on his Soviet control as well. As for the 'highly secret information' presented to the cabinet by Chamberlain on 3 March, the attorney general explained that: 'While he himself had no doubt as to the authenticity of the information, the evidence was not such as could be produced in a Court of Law or published.[124] The cabinet doubtless also shrank from giving the Soviet government the chance to claim that it was the victim of another, allegedly forged, 'Zinoviev letter'.

On 11 May Jix at last saw the chance of obtaining usable evidence of Soviet espionage. He received information (possibly *via* Monkland) that an employee of Arcos had procured a secret British Army signals training manual. Jix ordered a police raid on Arcos and the Russian trade delegation on the following day.[125] The raid, in fact, was to last three days, and Special Branch officers took another three days to sort through the files they had seized. But their haul was a disappointing one. The Soviet chargé d'affaires telegraphed to Moscow after the raid that there had been no 'very secret material at the Trade Delegation'. A month earlier, with the possibility of a police raid in mind (though he doubted that the Special Branch would enter the embassy itself) he had advised Moscow 'to suspend for a time the forwarding by post of documents of friends, "neighbours" and so forth from London to Moscow and vice versa'.[126] Macartney claimed that he had given Arcos advance notice of the raid; he showed Monkland a letter from another of his agents (codenamed 'Barton'), warning that the 'headquarters of the firm' was about to be raided.[127]

The Special Branch officers thus failed to find the documents for which Jix had ordered the raid. They did find proof that Arcos had recruited seamen for a Communist organisation and that the trade delegation had distributed communications from the Red International of Labour Unions. But there was no 'especially significant' document of the kind which the cabinet had earlier thought necessary 'to justify a sudden rupture'.

The cabinet found itself in a quandary when it met to discuss Anglo-Soviet relations on 23 May. Having decided to break off diplomatic relations, it had clearly to produce evidence to justify its decision. For this purpose the papers seized in the Arcos raid were insufficient. A cabinet committee concluded that the Arcos haul did not even prove 'the complicity of the Soviet Diplomatic Mission ... with the propagandist activities of [the trade delegation]'. Still lacking usable evidence of espionage, the cabinet concluded that it must at least give public proof that the Soviet legation had breached the normal rules of diplomatic behaviour. The only proof available was the telegrams exchanged between the legation and Moscow decrypted by GC & CS. These were, as the cabinet minutes euphemistically observed, 'secret documents of a class which it is not usual to quote in published documents'.[128]

Ministers had, however, one precedent to fall back on. To make its charges against the Russian legation stick, the cabinet decided to follow the appalling example of the 1923 Curzon ultimatum and quote intercepted Soviet telegrams. The first public reference to the intercepts was made by the prime minister on 24 May in a Commons statement on the Arcos raid. Baldwin read out four Russian telegrams which had, he drily observed, 'come into the possession of His Majesty's Government'. An opposition M.P. challenged Baldwin to say how the government had obtained the telegrams, but there was uproar (or, as *Hansard* put it, 'interruption') before he could finish his question. The speaker intervened and deferred further discussion until the debate two days later on the decision to end diplomatic relations with the Soviet Union.[129]

The debate, on 26 May, developed into an orgy of governmental indiscretion about secret intelligence for which there is no parallel in modern parliamentary history. Both Chamberlain and Jix followed Baldwin's bad example by quoting intercepted Russian telegrams. Chamberlain also quoted intercepted Comintern communications in order to show that 'the Zinoviev letter was not the only or the last [such document]'. Jix became quite carried away while accusing the Soviet trade delegation of running 'one of the most complete and one of the most nefarious spy systems that it has ever been my lot to meet'. 'I happen to have in my possession', he boasted, 'not merely the names but the addresses of most of those spies'.[130]

On the day of the debate Chamberlain informed the Russian chargé d'affaires of the decision to break off diplomatic relations because of 'anti-British espionage and propaganda'. Chamberlain gave his message an unusually personal point by quoting an intercepted telegram from the chargé d'affaires to Moscow on 1 April 'in which you request material to enable you to support a political campaign against His Majesty's Government'.[131]

Baldwin's government was able to prove its charge of Soviet dabbling in British politics. But the documents seized in the Arcos raid and the intercepted telegrams published in a white paper contained only a few cryptic allusions to the much more serious sin of espionage.[132] The government contrived in the end to have the worst of both worlds. It compromised its most secret and most valuable intelligence agency, GC & CS. And yet at the same time it failed to produce public evidence to support Jix's dramatic charges of 'one of the most nefarious spy systems that it has ever been my lot to meet'.

The effect of the government's publication of the Soviet intercepts on the intelligence services was traumatic. The Soviet Union responded by adopting the theoretically unbreakable 'one-time pad' for its diplomatic traffic. Between 1927 and the Second World War GC & CS was able to decrypt almost no high-grade Soviet communications (though it continued to have some success with Comintern messages). Denniston, the operational head of GC & CS, wrote bitterly that Baldwin's government had 'found it necessary to compromise our work beyond question'.[133] New entrants to GC & CS over the next decade were told the story of the loss of the Russian codes as a warning of the depths of indiscretion to which politicians were capable of sinking.

They were not, however, told the full story. What Denniston probably did not know was that pressure for the publication of Soviet intercepts had begun not with the politicians but with the intelligence chiefs themselves. Immediately after the First World War intelligence chiefs had been so alarmed by the threat of Soviet subversion that they considered the publication of intercepts 'imperative' to alert the British public to the danger in their midst. 'Quex'

Sinclair had argued in 1920 that *'even if the publication of the telegrams was to result in not another message being decoded, then the present situation would fully justify it'*.[134] In the course of the 1920s Sinclair learned greater discretion. But Baldwin's government did no more in 1927 than follow the earlier advice of the head of its secret service.

There was a sinister sequel to the ending of Anglo-Soviet diplomatic relations. While on his way back to Moscow by rail, Rosengolz, the Soviet chargé d'affaires in London, stopped at Warsaw Central Station on the morning of 7 June to breakfast with the Russian ambassador, Peter Voikov, in the station buffet. Just before Rosengolz's train left, Voikov was approached by a Russian monarchist exile, Boris Korenko, who shot him several times at close range, shouting 'This is for Nationalist Russia, not for the International!' The Soviet government was quick to declare (inaccurately) that 'a British arm directed the blow which killed Voikov' and that Britain was 'urgently conducting preparations for a war against the USSR'.[135]

Early in July the OGPU announced that it had uncovered 'a large espionage organisation managed and inspired by the well-known English intelligence agent Boyce'. The unfortunate Commander Boyce, the PCO in Helsinki, had been comprehensively deceived by the Trust before.[136] He may well have fallen victim to another OGPU deception in 1927. His chief assistant, the White Russian Colonel N.N. Bunakov, had also previously acted as the Trust's agent in Helsinki, apparently (though not certainly) unaware that it was run by the OGPU.[137] Boyce's most active agent within Russia was a former Tsarist naval captain, A.I. Hoyer, who collected intelligence on the Red Army, Navy and chemical industry in the Leningrad area, and also visited Odessa to inspect the Black Sea Fleet. The chief SIS courier, Anthony Khlopushin, crossed the Finnish border at pre-arranged points which seem suspiciously similar to the 'Finnish window' established earlier by the Trust as part of its attempts to lure Savinkov and Reilly across the frontier. Whatever the element of OGPU deception, Boyce's espionage network was probably penetrated at an early stage. Evidence at the trial included instructions and reports written in secret ink and exchanged between Boyce and Hoyer through the post. The American vice-consul at Reval thought that since their cover had been comprehensively blown by the arrest of Boyce's agents, the British government might be forced to close down their Passport Control Offices in Helsinki and elsewhere in the Baltic. The offices survived, but Boyce retired from SIS and was succeeded by his former deputy, Harry Carr.[138]

Though Kell welcomed the diplomatic breach with Russia, it had little effect on the Communist propaganda campaign in the armed services. MI5 reported 'a great advance in open propaganda' during 1927 but found it difficult to track down those circulating it. CPGB pamphlets were usually distributed to barracks at night but most of the night watches organised by

MI5 to catch the distributors were unsuccessful. Kell wrote after a fruitless night watch at Aldershot in July 1927:

> The great difficulty in making measures of this kind effective is that these efforts of the C.P. are spasmodic and not persistent, and, in view of past experience, it seems very probable that there will be no further instance of this kind for one, two, or even three months, when the same thing will occur again without warning.

The propaganda, he reported, did not appear 'to have any effect on the troops'.[139] After the sentencing of Wilfred Macartney and his Soviet control, Georg Hansen, in January 1928 to ten years' imprisonment each (modest sentences by later standards), Kell reported that open propaganda in the armed services 'gave place almost entirely to underground activity'. During 1928 MI5 investigated seventy-nine cases of soldiers or men seeking to enlist who were suspected of Communist activities of various kinds. Sixteen men were discharged and another two prevented from enlisting. Thirty-three men were 'cleared', either because the allegations against them were false or because they had 'given up Communism', and four cases were dropped. Twenty-four cases were still under investigation at the end of the year. Even judged by MI5's own statistics, the problem was clearly a manageable one.[140]

MI5's agents within the CPGB were also continuing to provide it with regular intelligence reports and documents from the party's King Street headquarters. Its most successful agent-runner by the later 1920s was an ex-naval officer recruited by Kell in 1925, Maxwell Knight, known in MI5 as 'M', who later achieved fame as a writer and broadcaster on natural history.[141] Knight was a popular eccentric who did not mind 'being considered a bit mad'. 'In a world where we are all tending to get more and more alike', he believed, 'a few unusual people give a little colour to life!' Knight's most obvious eccentricity was a passion for exotic pets which he claimed went back to a picnic lunch at the age of eight when he found a lizard and hid it from his parents in his box camera. For the remainder of his life he preferred 'queer or unusual pets', ranging from grass-snakes to gorillas, to cats and dogs. Visitors to his home might, as one of them recalled, 'find him nursing a bush-baby, feeding a giant toad, raising young cuckoos or engaging in masculine repartee with a vastly experienced grey parrot'. For several years Knight also had a pet bear named Bessie who 'excited a great deal of attention and admiration' when he took her, sometimes accompanied by a bulldog or a baboon, for walks near his Chelsea home.[142] 'High on the list of subjects which those who prefer to indulge in observations out of doors should embrace', wrote Knight, 'is the fascinating and essential one of the senses of animals'.[143] His experience of wild animals, he believed, taught him some of the fieldcraft he employed with MI5. Knight seems to have loved the mystery and intrigue of counter-intelligence work. Most of his agents whom he met in the lobbies of nondescript hotels or in other unremarkable rendezvous, usually unaccompanied by his exotic pets, knew him as 'Captain King' – ironically a name discovered in 1939 to be that of a Soviet spy in the Foreign Office.[144]

During the two years after the breaking of Anglo-Soviet relations in May 1927, the centre of government concern at Soviet subversion shifted from Britain to India. M.N. Roy boasted at the end of 1928: 'The advance made by the proletariat as a result of the revolutionary activities of the last two years is enormous'.[145] Petrie never took Roy's claims entirely at face value. On one occasion his agents found a list of non-existent Indian Communists drawn up by Roy to impress Comintern.[146] Roy also seems to have embezzled some of the Comintern funds entrusted to him for transmission to India. While he himself lived in some style in Paris and travelled freely, other Indian Communists complained of 'large sums' which had gone 'astray'. After a number of disagreements Roy was expelled from Comintern in 1929.[147] Petrie accepted, however, that despite Roy's tendency to make extravagant claims, Indian Communism had made remarkable progress during 1928. Philip Spratt, assisted by Ben Bradley, another CPGB member who arrived in India in September 1927, succeeded in founding a number of local Workers' and Peasants' Parties under Communist leadership and then, as Petrie's successor, Sir Horace Williamson put it, in 'welding' them together into an All-India Workers' and Peasants' Party. During 1927 and the first half of 1928 MI5, the Special Branch and DIB traced £1,030 forwarded to Spratt from Moscow via various addresses in England.[148]

During 1928 the enquiries by the all-party Simon commission into Indian constitutional reform rapidly raised the political temperature of the Raj. By omitting to include on it any Indian member, Baldwin's government made it appear a calculated insult to the Indian people. Even those Indians best disposed to Britain refused to have anything to do with it. In December the National Congress issued an ultimatum demanding self-government within a year. 1928 also saw a massive strike wave initially centred on the Bombay cotton mills which dragged on from April to October. DIB placed much – probably too much – of the blame for labour militancy on the Communists:

> By the end of 1928 ... there was hardly a single public utility service which had not been affected, in whole or in part, by the wave of communism which swept the country during the year.[149]

Petrie remained, however, remarkably well informed about the activities of the leading Indian Communists and the CPGB agents. As well as intercepting much Communist correspondence, DIB, doubtless with assistance from MI5 and the Special Branch, deciphered most of the devices employed to render that correspondence unintelligible – among them cryptic language, invisible ink, a transposition code and a figure cipher based on Palgrave's *Golden Treasury*. The 'cryptic writing', believed to be largely Spratt's invention, was intended to simulate correspondence between clergymen in which the correspondents referred to the Communist Party as the 'YMCA', the Workers' and Peasants' Parties as the 'Methodists', and addressed each other as 'Dear Brother in God'. All leading Communists were given pseudonyms (Spratt becoming 'Desmond' and Bradley 'Fred'), money became 'MSS', and 'send' and 'receive' were interchanged. Thus a message dated 14 June 1927 which read:

> You should receive some sort of MSS by the end of August. Ask Baker about it. It should not be sent directly by me or Ambrose.

actually meant:

> You should *send* some *money* by the end of August. Ask *Saklatvala* about it. It should not be *received* directly by me or *Muzaffar Ahmad*.[150]

Agent penetration of the Indian Communist Party also seems to have been extensive. One of the six Indian delegates to the sixth Comintern Congress in July 1928, Masood Ali, was shot in Moscow after being unmasked as a British spy. Intelligence notes on the CPI Congress in December 1928 strongly suggest that a police spy was present there also. At the end of the next important party meeting at Bombay in March 1929, the police arrested thirty-two leading Indian Communists and trade union leaders, including Spratt and Bradley, and began preparations for a mammoth conspiracy trial at Meerut which was to drag on for four years.[151]

Before committing the accused for trial, the district magistrate at Meerut summed up the conspiracy with which they were charged in words later commended by Petrie's successor, Sir Horace Williamson:

> Though the work [of the CPI] is to be executed in India, the policy is dictated from Russia; and a direct connexion has been traced between the councils of 'the mightiest world organisation' in the Winter Palace at Moscow and the hawker of pamphlets in a tent at a bathing fair on the banks of the Ganges.

Williamson was confident that the arrests had 'placed the authorities in a commanding position and created a vacuum in the leadership of the movement which was filled by very inferior material': a harsh judgment endorsed by several more recent Indian historians. The Communist movement disintegrated into what Williamson contemptuously dismissed as 'petty squabblings'. By the end of the year, as the Indian Congress made a dramatic declaration of independence and Gandhi began a new campaign of mass civil disobedience, the CPI seemed to have faded into irrelevance.[152] The alarm felt only two years earlier at the Soviet threat on the North-Western Frontier had also subsided. The chiefs of staff reached the sensible conclusion that the Russian munitions industry could not yet support 'a large-scale war'. From 1928 Soviet influence in Afghanistan was observed to weaken and the chiefs of staff watched with satisfaction as the Afghan government took what they considered 'a strong stand against Russian infiltration'.[153]

By the time Baldwin's second government fell from power after the general election of May 1929, the intelligence services could claim to have dealt successfully with the threat of Communist subversion in both Britain and India. By the end of the year, despite continued Comintern subsidies, the CPGB claimed no more than 3,200 members, many – perhaps most – of whom were unemployed. Throughout the 1920s the Red Menace was much exaggerated, though probably less by the intelligence services than by Tory diehards in and out of government. While Sinclair and Kell both had reputations as 'terrific anti-Bolsheviks', Thomson and Petrie were less alarmist than some of their political masters. There was never any prospect, whatever the supply of Red Gold, that the Communists, who lost their only Commons seat at the 1929 election, would dominate the British labour movement – still less that they would undermine the loyalty of the armed forces. During the second Baldwin government the Comintern executive steadily lost faith in the capacity of the CPGB not merely to lead a revolution but even to conduct a vigorous revolutionary debate. A prominent Comintern bureaucrat complained at the Tenth Comintern Plenum in 1929:

> How does it happen that all the fundamental problems of the Communist International fail to stir our fraternal British party? ... All these problems have the appearance of being forcibly injected into the activities of the British Communist Party ... In the British party there is a sort of special system which may be characterised thus: the party is a society of great friends.

At the end of the year Comintern ousted the 'great friends' and imposed a new leadership on the CPGB.[154]

In their secret war against Soviet subversion, however, the intelligence services were not simply tilting at windmills. Many British Communists were, as the miners' secretary, Frank Hodges, said in 1922, the 'intellectual slaves of Moscow'. Nor was their subservience simply intellectual. Soviet-dominated Comintern had a critical influence on the organisation of the CPGB, committing it from the first to total and unconditional support for the Soviet Union by illegal as well as legal means. Roy's complaint that Comintern's attitude to Indian Communism 'smacked of imperialism' applied also to its attitude to Britain. It sent the CPGB regular instructions as well as the regular subsidies which probably saved it from bankruptcy. When the British leadership did not please it, Comintern changed it and the CPGB dutifully approved the new leaders chosen for it.

Like the Roman Catholics in Elizabethan England, the Communists of the 1920s aroused both the hostility of the public and the suspicion of the authorities not merely because of their revolutionary potential (greatly exaggerated by their opponents as well as by themselves) but also because they appeared as the agents of a hostile foreign power. Despite their obedience to Moscow as the capital of the world's only worker-peasant state, most British Communists saw their allegiance, like Elizabethan Catholics, not as to a foreign government but to a universal church — the Communist International. Even in the 1920s, however, Russia was able to recruit spies and secret agents from CPGB members. Their activities mattered little in the 1920s when the Soviet Union — despite age-old British fears for the North-West Frontier — posed no serious threat to the British Empire. But the significance of Soviet espionage was to change dramatically once Stalin's brutal economic revolution turned the Soviet Union into a great military power. Though MI5 and the Special Branch scarcely underestimated the danger of Soviet subversion, they remained curiously traditional in their search for it, concentrating their attentions on the labour movement, the armed services, the CPGB apparat and agents from abroad. But there was enough in the experience of the 1920s to suggest that Soviet agents could also be recruited from within the establishment. Probably the ablest recruit of the decade was the young Cambridge graduate, Philip Spratt, whom DIB considered both 'the mentor' of Indian Communism and its most effective organiser.[155] The next generation of Comintern secret agents in Cambridge was to prove even more effective. Unlike Spratt, who was under surveillance even before he began his first secret mission, they were also to go undetected.

# 11 | DEPRESSION: THE MACDONALD YEARS

On 5 June 1929 Ramsay MacDonald became prime minister for the second time at the head once again of a minority Labour government dependent on Liberal support. Four months later Anglo-Russian diplomatic relations were restored with none of the rumpus which might have been predicted only two years before. Labour had the misfortune, however, to return to power on the eve of a world depression. In August 1931, unable to agree on expenditure cuts during the depression, the cabinet resigned. Most ministers expected the Labour government to be followed by a Conservative-Liberal coalition. To their surprise and indignation, Ramsay MacDonald remained in power at the head of an 'emergency' National Government composed of Conservatives, Liberals, and two Labour ministers, Philip Snowden and Jimmy Thomas, who accepted the expenditure cuts rejected by their colleagues. In October the National Government won a landslide election victory, reducing the Labour opposition to a rump of only fifty-two seats.

The financial crisis of 1931 served a curiously similar function to that of the Zinoviev letter of 1924: 'it provided an all-embracing excuse to divert attention from Labour's own failings'.[1] Once again, Labour claimed to have been intrigued out of office by a capitalist conspiracy, aided and abetted on this occasion not by the secret service but by its own prime minister. Obsessed by exaggerated theories of a 'bankers' ramp' and MacDonald's treachery, Labour failed to notice that it had been the victim of a smaller but still unpleasant conspiracy. As over the Zinoviev letter in 1924, the Conservative Party organisation had made disreputable use of secret intelligence for political advantage. In 1927 the Party chairman, J.C.C. (later Viscount) Davidson, had recruited the head of MI5's 'Investigation branch', Major (later Sir) Joseph Ball, to help him run 'a little intelligence service of our own', distinct from the main Central Office organisation. Ball employed against the Labour Party some of the same techniques of infiltration employed by MI5 in the CPGB. Davidson later boasted:

We had agents in certain key centres and we also had agents actually in the Labour Party Headquarters, with the result that we got their reports on political feeling in the country as well as our own. We also got advance 'pulls' of their literature. This we arranged with Odhams Press, who did most of the Labour Party printing, with the result that we frequently received copies of their leaflets and pamphlets before they reached Transport House. This was of enormous value to us because we were able to study the Labour Party policy in advance, and in the case of leaflets we could produce a reply to appear simultaneously with their production.[2]

In 1930 Ball became first director of the new Conservative Research Department, one of his assets being, in Davidson's view, that he 'had as much experience as anyone I know in the seamy side of life and the handling of crooks'. Though Ball covered his tracks well, he seems to have continued his secret infiltration of the Labour Party and maintained informal links with some of his former intelligence colleagues. He also went to elaborate lengths to defend the Conservative organisation against the techniques of infiltration he employed against Labour. All copies of reports produced by the new Research Department were numbered, marked 'Most Secret' (then the highest security classification in MI5 and SIS), and sent to senior Conservatives with receipts which they were expected to sign and returned in stamped, addressed envelopes. The response of Winston Churchill and others when presented with top secret reports on, for example, the pigmeat industry or the case for centralised slaughterhouses was sometimes so satirical that the system had to be abandoned after a few years.

Ball became, in Lord Blake's words, 'a quintessential éminence grise' whose influence on the affairs of the Conservative Party 'cannot be measured by the brevity of the printed references to him'. He took Neville Chamberlain's side in his leadership struggle with Baldwin, is said to have taught him fly-fishing, and quickly made himself an indispensable adviser when Chamberlain became party chairman in 1930. Ball's election strategy made a major contribution to the enormous size of the National Government's majority in the 1931 election.[3]

The depression and the expenditure cuts imposed by the National Government accelerated Britain's military decline. By 1933 Britain was incapable of sending an expeditionary force without unacceptable delay to meet a challenge from even a minor power outside Europe. Amid the encircling gloom and financial stringency which enveloped British defence policy, the service intelligence departments led an underprivileged and underfinanced existence on the periphery of defence planning. Since the recreation of the pre-1914 combined Directorate of Operations and Intelligence at the War Office in 1922 and the abolition of the post of DMI, the status of military intelligence had declined. The Intelligence Corps, which had been run down rapidly as soon as the war was over, expired altogether when the last units of the British Army on the Rhine returned home in December 1929.[4] To most ambitious officers intelligence appeared a backwater. With some honourable exceptions, commanding officers were apt either to leave their intelligence posts unfilled or to use their intelligence officers to keep the mess accounts.[5] The general ethos of the run-down interwar army distrusted serious intellectual effort and considered too great an interest in books 'unsound'. 'The whole show', complained General Ironside (later CIGS on the outbreak of war) in 1932, 'has got frightfully parochial'. The narrow horizons which depressed Ironside go far to explain the slowness of the War Office to come to terms during the 1930s either with France's military decline or with the rapid rise of the German Wehrmacht.[6]

Naval intelligence ran down almost as rapidly as its military counterpart after the First World War. Admiral John Godfrey, the able (though sometimes truculent) DNI appointed in January 1939, considered none of his predecessors since 'Quex' Sinclair's departure from the Admiralty in 1921 'of the calibre who could establish a great department'.[7] The DNI from 1927 to 1930 was a bluff, genial and increasingly odd Admiral, Sir Barry Domville, who complained that he was constantly receiving 'priceless documents from the numerous lunatics who were always paradoxically anxious to help me in collecting "intelligence"'. 'This type of work', he concluded, 'appeals apparently to the disordered mind. Not very complimentary, I found it!' He complained with much more reason at the duplication and wasted effort caused by the lack of coordination between the service intelligence departments and the rest of the intelligence community. The circulation of intelligence reports around the uncoordinated intelligence bureaucracy produced what Domville called 'the great paper game':

> As the information has probably already been exchanged amongst the various agents of their Departments at the collecting end, there results a bombardment at headquarters with the same literary ammunition from several directions, which, whilst giving a spurious corroboration, is really only effecting a duplication, as it is the same old tale arriving by a more devious route.[8]

Domville himself followed an increasingly 'devious route' and, in Godfrey's words, 'got on the wrong side of MI5'. During the 1930s he found Hitler 'absolutely terrific; absolutely A1' and set out to discover 'what Masons, Jews and other secret forces at work in our Society were up to'. In 1940 Domville was jailed in Brixton under Section 18b of the Defence of the Realm Regulations.[9]

For most of the interwar period Air Intelligence was even more run down than its naval or military counterparts. The Air Ministry had no representative at SIS until 1930 and no section at GC & CS until 1936. As in the War Office, Intelligence was submerged in a combined Directorate of Operations and Intelligence in which Intelligence came a poor second.[10] Until 1935 the Treasury refused the Air Ministry funds for its own intelligence staff to assess European airforces.[11] It was expected to rely instead on intelligence assessments from the War Office and the NID, neither of whom was much interested in the air. The Air Ministry had no confidence in either and looked with particular scorn on the NID which it regarded as 'a static information bureau ... notoriously required to have no views of possible enemy perspectives'. The Air Ministry thus resorted to 'an under-the-counter device'. A member of its planning staff, Wing-Commander R.G.S. 'Lousy' Payne, was told 'to concentrate on intelligence as his sole job'. According to Group-Captain (later Air-Marshal Sir) Victor Goddard, who became the first official head of European air intelligence at the Air Ministry in 1936, Payne 'became quite a master at the game and was soon awarded an assistant in his clandestine employment'.[12] The most serious gap in air intelligence between the wars was photographic reconnaissance. Though it had begun to emerge in the First World War as an intelligence tool of great potential it was abandoned altogether after the Armistice and not revived until the Italo-Abyssinian War of 1935.[13]

The secret intelligence services suffered from even greater neglect than most other areas of national defence. Arthur Henderson, who became foreign secretary in the second Labour government (1929–31), had paid close attention while home secretary in 1924 to intelligence reports on Soviet espionage and subversion in Britain. But he disliked the whole idea of British espionage and codebreaking, and preferred, like Ponsonby in 1924, to have no dealings with either SIS or GC & CS though he was responsible for both. Jovial and severe by turns, Henderson remained a devout Nonconformist lay preacher and a strict teetotaller. Sir Robert Vansittart, the permanent undersecretary at the Foreign Office from 1930 to 1937, claimed that 'He rated Secret Service like hard liquor, because he knew, and wanted to know, nothing of it'.[14] Hugh Dalton, Henderson's parliamentary undersecretary, was later to become wartime overlord of the Special Operations Executive (SOE). But in 1929 he had little sympathy for the intelligence services, suspecting 'that our present secret service personnel is excessive and that economy can with advantage be practised here'.[15] Sir John Simon, Henderson's Liberal successor in MacDonald's National Government (after a ten-week interim by Lord Reading), also appears to have been no friend of the intelligence community for most of his four years at the Foreign Office from 1931 to 1935. As an antimilitarist home secretary during the First World War, Simon had resigned in 1916 in protest against conscription. He returned to office in 1931, after fifteen years in the political wilderness, deeply committed to disarmament and to the cause of morality in international affairs. 'I as foreign secretary', he said in 1932, 'do not really see Great Britain involved in war for many years to come, probably the next fifty years'. That, he believed, 'is the sort of attitude a foreign secretary has to adopt'. He told Vansittart in December

1933: 'The loss of credit which the British Government will suffer in the eyes of the public if there is no international ... Disarmament Agreement will be something tremendous'. Not until after the final failure in April 1934 of the long drawn-out World Disarmament Conference at Geneva, first convened in February 1932, did Simon's mind begin to turn reluctantly to the problems of rearmament.[16]

Vansittart was much more interested in intelligence than his political masters. Unlike Henderson and Simon, he 'felt that we indulged in it all too little', and was probably the first permanent undersecretary to dine regularly with 'Quex' Sinclair.[17] SIS looked on Van as one of its chief supporters and when a newspaper campaign started against him in 1935 tried to discover who was behind it.[18] Feeling powerless to increase SIS's meagre resources, Van began – probably with Sinclair's approval – to cultivate his own intelligence sources, particularly in Germany, and built up what became known as his 'private detective agency'. Though the evidence is fragmentary, he also seems to have encouraged the efforts of Sinclair and his station chief in Rome, Claude Dansey, to build up an alternative to the passport control network. Van paid less attention, however, to the sometimes lamentable security of the Foreign Office and of British embassies abroad.[19]

The organisation of SIS headquarters remained much as Sinclair had found it in 1923. Operations were organised by 'G officers' who dealt directly with station chiefs and agents abroad. Intelligence reports received at Broadway were passed to 'circulating sections' headed by liaison officers from the Foreign Office and the service intelligence departments who decided what to forward to the departments they represented and advised on the priorities for intelligence collection. The heads of the political (Foreign Office), military and naval circulating sections remained unchanged throughout Sinclair's sixteen years as 'C'. Broadway contained in all less than twenty officers. Most were retired or seconded officers from the armed services; only one was a graduate.[20]

Sinclair's deputy (and eventual successor) was the army representative at SIS and head of the military section (later Section II), Colonel (later Major-General Sir) Stewart Menzies, an Old Etonian who had won no academic prizes at school but had been a prominent athlete and president of 'Pop' (the Eton Society). Menzies had entered intelligence work after being gassed in 1915 while serving with the Life Guards. Kirke, under whom he served in GHQ Intelligence, thought him 'a charming fellow' who would 'do well'. Menzies was remarkably well connected through both his mother and his wives. His mother, Lady Holford, was lady-in-waiting to Queen Mary. He married successively an earl's daughter, a baron's grand-daughter and a baronet's daughter previously married to a viscount. It was inaccurately rumoured within SIS that Menzies himself was the illegitimate son of Edward VII. Menzies knew the rumour and seems to have rather liked it. Despite his secret profession and what one of his colleagues considered 'an almost maniacal fondness for security', he was a well-known figure in London clubland between the wars. He held meetings and conducted some SIS business at White's, and also belonged to St James's and The Turf. Menzies had a life-long addiction to country sports and hunted with the Duke of Beaufort's hounds near his country house in Wiltshire until forced to stop after a fall well into his seventies.[21]

The head of the naval section (later Section III) in SIS was another cheerful – though less well-connected – extrovert, Captain Frederic Russel R.N., affectionately known as 'Barmy' to all in Broadway Buildings. Like Menzies, Russel was a traditionalist, proud of the fact that he had learned his seamanship under sail. Though popular, he was by general consent 'not a flyer'.[22]

The first head of the air section (later Section IV) in SIS, founded early in 1930, was Frederick Winterbotham, who had served as a scout pilot helping to pioneer photographic reconnaissance during the First World War until he was shot down in 1917. Winterbotham had a narrow escape. The German pilot who shot him down jovially observed after inspecting his bullet-ridden seat cushion, 'Just one more inch and you'd have been a soprano'. Winterbotham had read law at Christ Church, Oxford, and was the first graduate recruited to SIS headquarters. Temperamentally, however, he had much in common with his non-graduate colleagues. After the war he could not bring himself to settle down to an office job and looked instead for 'an outdoor life with hunting and sport'. But after he had spent a decade farming and stock-breeding in the Cotswolds, and failed to find better opportunities in Kenya or Rhodesia, a former girlfriend put him in touch with Archie Boyle, deputy head of intelligence at the Air Ministry, who offered Winterbotham his first job with SIS.[23]

The Foreign Office representative and head of the political section (later Section I) in SIS was, significantly, not a diplomat. When the Foreign Office chose its representative in 1921 it took the view that diplomats should have no direct involvement in espionage, and selected a former Indian Army officer, Major Malcolm 'Woolly' Woollcombe, who had entered military intelligence during the First World War and had been attached as an intelligence officer to the British delegation at the Paris peace conference. Woollcombe seems to have been overshadowed by his more successful father, Lieutenant-General Sir Charles Woollcombe. One of his SIS colleagues remembered him as 'a large, rather bumbling man'; another considered him 'rather indecisive'. The Foreign Office officials with whom he dealt were less critical and found him a methodical man with a rather school-masterly manner, conscientious, reliable and fair-minded, though not of the calibre required to reach the highest grades of the diplomatic service. Woollcombe remained as head of the political section until he suffered a breakdown during the Second World War and retired while still in his early fifties.[24]

The chief 'G officer' responsible for operations in Europe and the Near East in the later 1920s was Bertie Maw, formerly an SIS officer in the Balkans. He was a popular though not very influential figure, conspicuous in Broadway Buildings for both his club foot and infectious sense of humour. Maw retired in the early thirties and was succeeded as chief G officer by one of the more remarkable interwar SIS recruits, Lieutenant-Commander Reginald ('Reggie') Fletcher.[25] Fletcher's background was similar in many respects to those of most of his colleagues in Broadway Buildings. He joined the navy as a boy of fourteen in 1899, spent most of the First World War serving on destroyers, and had a ruddy, weather-beaten complexion from his years at sea. After the armistice he served under 'Quex' Sinclair as head of the Near Eastern section in NID. Fletcher also shared the common SIS addiction to London clubs and country sports. But in the early 1920s his career diverged sharply from those of his future colleagues in SIS as he entered politics and veered increasingly to the Left. Though coming from a Tory background, Fletcher was elected as a Liberal M.P. in 1923. He lost his seat in 1924, stood again unsuccessfully as a Liberal in a 1928 bye-election, then joined the Labour Party in 1929.[26] Admiral Sinclair no doubt saw Fletcher's recruitment (probably at about the time of the 1929 election) as a desirable way of rebuilding bridges with the incoming Labour administration after the ill-feeling caused by the publication of the Zinoviev letter. Like Maw, Fletcher ran SIS operations in Europe and the Near East.

Operations in the Far East against Japan were probably controlled by another naval officer, Lieutenant-Colonel Arthur Peel of the Royal Marines, who had served as assistant DNI to Sinclair after the war.[27] Fletcher left SIS to become M.P. for Nuneaton after the general election of November 1935. He seemed at the time one of the rising stars of the Labour Party and later became, as Baron Winster, minister of civil aviation in the post-war Attlee government. To those who knew him best, however, Fletcher seemed in but never really of the Labour Party, speaking in the Commons on naval and defence questions almost with the detachment of a cross-bencher.[28]

The head of the Passport Control Department which provided cover for most SIS station chiefs abroad was Major Herbert Spencer who had headed the department since its foundation in 1919. Spencer had his offices at 21 Queen Anne's Gate, the elegant building which also contained 'Quex' Sinclair's flat and backed on to Broadway Buildings. His own background was typical of many SIS officers. He had enlisted in the 13th Hussars in 1893, crossed to France with the British Expeditionary Force in 1914, moved into military intelligence work and became chief port control officer in MI5. Unsurprisingly, he was a member of White's and gave his interests as 'fishing, shooting, golf'.[29]

The head of counter-espionage in SIS (later Section V) was Major (later

Colonel) Valentine Vivian, who always signed himself by his initials in a spidery hand and thus became known as 'Vee-Vee' to his colleagues. Vivian was the son of a well-known Victorian portrait painter and had made his early career in the Indian police. While in India he had the misfortune (as it later transpired) to make friends with the orientalist and then Indian civil servant, St John Philby. St John's son Kim, who became Vivian's protégé in the wartime SIS, dismisses him scornfully in his memoirs as a timorous figure 'long past his best – if indeed he ever had one', with 'a reedy figure, carefully dressed crinkles in his hair, and wet eyes'. Others found him lean, elegant, courteous and meticulous – and noticed, as Philby apparently did not, that he had a glass eye. Vivian had a habit of standing at a right angle to those he met to shield the glass eye from their view. Unlike most of his colleagues at Broadway Buildings, he invariably wore army uniform and frequented none of the London clubs favoured by SIS officers. He was also, as Kim Philby acknowledged, of a more 'reflective temperament' than most at SIS head-quarters, with a tendency 'to discourse long and widely on SIS history, politics and personalities'. Malcolm Muggeridge, who served in SIS during the Second World War, found Vivian for all his methodical habits 'strangely romantic' and apt to relate 'anecdotes and tales which were much more like Ashenden than what it was really like'.[30]

Most SIS station chiefs abroad had a less romantic view of intelligence work than Vivian. Their cover as passport control officers condemned them to an underprivileged existence on the fringes of British embassies, where they were commonly regarded as an embarrassment rather than an asset by ambassadors who groaned inwardly even at the thought of their occasional presence at diplomatic cocktail parties.[31] A few ambassadors were openly hostile. Even on the eve of the Second World War Sir George Warner, British minister in the vital listening post at Berne, adamantly refused to allow the presence of a PCO and – significantly – was not overruled by the Foreign Office.[32] The original suggestion by SIS in 1919 that PCOs should be posted as second secretaries had been rejected by the Foreign Office on grounds which included the 'unsuitability of some of the personnel'. Some PCOs were given consular status instead but this move too was restricted by the consular service.[33] As early as 1922 the consul-general in New York appealed vainly for the suppression of the passport control office.[34]

The position of the PCOs remained, as the Foreign Office acknowledged, 'anomalous'. It was agreed in 1919 that PCOs would be 'attached' to British missions abroad but would 'not form part of the diplomatic personnel'. A decade later it was acknowledged that 'the precise effect of this ruling has never been very clear ...' SIS pressed intermittently but unsuccessfully for PCOs to be turned into 'proper diplomats', claiming that this would 'increase the security of both themselves and the Foreign Office in the work they are doing'. The Treaty Department of the Foreign Office, of which the passport control organisation was theoretically a part, argued that on the contrary PCOs should have 'no connection with H.M. diplomatic missions'. Attempts to agree on a coherent definition of the PCOs' status were still continuing in the early 1930s. In 1933, in order to exempt them from French income tax, they were eccentrically defined as men who, though not consular officers, were 'full-time salaried officers engaged in activities of a kind ordinarily entrusted to consular officers'. On that semi-farcical note, the discussion petered out. C.J. Norton, Vansittart's private secretary, argued in November 1933 that the discussion had revealed no 'clear way of regularising the position of PCOs without disadvantage in some respect ... Anomalies, as the British Common-wealth shows, are often best left alone'.

The PCOs themselves were less happy to let the matter drop. The anomalies of their underprivileged status exposed them to an unpredictable series of minor irritations in foreign capitals. There were controversies concerning, for example, Czech attempts to deprive the PCO in Prague, L.A. Hudson, of his right to duty-free alcohol in 1925; calls for the production of New York Passport Control files in an American court case in 1931; French demands in 1932 that Passport Control staff pay French income-tax; and the entitlement of the Brussels PCO, Captain H.A. Westmacott, to diplomatic immunity after a car crash in 1933.[35]

New recruits to SIS stations abroad were left largely to their own devices. When Leslie Nicholson, a former intelligence corporal in the BAOR, was recruited to run SIS operations in Prague under cover of an import-export business in 1930, he was told to his surprise that 'there was no need for expert knowledge': SIS required 'information on every subject under the sun, political, military, industrial, economic, social scandal in high places, any scraps of information that might fit into the overall jigsaw puzzle of intelligence from any country'. Nicholson's induction course consisted chiefly of training in codes, ciphers, communications and finance. But he was given no training in the fieldcraft required for recruiting and running agents or in other forms of intelligence gathering. When Nicholson asked for 'tips on *how* to be a spy', he was told he could spend two or three weeks en route to Prague at Vienna where the local PCO, Captain Thomas Kendrick, one of the most experienced station chiefs in SIS, would give him on the spot training.

'Could you give me some idea of how to begin?' asked Nicholson. '... Are there any standard rules? ... or could you give me some practical hints?'

Kendrick thought for a moment. 'I don't think there are really', he replied. 'You'll just have to work it out for yourself. I think everyone has his own methods and I can't think of anything I can tell you'.

Nicholson was appalled. He was further dismayed when Kendrick told him about his predecessors. Two had been recalled after brushes with the Czech police, one as a result of his periodic drinking bouts, the other after 'a row over a girl-friend'.

Nicholson arrived in Prague with only one lead – a file headed 'Pickles' given him by C before he left London. 'Pickles' was the codename for a new explosive allegedly being secretly developed by a Czech professor. Nicholson's contact was a young bon viveur with a florid complexion named Constantine who explained that the unnamed Czech professor had succeeded in 'partially splitting the atom' and come up with 'the most powerful explosive known to man'. The professor, when finally produced by Constantine, struck Nicholson as 'more than a little eccentric, in manner as well as in dress ... with a great mane of white hair, and a slightly mad look' but produced a pleasingly loud explosion at a demonstration in a wood near Prague. Constantine and the professor explained that they required money for further experiments. Having received well over a thousand pounds, they then demanded a thousand more. London refused. Nicholson remained for the rest of his life unaware that he had been the victim of what must certainly have been a confidence trick and convinced, on the contrary, that 'a great opportunity' had been lost:

> I suppose we shall never know whether, for the sake of a thousand pounds, we missed the chance of acquiring data which might have enabled us to split the atom before the Hitler war broke out.[36]

One of the first things impressed on all new recruits was that SIS was desperately short of money. Vansittart felt he had 'to work Henderson into his best mood' before slipping the secret service estimates among his papers for signature. Henderson would 'pause, sign and sigh, "you will be the death of me one day, Van"'. Sinclair was sometimes so short of funds that Vansittart found him forced to appeal to relatives for assistance.[37] As late as 1935 Sinclair complained that his total budget amounted only to the annual cost of keeping a destroyer in home waters.[38] PCOs abroad were kept on a tight financial rein. While serving in Prague and Riga during the 1930s Leslie Nicholson found his 'biggest headache ... the necessity of accounting for every single penny and trying to justify the expenses we had to render monthly':

> The whole system was ruled over by a retired naval paymaster, [Commander P. Stanley Sykes] known to everyone in the Service as 'Pay'. He treated public money as it if were his own and seemed almost to begrudge every penny we spent.

'Pay' Sykes was a former friend of Cumming who had been with SIS since the First World War. On his occasional trips abroad he unbent a little and struck Nicholson as a 'gay old dog' who liked to 'put up his eye-glass at the girls'. When 'Pay' came to inspect Nicholson's accounts in Prague in 1932, they spent an animated evening at 'an intimate cabaret':

> The main act was provided by pretty Hungarian twins who, in unison, performed a rather sexy double striptease. Pay's monocle rose and fell with regularity as his eyebrows lifted in approval or astonishment ... After some time the alcohol began to excite their Hungarian temperaments and to liven things up they started throwing empty glasses at the walls after downing the drinks. Soon most of the customers were under the tables with glass splinters flying everywhere. Pay and I were sitting on the carpet with our table held up in front like a shield and he was enjoying himself enormously. "By gum", he kept turning to me and shouting above the racket, "you fellows certainly see life!"[39]

Apart from such occasional nights out with 'Pay', SIS officers also enjoyed one illegal financial privilege. At least some of them paid no income tax on their modest salaries. When they ran into difficulty with Inland Revenue, 'Pay' Sykes instructed them to contact an 'indoctrinated' tax inspector who arranged matters for them.[40]

Sykes failed, however, to prevent a number of financial scandals. The eccentric accounting procedures of passport control officers, caused by their mixture of open and secret responsibilities, combined with the opportunities for a black market in British visas to produce tempting opportunities for embezzlement. The most lucrative opportunities for trafficking in visas came from the growing numbers of Jewish refugees and would-be emigrants to the British mandate in Palestine. In five years the Jewish population of Palestine more than doubled – from 175,000 in 1931 to almost 400,000 in 1936, the majority of the new immigrants coming from Poland and Central Europe. Most of the black markets in visas were run by local clerks recruited to run the genuine business of passport control while the PCOs themselves concentrated on intelligence work. No less than three cases of trafficking in visas arose in Warsaw between 1930 and 1936. Other 'irregularities' in visa accounts were discovered in the passport control offices of Nicosia, Vienna, Athens, Prague, Stockholm, The Hague, Rotterdam and Rome. During 1936 major scandals were to occur in both Warsaw and The Hague.[41]

PCOs were not supposed to engage in operations against governments of the countries in which they were stationed. Captain Kendrick in Vienna was, for example, largely concerned with collecting intelligence from Fascist Italy, while Claude Dansey in Rome was building up a network of informants in Germany.[42] 'Quex' Sinclair's main priority at the beginning of the 1930s was, as it had been since he took office, the USSR. Neither Henderson nor Simon shared Sinclair's world view but both stayed too aloof from SIS to attempt to determine its priorities. When Winterbotham joined SIS early in 1930 he was told that 'Target Number One' remained the Soviet Union. But Sinclair complained of being 'hard up for men for Russia'. In the increasingly hostile environment of Stalinist rule, SIS had no agents remotely capable of filling the intelligence gap left by the loss of the Soviet codes in May 1927. Winterbotham discovered that the skills of SIS's remaining Russian agents were limited to 'spotting the numbers on the caps of troops and watching ships go up and down the coast'. Far more useful to SIS was a White Russian general exiled in Paris who studied birth, death and marriage announcements in local newspapers from the Soviet Union and succeeded by 1932 in compiling what Winterbotham considered 'an almost complete order of battle of the Russian airforce'.[43] SIS also depended for much of its Soviet intelligence on its links with the intelligence services of states on Russia's borders: Finland, the Baltic States, Poland and Czechoslovakia. Harry Carr, the PCO in Helsinki from 1927 to 1941, built up a particularly close connection with Finnish intelligence, whose officers regularly visited both SIS and MI5 headquarters in London.[44]

Vansittart defined his three pet hates as 'Communism, Deutschism and homosexuality'.[45] The shift in SIS priorities during the early thirties from Soviet Communism to 'Deutschism', though prompted chiefly by the rise of Adolf Hitler, owed something to his influence. It owed something also to the influence of Reggie Fletcher, the G officer in charge of European operations. Fletcher was outraged by the rundown of the armed services despite government assurances that if the disarmament talks on which Sir John Simon pinned his hopes for the future failed, national defences would be strengthened. Over lunch and dinner in St James's and other London clubs, he urged friendly journalists to write articles denouncing the decline of the Royal Navy and promised to give them all 'the dope' they needed. NID, he declared, had 'no grey matter in it'. Admiral Sir James Troup, who became DNI in 1935, was, he claimed, 'an absolute child about intelligence'. But Fletcher's particular *bête noire* was the Air Ministry which he dismissed as 'a poor show ... full of discards from Army and Navy'. By the mid-thirties he claimed that the British aircraft industry had fallen 'up to seven years behind the latest practice as regards monoplane design, stressed skin construction, blind-flying instruments, variable pitch propellers, the retractable undercarriage, etc., etc.' In addition to the lethargy of the National Government he blamed the 'conservatism of the Air Ministry' with its preference for 'gentlemen administrators' rather than trained specialists, and the near monopoly and excessive profits enjoyed by a 'ring' of aircraft manufacturers.[46]

Perhaps the most sensitive operation during Fletcher's years with SIS concerned the prime minister himself. Even before the 'desolation of loneliness' which followed Ramsay MacDonald's break with the Labour Party in August 1931, he was deeply troubled by what his notebook discreetly calls 'private concerns'.[47] These concerns probably derived from an affair some years earlier with a continental *cocotte* to whom he had written compromising letters which she now threatened to reveal. It is also probable, though not certain, that SIS was used to purchase and retrieve the letters. Unsurprisingly the secret files which might cast light on the episode are not available and may have been destroyed. But the story was revealed to the historian and sometime deputy DNI Captain Stephen Roskill by Sir Walford Selby who, as principal private secretary to the foreign secretary from 1924 to 1932, was in contact with SIS and probably in a position to know the truth.[48] Fletcher's precise role in the affair remains a mystery. But, perhaps significantly, a friend found him in January 1933 'very down on Ramsay', claiming that he was 'notoriously ungrateful to his friends'.[49]

Despite its success in keeping its dealings on behalf of the prime minister, like most of its other operations, secret, SIS suffered one major public embarrassment. In 1932 Compton Mackenzie published a volume of reminiscences entitled *Greek Memories* which included some affectionate if satirical recollections of Cumming and First World War intelligence work. 'Quex' Sinclair was furious. In addition to revealing the contents of wartime telegrams received by the Foreign Office, Mackenzie had in Sinclair's view committed three more serious breaches of the Official Secrets Act. He had mentioned fourteen wartime intelligence officers (some of whom still had SIS connections); he had disclosed the secret acronym MI1c (still used by Menzies and the military section of SIS); and he had revealed that passport control was used as a cover for secret service work. MI5 and the Special Branch, doubtless inspired in part by a sense of rivalry with SIS, seemed less concerned. During the committal proceedings sympathetic Special Branch officers stood Mackenzie several rounds of pink gins and Ella Cook, a friend and former member of MI5, came to offer commiserations.[50]

Both the committal proceedings and the Old Bailey trial, each held partly *in camera*, contained moments of high farce. One of the wartime agents allegedly compromised by Mackenzie, Captain Christmas, turned out to have died ten years before; another, Sir C.E. Heathcote-Smith, included intelligence work in his *Who's Who* entry; a third, Pirie Gordon, had reviewed *Greek Memories* in *The Times*. The judge at the Old Bailey trial asked the attorney-general how recently Cumming, whose identity Mackenzie had revealed, had died. The attorney-general did not know. Neither did any other member of the prosecution. The defence was unable to help. Finally Mackenzie had to supply the answer himself and reveal that Cumming had died in 1923.

In the end Mackenzie was persuaded by his counsel to plead guilty and was fined £100 with £100 costs.[51] He took a terrible revenge. To pay his own much more substantial costs he wrote a satire of the secret service entitled *Water on the Brain*.[52] Sinclair and Kell, C and K, were satirised as the deadly rivals, N and P, whose obsessions with secrecy oscillate between farce and paranoia. Mackenzie demonstrated his inside knowledge of SIS by revealing that N was also known as 'The Chief', used green ink and shared his headquarters with codebreakers eavesdropping on the Russians (thinly disguised in *Water on the Brain* as 'a staff of confidential Russian scholars who sat in two-hour watches listening to the propaganda from Moscow which they dictated to stenographers in England'). Valentine 'Vee-Vee' Vivian, the SIS head of counter-espionage, whom Mackenzie probably blamed for his prosecution, is satirised as 'H.H.' Hunter Hunt, slow but 'devilish sure' and 'equally polite'. Just as Vee-Vee was later contemptuously dismissed by Philby as cringing and ineffectual, so H.H. 'would probably have apologised to his own shadow for being afraid of it'. Broadway Buildings, the SIS headquarters, are portrayed as 'Pomona Lodge'. When the name is published in a spy thriller, the secret service is forced to leave and its former HQ becomes 'an asylum for the servants of bureaucracy who have been driven mad in the service of the country'.

Like SIS, GC & CS lived on a shoestring. As Denniston complained, it 'became in fact an adopted child of the Foreign Office with no family rights, and the poor relation of the SIS, whose peacetime activities left little cash to spare'.[53] Though GC & CS occupied the same building as SIS and was under Sinclair's control, relations between the two secret agencies tended to be rather distant. GC & CS staff referred to SIS as 'The Other Side'. A diplomat who joined the Foreign Office in 1929 noted that SIS did not even attempt to collate intercepts with its own reports. Neither, until 1929, did the Foreign Office. The same young diplomat found the filing system for secret intelligence 'chaotic'. At his suggestion SIS reports were put henceforth into red folders and intercepts into blue. Any intelligence material 'entered' in the Foreign Office archives went into the green or 'most secret' files.[54]

After the loss of the Soviet codes in 1927 GC & CS could no longer provide the intelligence which had done most to bring it to the attention of both the Foreign Office and the cabinet. Before the Second World War GC & CS was also unable to decrypt any German traffic of importance. While the German armed forces relied on the Enigma machine cipher (all of whose variations remained unreadable by GC & CS until 1940) the German foreign ministry sent highgrade communications by either one-time pad, like the Russians, or a code known as Floradora. The basic Floradora code was reconstructed during the 1930s but was usually reciphered in a form which GC & CS succeeded in decrypting only in 1942. Telegrams in the basic code were, as Denniston acknowledged, on matters 'of little interest or value'. GC & CS had considerable success with Hungarian and Balkan codes but since most diplomatic traffic from this region passed over inaccessible continental landlines, Denniston doubted whether the quantity of material intercepted justified the enormous cryptographic effort involved. Austrian intercepts during the 1930s became too few to decrypt. The yield from French intercepts remained erratic. Because of the proximity of London and Paris, much French traffic went by diplomatic bag beyond the reach of the codebreakers. In 1935 the Quai d'Orsay introduced the first interwar French code to defeat GC & CS though some of its older and flimsier codes remained in use. GC & CS probably possessed the capacity to decrypt Scandinavian traffic but, as Denniston wrote later, 'the Foreign Office disclaimed any interest in Scandinavia, so this subject was dropped'.[55]

GC & CS sometimes sought the help of Foreign Office officials in an attempt to discover the likely content of intercepted telegrams as an aid to breaking the codes in which they were sent. One partly decrypted telegram from the Rumanian minister in London reporting a discussion in 1930 with Orme 'Moley' Sargent, the head of the Central Department, contained the phrase: 'As I was leaving, Mr Sargent said wittily ...' There followed a dozen groups which GC & CS was unable to decrypt. On being shown the telegram by a cryptanalyst, however, Sargent indignantly insisted that he had made 'no witticism to that bloody little man'. 'The GC & CS man', recalls an eye-witness, 'went sadly away'.[56]

GC & CS's main successes during the 1930s were with Japanese, Italian and Comintern traffic. By 1930 Japanese naval signals were being intercepted and decrypted in ships of the Royal Navy on the China Station by cryptanalysts trained by GC & CS. In 1934 a naval intercept station was founded by the Admiralty at Hong Kong (whence it was moved to Singapore after the outbreak of war). A substantial amount of Japanese military and military attaché traffic was also decrypted during and after the Japanese invasion of Manchuria in September 1931.[57] But while these intercepts served to improve British knowledge of Japanese troop movements they were not of major operational usefulness. The cabinet at first paid little attention to the Japanese invasion, then decided 'it was not worth the heavy cost of using coercion to impose one's will upon Japan'. Like most other British diplomats Vansittart felt that 'The Chinese had been asking for trouble, and they got it'. After the Japanese landing at Shanghai in February he forecast both resignedly and accurately:

> *We* are incapable of checking Japan if she really means business and has sized us up, as she certainly has done. Therefore we must eventually be done for in the Far East unless the United States are eventually prepared to use force.[58]

The Japanese intercepts thus merely helped Britain keep track of a menace to which she was in no real position to respond.

The largest volume of intercepts supplied by GC & CS during the 1930s was probably of Italian traffic. It was able to reconstruct the main Italian naval code book during the 1920s because of what Denniston called 'the delightful Italian habit of encyphering long political leaders from the daily press'. Until

1934 'the Intelligence value of the effort was slight'. During the Italo-Abyssinian War of 1935, however, the naval section of GC & CS was 'able to keep DNI fully informed of the strength and activities of the Italian Navy'. The Abyssinian and Spanish Civil Wars also generated a large volume of Italian military traffic which was, Denniston reported, 'tackled successfully'.[59] By 1935 GC & CS was 'beginning to make progress' with Italy's diplomatic ciphers as well.[60] Unknown to GC & CS, however, Italy's codebreakers, helped by glaring lapses in Foreign Office and embassy security, also had considerable success with British diplomatic traffic.[61]

The Foreign Office unwisely failed to seek the advice of GC & CS on its own code and cipher security. Until the war ciphering and deciphering was mostly done by King's Messengers between their voyages. Had GC & CS's advice been sought, it would have been highly critical of 'cipher Y' which was based on relatively straightforward transposition. Probably the best cipher in common use – 'K' – was always reciphered. But one of those who used it later recalled that 'the reciphering tables could be used again and again'.[62] GC & CS would have been unlikely to approve. Physical security in both the Foreign Offices and British embassies was even worse. From 1936 onwards the Foreign Office was to suffer a series of rude awakenings to the weakness of its own security. Not until the early months of the war, however, did it begin to grasp the full extent of its own failings.[63]

The most important innovation in intelligence gathering during Ramsay MacDonald's six-year term as prime minister concerned economic intelligence. The First World War blockade of Germany had left a residual awareness of the importance of economic warfare, an awareness subsequently strengthened by the Historical Section of the Committee of Imperial Defence (CID). The volume of the official history of the war dealing with the blockade was the only one not to be published because of its potential value to an enemy.[64] As a result of the work of its Historical Section, the CID set up in 1923 an Advisory Committee on Trade Questions in Time of War which by 1925 was considering methods of economic warfare.[65]

The man who emerged as the main authority on economic intelligence during the 1920s was Major (later Sir) Desmond Morton, a gunnery officer who had become Haig's A.D.C. after being seriously wounded while commanding a battery on the Western Front in 1917. Churchill met Morton while he was on Haig's staff and formed an instant and enduring friendship with this 'brilliant and gallant officer'. In 1919, as secretary of state for war, Churchill appointed Morton to what he considered 'a key position' in SIS. Their friendship developed further in 1922 when Churchill bought Chartwell Manor in Kent near Morton's home. During 1927 Morton produced a series of reports on 'Industrial Mobilisation Abroad' which attracted considerable interest from the CID in general, and in particular from Hankey who served as secretary to both the cabinet and the CID. The ending of the Allied

Control Commission in 1928 (hitherto a major source of information on the German economy), the onset of the Depression, and the growing international importance of the disarmament issue all combined to give greater priority to economic intelligence. In 1929 the CID set up the Industrial Intelligence in Foreign Countries Sub-Committee (FCI), which in turn recommended the establishment two years later of the Industrial Intelligence Centre (IIC) with Morton at its head and a brief 'to discover and report the plans for manufacture of armaments and war stores in foreign countries'. Until 1935 the IIC was funded from the Foreign Office secret vote which also financed SIS. In 1934 it moved to share the SIS headquarters in Broadway. Two years later, by now 'administratively attached' to the Department of Overseas Trade, the IIC moved to larger premises at 70 Victoria Street.[66]

In addition to receiving secret intelligence reports, the IIC also sought to collate information from the service ministries, the Foreign Office, the Treasury and the Board of Trade. It was ill-equipped for this herculean task with, until 1936, only three administrators and four clerical officers. The IIC owed its foundation to Hankey and the CID. Ramsay MacDonald's National Government seemed barely aware of its existence. Especially in its early years the IIC thus remained somewhat remote from the main stream of Whitehall economic planning.[67] When Morton complained that 'No-one loved us, and no-one gave us credit', he had the government particularly in mind. 'No politician in power', he wrote caustically, 'likes to be given information, backed by facts and calculations, which entirely upsets his whole policy'.[68]

Though Morton failed to gain the serious attention of any cabinet minister until Sir Philip Cunliffe-Lister (later Earl of Swinton) became secretary of state for air in 1935, he never lost the ear of his friend and neighbour, Winston Churchill. Churchill's constitutional position in relation to the intelligence community during his wilderness years was wholly remarkable. Unable to tolerate the lack of intelligence after he left office in 1929, Churchill sought it from Morton and no doubt from others. Early in the life of the first National Government, Morton consulted Ramsay MacDonald. 'Tell him whatever he wants to know, keep him informed', the prime minister replied. He put that permission in writing and it was endorsed by his successors, Baldwin and Neville Chamberlain. Astonishingly, Churchill was thus supplied on the instructions of three successive prime ministers with secret intelligence which he was to use as the basis of public attacks on their defence policies and of his own campaign for rearmament.[69]

Probably prompted by Morton, SIS began to pay greater attention during the early thirties to collecting economic intelligence. A number of British businessmen abroad, working for firms as varied as Unilever and Eno's Fruit Salts, were recruited as part-time agents. Other businessmen provided general economic information (not always amounting to secret intelligence) used in assessing the military potential of, in particular, Russia and Germany. Among armaments manufacturers there was a well established tradition, going back before the First World War, of providing Whitehall with foreign naval and military intelligence which came their way. Vickers, the leading British armaments firm, continued that tradition between the wars.[70] Several Vickers representatives had very close connections with SIS. The closest were probably those of Captain 'Eddie' Boxhall, who worked for Vickers in Bucharest, was regarded by them as probably the ablest of all their foreign representatives, and enjoyed a certain social status as the son-in-law of Prince Barbu Stirbey, administrator of the royal domains until he fell from favour in the 1930s. Boxhall was also appointed SIS station chief in Bucharest at the end of the First World War and seems to have retained that position until the next war when he served with SOE.[71] Among other Vickers' employees closely involved with SIS was their representative in Peru, Colonel Lembcké, who aroused unease within the Foreign Office in 1932 as a result of an 'extremely irregular arrangement' by which he sent intelligence reports to London via the diplomatic bag.[72] Three years later the managing director of Vickers shipyards, Sir Charles Craven, incautiously admitted in public that Vickers continued to supply Whitehall with any intelligence on foreign armaments which came its way.[73] Vickers also supplied more general economic intelligence. Probably the most valuable in the early 1930s came from its electrical engineering subsidiary, Metro-Vickers, whose managing director, Mr Richards, had been a military intelligence officer in North Russia during Allied intervention after the First World War. By 1926, Metro-Vic had eight of their engineers in Russian cities and the Urals who, it privately considered, had 'exceptional opportunities of judging the position in Russia'. Richards asked them to supply 'general information' on the Soviet economy which he almost certainly passed on to SIS and Desmond Morton: information which ranged from the state of the harvest to the progress of heavy industry. In the West such 'general information' would scarcely have qualified as secret intelligence, but in the increasingly paranoid atmosphere of Stalinist Russia it led eventually to the arrest of six British Metro-Vic engineers in March 1933 on wildly exaggerated charges of espionage and fabricated charges of sabotage. After a show trial sentenced two of the engineers to short prison terms, the British government retaliated with a trade embargo which was lifted in July when the engineers were released.[74]

Until 1933 the main priority of Morton and the IIC remained Soviet Russia.[75] The economic intelligence they collated encouraged a more realistic appraisal of Soviet military potential than the alarmist estimates of the Russian threat to India's North-Western Frontier peddled by Birkenhead and others at the time of the breach of Anglo-Soviet relations in 1927. The chiefs of staff correctly concluded, with the gift of hindsight, that, before Stalin's first Five Year Plan began in 1928, the Russian munitions industry 'could not have supported a large-scale war'. Though impressed by the rapid development of Soviet military potential under the first Five Year Plan, the chiefs of staff reported confidently in 1934 that 'the Red Army is below that of any first-class European Power, and definitely inferior to the combined British and Indian forces which we could put into the field'.[76] Within Europe, the main anxieties of the chiefs of staff were now focused on German rearmament. Morton and the IIC concluded well ahead of either the War Office or the Air Ministry that Germany was preparing for total war.[77]

The man who did most to extend SIS's business connections during the 1930s was Colonel (later Sir) Claude Dansey, subsequently assistant chief of the wartime SIS. Born in 1876 the eldest son of a captain in the Life Guards, Dansey had a notably disturbed late Victorian childhood which he managed to conceal from his SIS colleagues. After being taken away from Wellington College because of trouble with the drains which led to the death of two boys from suspected diphtheria, he was sent to a school in Belgium where he was seduced by Oscar Wilde's first male lover, Robert Ross. By the time he was fifty, Dansey had behind him a series of blood-stained adventures at the outposts of the pre-war Empire, fighting successively against the Matabele, Borneo rebels, Boers and the Mad Mullah; a succession of Anglo-American business ventures which ranged from oil to horse-racing; and an intelligence career spanning both MI5 and SIS. During the First World War he had served as head of MI5e, responsible for 'port intelligence' and the surveillance of civilian passengers, but seems to have been bored by the lack of action and office routine of much of his work. After the United States entered the war in April 1917, he spent six months working in Anglo-American intelligence liaison, then moved into MI1c, working for Cumming in Switzerland and the Balkans at the end of the war. During the 1920s he resumed his business career, failed to make his fortune, but established an impressive range of business contacts on both sides of the Atlantic while keeping informal links with SIS. In 1929, following the death of his main American business associate and the Wall Street Crash, Dansey returned to full time work for SIS as PCO in Rome.[78]

Dansey had probably the most pugnacious personality in SIS. According to one of his colleagues in the 1930s, 'there was nothing he'd enjoy more than having a scrap'. He believed that 'every man had his price and every woman was seducible'.[79] For intellectuals he had a loathing which continued undiminished until his death in 1947. He wrote in December 1945: 'I have less fear of Bolshies and Fascists than I have of some pedantic but vocal University Professor'. The 'Practical English' of the past were, he complained, being replaced by 'long haired "planners" injecting themselves into every-thing'.[80] Another of Dansey's pet hates, acquired during his frustrating years in MI5, were counter-espionage officers whom he regarded as time-wasters, diverting the energies of the secret service from active operations. He developed a particular contempt for Major Vivian, the head of counter-espionage in SIS. During the war Kim Philby was to observe with glee how 'Vee-Vee' 'cringed before Dansey's little minutes and shook his head sadly at his defeats, which were frequent'.[81]

Dansey's tough, decisive manner, the aura of secrecy which surrounded him, and the high affairs of state at which he hinted persuaded a surprising number of businessmen to give him various forms of assistance. During the early thirties, while PCO in Rome, Dansey used his business connections to build up a growing network of part-time agents with German contacts. It is probable that his unofficial empire-building was encouraged by Vansittart and that some of his German informants were also members of Van's 'private detective agency'. 'Quex' Sinclair doubtless welcomed Dansey's ability to extend the SIS network without making demands on his severely depleted funds.[82]

Two leading members of Dansey's network had worked for military intelligence during the First World War. Sigismund Payne Best, who now owned a pharmaceutical and chemical agency in Holland, began working part-time for Dansey soon after Hitler became chancellor of Germany in January 1933. So too did Best's wartime colleague, Rex Pearson, now working for Unilever in Switzerland. Most of the businessmen recruited by Dansey, however, were new to intelligence work. Among them were the former Conservative M.P., Frank Nelson (later knighted) who worked for Dansey in Switzerland and went on to organise the wartime SOE; Frederick 'Fanny' Vanden Heuvel, a Papal count as well as a director of Eno's Fruit Salts and later of Beecham's, whom Philby considered 'a smooth operator' despite his mauve spats; and William Stephenson, a wealthy Canadian businessman, whose visits to Germany as owner of the Pressed Steel Company enabled him to provide intelligence on the German steel industry and who went on to head wartime intelligence liaison with the United States. Dansey's wealthiest business friends were the Jewish diamond millionaires, Solly and Jack Joel, whom he had met in South Africa before the First World War. The rising tide of Nazi anti-Semitism made both happy to give Dansey financial support. But the businessman most closely involved with Dansey was the Hungarian Jewish film producer Alexander Korda, who moved to London in 1931 after twenty years of mixed success in Budapest, Vienna, Berlin, Hollywood and Paris, and a year later set up his own company, London Film Productions, which rapidly made him an international celebrity with films such as *The Private Life of Henry VIII*, starring the Oscar-winning Charles Laughton. The flamboyant Korda (later the first member of the film industry to receive a knighthood) was an Anglophile with a taste for the mystery of espionage as well as the glamour of film-making. His willingness to become involved with SIS also owed much to Dansey's success, chiefly through his wide range of business contacts, in helping to raise the finance for London Film Productions at a critical stage in Korda's career. It has been claimed that some of SIS's own exiguous funds were also directly invested in what proved to be a highly profitable enterprise. During the early thirties it is unlikely that Dansey's business contacts did much more than provide general economic intelligence and retail the gossip of the international business world. But in 1936 he was to use his growing network as the basis of a new and highly secret 'Z organisation' in SIS working independently of the passport control system.[83]

Like SIS and GC & CS, MI5's main problem in the thirties was shortage of resources. In 1930 Colonel Sir Vernon Kell and his deputy Lieutenant-Colonel Sir Eric Holt-Wilson had only five 'civil assistants' of officer rank at their Cromwell Road headquarters to deal with the main work of counter-espionage and the monitoring of Communist subversion in the armed services. Despite their 'civil' status all five came, like Kell and Holt-Wilson, from military backgrounds. Captain (later Major) Herbert H. Bacon and Major (later Lieutenant-Colonel) W. Edward Hinchley-Cooke had joined MI5 during the First World War; Major (later Colonel) W.A. Alexander arrived in the early 1920s; Lieutenant (later Major) H.F. Boddington joined in 1926; Captain A. Charles Butler came on a temporary secondment in 1926 and succeeded Joseph Ball in a permanent post a year later. Butler and Bacon went on to become heads of, respectively, A (Administration) and C (Security) Divisions in the expanded MI5 of the Second World War. In addition to its 'civil assistants', MI5 also had six officers to command the War Office Constabulary for which it was responsible, whose main duties were the security of War Office buildings. The chief constable was Lieutenant-Colonel J.S. Mellor.[84]

MI5's finances were chaotic as well as inadequate. The Treasury sometimes complained that it could not trace details of expenditure which MI5 had 'hidden away' in various parts of the War Office accounts. Some MI5 officers received War Office salaries while others were paid from the Secret Vote. Kell and Holt-Wilson oscillated between the two. They had ostensibly retired from the army on joining MI5 in, respectively, 1909 and 1912, and were paid until 1914 from the Secret Service Fund. On the outbreak of war they were formally recalled to 'General Staff appointments' and placed on the War Office establishment. In 1924, however, 'it was considered necessary to place them on the retired list for purposes of secrecy'. Both then went through the pretence of retirement and were paid from the Secret Vote until their real retirement in 1940.[85]

Midway between the wars, MI5 retained a rather traditional view of counter-espionage and counter-subversion which had evolved little during the 1920s. Largely because of their own military backgrounds and their lack of direct responsibility for 'civil' matters, the officers at MI5 headquarters continued to see Soviet subversion and espionage chiefly in military terms. They retained, in particular, an exaggerated concern at the long-term consequences of Communist propaganda in the armed forces. MI5 investigated 82 cases of soldiers suspected of various forms of Communist activity in 1929. Of these, 46 soldiers were 'cleared', 5 cases were dropped, 16 were 'still under investigation' at the end of the year, and 15 men were discharged (one fewer than in 1928). MI5 reported, however, that by the end of 1929 there had been an 'intensification' of both open propaganda and underground subversion. It traced much of this 'intensification' to secret instructions allegedly sent by Comintern's executive committee to the CPGB on 11 October 1929 urging it to set up cells within the armed services aimed at collecting secret information, agitating against commanding officers, and distributing anti-militarist propaganda. 'That espionage, as well as propaganda, is one of the dangers against which we have to guard', MI5 reported, 'cannot be too strongly emphasised'. It concluded in February 1930 that 'Communist efforts to tamper with H.M. Forces has [*sic*] increased and is still increasing':

> It is not suggested that as yet any serious harm has been done to the loyalty and discipline of the Forces generally, but in the case of certain of the more technical units, there is no doubt that this long continued and subtle propaganda is beginning to have a certain effect on both discipline and morale, which, if allowed to spread unchecked, will in the long run prove disastrous to the Forces as a whole.[86]

MI5's warnings against the dangers of subversion gained greatly in credibility after mutiny among ships of the Atlantic Fleet at Invergordon in September 1931. Though short-lived, the unrest in the navy caused a greater stir than any other disturbance within the armed forces since demobilisation after the First World War, and briefly raised the spectre of the Russian and German naval mutinies of 1917 and 1918 which had helped to topple both Tsar and Kaiser. It is now clear that the mutiny was a spontaneous protest by the lower deck against incompetently-planned and unfairly-distributed wage cuts. Trouble was quickly ended by reducing the cuts. But both Admiral Wilfred Tomkinson, senior officer (in effect acting C-in-C) of the Atlantic Fleet, and some of his officers, alarmed by the sudden discovery that as one of them put it, 'Twenty officers can't "make" a thousand do something if they don't want to', over-reacted to the whole affair. Tomkinson convinced himself that the mutiny was highly organised and must have been planned 'over a considerable period'. Fresh alarm was caused by an unauthorised signal said to have been exchanged between two ships of the Atlantic Fleet as they were steaming south from Invergordon on 18 September, allegedly referring to a mutiny planned at Portsmouth on the 22nd. The impact of the exaggerated reports of mutiny in the Atlantic Fleet was heightened by their arrival in the middle of a major financial crisis at the most critical moment in the life of the first National Government. The fears of foreign bankers that the government had lost its grip were strengthened, and the flight from the pound was, as Hankey told his diary, 'immensely stimulated'. On 17 September £10 million in gold was withdrawn from the Bank of England. Next day the figure rose to £18 million and the government was forced to make a hitherto unthinkable breach with financial orthodoxy and abandon the Gold Standard.[87]

On 21 September, the day that the bill ending the Gold Standard was rushed through all its stages in parliament, the cabinet heard an alarmist report on the progress of the mutiny, based largely on intelligence supplied by NID and MI5. The report was treated with extraordinary secrecy, excluded from the normal cabinet minutes, and summarised in a 'most secret' note which was then placed in a sealed envelope to be opened only by Hankey, his deputy or their successors. The cabinet was warned that

> ... the situation was extremely serious. There was a complete organization on the lower deck to resist the pay cuts, and the petty officers were now affected ... The intention now was for the crews to walk out of the ships on Tuesday morning [22 September] ... The marines afloat were implicated and ... the marines at the home ports were not to be trusted.

Most of this was nonsense. It is now clear that there were no plans for a further mutiny on the 22nd. But the grossly inflated estimates of naval unrest inevitably magnified fears of the opportunities for Communist subversion. The cabinet was told that 'The Communists were active in the ports and had sent some of the best agents there'.[88]

The CPGB had indeed hurriedly sent agents to the home ports, but their attempts to stir up trouble were sometimes comically inept. On 23 September Able Seaman Bateman, whose ship had arrived in Portsmouth from Invergordon, was approached in a fish and chip shop by a Communist named 'Shorty' Hutchings, posing as a journalist. Hutchings insisted on paying for Bateman's fish and chips, told him he wanted a story on Invergordon and arranged to meet him for drinks on the following day at the Park Hotel. Bateman turned up on the 24th together with a naval telegraphist named Bousfield who was, almost certainly, working for MI5. In the course of four hours' steady drinking at Hutchings' expense in the Park Hotel, he revealed according to later evidence in court, 'that he was a member of the Third International', and explained that 'he wanted sailors to come out on strike'. When Bateman and Bousfield demanded money, Hutchings said he would have to consult 'his superiors in London'. If they agreed, he would telegraph Bousfield: 'Mother ill. Come at once. Walter.' Before leaving, he assured Bousfield that if he lost his job with the navy, 'telegraphists were wanted in Russia, and he could get him a well-paid job there'.

After receiving the expected telegram from 'Walter', Bousfield travelled to London and met a *Daily Worker* journalist named William Shepherd at a house in Hampstead. Bousfield agreed to draft a seditious pamphlet to be distributed among sailors by Bateman and a non-existent friend named 'Smithson'. Shepherd promised to pay Mrs Bousfield £2 a week for the next year and make a further payment to Bateman. It was agreed that Bousfield would hand over the seditious pamphlet for printing to a man with a yellow handkerchief in his breast pocket whom he would meet in a Portsmouth pub. The two men duly met and the pamphlet was handed over in the lavatory at Portsmouth railway station. The man with the yellow handkerchief, who was immediately arrested, turned out to be George Allison, the unsuccessful agent sent to Bombay five years before, now acting general secretary of the British branch of the RILU, the National Minority Movement. In November Allison was sentenced to three years in jail and Shepherd to twenty months. For reasons which remain obscure no evidence was presented against Hutchings.[89]

The exaggerated fears of naval subversion provoked by Invergordon produced an extensive purge. One hundred and twenty men from the Atlantic Fleet suspected – sometimes on dubious evidence – of mutinous intentions were transferred to shore barracks. As soon as the National Government had been safely returned to power in the election on 28 October, they were discharged 'Services No Longer Required' and left outside the dockyard gates with thirteen shillings and a rail warrant. Commanders-in-chief at naval stations around the world were encouraged to pre-empt further trouble by discharging men 'whose conduct, character or lack of ability renders them undesirable for retention in the service': among them homosexuals and 'lower deck lawyers'.[90]

The immediate effect of Invergordon and the fears of further mutinies which followed was to increase MI5's powers. The attempts by civilian Communists to stir up naval unrest in the home ports seemed to prove MI5's arguments about the absurdity of dividing responsibility for monitoring civil and military subversion. Ever since the First World War Kell and his deputy Holt-Wilson had been agitating for '*one Centralised Security Service*':

> ... It is wasteful of energy to have more than one pack of hounds after each fox, and many of our present-day secret enemies go in for dangerous Civil propaganda and activities as well as espionage and mischief directly prejudicial to defence.

In September 1931, noted Kell exultantly, 'we took over Scotland Yard intelligence'. Responsibility for all 'investigations dealing with the Communist and foreign revolutionary movements' was transferred to MI5, which increasingly described itself as the Security Service. The Special Branch continued to make enquiries on Kell's behalf, when requested, and became more than ever 'a valuable camouflage' for MI5.[91]

As part of the transfer of responsibilities, MI5 acquired Scotland Yard's leading experts on subversion. Chief among them was Captain Guy Liddell, who went on to become head of MI5's wartime B (Counter-Espionage) Division, a talented amateur cellist with a deceptively ruminative manner and a subtle intellect. Even Kim Philby later remembered him with affection as 'an ideal senior officer for a young man to learn from':

> He would murmur his thoughts aloud, as if groping his way towards the facts of a case, his face creased in a comfortable, innocent smile. But behind the facade of laziness, his subtle and reflective mind played over a storehouse of photographic memories.[92]

But Liddell's private life was scarred by an increasingly unhappy marriage to Calypso Baring, younger daughter of Lord Revelstoke. Had he been a less patient man, one of his MI5 colleagues believes, 'he must surely have strangled Calypso'. Their marriage was eventually dissolved in 1943.[93]

As a by-product of the Statute of Westminster, which in December 1931 gave the self-governing dominions legislative independence, MI5's relationships with imperial intelligence services were redefined at a secret conference of security chiefs.[94] MI5 emerged from it, as from the readjustment of its relations with the Special Branch, with enhanced status. Kell's deputy, Holt-Wilson, claimed proudly:

> Our Security Service is more than national, it is Imperial. We have official agencies cooperating with us, under the direct instructions of the Dominion and Colonial Offices and the supervision of the local Governors, and their chiefs of police, for enforcing local Security Laws in every British Community overseas.
>
> These all act under our guidance for Security duties. It is our duty to advise them, when necessary, on all Security measures necessary for defence and civil purposes; and to exchange information regarding the movement within the Empire of individuals who are likely to be hostile to its interests from a Security point of view.[95]

MI5's main priority remained, however, Communist subversion in the armed forces. Its energy in continuing the search for naval subversion after the Invergordon mutiny ended by causing some concern in the Admiralty. On 30 June 1932 the Board of Admiralty decreed that agents should not in future go on board ships or 'undertake espionage work' away from home ports. In his later study of naval policy between the wars Captain Stephen Roskill found no evidence of any Communist activity in the navy save for a few cases of naval ratings attending CPGB meetings in Hyde Park in support of the miners during the prolonged strike of 1926.[96] MI5, however, continued to regard Communist subversion in all the armed services as a serious menace.

Its fears were strengthened by the fact that several of the Invergordon mutineers discharged in 1931, though previously apolitical, were recruited by the CPGB and became active in it. Len Wincott, one of the most prominent ex-mutineers, made a series of speaking tours, chiefly in the ports. He had, he discovered, 'the most valuable pass-key one could wish for: my own working class accent':

> Unlike the intellectual type who does not know the difference between slumming and helping, I did not have to prove my credentials by standing at the corner of the street with a flowing red tie for everybody to see and shouting 'Daily Worker' in an accent which would have got me a chair at Oxford without any exams.

In 1934 Wincott was told by the CPGB secretary Harry Pollitt that he 'was to go to the Soviet Union to work in the International Seamen's Club in Leningrad'. A few years later he was sent to a labour camp during Stalin's purges.[97] Fred Copeman, another Invergordon mutineer, also became a CPGB militant and commanded a British battalion in the Spanish Civil War. He too became disillusioned, noted the 'extremes of squalor and luxury side by side in Stalin's Russia', left the CPGB in 1939, and later became a leading member of the Moral Rearmament movement.[98]

In the aftermath of Invergordon both MI5 and the service ministries viewed with peculiar horror the crude tracts prepared by the CPGB for distribution to the armed forces, in particular the irregular issues of *Soldier's Voice* and its naval equivalent *Red Signal*. According to War Office and Admiralty statistics, during 1932 50,000 copies of seventeen different subversive pamphlets aimed at the services were distributed in twenty different locations. The basic message of many of them was summed up in the *Soldier's Voice* call to class war in May 1932:

> Let us use the knowledge of arms which they give us, when the opportunity presents itself, to overthrow their rule, and in unity with our fellow workers, to establish free socialist Britain.

The attorney general, Sir Thomas Inskip, complained that the authors of the tracts used 'comparatively harmless and ill-paid persons' to throw their tracts over barrack walls and push them 'into the hands of soldiers and sailors in places of refreshment or in music halls'.[99] The young Bristol Communist, Douglas Hyde, later news editor of the *Daily Worker*, recalled how bundles of *Soldier's Voice* were 'smuggled down from London' to be dropped by night over the wall of the local barracks:

> Since the risks were high, volunteers were called for, who then drew lots.

I volunteered but drew a blank. The unlucky one that night was caught in the act and disappeared into the neighbouring jail for eighteen months.[100]

MI5 read *Soldier's Voice* more attentively than the Bristol soldiers. In October 1932 it prepared a detailed report which, it claimed,

> irresistibly demonstrated the growing menace, which the Communist movement represents, not only to the maintenance of law and order, but to the stability of the Armed Forces, and earnestly represented that, if steps were not taken to deal with it at the present stage of its development, it would present a very much more difficult task in the future.

MI5 also drafted a Public Security Bill which it declared represented 'the minimum measure of legislation required'. It was remarkably broadly framed to prohibit

> Use or advocacy of the use of force, violence, intimidation, etc., for the purpose of procuring the alteration of the established law, form of Government, or constitution of the United Kingdom, or for the purpose of bringing into hatred or contempt the administration of justice, or for the purpose of interfering with the administration of the law, or with the maintenance of law and order.

MI5 proposed that it become an offence even to contribute to any society which aided or abetted any of these acts. And it proposed further clauses to prohibit 'inducing etc. any member of H.M. Forces to fail in duty, or commit a breach of discipline'.[101] Not surprisingly, the government was not convinced. But MI5 did not give up.

Early in 1933 new 'information of the highest importance' threw 'a flood of fresh light' on Comintern plans for 'seducing the Armed Forces of the Crown from their allegiance'.[102] That new light came from what Denniston considered one of GC & CS's most successful operations of the 1930s which identified 'a mass of unusual and unknown transmissions' as coming from 'a worldwide network of clandestine stations controlled by a station near Moscow'. A team of cryptanalysts led by Colonel (later Brigadier) John Tiltman successfully decrypted all Comintern radio traffic with England. A direction-finding team led by Leslie Lambert (well known to radio audiences as the popular raconteur 'A.J.Alan') and a more recent recruit named Kenworthy succeeded in tracking down the British transmitter in the Comintern radio network to a terrace house in a London suburb. Denniston considered this 'perhaps the earliest example' of direction-finding in the history of GC & CS.[103] MI5 was able to use the success of Lambert and Kenworthy as a further argument for new legislation. Had the terrace house in a London suburb contained obscene literature, it would have been easy to obtain a search warrant from a magistrate. But no powers of search existed for the 'far more dangerous literature' produced by Comintern.[104]

A few months later MI5's persistence finally paid off. On 9 October 1933 the first lord of the Admiralty told the cabinet, after receiving an MI5 report:

> ... Communist Agents known to the authorities had in their possession a pamphlet intended to be issued to the Fleet containing a gross incitement to mutiny. The state of the law was such, however, that nothing could be done to stop the issue of the pamphlet. After the event those proved to have issued it could be punished but probably it would only be possible to secure evidence against a distributor who would be a mere hireling. The existing law did not make it an offence to prepare such a pamphlet or to hold it before publication.

This instance of 'gross incitement to mutiny' brought to a head discussions which had been proceeding for some time on the need for new legislation.[105] Nine days later the cabinet considered the first draft of an Incitement to Disaffection Bill in a memorandum signed by the service ministers and the home secretary:

> The primary object of the Bill was to provide a summary method of dealing with attempts to seduce members of His Majesty's Forces from their duty and allegiance, the second main object being to empower Justices of the Peace to grant search warrants where they are satisfied that there is reasonable ground for suspecting that an offence under the Bill has been committed.[106]

The home secretary, Sir John Gilmour, reported 'a good deal of information ... which suggests that the Police Service contains at least a proportion of men who could not be relied on to withstand attempts to undermine their loyalty'. Over the next few months he tried, but failed, to persuade the cabinet to extend the bill to include attempts to subvert the police.[107]

The bill made its first appearance in the Commons on 10 April 1934. At the second reading six days later the Liberal Isaac Foot (father of the future Labour leader) asked 'what evidence there is that a single soldier has been influenced in his allegiance or that a single sailor has done more than deride these wonderful papers, "The Soldier's Voice" and "The Red Signal" ...'[108] None was produced. The National Government's huge parliamentary majority ensured none the less that the bill became law before the year's end. To the surprise of both its opponents and supporters, it led to only one prosecution. In 1937 a Leeds University student 'of extreme political views' was sentenced to twelve months in prison for suggesting to an RAF pilot that he steal an aeroplane and use it to help the Spanish Republicans. His sentence was drastically reduced on appeal.[109]

Though MI5 and the service ministries greatly exaggerated the importance of the crude, ineffective propaganda in the *Soldier's Voice* and the *Red Signal*, their concern at the threat of sabotage and espionage in dockyards and munitions factories had more justification. Between 1933 and 1936 there were six quite serious cases of sabotage to ships' machinery in naval dockyards (five in Devonport and one at Sheerness) which prompted a detailed investigation by MI5 of Communist activity in royal dockyards and naval ordnance works. In Devonport, the main centre of sabotage, an undercover MI5 case officer succeeded in winning the confidence of dockyard workers and becoming 'personally acquainted' with the members of a Communist cell. Early in 1936 MI5 recommended the dismissal of the cell leader, John Salisbury. In accordance with a procedure agreed between Kell and Sir Warren Fisher, the chairman of the Secret Service Committee, probably in the wake of the Invergordon mutiny, the MI5 recommendation was referred to and approved by a three-man committee headed by Sir Archibald Carter, permanent undersecretary at the Admiralty, assisted by one of his deputies and a Treasury official. Salisbury's dismissal caused little protest. Local officials of the TGWU were told in confidence some of the case against him (though it was not revealed to Salisbury), and Ernest Bevin, the TGWU general secretary, who had already had a number of bitter conflicts with Communists, said privately that 'nobody would attempt to defend Salisbury'.[110]

In October 1936 Kell recommended eight more dismissals: four from Devonport, one from Sheerness and three from the Naval Ordnance Works in Sheffield. In addition to studying MI5 files on the eight men concerned and photographs of their intercepted correspondence, the Carter committee also heard oral evidence from Kell and the MI5 case officer at Devonport who impressed them 'by his fair-minded attitude'. The Commitee believed it 'impossible, largely owing to the inability to disclose secret sources of information, to produce proof to satisfy a court of law'. But they concluded that in the case of the Devonport workers, Francis Carne, Alfred Durston, Henry Lovejoy and Edward Trebilcock:

> It is certain, beyond any reasonable doubt ... that all four men have been actively engaged in dangerous subversive propaganda, and not merely in the doctrinaire preaching of Communism as a political creed.
>
> There is also very strong suspicion, though not amounting to certainty, that they were intimately connected with acts of sabotage.
>
> None of the four has been very active since the dismissal of Salisbury, but there is good reason for believing that they have received orders from above ... We recommend that they should all be discharged.

The Committee also approved the dismissal of Henry Law, a shipwright at

Sheerness, who 'apart from other considerable activities ... took an active part in attempting to get the public to refuse cooperation in the experimental "black-out" at Sheerness in 1935'. But Sir Archibald Carter and his colleagues concluded that MI5 had not produced 'sufficiently definite evidence' to justify the dismissal of the Sheffield Ordnance workers: 'They are, however, suspicious characters, and a closer watch will be kept upon them.' On this occasion local trade union officials were not consulted and the five dismissals at Sheerness produced a flood of union protests. Bevin, acting both as chairman of the TUC and general secretary of the TGWU, wrote to the prime minister, Stanley Baldwin, calling for an independent tribunal. At a private meeting in the House of Commons Baldwin took at least some of the wind out of Bevin's sails. When Bevin argued that in the case of Alfred Durston 'there appeared to have been a miscarriage of justice', Baldwin read out compromising extracts from Durston's intercepted letters.[111]

MI5's most valuable agent on Soviet espionage in the arms industry was Olga Gray, the twenty-five-year-old daughter of a *Daily Mail* night editor in Manchester recruited by Maxwell Knight as a long-term penetration agent in 1931. At Knight's request Miss Gray joined the Friends of the Soviet Union and became in 1932 a typist for the Anti-War Movement, a Communist front organisation based in Gray's Inn Road. She gradually succeeded in winning the confidence of Percy Glading, the first of the CPGB agents sent to India in 1925, who now worked in the same building as secretary of another front organisation, the League Against Imperialism. Glading had formerly been employed at the Woolwich Arsenal and was engaged in developing an espionage ring among Arsenal workers. By 1934 Miss Gray was sufficiently trusted by Glading and Pollitt, the CPGB general secretary, to be used as a foreign courier, smuggling money to Indian Communists.[112]

MI5 continued, as in the 1920s, to have access to intercepted phone calls and correspondence sent and received by CPGB headquarters in King Street. In the course of the 1930s, as Maxwell Knight's network of agents infiltrating Communist and subversive groups expanded, he became head of an ultra-secret section of MI5 known as B5b, based at a house in Dolphin Square held in the name of 'Miss Coplestone'. His agents within the CPGB, most of whose names still remain hidden in MI5 files, included at least one 'close to', though not actually on, the Central Committee.[113] Knight's success owed something to the seductive force of his personality. Though he failed to consummate his first two marriages and his first wife committed suicide, he seemed to his wartime assistant Joan Miller to exude animal magnetism. 'He could', she believed, 'make men and women do anything'. Knight also had for a time a rather disturbing interest in the occult, going with Denis Wheatley to séances by the notorious Satanist Aleister Crowley to research black magic for Wheatley's novels.[114]

Knight's taste for the bizarre made it possible for him to use informants who might not have cooperated with a more conventional case-officer. One of the more unusual was the future Labour M.P., Tom Driberg, who had joined the CPGB during his last year at Lancing in 1924, and during his three years at Oxford used, in his own words, 'to liaise between the City Party and the few members in the University'. It is hard to believe, as has been claimed, that Driberg joined the CPGB 'on Knight's instructions' and that his Communism was always a mere front.[115] Driberg was single-minded about very little before the Second World War save his homosexuality and it is difficult to imagine him as a dedicated, disciplined MI5 informant. It is likely, as Joan Miller suggests, that 'he was more a casual agent' who would only 'turn in a bit of stuff' when Knight put pressure on him. Knight, she claims, was a bisexual and, for a time, 'crazy' about Driberg. Throughout the 1930s Driberg combined his Communism with a taste for good living and a job running the William Hickey column in the *Daily Express* which led, as he acknowledged, to a certain 'incongruity between his views and his surroundings'. The contradictions in Driberg's complex character were such that he probably managed to combine some residual sympathy for the CPGB with his role as an informer for MI5. His friends within the party included one in whom Knight had a particular interest: Douglas Springhall, leader of the Young Communist League and a recruiter for Soviet Intelligence who was himself convicted of espionage in 1943. Driberg was eventually identified as an MI5 informer, probably after a tip-off by Anthony Blunt (then working for MI5) and expelled from the party by Harry Pollitt in 1941.[116]

While running Olga Gray, Tom Driberg and his other agents within the CPGB and front organisations, Knight also tried his hand at writing thrillers. His first novel *Crime Cargo* tells how a group of American gangsters hijack a cruise ship, the S.S. *Falkland*, and are defeated by mainly British grit. The chief villains are unconvincing stereotypes: Emilio 'Toad' Binetti, Eddie the Swede, 'Fingers' Reilly, 'Lobo the Killer' and Dumb Louie. So are the minor characters who include a French maid, 'the trim Adèle' ('Oh, la, la! Show ze leg – 'ow funny you speak'), a Chinese cook ('You makee guests happy'), and 'a Negro factotum who could do anything from mixing cocktails to shining shoes'. Knight allows himself a very occasional injoke detectable only by other intelligence officers – for example the naive villain who signed himself with 'a simple "C"'. But the most revealing aspect of his indifferent first novel is the way in which the upright heroes, outraged by the baseness of their opponents, gradually conclude that they do not deserve civilised treatment. After 'Toad' Binetti and his gang have been rounded up, Captain Sandys of the *Falkland* addresses them in language which probably reflected Knight's own attitude to Communist subversives:

During your brief régime here you seemed to think that the way to treat women, or anyone else in your power, was to subject them to threats of treatment which a savage would despise. Right! Now I know the sort of language you understand, I intend to speak to you in it myself.

Sandys begins by giving Binetti 'a crack on the nose that pushed that feature badly askew' and continues in the same vein while other members of the gang are given 'a period of unadulterated hell' in the engine-room. But the essential decency of both heroes and heroines persuades them to stop short of inflicting permanent mutilation. When the 'usually placid' Freddie becomes overenthusiastic while teaching one of the villains a lesson, one of the heroines intervenes:

'That's enough, Freddie', said Susan.
'I wanted you to beat him up, but don't kill him – he's not worth it'.

Binetti and his gang are finally handed over not to 'some Yankee court where you can bribe your way back to freedom' but to British justice. After trial at the Old Bailey, Binetti is hanged at Liverpool prison. Knight thus managed to combine patriotic respect for the superiority of English Law over its foreign rivals with the suggestion that it was sometimes permissible to step outside it.[117] But he was not a successful novelist. After the publication of his second novel, *Gunmen's Holiday*, in 1935, either he or his publisher gave up.

Unlike Somerset Maugham and Compton Mackenzie, Maxwell Knight was much more successful as an intelligence officer than as a novelist. Even after the triumphs of the Double Cross system during the Second World War, MI5 still remembered his handling of the Glading case as one of the most professional in its history, though it failed in the end to yield quite the results hoped of it.[118] During 1935 Olga Gray's career as an MI5 penetration agent was interrupted by illness but by 1937 Percy Glading had at last begun to involve her directly in espionage. In February of that year Miss Gray was asked to rent a flat in Kensington to be used as a safe house. In April the flat was visited by a Russian agent using the cover name 'Peters', whom Glading referred to as 'an Austrian who had served during the war in the Russian cavalry'. On the basis of that and other information, MI5 was able to identify Peters as the cosmopolitan NKVD officer, Theodore Maly, who operated under a number of aliases.[119] In August 1937 two more Soviet agents, using the names 'Mr and Mrs Stephens' turned up at the Kensington flat, and Miss Gray was taught how to assist 'Mrs Stephens' in photographing secret documents. Miss Gray was able to note the reference number of a document photographed in October which enabled MI5 to identify it as the plan of a new 14-inch naval gun. The 'Stephens' were observed to leave London for Paris, en route for Moscow.

For the moment MI5 ordered no arrests, preferring to wait until it had unravelled more of the espionage taking place in the Woolwich Arsenal. With the gift of hindsight, however, it probably wished it had arrested the 'Stephens' before they had left the country. After their departure Glading's connections with Moscow were temporarily disrupted by Stalin's purges, then at their height; Maly and possibly the 'Stephens' perished in them.[120] Early in 1938 Glading told Miss Gray that he was running short of money, had 'got the stuff parked all over London' ready to be handed over, and led her to expect that another Soviet agent was on his way to London. On 20 January the agent's arrival seemed imminent. Glading told Miss Gray to 'get the flat ready for something important' and said next day that there was 'urgent photography to be done'. On the evening of 21 January the Special Branch arrested Glading at Charing Cross Station just as he was receiving a brown paper parcel from another man. The arrests proved to be premature for Glading's contact turned out to be not his new Soviet control but Albert Williams, a hitherto unidentified spy working as an examiner under the chief inspector of armaments at Woolwich Arsenal. Soon afterwards two of Glading's other contacts in the Arsenal who had already been identified, George Whomack and Charles Munday, were also arrested. Evidence at their trial at the Old Bailey in March included a mass of incriminating documents and photographic material found at the homes of both Glading and Williams. Glading was given six years' imprisonment, Williams four and Whomack three: all light sentences by contemporary standards. For reasons which remain obscure, the prosecution presented no evidence against Munday, who was acquitted. Olga Gray was congratulated by the judge for her 'extraordinary courage' and 'great service to her country', and left to start a new life in Canada under a new name.[121]

During the early 1930s MI5 and the Special Branch began for the first time to pay serious attention to right-wing as well as left-wing subversion. They had taken a passing interest in the small Fascist splinter groups of the 1920s but rightly regarded them as of little significance.[122] MI5 took a closer interest in the British Union of Fascists (BUF) founded by Sir Oswald Mosley in October 1932. But it was not until street fighting between black-shirted Fascists and Communists, chiefly in the East End of London, began to grow in the spring of 1934 that Kell prepared his first full-scale report on 'The Fascist Movement in the United Kingdom'. Early in May he wrote to about 150 chief constables in England, Scotland and Wales asking for details at regular intervals of BUF membership and 'their opinion as to the importance to be attached to this movement in their areas'. From their replies he concluded that 'the Fascists have been more active and successful in the industrial areas and that their achievements in the majority of the Counties may be regarded as negligible'. But there were 'three important questions' which Kell confessed himself unable to answer for the moment:

1. Has the British Union of Fascists, apart from open and public activity,

any secret organisation in being, or under preparation, which would enable them to take effective action in an emergency?

2. Have they any intention of attempting to influence the Armed Forces by direct propaganda or otherwise?

3. Are their financial resources supplied in any way from foreign (i.e. Italian or German) sources?

For the moment MI5 believed that the opportunity for a Fascist coup was still far away, but it detected 'various tendencies' which were 'bringing Sir Oswald Mosley and his followers more to the front of the stage'. Their propaganda was 'extremely clever'.[123]

The Fascist threat, such as it was, appeared to reach its peak at the Olympia rally in June 1934, extravagantly proclaimed beforehand by the BUF as 'a landmark, not only in the history of fascism, but also in the history of Britain'. Most of the choreography for the rally was borrowed from Hitler and Mussolini. Mosley marched to the platform lit by a spotlight through a forest of Union Jacks and BUF banners while uniformed Blackshirts gave the Fascist salute and chanted 'Hail Mosley!' Fights between hecklers and Fascist stewards started almost as soon as Mosley began to speak. They continued intermittently for the next two hours. 'The Blackshirt spirit', declared Mosley afterwards, 'triumphed at Olympia. It smashed the biggest organised attempt ever made in this country to wreck a meeting by Red violence'. The Communist *Daily Worker* also claimed victory: 'The great Olympia counter-demonstration of the workers against Blackshirts stands out as an important landmark in the struggle against Fascism in this country'.[124] Though virtuously disclaiming all responsibility for the violence, both the BUF and the CPGB, in MI5's view, used 'illegal and violent methods': 'In fact, both ... were delighted with the results of Olympia'.[125]

After Olympia the cabinet briefly turned its mind to ways of preventing further rallies in which Fascists paraded in political uniforms. But the problems of framing new legislation to prevent such rallies were complicated by the difficulty of defining 'political uniforms'. Encouraged by reassuring MI5 reports, the cabinet gradually lost its sense of urgency. Kell concluded in October:

> It is becoming increasingly clear that at Olympia Mosley suffered a check which is likely to prove decisive. He suffered it, not at the hands of the Communists who staged the provocations and now claim the victory, but at the hands of Conservative MPs, the Conservative Press and all those organs of public opinion which made him abandon the policy of using his "Defence Force" to overwhelm interrupters.

The BUF had been publicly disowned a month after Olympia by the press baron, Lord Rothermere, its most prominent Conservative supporter. Mosley himself was said by MI5 to be in a state of 'acute depression' and the deputy leader of the BUF, Dr Robert Forgan, who later left the movement, was believed 'to have doubts as to his leader's sanity'.[126] MI5 reported in March 1935 that, according to a trustworthy source (probably an agent in the BUF), Fascist 'cells' had been formed in 'various branches of the Civil Service'. But the general tenor of Kell's intelligence continued to be reassuring. Reports to MI5 from chief constables showed that in all major cities except Manchester BUF membership had declined, branches had closed, sales of the *Blackshirt* had dropped, and enthusiasm had cooled.[127]

Mosley had begun receiving subsidies from Mussolini in the summer of 1933.[128] But though Kell was on the lookout for such subsidies, he failed for the next two years to find any evidence of them. At last, in October 1935, soon after the outbreak of the Italo-Abyssinian War, MI5 triumphantly reported secret evidence that Mussolini had agreed to pay the BUF £3,000 a month. The main intermediary was Mosley's 'chief of staff', Ian Hope Dundas, who stayed on in Rome giving weekly news broadcasts in English in support of the Italian cause. Mosley meanwhile began an intensive campaign in Britain under the slogan 'Mind Britain's Business', condemning the economic sanctions applied against Italy after her invasion of Abyssinia. MI5 believed that the details of Mussolini's subsidies to the BUF were known only to a small inner circle of Mosley's followers, one of whom went regularly either to France or Switzerland to collect the money in pound notes.[129] Mosley later concluded, probably correctly, that MI5's chief informer within the BUF was the former Conservative M.P., W.E.D. (Bill) Allen, who later served in SOE. But Allen may not have been MI5's only source. By 1935 the secret of the Italian subsidies was poorly kept by the BUF leadership. Forgan warned Mosley that the subsidies were 'known to a number of people who are not in our confidence'. One BUF member, to Mosley's annoyance, mentioned the Italian money in correspondence from Rome which may well have been intercepted.[130]

Mussolini's subsidies did little or nothing to arrest the steady decline of the BUF during the two years after the Olympia rally. A German agent, Colin Ross, visited England in April 1936 to report on the state of the British Fascists. According to the Special Branch, which kept him under close surveillance, Ross concluded that the BUF had 'a fine policy and a splendid leader, but absolutely no organisation'. There were signs, none the less, of growing German influence among the Blackshirts. In July the BUF changed its full title to the 'British Union of Fascists and National Socialists'. 'Mosley', MI5 reported, 'has also shown a closer approach to the German spirit in his more pronounced attacks on the Jews during recent months'.[131] MI5 emphasised the growing influence within the BUF of the pro-Nazi William Joyce who, it believed, had greater influence on militant Blackshirts than Mosley himself. It continued for several years to rely on a rather optimistic appreciation of Joyce by 'someone who knows him well', written late in 1934, which claimed that though he was 'a rabid anti-Catholic' and 'a fanatical anti-Semite' with 'a mental balance ... not equal to his intellectual capacity', it was unlikely that anything 'could occur to shake his basic patriotism'. In fact Joyce took German citizenship in 1940 and became known to the British people as 'Lord Haw-Haw', broadcasting Nazi propaganda in English for most of the war.[132]

Mosley's increasingly pro-German attitude inevitably raised suspicions in MI5 that, despite Ross's unfavourable report, the BUF might be receiving funds from Hitler as well as Mussolini. But though MI5 concluded that Mosley had made 'some advances' in the hope of Nazi subsidies, it could find no evidence that any had arrived. Mussolini too appeared to be losing confidence in the British Fascists. MI5 reported in July 1936 that the monthly Italian subsidies had been cut from £3,000 to £1,000, and that the BUF was in 'general decline'. Though it also recognised that Mosley's 'more pronounced attacks on Jews' had struck a chord in parts of the East End, MI5 seems to have underestimated the potential threat to public order:

> It is true that in the East End Fascist speakers have had a better welcome than elsewhere, but there is a good deal of anti-semitic feeling there and anti-semitic speeches are therefore welcome. There does not seem to be any reason for believing that public opinion in the East End is becoming seriously pro-Fascist.[133]

For several months both the government and the Metropolitan police, like MI5, underestimated the growing tension in the East End. On 4 October plans by four columns of Blackshirts to march to meetings in Shoreditch, Stepney, Bethnal Green and Limehouse led to the 'Battle of Cable Street' when anti-Fascists threw up a barricade in the Blackshirts' path, fought with police and forced Mosley to divert his march along the Embankment. The day produced, according to the Special Branch, 'undoubtedly the largest anti-Fascist demonstration yet seen in London'. It also led the government to recover the sense of urgency it had lost after the Olympia rally two years before. The home secretary told the cabinet: 'There cannot be the slightest doubt that the Fascist campaign ... is stimulating the Communist movement so that the danger of a serious clash is growing'. A Public Order Act prohibiting political uniforms and empowering the police to forbid political processions was rushed through parliament and came into effect on 1 January 1937.[134]

The battle of Cable Street, quickly condemned by the BUF as 'the first occasion on which the British Government has surrendered to Red Terror', gave Mosley just the publicity he was looking for. MI5 reported that at meetings organised by Mosley in the East End immediately afterwards, before the Communists had 'time to organise opposition', 'the display of pro-Fascist sentiments on the streets surprised a number of experienced observers'. But the BUF resurgence was short-lived. MI5 believed that 'the Fascists instead of keeping the situation at boiling point ... allowed it to subside again during the latter part of October and November'. At the end of November 1936 MI5 put BUF membership at 'a maximum of 6,500 active and 9,000 non-active members'; the Special Branch put it rather higher at a total of nearly 20,000.[135] The Commissioner for the Metropolitan Police reported a few months later: 'The Public Order Act of 1936 seems to have killed the wearing of political uniforms without any need for prosecution'. With the banning of the Blackshirts the BUF dwindled steadily into insignificance.[136]

But while the Fascist menace declined at home, it rose dramatically abroad. By the time the British Blackshirts lost their shirts, Germany had, for the first time since the First World War, replaced Soviet Russia as the main target of British foreign intelligence.

# 12 | APPEASEMENT: THE ROAD TO MUNICH

One of the many by-products of German rearmament under the Nazi régime was a modest revival of British government interest in its intelligence services. That revival can be dated quite precisely to the spring of 1935. On 16 March Hitler announced the introduction of conscription. On the 25th he boasted to Sir John Simon, now nearing the end of his term as foreign secretary, that the Luftwaffe had already 'reached parity' with the RAF. What the Führer meant by this extravagant boast was not immediately clear since the Germans had recently produced three conflicting estimates of British air strength. After a fortnight's delay the British air attaché in Berlin was at last given an official German explanation. 'Herr Hitler's claim', he reported, 'was to approximate parity with our existing First-line strength ... which strength he had assumed to be 800–850 aircraft'. Sir Edward Ellington, the taciturn chief of the air staff, was unruffled, but gave a warning for the future:

> It is possible that this belated elucidation, which is still somewhat vague, is an afterthought to explain away what was, in fact, a mistaken statement on the part of Herr Hitler ... There is no ground for alarm at the existing situation. Whatever first-line strength Germany may claim we remain today substantially stronger *if all relevant factors are taken into account.* But the future, as opposed to the present, must cause grave concern.[1]

Churchill, now in the middle of his wilderness years on the back benches, was more alarmist. Hitler, he wrongly believed, had actually understated his case and was already 'much stronger than we are'.[2]

The cabinet was understandably confused. On 17 April it instructed the Ministerial Committee on Defence Policy and Requirements (DPR)[3] to work out the truth of Hitler's claims. The committee quickly discovered that one of its 'greatest difficulties' was the shortage of intelligence on the German air force. Its investigation 'brought out very clearly the need for increased financial provision for Secret Service funds'. But it considered an immediate supplementary estimate on the Secret Service vote 'most undesirable', no doubt because of the unwelcome publicity which would result. The Committee therefore 'requested the Foreign Office and the Treasury to consult together with a view to finding some other means of provision' – in other words to cook the books and divert non-secret funds to secret purposes.[4]

The Defence Requirements Sub-Committee (DRC) of the CID underlined the need for greater intelligence spending. German naval rearmament, it reported, provided a recent example of a major issue 'on which our Intelligence proved defective'. SIS in particular urgently required more funds:

If [its] allowance is not augmented, and very largely augmented, the organisation cannot be expected to fulfil its function, and this country will be most dangerously handicapped. It is difficult to assign an exact figure to this service, on which increased demands are continually being made; but nothing less than £500,000 will be really adequate.

That conclusion was endorsed in principle by the ministerial DRC in January 1936 and by the cabinet a month later. But it was agreed that the secret vote could only be raised gradually: a decision doubtless dictated by fear of public comment as well as by the need for economy. There is no record of any subsequent discussion of the intelligence budget by either the cabinet or any ministerial committee before the Second World War.[5] With the tacit consent of the remainder of the cabinet the affairs of the intelligence services were left in the hands of a handful, at most, of senior ministers and their advisers. With their approval and without debate in parliament the secret service vote was raised from £180,000 in 1935 to £250,000 (with a supplementary vote of £100,000) in 1936, £350,000 in 1937, £450,000 in 1938, and £500,000 in 1939.[6]

Not all the secret vote went to SIS. On the other hand SIS had access to funds, in particular from passport control, other than the secret vote. Its labyrinthine budget contained so much deliberate mystification that even SIS no longer knows what it amounted to in the 1930s. Despite the increased budget, however, there is no doubt that right up to the outbreak of war SIS was hampered by shortage of funds. Until 1939 it was unable even to afford wireless sets for its agents.[7]

The budgetary problems of SIS were compounded by financial scandals. The eccentric accounting procedures of passport control offices, with their mixture of open and secret responsibilities and the possibility of trafficking in British visas, continued to offer tempting opportunities for embezzlement.[8] In July 1936 three Polish clerks in the Warsaw passport control office were arrested on a charge of extorting money from prospective Jewish emigrants to Palestine. The British ambassador to Poland was anxious to prevent the PCO, Major J.P. Shelley, and his assistant, Captain H.T. Handscombe, from appearing in court 'since they might well be asked questions about the internal affairs of the Passport Control Office which it would be inexpedient for them to answer'. A far more serious scandal came to light two months later in The Hague where the PCO himself, Major H.E. Dalton, had been embezzling fees paid by Jewish refugees, allegedly to finance an expensive love affair. Best had suspected him of extortion from Dutch firms at the very beginning of his intelligence career in Holland during the First World War. Dalton's assistant, John ('Jack') Hooper, discovered his embezzlement in the mid-thirties, and forced him to share the proceeds by threatening to expose him. In the end the pressure became too much for Dalton and he shot himself in September 1936. A subsequent investigation revealed that he had stolen several thousand pounds of government money. Hooper confessed his own part in the fraud and was dismissed but escaped prosecution for fear of the public scandal which his trial would cause. To 'Quex' Sinclair's relief, no newspaper linked either the arrests in Warsaw or Dalton's suicide in The Hague with SIS.[9]

The passport control organisation in The Hague never recovered from Dalton's suicide. Dalton's successor, Major 'Monty' Chidson, though a fluent Dutch speaker who later had a more successful wartime intelligence career,[10] was not a success in the Netherlands. He became involved in a number of personal disputes and had a public quarrel with Sigismund Payne Best, who was engaged in intelligence work for Claude Dansey. Best later complained:

I met [Chidson] at a Legation Ball where he welcomed me with shouts of 'Hallo, here is old Best the arch spy – I know all about you' etc., etc. The last I saw of him he was vomiting on some lady's lap.[11]

Chidson's most disastrous action in The Hague was to recruit a young Dutch agent with a German wife, Folkert van Koutrik, whom he told to shadow an Abwehr agent in The Hague, Traugott Protze. The inexperienced van Koutrik was quickly identified by Protze and recruited as a double agent working for the Abwehr. Protze also succeeded in recruiting Dalton's former assistant, 'Jack' Hooper.[12] In the early months of the war the German penetration of the passport control office at 57 Nieuwe Parklaan in The Hague was to have disastrous consequences for SIS.[13]

'Monty' Chidson was recalled from The Hague in 1937. His successor was Major Richard Stevens, a forty-four-year-old Indian Army officer whom Best believed to be filling in time before promotion to lieutenant-colonel.[14] By his own later admission, Stevens was not a success:

I had never been a spy, much less a spymaster. My intelligence work, mainly the evaluation of military reports on the deployment of armed native tribesmen, was done solely on the Northwest Frontier ... I agreed to go to The Hague as long as my superiors realised that I thought myself to be lacking in experience and training for the assignment and was, in my own eyes, altogether the wrong sort of man for such work.[15]

SIS's problems in the mid-thirties were not limited to The Hague. Captain Rex Howard RN, who succeeded Reggie Fletcher as chief G officer in charge of operations when Fletcher entered the Commons after the 1935 election, was one of the most popular officers in Broadway. His ability did not match his popularity. David Footman, one of the ablest SIS recruits of the thirties (later head of political intelligence and a Fellow of St Antony's College, Oxford), found him 'a very, very decent chap who hadn't got the brains of Fletcher'. Howard did, however, make it a rule that all station chiefs should return to Broadway two or three times a year to review their past intelligence reports and future priorities.[16]

During the mid-thirties SIS also found its intelligence-gathering impeded by increasing pressure on the overt side of passport control from the growing number of Jewish and other refugees from persecution in Central Europe. Captain Frank Foley, the PCO in Berlin since 1920, reported as early as March 1933: 'This office is overwhelmed with applications from Jews to proceed to Palestine, to England, to anywhere in the British Empire'. 'The position of the Jew in Germany, even if he possesses capital, is ... a desperate one', he wrote in 1935. 'He is being ruined economically and at the same time he is unable to emigrate as he cannot obtain the release of even a moderate proportion of his capital sufficient to enable him to do so'. Much of Foley's time was spent dealing with the refugee problem. 'It is', he concluded, 'useless to talk to the German Government whose declared object is to destroy [the Jews] body and soul'. After the Anschluss with Austria, the problems of the Vienna passport control office became equally severe. Captain Kendrick, the PCO, reported that his staff were 'so overwrought that they will burst into tears at the slightest provocation'. 'In order to conduct the work of the Passport Office as applicants desire', wrote the consul-general in Vienna, 'we should need a staff of 40 people and a building like the Albert Hall ...'[17]

Foley had been a Zionist sympathiser since the First World War and had built up an intelligence network of well-placed Jewish businessmen, among them Dolf Michaelis, the banker, and Wilfrid Israel, the British-born heir to a famous business dynasty, who maintained clandestine contacts with a number of Nazi administrators during the early years of the Third Reich. Though achieving only limited success as an intelligence officer, Foley was much more successful in helping German Jewry. According to one of the surviving members of his Jewish intelligence network, Hubert Pollack, 'The number of Jews saved from Germany would have been tens of thousands less had Captain Foley not sat in the consular office in the Tiergartenstrasse'. Pollack's evidence was confirmed by other testimony at the trial in Jerusalem of Adolf Eichmann, the administrator of the Final Solution, in 1961–2.[18]

In 1937 Maurice Jeffes, formerly PCO in Paris, succeeded Major Herbert Spencer as director of the Passport Control Department. 'I do not suppose', writes Kim Philby patronisingly, 'that he would have claimed to be more than a capable, if colourless administrator'. Jeffes was colourless only 'in a purely metaphorical sense'. While giving him an inoculation before a trip abroad, the SIS doctor (whose other clients included the Savoy Hotel) had used the wrong serum with the result, according to Philby, that his face turned 'a strange purplish blue'. Malcolm Muggeridge, who joined SIS during the war, discovered that Jeffes 'kept his office in a permanently twilit condition with the curtains closely drawn, in order to counteract as far as possible the extraordinary colour of his face'. Both Philby and Muggeridge found that 'it was impossible not to like him'.[19] On taking over as director of passport control, Jeffes quickly discovered that 'the refugee situation' had 'completely revolutionised' its work. Visas issued by passport control and consular offices abroad under his direction rose to 144,327 in the 1937/8 financial year and to 212,268 in 1938/9.[20]

The problems of the PCO network caused by its limited resources, shortage of outstanding talent, the refugee problem, the scandals at The Hague and Warsaw, its increasingly transparent cover and the growing demand within Whitehall for intelligence from Nazi Germany, persuaded 'Quex' Sinclair, almost certainly in consultation with Vansittart, to try to devise an alternative method of channelling secret intelligence back to London. The solution was suggested by Claude Dansey's network of business contacts built up during his years as PCO in Rome (1929–36).[21] Late in 1936 this network became the basis for a new top-secret 'Z organisation' headed by Dansey, which was kept secret from all SIS headquarters staff except Sinclair himself. Within Broadway Buildings Dansey was widely believed to have been sacked from Rome after a financial scandal and to have gone to live abroad.[22] (An audit in 1937 did indeed reveal 'irregularities' in the accounts at the Rome passport control office.)[23] David Footman later recalled the 'shock' with which he and other Broadway officers discovered the existence of the Z organisation for the first time on the eve of war.[24]

Dansey's headquarters were an eighth-floor suite in the huge Bush House office block in the Aldwych, little more than a mile from Broadway, which also housed the BBC world service and the Russian news agency Tass. Next to the Z organisation suite were the offices of Geoffrey Duveen and Company Ltd, run by a barrister friend of Dansey who provided him with a hidden back entrance to his own office and various other forms of assistance. Immediately below was the Joel brothers diamond company which gave the Z organisation cover as part of its own export department as well as providing some of the finance for it.[25] Dansey enjoyed the sense of mystery which he generated. In addition to styling himself 'Z', he had a passion for aliases and carried bogus visiting cards inscribed with such names as Captain Charles Pomfret-Seymour, CBE, DSO, RN. Unhappily, as his staff complained, he sometimes forgot which alias he was using.[26]

Dansey's deputy, chosen in consultation with 'Quex' Sinclair, was Commander Kenneth Cohen, who had retired from the navy in 1935 at the age of thirty-five for a well-paid London job in civil engineering which he found increasingly dull. He remained in occasional contact with NID, chiefly as a Russian interpreter, and early in 1937 received an invitation through NID to a mysterious meeting with Claude Dansey. Afterwards he was summoned to another secret meeting with Sinclair at his flat in Queen Anne's Gate. Cohen was struck by Sinclair's way of barking out a few phrases at a time and by his 'tremendous outward persona', though he later came to feel there was less behind the impressive façade than at first appeared. The meeting ended with Cohen's appointment as Dansey's assistant (codenamed Z-2).[27]

The Z organisation was set up essentially to obtain intelligence from Nazi Germany and, to a lesser extent, from Fascist Italy. It was intended from the outset not merely to provide an alternative to the PCO network but to replace it entirely if it were overrun by the enemy in time of war. Dansey's two main bases for operations against Germany were the same as Cumming's during the First World War: Switzerland in the south and the Netherlands in the north. In Zurich, his main Swiss station, his representatives were the First World War intelligence veteran, Rex Pearson of Unilever, and Basil Fenwick of Royal Dutch Shell. Other Z agents in Switzerland included 'Fanny' Vanden Heuvel in Berne, Sir Frank Nelson in Basle, and Victor Farrell in Geneva. The Swiss base was of particular importance because of the British ambassador, Sir George Warner's, hostility to SIS and his refusal to allow a PCO to be stationed at the Swiss capital, Berne;[28] he was, almost certainly, unaware that Dansey had organised an alternative SIS network. The Z organisation's most valuable source in Switzerland was probably Dansey's friend, Colonel Roger Masson, the Swiss intelligence chief, but fear of compromising Swiss neutrality limited contacts between them. As soon as war broke out, Dansey planned to move his headquarters from Bush House to Zurich.[29]

Dansey's main representatives in the Netherlands were two First World War intelligence veterans: Sigismund Payne Best in The Hague and Best's old enemy Richard Tinsley in Rotterdam. Best was the more active of the two. One of the firms which provided Dansey with cover was the pharmaceutical and general import-export firm Menoline Ltd of whose Dutch subsidiary Best was a director.[30] Best's business career and his second marriage, after the death of his first wife, to a well-known Dutch portrait painter together gave him a wide variety of contacts in fashionable Dutch society. Prince Henry, the consort of the Queen of Holland, used to call each Friday afternoon at the Bests' house for tea and cards. Best later remembered him as a man of simple tastes: 'We had a fireplace, and he had a great desire to make toast. He would toast a whole loaf of bread, which was, of course, too much to eat and had to be thrown away.' Prince Henry was the brother of the Grand-Duchess Elizabeth of Oldenburg and through him Best met many members of the former ruling houses of Mecklenburg and Oldenburg, and stayed frequently with them. Grand-Duchess Elizabeth, her son Nicklaus and his wife Helen, unlike some other members of their family, were resolute anti-Nazis and Best made no secret of the fact that he was 'engaged on Intelligence work ... certain that I could count upon their assistance in the event of war'.[31]

Other part-time agents of the Z organisation included the journalist John Evans in Prague; Frederick Voight, the Central European correspondent of the *Manchester Guardian*, in Vienna; Vincent Auger, who operated under London Films cover in Berlin; and the intelligence veteran Graham Maingot in Rome. Of the various firms which provided the Z organisation with cover and other forms of assistance, the most important remained Korda's London Film Productions. Andrew King, who was recruited from Cambridge through the University Appointments Board as the organisation's courier, was one of a number of Dansey's agents who spent an enjoyable two months at Denham Studios learning the rudiments of the film business. The principal intelligence sources of the Z organisation were refugees from Nazi persecution, some of them financed by Korda. Winterbotham was later very critical of the intelligence they provided; he recalled one case in which a refugee reported the construction of an underground airfield in an area he knew to be a swamp.[32] The most important of the refugees was probably Dr Klaus Spiecker, a senior civil servant under the Weimar Republic who ran the anti-Nazi Deutsche Freiheits Partei from Paris. Kenneth Cohen later remembered Spiecker as 'a valuable middle order source'. But the Z organisation was in general more remarkable for the speed and secrecy with which it was constructed than for the intelligence it produced. 'What it achieved was', in Cohen's opinion, 'very limited'.[33]

As well as encouraging Sinclair to develop the Z organisation, Vansittart also developed – particularly during his last two years as permanent undersecretary (1936–7) – his own 'private detective agency' dealing in German intelligence.[34] Van, more than any other Whitehall mandarin, stood for rearmament and opposition to appeasement. By far the most important British member of his network was Group Captain Malcolm Christie MC, DSO, a German-educated First World War pilot who had served as air attaché in Berlin from 1927 to 1930 before beginning a business career. Christie seemed to have stepped straight from the pages of John Buchan. He was a man of remarkable bravery who once crashed his damaged aircraft into a hangar rather than endanger ground staff. Like Van, he rather enjoyed the romance of cloaks and daggers; in their correspondence during the Munich crisis the two men adopted the pseudonyms 'Mr Gilbert' (Van's second Christian name) and 'Barclay' (the surname of Lady Vansittart's first husband).[35]

Christie owned a house on the German-Dutch border which he used as base for his undercover work. He moved easily among official circles in Berlin, and was well acquainted with both Goering, whom he had got to know at university in Aachen, and Goering's state secretary, Air General (later Field-Marshal) Erhard Milch. From time to time Goering summoned Christie to long 'man to man' talks on Anglo-German relations.[36] Christie's main secret informants in the mid-thirties are listed in a cryptic note of about 1938 preserved among his papers:

> Gord of little value now – sacred and doubting. Best informed sources X and Dr Y per Catholic Church, General Staff and Adolf's immediate entourage. Z with roots in Paris, General Staff and Embassy. Debts now paid off.

'Gord' was Carl Goerdeler, the anti-Nazi burgermeister of Leipzig from 1930 to 1937; Van's faith in him later revived. 'X' was a senior official (still unidentified) in the German air ministry who was Christie's chief informant on the Luftwaffe. 'Dr Y' remains a mystery. 'Z' was Hans Ritter (usually called K or 'The Knight', the English translation of his German surname), the Junkers aircraft company representative in Paris and adviser to the German Paris embassy. Among Christie's other informants at various times were Robert Bosch, founder of the Bosch precision machines and electrical equipment company; a certain 'Fish' said to supply information from 'only the highest proven sources'; and 'Johnnie', a German diplomat and former staff officer – probably Hans 'Johnnie' von Herwarth, later West German ambassador to Britain.[37]

Christie began sending Vansittart reports from his informants in December 1933. Over the next eighteen months Van came to regard him as 'the best judge of Germany that we shall ever get'. His 'private detective agency' was otherwise chiefly composed of German opponents of Hitler, among them Carl Goerdeler and Robert Bosch, who sometimes made contact with Van directly as well as via Christie; Theodor Kordt, counsellor at the German embassy in London; his brother Erich, senior counsellor at the German foreign ministry; Klop Ustinov (father of Peter), one-time press attaché at the German embassy; and Wolfgang zu Putlitz, junior secretary at the German embassy who escaped to England from Holland soon after the outbreak of war. Van later described his German sources as 'a few brave men' who 'knew that I realised a war to be nearing':

> They thought that, if they fed me with sufficient evidence, I might have influence enough to arouse our Government and so stop it. Of course they were wrong, but we tried.

But Van later had some doubts about the aims of some of his German informants. He said of Theodor Kordt:

> ... I gradually discovered that what he really wanted was a German maximum without war with *us*. His real game was to get a free hand in expansion east, and expansion to the limit, including Russia ... Kordt was riddled with the notion of expansion. Otherwise he was a decent, humane man, and emphatically not a Nazi.

Van came to feel much the same about Goerdeler. Putlitz was a rather different character who, in Van's view, 'went sadly astray after the war' by entering the East German foreign service.[38]

As well as taking a close interest in SIS and founding his own 'private detective agency', Vansittart also developed links with MI5. Within MI5 his closest contact was Dick White, probably the ablest of Kell's interwar recruits and a future head of both MI5 and SIS. After graduating from Christ Church, Oxford, White had spent several years in the USA at the Universities of California and Michigan. He was recruited by Kell in 1935 to keep track of German émigrés with Nazi sympathies resident in Britain. Before beginning work in MI5 late in 1936, White spent several months in Germany in Munich and Berlin perfecting his knowledge of the German language and building up an impressive range of German contacts. Among them was a member of the official German press agency, the Deutsche Nachrichten Büro who shortly afterwards was posted as assistant to the Büro chief in London, Fritz Hesse, and became one of White's most valuable sources. MI5, and White in particular, frequently acted as a channel of communication between the anti-Nazis in the German embassy and the Foreign Office. White ensured that Van was fully informed of all the German intelligence that came MI5's way, finding him always eager – sometimes overeager – to receive it. Van also took a close interest in MI5's attempts during the thirties to open foreign diplomatic bags with the help of a secret department of the Post Office. Half a century later, no aspect of interwar MI5 work remains more sensitive. Though there is no evidence that MI5 had significant success in intercepting German and Russian diplomatic bags, it seems to have had some success with the Italian, Japanese and Balkan embassies.[39]

Vansittart's passion for secret intelligence and his increasing attention to his own network of informants added to his growing reputation in Whitehall as an overmighty official. Sir John Simon, Van claimed later, never 'liked him' and was the 'snakiest' of foreign secretaries. But he was also a rather colourless and remote figure at the Foreign Office whose sometimes indecisive personality was overshadowed by Van's. When Baldwin succeeded MacDonald as prime minister in June 1935, Simon was replaced by the former MI1c station chief Sir Samuel Hoare. 'At last', claimed Van, 'I've got a Foreign Secretary I can work with'. Both ill at ease and in poor health during his term at the Foreign Office, Hoare seemed content to be overshadowed by his permanent undersecretary. He wrote modestly: 'Vansittart's fertile mind and unequalled knowledge of European politics and personalities were invaluable to me, whilst my more conventional methods may have been useful to him as a supplement to his sparkling *tours de force*'. Hoare lasted only six months as foreign secretary, discredited by the Hoare-Laval plan of December 1935 (largely devised by Van) which was widely interpreted as the sacrifice of Ethiopian independence to Italian imperialism. Van's reputation suffered along with Hoare's. But the most dangerous threat to his authority came from Hoare's thirty-eight-year-old successor as foreign secretary, Anthony Eden. 'The truth is', Eden believed, 'that Vansittart was seldom an official giving cool and disinterested advice ... He was himself a sincere, almost fanatical crusader, and much more a Secretary of State in mentality than a permanent official'. Determined not to be overshadowed like his predecessors, Eden took office 'with the unconcealed aim of easing Van out'.[40]

Aware of his declining authority in 1936 and 1937, Vansittart tried vainly to bolster his position by multiplying his warnings of German ambitions and by emphasising the importance of his intelligence contacts in providing an insight into Nazi policy. Hankey, like many others in Whitehall, believed Van was 'apt to get rather jumpy. He pays too much attention to the press of all countries and to S[ecret] S[ervice] information – useful pointers in both cases, but bad guides'.[41] The accession of Neville Chamberlain to the premiership in May 1937 was another blow to Van's prospects of survival. Chamberlain was so suspicious of Van's contacts with Churchill and other opponents of appeasement that he took the extraordinary decision to have him tailed for a time by MI5. SIS and Sinclair in particular remained among Van's firmest supporters. As soon as news reached Broadway on 12 December 1937 that Chamberlain had decided to replace Vansittart as permanent undersecretary by Sir Alexander Cadogan and given him the high-sounding but less influential post of chief diplomatic adviser, Sinclair hurried round to Van's luxurious London home at 44 Park Street. He paced up and down the drawing room, clenching his fists and repeating 'Van, this is disastrous!'[42]

Vansittart seems to have tried to keep control as chief diplomatic adviser of SIS and GC & CS. Though he failed, he retained his private detective agency, remained in close touch with the intelligence services (especially with Sinclair and White), and increasingly stressed intelligence reports in his analyses of German policy. Cadogan never equalled Van's growing passion for the secret world. Initially he struck one senior intelligence officer as 'one of the old school who did not really like intelligence'. But Sinclair's forebodings of December 1937 were not to be fulfilled, and he quickly won Cadogan's confidence. Within a few weeks of becoming permanent undersecretary, Cadogan was noting in his diary that Sinclair was coming round to the Foreign

Office 'with interesting information'. He came to enjoy Quex's company over lunch and dinner in London clubs and found that he played an acceptable hand of bridge – making up for some lack of subtlety by the briskness of his play.[43]

Thanks largely to the influence of Sir Joseph Ball, Chamberlain displayed a greater interest in intelligence as prime minister than either MacDonald or Baldwin. The Foreign Office, however, rightly suspected him of using Ball as an intermediary with the Italian embassy in order to bypass the foreign secretary, Anthony Eden, and secure some understanding with Fascist Italy as a step towards a broader settlement with Nazi Germany. Ball's contact in the Italian embassy was its legal adviser Adrian Dingli, a Gray's Inn lawyer of Italian and Maltese extraction who had previously worked for MI5. From July 1937, two months after Chamberlain succeeded Baldwin, Ball and Dingli acted intermittently as a secret channel of communication between the prime minister and Count Grandi, the Italian ambassador. On occasion Ball saw Grandi and Dingli saw Chamberlain.[44] Precisely what these backstairs intrigues amounted to remains obscure. Even Chamberlain was confused about what they were, while Grandi confessed to having 'ornamented' his own version of events which was further embroidered by Count Ciano, the Italian foreign minister.[45] Dingli's unpublished memoirs doubtless exaggerate his own role. Ball's own version of events, on the other hand, probably underrates the extent of his secret dealings. He claimed that he 'only saw Grandi once, and the conversation was then entirely general'.

Ball's secret contacts with the Italian embassy helped to fuel Eden's growing irritation with the prime minister. On 20 February 1938 he resigned in a blaze of publicity in protest against Chamberlain's anxiety to secure an Anglo-Italian agreement. On the same day Ball met Dingli secretly at Waterloo Station, got into a taxi with him and was then informed that Italy was prepared to withdraw her 'volunteers' from the Spanish Civil War. Ball quickly told Sir Horace Wilson, Chamberlain's chief industrial adviser and confidant on many other matters, who passed the news on to the prime minister.[46] The offer conveyed by Dingli helped prepare the way for the Anglo-Italian agreement of April 1938 by which each side undertook to respect the Mediterranean status quo. The secret Anglo-Italian channel of communication through Ball and Dingli functioned again later in the year during the Munich crisis and during final preparations for Chamberlain's visit to Rome in January 1939.[47] But Ball eventually concluded that Dingli was playing a double game and had his correspondence intercepted. It was then discovered that Dingli was writing a book about his secret dealings with Whitehall. According to Ball, 'The half a dozen typewritten copies of the book were seized, and Dingli shortly afterwards committed suicide, after being involved in a serious case of embezzlement'.[48]

Though occasionally irritated by Chamberlain's encouragement of backstairs diplomacy, Viscount Halifax, Eden's successor as foreign secretary, was usually content to follow the prime minister's lead on policy to Germany and Italy. Halifax accepted the Foreign Office without enthusiasm and had little influence on pre-war foreign policy. His parliamentary secretary, R.A. Butler, noted ironically that, when faced with new proposals, he would 'commune with himself, with his Maker, and with Alec (Cadogan). So plenty of time elapsed before he took a decision.'[49] It is doubtful whether any of the independent intelligence initiatives by Chamberlain's entourage had any greater significance than Ball's bizarre dealings with Dingli, but they continued to create an intermittent atmosphere of backstairs intrigue which the Foreign Office found understandably disconcerting. MI5 was also suspicious. On 28 November 1938 Kell himself called at the Foreign Office to show Cadogan secret evidence that a member of the Number Ten staff named George Steward had been in secret touch with Fritz Hesse, the press adviser to the German embassy whose office contained an MI5 source, allegedly suggesting that Britain would 'give Germany everything she asks for the next year'. Cadogan was reluctant to repeat Kell's message to Halifax, who was 'getting rather fed up', for fear it would prompt his resignation, but decided he had to do so. 'We must stop this sort of thing', he told his diary. When Halifax tackled the prime minister next day, Chamberlain appeared 'aghast'. Halifax believed that Steward had acted independently of Ball. Cadogan was 'not so sure', and also suspected Sir Horace Wilson of complicity in the affair, but he agreed with Kell that Steward should be 'spoken to' by Wilson. 'This', he believed, 'will put a brake on them all'.[50]

During the period of German expansion leading up to the Munich crisis of September 1938 when Britain and France sought vainly to contain Hitler's ambitions by a policy of appeasement and thus secure, in Chamberlain's ill-fated phrase, 'peace for our time', the intelligence services were faced with two main problems: to assess the threat posed by German rearmament, and to provide advance warning of the series of German forward moves which began with the remilitarisation of the Rhineland in March 1936. The problems of German rearmament rapidly exposed both the lack of coordination in intelligence collection and the confusion of intelligence assessment. The Air Ministry, Admiralty, and War Office each independently assessed the growth of German forces by, respectively, air, sea and land, as revealed by public sources of information, service attachés and other official reports, and secret intelligence. The Chiefs of Staff (COS) then considered these separate assessments and the economic intelligence gathered by the IIC. But instead of coordinating the various assessments in more than the sketchiest outline, they tended simply to accumulate a mass of only partly digested detail.[51] The service assessments and the COS appreciations were themselves always liable to be challenged elsewhere in Whitehall, especially by the Foreign Office, but there was no adequate machinery for resolving the contradictions which resulted.

The worst contradictions arose over the threat posed by the Luftwaffe. An apocalyptic vision of aerial warfare was widely diffused both within Whitehall and among the public at large.[52] Baldwin told the Commons in an oft-quoted speech of November 1932: 'No power on earth can protect the man in the street from being bombed. Whatever people may tell him, the bomber will always get through.' Added to the general, fearful vagueness about the menace of the Luftwaffe were the formidable statistical and technical problems of calculating its strength. Until 1938 there was a large but variable gap between the nominal establishment of German squadrons and their real operational strength. The figures for German aircraft production in themselves were dangerously misleading since the majority of pre-war planes were trainers unsuitable for combat. But modern factories turning out twin-engined trainers were easily transformed by the imagination of uncritical observers into production lines for first-line aircraft.[53] Air Ministry intelligence found most SIS agents 'notoriously lacking' in the technical knowledge needed for accurate reporting on German aircraft strength.[54]

Hitler's claim to have reached 'parity' with the RAF in the spring of 1935 quickly brought to a head the clash of rival intelligence estimates within Whitehall. Air Ministry intelligence put the number of trained German pilots at 4,000. But in May 1935 Cunliffe-Lister, chairman of a new Air Parity Subcommittee set up by the DRC (and shortly to become both minister of air and Earl Swinton), challenged the Air Ministry figures. Probably influenced by Winterbotham, head of Air Intelligence in SIS, he put the figure at 8,000. A meeting of the Air Parity Subcommittee attended by 'Quex' Sinclair himself failed to resolve the conflict of estimates.[55]

The air staff remained confident of their own superior expertise in interpreting the intelligence they received. In addition to reports from SIS, air attachés and French intelligence, they possessed a number of sources of their own. Part of the work of Air Intelligence was 'the daily interviewing of travellers, industrialists, refugees and others who had first-hand information to give to "someone in the Air Ministry"'. The most valuable of these informants was probably Sir Roy Fedden, the doyen of British aircraft-engine designers. After the First World War Fedden had trained a generation of German engineering apprentices at the Bristol aircraft factory at Filton. During the 1930s his former pupils, now designers and production-engineers for the Luftwaffe, 'missed no opportunity, Nazi secrecy notwithstanding, to show their father-in-technology, when he visited Germany from time to time, precisely what they were achieving'.[56]

But until the autumn of 1936 the intelligence assessments of the air staff were more conditioned than they realised by memories of their own struggles in building up the RAF as an independent force and by the erroneous belief that once the Luftwaffe reached a front-line strength of 1500 aircraft, it would be forced to slow down its hectic expansion and go through a period of consolidation. There were powerful voices in Whitehall who doubted the ability of Air Intelligence or the Air Ministry to grasp what was going on in Germany. When Sir Warren Fisher retired as permanent head of the Treasury in 1938 he complained bitterly that 'For some years we have had from the Air Ministry soothing-syrup and incompetence in equal measure'. But the most persistent critic of Air Intelligence was the Foreign Office. Vansittart believed that 'Air policy' in its broadest aspects had become too serious a matter to leave to the inferior intellects of service specialists. The Foreign Office could not afford to trust the judgment either of the Air Ministry or of the service chiefs in general:

> Prophecy is largely a matter of insight. I do not think the Service Departments have enough. On the other hand they might say that I have too much. The answer is that I know the Germans better.

Van placed most trust in the secret reports on the Luftwaffe sent him by Group Captain Christie, but was slow to send his reports to the Air Ministry and concealed Christie's identity when he did so. The first of Christie's assessments of the Luftwaffe to reach the Air Ministry arrived in February 1936 and gave the projected German air force strength for 1 April 1937 and 31 December 1938 together with figures for current aircraft production. Air Intelligence gave it a sceptical reception. Ellington, the chief of the air staff, loftily wrote off Christie's report as 'someone's deductions' from only part of the information already at the Air Ministry's disposal. Swinton, the secretary of state for air, knew better, scrawled 'NO' in red ink on Ellington's report, and summoned him to his office.[57]

A protracted dispute followed between Foreign Office and Air Ministry over the figures supplied to Christie by 'X', his source within the German Air Ministry. Air Intelligence prepared a questionnaire for 'X', criticising his figures. 'X' replied in March 1936 defending them as 'official and correct' and giving new technical information on engine modifications to the Dornier 17 bomber. AI3(b), the German section of Air Intelligence, dismissed 'X's' reply as 'unsubstantiated'. After a further report from X it added: 'We do not believe that Germany with her ability and love of good organisation would adopt the methods which "X" states she has adopted'. The director of Air Intelligence wrote more guardedly that while it was impossible to accept 'X's' conclusions without knowing his source, he was to be encouraged to pass on further information.

In the autumn of 1936 Air Intelligence and the Air Ministry performed a volte-face. The flow of intelligence from Christie and other sources gradually compelled them to abandon their conviction that after reaching a front-line strength of 1500 aircraft, the Luftwaffe would be forced to slow down and consolidate. The air staff informed the CID in October 1936 that they now believed Germany to be aiming at the greatest possible expansion. Desmond Morton, previously a critic of Air Intelligence estimates, agreed. The final IIC report for 1936 predicted an acceleration of the German aircraft building programme. Even with the acceleration of British building programmes, the air staff no longer believed that the RAF over the next few years could keep pace with the Luftwaffe.[58]

By 1937 both Air Intelligence and the Foreign Office had agreed on reasonably accurate estimates of present and projected German air strength. But the Air Ministry, having earlier underestimated the German threat, now veered to the opposite extreme. It exaggerated both the immediacy of the Luftwaffe menace and the capacity of its bombers to deliver a knock-out blow. Others in Whitehall were even more alarmist. 'For the first time in centuries', wrote Sir Warren Fisher in April 1938, 'our country is (and must continue to be) at the mercy of a foreign power'. In reality the Luftwaffe was still incapable of launching anything approaching the London Blitz. Not until 1939 did it acquire the new generation of aircraft and enough trained airmen to make it an actual rather than a potential menace. And not until 1940 did it acquire the forward bases in France and the Low Countries from which it began the Battle of Britain. Hankey, the cabinet secretary, showed better judgment than Fisher or Vansittart when he wrote in 1934: 'The Cabinet are overrating the *imminence* of the German peril. The peril is there all right, but will take more than five years to develop in the military and air sense'.[59]

Military intelligence estimates during the first five years of Nazi rule followed the same basic pattern as those of Air Intelligence: an initial underestimation of German military potential, an about-turn in the autumn of 1936, followed by an overestimation of the immediate German menace. Both the War Office and the Industrial Intelligence Centre were misled by the comparatively slow start to German rearmament and jointly predicted in July 1935 that the Wehrmacht would expand at a maximum rate of 8 or 9 divisions a year to a peak of 90 to 100 divisions in 1943. Until September 1936 the German intelligence section in the War Office viewed the revival of the German army without serious concern for two reasons. First, it saw the army as a moderating influence on Nazi hotheads. General (later Field-Marshal Sir) John Dill, the director of Military Operations and Intelligence (1934–6), concluded after a tour of inspection in Germany in September 1935 that the army 'appears to have escaped the danger of political infection ... and is now probably the most important factor in stabilising conditions inside Germany'. Secondly, military intelligence trusted Hitler's declaration that the German army would not exceed a peacetime strength of 36 divisions, and considered that strength not unreasonable.[60]

That comforting illusion was shattered by the announcement in September

1936 that Germany had broken the 36 divisions limit. Thereafter order of battle intelligence on the German army was reasonably accurate. During the Munich crisis of September 1938 military intelligence estimated the German army at 79 divisions in all (including the reserve and Landwehr) as compared with an actual strength of 75 divisions.[61]

Hitler's first two major military moves – the invasion of the demilitarised Rhineland in March 1936 and of Austria two years later – were both foreseen as possibilities in Whitehall, but their timing was not. No intelligence service could have worked out the timing long in advance since Hitler took the final decision for invasion barely a fortnight before the march into the Rhineland and only a few days before the *Anschluss* with Austria. On each occasion, however, the Foreign Office received a last-minute warning. On the evening of 6 March 1936 Christie was given details in Paris by Hans Ritter, then an adviser to the German embassy, of the Rhineland *Einmarsch* planned for the following day. Shortly after midnight Christie telephoned Van at his Park Street home with accurate intelligence both about the invasion which began a few hours later and the German diplomatic offensive which was to follow.[62]

After the remilitarisation of the Rhineland in contravention of the Versailles treaty, there were numerous indications that Hitler's next moves would be against Austria and Czechoslovakia. Some of the more remarkable intelligence came once again from Christie, who was invited by Goering to a two and a half hour 'man to man' talk in Berlin on 3 February 1937:

> ... I asked the General straight out 'What is Germany's aim in Europe today?' Goering replied 'We want a free hand in Eastern Europe. We want to establish the unity of the German peoples (Grossdeutschegemeinschaft)'. I said 'Do you mean to get Austria?' Reply 'Yes'. I said 'Do you mean to get Czechoslovakia?' Reply 'Yes'.[63]

Hitler was in less of a hurry than Goering. He did not decide to go ahead with the *Anschluss* until the decision by Schuschnigg, the Austrian chancellor, on 9 March 1938 to hold a referendum on the 13th which he believed would produce a majority against union with Germany. Curiously, the first warning of Operation 'Otto', the German invasion, reached the Foreign Office from Cairo. On 9 March General (later Field-Marshal) Walter von Reichenau was in Cairo attending a meeting of the Olympic Games Committee when he received an urgent summons to return to Germany. Before leaving Cairo, Reichenau telephoned the German minister, Fritz Titze, to tell him the *Anschluss* was now imminent. Their conversation was intercepted and a report of it telegraphed to the Foreign Office.[64] At 5.30 a.m. on Friday 11 March Schuschnigg was woken with the news that Germany had closed the frontier and was massing troops. Next day the Wehrmacht crossed the border, leaving in their wake a trail of stranded vehicles ill prepared for the improvised invasion.

During his intercepted telephone conversation with Titze, von Reichenau had boasted that after the *Anschluss*, Germany would soon use unrest among Sudeten Germans as an excuse to 'walk in' to Czechoslovakia.[65] Christie sent the same message from Germany. Goering, he reported, was calling for a 'lightning war' against the Czechs:

> The crucial question is How soon will the next step against Czechoslovakia be tried? ... The probability is that the delay will not exceed two or three months at most, unless France and England provide the deterrent, for which cooler heads in Germany are praying.[66]

In reality Hitler did not approve plans for Operation 'Green', the invasion of Czechoslovakia, until 30 May 1938, and the Wehrmacht was given until 1 October to complete preparations.[67] As early as mid-May, however, misleading intelligence reports convinced SIS, the Foreign Office, and the prime minister that a German attack was imminent. The most important of these reports came from Paul Thümmel, a disaffected officer in the Abwehr, German military intelligence. Thümmel had offered his services to Czech military intelligence in 1936, saying that he was doing so not merely because he needed money but also because he had a Slav fiancée and hated the Nazi régime. General Frantisek Moravec, the head of Czech military intelligence, was 'not impressed'. 'Spies, being human', he believed, 'often invent a better-sounding motive if their sole reason for betraying their country is money'. He was, however, enormously impressed with the excellent intelligence on German battle order and mobilisation plans which Thümmel sold to the Czechs. Thümmel never revealed his real name to the Czechs, and Moravec never tried to discover it for fear of compromising his intelligence work. He was known to the Czechs only as agent A54. Thümmel was later to supply SIS directly with first-class political and military intelligence for the first two years of the war. But until the German occupation of Prague in March 1939 he passed intelligence only to the Czechs, who forwarded some of it to SIS via the PCO in Prague, Major Harold 'Gibby' Gibson.[68] On the night of 12–13 May Thümmel met Czech intelligence officers secretly at Louny police station in the Sudetenland. His report, summarised in a Czech intelligence memorandum, was on this occasion more alarmist and less accurate than usual:

> The Germans are preparing a campaign of provocation and sabotage which will erupt on the eve of the Czech local elections on 22 May. In the last few days, arms, explosives and munitions have been smuggled into Czechoslovakia. The explosives and munitions are concealed in glass jars and tins of jelly and stewed fruit. Secret arms depots have been set up in two towns in Northern Bohemia.

Shock troops, mainly led by high-ranking officers of the SS and SA, are waiting to invade Czech territory . . .

Officials of the Henlein Sudeten Party are to listen regularly to German broadcasts. As soon as they hear the password 'Amtsverwalter' – and it is expected within three days – they are to declare a state of alert. This will be a signal for sabotage: destruction of railway lines, main roads and bridges, and armed attacks on frontier posts and Czech sentries.

This action is expected to come to a head on 22 May, when the 'tortured Sudeten Germans' will call for help from their German brothers.

Sudeten German Freikorps troops, supported by SS groups, will then invade Czechoslovakia in the region between Decin and Bilina which is the centre of subversive activity.[69]

Moravec claimed that only Czech precautions taken after Thümmel's warning averted large-scale sabotage by Sudeten Germans.[70] In order to obtain as much British support as possible, he may well have overstated the immediate danger of German attack. It is highly doubtful whether plans for sabotage on the scale suggested by Thümmel had in reality yet progressed beyond the drawing board.

Thümmel's sensational revelations forwarded to Broadway by 'Gibby' Gibson were, however, accompanied by reports from Christie to Vansittart of invasion plans which may well have accurately reflected German intentions for the autumn but were wrongly thought to be imminent.[71] Simultaneously both SIS and Czech military intelligence reported German troop manoeuvres on the border which also pointed to an early invasion.[72] The reports were wrong. After extensive reconnaissance along the Czech frontier, the British military attachés in Berlin and Prague jointly reported no evidence of unusual troop movements. But in the highly charged atmosphere produced by Thümmel's revelations and the agitation by Sudeten Germans, both the Czechs and SIS seem to have exaggerated the significance of routine German manoeuvres.[73]

Major-General (later Lieutenant-General Sir) Henry Pownall, the Director of Military Operations and Intelligence (1938–9), wrongly believed Czech claims and British intelligence reports rather than the military attachés' personal observations. The Germans, he insisted, '*were* up to some monkey tricks'. Sinclair reported, and Pownall believed, that Germany abandoned its plans for an invasion on 23 May only in the face of a British warning and the Czech mobilisation of 170,000 men:

The result is that the Germans are mighty sore about [it], the more so that French newspapers proclaim it as a diplomatic victory for England, giving all the credit to British (and French) diplomacy and none to Germany's (alleged) moderation.[74]

If the Germans were, as Pownall claimed, 'mighty sore', it was chiefly because they had never planned a coup in the first place. Chamberlain never doubted, however, that the intelligence had been accurate. He wrote on 28 May:

> The more I hear about last week the more I feel what a 'd-d close run thing' it was ... I cannot doubt in my mind (1) that the German Government made all preparations for a coup, (2) that in the end they decided after getting our warnings that the risks were too great ...[75]

Several times more before the outbreak of war the prime minister was to be deceived by false reports of impending German coups.[76]

The gratifying illusion that a British warning had stopped the German dictator in his tracks had an enduring influence on British policy. Chamberlain feared that the blow to Hitler's prestige in May 1938 had been too great for him to yield to such a public warning a second time. Even on the eve of war in August 1939 there was reluctance in Whitehall to send a formal warning for fear that it would be counter-productive, and the desire to find a formula which was unprovocative as well as firm contributed to the delay in sending it.[77]

The apparent British diplomatic victory of May 1938 appeared to be a triumph for 'Quex' Sinclair as well as the prime minister, for without the forewarning of Hitler's alleged plan of attack there might, it seemed, have been no time to turn him back. The effect of this illusory triumph during the sixteen months of peace which remained was to move Sinclair closer to the centre of policy-making than ever before. In the numerous crises which led up to war he had the ear of both the prime minister and the foreign secretary. During the Munich crisis he was to offer not merely intelligence appreciations but also wide-ranging policy recommendations.[78] Though its position was thus paradoxically strengthened by the bad intelligence it provided in May 1938, SIS was not universally appreciated in Whitehall. Sinclair had to face mounting criticism from the service ministries on the quality of SIS military, naval and air intelligence. In July 1938 he was forced to concede the truth of some of the criticisms. SIS was able to provide good intelligence on German naval construction, thanks chiefly to information from a naval engineer, Dr Otto Krueger, channelled through the passport control organisation in the Netherlands. But Sinclair acknowledged that SIS military and economic intelligence from Germany was otherwise no more than fair. He also admitted that SIS political reports had accepted too uncritically both Nazi and anti-Nazi propaganda. Sinclair justly complained, however, that he was caught with only limited resources between the conflicting demands of the service departments who wanted less political (as opposed to military) intelligence and the Foreign Office who wanted more.[79]

Intelligence reports before the Munich crisis of September 1938 were both fuller and more accurate than before any of Hitler's previous coups. The first SIS reports, probably deriving chiefly from the Czechs, on Operation 'Green' – Hitler's plans for the invasion of Czechoslovakia – arrived in Whitehall early in July. Further warnings followed from Vansittart's intelligence network later in the month. Though Operation 'Green' was not scheduled to begin until 1 October, they wrongly pointed to a German attack at any time from the end of August onwards. Early in August two independent and, in substance, probably accurate reports arrived of a meeting at Berchtesgaden when the Führer had reaffirmed his determination to attack after the harvest was in, regardless of all risks and obstacles. Further corroboration of the invasion plans came from Carl Goerdeler and from military dissidents.[80]

General Ludwig Beck, the German chief of staff, was horrified by the military adventurism of Operation 'Green' and the world war he feared would result from it. Having tried and failed to prepare a mass resignation of the high command – in effect a general strike of the generals – if Hitler went ahead, he resigned on 18 August. Beck's successor, General Franz Halder, and the commander-in-chief of the Wehrmacht, General Walter von Brauchitsch, turned to conspiracy and considered plans for the army to arrest the Führer if he tried to declare war on France and Britain. Chamberlain and Halifax learned something of the conspiracies within the high command but doubted both the determination and the organisation of the conspirators. They were probably right to do so. In August General Ewald von Kleist visited London as an emissary from some of the plotters to seek British support and urge firmness in dealing with Hitler. With the approval of Chamberlain and Halifax he was seen by Vansittart and Churchill. After a few days he was followed by another military emissary, Colonel Hans Boehm-Tettelbach. Each envoy, however, damaged his credibility by being unaware of the other's visit. Chamberlain scornfully compared them to day-dreaming Jacobites at the court of Louis XIV of France, promising to restore the Stuarts if only Louis was 'sufficiently threatening' to William III.[81]

Fears of an imminent German move against the Czechs were strengthened by the first direct Nazi attack on the PCO system. On 17 August Captain Kendrick, the SIS station chief in Vienna, was arrested near Salzburg while on his way to Munich. He was, as the *Times* report acknowledged, driving 'partly through or near territory where German manoeuvres were understood to be in progress'. Several further arrests followed of others alleged to be spying on German troop movements. After the intervention of Sir Nevile Henderson, the British ambassador in Berlin, Kendrick was released, expelled and flew back to England on the 22nd. The Germans claimed, though Kendrick denied, that he had confessed to espionage before his expulsion.[82] Since the Germans had been well aware for some time that passport control was used as a cover for SIS work and had been able, had they wished, to arrest Kendrick ever since the *Anschluss* in March 1938, his arrest five months later appeared to suggest either a determination to expose SIS activities and secure a propaganda victory or the desire to prevent him collecting intelligence on Operation 'Green'. Both interpretations seemed ominous. Immediately after Kendrick's expulsion, his staff were withdrawn from Vienna. Soon afterwards the station chiefs in Berlin and Prague, Major Foley and Major Gibson, were temporarily recalled to London for fear that Operation 'Green' might be accompanied by a further onslaught on SIS.[83]

Cadogan arrived back from a disturbed French holiday at the beginning of September to find 'enough in the Secret Reports to make one's hair stand on end'. 'It's obviously touch and go', he believed, 'but not gone yet'. On 6 September Whitehall received the most impressive warning yet. Theodor Kordt, the German chargé d'affaires, previously one of Vansittart's 'private detectives', and, in Cadogan's view, a brave man who 'put conscience before loyalty', paid a secret visit to 10 Downing Street, was admitted through the garden gate and warned Chamberlain's intimate adviser, Sir Horace Wilson, that Hitler had decided to invade Czechoslovakia. Next day he returned to Number 10 and repeated the same message to Lord Halifax. But whereas Kleist and some previous informants had given approximately the correct date planned for Operation 'Green' at the beginning of October, Kordt erroneously pointed to 19 or 20 September. On 12 September, the day after Hitler had demanded at a Nuremberg rally 'self-determination' for the Czech Sudeten-land and an 'end to slavery' for the Sudeten Germans, SIS reported – also wrongly – that all German missions had been told that the invasion had been scheduled for the 25th. The Foreign Office concluded that Hitler might attack on any date between the 18th and the 29th.[84]

During his secret visits to Number 10 on 6 and 7 September, Kordt called for a firm statement to be 'broadcast to the German nation' that Britain would help the Czechs resist a German attack. He failed to convince his listeners. On the 8th Chamberlain announced to an inner circle of advisers – Halifax, Horace Wilson, Simon and Cadogan – a secret 'Plan Z' for him to visit Hitler in person to try to settle the crisis without war. To Vansittart, brought into the meeting at Halifax's request after Plan Z had been announced, 'it was Henry IV going to Canossa again'. But Van had become a voice crying in the Whitehall wilderness. 'We argued with him', Cadogan told his diary, 'and I think demolished him'.[85] Some at least of the prime minister's sense of urgency derived from the faulty intelligence which had given Whitehall a mistakenly accelerated timetable for Operation 'Green'. Chamberlain feared that if he waited beyond mid-September, the Czech invasion might have begun and he would arrive in Germany too late. On 15 September he made his first dramatic flight to Munich to parley with the Führer at his grandiose mountain retreat at Berchtesgaden. *Le Matin* caught the mood of both the French and British press when it applauded the courage of 'a man of sixty-nine making his first aeroplane journey ... to see if he can banish the frightful nightmare which hangs over us and save humanity'. Within Van's entourage, Chamberlain's shuttle-diplomacy gave rise to a cynical ditty:

> If at first you can't concede
> Fly, fly, fly again.

After three round-trips by air and a shambling four-power conference at Munich, Chamberlain returned to London and a hero's welcome on 30 September, brandishing the piece of paper which gave the Czech Sudetenland to Germany and, he claimed, meant not only 'peace with honour' but 'peace for our time'.

The main problems of intelligence before and during the Munich crisis were, as so often, chiefly problems of analysis and use rather than problems of collection. Intelligence was analysed against the background of highly questionable assumptions which somehow escaped serious challenge either in Whitehall or Broadway. The most dubious assumption concerned the strength of Czech resistance. The chiefs of staff told the cabinet in March 1938:

> No pressure that we and our possible Allies can bring to bear, either by sea, or land or in the air, could prevent Germany from invading and overrunning Bohemia and from inflicting a decisive defeat on the Czechoslovakian Army.

Not a single minister disputed that sweeping and unqualified assertion. Chamberlain and Halifax, his foreign secretary, made it the basis of their policy. France as well as Britain put pressure on the Czechs to make concessions to Hitler.[86] But while the French were prepared to make a stand if Hitler rejected reasonable concessions, Chamberlain, Halifax and the chiefs of staff believed, like Sinclair, that war must be avoided at all costs. At the moment when it mattered most, the service chiefs and SIS were as ardent appeasers as the government. SIS insisted that Czech security would actually be improved by the loss of the Sudeten Germans.[87]

The arguments for appeasement at all costs flew in the face of much of the intelligence available. The War Office's own battle order intelligence showed that the German army was badly outnumbered on the French frontier and possessed only a limited numerical advantage over the Czechs.[88] Brigadier Stronge, the military attaché in Prague, wrote later: 'The more I saw of the [Czech] troops in 1938, the General Staff and the whole of the military ensemble, the more convinced did I become that here was a force capable of defending its frontiers and willing to do so at any cost'.[89] With Allied support he believed the Czechs could hold out for three months, and his views were supported by the French. But Chamberlain and the chiefs of staff preferred the much more pessimistic forecasts of Mason-Macfarlane, the military attaché in Berlin, based on only a fleeting visit to Czechoslovakia and little knowledge of her defences.[90]

The role of the intelligence community during the Munich crisis was not limited to intelligence collection. Probably to a greater degree than ever before, 'Quex' Sinclair was anxious to influence policy-making. SIS policy during the crisis was set out in a 'most secret' memorandum of 18 September, 'What Should We Do?', possibly drafted and certainly approved by Sinclair himself.[91] SIS argued strongly that the Czechs should be pressed to accept 'the inevitable' and surrender the Sudetenland. They should 'realise unequivocally that they stand alone if they refuse such a solution'. Britain, for her part, should continue with a policy of calculated appeasement. She should not wait until German grievances boiled over and threatened the peace of Europe. Instead the international community should take the initiative and decide 'what *really legitimate* grievances Germany has and what surgical operations are necessary to rectify them'. Some of Germany's colonies, confiscated after the last war, should be restored. If genuine cases for self-determination by German minorities remained in Europe they should be remedied:

> It may be argued that this would be giving in to Germany, strengthening Hitler's position and encouraging him to go to extremes. Better, however, that realities be faced and that wrongs, if they do exist, be righted, than leave it to Hitler to do the righting in his own way and time – particularly if, concurrently, we and the French unremittingly build up our strength and lessen Germany's potentialities for making trouble.

SIS was under no illusion, however, either that Hitler could be depended upon to keep his promises or that Germany would be satisfied simply by rectifying her legitimate grievances. British security depended on comprehensive and rapid rearmament:

> If we emerge from the crisis without war, we should take the lesson to heart. In all the potential enemy countries, the 'axis' ones, force is the keynote of policy, and our own policy should rest on the capacity to retaliate with adequate force. Platitudinous though it may be, our only chance of preserving peace is to be ready for war on any scale, without relying too much on outside support.

Though Britain could not 'really trust any foreign country', SIS recommended 'a permanent defensive alliance' with France, combined with pressure on

France to rearm as rapidly as possible. The Italians were 'fickle and unscrupulous' but the Rome-Berlin axis could be weakened by 'playing up to their pride' and recognising the Italian Empire in Ethiopia. Similarly, in order to improve relations with Japan, Britain might go some way 'even at the sacrifice of some principle, in recognising – for it has to be recognised – Japan's special position in East Asia'. The feelings aroused among Americans by the Munich crisis should be used to try to strengthen relations with the USA. In south-eastern Europe Britain should offer financial and economic aid to make the states of the region less dependent on Germany 'short of committing ourselves to supporting them actively'. Britain should, however, move as close as possible to an alliance with Turkey. To strengthen her position in the Middle East, Britain should 'go an appreciable way to satisfying the Arab world' over Palestine. The best solution would be 'Jewish cantonisation' in an Arab state; at worst there should be 'a mere token State for the Jews, with rigid safeguards against Jewish expansion'. SIS added, almost as an afterthought:

> P.S. *Russia*: We can never bank on this country but, to keep on the right side of this devil, we must sup with him to some extent, adapting the length of our spoon to circumstances at any given moment.

Sinclair emphasised the need, however, not to antagonise Germany. There should be no attempt at encirclement or an anti-German front which would give Hitler the opportunity to complain of hostile combinations, 'for if he has that pretext it is a rallying cry and, in his eyes, justification for various dynamic and dangerous measures'. In sum, Britain should try to ensure *'that Germany's "style is cramped", but with the minimum of provocation'*.

'Quex' Sinclair's emergence as policy adviser as well as intelligence supplier and analyst was further evidence of the enhanced interest in intelligence shown by the prime minister and the Foreign Office during the gravest crisis they had experienced since the First World War. When Cadogan prepared a broad review of British policy after the Munich crisis was over, he drew on the SIS paper.[92] Though Sinclair had been outraged by Vansittart's replacement at the end of 1937, his policy by the time of Munich differed sharply from Van's. Much in his paper accorded with the existing thinking of Chamberlain, Halifax and Cadogan, and doubtless served to reinforce it.

The handing over of the Sudetenland to Germany by the Munich agreement of 30 September 1938 left the dismembered Czechoslovak state at the mercy of the Third Reich. It deprived the Western Allies of the wartime support of the Czech army, which in September 1938 was almost half as large as the Wehrmacht. With a population less than half that of Greater Germany and with a far less vigorous economy, France could not hope for a better opportunity in future to fight Germany on even terms. The few divisions

Britain had ready for service overseas (two in 1938, four by August 1939) could do little to plug the growing military gap. It has been persuasively argued that 'In 1939 Britain and France were strategically in a much worse position than before 30 September 1938'.[93]

Underlying the exaggerated defeatism of British ministers, service chiefs and SIS during the Munich crisis was a faulty assessment not merely of the potential strength of Czech resistance but also of the threat from the Luftwaffe. Chamberlain gave the cabinet an emotional account of how, returning from his second visit to Hitler, he had flown up the Thames to London, imagining a German bomber flying the same course:

> ... He had asked himself what degree of protection they could afford for the thousands of homes which he had seen stretched out below him and he had felt that we were in no position to justify waging a war today.

'We thought of air warfare in 1938', wrote Harold Macmillan later, 'rather as people think of nuclear warfare today'.[94] By the time the Munich crisis began, the delusion that Germany possessed the power to shatter London from the air and Czech resistance on the ground with simultaneous knock-out blows was so firmly rooted as to be invulnerable to much contrary intelligence. Accurate estimates of the size of the Wehrmacht and the Luftwaffe had less influence than ill-informed guesses of their ability to annihilate opposition.

Hitler, by contrast, was able to use good intelligence as one ingredient in his triumphantly successful policy of intimidation. His state secretary, Weizsäcker, boasted, with some (but probably not enormous) exaggeration, that the German government could read half the telegrams sent to Berlin embassies. Because Czech telephone communications to London and Paris passed through Berlin, Germany was able to intercept those too. Hitler boasted soon afterwards that by tapping Czech telephone calls, 'I have been able almost every day to confirm the effect of our propaganda'. That propaganda, Hitler immodestly explained, had won an 'enormous' victory: 'We have acquired one million people with over 100,000 square kilometres'. In the final stages of the Munich negotiations Hitler even made transcripts of Czech telephone calls available to the Foreign Office, hoping to disconcert Neville Chamberlain with the insulting references to himself. Jan Masaryk, the Czech minister in London, told Eduard Beneš, the Czech president: 'It is unfortunate that this stupid, badly informed little man is the English prime minister, and I am convinced ... that he won't be much longer'. Chamberlain may also have received evidence from transcripts of the telephone taps supplied by either German or British intelligence (or possibly by both) that the Czechs were secretly discussing the crisis with Churchill. 'Winston', he complained, 'was carrying on a regular conspiracy against me with the aid of Masaryk the Czech

Minister'.[95] Soon after the Munich crisis the prime minister was further put out to find himself 'ridiculed' by 'contemptuous references' in German intercepts decrypted by GC & CS.[96]

The German intercepts which offended Chamberlain were exceptional. Throughout the 1930s GC & CS failed to crack German high-grade codes and ciphers and provided only a limited amount of intelligence from its attack on lower grade systems. GC & CS had much more success with the other member of the Rome-Berlin axis. Italy's code and cipher security was poor. The greatly increased volume of Italian traffic during the Ethiopian and Spanish Civil Wars enabled GC & CS to master Italian ciphers 'all but completely'.[97] Though the decrypts supplied by GC & CS threw 'useful light' on Italy's intentions and the movements of her armed forces before and during her conquest of Ethiopia (1935–6),[98] they probably did little to modify British policy. The hope of retaining Italy as an ally against Germany and the weakness of the Royal Navy in the Mediterranean at a time when it was preoccupied by the Japanese menace in the East undermined from the start British opposition to Italian designs on Ethiopia.

The naval section of GC & CS also felt strongly that its decrypts were poorly used by the NID. Intelligence on both Italian warships and forts in Libya and East Africa which 'Nobby' Clarke considered 'of priceless value' was considered by the Admiralty as 'too secret to use'. The confidential briefings sent to naval commanders thus sometimes included 'demonstrably false information gathered from captains of merchant vessels and other less trustworthy sources'. What most exasperated Clarke and his colleagues, however, was the reintroduction by Rear Admiral J.A.G. Troup (DNI from 1935 to 1939) of the practice, abandoned in 1917, of requiring the full text of all decrypts to be sent to him. In Clarke's view:

> Apart from the increased labour which this necessitated, the scheme was quite useless as the majority of the messages were of no possible interest and many were so full of blanks that they were merely dangerous to those who would fill in the blanks in a way which the cryptographers could tell them were wrong. This was a throw back to [Room 40] when cryptographers were regarded for a long time as mere crossword puzzle solvers and not as the experienced intelligence officers which years of training and experience had made them.[99]

Italian naval and military intercepts continued to be plentiful after the conquest of Ethiopia as a result of Mussolini's intervention in the Spanish Civil War (1936–9). Neither Italian nor Spanish intercepts, however, provided any clear indication of the likely victor until the closing months of the war. SIS confessed as late as September 1938, only five months before Franco's government was recognised by Britain: 'We cannot spot the winner yet ... The outcome must be largely a matter of speculation'.[100] The Italian intercepts did, however, provide important insights into Mussolini's policy during the war. They were studied in Whitehall with particular care during the summer of 1937 when a number of Italian destroyers, submarines and aircraft, sent to assist Franco's Nationalist forces, began a brief but extraordinary period of Mediterranean piracy. On 1 September a torpedo narrowly missed the Royal Navy destroyer *Havock* on patrol in the Western Mediterranean. Next day the cargo vessel *Woodford*, flying the British flag, was torpedoed off Valencia. In both cases the secret attacker was an Italian submarine. The Admiralty knew from intercepts where the Italian submarines were operating and believed 'it should not be too difficult for a flotilla of destroyers to locate an offender'. Its Plans Division suggested sending a flotilla to deter further attacks. If the deterrent did not work 'the sinking of one submarine would', it believed, 'settle any further apprehension for our shipping and for Great Britain's honour'.

Instead, the attacks on shipping were referred to an international conference which opened at Nyon, near Geneva, on 10 September. The nine powers represented agreed to institute naval controls in the areas where attacks had taken place. Even before the conference opened, however, Italian intercepts decrypted by GC & CS already indicated that Italy had had second thoughts. On 14 September the Foreign Office telegraphed the British delegates at Nyon – Eden, the foreign secretary, Chatfield, the first sea lord, and Vansittart – with the news (obtained from intercepts) that Italian submarines had been ordered to cease all attacks.[101]

Sadly, Whitehall had no idea that Italy's intelligence about Britain was probably even better than its own about Italy. Italy's most fruitful source appears to have been the British embassy in Rome. Thefts of documents from the embassy, which seem to have begun on a small scale in 1924,[102] began to be organised on a regular basis in 1935 by the 'P Squad' of Italian Intelligence which specialised in the *prevelamento* (withdrawal) of secrets from foreign diplomatic missions. The mole within the embassy was a long-serving chancery servant, Secondo Constantini, remembered by Lord Gladwyn (then Gladwyn Jebb), who served in Rome up to the Ethiopian War, as 'a very nice, agreeable, intelligent man' whom British diplomats regarded 'as a sort of friend of the family'. Constantini regularly passed to the head of the 'P Squad' documents and ciphers which were photographed and replaced in the embassy in the space of about an hour and a half before they had been missed.[103]

Italian Intelligence also appears to have had a source within the Foreign Office. Ironically one of the documents apparently leaked from the Foreign Office was a 1936 memorandum by Eden, complaining, *inter alia*, of 'serious leakages of information obtained by His Majesty's Ambassador at Berlin', Sir Eric Phipps, which threatened to 'prejudice his own position and the sources of his information'. Count Ciano, the Italian foreign minister, obligingly gave a copy to Hitler together with a telegram from Phipps denouncing the German government as dangerous adventurers. Hitler was said to be disagreeably impressed. On another occasion early in 1939 Ciano handed the Yugoslav prime minister copies of two despatches from the British minister in Belgrade to the Foreign Office.[104]

Italian policy throughout the Ethiopian crisis was, in the opinion of Professor Toscano, the doyen of Italian diplomatic historians, 'largely based' on British intercepts which revealed both the conflicts between Italy's opponents and the extent of British military unpreparedness. Among many British documents in Mussolini's possession was a copy of the Maffey report of June 1935 which concluded that British interests in and around Ethiopia were not sufficient to justify opposition to Italian conquest. In February 1936 at a crucial stage in the Ethiopian war, when the British government was considering oil sanctions, Mussolini – to the acute embarrassment of the Foreign Office – published the Maffey report in the *Giornale d'Italia*. Mussolini's confident response to the arrival of the Home Fleet in the Mediterranean is known to have been influenced by a somewhat alarmist telegram from the Fleet Admiral to the Admiralty, complaining of problems with the crew and dangerously inadequate munitions. Similarly, the collapse of the Anglo-Italian 'Gentlemen's Agreement' of January 1937 reflected Mussolini's anger at the evidence in further intercepts of British attempts to block an Italian understanding with Yugoslavia.[105]

Until the beginning of 1937 the British ambassador in Rome, Sir Eric Drummond (soon to become Lord Perth), remained convinced that, despite the publication of the Maffey report in the Italian press and other embarrassments, no documents were leaking from his embassy.[106] He was forced to change his mind after the theft in January 1937 of a diamond necklace belonging to his wife from a locked red box in his own apartment next to the Chancery. Vansittart and Drummond now jointly decided on a long-overdue investigation of Rome embassy security. Since the Foreign Office as yet possessed neither a security department nor even a single security officer, he was forced to appeal to Major Valentine Vivian, the head of counter-espionage in SIS. Vivian modestly disclaimed any expertise in questions of embassy security but, since he did not believe 'that such a thing as an expert in security measures exists', agreed to carry out the investigation.[107]

Vivian arrived in Rome on 8 February. Next day, accompanied by the head of chancery, Andrew Noble (later a baronet), he made 'an experimental tour' of embassy buildings during the long lunch and siesta period which extended each day from 1.15 to 5 p.m. The tour confirmed his worst fears:

> Having arrived in the Ambassador's compound we found the window of
> Mr Noble's own room in the Chancery (which, according to Standing

Orders, should have been locked by Picton [the head chancery servant])
unlocked and standing invitingly open. We entered all the Chancery rooms,
making no effort to reduce noise, but were left completely undisturbed for
about half-an-hour before one of the Chancery servants came to investigate.

The experiment shows, I think, that it would not be impossible or even
difficult for unauthorised persons to enter and spend long periods in the
Chancery or Registry rooms ...

Closer inspection revealed a series of basic lapses in physical security. The
previous first secretary had among his papers a note 'which should never have
been made at all' of the combination number of the chancery safe, though
this had since been changed; the doors to the presses could 'be fairly simply
removed with the assistance of a screwdriver'; the same key fitted all the
embassy red boxes and no less than six copies of it 'must have been at the
disposal of native servants'; the embassy was entirely unaware that its telephones might be bugged, and, 'somewhat significantly', a new telephone had
recently been installed in the cipher room. Noble, whom Vivian found the
most security-conscious of the embassy staff, agreed with him that 'security
was virtually non-existent'.[108]

What most concerned Major Vivian were the four chancery servants, all
either of Italian nationality or domiciled in Italy. All, he believed, had many
opportunities for removing embassy documents and taking wax impressions
of keys, and would find it 'very hard to resist' pressure to do both from the
Italian authorities.[109] The ambassador himself was concerned about Picton,
the chief chancery servant, whom he agreed was 'entirely unsuited for the
post': 'Though a water colour artist of some merit, he is a weak character,
and a vague and incurable muddler of everything he does from keeping
accounts to buying railway tickets or handling customs forms'.[110] Vivian,
however, was far more concerned by Picton's deputy, Constantini, whom he
rightly suspected of responsibility for the removal of classified documents
from the embassy:

S[econdo] Constantini is an Italian subject and has been employed in the
Chancery for twenty-one years. He might, therefore, have been directly or
indirectly responsible for any, or all, of the thefts of papers or valuables
which have taken place, or are thought to have taken place, from this
Mission. He was, I understand, not quite free of suspicion of being himself
concerned in a dishonest transaction for which his brother, then also a
Chancery servant, was dismissed a short while ago. Moreover, though the
Diplomatic Staff at the time did not connect him with the matter, I am
clear in my own mind that the circumstances of the loss of two copies of
the "R" code from a locked press in the Chancery in 1925 point towards
S. Constantini, or his brother, or both, as the culprits.[111]

From the Rome embassy, Vivian went on to inspect the legation to the Vatican. He was stunned to discover that it was housed in part of a building in the Via San Nicola da Tolentino, owned and otherwise used by the Italian armed forces. The legation premises, reported Vivian, 'are entirely unoccupied at night, are quite unsuitable for their purpose and afford no protection whatever for the documents they house'. Visiting the legation at night, as 'an experiment', he found a red box on a table, unlocked it and discovered the legation keys giving access to most of the files. Vivian called for the legation's 'early removal to other, less blatantly insecure premises'.[112] The envoy to the Vatican, Mr Osborne, failed to see the force of Vivian's arguments. The fact that the rest of the building was occupied by the Italian armed forces was, in his view, a protection against burglary. 'That Italian authorities themselves would take, or suborn others to take, our papers did not seem to occur to him'. Vansittart minuted savagely: 'The Vatican mission is a scandal'.[113]

Five months later, in July 1937 Vivian visited the embassy at Berlin. Sir Nevile Henderson, the ambassador, had little greater grasp of embassy security than Sir Eric Drummond in Rome and was notoriously indiscreet in his telephone conversations. 'The Germans', it has been unkindly suggested, 'did not need a key to British ciphers. They only needed to lure Sir Nevile Henderson to the telephone'.[114] The Berlin embassy porter was a German, the ambassador's residence had no proper guard and, during Henderson's annual two-month leave, the whole embassy was, outside working hours, virtually at the mercy of the German porter. Vivian concluded:

This means, in fact, that the Gestapo could, if they were so minded, introduce nightly and for a practically unlimited period each night any number of lock-smiths and experts in safe-breaking, thereby having continuous access to current papers, telegrams and prints without leaving any trace ...

There is, of course, no evidence that the porter has admitted Gestapo agents, but, having in view the situation in Berlin and the German mentality, it would be sheer lunacy not to act on the assumption (a) that the porter is in the pay of the Gestapo, (b) that the latter have at their disposal as expert lock-pickers as the criminal or professional world can produce.[115]

Vivian drew a number of general conclusions from the dreadful lapses of embassy security at Rome and Berlin. The first was the need to impress on British diplomats that Germany, Italy, Japan and Russia should be treated as 'enemy countries' for intelligence purposes:

It must be assumed, in the absence of proof to the contrary, that the Intelligence sections of these countries will have established the most complete arrangements for taking advantage of every opportunity afforded by (a) Venality or openness to pressure on the part of Embassy personnel, (b) Inadequacy of watch and ward arrangements, (c) Occasional or habitual carelessness in the handling of keys, and (d) Imprudent handling of various categories of papers.

It follows that, if an Embassy Staff contains natives of the country or persons belonging to the British community domiciled in the country, the task of the 'enemy' Intelligence will be obviously much simpler and the danger to State secrets much greater.

The first priority was therefore 'the replacement of certain native or domiciled members of the staff by 100 per cent British subjects recruited from the United Kingdom'. This was particularly urgent in the Rome embassy where there were 'ample indications' that 'at least one traitor' was at work.[116] Vansittart noted on the file that the replacement of the four chancery servants at Rome was 'essential'. Drummond commended Vivian's report as 'very sensible and well-balanced'.[117]

Though Eden sent a circular to British missions incorporating 'certain valuable suggestions' made by Vivian on embassy security,[118] any sense of urgency seems to have been quickly lost. Foreign chancery servants were not dismissed. A Foreign Office minute on a report by Drummond in May 1937 concluded: 'It results from this that the servants are pretty certain to be crooks, but the Amb[assado]r thinks that he can limit their activities'.[119] Most remarkably of all, Signor Constantini, whose guilt Drummond could not really credit,[120] retained his job in the Chancery. As a reward for his long and supposedly faithful service he and his wife were invited to London in May 1937 as the guests of His Majesty's Government at the coronation of King George VI. So Constantini was able to go on handing documents from the British embassy to the Italian 'P Squad' until Italy declared war in June 1940. Some of these documents also found their way to the Soviet embassy. Even when Italy went to war, Constantini was not dismissed. Though now an enemy national, he was employed by the Vatican legation. Not until the Allied armies entered Rome in the summer of 1944 was Constantini finally unmasked as a spy and dismissed.[121]

Vivian's investigations produced some improvements in physical security but did little to change attitudes. The general air of complacent defeatism about security within the Foreign Office was epitomised during 1937 in minutes by Vansittart's private secretary, Clifford Norton. The theft of Lady Drummond's necklace had, he reported, left the Rome embassy 'very much alive to dangers' and perhaps more security-conscious 'than any other Mission'. 'Thorough consideration' in the Foreign Office had led to the comforting, and equally misguided, conclusion that the Italians could not 'read our ciphers'. The general problems of embassy and Foreign Office security were 'the subject of many discussions per annum with the heads of the Secret

Service and of MI5'. 'Problems of accommodation and finance' made impracticable any further major steps 'to make the F.O. safer'. But Norton concluded that such steps were in any case unnecessary: 'All reasonable precautions are taken: absolute security is impossible'.[122]

Though Britain had at least intermittent access to good intelligence from both Germany and Italy before the Second World War, she was on balance losing the intelligence war against both. The intelligence war with the Soviet Union was an even more unequal struggle. Once the Great Terror started in 1936, Viscount Chilston, the British ambassador, almost despaired of discovering anything of importance. 'He gets no information', noted Neville Chamberlain in 1937, 'and the condition of the country is a mystery to him'. In October 1938, shortly before he left Moscow, Chilston sadly concluded that 'it is impossible to obtain even an inkling of what is discussed within the [Kremlin's] walls'.[123] SIS had no PCO in Moscow. A proposal to appoint one in 1936 in the hope of improving both the flow of intelligence and the visa system collapsed in the face of Chilston's vigorous protests:

> I know from considerable past experience that even in a normal European capital the presence of a 'Passport Control Officer' is liable to cause serious embarrassment to the Mission; and I need not tell you that the embarrassment would be infinitely greater here ... Anybody who went anywhere near the Passport Control Officer would be liable to get into very serious trouble; and I myself should much dislike the necessity of affording him 'cover', since I feel convinced that the disadvantages, in the form of increased suspicion and general hostility, would far outweigh any practical advantages which might be secured by his presence.[124]

MI5's operations against the CPGB and Soviet espionage in Britain during the later thirties were far more successful than those of SIS in the Soviet Union. But its very success in penetrating CPGB headquarters and monitoring Soviet espionage and Communist subversion in munitions works and naval dockyards may well have helped to blind it to newer forms of Soviet penetration. By 1937, taking advantage of slack security in the Foreign Office, the NKVD (formerly OGPU) had recruited at least one agent in the Communications Department who went undetected until compromised by a Soviet defector to the USA shortly after the outbreak of war.[125] Most dangerous of all was the NKVD's recruitment, through the intermediary of the Comintern intelligence apparat, of long-term penetration agents (since known as moles) beginning at Cambridge in the mid-thirties. Unlike the first of the Cambridge Comintern agents, Philip Spratt, recruited almost a decade before, the new generation of Cambridge moles were told to break all visible ties with the CPGB. Kim Philby and Guy Burgess, the two earliest recruits (probably during the 1933–4 academic year), both adopted neo-Fascist poses.

NKVD had a remarkably patient and far-sighted strategy for placing agents in the commanding heights of the British establishment. The Soviet control who attempted unsuccessfully to turn the young Oxford graduate, Jenifer Fischer Williams (later Mrs Hart), into an NKVD agent in 1938, told her that nothing would be expected of her for ten years. During the brief period before Miss Fischer Williams broke off contact with him, he was chiefly concerned to ensure the success of her career in the Home Office, following with meticulous detail even her membership of the music society.[126] By Munich the NKVD strategy had already achieved two striking successes. The first, unsurprisingly, was in the Foreign Office, where Donald Maclean began work in 1935 and quickly established himself as a high-flyer with a reputation for 'plenty of brains and keenness'. Lord Gladwyn remembers him being spoken of as a possible permanent undersecretary of the future. In 1937 Guy Burgess, then a BBC producer, succeeded in winning the confidence of David Footman, deputy head of political intelligence in SIS, and persuaded him to give a talk on Albania for the Home Service. A year later, thanks probably to his contact with Footman, Burgess himself was recruited by a newly established section of SIS.[127] Ironically, during Stalin's purges bogus evidence was frequently produced at show trials alleging that SIS had highly placed moles in the Soviet administration. 'Quex' Sinclair must frequently have wished that the evidence were true.

In the intelligence battle against her three main European rivals, Germany, Italy and Russia, Britain began with the built-in disadvantage that secrets are easier to protect in authoritarian than in open societies. But the Foreign Office made an inevitable handicap far worse by the sometimes comic amateurism of its security both at home and abroad. The Foreign Office also bears the major responsibility for the weaknesses of both intelligence collection and intelligence analysis. The principal problem of intelligence collection was the shortage of both men and money devoted to it. Had successive foreign secretaries taken their responsibilities for SIS with appropriate seriousness they would scarcely have allowed a situation in which Sinclair had sometimes to appeal to relatives for money and was still unable at the time of Munich to afford wireless sets for his agents. Nor would they have shown so little interest in the quality of recruits to SIS. At a time when the Foreign Office remained anxious to recruit some of the ablest graduates straight from university, it remained apparently content that SIS should recruit almost none – and that some of its leading officers should, like Dansey, be positively anxious to exclude graduates from their ranks. Amazingly, Soviet intelligence was thus able to begin recruiting in Oxbridge several years before SIS. Probably no pre-war recruit to SIS was as able as Kim Philby, Donald Maclean or Anthony Blunt. Had the Foreign Office taken any serious interest in the appointment of SIS station chiefs, it would scarcely have tolerated either the disastrous sequence of Dalton, Chidson and Stevens in what, by the outbreak of war, was probably the chief link in the PCO network gathering German intelligence.

The main problems of interpreting the raw intelligence supplied by Britain's under-funded intelligence services arose from the fragmented structure of the intelligence community and the multiplicity of government departments with which it dealt. From 1935 onwards the progress of both the Ethiopian War and German rearmament produced a growing awareness of the need to collate, evaluate and coordinate the diffuse and sometimes conflicting information flowing into Whitehall from a wide variety of secret and non-secret sources. Major-General (later Field-Marshal Sir) J.G. Dill, the Director of Military Operations and Intelligence, wrote inelegantly but accurately in July 1935 'of the increasing tendency for certain specific aspects of intelligence to develop, in which two or more separate departments are equally interested, with the result that the danger of uneconomical duplication in the collation and recording of such intelligence is tending to increase'. Over the next few years the main support for a machinery to coordinate intelligence assessment came from the cabinet secretary and the service chiefs, and the main resistance issued from the Foreign Office. Late in 1935 discussions by the deputy chiefs of staff chaired by Sir Maurice Hankey as secretary of the CID recommended the establishment of an Inter-Service Intelligence Committee (ISIC). Though approved in January 1936 by the chiefs of staff and the CID, the ISIC was stillborn. It was replaced in June 1936 by the Joint Intelligence Sub-Committee (JIC) of the chiefs of staff which normally met at least once a month and included Morton, the head of the IIC, or his deputy.[128]

Not until the eve of war, however, did the JIC begin to fulfil the role for which it had been intended. Its slow development was due partly to the continued parochialism, despite their previous good intentions, of the service intelligence departments and the service ministries. Each service department continued to make, in collaboration with the IIC, its own individual assessment of German rearmament. The Joint Planning Staff (JPS) of the chiefs of staff, who had been intended to seek intelligence assessments on inter-service questions from the JIC, usually failed to do so.[129] Without Foreign Office participation no attempt at intelligence coordination could in any case hope to succeed. And until Munich, jealous of its monopoly of political intelligence and determined that the service departments should not infringe its prerogatives, the Foreign Office remained totally aloof.

Munich gave a new urgency to the problem of intelligence coordination. At the first post-Munich meeting of the JIC, which considered a new European strategic appreciation, the Foreign Office felt that it could no longer stay entirely aloof and for the first time sent a representative.[130] Brigadier (later Major-General) Frederick Beaumont-Nesbitt, the Deputy Director of Military Intelligence and chairman of the JIC, wrote a secret memorandum attacking the 'overlapping and wasted effort' in analysing political intelligence:

All various political intelligence sources ranging from press to 'Most Secret reports', with only few exceptions, are received by each Intelligence Directorate. How the latter deal with them is their affair; but every item has to be examined – if merely superficially – and its value assessed. This in itself means time; and frequently, where the Service Departments are concerned, it must mean wasted time. For much of this information is quite outside their province ...

Under the present system such a state of affairs is inevitable, since no single Department is responsible for first assimilating this mass of material and for subsequently passing it on to other interested parties in an easily digested form. It is not the task of the FO; though it is this Department which requires, and takes, the lion's share ... Yet every Department, for its own purposes, must, at the moment, be prepared to analyse the international political situation. There may be as many readings of the situation as there are commentators ... [And] there is always the possibility that the political assumptions will be found not to be in accordance with FO views.

Beaumont-Nesbitt therefore proposed a strengthened JIC under Foreign Office chairmanship whose 'principal task would be to sift all that Political Intelligence material, which hitherto has been dealt with by several departments' and end the confusion.[131]

Sinclair's deputy, Colonel Stewart Menzies, representing SIS, found 'the basic idea underlying this scheme ... sound and necessary':

Our own constantly recurring experience of being called upon for ad hoc notes on various aspects – which can only be one-sided – is our strongest proof that such machinery is badly needed.[132]

The Foreign Office was much less enthusiastic. It had yet to be fully converted to the principle of the coordinating of intelligence with the service ministries, and remained fearful of losing its monopoly as the sole authorised purveyor of political intelligence. As a result its participation in JIC meetings remained erratic until the summer of 1939. Cadogan professed himself 'horrified' by Beaumont-Nesbitt's proposals:

We sh[oul]d have an outside C[ommit]tee (in which F.O. w[oul]d be rep[resente]d it is true) sifting all the inf[ormatio]n rec[eive]d from various sources and pontificating upon it. And Heaven knows what conclusions they would reach.

But Cadogan was forced to admit that the existing system of intelligence assessment was chaotic:

There are ... a number of sources of inf[ormatio]n, including our official tel[egram]s & despatches and S.I.S. reports, copies of all of which are simply flung round, without comment, to the various Dep[artmen]ts, who have varying ability to test and appraise them. The result is that they all exercise their ingenuity upon them with, no doubt, conflicting conclusions.

That, Cadogan now acknowledged, was 'a situation that must be remedied'.[133] The remedy, however, was still far from complete by the outbreak of war.

# 13 | RUMOURS OF WAR AND WAR

Munich is nowadays remembered as a German triumph and an Anglo-French humiliation. Hitler did not see it quite that way. He was secretly dismayed that the crisis had ended without the war which he had planned to destroy Czechoslovakia and that Chamberlain had manoeuvred him into accepting a peaceful settlement. For the remainder of his life he continued to believe that he should have gone to war in September 1938.[1] 'Quex' Sinclair correctly reported that the Führer was 'depressed' by the Munich agreement. SIS, however, was over-optimistic. Hitler, it alleged, 'resented the popularity acquired by Mr Chamberlain in Germany as detracting from his own'. Though 'the bulk of the nation, largely unwillingly but resignedly, would have followed the Führer into war', SIS claimed that 'the Gestapo would have had to deal with some 20–30,000 saboteurs'.[2]

Until mid-December 1938 SIS continued to believe that Hitler's immediate ambitions lay not in the West but in the East, especially the Ukraine. 'At present', it reported, 'he is devoting special attention to the Eastward drive, to securing control of the exploitable riches of South, and possibly more, of Russia'.[3] Chamberlain was not much alarmed. A Russo-German conflict over the Ukraine, he told the cabinet, was no concern of Britain's.[4] Ten days before Christmas, however, Whitehall began to be disturbed by a series of intelligence reports that Hitler's first move might be not 'the Eastward drive' but a surprise attack in Western Europe. One of the consequences of these reports was to keep Sinclair close to the centre of policy-making with the ear of both Chamberlain and Halifax as well as regular access to Cadogan. At moments of crisis he had a habit of dressing in the admiral's uniform he had originally discarded for civilian clothes on becoming C. The intelligence supplied by SIS and other secret sources during the less than nine months of peace which remained varied from excellent to dreadful. Whitehall found the greatest difficulty in distinguishing between the two. As Captain (later Admiral) J.H. Godfrey discovered on becoming DNI in January 1939, 'There were so many authentic rumours about Germany's intentions that, whatever happened, *someone* could say "I told you so".[5]

Sinclair failed to realise that one of the main sources of what eventually turned out to be 'unauthentic rumours' was his own opposite number in Germany, Admiral Wilhelm Canaris, head of the Abwehr. Canaris has been fairly described as 'the Hamlet of conservative Germany', a man with a subtler and more complex, if less decisive, mind than Sinclair. In the course of 1938, repelled by the brutality of Nazism, Canaris turned against the Führer. But after the failure of the conspiracies within the high command, he devised a more devious form of opposition. After Munich he seems to have hoped to stir the British into stiffer resistance to Hitler's ambitions by planting bogus intelligence of impending German attacks. Though Canaris's intelligence plants did much to galvanise the British into giving a series of guarantees to resist Nazi aggression in the spring of 1939, those guarantees failed to restrain Hitler from embarking on a war which Canaris feared Germany could not win. Canaris's motives were, however, rarely clearcut. His patriotic dread of German defeat was probably more powerful than his loathing of Adolf Hitler. Some of his intelligence plants may have been part of a war of nerves designed to test the enemy's resolve.[6]

Colonel (later Major-General) Hans Oster, who became Canaris's chief of staff in 1939, was a far more committed anti-Nazi and more anxious than Canaris to stiffen British opposition to Hitler. Once war broke out, he became one of the organisers of the underground resistance, later helping a number of Jews to escape the gas chambers. During the Phoncy War which preceded Hitler's invasion of the Low Countries in May 1940, Oster several times gave the Dutch military attaché in Berlin and the Vatican secret last-minute warning of the intended dates of the German offensive in the West. Sadly, his warnings were given insufficient weight in Whitehall, both because some of the pre-war warnings of German offensives had proved to be false alarms and because Hitler's plans for an offensive during the Phoney War were several times postponed.[7] After the abortive bomb plot against Hitler in July 1944 both Oster and Canaris were arrested and later executed.

Other German dissidents within the armed and foreign services preferred more straightforward warnings than the intelligence plants used by Canaris. In June 1939 Lieutenant-Colonel Count Gerhard von Schwerin, the anti-Nazi head of the British section of the German war ministry intelligence department, came on a visit to England, his movements and conversations closely monitored by MI5. Like Canaris, Schwerin believed that 'Germany would not win a long war'. His main message, repeated in conversations with – among others – Godfrey, the DNI, and General Marshall-Cornwall, director-general of air and coast defence, never varied:

War must result in the near future *unless* we can convince Hitler that we mean business ... Hitler took no account of words, only of deeds and Hitler was the only person that had to be convinced, no one else counted.

Schwerin suggested, without success, three dramatic actions to bring home to Hitler the seriousness of British intentions: a naval demonstration, bringing Churchill ('the only Englishman Hitler is afraid of') into the cabinet, and stationing the RAF 'striking force' in France.[8] Other German dissidents such as Carl Goerdeler and Theodor Kordt usually sent the same basic message: that the only chance of stopping Hitler on the road to war was resolute and visible Western opposition. The dissidents had something of a mixed reception in Whitehall. Vansittart repeatedly emphasised their warnings and those from his own informants, but suffered from a reputation as an alarmist. Cadogan, who had felt boundless admiration for Theodor Kordt in September 1938, did not 'quite trust' him by May 1939. He trusted some of Van's informants even less.[9]

Between mid-December 1938 and mid-April 1939 Whitehall received no less than twenty warnings from a variety of secret sources of impending Axis aggression.[10] The first major scare resulted from an approach to Ivone Kirkpatrick, then finishing a tour of duty as first secretary at the Berlin embassy. On 11 December Kirkpatrick received an urgent request for a meeting from a retired German high official who began by insisting that his life was in danger and demanded elaborate precautions to protect his identity. Since he claimed that British ciphers had been broken (as indeed some had), he made Kirkpatrick promise not to telegraph his warning from Berlin but to deliver it in person to the Foreign Office. He had, he said, 'first-hand information' from the German ministries of war and air that Hitler had ordered preparations for an air attack on London to be completed in three weeks' time. According to Kirkpatrick's later recollection, his informant told him Hitler had not definitely decided to bomb London, but wished 'to be in a position to do so if he feels so inclined'.[11] A diary entry by Cadogan, to whom Kirkpatrick reported in London on 15 December, is more positive. Kirkpatrick, he wrote, had been told 'that Hitler will bomb London in March!' The 'first-hand information' supplied by the German official was certainly false and possibly an intelligence plant prepared by Canaris, but Cadogan, Halifax and Chamberlain all took the story seriously. The cabinet was summoned at 10 a.m. on the day following Kirkpatrick's return and decided to summon the anti-aircraft regiment from Lichfield and place its guns at Wellington Barracks in full view of the German embassy.[12] Illusory fears of a sudden knock-out blow by the Luftwaffe lingered into the New Year. In mid-January 1939 MI5 was told by what Vansittart considered a 'good German source' of plans for 'a sudden and unannounced air attack on London'. Simultaneously SIS reported, also erroneously, that Hitler and his advisers believed that London 'could be destroyed in a couple of days by unceasing bombing attacks, in reply to which "the miserable English anti-aircraft defences" would only be able to cause the loss of 100 or perhaps 150 bombers':

> ... There is incontrovertible evidence that at any rate many of the Führer's entourage are seriously considering the possibility of a direct attack on Great Britain and France during the next few months – perhaps during the next few weeks. It does not even seem to be at all unlikely that the Führer himself is thinking on such lines as these. At any rate all our sources are at one in declaring that he is barely sane, consumed by an insensate hatred of this country, and capable both of ordering an immediate aerial attack on any European country and of having his command instantly obeyed.[13]

By mid-January 1939 further false intelligence had accumulated pointing to German preparations for a surprise attack on Holland and possibly Switzerland as well. 'Germany', wrote Vansittart, 'is obviously picking a quarrel with Holland'. Despite a personal dislike for his predecessor which at times amounted to loathing, Cadogan agreed that there was a 'vital' danger of a German invasion of Holland either 'out of the blue' or after a brief crisis.[14] At least some of the intelligence reports which so misled both Vansittart and Cadogan may well have been planted on SIS through the PCO network in the Netherlands which the Germans had successfully penetrated several years before. The cabinet foreign policy committee, meeting on 23 January, took the intelligence plants at face value. It agreed, at Halifax's suggestion, to warn President Roosevelt of the threat to Holland. Vansittart further proposed to 'encourage both Holland and Switzerland to remove their remaining gold reserves out of harm's way', thus 'diminishing the temptation for Hitler to attack in the West'. The years of appeasement were now clearly at an end. Both Chamberlain and Halifax agreed that Britain must support the Dutch against a German attack.[15]

The foreign policy committee met again on 26 January. It recommended joint staff talks and planning with France and Belgium, an Anglo-French undertaking to resist a German attack on Holland or Switzerland, and informal talks with the Dutch. On 1 February the cabinet approved these proposals, thus recognising a reality it had struggled to evade since the First World War: that British security had to be defended on the continent of Europe as well as on the high seas, and that continental defence required firm commitments to continental allies. It was deeply ironic that this major turning point in British defence policy owed its immediate origins not to the German invasion of Austria or to the threatened invasion of Czechoslovakia but to a quite illusory threat to Holland based on false intelligence.[16]

February 1939 brought a temporary lull in the war scares of the past two months. Sinclair came to the conclusion that earlier 'alarmist rumours' had been 'put forward by Jews and Bolshevists for their own ends'. His station chief in Paris, Commander 'Biffy' Dunderdale, reported that the Deuxième Bureau was 'entirely calm' and discounted rumours of surprise attacks.[17] Cadogan too had had enough for the moment of 'alarmist rumours'. When Vansittart continued to produce them, Cadogan denounced him to his diary as 'a prize ass' who 'out-Cassandras Cassandra in a kind of spirit of pantomime'. But he had also lost confidence in Sir Nevile Henderson, who returned to his post as ambassador in Berlin on 13 February after four months' sick leave and was, in Cadogan's view, 'completely bewitched by his German friends'. When Henderson reported that the German compass was 'pointing towards peace'[18] and appeared to pour scorn on the intelligence reports of the last few months, Cadogan came to the defence of SIS:

> Our agents are, of course, bound to report rumours or items of information which come into their possession: they exercise a certain amount of discrimination themselves, but naturally do not take the responsibility of too much selection and it is our job here to weigh up the information which we receive and try to draw more or less reasonable conclusions from it. In that we may fail and if so it is our fault, but I do not think that it is fair to blame the SIS. Moreover, it is true to say that the recent scares have not originated principally with the SIS agents in Germany, but have come to us from other sources.[19]

'All the information I get', wrote Chamberlain cheerfully on 19 February, 'seems to point in the direction of peace'. Vansittart, however, continued to point in the opposite direction.[20] Next day he sent Halifax a report from his 'private detective agency' that Hitler had decided to liquidate Czechoslovakia. Though Christie remained his main English 'detective', Van was by now also receiving well-informed reports from the disillusioned secretary of the Anglo-German Fellowship, T.P. Conwell-Evans, formerly an admirer of Hitler but now an active opponent of appeasement. According to Conwell-Evans:

> Hitler had decided to devour the remains of Czechoslovakia in the very near future. The method which Hitler intends to adopt is to stir up a movement for independence among the Slovaks. Czech resistance to these claims will then give Hitler the opportunity to intervene *manu militari*, or in other words to invade the remains of Czechoslovakia.

By early March Van's 'detectives' were predicting a German coup during the week of the 12th to the 19th.[21] Henderson, predictably, was not impressed and continued to inveigh against 'wild stories of attacks in various directions'. By 11 March, however, the 'wild stories' were supported by both MI5 and SIS. Probably as the result of intelligence from an MI5 informant in the

German embassy, Kell himself called at the Foreign Office on the 11th 'to raise [Cadogan's] hair with tales of Germany going into Czechoslovakia in [the] next 48 hours'. After dinner Cadogan's private secretary, Gladwyn Jebb, rang up with further 'hair-raising' reports from SIS of a German invasion planned for the 14th. On the 13th SIS sent a further report that the Germans were about 'to walk in'. But Cadogan considered the situation 'still v. obscure' and neither Chamberlain nor his foreign secretary were yet convinced by the intelligence warnings. As late as 13 March Halifax believed that 'rumours and scares have died down', and could see no evidence that the Germans were 'planning mischief in any particular quarter'. But he added as an afterthought: 'I hope they may not be taking, even as I write, an unhealthy interest in the Slovak situation!' The German interest by now was very unhealthy indeed. On 15 March Hitler's troops occupied Prague and announced the annexation of Bohemia and Moravia. Slovakia became a vassal state, and Hungary occupied the Carpatho-Ukraine to the east of Slovakia. Van was bitter at the rejection of his warnings. 'Nothing seems any good', he wrote morosely on 15 March, 'it seems as if nobody will listen to or believe me'. Cadogan admitted to his diary that he had been wrong and Van's informants right:

> I must say it is turning out – at present – as Van predicted and as I never believed it would. If we want to stem the German expansion, I believe we must try to build a dam *now*.[22]

Dam-building began almost at once, prompted by a further series of German invasion scares. The next scare came only two days after the German entry into Prague. On 17 March the Rumanian minister in London, Virgil Tilea, told Halifax that his country had received 'something very much like an ultimatum' to submit to German economic domination, failing which there was the danger of 'an almost immediate' invasion. Simultaneously Vansittart (his credibility improved by the most recent German coup) reported that in the event of war the Hungarian government had undertaken a few days earlier to allow German troops to pass through Hungary and to assist in crushing Rumanian resistance. SIS also reported German plans 'for a drive through Hungary to Rumania, in concert with Bulgaria, accompanied by defensive action only in the West'.[23]

It seems unlikely, however, that there ever was a German ultimatum. The Rumanian foreign minister insisted that economic negotiations with Germany were proceeding 'on completely normal lines', and that '*for the moment* there was no threat to Rumania's political or economic independence'. Sinclair warned the Foreign Office on the morning of 18 March that Tilea's report of an ultimatum might be false. He probably based that judgment on the intercepted instructions of the Rumanian foreign minister and Tilea's own report to Bucharest of his conversation with Halifax, neither of which made any reference to an ultimatum.[24] Tilea stuck to his story, insisting to the Foreign Office that it had come from a reliable private source, 'the general manager of a big Rumanian industrialist, who had come specially to Paris to pass the news on to him'. The truth is probably that Tilea, with the encouragement of King Carol of Rumania, greatly exaggerated the immediate German threat in order to secure a promise of British support. In this he was triumphantly successful.[25]

On Saturday 18 March the cabinet met hastily in emergency session, considered reports of the German threat to Rumania, and approved approaches to Russia, Poland, Yugoslavia, Turkey, Greece and Rumania 'with a view to obtaining assurances from them that they would join with us in resisting any act of German aggression aimed at obtaining domination in south-east Europe'. By 27 March it was clear that there was no prospect of bringing Poland and Russia together. The immediate British aim therefore became a mutual assistance pact between Britain, France and Poland in support of Rumania. Only four days later, however, on 31 March, Neville Chamberlain suddenly announced the government's decision to give Poland a unilateral and unconditional guarantee. 'A continental commitment with a vengeance!' commented Pownall, the Director of Military Operations and Intelligence. 'But', he added, 'I'm sure it's the right policy. The only way to stop Hitler is to show a firm front'.[26]

The immediate cause of Chamberlain's dramatic announcement was the mistaken fear of an impending German coup in Poland similar to the equally unfounded Rumanian scare a fortnight earlier. After Hitler's annexation of the predominantly German Memel region in Lithuania on 22 March, rumours spread across Europe that his next move would be the seizure of Danzig or an attack on Poland. SIS received 'various reports' (all erroneous) that German military preparations for an attack were to be concluded by 28 March – a date about which it was particularly confident: 'This is the only case in which [SIS] have been able to substantiate rumours of definite dates fixed for action'. On 29 March Chamberlain received dramatic confirmation of an imminent German coup. At 6 p.m. that evening Ian Colvin, the twenty-six-year-old Berlin correspondent of the *News Chronicle* and probably a member of Vansittart's 'private detective agency', was escorted by Halifax and Cadogan into the prime minister's room at the Commons. Also present was a mysterious figure whom Colvin believed to be 'Quex' Sinclair himself. Colvin provided what Cadogan called 'hair-raising details' of an imminent German attack on Poland. A victualling contractor to the German army had been ordered to provide the same amount of rations as he had supplied in September 1938 to prepare for an invasion of Czechoslovakia, and to deliver them by 28 March to 'forward dumps in an area of Pomerania that formed a rough wedge pointing towards the railway junction of Bromberg in the Polish corridor'. All Colvin's information pointed to an 'attack on the Polish Republic in twelve hours, three days, a week or a fortnight'. After Colvin had left, Halifax stayed behind with the prime minister. The two men 'then and there decided' on an immediate Polish guarantee. Halifax, Cadogan and R.A. Butler, parliamentary undersecretary for foreign affairs, stayed up until the early hours drafting a declaration for consideration by the cabinet on the following morning. Colvin's evidence was, however, less decisive than he believed. Halifax and the Foreign Office had already accepted the case for a Polish guarantee and had gained Chamberlain's approval 'in principle'. Colvin's evidence was used by the Foreign Office to force the pace, impress the prime minister and convince the cabinet.[27]

The Polish guarantee began a diplomatic revolution. It was followed by Anglo-French guarantees to Greece and Rumania on 13 April, to Turkey on 12 May, and by the beginning of Anglo-French negotiations with the Soviet Union in mid-April for a treaty of mutual assistance (which was, however, never to materialise). That diplomatic revolution and the introduction of limited conscription on 20 April took place against the background of a further series of German intelligence plants and false alarms suggesting plans for surprise attacks on London and the Royal Navy. During March fears revived of a German 'bolt from the blue in the air'. By the 23rd 83 anti-aircraft guns and 52 searchlights were in position around the capital.[28] There were equally mistaken reports of a U-boat menace. On 27 March NID reported on the basis of SIS and other intelligence:

There may be up to 15 German submarines abroad, whose permanent position is unknown, but their probable areas of operations are:-
1. North West African coast and Cape Verde Islands
2. Coast of Brazil
Six more are standing by in Germany to proceed abroad. Information received indicates that German subs are probably mounting a continuous patrol in the areas mentioned, and the boats are returning about every three months.

The report of a submarine threat in the South Atlantic was wholly wrong and the Admiralty was wholly deceived by it. Although existing Admiralty estimates of U-boat strength showed that patrols on the scale alleged were impossible, NID simply revised these estimates upwards in order to make an otherwise incredible menace credible. Traffic analysis and direction-finding by the German naval sub-section at GC & CS (founded in May 1938) also failed to find any trace of U-boat patrols in the South Atlantic but attempts by 'Nobby' Clarke, the head of the sub-section, to 'scotch' the NID report went unheeded.[29]

On 3 April there was another false alarm. The Foreign Office circulated warnings from the Berlin embassy of a possible attack by the Luftwaffe on the Home Fleet in harbour during the following Easter weekend while most of the seamen were on leave. Simultaneously, one of Vansittart's informants reported – also inaccurately – that U-boats were patrolling in the Channel and the Thames estuary.[30] Halifax asked Earl Stanhope, the First Lord of the Admiralty, to make it tactfully clear that 'the Navy was always ready and was not to be caught out'. Tact was not Stanhope's strong point. On 4 April he recorded an alarmist statement on the BBC telling listeners that 'Shortly before I left the Admiralty it became necessary to give orders to man the anti-aircraft guns of the Fleet so as to be ready for anything that might happen'. The Foreign Office was horrified, Chamberlain was consulted, and the broadcast was stopped. But the story reached the papers and 'a fine row' followed in the Commons. 'Why do we keep exhibits like Jim [Stanhope] in the Cabinet!!', Cadogan plaintively asked his diary.[31]

The German intelligence plants culminating in the embarrassing farce of Stanhope's censored speech served to distract the Foreign Office from the more immediate problem of Mussolini's ambitions in the Adriatic. Little distraction was, however, needed. The Southern Department of the Foreign Office, whose responsibilities included Italy and Albania, remained convinced in mid-March that 'Italian designs on Albania have been put into cold storage'. In reality Mussolini was prompted by Hitler's coup in Prague to go ahead with the occupation of Albania. On 22 March SIS produced a report from a 'secret source in Italy' suggesting an Italian move against Yugoslavia, probably accompanied by a landing in Albania. But SIS could not vouch for the accuracy of its report and Prince Paul of Yugoslavia dismissed it as 'out of date'. Early in April a contact in the German embassy gave Dick White of MI5 much more detailed intelligence on Italian preparations for an Albanian coup. But when White took the information to the Foreign Office he was given a sceptical reception. On 3 April, Sir Andrew Noble of the Southern Department (formerly head of chancery in Rome) still believed 'that Italy is not going to pounce on Albania just now'. At a cabinet meeting on the 5th Halifax also discounted rumours of an Italian invasion. Two days later, on Good Friday, while the Royal Navy was on the alert against an imaginary threat from the Luftwaffe, Italy occupied Albania. After attending a three-hour Good Friday service Halifax met Cadogan and 'decided we can't *do* anything to stop it'.[32] Chamberlain took the invasion as a personal affront. 'It cannot be denied', he told his sister, 'that Mussolini has behaved to me like a sneak and a cad'.[33]

The hopeless confusion of Easter 1939, when the Admiralty stood ready to repel an imaginary German attack and the Foreign Office was caught off its guard by a real Italian invasion, brought to a head the problems of intelligence assessment. The chiefs of staff now demanded that, as a minimum response to these problems, all intelligence – both political and military – which required quick decisions should be collated and assessed by a central body on which the Foreign Office would be represented.[34] Though still concerned to keep its undivided control of political intelligence, the Foreign Office was also conscious that intelligence assessment had become intolerably confused. Halifax had felt since the beginning of the year 'that they were all moving in a mental atmosphere much like the atmosphere with which a child might be surrounded in which all things were both possible and impossible, and where there were no rational guiding rules'.[35] Cadogan was 'daily inundated by all sorts of reports' and found it virtually impossible to sort the wheat from the chaff. The Foreign Office took seriously a whole series of intelligence plants and false alarms but disregarded accurate intelligence before the German occupation of Prague and the Italian invasion of Albania. Cadogan confessed that even when he correctly identified accurate intelligence reports, 'It just happened that these were correct; we had no means of evaluating their reliability at the time of their receipt'. After the traumatic Easter weekend Cadogan held meetings with both Sinclair and his senior officials to discuss the 'sifting' of SIS reports. Probably as a result of these meetings the Foreign Office gave way to service pressure for a Situation Report Centre (SRC) where the service directors of intelligence under a Foreign Office chairman would jointly assess intelligence and issue daily reports 'in order that any emergency measures which may have to be taken should be based only on the most reliable and carefully coordinated information'.[36] After two months the SRC proposed its own amalgamation with the Joint Intelligence Committee (JIC). In July the Foreign Office, hitherto only an irregular attender at the JIC, agreed. In the reorganisation which followed the JIC acquired both the basic structure and the responsibilities it retained throughout the war, with the three service directors of intelligence or their deputies meeting under a Foreign Office chairman. Their responsibilities included:

(i) The assessment and co-ordination of intelligence received from abroad with the object of ensuring that any Government action which might have to be taken should be based on the most suitable and carefully co-ordinated information obtainable.

(ii) The co-ordination of any intelligence data which might be required by the Chiefs of Staff or the Joint Planning Sub-Committee for them.

(iii) The consideration of any further measures which might be thought necessary in order to improve the efficient working of the intelligence organisation of the country as a whole.[37]

On the eve of war Whitehall had thus at last acquired a vision of the intelligence community as a whole which was to be of enormous importance for the conduct of the war. But neither the SRC nor the reorganised JIC which absorbed it achieved any overnight pre-war miracles. During the final months of peace there were three major failures of intelligence assessment. Whitehall badly misjudged the danger of a Nazi-Soviet pact; the ability of the German economy to withstand the strains of war; and the Polish crisis which led to the outbreak of war.

It is still unclear whether the Anglo-French negotiations with the Soviet Union for an anti-Nazi pact were a genuine missed opportunity or a lost cause from the outset. Germany was eventually able to outbid Britain and France by offering German-Soviet control of the Baltic states and Poland. Had Whitehall grasped the danger of a Nazi-Soviet pact it would at the very least have moved more quickly. On the British side, however, talks began without either enthusiasm or a sense of urgency. Halifax and Cadogan were 'on balance' in favour of an accord. Chamberlain had an even more 'profound distrust' of Russia. Cadogan wrote in his diary on 20 May: 'In his present mood, P.M. says he will resign rather than sign alliance with Soviet. So have to go warily'.[38] Chamberlain complained to the improbably named leader of the British mission during the final round of talks in Moscow during August, Admiral Sir Reginald Aylmer Ranfurly Plunkett-Ernle-Erle-Drax, that 'the House of Commons had pushed him further than he wished to go'.[39]

Sinclair, who kept his reputation as 'a terrific anti-Bolshevik', was, if anything, even less enthusiastic than Chamberlain. Though he had a growing respect for the Russian secret service whom he considered 'experts at espionage', and was impressed by their apparent ability to bug every conference room and hotel bedroom in Moscow, Quex had a much lower opinion of the Red Army. With its high command decimated during the purges, he believed that Russia 'could do nothing of real value' as an ally.[40] He saw the allied negotiations with the Russians as a new and dangerous form of appeasement, and gave Drax a pessimistic briefing on 1 August before he set out for Moscow:

> Quex explained that the political negotiations were not going well. 'When they started', he said, 'the Russians were here and the British were here', holding up his two hands about eighteen inches apart. 'Now', he said, 'the Russians are here and the British are here'. His right hand representing Russia, remained unmoved; his left hand, representing Britain, had moved across to within two inches of the right. I gathered that appeasement had done its worst. He did not appear to be optimistic as to the outcome, and his final comment was this: 'It's an infernal shame that they should send you to Moscow to try and clear up the mess that has been made there by the politicians'.

There was more than a hint of farce about poor Drax's trip. He was horrified to discover that the government had hired for his voyage an ancient merchant vessel capable of steaming at less than half the speed of a modern cruiser. On arrival he suddenly remembered that he had not been provided before departure with any official credentials: 'One naturally felt, though without showing it, a trifle non-plussed when asked to produce them. The only thing to do was to wire home ...'.[41]

By the time Drax arrived in Moscow on his ill-fated mission in August, there had been recurrent reports of a Nazi-Soviet rapprochement for over three months. Some of the earliest and most remarkable came from a Soviet defector to the United States, Samuel Ginsberg alias Walter Krivitsky, formerly NKVD *rezident* in the Netherlands. The State Department, like the Foreign Office, had as yet little experience in dealing with defectors and paid little attention to what he had to say about Soviet policy. In April 1939, however, he began publishing articles in *The Saturday Evening Post* in association with another Russian Jewish émigré, Don Levine, who had a well-established reputation as a sensation-seeking journalist. Among Krivitsky's revelations, partially ghosted by Levine, was the sensational claim that Stalin had been aiming at a pact with Hitler since 1934. In order to justify the $5,000 an article he had extracted from the *Saturday Evening Post*, Levine appears to have pushed this and other of Krivitsky's arguments to a level of exaggeration which damaged their plausibility. Krivitsky further damaged his own credibility by allowing himself to be inaccurately described as a former general in Soviet military intelligence (GRU) who controlled at various moments 'the main keys to Stalin's foreign policy'.[42]

Air Intelligence and the chanceries of the Moscow and Washington embassies thought that, despite the exaggerated sensationalism of the articles, there might be something to the allegations of a Nazi-Soviet rapprochement. The Northern Department of the Foreign Office, which was responsible for Russian affairs, was much more scornful of 'the self-styled general' and dismissed his revelations as 'a lot of very good Russian dreaming', 'mostly twaddle', 'rigmarole' and 'nonsense'. The main problem of the Northern Department was its difficulty in believing that Hitler and Stalin could ever come to terms at all. Krivitsky's revelations were 'directly contrary' to all its 'other information' and therefore incredible. Though the Department eventually conceded that there might be 'a few grains of sense in this rigmarole', its head, Laurence Collier, concluded:

> On the whole we do not consider that these would-be hair-raising revelations of Stalin's alleged desire for a *rapprochement* with Germany are worth taking seriously.[43]

The Northern Department also failed to take seriously other reports of a Nazi-Soviet rapprochement. On 6 May Carl Goerdeler sent a warning to

Frank Ashton-Gwatkin, economic counsellor at the Foreign Office, that the German high command had received a 'new and unexpected' offer from the Soviet Union. According to another report from Berlin, Goering's A.D.C., General Bodenschaft, was speculating about a major change in German-Soviet relations. Both reports were dismissed by SIS and the Foreign Office, rightly at this stage, as 'wishful thinking' and 'rash assumptions'.[44] Vansittart was almost alone in Whitehall in believing that 'there is no time to be lost in this Russian business'. By the time the cabinet belatedly approved the principle of an Anglo-Franco-Soviet pact in mid-May, Van was seriously alarmed by the danger that Germany and Russia would come to terms. But his repeated warnings were undermined both by his continuing reputation as an alarmist (only slightly dented by his success in predicting the Prague coup) and by the doubtful nature of the early evidence he produced. On 17 May Van sent Halifax a warning from Christie, based on 'an entirely reliable source', that Hitler had been negotiating with Stalin through the Czech General Sirovy and proposed helping Russia to partition Poland, take Bessarabia, dominate the Dardanelles and invade India. Though the 'Sirovy mission' was also mentioned in a letter from Sir Nevile Henderson, Christie's report was at the very least wildly exaggerated; it was dismissed by J.M. Troutbeck, formerly first secretary in Prague, as 'pure myth'. On 21 May Van telephoned Cadogan 'in a flap' with intelligence from a 'secret German source' that Julius Schurre, an official of the Economic Policy Department in the German Foreign Ministry, was leaving for Moscow next day to negotiate a commercial agreement. Van's secret source, Helmut Wohlthat, economic adviser to the German four-year plan, was well placed but unreliable. Like some other opponents of Hitler, he seems to have deliberately exaggerated a German threat in order to provoke as strong a British response as possible.[45]

From mid-June onwards Christie was sending Van at least weekly intelligence reports on German preparations for war with Poland and alliance with Russia. On 15 June Van received the same warning at the Kensington home of Cornwell-Evans from the anti-Nazi diplomats Erich and Theo Kordt. Only an Anglo-Soviet alliance, they argued, could hold Hitler back. Van replied, over-optimistically, that an alliance was on the way. Cadogan was suspicious of most of Van's sources and by now did not trust either of the Kordts.[46]

Van's increasingly agitated reports from his private detective agency were only part of what MID called an 'unusually large number of rumours' during June of a Russo-German rapprochement. 'I feel intuitively', wrote Sir Nevile Henderson on 13 June, 'that the Germans are getting at Stalin'. Canaris was said to have confirmed that they were. But intelligence reports did not add up to a coherent picture. MID pointed to contradictory evidence, much of it from SIS:

... At least one most secret report indicat[ed] that the Germans held the view that the elimination of Stalin was essential for their plans. Another most secret report from a reliable source on the Russian side stated that Stalin was very bitter on account of German intrigues in the Ukraine and that, so long as he remained, no question of a rapprochement was possible. A further report early in June stated that although certain sections of influential Soviet opinion might be against active cooperation with the Western Powers, yet the feeling against Germany was still very bitter.

The War Office was, however, prudent in its overall assessment. It recognised the possibility of a Russo-German commercial agreement (which was indeed under discussion) and concluded that, despite 'immense ideological difficulties', the danger of a more general rapprochement could not be discounted. The Foreign Office remained much more sceptical. Frank Roberts of the Central Department thought it 'in the Russian interest to frighten us with the bogy of an agreement with Germany'. The Northern Department believed it more likely that Russia would retreat into isolation than sign an accord with Germany if her talks with England and France broke down. Chamberlain dismissed all reports of a Nazi-Soviet pact. He assured the cabinet's foreign policy committee on 10 July that 'it would be quite impossible in present circumstances for Germany and Soviet Russia to come together'.[47]

The signature of the Nazi-Soviet pact on 23 August thus caught Whitehall badly off its guard. The Russians, wrote Pownall indignantly, were 'really the limit in double-crossers':

> We knew they were pretty crooked but a skein of wool is a straight line compared to them! ... We had no previous information – though a few vague indications – that the Russians were double-crossing us.[48]

The Commons were hurriedly recalled from their summer recess on 24 August. The parliamentary undersecretary at the Foreign Office, R.A. Butler, was asked by M.P.s what 'our intelligence was up to'.[49] He put the same question to the Foreign Office. Laurence Collier, the head of the Northern Department, replied with a 'paper of secret intelligence on the subject of German-Russian intrigues'. Intelligence direct from Soviet sources, wrote Collier, was scarce and 'notoriously difficult' to obtain. Intelligence from German sources was 'much more plentiful' but 'contradictory'. Reports from third parties 'usually came from persons of questionable reliability':

> In general, we find ourselves, when attempting to assess the value of these secret reports, somewhat in the position of the Captain of the Forty Thieves when, having put a chalk mark on Ali Baba's door, he found that Morgiana had put similar marks on all the doors in the street and had no indication to show which mark was the true one. In this case there were passages ...

in many of our reports which told against the probability of a German-Soviet rapprochement. We had no indications that these statements were in general any less reliable than those in a contrary sense: and from an impartial consideration of Soviet interests, as far as we could estimate them by trying to put ourselves in the position of the Soviet government, it seemed to us likely that they were reliable – at least to the extent that isolation, rather than a rapprochement with Germany seemed indicated as the probable alternative policy to one of agreement with France and this country.[50]

The Foreign Office had, in other words, concluded that from the Soviet point of view isolation made more sense than a pact with Germany. It had therefore tended to give more weight to reports which agreed with that conclusion than to those which did not. Van, largely isolated in his role of chief diplomatic adviser, started from quite different assumptions and weighted the reports quite differently. In its own post-mortem, however, the Foreign Office put the blame on the suppliers of intelligence rather than on the analysts. 'The fact remains', wrote Sir Orme Sargent (later to succeed Cadogan as permanent undersecretary), 'that we were never told that the Germans and Russians had started negotiations with one another – which was the only thing that mattered'.[51]

The Americans, however, *were* told. Their source was an anti-Nazi diplomat in the German embassy at Moscow, Hans Heinrich ('Johnnie') Herwarth von Bittenfeld. On 16 May Herwarth met his friend 'Chip' Bohlen of the United States embassy at an American dacha in the country. As they went riding in the fields round the dacha, Herwarth revealed that a major shift in German policy to Russia was underway and that he was arranging a meeting between Schulenburg, the German ambassador, and Molotov, the Soviet foreign minister. Over the next three months Bohlen drafted a series of long-hand reports of the intelligence supplied by Herwarth on the progress of German-Russian relations. Bohlen found this an inconvenient method since his handwriting was 'virtually illegible' even to himself, but he refused to dictate for fear that his office was bugged. His reports were telegraphed in the highest security classification available direct to the Secretary of State, Cordell Hull. The American embassy revealed none of Herwarth's information to British or French diplomats in Moscow, believing that 'the risk to the source was too great'.[52]

Unknown to Bohlen, Herwarth both intended and expected his information to reach the British and French. Unhappily his close friend in the British embassy, Fitzroy Maclean, had left some time before Russo-German talks began. In the second week of July Herwarth discussed the prospect of a Nazi-Soviet pact in 'cautious tones' with Maclean's successor Armin Dew, but amid the welter of rumours in the Moscow diplomatic colony the significance of Herwarth's cautious warning seems not to have been grasped by the British embassy. The further Anglo-French negotiations for an anti-German pact with Russia progressed, the more difficult Herwarth found it to arrange regular secret meetings with British or French diplomats. He therefore decided to concentrate on keeping Bohlen informed of the progress of Russo-German negotiations. 'I was pretty sure', wrote Herwarth later, 'that by informing the Americans, word would reach Paris and London, since I knew that their Foreign Offices both maintained confidential contact with Washington'.[53]

But the State Department did not confide in the British and French ambassadors in Washington until the eleventh hour. During a ball at the German embassy on the evening of 15 August Herwarth led Bohlen over to a corner of the ballroom. As they drank champagne against the background of the dance music, Herwarth revealed that the political basis of a Nazi-Soviet pact had just been agreed – even earlier than he had expected.[54] Two days later, on 17 August, Sumner Welles, the American undersecretary of state, summoned the British ambassador in Washington, Sir Ronald Lindsay, and broke the news to him. Lindsay immediately telegraphed to London. His telegram arrived in the Foreign Office Communications Department at 9.30 a.m. on the 18th. There followed a mysterious delay. The deciphered telegram did not reach the Central Department to which it was addressed until the 22nd. Frank Roberts minuted, with considerable understatement: 'It is a great pity that this tel[egram] was not decyphered until 4 days after receipt, with the result that we were taken by surprise this morning'.[55] Less than a month later the Foreign Office discovered a Soviet mole at work in the Communications Department and concluded that the telegram had been deliberately delayed by him.[56]

A second great intelligence failure during the final months of peace was the assessment of Germany's ability to sustain a major war. Since 1934 the IIC, collating information from published sources, other intelligence services, the service ministries, the Board of Trade and other government departments, had prepared a number of assessments which exaggerated both the achievements and efficiency of the Nazi economy. It emphasised the 'incredible rapidity' of German rearmament, the efficiency of German industry and the 'rigid, centralised government control of everything which forms the foundation of the totalitarian state'. The Berlin embassy commented on one IIC report that it showed 'rather too much tendency to attribute to Germany in every respect the sort of Machiavellian super-intelligence which is easier to imagine than to create'.[57] But the exaggerated belief of Morton and the IIC in a totalitarian government gearing all its resources to war even in peacetime led many in Whitehall to the erroneous conclusion that Germany would go to war with her economy already fully stretched. There were some highly optimistic claims that the German economy was rapidly becoming badly overstretched even in peacetime. According to a report to the cabinet foreign policy committee in November 1938 (almost certainly from Carl Goerdeler), Dr Schacht, the finance minister, was predicting financial chaos.[58] Halifax told the same cabinet committee on 23 January 1939:

> The recent dismissal of Dr Schacht supported the theory that the financial and economic condition of Germany was getting desperate and was compelling the mad Dictator of that country to insane adventures.[59]

The general conclusion reached by the IIC was that Germany probably possessed reserves of food and the main raw materials to meet one year's peacetime needs. Assuming the continued import of Swedish iron-ore and the maintenance of her main overland trade routes, Germany could probably maintain her existing level of industrial production for fifteen to eighteen months. But when war broke out in September 1939 it was expected that from the spring of 1941 Germany's supply difficulties would become steadily more severe. Remarkably the Treasury played little or no part in economic intelligence assessments, and stayed almost completely aloof from the IIC. Unlike the IIC, it believed that Germany was better prepared for a long war than Britain, whose prospects would be 'exceedingly grim' without massive American assistance. The chiefs of staff preferred the more reassuring IIC assessment to the pessimism of the Treasury.[60] In the event Germany's series of lightning victories were to make it unnecessary for her even to go over to a full-scale war economy for more than two years.

The final peacetime intelligence failure was to misread the German-Polish crisis which led to the outbreak of war. Rumours of German plans for a Polish invasion had continued throughout the spring and early summer of 1939. Colonel Beck, the Polish foreign minister, described one such rumour on 1 July as the 'forty-ninth of its kind'. Hitler intended, as he told his generals on 23 May, to attack Poland 'at the first suitable opportunity'. The Nazi-Soviet pact provided just that opportunity. 'Now', Hitler told his high command, 'I have Poland just where I want her!'[61]

While Sinclair was taking an early summer holiday in June, apparently expecting trouble in a few months' time, Major Woollcombe, the head of the SIS political section, accurately concluded that there was probably no way of settling Hitler's demand for the Baltic port of Danzig without recourse to war:

> ... Even if Hitler were to give undertakings regarding non-militarisation, Polish trade facilities, etc., his word is so utterly valueless and his ulterior motives regarding Poland so sinister ... If we have to honour our guarantee, we will no doubt get a loyal and brave return from the Poles ... We would not be fighting only for Danzig, any more than Hitler would be.[62]

The first detailed intelligence on Hitler's plans to attack Poland came on 17 August in a report to Vansittart from Christie who had been given details of recent Italo-German talks at which these plans had been discussed.[63] On the evening of the 18th Cadogan wrote a caustic note in his diary of a visit from Van 'in a high state of excitement':

> I asked him to come round, and gave him cold supper. I have never seen a man nearer nervous collapse. *His* source [Christie] has told him H[itler] has chosen war, to begin between 25th and 28th. I have my suspicions of his source. Still, one can't ignore it. Spoke to H[alifax] who will be here noon tomorrow. Agreed *not* to send for P.M., yet. Eventually calmed Van down a bit and packed him off about 11. This is the beginning of the 'War of Nerves'. And I have seen the first casualty!

Cadogan had heard so many dates for so many German coups since the beginning of the year that, though he could not ignore it, he felt 'naturally sceptical' about Van's latest information. He simultaneously received more reassuring news from Sinclair. SIS sent a report from a 'very good source' that Hitler's railway chief had told him on the 16th that he could arrange transport either for the forthcoming Nuremberg rally or for mobilisation but not for both. According to a further, unconfirmed SIS report, Hitler opted for the rally. But on the 19th Sinclair and Van reported ominously that those coming to the Nuremberg rally would have to travel on foot or by car, 'the railways being absorbed by troop transport'.[64]

Both SIS and many others in Whitehall had an exaggerated belief in the conflict within the Nazi leadership between 'radicals' like Ribbentrop, the foreign minister, who aimed at limitless expansion, and 'moderates' led by Goering, anxious for agreement with the Western democracies.[65] Whitehall's final illusory hopes for peace were centred largely on the influence of the German moderates and the Italians. Sinclair received a report that Goering was willing to come to London to talk to Chamberlain. The prime minister agreed on 21 August and secret arrangements were made for a meeting on the 23rd. But Goering failed to turn up and Hitler was said to have decided against the visit.[66] Reports continued to arrive that while the Nazi-Soviet pact was being concluded in Moscow, 'all German military preparations [were] going forward'. Sinclair and Cadogan were still in two minds about the outcome. When Halifax asked 'Do you think this means war?' on the 23rd, Cadogan gave the schizophrenic reply: 'Yes: I think it does, but I believe it doesn't'. Sinclair, he noted in his diary, 'felt the same way'.[67] Both by now were badly confused by the classic problem of distinguishing the key intelligence signals from misleading or irrelevant background noise.

In a secret speech to his generals at Obersalzberg on 22 August, Hitler

announced that 'the destruction of Poland' would begin early on the morning
of the 26th:

> So in a few weeks hence I shall stretch out my hand to Stalin at the
> common German-Russian frontier and with him undertake to redistribute
> the world ... After Stalin's death – he is a very sick man – we will break
> the Soviet Union. Then there will begin the dawn of the German rule of
> the earth.

Goering, whom Sinclair vainly hoped would meet Chamberlain next day in
an effort to secure the peace, jumped on a table and danced in celebration.[68]

Hitler was confident that with the conclusion of the Nazi-Soviet pact Britain
and France would not fight for Poland. He dismissed Chamberlain and the
French prime minister, Daladier, as 'poor worms' who were 'too cowardly to
attack' and lacked the nerve to 'go beyond a blockade'. But on this occasion
Hitler too had miscalculated. He discovered on the afternoon of 25 August,
probably from intercepts, that a formal Anglo-Polish treaty was at an advanced
stage of preparation. To Hitler's displeasure Mussolini was also reluctant to
go to war and demanded large military supplies. That evening the invasion
planned for the following morning was stopped in its tracks. The news that
the attack on Poland had been postponed was misinterpreted in Whitehall as
evidence that Hitler's resolve was 'wobbling'. In reality the Führer was simply
allowing himself a few more days to try to break the nerve of the 'poor worms'
in London and Paris and steel the nerve of his reluctant ally in Rome. Western
leaders tried to avoid war by pressure on Poland to be conciliatory, by attempts
to use Mussolini as a mediator, and by secret talks with a Swedish intermediary,
Birger Dahlerus. But they were not prepared for another Munich.[69]

Dahlerus's messages from Berlin did not amount to much, noted Cadogan,
'unless one can infer from them that Hitler has cold feet'.[70] For a few days
there were encouraging, but illusory, signs that the Führer was having second
thoughts. On 27 August Carl Goerdeler's friend, the refugee educationalist
Dr Reinhold Schairer, turned up at the Foreign Office with news from
Goerdeler that the Rome-Berlin Axis had virtually collapsed, that petrol and
other war materials were in short supply, and that Hitler's high command
was pressing him to avoid a two-front war. Sinclair personally confirmed
Goerdeler's information. According to an SIS report just received, General
Halder, chief of the German general staff, and Admiral Raeder, commander-
in-chief of the navy, 'convinced that the British and French would fight', had
warned Hitler on the 22nd against the danger of fighting on two fronts.
Further confirmation came from the counsellor of the German embassy, Dr
Ewart von Selzam, who told William (later Baron) Strang, head of the Central
Department, that news of the Anglo-Polish treaty had come as a 'bombshell'
and left Berlin uncertain what to do next.[71] At Sinclair's request the Foreign

Office agreed to send his personal assistant, David Boyle, on a secret mission to Berlin by the ambassador's plane on the 28th, probably to investigate the dissensions in the German high command.[72]

Further hopeful news followed. On 28 August Sinclair reported 'news of trouble with reservists in Germany'. Next day his assistant David Boyle flew back from Berlin with 'some interesting – and not unhopeful – news', apparently confirming earlier SIS reports of dissensions in the high command.[73] Further apparent confirmation of these dissensions came on the night of 28 August in a message to Ashton-Gwatkin from Goerdeler, who was now in Stockholm. Gwatkin was convinced that Goerdeler was 'a palpably honest man' who represented the ideas and policies of the General Staff:

Hitler is no longer the only person who counts in Germany. Even Hitler cannot make war without full consent of his generals.

Goerdeler reported that the generals had prevented an attack on Poland planned for the 26th.[74] Two days later, on 30 August, he sent an optimistic telegram to the Foreign Office:

Chief manager [Hitler]'s attitude weakening. Remain completely firm. No compromise. Take initiative only for general settlement under strong conditions.[75]

Cadogan simultaneously received other reports of 'trouble in Germany'. 'I can't help thinking', he wrote, '[that the] Germans are in an awful fix. In fact it's obvious even if one discounts rumours of disturbances'.[76] On the 31st Henderson telegraphed the news from Berlin of the creation of a Ministerial Council for the Defence of the Reich chaired by Goering but excluding Hitler. Following the exaggerated reports over the past few days of dissension within the high command, some senior Foreign Office officials jumped to a hopelessly optimistic conclusion. Sir Orme Sargent believed that 'a Palace revolution must have occurred' and that Goering and the generals had taken charge from Hitler. On this occasion Sinclair was better informed. The new Ministerial Council was, he reported, 'the coping stone of the German war preparations'.[77] Cadogan, however, refused to give up hope. 'It *does* seem to me', he wrote at about midnight on 31 August, '[that] Hitler is hesitant and trying all sorts of dodges, including last-minute bluff'.[78] A few hours later, at dawn on 1 September, as German troops crossed the border into Poland, Cadogan's last hopes of peace were dashed. Two days later Britain was at war.

The Second World War, like most of its predecessors, found Britain at best half ready. The intelligence services and the machinery of intelligence assessment were no exception. Whitehall knew so little about Germany's immediate plan of campaign that it feared the Luftwaffe might attempt an immediate 'knock-out blow' against the capital. At eleven-fifteen on Sunday morning 3 September, barely a quarter of an hour after the prime minister had broadcast the news that the nation was at war, the air-raid sirens wailed over London. In the War Office the entire staff from top brass to junior clerk filed down to the shelter in the basement. There they listened apprehensively to a series of muffled explosions above them which a former military attaché with first-hand experience of air-raids during the Spanish Civil War identified alternately as bombs and anti-aircraft fire. When the all-clear sounded, the War Office staff emerged from the basement and discovered with astonishment that there had been no air-raid at all, and that the 'explosions' had been caused by the noise of slamming office doors echoing down the lift shafts.[79]

The farcical start to the war in the bowels of the War Office was followed almost immediately by a major security scandal at the heart of the Foreign Office. On 4 September Cadogan received a 'very unpleasant' telegram from the Washington embassy which gave him 'a line on the "leaks" of the last few years'.[80] He immediately ordered a secret joint investigation by Brigadier 'Jasper' Harker, the head of MI5's B (Counter-espionage and counter-subversion) division and Colonel Vivian, the head of Section V (Counter-espionage) in SIS. The 'line on the "leaks"' came from the Soviet defector to the United States, Walter Krivitsky, whose credibility had been much improved by the signing, as he had predicted, of the Nazi-Soviet pact. His information enabled Harker and Vivian to trace the source of the leaks to a Soviet mole in the Communications Department. Cadogan was appalled by the 'awful revelations of leakage' which they uncovered. The chief suspect was a cipher clerk, Captain John King, whom Harker and Vivian subjected to 'a "Third Degree" examination' on 25 September. Cadogan wrote in his diary next day: 'I have no doubt he is guilty – curse him – but there is no absolute proof'.[81] Doubtless unaware of the weakness of the case against him, King cracked under further interrogation. At a trial *in camera* at the Old Bailey in October, kept secret for the next twenty years, King was sentenced to what now seems the modest sentence of ten years' imprisonment.[82] Harker and Vivian suspected others but failed to find enough evidence for a prosecution. Two officials were, however, sacked for 'irregularities'. Cadogan agonised for the remainder of the year about how to remedy the appalling lapses of security uncovered by Harker and Vivian. 'I *shall* be glad when it's over!', he wrote despondently on 30 November. Halifax decided that he had no option but to start the Communications Department again from scratch and move its remaining members to other jobs. Halifax broke this 'most painful' news to the Department on 1 December and, in Cadogan's view, 'he did it very well'.[83]

As well as grappling with the problems of its own security, Whitehall also found continuing difficulty in distinguishing good from bad intelligence. In the autumn of 1939 it received two major intelligence windfalls, one genuine and extremely valuable, the other bogus and dangerously misleading. Initially it paid little attention to the first but was badly deceived by the second. In October 1939 the British naval attaché in Oslo received an anonymous letter offering secret German scientific and technical information and asking for one of the BBC news broadcasts in German to begin with the uncharacteristic phrase 'Hallo, hier ist London' if it was desired to take the offer up. The broadcast was duly made and in the first week of November a packet containing seven typed pages and a sealed box was delivered to the naval attaché.

From Oslo the packet was forwarded to SIS headquarters in London, where it landed on the desk of the twenty-seven-year-old physicist Dr. R.V. Jones, who had joined the air section under Group-Captain Winterbotham at the outbreak of war and was the only man in SIS with the scientific knowledge even to attempt to evaluate its contents. Jones opened the sealed box gingerly, fearing that it might contain a bomb, and discovered instead a newly-developed electronic proximity fuse for an anti-aircraft shell. An accompanying typescript contained, in addition to details of the fuse, information on the use of the Junkers 88 as a divebomber, on methods of attack on bunkers during the Polish campaign, on torpedoes, on radar development, on the first German aircraft carrier, on a bomber guidance system later used in the 'Battle of the Beams', on remote-controlled gliders, on the early stages of rocket development, and on the secret testing ground at Peenemünde. When tested at the Admiralty Research Laboratory, the proximity fuse was found to be better than any available in England. But though some of the accompanying information could also be corroborated and R.V. Jones had no doubt that the 'Oslo report' was genuine, he could find no one else in the service ministries or SIS to take it as seriously as himself. He was told by some to whom he showed it that it was too good to be true, that the genuine information had been inserted simply to conceal a larger hoax. None of the ministries even bothered to keep a copy in their files. Its accuracy, however, was established in almost every detail as the war progressed. 'In the few dull moments of the war', Dr Jones would sometimes turn up his copy of the Oslo report 'to see what should be coming along next'.[84]

Sadly, in the autumn of 1939, Whitehall paid far more attention to an intelligence plant in the Netherlands than to the Oslo report. The passport control office in The Hague had never recovered from the suicide of Major Dalton in 1936.[85] Remarkably, his corrupt assistant, 'Jack' Hooper, who had been recruited by the Abwehr, was taken back on the SIS payroll by the PCO, Major Richard Stevens, on the eve of war. Though Hooper confessed that he had been playing 'a little ball' with the Abwehr, SIS did not realise that his information had enabled the Germans to track down Stevens's best German agent, Dr Otto Krueger, a consultant engineer providing valuable intelligence on German naval construction. Krueger was arrested on 7 July and committed suicide in his cell the day after Britain went to war.[86] Hooper was probably unaware that another member of Stevens's organisation in The Hague, Folkert Van Koutrik, was also working as a double agent for the Germans.[87] At the outbreak of war Van Koutrik revealed that a German diplomat in The Hague, whose name he could not identify, had been passing information to the British. The diplomat concerned, Wolfgang zu Putlitz (formerly stationed in Britain where he had passed information, usually via the male lover he employed as valet, to both Vansittart and MI5), was startled to be informed by the German minister, who wrongly regarded him as above suspicion, that someone in the legation was working for the British. Shortly afterwards he and his valet escaped to Britain.[88]

War gave both Van Koutrik and his German masters new opportunities. Hitherto the passport control organisation run by Major Stevens and the Z organisation under Sigismund Payne Best had been kept entirely separate. On the eve of war, however, as Dansey was preparing to move himself and his headquarters staff to battle stations in France and Switzerland, he ordered Best to join forces with Stevens who would henceforth handle his communications and supply him with funds.[89] Collaboration with the penetrated passport control network inevitably compromised the Z organisation also. The Sicherheitsdienst (SD), the SS Security Service, which had taken control of the infiltration of SIS in the Netherlands from the Abwehr, had now to decide whether to use its penetration to mount a long-term deception passing on bogus intelligence, or to aim for a spectacular short-term victory over SIS. Reinhard Heydrich, the able and ruthless head of the SD, an expert in both dirty tricks and mass persecution, chose the second option.[90] His decision led directly to the capture of both Best and Stevens at the Dutch border town of Venlo on 9 November.

The 'Venlo incident' was one of the most embarrassing episodes in the history of SIS. Though Best and Stevens were quickly used as convenient scapegoats, and the inexperienced Stevens in particular emerges from the affair with little credit, Venlo would scarcely have been possible without serious misjudgments by SIS headquarters and Whitehall as a whole. Best indeed showed greater initial caution than some of his superiors. The bait which eventually lured both him and Stevens to Venlo was first laid by Dr Franz Fischer, an SD informer in the Netherlands operating under cover as a Catholic refugee while he sent Heydrich reports on genuine German refugees. Fischer succeeded in winning the confidence of one of Dansey's main informants, Dr Spieker, the refugee Catholic politician in Paris. Dansey in turn recommended Fischer to Best in the autumn of 1938. Best was suspicious. According to his own later account, his enquiries convinced him that 'some of the people with whom he consorted were certainly wrong-uns'. Dansey insisted that Fischer was 'in a position to obtain information of vital importance through his contacts with airforce officers', but agreed to deal with Fischer through his London headquarters rather than through Best. When Dansey moved to battle-stations abroad on the outbreak of war, Best was pressed to take over as Fischer's case-officer. 'So', wrote Best later, 'I had the damn fellow up to my office and spent a morning interrogating him'. He wrote a report to Dansey reiterating some of his previous suspicions but was assured that 'Dr Spieker knew Fischer well and that he was quite trustworthy': 'I was therefore to continue to use him but, of course, must take every precaution'. Major Hatton-Hall, soon to succeed Menzies as head of the SIS military section, visited The Hague to emphasise the importance of maintaining contact with Fischer.[91]

Fischer claimed to be in contact with a Luftwaffe major named Solms who had important intelligence on a military conspiracy against Hitler which he wished to deliver personally to Best. Hatton-Hall insisted that Solms, who had previously been in contact with Dr Spieker (and was in reality an Abwehr officer named Johannes Traviglio), had always shown himself most reliable.[92] Best met Solms – 'a big, bluff, self-confident fellow, a Bavarian, and inclined to talk as big as he looked' – at a small hotel in Venlo:

> I very soon discovered that he was not nearly as knowledgeable as he pretended, and came to the conclusion that he was little more than an errand boy for more important people in the background. Indeed, he eventually admitted that he could not say much until he had reported to his chief about our meeting ... At our second meeting [at the beginning of October] he impressed me much more favourably; he was calmer, less boastful and seemed to be acting under definite instructions ... He answered one or two questions on technical air force matters which I put to him and, in the end, told me that there was a big conspiracy to remove Hitler from power in which some of the highest ranking army officers were involved. He could give me no details, as the ringleaders would only deal with me direct.[93]

Before they parted, Best gave Solms a code by which the 'ringleaders' of the conspiracy could identify themselves in communications with him. In order to disarm lingering British suspicions, the SD shrewdly decided to display some suspicions of its own. Ironically, the SD hit upon the same stratagem as the author of the Oslo Report. On 6 October Best received via Fischer a coded message that General von Wietersheim, allegedly one of the leading conspirators, wished to meet him in Holland but asking Best to prove his credentials by arranging for a particular news item to be broadcast on the German service of the BBC. The item was duly broadcast twice a few days later.[94]

By now most of Best's doubts about the German dissidents had disappeared.

He believed he 'might be on to quite a big thing' and took Stevens fully into his confidence. 'From that time on', wrote Stevens later, 'we worked together as partners'.[95] Stevens himself had no doubts. The British naval attaché in The Hague, Captain (later Vice-Admiral) B.B. Schofield, in whom Stevens confided, found him 'very wound up about the whole business, but he refuted any suggestion that it might be a trap, so I could do nothing but wish him luck'.[96] Because of the close watch kept by the Dutch on the German frontier and the Germans who crossed it, Best and Stevens took into their confidence the Anglophile chief of Dutch military intelligence, Major General van Oorschot, who assigned one of his officers, Lieutenant Klop, to help smooth arrangements for meetings with the German conspirators. In subsequent dealings with the Germans, Klop, who spoke perfect English, posed as a British officer, Lieutenant Coppens.[97]

On 19 October Best and Stevens received a message via Fischer that General von Wietersheim would be at the small frontier village of Dinxperlo at 10 a.m. next day. In the event the general failed to arrive but sent two alleged emissaries, Captain von Seidlitz and Lieutenant Grosch, whom Fischer claimed to know well. The emissaries explained that the general had been nervous about the problems of crossing the frontier to make contact with the British, and had sent them to spy out the land. They were in reality two junior SD officers, von Salisch and Christensen, sent by the head of the SD counter-espionage section, Walter Schellenberg, who was now directing the operation on the German side. Ironically, in view of the later fate of Best and Stevens, Salisch and Christensen found themselves surrounded by Dutch police while talking to the British at a house in Arnhem. Klop persuaded the police, who rightly suspected German espionage, to depart, and the talks continued.[98] Salisch and Christensen asked what England's peace terms would be. Best replied, 'The status quo prior to Munich'. The 'conspirators' explained their plans to take Hitler prisoner and form a new 'democratic' government. Hitler would initially be the nominal head of the new government to ensure its popular support, but would later be eliminated.[99]

'Quex' Sinclair by now was ill with cancer, but still at work. Cadogan, who had grown rather fond of him, noted sadly on 19 October that he was clearly 'going downhill'. On the 23rd Sinclair brought a report on Best's and Stevens's dealings with the alleged German conspirators. Cadogan was initially suspicious about what he called Sinclair's 'German General friends'. 'I think they are Hitler agents', he confided to his diary. But Cadogan's doubts were not shared by Chamberlain, Halifax and the SIS leadership. Within a few days Cadogan too had concluded that the German conspirators were genuine, and spent much time over the next fortnight drafting and redrafting statements of British peace terms to be used by Best and Stevens.[100] Nor was there any sign of major doubts at SIS headquarters. Colonel Stewart Menzies, Sinclair's deputy and eventual successor, was an enthusiastic supporter of negotiations with the

German 'conspirators'. According to Best, Menzies was reluctant even at the end of the war to believe that the approaches from the German conspirators had been wholly bogus, and told him in 1947:

> I know that mistakes were made but don't you think that possibly there was some truth in Fischer's and Solms' stories and that they were really, like you, victims of circumstance and that the Gestapo only got wind of the affair later?[101]

On 30 October Schellenberg decided to come to meet Best and Stevens himself, posing as 'Major Schaemmel'. He drove across the frontier at Arnhem in a car driven by 'Grosch' and accompanied by his friend Professor Max de Crinis, who took the role of 'Colonel Martini', one of the leading conspirators. Once again the Dutch police were suspicious and the German party was stopped and searched. Klop took the opportunity to go through their belongings and check their papers, found everything in order, then drove the Germans to The Hague where they met Best and Stevens. Though 'Schaemmel' struck Best as having 'a babyish sort of face' covered with duelling scars, he quickly emerged as the spokesman of the group. Hitler, he insisted, 'must be got rid of'. But if he were assassinated, chaos would follow. The plan was therefore to imprison him and force him to authorise a military junta to start peace negotiations. First, however, the conspirators must know whether Britain and France were prepared for 'a peace which is both just and honourable'.[102]

Cadogan felt that this message 'doesn't get us much further', but was anxious to keep the conspirators 'on hook'. 'There's *something* going on in Germany', he concluded. 'That's about all one can say'. He spent an hour with Halifax and Chamberlain on the evening of 31 October drafting a reply to Schaemmel's enquiry. When the prime minister and foreign secretary informed the rest of the war cabinet next day, they found themselves embarrassed both by their previous failure to mention contacts with the conspirators and by the evident distaste of some ministers – Churchill in particular – for any dealings with them. Cadogan found Chamberlain 'frightened' by the strength of cabinet reaction. He tried to persuade Halifax, who was also somewhat shaken, that 'the first impact was bound to be unfavourable and arouse suspicion', and that he should not be deterred by it. Cadogan wearily redrafted – 'for the nth time' – a reply to the conspirators. But Churchill was away till the evening of the 5th and such was the strength of his suspicions that neither Chamberlain nor the war cabinet dared sanction any reply 'without his approval'. Cadogan found this 'awkward' since the conspirators had apparently grown impatient by the 3rd, were asking for an answer and seemed 'to expect "negotiations"'.[103]

The situation was further complicated by a succession struggle in SIS. On 29 October Sinclair had an operation for cancer and the surgeons pronounced his case 'hopeless'. Though Cadogan thought he might still 'go on for some time', Sinclair died on 4 November.[104] Dansey hurried back from Switzerland to challenge Menzies for the succession. Rear-Admiral Godfrey, the DNI, and other outside candidates were also canvassed in Whitehall.[105] At the time of Sinclair's death Cadogan was '*not* satisfied' that his fellow Old Etonian Menzies was the right man to succeed him. But Menzies resolved some of Cadogan's doubts and stole a march over his rivals by producing, on the day following Sinclair's death, a sealed letter from 'Quex' recommending him as his successor.[106]

On the morning of 6 November, while Menzies was struggling to secure the succession to Sinclair, Halifax called on Churchill and obtained his consent to the wording of a reply to the German conspirators. Though the reply was phrased in terms intended to keep the conspirators 'on hook', they were to be told that Hitler must be removed in advance of peace negotiations. Chamberlain was in optimistic mood and seems to have interpreted the German approaches as evidence of growing awareness by the enemy that 'they *can't* win'. 'I have a "hunch"', he wrote on 5 November, 'that the war will be over by the spring'.[107]

Best and Stevens arranged to meet representatives of the conspirators to pass on the British reply at the frontier town of Venlo on 7 November. Since Schaemmel and Grosch, who accompanied him, claimed they could no longer take the risk, after their earlier experiences with the Dutch police, of coming into the centre of Venlo, the meeting was arranged at a café which, though on Dutch soil, was sited between the Dutch and German customs barriers. At the meeting Schaemmel and Grosch declared themselves disappointed with the British reply but said that the general at the head of the conspiracy would meet Best and Stevens next day, bringing secret papers with him. Next day, however, Schaemmel returned to the café to explain that the general had been obliged to attend a staff meeting in Munich. Stevens and Best agreed to return again on the following afternoon. They were unaware that an SS snatch-squad had been waiting to kidnap them on both the 7th and the 8th but had been deterred from moving in by the presence of large numbers of Dutch police and the fear of provoking a battle on the border. On the 9th however, Klop drove to the café with Best and Stevens without waiting for the local police to take up position. By the time the police arrived Best and Stevens had been bundled over the border into Germany. Only Klop had time to open fire but was mortally wounded.[108]

SIS was at first uncertain what had happened to Best and Stevens. First reports suggested both had been 'bumped off'. For a fortnight neither SIS nor the Foreign Office guessed that the 'conspirators' were part of an SD plot. Cadogan speculated that 'the Generals' behind the conspiracy might have succeeded in 'exercising some restraining influence' on Hitler and preventing a German invasion of Holland. Radio messages from the conspirators, making no mention of the Venlo capture, continued to reach SIS. Cadogan noted naively on 15 November: 'The Generals are still alive – and apparently unaware of the frontier incident'. On the 18th he submitted a 'fairly meaningless' message from the conspirators to the prime minister, who took it sufficiently seriously to prepare a draft reply. After a fortnight Schellenberg tired of continuing the charade and radioed a mocking message on the 22nd using the conspirators' callsign to tell SIS it had been duped. 'So that's over,' Cadogan noted in his diary, though he still thought it possible that the conspirators had been genuine at the outset but had been 'taken over' by the Gestapo.[109]

The Germans added to SIS's humiliation by turning the Venlo incident into a propaganda victory as well as an intelligence coup. Best and Stevens were declared to have masterminded an assassination attempt on the Führer by a Communist cabinet maker. When the Germans invaded Holland in May 1940 the support given by Van Oorschot and Dutch Intelligence to SIS in Holland was used as one of the pretexts to justify their aggression. From the German point of view, however, the Venlo incident, though a brilliant tactical victory, was a strategic failure. SIS's slowness in realising that the conspirators were bogus even after the capture of Best and Stevens is evidence of how easily Schellenberg could have inaugurated a long-term system of deception similar to that later so successfully employed by the British against the Germans. Instead, he threw away at Venlo a major intelligence asset for a mere propaganda victory.

The Venlo incident had come at a highly inconvenient moment for Menzies personally. But though it disturbed his campaign to succeed 'Quex' Sinclair, it did not disrupt it. Once back in London, Dansey quickly discovered that he lacked the support to challenge Menzies and threw his weight behind him. Fortified by Sinclair's posthumous support and the vigorous opposition of Major Woollcombe, the Foreign Office representative in SIS, to an outside appointment, Menzies became the Foreign Office candidate. Churchill intervened in the succession struggle, probably to press the claims of Godfrey, the DNI. 'He ought to have enough to do', complained Cadogan, 'without butting into other people's business'. Godfrey was, in any case, reluctant to leave the Admiralty, and after almost a month's lobbying in Whitehall Menzies won the succession battle. Halifax told him of his appointment as chief of SIS on 29 November. Soon afterwards Menzies made Dansey his assistant chief, and the Z organisation was amalgamated with what remained of the PCO network.[110]

While the Germans were planning their remarkable coup at Venlo, MI5 was simultaneously beginning to penetrate the Abwehr with double agents of its own. At the beginning of the war, possibly influenced by his talks with the

French on the use of double agents, Dick White, then working in B division, wrote an influential memorandum arguing that spies captured in England should, if possible, be 'turned round' rather than executed, and used to send false information to the enemy.[111] Though the initial results achieved by MI5 were much more modest than Schellenberg's spectacular deception of SIS, the long-term consequences of that penetration were far more important. Unlike Schellenberg and the SD, MI5 and the other sections of the intelligence community eventually involved in what became known as the 'double-cross system' were content to play a long and patient game for very high stakes indeed. The agent whom MI5 considered the 'fons et origo' of the double-cross system was Arthur Owens (codenamed SNOW), an electrical engineer who emigrated to Canada as a child and had returned to live in London. Early in 1936 he had begun to work part-time for SIS, reporting on his business tours of German shipyards. Later in the year however, MI5 discovered a letter from Owens in a routine check of correspondence addressed to Box 629, Hamburg, a cover address known to be used by the Abwehr. Soon afterwards Owens confessed that he had joined the Abwehr but claimed that he had done so only to penetrate it in the interests of SIS. Though he continued to supply SIS and MI5 with details of some of his dealings with the Abwehr, and on one occasion a radio transmitter supplied by it, he was regarded with understandable suspicion. Colonel 'Tar' Robertson, Owens's MI5 case officer, decided to leave him on a loose rein in the knowledge that if war came he could be arrested under emergency regulations. However much Owens concealed from MI5, it is clear that he also defrauded the Abwehr, claiming to have at least a dozen sub-agents in England whom MI5 concluded probably all 'existed only in SNOW's imagination'.

In August 1939 Owens left for Hamburg together with his mistress (an Englishwoman of German extraction) and a man whom MI5 believed he intended to recruit for the Abwehr. On 4 September, soon after his return to England, he arranged a meeting with a Special Branch inspector at Waterloo Station. To his surprise, he was served with a detention order and taken to Wandsworth Prison. Once in prison, Owens quickly offered 'Tar' Robertson a bargain. In return for his liberty he volunteered to reveal the whereabouts of his wireless transmitter and communicate with the Abwehr under MI5 control. Robertson agreed. Owens's transmitter was installed in his cell and, after some difficulty, he succeeded in sending a cryptic but momentous message to his Abwehr control, Major Ritter, which was to mark the beginning of the 'double-cross system':

> Must meet you in Holland at once. Bring weather code. Radio town and hotel Wales ready.

The 'weather code', Owens explained, was for transmitting the daily weather reports he was expected to send. The reference to Wales related to an assignment given him by the Abwehr to recruit a Welsh nationalist to organise sabotage in South Wales. Later in September Owens met Ritter in Amsterdam and arranged a further meeting in October to which he promised to bring a Welsh saboteur. For this second meeting MI5 provided a reliable Welsh nationalist, Gwilym Williams, a retired Swansea police inspector who posed as an explosives expert and made a favourable impression on the Abwehr. At the very moment when the heads of the SIS organisation in the Netherlands were falling victim to an elaborate German deception plan involving bogus German dissidents, the Germans were thus themselves being deceived – also in the Netherlands – by bogus British traitors sent by MI5.

Owens and Williams returned to England with money, an Abwehr code, microphotographed instructions, detonators hidden in a block of wood, and information on how to contact two other German agents already in Britain. MI5 quickly rounded up both the German agents. The first, Mathilde Kraft, a German woman living near Bournemouth, was sent to Holloway. The second (codenamed CHARLIE by MI5) was a British-born photographer of German parents, who had been pressured into working for the Abwehr by threats to a German relative and was easily turned into a double agent by MI5. The code supplied to Owens and Williams turned out to be extremely valuable in helping GC & CS to discover the basic construction of Abwehr codes which were later regularly broken and assisted the capture of other Abwehr agents.[112] The double-cross system inaugurated by Arthur Owens from a Wandsworth prison cell in September 1939 was eventually to grow into a great system of deception which played a crucial role in the D-day landings. No one at the start of the war, however, could possibly foresee its vast potential. The early achievements of the double-cross system could scarcely compensate in November 1939 for the public humiliation of the Venlo coup.

When Halifax told Menzies of his appointment as Sinclair's successor on 29 November, he raised with him 'the possible need of reviewing [SIS] organisation'. The Foreign Office, however, had still to resolve its own security problems. Cadogan continued to be plagued by the problems of establishing a secure Communications Department.[113] The new year brought further unpleasant revelations of security lapses. In January 1940 Krivitsky came to London to be debriefed by MI5 and SIS on Soviet espionage in Britain. At a meeting with Gladwyn Jebb, then Cadogan's private secretary, Krivitsky claimed that 'a young man in the Foreign Office of good family' was working for the NKVD. With the advantage of hindsight, Lord Gladwyn believes that the NKVD agent referred to may have been Donald Maclean. But at the time Krivitsky's clues were vague and the Foreign Office had no shortage of young diplomats 'of good family'.[114]

Krivitsky's further revelations were, in any case, overshadowed by a report from SIS on 26 January that secret Foreign Office documents had been passed to Germany on the eve of war from the Central Department. Cadogan wrote miserably in his diary: 'I can trust *no-one*'. Though the truth of the SIS report seems never to have been fully resolved, it persuaded Cadogan to take the long overdue step of appointing a chief security officer.[115] But William Codrington, the retired diplomat (and brother of one of Dansey's earliest recruits to the Z organisation) who accepted the new post on 8 February was given neither a salary nor, until 1944, any assistant. Not until after the war did the Foreign Office at last establish a Security Department.[116]

The most serious and continuous intelligence problem during the six months of Phoney War which followed Germany's conquest of Poland in September 1939 was the problem of intelligence assessment which had bedevilled British policy-making during the pre-war crises with Germany. The Joint Intelligence Committee (JIC) which had been charged under its Foreign Office chairman, Victor Cavendish-Bentinck (later Duke of Portland), with 'the assessment and co-ordination of intelligence' as well as the consideration of measures 'to improve the efficient working of the intelligence organisation of the country as a whole', was unable to perform any of these tasks adequately during the Phoney War. Indeed the chiefs of staff did not give it the opportunity to do so. From the day the war began they had the Joint Planning Staff (JPS), but not the JIC, always close at hand in a nearby room during their meetings. For the first six months of the war the JIC was not shown JPS papers before they went to the chiefs of staff. The JIC was neglected even by the three service directors of intelligence: not until February 1940 were all three present at one of its meetings. As well as being neglected, the JIC was also overburdened with the administrative problems of setting up the Middle East Intelligence Centre (MEIC) and the Inter-Service Security Board (ISSB), established in March 1940 to oversee the security and deception aspects of military planning. Lacking any assessment staff of its own, the JIC could do little more than collate intelligence pre-selected for it by the departments who supplied the intelligence. During the Phoney War it was rarely asked for intelligence appreciations more substantial than its daily situation reports. Those that it prepared were unimpressive. When asked in December 1939 to review Germany's probable plans for the spring of 1940, the JIC simply listed a series of options and rather feebly concluded: 'Which of these courses Germany will select will depend less upon logical deduction than upon the personal and unpredictable decision of the Führer'. The response of the JPS was mildly contemptuous. The JIC, it concluded, had failed to reveal anything new about German intentions or to discern the strategic considerations which influenced German planning. The Joint Planners also bemoaned 'the lack of satisfactory intelligence in respect of the German industrial situation since the outbreak of war'. With good intelligence on 'the kind of war material being produced in Germany' and on the output of aircraft and offensive weapons, 'a valuable indication of enemy intentions might be obtained'.[117]

The end of the Phoney War in the spring of 1940 provided further depressing evidence of the deficiencies of intelligence assessment. It was generally believed within both the Admiralty and Whitehall as a whole that Germany lacked the capacity to mount an invasion of Scandinavia. Partly as a result, intelligence which pointed to a German invasion was discounted until it was too late. By 11 March the Foreign Office had received a warning from Forster, the Gauleiter of Danzig, that Hitler was planning an attack on Denmark and Norway. But though Forster struck Cadogan as both 'frank' and 'a gentleman', his warning was disregarded by the Foreign Office and left out of all intelligence assessments.[118] On 14 March the war cabinet cancelled plans for British forces to take control of northern Norway at the very moment when Germany was stepping up its own preparations for an invasion. On 7 April NID signalled to the commander-in-chief of the Home Fleet:

> Recent reports suggest that a German expedition is being prepared. Hitler is reported from Copenhagen to have ordered the unostentatious movement of one division in ten ships by night to land at Narvik with simultaneous occupation of Jutland. Sweden to be left alone. Moderates said to be opposing the plan. Date given for arrival Narvik was 8th April.

The reports were accurate but failed to impress NID. 'All these reports', it warned the C-in-C, 'are of doubtful value and may well be only a further move in the war of nerves'.[119]

The almost total surprise in Whitehall caused by the German invasion of Norway on 9 April was the result both of false assumptions about German military capacity and of a failure to collate intelligence which might have undermined these assumptions. Not merely was there poor coordination between different ministries. There were some remarkable failures of communication even within individual service intelligence departments. In the Admiralty, NID I, which dealt with German intelligence, failed to forward SIS and diplomatic reports of German designs on Scandinavia to the NID Operational Intelligence Centre which was responsible for studying enemy ship and aircraft movements. Things were just as bad in the War Office. MI2, whose responsibilities included Scandinavia, and MI3, which dealt with German intelligence, failed to compare notes or exchange information. MI2 was told about plans for British intervention in Norway but MI3 was not.[120]

The German Blitzkrieg which began on 10 May and overran the Low Countries and France in the space of only six weeks exposed once again the deficiencies both of intelligence assessment and of the use made of it. Field-Marshal Lord Gort, VC, the commander-in-chief of the British Expeditionary

Force (BEF), had a legendary reputation for bravery under fire but no experience of commanding any unit larger than a brigade. Pownall, who became Gort's CGS, found him 'quite splendid' and 'not at all rattled' once the German onslaught began.[121] Though Gort's defiant toughness helped to make possible the escape of most of the BEF from Dunkirk, he had a limited grasp of international politics and not much understanding of intelligence. His able DMI, Major-General Mason-Macfarlane, previously military attaché in Berlin, had 'a strange mixture of respect and contempt' for the commander-in-chief. One of Mason-Macfarlane's officers later recalled an occasion when Gort suddenly thrust his head round his DMI's door:

> 'Bulgarians?' Gort said. 'Good chaps, aren't they?'
> 'No, Sir, not very good', Mason-Mac replied.
> 'Oh! Bad chaps, eh? Pity, pity!' said the Commander-in-Chief, and vanished.
> Mason-Mac said nothing, but turning to me he spread his hands wide in a gesture of resignation.

'Mason-Mac' himself suffered both from a back injury, whose pain he tried to dull with armagnac, and from the after-effects of an accident while pig-sticking in India which may have left him impotent. His staff-officer, Lieutenant-Colonel (later Field-Marshal Sir) Gerald Templer, who was responsible for security and counter-espionage, noticed a fierce temper which Mason-Mac, charming and irascible by turns, had difficulty in keeping under control:

> I spoke to him pretty straight, but I had to watch what I said, because I always thought him quite capable of pulling a knife or a pistol on me.[122]

By the early months of 1940 Mason-Mac had assembled an intelligence staff in France of 80 officers and 120 other ranks. In addition to his intelligence duties proper, he was also responsible for censorship of mail, telegrams and newspapers, for dealing with sixty press correspondents, for handling visiting VIPs from Britain and abroad, and for developing liaison arrangements with the RAF and the French.[123] Mason-Mac's overburdened intelligence branch paid little attention, however, to the morale of their allies. Once the German Blitzkrieg began French demoralisation quickly became obvious. But BEF intelligence and liaison officers were reluctant to appear defeatist by criticising their allies before the battle had even begun. The problems of French morale were emphasised only by Brigadier-General Spears, Churchill's semi-official liaison officer, and by the Duke of Windsor, who was unfavourably impressed by several visits to French armies in the winter of 1939–40.[124] Though somewhat inattentive to French morale, Mason-Mac devised a remarkable scheme in April 1940 to deal with British expatriate defeatists who were going the rounds of Paris cocktail parties calling for a negotiated peace. Mason-Mac glowered over reports of the cocktail party conversations, then told Gerald Templer and his fellow intelligence officer, Ewan Butler:

> Right! I'll tell you what we'll do – just the three of us, myself, you, Gerald, and Ewan here. We'll go down to Paris and kidnap two or three of these charmers. We'll drive them out into the Bois de Boulogne, strip them and let them make their way back into Paris as best they can. At the same time we'll put about a story in the right places explaining why these people have been dealt with in this fashion. Go and work out a plan.

Templer and Butler listened with growing alarm, saluted and went off to 'comply with orders'. Somewhat to their relief, the Blitzkrieg began before Mason-Mac's plan had been acted on.[125]

Though its precise timing was not foreseen, the launching of Hitler's western offensive on 10 May 1940 came as no surprise. Military intelligence had warned repeatedly that 'Germany is in a position to invade Holland and Belgium at the shortest possible notice'. Fragments of plans for a German offensive on a broad front between the North Sea and the Moselle had been captured by the Belgians in January from a German officer who had crash-landed on Belgian territory. Though the Belgians in general held the British and French at arm's length in order to emphasise their neutrality, on this occasion they handed over a rather inadequate précis of the captured documents. The Germans, however, turned the lost documents to their advantage. Deducing that the Allies would be confirmed in their belief that the German objective was the Channel coast of the Low Countries, the Germans changed their plans to direct their main thrust through the Ardennes with the aim of cutting off Allied armies north of the Somme. At the beginning of May, the Allies possessed intelligence which, with the dangerous gift of hindsight, should at least have persuaded them to consider the possibility of an Ardennes offensive. They did not do so. On the British side failure to collate the intelligence available helped the Germans achieve tactical surprise. Abwehr wireless traffic intercepted by MI5's Radio Security Service which concerned the area of the German offensive was either ignored by, or never communicated to, the German section of military intelligence. There is good, but not conclusive, evidence that the Abwehr traitor, Paul Thümmel, warned on 25 March 1940 that the main German thrust in the West would come through the Ardennes, and on 1 May that the offensive would begin on the 10th.[126] That the evidence which pointed to an attack through the Ardennes was so disregarded was due chiefly to the long-held conviction by the French high command, not seriously challenged by the British chiefs of staff, that the

Ardennes were impassable. General Gamelin, the French commander-in-chief, left his weakest armies on the Meuse with no organised reserve behind them in what proved to be the path of the German assault. In only five days' fighting Allied defences were breached beyond repair.[127]

The overstretched intelligence branch of the BEF was overwhelmed with equal speed. Though the intercept stations in France were able to provide substantial intelligence on the progress of the battle from decrypted German tactical signals transmitted either in plain language or low-grade hand ciphers which could be broken on the spot, they could not find time to pass intercepts on to GC & CS. Communications even between the intercept stations and the intelligence staff at GHQ and army headquarters also began to break down as soon as the battle began. The confusion was compounded by Gort's disastrous decision to break up his GHQ intelligence staff. When the German offensive began on 10 May, Gort and Pownall moved to advance headquarters at Wahagnies near Brussels, Mason-Mac and others were stationed in a village some miles distant, while the bulk of the intelligence staff were left fifty miles away at Arras. Inevitably, the intelligence which managed to pass through these lengthy and confused lines of communication was often out of date by the time it reached fighting formations at the battle front. On 18 May the German advance south of the BEF forced GHQ's intelligence staff back to Hazebrouck, and by its own admission 'all effective work' came to an end. Mason-Mac was relieved of his post as DMI and sent to command a scratch force – 'Macforce' – with Templer as his chief of staff to help protect the rear of the BEF. He had, as he later complained, 'no staff, no signals, no nothing, in a sector in which all the roads were blocked by refugees streaming in all directions and with French troops retiring in a state of complete disorder'. Had Mason-Mac remained as DMI, concludes the official historian of the campaign, 'Lord Gort might not so often have been without adequate information'. With the intelligence staffs attached to British formations unable to function during the retreat of the BEF, the task of supplying even tactical intelligence passed from France to London.[128]

At a critical moment in its rearguard action the BEF did, however, receive one intelligence windfall of possibly major importance. On 25 May a patrol captured a German staff car which had ventured too close to the British line, and recovered from it two top secret German documents. The first contained the German 'Order of Battle and Commands' as of 1 May, together with details of army groups, armies, corps and divisions, their commanders and chiefs of staff. According to the official historian of the campaign, military intelligence thus acquired 'for the first time an authoritative picture of the German Army, a grasp of its composition which was never subsequently lost'. The second captured document was even more valuable. It revealed that the German Sixth Army had been ordered to send two corps into a gap between the BEF and the Belgian army left by the Belgian retreat. Without waiting to seek authority from the French commander, Gort ordered into the gap two divisions who were preparing to attack elsewhere. In so doing, concludes the official history, 'he saved the British Expeditionary Force'. Only a few hours later the two British divisions would have arrived too late, the BEF would have been cut off from the Channel, and the Dunkirk evacuation which rescued 338,000 Allied troops would have been impossible.[129]

# 14 | WINSTON CHURCHILL AND THE MAKING OF THE BRITISH INTELLIGENCE COMMUNITY

Winston Churchill took office at the head of a coalition government on the very day, 10 May 1940, that the Phoney War ended and Germany began her Western offensive. Though the next few weeks brought Britain to the brink of military disaster, they also began a remarkable revival in the fortunes of her intelligence community. Churchill had a greater faith in, and fascination for, secret intelligence than any of his predecessors. During his early adventures at the outposts of empire he had acquired a fascination for cloaks and daggers which never left him. While home secretary in 1910–11 he had followed closely the early development of MI5. As first lord of the Admiralty in 1914 he had been personally involved in the founding of Room 40 and the revival of British codebreaking after a gap of seventy years. During the 1920s he attached a higher priority to Soviet intercepts than any other minister. Whilst in the political wilderness during the 1930s his contacts with Desmond Morton and other intelligence officers gave him the ammunition to attack the government's rearmament policy. Churchill returned to office on the outbreak of war wrongly convinced that British intelligence remained 'the finest in the world'. He could not believe that the government's failure to foresee so many of Hitler's actions was really 'the fault of the British Secret Service'. He wondered aloud 'whether there is not some hand which intervenes and filters down or withholds intelligence from Ministers'. As prime minister Churchill was often to insist on seeing 'authentic documents ... in their original form'.[1]

Churchill's faith in the supremacy of British intelligence, sadly deluded during the 1930s, was none the less prophetic. For, by an astonishing coincidence, the most valuable intelligence source in British history began to come on stream less than a fortnight after he became prime minister. On 22 May the codebreakers of GC & CS, now established in their wartime home at Bletchley Park, succeeded in breaking the German air-force version of the Enigma machine cipher. From that date onwards it was able to read current German traffic using the air-force Enigma almost without a break for the remainder of the war.[2] Though Churchill followed a wide range of intelligence activities with close attention, no section of the intelligence community captured his imagination more than Bletchley Park. He called the cryptanalysts 'the geese who laid the golden eggs and never cackled' or simply his 'hens', and arranged for a daily box of enemy intercepts to be sent to him from Broadway Buildings. Sometimes the buff-coloured box was personally delivered by Menzies himself. Churchill alone in Downing Street possessed the key to it which he kept on his personal keyring. Even his private secretaries had no idea what mysterious secrets the box contained. At the prime minister's personal insistence the Whitehall circle who shared the secret of his 'golden eggs' was limited to about thirty of those most closely concerned with the direction of the war, and included only half a dozen of his thirty-five ministers.[3] Within the Foreign Office only Cadogan and Victor Cavendish-Bentinck, the chairman of the JIC, were privy to the secret. Though the Foreign Office was responsible for GC & CS, even Cadogan did not visit Bletchley Park until January 1941. He found it 'a good show' and confessed to his diary that he would like to spend a week there 'so as to try to understand it'.[4] At first, the Enigma decrypts were referred to by the codeword 'Boniface' in order to suggest, if the enemy caught wind of them, that they derived from a secret agent rather than from cryptanalysis. By 1941 they were commonly known to the small circle of initiates as 'Ultra'.[5]

Ultra was an Allied rather than a purely British triumph: the culmination of a decade of intelligence work involving the Poles and the French as well as the British. The first breakthrough was made by Marian Rejewski, a brilliant mathematician from Posnan University who joined the cryptographic service of the Polish general staff in 1932. By studying a commercial version of the Enigma machine cipher and thousands of unsolved German intercepts, Rejewski succeeded in laying the theoretical foundations for the solution of Enigma. But without the assistance of espionage the successful application of that theory could well have taken many years. In December 1932 he received the instructions for operating the German Enigma, four diagrams of the machine's construction, and two tables of the keys used in October and December 1931.[6] Though Rejewski did not know it, the source of these stolen documents was a German traitor, Hans-Thilo Schmidt, in the Reichswehr cipher office. In October 1931 Schmidt had offered his services to French intelligence, who gave him the codename 'Asché' or 'HE'. His motives were purely mercenary. Captain (later General) Gustave Bertrand, head of the codebreaking section of French Intelligence, said cynically: 'He was fond of money; he also needed it because he was fonder still of women'. French cryptanalysts concluded that, despite the information in Schmidt's documents, Enigma remained unbreakable. Bertrand therefore decided to give copies of the documents to Colonel Gwido Langer, head of the Polish cryptographic service, with whom he had close contacts. It was agreed that Bertrand would pass on Schmidt's documents and Langer, in return, would share the results obtained from them. Though Bertrand visited Warsaw nine times between 1931 and 1937 to deliver documents on Enigma, Langer failed to keep his part of the bargain. He did not reveal to Bertrand that as early as January 1933, with the help of the latest batch of Schmidt's documents, Rejewski had succeeded in decrypting a series of Enigma intercepts. After that success Rejewski was joined by two other able cryptanalysts, Jerzy Rozycki and Henry Zygalski. Over the next few years they developed a series of improved code-breaking techniques, including several versions of the 'cryptographic Bombe', an electro-mechanical device for the rapid scanning of tens of thousands of possible Enigma combinations. According to later, but probably reliable, Polish evidence, by early 1938 the Poles were able to decrypt about three-quarters of current Enigma intercepts. The Germans, however, were simultaneously developing more sophisticated versions of the Enigma machine which by the end of 1938 had defeated Rejewski's team of cryptanalysts.[7]

As war grew near, Polish military intelligence decided to share the results achieved by Rejewski's team with both the French and British 'in the hope that working in three groups would facilitate and accelerate the final conquest of Enigma'. On 25 July 1939 a historic meeting of allied cryptographers took place at a secret hide-out in the Pyry forest near Warsaw. Colonel Bertrand and one of his cryptanalysts came from Paris. The British delegation was composed of Alistair Denniston, 'Dilly' Knox, who had been at work on Enigma for some years, and Commander Humphrey Sandwith, head of the Interception Service at the Admiralty.[8] The Poles held nothing back. They revealed their codebreaking methods, their reconstruction of the Enigma, and the 'bombes'.

Not the least important result of the Pyry meeting was psychological – to convince the participants that success was possible. During the Spanish Civil War Knox had broken a simplified version of Enigma used by Franco's forces as well as his Italian and German allies. He also made some progress in analysing German naval Enigma but when the Germans introduced new variations in April 1937 had 'to admit defeat'.[9] Denniston then felt gloomy about the prospects of ever breaking Enigma. 'Quex' Sinclair was gloomier still. The lack of German intercepts during the Munich crisis led him to doubt whether the volume of German traffic in wartime would be sufficient even to break hand ciphers. He wrote in October 1938:

> The recent crisis appears to have shown that as soon as matters become serious, wireless silence is enforced, and that therefore this organisation of ours is useless for the purpose for which it was intended.[10]

Despite the revelation of the Polish successes at the secret meeting in the Pyry forest, many at GC & CS remained pessimistic about the solution of Enigma. Frank Birch, who became head of the naval section at Bletchley

Park, encountered a widespread belief at GC & CS when war broke out that '*all* German codes were unbreakable': 'I was told it wasn't *worthwhile* putting pundits on to them'. He wrote to Denniston at the end of 1940: 'Defeatism at the beginning of the war, to my mind, played a large part in delaying the breaking of codes'.[11] But not everyone at GC & CS was defeatist. The achievements of Rejewski's team gave some of the younger cryptographers as well as the ailing 'Dilly' Knox new hope.

In August 1939 the Poles sent two of their reconstructions of the Enigma machine to Paris. On the 16th Bertrand crossed the Channel to deliver one in person, accompanied by 'Uncle' Tom Greene, the deputy head of the SIS Paris station, and was welcomed at Victoria Station by Stewart Menzies, wearing the rosette of the Légion d'Honneur in his buttonhole. When Poland was overrun in the following month Rejewski and his colleagues fled first to Bucharest, where they tried unsuccessfully to attract the interest of the British embassy, and then to France, where they joined forces with Bertrand's team of cryptologists at a secret address codenamed 'Bruno', fifteen miles east of Paris. GC & CS, meanwhile, as well as developing an improved version of the bombe, used the information supplied by the Poles in July to improve a manual sorting system based on large numbers of sheets with punched holes. In mid-December a British emissary visited Bruno to deliver one set of the sheets. He returned in great excitement at the turn of the year with the news that Bruno had broken the German army Enigma key for 28 October on the sheets he had taken with him. For the next six months until Bertrand's cryptologists dispersed after the Fall of France, GC & CS and Bruno worked in close collaboration. But, thanks to its growing advantage in manpower and resources, the initiative passed increasingly to GC & CS at its wartime home in Bletchley Park. On 22 May, twelve days after Churchill became prime minister, thanks both to new methods of cryptanalysis and to a much improved bombe, Bletchley began to decrypt regularly the Luftwaffe version of Enigma. It did so currently, or nearly currently, for the remainder of the war. A year later, in the spring of 1941, it mastered the naval Enigma. In the spring of 1942 it conquered the army Enigma. In addition it solved a whole series of hand ciphers, some of which provided 'cribs' which helped in the rapid solution of the daily change in settings of the Enigma machines.[12]

Without the expertise painstakingly built up at GC & CS on minimal resources by Denniston between the wars, Bletchley Park's wartime triumphs would have been impossible. But equally the enormous problems posed by the solution of Enigma would have been too much for the diminutive interwar cryptographic unit in Broadway Buildings. The 'Most Secret Ultra' – later 'Top Secret Ultra' – intelligence obtained from the Enigma decrypts was made possible only by a major new intelligence recruitment.[13]

That recruitment had begun two years before the outbreak of war. In 1937 Sinclair told Denniston that he was now 'convinced of the inevitability of war' and 'gave instructions for the earmarking of the right type of recruit to reinforce GC & CS *immediately* on the outbreak of war'. Treasury approval was gained for an additional wartime establishment of 86: '56 seniors, men or women, with the right background and training (salary £600 a year) and 30 girls with a graduate's knowledge of at least two of the languages required (£3 a week)'. Denniston quickly ran into difficulty as he began recruiting in the universities:

> It was naturally at that time impossible to give details of the work, nor was it always advisable to insist too much in these circles on the imminence of war. At certain universities, however, there were men now in senior positions who had worked in our ranks during 1914–18. These men knew the type required.[14]

The most active recruiter among those former members of Room 40 who 'knew the type required' was Frank Adcock, now Professor of Ancient History at Cambridge. Adcock went about his work with great enthusiasm and even greater secrecy. Among those recruited to Bletchley Park by Adcock and his former King's colleague, Frank Birch (who had left Cambridge for the theatre), were ten other Fellows of King's. Probably Adcock's first recruit, however, was a Fellow of Corpus Christi, E.R.P. 'Vinca' Vincent, the forty-three-year-old professor of Italian who had perfected his German while interned in Germany during the First World War. Vincent later recalled an invitation to dinner with Adcock in the spring of 1937:

> We dined very well, for he was something of an epicure, and the meal was very suitably concluded with a bottle of 1920 port. It was then that he did something which seemed to me most extraordinary; he went quickly to the door, looked outside and came back to his seat. As a reader of spy fiction I recognised the procedure, but I never expected to witness it. He then told me that he was authorised to offer me a post in an organisation working under the Foreign Office, but which was so secret he couldn't tell me anything about it. I thought that if that was the case he need not have been so cautious about eavesdropping, but I didn't say so. He told me war with Germany was inevitable and that it would be an advantage for one of my qualifications to prepare to have something useful to do.

Soon afterwards Vincent was summoned by telephone to Broadway Buildings. He returned at intervals over the next two years to practise work on some of the cryptographic problems which he was expected to encounter when war came. Though he found little of his training much use in wartime, he 'picked up the jargon and got to know some of the people'.[15]

GC & CS also arranged several short courses designed to give potential wartime recruits 'a dim idea of what would be required of them'. Thus partially enlightened, the recruits were able to 'earmark, if only mentally, further suitable candidates'.[16] Following the traditions of Room 40, the pre-war university recruiting drive was centred on arts faculties. It was not until late 1938 that GC & CS, probably prompted by the problems posed by Enigma, set out to recruit its first mathematician. The new recruit, Peter Twinn, who had graduated from Oxford a few months earlier, was told after his recruitment:

> that there had been some doubts about the wisdom of recruiting a mathematician as they were regarded as strange fellows notoriously unpractical. It had been discussed whether, if some scientific training were regretfully to be accepted as an unavoidable necessity, it might not be better to look for a physicist on the grounds that they might be expected to have at least some appreciation of the real world.

Twinn's postgraduate work in physics since his graduation may have lessened apprehension in GC & CS at the prospect of recruiting a mathematician. In the event he found his new job 'fascinating' and his colleagues congenial.[17]

Though the first wave of what Denniston called the 'professor types' who arrived at Bletchley Park on the outbreak of war was composed mainly of linguists, classicists and historians, it also included two brilliant Cambridge mathematicians: Alan Turing of King's and Gordon Welchman of Sidney Sussex College. During the first year of the war it was Turing and Welchman, building on the earlier work of the Poles and the French, who made the crucial breakthroughs in the solution of Enigma. Turing and Welchman may have been recruited, however, less because of their distinction as mathematicians than because of their skill at chess. 'Someone', wrote Vincent later, 'had had the excellent idea that of all people who might be good at an art that needs the patient consideration of endless permutations, chess-players filled the bill'. Among other chess players who arrived at Bletchley Park in the winter of 1939–40 were Dennis Babbage, Stuart Milner-Barry and Hugh Alexander. The mathematicians at Bletchley Park so quickly established themselves as indispensable, however, that during the first weeks of the war the recruiting drive was extended to mathematicians without a reputation for chess.[18]

The 'emergency list' prepared by GC & CS before the war included clever undergraduates (again mostly from arts faculties) as well as more senior 'professor types'. Towards the end of the Easter (summer) term 1939 Denniston wrote to the heads of about ten Cambridge and Oxford Colleges, asking to interview about half a dozen of the ablest men in each for war work. Harry Hinsley (later the official historian of British wartime intelligence) was then not yet twenty-one, at the end of his second year at St John's College, and had just taken first-class honours in Part I of the Cambridge Historical Tripos. He remembers being interviewed at 10.45 a.m. one morning in St John's by Denniston, Colonel (later Brigadier) J.H. Tiltman (head of the military section at GC & CS), and 'one other shadowy figure' whose identity he can no longer recall:

> The kind of questions they asked me were: 'You've travelled a bit, we understand. You've done quite well in your Tripos. What do you think of government service? Would you rather have that than be conscripted? Does it appeal to you?'

The only government service mentioned, however, was the Foreign Office. Hinsley was one of about twenty Oxbridge undergraduates earmarked in this way for wartime work at Bletchley Park. Unlike the 'professor types' they were given no inkling of the secret world which awaited them. Not until Hinsley arrived at Bletchley Park did he discover even the existence of the organisation which had recruited him several months before.[19]

GC & CS lacked the administrative expertise to cope adequately with its fourfold expansion in the first sixteen months of the war. By the beginning of 1941 it was, by Whitehall standards, poorly organised. But the very amateurism of the early Bletchley Park was central to its success in at least two ways. The belief of Denniston, Tiltman and others in the ability of the highly intelligent and well-educated to grapple successfully even in their late teens with unfamiliar problems of great complexity enabled GC & CS to assemble with great speed perhaps the ablest team of cryptographers and intelligence analysts in British history. A more 'professional' service or civil service department would have been unlikely to show quite such faith in such raw recruits. When Winston Churchill arrived to inspect Bletchley Park as prime minister, he is said to have told Denniston: 'I told you to leave no stone unturned to get staff, but I had no idea you had taken me literally'. BP's informality meant that it was able to exploit the talents of unconventional and eccentric personalities who would have found it difficult to conform to military discipline or civil service routines. Alan Turing, possibly Bletchley's most gifted code-breaker, is a case in point. He kept his coffee mug chained to a radiator to prevent theft, sometimes cycled to work wearing a gas mask to guard against pollen, changed his life savings into silver ingots and buried them in the Bletchley Woods. Sadly, he failed to find them when the war was over. Bletchley's early amateurism and tolerance of eccentricity was crucial to the creative anarchy of its working methods which took little account of rank and hierarchy. Ignoring bureaucratic demarcation lines, the staff of GC & CS had begun by early 1941 to move on from their interwar roles as cryptanalysts and translators to offer intelligence appreciations as well.[20]

The brilliantly successful recruiting drive to Bletchley Park was only one part of the last-minute mobilisation by all sections of the intelligence community on the eve of, and at the beginning of, the Second World War. The service intelligence departments, however, were slower off the mark than GC & CS. When the able, highly strung Captain John Godfrey became DNI in January 1939 he found the intelligence cupboard 'distressingly bare'. NID contained only fifty men and women, insufficient even for its peacetime duties. Within three years it was to grow to over a thousand. Among the first to offer Godfrey help was his First World War predecessor, 'Blinker' Hall, and Godfrey felt he could 'do no better than follow [Hall's] example' in looking for new recruits. Like Hall, who had chosen the stockbroker Claud Serocold to assist him, Godfrey decided to select a personal assistant from the City. Sir Montague Norman, the Governor of the Bank of England, Lionel and Anthony de Rothschild, Olaf Hambro and Sir Edward Peacock were all '100% cooperative' in helping Godfrey 'find staff and make useful contacts'. Norman and Peacock together found Godfrey his personal assistant and chief intelligence planner, the maverick stockbroker Ian Fleming – recruited, appropriately, over an epicurean lunch at the Carlton Grill. By mid-summer 1939 Fleming and about twenty other civilians were ready to join NID when, as Godfrey put it, 'the balloon went up'. As well as the civilians, Godfrey recruited several naval veterans of Room 40: among them Jock Clayton (later Rear-Admiral) who was called from retirement to head the Operational Intelligence Centre (OIC) which monitored the naval movements of potential enemies, and Paymaster Captain Thring who was put in charge of the OIC's U-boat tracking room.[21]

Godfrey gradually reached the heretical conclusion that 'In intelligence operations we should rely more on the civilian than on the regular navy officer'. By 1941 the U-boat tracking room, arguably the most vital section of naval intelligence, was wholly staffed by civilians and headed by the future judge, Rodger Winn. As at Bletchley Park, the relative informality of NID, which failed to observe the traditional rigours of naval hierarchy and discipline, was one of the secrets of its success. Godfrey himself described the atmosphere in Room 39, NID's coordinating section, as rather 'like that of a commune'. It became so noisy that he had a green baize door installed between Room 39 and his own office:

As far as I know it never had a head, nor would a "head", in the way that the word is usually accepted in the service, have been tolerated ... "Room 39" consisted at one time of two stockbrokers, a schoolmaster, a K.C. relieved by a most eminent barrister, a journalist, a collector of books on original thought, an Oxford classical don, a barrister's clerk, an insurance agent, two regular naval officers, an artist, two women civilian officers, and several women assistants and typists. Ian [Fleming] had a brainwave and some other specimen arrived for trial and if he did not suit was mysteriously spirited away.[22]

But neither NID as a whole nor the OIC was an instant wartime success. NID was able to provide little help with current operations during the Phoney War. The OIC gave no warning of early attacks by German warships or U-boats. Not until German radio revealed that a U-boat was responsible for the sinking of the *Royal Oak* in Scapa Flow in October 1939 did NID discover how it had happened. Even then an Admiralty Board of Enquiry refused to believe that the attack route used by the U-boat was possible. Gradually, however, greater experience and the priceless Ultra intelligence on German naval movements turned the OIC into the nerve centre of the Admiralty and gave it a crucial role in winning the war against the U-boats.[23]

The intelligence cupboard in the War Office at the beginning of 1939 was as bare as that in the Admiralty. Most army officers shunned intelligence appointments as a threat to their promotion prospects. It was vaguely hoped before Munich that regular officers already qualified as interpreters or receiving language training would be sufficient to meet wartime intelligence staff needs for both the War Office and service overseas. Ten-day courses were held yearly in Commands to equip young regimental officers for intelligence duties at brigade and battalion level, but they were later acknowledged to have been 'of a low standard'. Plans for reviving the Intelligence Corps when war broke out lay almost forgotten in War Office files until September 1938. 'Military complacency', according to an Intelligence Corps historian, 'was not really shaken until the Munich crisis'. Immediately after the crisis the War Office began a search for new intelligence recruits. During the next few months several hundred linguists and other specialists from the newly-formed Army Officers Emergency Reserve (AOER) were summoned for interview.[24]

The War Office, however, was still prepared to devote only the most niggardly resources to the training of wartime intelligence officers. In March 1939 Brigadier Martin, the deputy DMI, summoned the joint managing director of Fortnum and Mason, Eric Shearer, and surprised him with the news that he had been chosen, in the event of war with Germany, to become Commandant at Minley Manor near Camberley, which was to be the School for Intelligence Training for the whole army. Shearer was an ex-Indian army officer who had served for several years in MID during the 1920s and had left the War Office for a business career in 1929. 'Stifling back any sign of surprise' at the news of his appointment, he insisted on beginning a preparatory intelligence course in London immediately in order to 'brush up' his own 'military education', train the wartime staff of Minley Manor, and prepare at least fifty 'high-grade men' for intelligence staff appointments immediately on the outbreak of war. The War Office agreed, seconded Lieutenant-Colonel Gerald Templer to assist him, arranged for Shearer to use the Royal United

Service Institution for his intelligence course three evenings a week, and gave him a bus for weekend exercises. But Shearer was given no peacetime salary and was expected to pay most of his own expenses, even though he worked until the early hours of most mornings at his Bruton Street flat devising an intelligence training course. To assist him he persuaded three other ex-officer friends to train as instructors; the War Office found two more. All, however, had less experience than Shearer and were only able to work part-time. Shearer himself resigned as chief executive at Fortnum and Mason, and was given an undemanding 'cover' job by his friend Edward Molyneux, the London couturier and veteran of Room 40.[25]

As a result of Shearer's efforts sixty of his trainees were ready for appointment as intelligence staff officers when the war began. Fifteen French linguists had also been trained by the former First World War intelligence officer, Sir Edward Spears M.P., for liaison duties with the French. Thanks to the last-minute courses improvised by Shearer and Spears, 'mobilisation of the Intelligence Staff was just, but only just, achieved' in September 1939. So fine was the margin that when Mason-Macfarlane, as DMI of the BEF, was granted four additional intelligence officers during the first week of mobilisation, only three could be found. A telegram was sent to a member of the AOER asking if he would fill the fourth vacancy. He reported to the War Office the same evening, obtained a uniform from Moss Bros., and joined Mason-Macfarlane next day.[26]

On 3 September 1939 Shearer and his instructors assembled on the pavement outside White's Club in St James's Street, dressed in khaki tunics and riding breeches; Shearer later explained the breeches by saying that he was 'still, at heart, a cavalryman'. They then set off in two cars for Minley Manor to start the first of the wartime courses on military intelligence. 'Neglected in peace time', wrote Shearer later, 'the demand for officers trained in Intelligence duties was now overwhelming'. His staff worked flat out running five-week courses for fifty officers at a time, with barely a breathing space between courses. Shearer himself was promoted as DMI at GHQ Cairo in January 1940 and succeeded by Colonel K.V. Barker-Benfield.[27] During the six months after his departure the School of Military Intelligence moved to new quarters first near Aldeburgh, then in Swanage.[28]

Despite the heavy demands on it, the School's resources were meagre. In October 1939 Major (later Brigadier) T. Robbins, one of the graduates of the first course at Minley, was made instructor on the German Army and POW interrogation. Finding no material on the German Army available from the War Office, and the Staff College library both 'scanty and out of date', he resorted to direct action. Early in 1940 he visited Brussels, wearing a bowler hat and carrying the tightly-rolled umbrella he had used in the City between the wars as civilian disguise in order not to offend the neutral Belgians, then combed the bookshops for military text books in German which were sent back to England by diplomatic bag. Plans for a tour of Dutch bookshops in May were, however, wrecked by the German invasion. Not until June did Robbins receive authorisation to open an Interrogation Wing in the School of Military Intelligence:

> It had taken many months of representation to the War Office, the overcoming of every form of irrelevant objection, to convince our superiors that immediate interrogation of prisoners of war and examination of the documents, letters etc. found on them would provide a reliable source of tactical information.

Since the War Office possessed no manual on interrogation or document examination, Robbins had to base his course on what he remembered of his experience as intelligence officer on the Western Front during the last two years of the First World War.[29]

In an attempt to bring some order into recruitment of intelligence officers, a special subsection, MI1x, was set up at the War Office on the outbreak of war to deal with selection, training and posting. It inherited a pre-war list prepared by MID of 400 possible intelligence recruits, most of whom turned out to be dead, abroad or otherwise unavailable. MI1x rapidly established its own up-to-date card index of linguists and other specialists thought to be suitable for intelligence work, and found itself supplying recruits not merely to military intelligence but also to SIS, MI5, and later to SOE.[30]

The Intelligence Corps itself was not formally re-established until 15 July 1940 after prolonged lobbying by Major (later Brigadier) Jeffries of MI1x. Despite the support of the DMI, General Beaumont-Nesbitt, Jeffries was unable for several months to find a suitable headquarters and training ground. He 'persisted to the point of being a nuisance':

> The D.M.I. then took me to the Secretary of State and I was finally told that no official action or billeting orders could be given, but that if I liked to take private action myself I could do so provided I involved no-one officially. I went back to my room in the War Office, where I worked with a G.S.O.3, Capt. (now Lieut-Col.) Sir John Russell. He was well known at Oxford, a live wire, and a former President of the Union. I told him to go to Oxford, use any means he possibly could and not come back until he had a college for the newly founded Corps. He went off at once and returned five days later with two colleges in his hand. Oriel for the Staff H.Q. for all officers in the Corps, and all training, living quarters and messing. Pembroke for the Commandant (not yet appointed) and his office.

Jeffries was promoted colonel and appointed commandant of the Intelligence

Corps founded largely through his own initiative.[31] The high proportion of new recruits to the Corps and the small leaven of regular officers caused some early problems in the field. There were frequent complaints about intelligence officers' lack of military knowledge coupled with what one Intelligence Corps historian euphemistically calls 'allusions to long haired intellectuals'. Toleration increased as it was recognised that, in the words of the same historian, 'men of this type will be present in fairly large numbers in the Intelligence organisation in war, for they are the kind that study languages and other subjects of Intelligence interest and travel extensively'.[32]

MI5 also had a substantial infusion of intellectuals (not usually long haired). Some were provided by MI1x and the Intelligence Corps, but most were recruited direct. Unlike GC & CS, however, MI5 had failed to prepare for its wartime expansion by earmarking potential recruits and providing some preliminary training. Its wartime expansion, which began in earnest only in 1940, was thus highly improvised. Outside Whitehall, its main contacts were with the law. Its wartime recruits included six future judges – Patrick Barry, Edward Cussen, Helenus 'Buster' Milmo, Henry 'Toby' Pilcher, Blanshard Stamp, and John Stephenson – and a series of other able barristers and solicitors. Among the solicitors was Martin Furnival Jones, later director-general of MI5 from 1967 to 1972. MI5's academic contacts (mostly in Oxford) provided such distinguished recruits as Herbert Hart (later Oxford professor of jurisprudence and principal of Brasenose College), Christopher Cheney (later Cambridge professor of medieval history), J.C. Masterman (later provost of Worcester College and vice-chancellor of Oxford University), Victor (later Lord) Rothschild, and Anthony Blunt (later Keeper of the Queen's Pictures). One of the distinguished lawyers who joined MI5 in 1940 later commented that the calibre of the wartime recruits was, on average, 'too high'. In retrospect Dick White agreed. 'In the national interest', he told Masterman, 'I think that we appropriated too much talent. The demand for men of ability in other departments was enormous and perhaps we were a bit greedy'.[33]

The new recruits were generally unimpressed by MI5's top leadership at the beginning of the war. Kell was sixty-seven in 1939, had been in office for thirty years, and was in failing health. Sir Eric Holt-Wilson, who had been Kell's deputy since 1917, appeared stuffy and uninspiring. 'Jasper' Harker, the director of B division, struck one – and perhaps most – of the new recruits as 'the lightest of lightweights [who] sought to compensate by a synthetic assurance what he lacked in natural authority'.[34] The second rank of MI5 leadership contained men of much greater ability. Three in particular impressed the new recruits. Guy Liddell, who succeeded Harker as director of B division in June 1940, was a man of broad culture as well as high professional skill. He had been deserted by his aristocratic wife Calypso who had taken their children to the United States. As a result he was left vulnerable in his private life and was incautious in his wartime friendships with, among others, Guy Burgess. But his personal vulnerability seems not to have impaired either his professional skill or his standards of discretion.[35] Liddell's deputy, Dick White, had already established a reputation as the highest flier among the younger professionals within MI5. The third MI5 professional who particularly impressed the new recruits was 'Tar' Robertson, head of the double agents subsection B1(a). J.C. Masterman, who served under him, found him 'in no sense an intellectual' but 'a born leader gifted with independent judgment' and 'extraordinary flair': 'Time and again he would prove to be right in his judgements when others, following their intellectual assessments, proved to be wrong'.[36]

But the sheer speed of MI5's wartime expansion, though it provided both a large number of able recruits and rapidly produced a successful blend of amateur and professional, carried one potentially grave disadvantage. With the personnel and resources available it was probably impossible to vet thoroughly all the new recruits. Even the vetting that was possible, however, was not always completed. Early in the war, for example, Harker asked a young Oxford graduate in the Home Office, Jenifer Fischer Williams (who married Herbert Hart in 1941), to recommend the names of suitable recruits to MI5. Harker was unaware that Miss Fischer Williams had been a secret member of the CPGB until less than a year before and that the NKVD had tried to recruit her as a Soviet mole.[37] Though the NKVD approach failed, Harker's action provides a graphic illustration of the risks taken during MI5's rapid wartime expansion. In the case of Anthony Blunt, evidence of his past Communist associations was actually available to MI5. But so far removed did the cultivated, slightly snobbish Blunt appear to be from the Communists kept under surveillance before the war that the evidence was not rigorously examined. Having been expelled from the Minley Manor training course in the autumn of 1939 when evidence emerged of his past Communist associations, Blunt remarkably succeeded in talking his way back into military intelligence and thence, a few months later, into MI5.[38]

At a time when the overwhelming priority both of the Security Service and the nation as a whole was defence against the threat of a German invasion it is perhaps unreasonable to expect MI5 to have been fully alert also to the threat of Soviet subversion. The rapid expansion of MI5, though providing an opening to at least one Russian mole, triumphantly achieved its primary object of equipping MI5 for the war with Germany. Like GC & CS and OIC, MI5 owed much of its wartime success to its comparative freedom from both bureaucratic routine and military hierarchy. Masterman was later to write nostalgically in his memoirs:

In joining M.I.5 I became one of a team, a team of congenial people who worked together harmoniously and unselfishly, and amongst whom rank counted for little and character for much.[39]

SIS never succeeded in generating quite the same wartime atmosphere. The published reminiscences of wartime recruits betray few signs of the affectionate respect felt by Masterman for the pre-war professionals of MI5's B Division. The hallowed rituals of SIS – the green light bulb outside C's room, the special green ink reserved to him alone, the ubiquitous use of sometimes pointless codenames – struck some of the newcomers as richly comic. When Malcolm Muggeridge and Graham Greene, among others, were given training on secret inks which included instructions on obtaining the raw material for an ink codenamed BS (birdshit), their reactions were sometimes understandably satirical.[40] The recollections of Hugh Trevor-Roper (now Lord Dacre) are more caustic. He considered the established hierarchy as 'of very limited intelligence' and the professionals 'by and large pretty stupid – and some of them very stupid'. Within the ranks of the professionals he observed tensions between two groups:

There were the metropolitan young gentlemen whose education had been expensive rather than profound and who were recruited at the bars of White's and Boodle's by Colonel Dansey, and there were the ex-Indian policemen who were recruited, through the Central Intelligence Bureau in New Delhi, by Colonel Vivian. The former ran the espionage, the latter the counter-espionage. Neither class had much use for ideas. The former had seldom heard of them ...; the latter regarded them as subversive.

The rivalries between those responsible for espionage and the growing counter-espionage department (Section V) were made worse by the bitter personal animosity between Dansey and Vivian. Dansey had stolen an early march over his rival by becoming Menzies's assistant chief (ACSS) soon after the new C took over. But as counter-espionage and the double-cross system expanded, Vivian gained revenge by acquiring the ambiguous title of deputy chief early in 1941, thereafter signing his new initials (DCSS) in a distinctive shade of red ink.[41]

Tensions within SIS between pre-war professionals and wartime amateurs were much more acute than in MI5. According to Lord Dacre:

The amateurs regarded the Service as existing to help win the war. It was this need alone which had brought them into it, and naturally they did not look beyond that immediate aim. Consequently, they were impatient of the mandarins with their complacent airs and their sacred 'procedure'. The professionals, on the other hand, preened themselves on their 'long-term views'. They looked beyond the war. Indeed, it seemed to us, they sometimes regarded the war as a dangerous interruption of the Service; and they sighed for the time when they would get rid of those irreverent amateurs with their disruptive 'short-term' views, their carelessness of the delicate health of a venerable system.

Lord Dacre's judgement on the pre-war professionals, though not charitable, is understandable in the light of his own experiences. His own 'irreverent thoughts and dangerous contacts' led to him being 'secretly denounced as being probably in touch with the Germans'. He was subjected to a secret 'trial' at which Colonel Vivian called for his dismissal. Menzies, who acted as judge, found in favour of the defendant but, in Lord Dacre's words, 'It was a narrow squeak'.[42]

Unlike Trevor-Roper, Muggeridge and Graham Greene, one of the wartime recruits went out of his way to curry favour with the SIS professionals. That recruit was a Soviet double agent. Kim Philby saw in the wartime tension between amateurs and professionals a remarkable opportunity to worm his way to the top of SIS. He almost succeeded. Philby was the only new recruit decorated for his wartime work. He was, in Trevor-Roper's view, being groomed as a future C.[43]

Lord Dacre's overall judgment on the wartime SIS is probably too harsh. Later in the war its agents were to gain important intelligence about both V rocket development at Peenemünde and heavy water plants in Norway. But there is little doubt that its wartime leadership was not of the calibre of some of the senior professionals in MI5 and GC & CS. Menzies was fortunate that his position as head of SIS also gave him overall responsibility for Bletchley Park. He sometimes delivered the most important decrypts to the prime minister personally and accompanied those privy to the 'Ultra secret' on visits to GC & CS where he was able to bask in its reflected glory. When Bletchley Park's three leading codebreakers, Turing, Welchman and Alexander, were summoned to the Foreign Office in July 1941 to be congratulated on their achievements and rewarded with £200 apiece, they were presented by Menzies and introduced as his 'Brains Trust'.[44]

While GC & CS expanded greatly in size and even more in influence, SIS operations actually contracted during the first eighteen months of the war. The closure of its Berlin and Vienna stations on the outbreak of war was followed a month later by the demise of the Warsaw station after the German conquest of Poland. During the Russo-Finnish 'Winter War' of 1939–40 the Helsinki and Baltic stations were forced to take refuge in Stockholm. The German Blitzkrieg victories in the spring and early summer of 1940 and the Italian entry into the war in June deprived SIS of its stations in Oslo, Copenhagen, Paris, Rome, Brussels and The Hague. By the spring of 1941 all the Balkan stations had been forced to retreat to Istanbul. Within Europe

SIS was thus thrown back on the neutral capitals of Madrid, Lisbon, Berne and Stockholm. But in Madrid SIS operations were at first severely restricted by the insistence of the British ambassador, Sir Samuel Hoare, a former MI1c station chief, that nothing be done to offend Franco and encourage him to join forces with Hitler. Hoare was, however, content for his naval attaché, Commander Alan Hillgarth, working in cooperation with SIS, to bribe some of Franco's generals to encourage them to remain neutral. Cadogan thought Hillgarth 'rather a charlatan but, like Sam [Hoare], rather an effective one'.[45]

The loss of the SIS stations and agent networks over most of Europe was partly compensated by liaison with the intelligence services from occupied countries which moved their headquarters to London. After the Fall of France it was this liaison which gave SIS most of its intelligence from occupied Europe. Czech intelligence, the first to move its headquarters to London, also provided SIS with its best source during the early years of the war, the senior Abwehr officer, Paul Thümmel. Though Thümmel's warnings of an impending German thrust through the Ardennes in the spring of 1940 attracted little attention, much greater attention was paid to intelligence supplied by him in the second half of 1940 on plans for, and the postponement of, Operation Sealion, the German invasion of Britain. On 29 September Thümmel also correctly predicted the German entry into Rumania early in October. In December he began supplying information about German plans for the invasion of Yugoslavia and Greece in the spring of 1941. Czech writers have claimed that late in March 1941 Thümmel gave detailed information on Operation Barbarossa, the German invasion of Russia originally planned for 15 May and finally launched on 22 June. His warnings may, however, have been later and less precise than since suggested by the Czechs. On the debit side Thümmel also provided reports on German plans for attacks on Spain and Turkey which proved to be misleading. But his record as an Allied agent during the first two years of the war remains a remarkable one.[46]

SIS also established a good working relationship with Polish intelligence HQ which had decamped first to Paris and then to London, and maintained wireless contact with a substantial network of agents in occupied Poland and smaller networks elsewhere. The Polish government in exile agreed to give SIS all the intelligence it received save that solely concerned with Polish internal affairs. Among the intelligence supplied by the Poles was a series of reports on German preparations for Operation Barbarossa though the significance of these reports, as of similar reports from other sources, was not at first appreciated.[47]

The Poles and Czechs were the only exiled intelligence services allowed full autonomy in dealing with their agent networks. SIS insisted on controlling the communications, logistics and funds of all other Allied intelligence headquarters in London. With the Norwegians Menzies succeeded in establishing a reasonably harmonious working relationship. The SIS liaison officer, Commander Eric Welch, was married to a Norwegian, had worked in Norway before the war, and had the local knowledge required to win the confidence of both the Norwegian military intelligence staff in Britain and the Milorg resistance group in Norway.[48]

Dealings between SIS and other exiled intelligence services were far more fraught. Relations with the Dutch had already been soured by the Venlo débâcle and by the evidence it provided of Anglo-Dutch intelligence collusion which was exploited by the Germans in an attempt to justify their invasion in May 1940. They suffered further serious damage when the first joint SIS-Dutch operation organised from London ended in disaster in October 1940 with the German capture of its Dutch leader and several members of the Dutch Resistance.[49]

Relations with the French posed even greater problems. In the summer of 1940 SIS suddenly found itself confronted with two Frances: de Gaulle and the Free French continuing the fight from London, and the Vichy régime of Marshal Pétain which had signed an armistice with Germany but with which the Foreign Office was reluctant to lose all contact. SIS responded by establishing two separate French sections: one under Commander 'Biffy' Dunderdale, formerly station chief in Paris, to liaise with the Free French; the other under Commander Kenneth Cohen, formerly of the Z organisation, to revive intelligence contacts with Vichy. There followed an inevitable series of demarcation disputes between the two.[50]

De Gaulle bitterly resented SIS's restrictions on the autonomy of his own intelligence organisation and its ability to run operations of its own on French territory. Both SIS and MI5, for their part, were appalled by de Gaulle's repeated and sometimes elementary breaches of security. During preparations for the Anglo-Free French Dakar expedition in the autumn of 1940, MI5 reported that while purchasing his tropical wardrobe at Simpson's in Piccadilly, de Gaulle had explained quite openly that he was leaving for West Africa. At dinner in a Liverpool restaurant Free French officers also drank to the toast 'Dakar'.[51] Despite British complaints, de Gaulle's attention to security continued to be intermittently lackadaisical. Early in 1941 Menzies warned Brigadier-General Sir Edward Spears, liaison officer with the Free French, that de Gaulle had mentioned the dates of another African trip in a 'phone call to the United States. He added: 'As the transatlantic telephone is obviously not a secret form of communication, it is reasonable to assume that this news will be in the possession of the Axis'. Spears, who was due to accompany de Gaulle on his African travels, was understandably put out. He assured Menzies that he had made no 'suicide pact' with de Gaulle: 'if he wants to commit "Hara Kiri" he must do so by himself'.[52]

The problems of intelligence liaison with the Free French reached an astonishing climax on New Year's Day 1941 with the arrest of the commander-in-chief of the Free French navy, Admiral Muselier, on suspicion of treason. MI5 had obtained four documents, allegedly emanating from the Vichy consulate in London, which appeared to show that Muselier had betrayed the plans for the Dakar expedition to Vichy through the intermediary of the Brazilian embassy, was plotting to hand over the Free French submarine *Surcouf* to Vichy, and had been paid £2,000 to sabotage recruiting to the Free French navy. Churchill, according to Cadogan, wanted to hang Muselier 'at once', but MI5's case against the admiral quickly began to crumble. Cadogan noted in his diary on 3 January that Guy Liddell, the director of B division, was 'not very enlightening' about the evidence, and that de Gaulle had 'worked himself up into being a passionate advocate' of Muselier. On the 8th de Gaulle summoned Spears, told him he was now certain of Muselier's innocence, and that if the admiral were not released within twenty-four hours, 'all relations between Free France and Great Britain would be broken off, whatever the consequences which might ensue'. On the same day Adjutant Collin of the Free French security service confessed that the documents which had led to the admiral's arrest were forged and had been used by himself and his colleague Commandant 'Howard' in order to discredit Muselier against whom they had a grudge. 'Howard' then confessed as well. To make matters worse, de Gaulle wrongly suspected that both Collin and 'Howard' had been planted on the Free French security service by the British. Even after Muselier had been freed and Churchill had apologised in person, de Gaulle's suspicions of a British intelligence plot lingered on. Ironically, just over a year later de Gaulle himself placed Muselier under house arrest and complained to the British that he 'indulged in drugs' and was 'morally unbalanced'. Another violent altercation followed. But on this occasion the British took Muselier's side against de Gaulle and tried vainly to prevent him being sacked as commander-in-chief of the Free French navy.[53]

Potentially the most important part of SIS's intelligence liaison work was with the United States. In May 1940, possibly at the urging of Churchill himself, Menzies appointed the Canadian millionaire businessman and former First World War fighter pilot, William 'Little Bill' Stephenson (later knighted) as PCO in New York. Like his First World War predecessor in New York, Sir William Wiseman, Stephenson was an ex-boxer. He was a former amateur lightweight world champion, known as 'Captain Machine Gun' because of the speed of his punches. Through his friend, the American world champion boxer Gene Tunney, he made the acquaintance of Edgar Hoover, the head of the FBI. Stephenson's clubbable personality, business contacts and remarkable capacity for dry Martinis won him a wide range of American friends and acquaintances. His business trips to Germany in the mid-thirties also led him into part-time intelligence work observing German rearmament first for Winston Churchill, then for the IIC and SIS.[54]

Stephenson's New York office, which eventually took up residence on the sixth floor of the Rockefeller Center on Fifth Avenue with the title British Security Coordination (BSC), was responsible for keeping track of enemy activities against the British war effort in the Western hemisphere, for devising countermeasures, and for providing liaison between American intelligence and all sections of the British intelligence community. One of Stephenson's first and most important acts as head of BSC was to arrange an informal visit to London by President Roosevelt's special envoy, Colonel 'Wild Bill' Donovan, later first head of OSS, the wartime predecessor of the CIA. After the Fall of France the Departments of State and War, like Joseph Kennedy, the American ambassador in London, were pessimistic about Britain's chances of survival. At Stephenson's request Donovan was shown the red carpet – indeed a whole series of red carpets – in an attempt to convince him otherwise. During a three-week stay in July and August 1940 Donovan was granted an audience with King George VI, received by Churchill, and taken to meetings with Menzies and most other intelligence chiefs. He confided to Admiral Godfrey, the DNI, that before leaving the United States he had been warned that the British were difficult, secretive and patronising. Donovan found them 'quite the opposite' and remarkably willing to share secret intelligence with him. Stephenson cabled SIS headquarters soon after Donovan's return: 'Donovan believes you will have within a few days very favourable news, and thinks he has restored confidence as to Britain's determination and ability to resist'. The 'very favourable news' was the Destroyers Deal of 2 September by which Britain received fifty First World War American destroyers in return for leasing the United States naval and air bases in the Caribbean and Western Atlantic: the forerunner of the Lend-Lease Act of March 1941 which made the United States the 'arsenal of democracy' eight months before the American entry into the war. It was, as Churchill acknowledged in his memoirs, 'a decidedly unneutral act by the United States' whose 'effects in Europe were profound'. Stephenson told SIS that without Donovan's help the Destroyers Deal could not have been concluded. Lord Lothian, the British ambassador, agreed that 'Donovan helped a lot'.[55]

Donovan also urged on Roosevelt 'full intelligence collaboration'. The President himself personally assured Stephenson that he would be given every assistance in obtaining intelligence on any subjects he chose. Roosevelt's willingness to embark on an informal intelligence alliance had much to do with the admiration he had formed for 'Blinker' Hall as assistant secretary of the navy at the time of the Zimmermann telegram. 'Of course, Hall had a wonderful intelligence service, but I don't suppose it's much good now', Roosevelt told Admiral Godfrey in 1941. As Godfrey listened to an elaborate but mythical description of British espionage in the First World War, he realised that Hall had spun a series of fantastic tales which the president had swallowed whole.[56]

The cooperation between Stephenson and Donovan – 'Little Bill' and 'Wild Bill' – was eventually to form the basis of a full-scale Anglo-American intelligence alliance. Stephenson himself became the first non-American to receive the United States' highest civilian decoration, the Medal of Merit. But BSC did not achieve the instant, dramatic success suggested by some sensational accounts of Stephenson's career as the 'man called Intrepid'. Nor did it have much to do with the Anglo-American collaboration in sigint which developed out of contacts between Denniston and the great American cryptographer William Friedman. In its early stages the American intelligence forwarded to London by BSC on the Axis powers and occupied Europe added little to what Whitehall already knew. Morton commented on one set of confusing American secret reports received in the summer of 1941: 'The Book of Revelations read backwards would be more helpful'.[57] Though Stephenson remained in close touch with Donovan, during 1941 he was sometimes at odds with both the FBI and the State Department. Until Pearl Harbor brought the United States into the war, in December, he took a number of rather dangerous risks in an attempt to undermine American neutrality. He commissioned a series of forged documents purporting to reveal nefarious German designs in the New World which were quoted not merely by the American press but also by President Roosevelt in a broadcast to the American people. On this occasion Stephenson covered his tracks. But his attempts to discredit Adolf Berle, the mildly Anglophobe assistant secretary in the State Department, backfired. An inept attempt by a BSC agent named Paine to 'get the dirt' on Berle was discovered by the FBI and Stephenson had hastily to get Paine out of the country.[58]

Particularly during the first eighteen months of the war, SIS sometimes found relations with its consumers more difficult than with its allies. Complaints by the service ministries as well as demands by Menzies for more money led Chamberlain in December 1939 to order an investigation by the former cabinet secretary Lord Hankey, now minister without portfolio. Hankey reported in March 1940 that all the service departments complained about the shortage and imprecision of SIS reports and wanted better evidence of their reliability. The same grievances were still being voiced a year later. Menzies, for his part, complained that the service departments often ignored SIS intelligence in their own summaries and appreciations. In his report of March 1940 Hankey concluded that the Foreign Office did not share the criticisms of the service departments.[59] But dissatisfaction was growing in the Foreign Office also. Cadogan complained in May 1940 that SIS was badly in need of overhaul. In September the young diplomat Patrick Reilly (later ambassador in Moscow and Paris) was moved into Broadway Buildings as Menzies's assistant chief staff officer to keep a closer watch on SIS activities.[60]

For all its failings, however, SIS did help to pioneer two major wartime intelligence activities. To its chagrin it lost control of both in the first year of the war. The first major wartime achievement by SIS was to pioneer new methods of photo reconnaissance by air (PR) which was to establish itself during the war as a form of intelligence gathering second in importance only to sigint. The coming of the Italo-Abyssinian war in 1935 had led to the revival of PR after a seventeen-year break, but the techniques employed in the Eastern Mediterranean and the Red Sea of oblique angle photography from the perimeter were of little use against targets deep inside Germany. From 1936 onwards, however, the Deuxième Bureau of the French airforce began photographing military targets along the Franco-German border. Frederick Winterbotham, head of the air section in SIS, was told by his opposite number in the Deuxième Bureau, Georges Ronin, that he had employed an elderly Paris portrait photographer with a large wooden camera to take photographs over the side of an aeroplane while being flown down the Rhine. The results achieved by this rather primitive technique aroused the interest of SIS. Winterbotham had been one of the pioneers of PR during the First World War until he was shot down after a series of perilous sorties. In 1938 he proposed cooperation between SIS and the Deuxième Bureau in clandestine high-altitude PR using a high-speed aircraft to minimise the dangers of detection and interception. It was agreed to set up a commercial front organisation, the Aeronautical Research and Sales Corporation, with offices in Paris and London, to run the combined Anglo-French secret operation. Though the original plan may have been for a French crew to carry out most of the reconnaissance flights, the first PR missions were led by F. Sydney Cotton, an extrovert Australian pilot and adventurer with business connections in Germany, recruited by Winterbotham. The plane chosen for the missions was an American Lockheed 12A, with a hole cut in the bottom of the fuselage to take three concealed cameras initially operated by an assistant who signalled to Cotton by tugging strings attached to his elbows. The main problems previously encountered in attempts at high altitude reconnaissance had been condensation and frost on the camera lens which made photography impracticable. Unlike its British rivals, however, the Lockheed had a heated cabin, and Cotton and Winterbotham discovered that its hot air system could be used to keep both the windscreen and the camera lens clear. For the first time high altitude PR thus became a practical possibility. 'It was', wrote Winterbotham later, 'as simple as that. I find it almost impossible to describe my elation at this chance discovery'.[61]

By the end of April 1939, when his collaboration with the French ceased, Cotton had photographed large areas of Germany and the Mediterranean while ostensibly on business flights. He then moved to England, operating from Heston aerodrome in a second Lockheed painted pale duck-egg green to lessen detection, carrying extra fuel tanks which more than doubled its range, and fitted with improved cameras. During the three months before the outbreak of war Cotton covered further areas of both Germany and the Italian Empire. His most remarkable coup was probably his visit to an international air show at Frankfurt late in July where he succeeded in taking the commandant of Tempelhof Airport on a joyride over sensitive areas, secretly taking photographs all the way with cameras operated by a button under the pilot's seat.[62]

Until the outbreak of war the Air Ministry refused to have anything to do with Cotton's activities for fear of being discovered to be involved in espionage. Once war began its attitude changed and on 23 September 1939 SIS formally surrendered control of Cotton's unit to the ministry. Cotton himself became a wing commander based at Heston and charmed two scarce Spitfires out of Air-Marshal Dowding, the commander-in-chief of Fighter Command. The Spitfires were stripped of their armaments to increase their speed and range, painted duck-egg green, and fitted with wing cameras whose lenses were kept clear by heat from the engine exhausts. With a range of 1,250 miles, a cruising speed of almost 400 miles per hour and a ceiling of 36,000 feet, the modified Spitfires were almost invulnerable to enemy attack. Cotton's unit was given the official title 'No. 2 Camouflage Unit' in November 1939, followed by the more appropriate name 'Photographic Development Unit' (PDU) in January 1940. Cotton himself gave the leading members of his hand-picked team a badge bearing the cryptic symbols 'C.C.11'. 'C.C.' stood for 'Cotton's Crooks'; '11' referred to the 'eleventh' commandment: 'Thou shalt not be found out'.

The PDU's main initial problem was a severe shortage of photographic interpreters. There were initially only two photographic interpreters in the entire BEF. Cotton therefore turned for help in December 1939 to private business. One of his friends, 'Lemnos' Hemming, who had worked for him on aerial surveying in Newfoundland twenty years before, now ran an aerial survey business at Wembley called the Aircraft Operating Company with advanced photogrammetic equipment and photographic interpreters. Hemming had offered his services to the Air Ministry but had been turned down despite the fact that his equipment was the most advanced in Britain. The photogrammetic expert at the Aircraft Operating Company, Michael Spender (brother of the poet Stephen Spender and the artist Humphrey Spender), was able to use the Swiss 'Wild' machine to calculate the dimensions of objects which appeared on Cotton's high-altitude photographs with unprecedented accuracy.[63]

The Air Ministry, however, remained suspicious both of 'Cotton's Crooks' and of their collaboration with the Aircraft Operating Company. Until the fall of France the ministry continued to pin most of its faith for long-range reconnaissance on twin-engined Blenheim bombers which, unlike the unarmed Spitfires of the PDU, were believed to be capable of fighting for airspace. The heavy losses suffered by the Blenheims both before and during the campaign in France finally decided the issue in favour of the unarmed but much faster Spitfires. 'After careful consideration', the Air Ministry decided that the PDU 'should now be regarded as having passed beyond the stage of experiment and should take its place as part of the ordinary organisation of the Royal Air Force'. On 18 June the PDU became an operational unit of the RAF under the commander-in-chief Coastal Command and was given the name which it retained for the remainder of the war: the Photographic Reconnaissance Unit (PRU). Soon afterwards the Aircraft Operating Company was taken over by the Air Ministry and subsequently renamed the Photographic Interpretation Unit (PIU). Thanks largely to the university contacts of the photogrammetic expert, Michael Spender, the PIU recruited a number of able academics to work on interpretation. Two of the first recruits in the summer of 1940 were 'Bill' Wager, later Professor of Geology at Oxford, and Glyn Daniel, later Disney Professor of Archaeology at Cambridge. They were joined in the autumn of 1940 by the elderly Cambridge botanist Hamshaw Thomas who had worked as a photographic interpreter in the First World War. Like Bletchley Park, the PIU owed much of its success to a combination of academic talent and freedom from bureaucratic routine. Despite early Air Ministry resistance it also secured a growing number of able WAAF photographic interpreters. Cotton had been an early supporter of the WAAFs, believing, as one of them later recalled, that the skills of a good housewife could be readily transferred to PI. 'Looking through magnifying glasses at minute objects in a photograph', he concluded, 'required the patience of Job and the skill of a good darner of socks'.[64]

On the very day that PRU was established as an operational unit of the RAF, Cotton received a letter announcing that he was being replaced as commander of the unit by Wing-Commander (later Air-Marshal Sir) Geoffrey Tuttle DFC. Cotton attributed his dismissal, which he denounced as 'cowardly in the extreme', to bureaucratic jealousy and inter-departmental rivalry. There was more to it than that. Winterbotham, who remained in touch with Cotton during the Phoney War, received numerous complaints about his behaviour in France through the SIS Paris station and the Deuxième Bureau. Some of the complaints were comparatively trivial. Cotton was said to have 'dressed up in funny hats in the French Mess' and 'really played the fool' in the company of women. Other complaints were more serious. Cotton was alleged to have been concerned in running a Paris brothel and to have tried to use a Lockheed to fly a French textile magnate from Bordeaux to Britain after the French collapse instead of looking after essential equipment and personnel.[65] Whatever the exact truth of all these allegations, the decision to find a less controversial commander for the PRU is understandable. Cotton's brief but colourful career as commander of the PDU had none the less entirely vindicated the attempt by Winterbotham and SIS to improve pre-war methods of aerial reconnaissance. Had there been no alternative in the summer of 1940 to the long-range reconnaissance by Blenheim bombers hitherto favoured by the Air Ministry, the prospects for PR would have been bleak indeed.

SIS's second major innovation at the beginning of the Second World War was in the use of sabotage. Prompted by the *Anschluss*, it had founded its first specialist dirty tricks department – Section D (for 'Destruction') – in March 1938. The tricks – delicately described as ways 'of attacking potential enemies by means other than the operations of military force' – were not, however, to be tried in peacetime. Until the balloon went up, the new Section was simply 'to investigate every possibility'. Its head (codenamed 'D') was the larger than life figure of Major (later Major-General) Laurence Grand, tall, thin, black-moustached, with a red carnation always in his button-hole. Some found him an inspiring leader. Others had their doubts. Kim Philby, who joined Section D in the summer of 1940 (eighteen months after his fellow Soviet agent, Guy Burgess), watched cynically as Grand's mind 'ranged free and handsome over the whole field of his awesome responsibilities, never shrinking from an idea, however big or wild'. The official historian of *SOE in France* also confesses a degree of scepticism about plans such as that 'to destroy the telecommunications of the southern Siegfried line through the agency of two left-wing German expatriates, one stone deaf and the other going blind'.[66]

'Other means' of attacking enemies in wartime were also investigated by the small research section (originally manned only by one officer and a typist) of the general staff at the War Office, GS(R), founded at about the same time as Section D. The first head of GS(R) chose army education as his subject of research but his successor at the end of 1938, Major J.C.F. Holland, a less dashing figure than Grand but also a chain-smoker, concentrated instead on guerilla warfare. He agreed with Grand that his section would concentrate on types of warfare which could be tackled by troops in uniform while Section D would deal with unavowable, undercover operations. After the German occupation of Prague in March 1939, Grand was summoned to a secret meeting at the Foreign Office and authorised to begin preparations for sabotage and propaganda in the Czech borderlands, Austria, and areas threatened by German expansion in eastern and south-eastern Europe. Simultaneously GS(R) was incorporated into MID with the new title MIR, and Holland was given an assistant, Major (later Major-General Sir) Colin Gubbins. 'If guerilla warfare is coordinated and also related to main operations', MIR concluded in June 1939, 'it should, in favourable circumstances, cause such a diversion of enemy strength as eventually to present decisive opportunities to the main forces'. Gubbins prepared three handbooks, *The Art of Guerilla Warfare*, *Partisan Leader's Handbook*, and *How to Use High Explosives*, the last kept constantly up to date during the war, and widely distributed to resistance groups in several languages. During the summer of 1939 Holland briefly moved his small staff into offices next to Section D, and cooperated with Grand in organising basic training on guerilla warfare for potential recruits – explorers, linguists, mountaineers, businessmen with foreign contacts. But by the outbreak of war Holland had become disturbed by what he regarded as Grand's wildcat schemes, and the two sections parted company.[67]

Section D expanded rapidly after the outbreak of war, claiming an officer strength of 140 by July 1940 – more than the main body of SIS. (75 were actually counted in August.)[68] One of the wartime recruits, Bickham Sweet-Escott, has left a graphic account of a job interview which was probably typical of many. 'For security reasons', his interviewer told him, 'I can't tell you what sort of job it would be. All I can say is that if you join us, you mustn't be afraid of forgery, and you mustn't be afraid of murder.' Late in 1939 the expanding Section D moved its headquarters to offices over St Ermin's Hotel, next to Caxton Hall. On the fourth floor Grand established a storeroom full of explosives which were dispatched by courier to agents abroad. The explosives expert in charge had previously been successively test-pilot, gun-runner and boxing promoter. He was the only man Sweet-Escott ever met who 'habitually and quite naturally talked in rhyming slang, and spoke always of touching his titfer'. In 1940, possibly at the suggestion of Guy Burgess, Grand also established a training school for foreign saboteurs at Brickendonbury Hall, a former school with spacious grounds near Hertford. 'Guy Fawkes College', as Burgess christened it, gave him ample scope for the practical jokes which, later in 1940, helped to terminate his career in British (though not Soviet) intelligence.[69]

If Grand achieved little else, he at least accustomed some senior civil servants and ministers to the unheard-of idea that a secret department specialising in sabotage and subversion could contribute to the British war effort.[70] After hearing details of one sabotage scheme in November 1939, even the highly respectable Cadogan found himself, to his surprise, 'rather inclining to press the button!'[71] Whitehall's initial interest in Grand's often over-optimistic schemes stemmed chiefly from an exaggerated belief in Germany's economic vulnerability. Both Chamberlain and Halifax began the war believing that economic pressure rather than military defeat would bring Germany to her knees. 'Time', said Halifax, 'is on our side'. The Ministry of Economic Warfare (MEW), which was set up on the outbreak of war and absorbed Morton's IIC, agreed. Its first minister, R.H. Cross, declared quite inaccurately in January 1940 that the first four months of the war, though mostly 'phoney', had caused the German economy as much strain as the first two years of the Great War. The MEW was understandably christened by its opponents the 'Ministry of Wishful Thinking'.[72]

The German war effort was believed to be critically dependent on two imports, Swedish iron ore and Rumanian oil, and it was these which formed the main targets for Grand's sabotage schemes. Section D's first priority at the outbreak of war was Swedish iron ore. Stopping these imports, wrote Churchill in December 1939, offered the best prospect 'for many months to come' of achieving the equivalent of 'a first-class victory in the field or from the air' against the enemy: 'It might indeed be decisive'. The MEW believed it would be. A variety of overt and covert operations were considered, ranging from laying minefields off the Norwegian port of Narvik (through which most Swedish iron ore exports passed in the winter months) to various schemes for sabotage. The first target for sabotage was the Swedish port of Oxelösund where the Germans were believed to have stockpiled supplies of iron ore.[73] Grand picked a two-man team for the Oxelösund operation: William Stephenson, the future head of British Security Coordination in New York, and Alfred Rickman, author of a book on *Swedish Iron Ore* published in September 1939 who was now a demolition expert with Section D. By the beginning of 1940 SIS was impatient to go ahead, and Cadogan had to order Menzies to 'wait for proper authority'. On 17 January Menzies briefed the prime minister and senior members of the war cabinet, and apparently gained permission to proceed. The prospects for successful sabotage were, Cadogan believed, 'quite satisfactory and hopeful'. The necessary plastic explosive, the first to be used in wartime operations, had probably already been removed from Grand's fourth-floor storeroom and sent to Stockholm by diplomatic bag where, without the knowledge of the minister, it was stored in the cellar of the British legation. According to Stephenson, Rickman alarmed him by insisting on carrying a loaded revolver at all times, even in bed, and accidentally discharging it in his hotel room. The scheme collapsed when the Swedish police discovered the saboteurs' attempts to recruit local assistants. Though Stephenson escaped, Rickman was arrested. Further sabotage schemes were cut short by the German invasion of Denmark and Norway in April 1940.[74]

Section D's second main objective during the Phoney War was to deprive Germany of her imports of Rumanian oil. MIR had similar ideas and sent out three officers in plain clothes who were given diplomatic cover at the Bucharest legation where they disconcerted the staff by 'playing casually with detonators' in their office and 'drinking very much more than was good for them'. The officers, Stanley Green, formerly employed in the Rumanian oil business, Tim Watts, a chemist from ICI, and the writer Geoffrey Household, best known for his thriller *Rogue Male*, devised three plans for the devastation of the oil fields in the event of the German invasion which was thought to be imminent. The first plan assumed the active assistance of the Rumanian army; the second merely assumed Rumanian connivance. The third scheme (which unlike the other two was not communicated to sympathetic officers on the general staff) was a plan to sabotage the oilfields in the event of Rumanian opposition. With the

Fall of France and the evacuation of the BEF from Dunkirk all prospect of Rumanian cooperation disappeared and MIR fell back on Plan 3. Shortly before it was due to go ahead word of it leaked out (possibly from an oil merchant in London), two military sentries were posted at each intended target, and the plan was called off.[75]

While MIR was plotting to destroy Germany's Rumanian oil supplies at source, Section D was simultaneously devising alternative plans to sabotage their transport down the Danube. The best point for sabotage appeared to be the 'Iron Gates' at the bottom of the eight-mile long Kazan Gorge in Yugoslavia, probably the most dangerous navigable cataracts in Europe. Close to the outbreak of war George Taylor, a forceful Australian business-man recruited by Grand to Section D (and later head of SOE's Balkan Section), visited Belgrade and recruited a locally-based South African arms dealer named Julius Hanau (predictably codenamed 'Caesar') for a scheme to block the Iron Gates by using explosives to collapse a cliff bordering the gorge into the river.[76] Grand's friend, the mining magnate Chester Beatty, gave Hanau the services of several mining engineers who reported that the scheme should block the Danube for several months at least. Hanau obtained local support for the scheme from opponents of the ruling Yugoslav régime and by bribing local officials. By mid-December 1939 the tunnelling required to mine the cliff was, according to SIS, 'well on the way to completion' when it was discovered by the police; 'the Yugoslav government intervened, stopped the work and took over the mines which had already been laid'.[77]

The most extraordinary schemes to block the Iron Gates were probably those devised during the winter of 1939–40 by Mervin Minshall, a self-styled refugee from the establishment who had dabbled in intelligence work during the 1930s (narrowly escaping poisoning, or so he believed, by 'Goering's top agent', 'the beautiful Lisa', with whom he had an affair) and was taken on first by NID, then by Section D, soon after the outbreak of war. Of all SIS agents, the buccaneering Minshall probably came closest to the fictional stereotype of James Bond and may well have given his friend and Bond's creator, Ian Fleming, some of his raw material. By his own (never understated) account, Minshall actually exercised his licence to kill while travelling on the Orient Express and had his intelligence work frequently interrupted by a succession of demanding women such as the 'dish' who burst naked into his hotel room at Bucharest, claiming to bear a message from the British legation, threw herself full length on the bed, and beckoned in Minshall's direction. It seemed to Minshall 'a funny way of bringing a message from the British Legation. Assuming she was from the Legation'. The enemy was less fortunate. Minshall succeeded in having the German naval attaché 'black-balled' from 'the best brothel in Bucharest'. To the understandable alarm of British legation staff, whom Minshall found 'scared stiff' by his adventurous schemes, he was given diplomatic cover as vice-consul in Bucharest and supplied with plastic explosive through the diplomatic bag. His first scheme, to disrupt Danube navigation by bribing 40 of the 50 Iron Gates pilots to leave the country for 500 gold sovereigns each and having the remainder 'unobtrusively bumped off', fell through for lack of sovereigns. Minshall then devised a scheme to sail barges down the Danube with a score of naval ratings improbably disguised as art students and sink the barges to block the Iron Gates. But after German agents had tricked his crews into going on shore leave while they stole their fuel, he concluded that 'at every turn I had been out-thought and out-witted by the Nazis'. *The Times* ridiculed German claims on 8 April 1940 that 'an agent of the British Secret Service camouflaged as a Vice-Consul' had been foiled in an attempt to block the Iron Gates. On this occasion, however, as Minshall acknowledged, 'Goebbels was turning out the truth, the whole truth and nothing but the truth'.[78]

What Cadogan called the 'eternal question of denying supplies of oil to Germany' continued to preoccupy both the cabinet and SIS. Grand's favourite alternative to the Iron Gates scheme was to blow up the Yalomitza bridge linking Bucharest to the Ploesti oilfields. Both the British minister in Bucharest, Sir Reginald Hoare (brother of Samuel), and the Foreign Office were understandably nervous. Late in 1940 the Yalomitza bridge sabotage scheme was first approved and then abandoned for fear that Hoare might be 'exposed to danger as a result'.[79] Secret negotiations also dragged on with sections of the Yugoslav general staff to persuade them to sabotage the Iron Gates themselves. A few days before the German invasion of April 1941, General Simovic, who had just led a successful coup d'état, assured the British minister that plans to sabotage the locks below the Iron Gates were ready to go ahead, but in the chaos of invasion the scheme misfired.[80] Though a number of barges were sunk in an attempt to put the locks out of action, the Danube was only partially and temporarily blocked. No other significant acts of sabotage interfered with the eleven-day German conquest of Yugoslavia. According to Menzies, the Yugoslavs were 'very uncooperative'.[81]

Despite the failure of Section D's main schemes in both Scandinavia and the Balkans, the German conquest of France and the Low Countries in the six-week Blitzkrieg which began on 10 May 1940 increased Whitehall's interest in both sabotage and subversion. The failure of regular warfare was now to be redeemed by irregular warfare. Instead of enlarging the SIS field of operations as Menzies must have hoped, however, the adoption of this strategy was to remove sabotage and subversion from SIS control. The chiefs of staff reported to the war cabinet on 25 May that, if France fell, 'Germany might still be defeated by economic pressure, by a combination of air attack on economic objectives in Germany and on German morale and the creation of widespread revolt in her conquered territories'. In order to rouse occupied Europe to rebellion – a task 'of the very highest importance' – it was urgently necessary to found 'a special organisation'. For once, the chiefs of staff succeeded in firing Churchill's imagination. After a month of inter-departmental wrangling, a meeting at the Foreign Office attended by Menzies agreed on 1 July that 'the multiplicity of bodies dealing with sabotage and subversive activities' must be replaced by 'a Controller armed with almost dictatorial powers'. The brash, dynamic Labour politician, Hugh Dalton, minister of economic warfare in Churchill's coalition government, was already lobbying hard for the position of 'Controller'. Cadogan complained that Dalton was 'ringing up hourly to try to get a large finger in the Sabotage pie', but believed that he was 'the best man' for the job (though he later changed his mind). Halifax, as one of his colleagues told him, would 'never make a gangster'. Dalton had the appearance of a man who would. He was rashly confident that by the end of the year 'the slave lands which Germany had overrun' would rise in revolt, and that Nazism might then 'dissolve like the snow in spring'. 'Regular soldiers', he complained, 'are not men to stir up revolution, to create social chaos or to use all those ungentlemanly means of winning the war which come so easily to the Nazis'. He was.[82]

On 16 July Dalton had his wish. Churchill gave him control of 'a new instrument of war', which was christened a few days later the Special Operations Executive (SOE). 'And now', the prime minister told him, 'set Europe ablaze'. In reality, during Dalton's two years in charge of SOE, Europe was 'too damp to do more than smoulder'.[83] SOE absorbed both Section D and MIR, whose heads returned to their regiments. It also took over from the Foreign Office its semi-secret propaganda department EH (so called after its London headquarters, Electra House on the Embankment) which was developing 'black' propaganda; a year later, however, that section left to become the Political Warfare Executive (PWE). The first executive head of SOE was Sir Frank Nelson, a former India merchant and Conservative M.P. who had worked for the Z organisation in Switzerland. The chair at SOE council meetings was taken by Dalton's aide, Gladwyn Jebb (previously Cadogan's private secretary), who also had the thankless task of liaising with the Foreign Office and SIS.[84]

Inevitably SIS did not take kindly to losing its sabotage section and its near-monopoly of clandestine operations overseas. It resented having to compete with SOE for scarce transport and other resources, and successfully insisted until 1942 on running SOE's wireless communications for it.[85] Behind the personal and inter-departmental rivalries which soured relations between SIS and SOE, Bickham Sweet-Escott rightly observed a broader conflict of interest between intelligence gathering and sabotage:

For the man who is interested in obtaining intelligence must have peace and quiet, and the agents he employs must never if possible be found out. But the man who has to carry out operations will produce loud noises if he is successful, and it is only too likely that some of the men he uses will not escape.[86]

Though some of the rivalry between SIS and SOE abated as the war progressed, the conflict of interest between them could never be completely resolved. Churchill became resigned to 'the warfare between SOE and SIS' as 'lamentable but perhaps inevitable'.[87]

Much of the original impulse for SOE came from the conviction that the German victories had demonstrated the enormous power of subversion and sabotage. The sheer rapidity of the German Blitzkriegs was mistakenly ascribed to the assistance of large 'fifth columns' working behind the lines. Sir Nevile Bland, the British minister in the Netherlands, argued that the rapid collapse of the Dutch, who surrendered after only five days' fighting on 15 May, had been made possible by the cooperation between the fifth column and German parachutists. He cited as an example a report, reminiscent of the spy scares of the First World War, that a German maid had led the parachutists to one of their targets. Bland warned of the same danger threatening Britain from the 'enemy in our midst': 'Every German or Austrian servant, however superficially charming and devoted, is a real and grave menace ...' There was, he claimed, a fifth column of German and Austrian residents who, as soon as the signal was given, would 'at once embark on widespread sabotage and attacks on the civilians and the military indiscriminately'. When Bland's report was presented by Halifax to the war cabinet on 15 May, Churchill declared that 'urgent action' was required.[88] He later told the Commons:

After the dark, vile conspiracy which in a few days laid the trustful Dutch people at the mercy of Nazi aggression, a wave of alarm passed over this country, and especially in responsible circles, lest the same kind of undermining tactics and treacherous agents of the enemy were at work in our Island.[89]

The danger of German invasion during the months which followed the Fall of France provoked an attack of spy mania not much less virulent than that which preceded and accompanied the First World War. A Home Intelligence report to the Ministry of Information concluded on 5 June: 'Fifth Column hysteria is reaching dangerous proportions'. The broadcasts from Bremen by Oswald Mosley's former lieutenant, William Joyce (better known as 'Lord Haw Haw') were widely believed to prove the existence of an army of German informants. It was rumoured in Wolverhampton that Joyce had referred in a 9.15 p.m. broadcast to a town clock which had stopped only twenty minutes earlier. According to another version of the same unfounded rumour Joyce had said, 'We know all about Banstead, even that the clock is a quarter of an hour slow today'.[90]

Though there were a few prosecutions of rumour-mongers, cases of Fifth Column hysteria occurred among the authorities themselves. The Vice-Admiral commanding the port of Dover reported in May 'numerous acts of sabotage and Fifth Column activity'. General Ironside issued an extraordinary warning, shortly before being replaced as C-in-C Home Forces in July, that there were 'people quite definitely preparing aerodromes in this country' for the invader. According to a pamphlet put out by the Ministry of Information:

> There is a fifth column in Britain. Anyone who thinks that there isn't, that it 'can't happen here', has simply fallen into the trap laid by the fifth column itself. For *the first job of the fifth column is to make people think that it does not exist.* In other countries the most respectable and neighbourly citizens turned out to be fifth columnists when the time came.[91]

During his investigation of the intelligence services a few months earlier, Hankey appears to have been unimpressed by MI5's leadership. MI5's problems were further increased by its failure to deal with a largely imaginary fifth column. Counter-espionage and counter-subversion, Churchill complained, were 'not working smoothly'.[92] The final nail in Kell's coffin may well have been MI5's search of the German embassy which had been left in the care of the Swiss. On 4 June Cadogan got the Swiss minister to agree to what was doubtless intended to be a discreet search of the embassy premises, but the minister returned two days later to complain of an 'MI5 irruption into the German embassy'. Outraged by the clumsiness of the search, Cadogan 'worked over Kell on the telephone'.[93] On 10 June Kell was dismissed. His diary entry that day was slightly less terse and uninformative than usual. Kell wrote: 'I get the sack from Horace Wilson [the permanent head of the civil service]', added his dates of service '1909–1940', and drew a line. Then he vented his feelings on the Italians: 'Italy comes into the war against us. Dirty Dogs'. Kell's deputy, Sir Eric Holt-Wilson, who had served under him since 1912, was also sacked.[94]

To iron out what he called the 'overlaps and underlaps' in the various agencies dealing with counter-espionage and counter-subversion, Churchill founded the Security Executive which was formally constituted by the war cabinet on 28 May. Its first head was the former minister of air, Lord Swinton, whom Churchill instructed to 'find out whether there is a fifth column in this country and if so to eliminate it'. As deputy chairman Swinton brought in the former MI5 officer Joseph Ball from Conservative Central Office. Swinton took, from the start, a close interest in the organisation and running of MI5, bringing in an expert from Burroughs Business Machines to improve Kell's vast, rather ramshackle card index of suspected subversives and enemy sympathisers.[95] His early criticisms of MI5 organisation doubtless contributed to Kell's abrupt dismissal. Swinton also took a keen interest in the appointment of Kell's successor. 'Jasper' Harker, who took over as acting director-general, lacked the powers of leadership to inspire confidence among MI5's able wartime recruits. One of them described him as 'a sort of highly-polished barrel which, if tapped, would sound hollow (because it was). Swinton saw through him in a flash'. On Swinton's recommendation the sixty-one-year-old former head of DIB, Sir David Petrie, was summoned from semi-retirement to take over as director-general in November 1940 with Harker as his deputy. Cadogan considered his appointment 'a bad move' but MI5 and, in the end, most of Whitehall disagreed. The young recruit who thought Harker lightweight had much greater respect for Petrie:

> Solid in appearance and in mind, he made it his business to know the essentials of his job, but did not hesitate to delegate. I doubt if he had more than a B + mind but he used it, made few – if any – mistakes, and combined courtesy with firmness.

Another MI5 officer found Petrie 'one of the best man managers I ever met'.[96]

The Security Commission's main priority during the interregnum at MI5 was to coordinate action against the alien refugees who were believed to be the principal recruiting ground for the Fifth Column. At the outbreak of war 415 enemy aliens on the MI5 blacklist of suspected Nazi sympathisers had been arrested. Six months later the total number of aliens interned had grown close to 2,000. But when fears of a fifth column mounted as the Germans overran France and the Low Countries, the Home Office resisted pressure for further arrests. The home secretary Sir John Anderson, anxious to avoid the anti-alien hysteria of the First World War, told the cabinet that none of the intelligence services had found any evidence of Nazi plans to infiltrate German and Austrian refugees. Nor, as a group, were the refugees potentially dangerous. He sensibly argued that while wholesale internment would be popular in the short term, the 'inevitably poor treatment' of internees would produce a sympathetic backlash. The chiefs of staff, however, insisted that alien refugees were 'a most dangerous source of subversive activity': 'The most ruthless action should be taken to eliminate any chances of fifth column activities'.[97] Churchill sided with the chiefs of staff rather than with the Home Office. 'In existing circumstances', the war cabinet minutes record, 'he thought it important that there should be a very large round-up of enemy aliens and suspect persons in this country'. Most ministers agreed.[98] With the support of MI5, Swinton and the Security Executive energetically supervised the 'round-up'. The result, as the Foreign Office noted, was to raise 'MI5 from their former advisory position to what is in effect an executive function, so that it is in fact their view rather than that of the Home Office which over matters of internment and detention in the long run prevails'.[99]

During the three month period from May to July 1940 about 22,000 Germans and Austrians, and about 4,000 Italians were interned. After Swinton and the Security Executive had emphasised 'the danger of retaining alien internees in this country' where they might help the invader, deportations to Canada began. And then the reaction Anderson had predicted started to set it. On 2 July the *Arandora Star*, carrying 1200 German and Italian internees across the Atlantic, was torpedoed and sank with heavy loss of life. A subsequent report to the cabinet revealed that a number of the Italian deportees who appeared on an MI5 list of 'dangerous characters' because of their alleged fascist associations had in fact no such associations. One of those drowned at sea had lived in England for twenty years and was secretary of the Italian section of the League of the Rights of Man. Not surprisingly the cabinet decided not to publish the report. R.T.E. Latham, Fellow of the All Souls and temporary clerk in the Refugee Section at the Foreign Office, denounced the 'dunderheaded attitude of "the military" ' and 'incompetence in MI5 as the cause of our recent crude, cruel and foolish treatment of every kind of alien'. As the invasion scares declined, the number of internees also began to fall. By the end of the year Churchill had lost his earlier enthusiasm for 'a very large round-up'. He wrote in January 1941:

> I have heard from various quarters that the witch-finding activities of MI5 are becoming an actual impediment to the more important work of the department. I am carefully considering certain changes, not only in MI5 but in the Intelligence and Secret Service control ... I have no doubt that there is a certain amount of risk that some bad people may get loose but our dangers are so much less now than they were in May and June ... that I am sure a more rapid and general process of release from internment should be adopted.[100]

But if some of MI5's energies in the summer and autumn of 1940 were unnecessarily diverted into what Churchill called 'witch-finding activities', that period also saw a major expansion of the brilliantly successful double-cross system. Paradoxically the near isolation of Britain from the Continent after Dunkirk made MI5's task easier. Hitherto there had been many possible routes for German agents entering Britain. After June 1940 legitimate entry was possible only from Sweden and Portugal. Since MI5 was able to keep these two routes under close surveillance, the Germans were forced to use clandestine methods. During the three-month period from September to November 1940 over twenty-five agents landed by parachute or small boat, most of them inadequately trained and poorly equipped. MI5 found them 'an easy prey'. They were all the easier to detect since their forged identity documents were based on misleading information supplied by the SNOW (Owens) group of double agents. A high proportion of the new wave of German spies were also successfully turned round into double agents working under British control. The most successful was probably a twenty-six-year-old Dane, Wulf Schmidt (codenamed TATE by MI5 because of his resemblance to the famous music hall comedian), who parachuted into Cambridgeshire on the night of 19 September 1940 and was arrested by the local Home Guard the following morning. Schmidt appeared to be a convinced Nazi and told his MI5 interrogators that the German invasion was now at hand and the tables would shortly be turned. After almost a fortnight's interrogation, however, Schmidt broke down and agreed to become a double agent. 'Nobody ever asked me why I changed my mind', he said after the war, 'but the reason was really very straightforward. It was simply a matter of survival. Self-preservation must be the strongest instinct in man.' The same instinct no doubt motivated most other double agents. Schmidt exchanged wireless messages with his German control in Hamburg continuously from October 1940 until May 1945. His German controls were so pleased with his reports that they described him as a 'pearl' among agents, sent him large sums of money, and had him awarded the Iron Cross, First and Second Class. A few hours before Hamburg fell to the Allies on 2 May 1945, his control appealed to him by radio to keep in touch.[101]

As the double-cross system expanded MI5 increasingly required the cooperation of other sections of the intelligence community. From December 1940 GC & CS was able to decrypt Abwehr communications almost continuously. SIS was needed to help recruit and give assistance to double agents in neutral capitals. The ablest double agent recruited by SIS was Dusko Popov (codenamed TRICYCLE), a young Yugoslav in the Abwehr who contacted the SIS station at Belgrade. In December 1940 Popov travelled to London via Lisbon, telling the Abwehr that he was going to collect intelligence from a friend in the Yugoslav legation but with the real intention of making contact with MI5. Once in London Popov became the centre of a considerable network of other agents helping to operate the double-cross system. By cutting across the demarcation line which confined MI5 to British soil and SIS to foreign territory, the double agents thus necessitated closer cooperation between the two services than ever before. In order to run double agents successfully, MI5 also needed to know what information to give them – information that would both impress and deceive the enemy. To assemble that information B division in MI5, whose counter-espionage duties included the double agents, required the cooperation of the whole intelligence community. In September 1940 the 'Wireless Board' was set up to select intelligence for the Abwehr. On it sat Guy Liddell (who had succeeded Harker as head of B Division), Stewart Menzies and the three service directors of intelligence. This elevated committee, however, inevitably lacked the time to provide the detailed, sometimes daily, operational guidance which became necessary as the double cross system expanded in the autumn and winter of 1940. The Wireless Board therefore delegated the day-to-day supervision of the double agents to the Twenty Committee, so called because the Roman numeral for twenty (XX) is a double cross. The Twenty Committee held its first meeting on 2 January 1941 and thereafter met weekly for the remainder of the war.[102] It contained representatives of SIS, the three service intelligence departments, GHQ Home Forces, the deception department of the Air Ministry and the Security Executive under an MI5 chairman, the history don J.C. Masterman, formerly Dick White's tutor at Christ Church, Oxford. Masterman preceded the first meeting with what he later called 'a small but important decision, to wit that tea and a bun should always be provided for members':

> In days of acute shortage and of rationing the provision of buns was no easy task, yet by hook or crook (and mostly by crook) we never failed to provide them throughout the war years. Was this simple expedient one of the reasons why attendance at the Committee was nearly always a hundred per cent?

Despite some early tension between MI5 and SIS and the difficulties of reconciling the sometimes conflicting interests of deception, security, and intelligence gathering, the Twenty Committee worked remarkably smoothly. At only one of its 226 meetings was a disagreement pressed to a vote.[103] Initially, the Twenty Committee feared that there might be a large body of German spies in Britain of which it knew nothing. But from its very first meeting it began to grasp the astonishing truth that, in Masterman's words, '*we actively ran and controlled the German espionage system in this country*'.[104]

Following the successful inauguration of the Twenty Committee, a further attempt was made to strengthen intelligence coordination by bringing SIS more into line with the needs of the service intelligence departments. On 19 March 1941 Cadogan arranged a meeting at the Foreign Office to 'drag' the service intelligence directors 'into the open' and make them expand on their complaints of 'not enough intelligence' to Menzies personally. Cadogan was disappointed with the discussion which followed. The service directors pulled their punches, while Menzies was 'as usual, a bad advocate in his own behalf'. 'He babbles and wanders', wrote Cadogan, 'and gives the impression he is putting up a smokescreen of words and trying to put his questioners off the track'. But during the remainder of the year Menzies gradually yielded to pressure for the service departments to have a greater say in the running of SIS. In January 1942 he finally agreed to the appointment of three 'deputy directors' (nicknamed 'the commissars') in SIS from the services: the marine Colonel John Cordeaux to represent NID, Brigadier W.R. Beddington for

MID, and Air-Commodore 'Lousy' Payne for AI. Cadogan was surprised that Menzies had conceded so much. He himself would have been quite content with three service 'advisors' but felt he 'couldn't be more royalist than the King'.[105]

SIS was now clearly less influential than the system of photographic reconnaissance (PR) it had helped to create. The rapidly growing demand for the services of the PRU after its foundation in June 1940 inevitably produced conflicts of interest. The Admiralty in particular repeatedly complained that naval requests for PR were given too low a priority. Within NID there was talk for a time of developing a rival PRU within the Fleet Air Arm. During 1941, however, there was steady progress towards the coordination of PR on an interservice basis. The first major step was the transformation of the Photographic Interpretation Unit (PIU) into the Central Interpretation Unit (CIU) in January 1941. In April the CIU moved to Medmenham, the eighteenth-century headquarters of the Hell Fire Club, where it was based for the remainder of the war. Though Medmenham was administratively part of Coastal Command, it operated as an independent interservice unit, supplying operational intelligence, charts, plans and models to all three services. Reconnaissance proved more difficult to integrate than interpretation. By the beginning of 1941 three separate PRU units had emerged: No. 1 PRU, the original unit responsible for meeting the needs of the Admiralty and the Combined Intelligence Committee which monitored invasion threats; No. 2 PRU, based in Egypt, which covered the Middle East; and No. 3 PRU, responsible to Bomber Command. In the summer of 1941, despite recurrent grumbling from Bomber Command, No. 3 PRU merged with No. 1 to form a single unit. By now the problems caused by competing interservice demands for PR had begun to ease as both the supply and range of reconnaissance aircraft increased. The number of PR sorties increased from an average of 4.1 a day in April 1941 to 9.6 a day a year later. By the spring of 1942 there was no longer any shortage of PRU aircraft. The British armed forces had come to accept – and expect – high-quality photographic intelligence as a standard part of operational planning.[106]

The most important move towards improved coordination within the greatly expanded wartime intelligence community concerned the Joint Intelligence Committee, for only the JIC was charged with overseeing 'the efficient working' of the whole community. During 1940 it proved clearly inadequate to that task.[107] The first attempt by the chiefs of staff to remedy the failings of the JIC only made matters worse. Instead of giving the JIC more resources they hived off its responsibility for the main enemy appreciations. In November 1940 the chiefs of staff set up the Future Operations (Enemy) Section (FOES) with instructions to put itself in the enemy's shoes and produce regular assessments of enemy intentions. When Major-General Francis Davidson became DMI in December 1940 he was quick to protest against the 'complete nonsense' of depriving the JIC of one of its most important functions. An 'unbelievable episode' on 11 February 1941 appeared to prove his point. At 12.45 p.m. Davidson was telephoned by the Director of Plans and told to present the chiefs of staff at 5.30 p.m. with a detailed appreciation, including routes and timings over the next few months, of the German drive towards the Mediterranean as far as Athens and Salonica. Davidson considered this a 'pretty fast ball' to receive just before lunch. On turning up at 5.30 p.m. with maps and a hastily typed report, he was kept waiting until 6 p.m. and then told by the chiefs of staff to deliver his appreciation in 'only 3 to 4 minutes'. Davidson retorted that 'a worthwhile appreciation would require at least 10 minutes', spoke for ten minutes, and was then asked to 'repeat the dose' at 7.30 p.m. before a meeting of the Defence Committee chaired by the prime minister. He gave as his 'best guess' for the date of the German arrival in Athens 21 April, which Churchill described as 'unduly rapid'. In fact he was only six days out: the Germans entered Athens on 27 April.[108]

The experience of that remarkable day prompted Davidson to write a strongly worded memorandum entitled 'Give Us the Tools', arguing that appreciations of the kind he had been asked for at a few hours' notice should be the responsibility of a strengthened JIC. The chiefs of staff agreed, disbanded the FOES, and established the Axis Planning Staff (APS) – soon retitled the Joint Intelligence Staff (JIS) – as a subcommittee of the JIC charged with coordinating, assessing and disseminating strategic intelligence. Fortified by the JIS, the JIC was able at last to apply itself to coordinating the policy and administration of the intelligence community as a whole. On 22 April 1941 the chiefs of staff, who had met the JIC only twice during the second half of 1940, decided in future to meet them on a weekly basis.[109]

The founding of the JIS and the enhanced authority of the JIC worked no instant miracles. The JIC, like Whitehall as a whole, was slow to grasp the significance of intelligence on German preparations for Operation Barbarossa, the invasion of Russia begun on 22 June. Even in mid-May, when preparations for a German attack were unmistakable, it was confidently believed that Hitler would decide whether to go ahead only after the conclusion of Russo-German political negotiations. The JIC reported on 23 May that the advantages to Germany of reaching agreement with Russia were 'overwhelming'. GC & CS disagreed. Impressed by detailed evidence such as the secret movement of POW cages which seemed to have little to do with any policy of intimidation, it regarded a surprise German invasion as a probability by 14 May and a virtual certainty by the end of the month. In Whitehall, however, there was still diplomatic evidence which pointed in a different direction. Not until 12 June, only ten days before the invasion began, did the JIC finally conclude that 'Hitler has made up his mind to have done with Soviet obstructions and intends to attack her'. That it had finally reached this conclusion despite its long-held conviction of the 'overwhelming' advantages for Germany of a negotiated settlement with Russia was due to the emergence, with the creation of the JIS, of machinery which made it possible for the first time to assess in one place all the evidence provided by the whole intelligence community.[110]

Behind the growing coordination both of the intelligence community and of intelligence with the war effort it is possible to detect, though not always to document in detail, the powerful influence of the prime minister himself. Churchill's greatest achievement as war leader, apart from the sheer inspiration which his leadership provided, was the unified direction which he gave to the conduct of the war. Few of the bitter clashes between 'frocks' and 'brass hats' which had bedevilled Lloyd George's government during the First World War reappeared during the Second. On becoming prime minister Churchill had also become minister of defence. Within the war cabinet he set up a defence committee with himself as chairman, the Labour leader Clement Attlee as vice-chairman, attended by the service ministers, the chiefs of staff and other ministers as required. Attlee believed that it was thanks to 'Winston's knowledge of military men, his own military experience and flair, his personal dynamism and the sweeping powers that any prime minister in wartime can have if he chooses to use them' that 'the deadly problem of civilians-versus-generals in wartime was solved'.[111] Churchill used the same energy and flair in gearing intelligence to the war effort. As soon as he became prime minister he ordered the chiefs of staff to review the ways by which intelligence was used in operational decisions.[112] He was not satisfied with the result. Twenty years earlier, as secretary of state for war in 1920, Churchill had made the revolutionary suggestion that all the branches of British intelligence be combined in a single secret service.[113] On Guy Fawkes Day 1940 he shocked his chiefs of staff with a similar proposal. How, he asked provocatively, was intelligence as a whole organised, and who was the man responsible for it? The chiefs replied that the attractions of a single secret service were outweighed by 'many grave disadvantages': 'it seems to us very undesirable that a drastic reorganisation of this magnitude should be attempted at the very moment when we are fighting for our lives'.[114] The prime minister did not give up. He announced in January 1941 that he was 'carefully considering' the whole question of 'Intelligence and Secret Service control'.[115] The strengthening of the JIC and the emergence of the JIS over the next few months reflected Churchill's sustained pressure for a coordinated intelligence community and system of intelligence assessment. The intelligence services were in no doubt of the prime minister's personal interest in them. Four of the leading cryptanalysts at Bletchley Park – Turing, Welchman, Alexander and Milner-Barry – wrote direct to Churchill on 21 October 1941 to tell him that their work was being held up by staff shortages and other 'unnecessary impediments'. As soon as he received their letter on the 22nd, Churchill minuted: 'Action This Day. Make sure they have all they want on extreme priority and report to me that this had been done'.[116]

Unlike any of his predecessors, the prime minister was sometimes in danger of showing too much enthusiasm for secret intelligence. He was apt to spring on the chiefs of staff or others undigested snippets of intelligence gathered from his daily box of intercepts supplied by GC & CS. Even when abroad he was determined to remain in close and detailed touch with the very latest intelligence reports. Before leaving for the Casablanca conference in January 1943 he ordered Menzies to 'repeat all really important messages to me textually'. A week later he signalled from Casablanca: 'Why have you not kept me properly supplied with news? Volume should be increased at least five-fold and important messages sent textually'.[117] But the blemishes in Churchill's sometimes overenthusiastic tactical handling of intelligence were far outweighed by his grasp of its strategic importance. No British statesman in modern times has more passionately believed in the value of secret intelligence. None has been more determined to put it to good use. Churchill's early vision of a unified secret service was never to be realised. But it was under his inspirational leadership and in the finest hour of his long career that the fragmented intelligence services acquired at last that degree of coordination which turned them into an intelligence community.

# 15 | EPILOGUE: WAR AND PEACE

Intelligence did not decide the outcome of the war. Once the Red Army had weathered the shattering initial shock of the German invasion and the United States had been thrust abruptly into the conflict by the Japanese surprise attack at Pearl Harbor in December 1941, the much greater military resources of the Allies made ultimate victory for the Axis powers impossible. But if the successes of Allied intelligence did not win the war, they undoubtedly shortened it – and in so doing saved millions of lives. Good intelligence made possible at least three major Allied victories. Without Ultra, Rommel would probably have reached Cairo in the summer of 1942. Thanks, however, to the intelligence which the German intercepts provided on the movements of both Rommel and the ships bringing his supplies, General Auchinleck was able to bar the German advance at the first battle of El Alamein in July. His victory was less spectacular than Montgomery's four months later but probably even more important. Intelligence was vital also in the battle of the North Atlantic, the longest and most complex in the history of naval warfare. At the climax of the battle in the spring of 1943 German U-boats came very close to breaking the lifeline between Britain and North America. What probably tipped the balance, once again, was Ultra. Victory in the North Atlantic cleared the way for the immense shipments of American forces and supplies which in the summer of 1944 were to make possible Operation Overlord, perhaps the biggest intelligence success in the history of modern warfare.[1]

Without command of both sea and air, the D-day landings on the Normandy beaches would have been unthinkable. On the ground, however, the seven divisions of the initial Allied assault faced fifty-nine German divisions in occupied France. Overlord's success depended on the ability of the double cross system to fool the Germans into believing that the Normandy landings were only a feint and that the real attack would come in the Pas de Calais. But the double cross system depended in turn on Ultra which showed what baits the Germans were swallowing from the double agents in Britain and other methods of deception. They swallowed an enormous amount. By 1

June, five days before D-day, German intelligence believed there were almost ninety Allied divisions in Britain as against a real total of only forty-seven. At 1 a.m. on 6 June GARBO, perhaps the most successful of all the double agents, radioed to his Abwehr control that Allied forces had embarked for Normandy. The message arrived too late to assist the German defence but raised still higher GARBO's reputation with German intelligence. On D-day plus three, 9 June, at a time when the Allied assault could still have been driven back into the sea, GARBO sent his control another urgent message with a request that it be passed immediately to the German high command. 'The present operation', he insisted, 'though a large-scale assault, is diversionary in character'. At a crucial moment GARBO thus reinforced the German belief that the main assault was still to come in the Pas de Calais. When his message arrived, the crack 1st SS Panzer Division, together with the 116th Panzer Division, was on its way to Normandy. After reading the message Hitler ordered them back to the Pas de Calais and awarded GARBO the Iron Cross, Second Class. No incident better epitomises the ascendancy of the British intelligence community over its German opponent. Venlo had been well and truly avenged.[2]

The Second World War was followed, like the First, by a rundown and limited reorganisation of the intelligence community. Because of its wartime successes and the speedy transition from war to cold war, the rundown was less severe after 1945 than after 1918. GC & CS, which had been renamed GCHQ (Government Communications Head-Quarters) in a reorganisation which followed Denniston's departure in 1942, moved from Bletchley Park first to Eastcote in the London suburbs, then, a few years later, to new headquarters at Cheltenham. Denniston's successor, Commander Edward Travis, was rewarded at the end of the war with a knighthood, though sadly – in keeping with the interwar neglect of GC & CS – Denniston received no further recognition after a CMG in 1941. As after the First World War, GCHQ's priorities shifted from German to Soviet communications, which had been almost entirely neglected during the war itself. Once again the attack on Soviet diplomatic traffic yielded a measure of success. Though the scale of the success remains a highly classified secret, Soviet intercepts (codenamed Vinona) provided the clues which led to the arrest of the atom spy Klaus Fuchs in 1950 and to the attempt to arrest Donald Maclean a year later, foiled by his flight to Moscow with Guy Burgess.[3]

Thanks partly to the reflected glory of Bletchley Park, SIS emerged from the Second World War without the major overhaul it needed. Sir Stewart Menzies, knighted in 1943, remained Chief until 1951, regarded even by his admirers as an intelligence officer 'of the old school'. In 1946 SOE was wound up and its responsibilities for covert action handed over to SIS which formed a new Special Operations Branch and Political Action Group.[4] SIS's new duties added to the administrative confusion of its transition from war to peace. Nowhere was the confusion greater than in the Middle East where the SIS organisation concluded that its existing cover name, Inter-Service Liaison Department (ISLD), had been blown and adopted the new name Combined Research and Planning Office, Middle East (CRPO). After several large consignments of intelligence documents despatched from Cairo had failed to arrive at the CRPO office in Jerusalem, Captain Alistair Horne of MI5 (later to become a leading military historian) was called in to investigate. He discovered 'train loads of top secret documents ... sitting in the office of an utterly baffled Jewish sergeant in Jerusalem who worked for a thing called Command Regimental Pay Office, Middle East', whose initials were also CRPO.[5]

To a much greater extent than before the war, the energies of SIS during the Cold War were drawn into covert action. 'You can't 'ave Austria, Turkey or the Straits', the Labour foreign secretary, Ernest Bevin, told his Soviet opposite number, Molotov: 'You stay be'ind your iron curtain'. SIS was ill-equipped with both the men and money needed to assist in enforcing this injunction. Some of its part-time agents, bred by John Buchan out of G.A. Henty, trained in para-military arts at Fort Monkton near Gosport, horrified the shrewder professionals in SIS. But 'the times were against the professionals' – save, of course, for Kim Philby, well placed to sabotage anti-Soviet covert action as he continued his ascent towards the Chief's office which his Soviet controls must surely have felt was coming within his grasp.[6]

MI5 emerged from the war in better shape than SIS, trailing clouds of glory from the double cross system but handicapped by the suspicion of the Labour government as well as by its diminished resources. When Petrie retired in 1946, all the internal candidates for the directorship were passed over in favour of a former chief constable, Sir Percy Sillitoe. A year later Guy Liddell succeeded Jasper Harker as Sillitoe's increasingly disillusioned deputy. Sillitoe made no secret of his dislike for 'Oxbridge types' and 'long-haired intellectuals'. Since four of the directors of MI5's six post-war divisions (Dick White, Roger Hollis, Martin Furnival Jones – all future directors – and Graham Mitchell) were 'Oxbridge types' and a fifth (Alex Kellar, who had studied at the universities of Edinburgh, Yale and Columbia) also qualified as an intellectual, the omens for Sillitoe's seven-year term as director were not promising. Even a sympathetic biographer records 'the derision which ... apparently infected the greater number of Sillitoe's staff'. His son remembers one occasion when, convinced that his directors were trying to humiliate him by quoting Latin epigrams he could not understand, Sillitoe stormed out of MI5's Curzon Street headquarters, white-faced with rage:

When we got into the car I asked, 'What was that all about?' He said, 'One word – bastards!' He would return home to the flat in Putney night after night and tell my mother, 'Dolly, I can't get to grips with a brick wall!'[7]

As the Labour government became increasingly concerned (like its predecessor in 1924) with what the cabinet minutes called 'Communist endeavours to cause industrial unrest', it overcame its early suspicions of the Security Service and made increasing use of it. Clement Attlee became the first prime minister to visit MI5 headquarters and held several discussions with its senior staff on Communist subversion.[8] MI5 also emphasised the increased opportunities for Soviet espionage generated by the war:

> The attack by Germany on Russia in June 1941 caused a very considerable increase in the membership of the Communist Party in this country and some alteration in the social status of this membership which, from this date, showed an increased, though still small, number of people drawn from the professional classes. This point is important as regards the possibility of leakage of information to the Communist Party as the higher educational level of the new membership tended to give these members access to information of greater importance.
>
> The ever-increasing demands for man-power in war production, together with the co-operative attitude towards the war adopted by the Communist Party, tended to make Government Departments less inclined to exclude Communists from secret work and, in fact, members of the Communist Party are known to have been placed in positions where they had access to information of considerable secrecy. Many Communists are known to have volunteered to the Communist Party Headquarters information about British war production, projects and weapons, with the intention that this information should be passed on to the Russians. In addition, certain members of the Communist Party are known to have carried out espionage activities, the products of which were almost certainly destined for the Russians.[9]

Not till the net began to close on Burgess and Maclean in 1951, however, did MI5 begin to grasp the threat posed by pre-war Soviet moles in Whitehall who had long abandoned overt Communist connections.

MI5's main postwar successes were probably imperial rather than national, in assisting counter-insurgency campaigns during the retreat from Empire. Its most important contribution was probably in Malaya where the Communist Party embarked on a guerilla war in 1948. In the early stages of the emergency, as the Director of Operations, Lieutenant-General Sir Harold Briggs, admitted in 1950, intelligence was 'our Achilles heel'. A dramatic change followed the appointment in 1952 of General (later Field-Marshal) Sir Gerald Templer to the combined post of High Commissioner and Director of Operations.

'The emergency', Templer insisted, 'will be won by our intelligence system – our Special Branch'. He entrusted the reorganisation and expansion of his Special Branch, which became the sole Malayan intelligence agency, to senior officers of MI5 who also worked with him in planning his operations. Both Sillitoe and Dick White, who succeeded him as director-general of the Security Service in 1953, made personal tours of inspection during the emergency. Templer's leadership and the close coordination of the reorganised Special Branch with the security forces turned the Malayan campaign into probably the most successful counter-insurgency operation of modern times. By the time the Communist leader Chin Peng emerged from the jungle in 1955 in a vain attempt to seek an amnesty from the Malayan government, it was clear that he had lost the war.[10]

Among the most important legacies of the Second World War to the post-war British intelligence community were close, though very different, connections with the intelligence communities of both the superpowers. The Anglo-American intelligence collaboration begun even before Pearl Harbor had blossomed into a full-scale intelligence alliance of unprecedented intimacy. At Bletchley Park American cryptographers worked alongside their British colleagues. During the Battle of the Atlantic the OIC in the Admiralty exchanged intelligence almost daily with its Washington counterpart. American commands in European and Mediterranean theatres received the same Ultra intelligence as their British counterparts. The relations of SIS and SOE with the American OSS, though not always smooth, were 'always close and eventually harmonious'. By D-day there had been a complete merger of British and American strategic PR from bases in the United Kingdom.[11]

Operation Overlord in the summer of 1944 and the deception programme, Operation Fortitude, which accompanied it, were striking evidence of the closeness of the intelligence alliance. On becoming Supreme Commander Allied Forces in Europe at the end of 1943 General Eisenhower had quickly asked for the British general, Kenneth Strong, as his chief intelligence officer. Ike was so determined to secure Strong's services that when his request was refused by Alan Brooke, the CIGS, he appealed directly to Churchill, who agreed. Unlike any of Monty's intelligence officers, Strong had unrestricted direct access to both Eisenhower and his chief of staff, and the right to sack on the spot any intelligence officer, American or British, whom he believed not up to the job. 'The best time in a man's life', Strong enthused, 'is when he gets to like Americans'.[12]

The aspect of the wartime intelligence alliance with most importance for the future concerned sigint. The wartime BRUSA agreement to share sigint of May 1943 formed the basis of the still secret UKUSA agreement of 1947 which also included Canada, Australia and New Zealand, and divided the world into spheres of cryptographic influence covered by each signatory's listening posts. During the war Britain had been the senior partner in the intelligence alliance. The UKUSA pact was to turn her into the junior partner. Peacetime Britain became a victim of her own wartime cryptographic success. In 1942 Bletchley Park had invented the world's first electronic computer, codenamed Colossus. But a system of communications intelligence based on huge banks of computers, intercept stations around the globe and sigint personnel running eventually into six figures was simply too expensive for post-war Britain to take the lead. America's wealth gave her, for the first time, the intelligence as well as the military leadership of the Western world. The United States is said to have helped finance even some of the monitoring stations constructed on British territory. Under the BRUSA and UKUSA agreements the United States had control only over the American end of the transatlantic sigint link, leaving the British end to GCHQ. But it was a sign of the growing dominance of American investment that the United States attempted – unsuccessfully – in 1954 to take direct control of the British terminal also. Increasingly GCHQ made a habit of using pressure from its American equivalent, NSA, to argue the case within Whitehall for a larger sigint budget. Sir Leonard 'Joe' Hooper, the director of GCHQ from 1964 to 1973, confessed to the director of NSA, General 'Pat' Carter, that while lobbying for its two hundred-foot satellite dishes at Goonhilly in Cornwall, he had 'leaned shamefully on you, and sometimes taken your name in vain, when I needed approval for something at this end'. He added that the two dishes deserved to be christened 'Pat' and 'Louis' in honour of Carter and his deputy Louis Tordella. 'Between us', Hooper told Carter, 'we have ensured that the blankets and sheets are more tightly tucked around the bed in which our two sets of people lie and, like you, I like it that way'.[13]

Anglo-American collaboration in post-war espionage and covert action ran less smoothly than in sigint. OSS was disbanded at the end of the war and replaced in 1946 by the Central Intelligence Group (CIG) which became the Central Intelligence Agency (CIA) a year later. President Truman celebrated the founding of the CIG with a White House lunch at which the guests of honour were the first Director of Central Intelligence (DCI), Admiral Sidney Souers, and the President's chief of staff, Admiral William Leahy. Truman solemnly presented his guests with black cloaks, black hats and wooden daggers, then called Leahy forward and stuck a large black moustache on his upper lip.[14] The cloak and dagger image fitted at least some of the joint Cold War operations undertaken by SIS and CIA.

In the course of 1948 Stalin engineered a Communist coup in Prague, blockaded West Berlin, and stepped up his assistance to Communist rebels in Greece. Impressed by the difficulties of a covert counter-attack in Central Europe, both SIS and CIA were attracted by the apparently more encouraging prospects in the Balkans following Tito's break with Stalin. Probably towards the end of 1948 Bevin authorised the use of covert action in an attempt to detach Albania, like Yugoslavia, from the Soviet orbit. The attempt began in earnest in October 1949 with the seaborne landing in Albania of the first teams of armed British-trained agents. It ended ignominiously in a great show trial at Tirana in April 1954 and a reign of terror throughout Albania. As SIS liaison officer with the CIA in Washington from October 1949 until his recall in May 1951, Kim Philby did much to sabotage Albanian operations. He alerted the KGB to the seaborne landings in October 1949, to cross-border infiltration in the summer of 1950, and to the first CIA parachute drop in November 1950. Even without Philby, however, covert action in Albania was probably doomed. Security both in the SIS training camp in Malta and among the rival groups of Albanian émigrés was sometimes slapdash. Albanian intelligence eventually devised its own double-cross system. The Albanian dictator, Enver Hoxha, later boasted:

> We forced the captured agents to make radio contact with their espionage centres in Italy and elsewhere, hence to play our game ... The bands of the criminals who were dropped in by parachute or infiltrated across the border at our request came like lambs to the slaughter ...[15]

While the Albanian operation was turning sour, the Anglo-American intelligence alliance was disturbed by revelations of Soviet penetration of British security. The discovery of the atom spies, Klaus Fuchs and Nunn May, whose communist past had gone undetected by MI5, alarmed the CIA. It was even more perturbed by the flight of Guy Burgess and Donald Maclean to Moscow in May 1951. At the moment of his flight Maclean was head of the American desk in the Foreign Office. Until a few weeks before Burgess had been second secretary at the Washington embassy, staying at the home of the SIS liaison officer, Kim Philby. At the insistence of the CIA, Philby was recalled from Washington and officially retired from SIS with a £4,000 golden handshake paid in instalments. But Menzies was convinced of Philby's innocence and got rid of him with what Philby called 'obvious distress'. Menzies's deputy, Major-General John 'Sinbad' Sinclair (later knighted), who succeeded him as 'C' at the end of 1951, also refused to believe in Philby's guilt and eventually re-engaged him in 1956 as a freelance agent in Beirut working under journalistic cover. The new 'C', wrote Philby cynically, though 'not overloaded with mental gifts (he never claimed them), was humane, energetic and so obviously upright that it was impossible to withhold admiration ... It was distasteful to lie in my teeth to the honest Sinclair.'[16] By 1953 another SIS officer, George Blake, was also working for the KGB as a remarkably successful double agent.

The Philby affair produced tensions between SIS and MI5 as well as in the Anglo-American intelligence alliance, for the leadership of MI5 shared the CIA's belief that Philby was a double agent. Post-war collaboration between SIS and MI5 never approached their close wartime cooperation in running the double-cross system. When Harold Macmillan became defence minister in 1954, convinced that 'the first essential' in the Cold War was good intelligence, he was dismayed at the lack of coordination between SIS on the one hand and MI5 and the Imperial security services on the other:

> No one is wholly responsible – it's partly Defence, partly Colonial Office, partly Foreign Office. There's no central anti-Communist organisation with any drive in it. 'Cold War' alarms me more than 'Hot War'. For we are not really winning it, and the Russians have a central position ... and a well-directed effort with strong representation (through the Communist Party) in every country.[17]

In the early 1950s the main focus of SIS covert action shifted to the Middle East. The most successful action, at least in the short term, was Operation Boot, mounted in cooperation with CIA's Operation Ajax, which in August 1953 helped to overthrow the anti-Western prime minister of Iran, Mohammed Mossadeq, and bring back the Shah in triumph from exile in Rome. Though the main responsibility for the Iranian operation was later claimed by Kim Roosevelt (cousin of FDR) of the CIA, SIS alleged that 'Roosevelt really did little more than show up in Iran with CIA funds to encourage agents the British had organised and then released to American control.' The Shah never forgot his debt to SIS; until his fall in 1978 the station chief in Teheran had much easier access to him than the British ambassador.[18] Churchill, now seventy-nine, in the middle of his four-year term as peacetime prime minister (1951–5) and in failing health, summoned up much of his old enthusiasm for cloaks and daggers as he followed the fortunes of Operations Boot and Ajax. On his way home from Teheran, Kim Roosevelt called in Downing Street to brief Churchill in person. He found him propped up in bed, recovering from a stroke but anxious to hear the 'exciting story' Roosevelt had to tell. 'Young man', said Churchill when the story was finished, 'if I had been but a few years younger, I would have loved nothing better than to have served under your command in this great venture'.[19]

But Churchill's great powers were waning fast. 'In the midst of the war', he said, 'I could always see how to do it. Today's problems are elusive and intangible'.[20] His vision of the intelligence community, central to his role as war leader, was becoming blurred in peacetime. Churchill's increasing deafness led in 1954 to one remarkable moment of black comedy in the history of GCHQ. While installing microphones and a loudspeaker in the cabinet room to help the prime minister hear what his ministers were saying, GCHQ technicians slipped up, and an astonished taxi-driver heard the cabinet meeting broadcast live over his cab radio as he was driving down Whitehall.[21]

'Sinbad' Sinclair's term as 'C' is remembered by some survivors of the period as 'the horrors'. SIS was drawn into increasingly unrealistic plans to bolster Britain's declining influence in the Middle East by covert action – plans which seem to have captured the imagination of Sir Anthony Eden during his disastrous twenty-one month term as prime minister after Churchill stepped down in April 1955. Even before the Suez crisis SIS was developing a madcap scheme, codenamed Operation Straggle, to engineer a coup in Syria. In March 1956 CIA representatives listened in dismay in the sixth-floor conference room at Broadway Buildings as Sinclair's deputy, George Young, outlined plans for Turkey to provoke frontier incidents, for Iraq to stir up Syrian desert tribes, and for Lebanese Christians to infiltrate across the Syrian border as the prelude to full-scale Iraqi invasion. They were still more dismayed at SIS plans to topple President Nasser in cooperation with the Israelis (crudely described as the 'snipcocks').[22] The lowest point in 'the horrors' was probably a plan to assassinate Nasser. Eden's foreign secretary, Selwyn Lloyd, discovered the plot only at a late stage in its preparation and concluded that SIS was no longer fully under political control. It seems more likely, however, that the assassination plan – mercifully never implemented – had the personal blessing of the prime minister.[23]

British collusion with France and Israel in the Suez War late in 1956 – the one really indecent episode in an honourable retreat from Empire – did substantial short-term damage to the Anglo-American intelligence alliance as to the rest of the special relationship. The newly-begun American programme of aerial reconnaissance by high-flying U2 aircraft was used to monitor Anglo-French preparations in the Mediterranean for the attack on Egypt. On 30 October Gary Powers, later to achieve notoriety as the U2 pilot shot down over Russia, photographed the first shots fired by Israeli troops as they moved across the Sinai desert.[24] NSA was also able to monitor the development of the Suez crisis by decrypting some of the diplomatic and military traffic of Britain, France and Israel. Ironically, (Sir) Eric Jones, who had recently succeeded Sir Edward Travis as head of GCHQ, was on a visit to NSA on the eve of the Suez War. While sailing back to England on board the *Queen Mary*, he wrote mournfully to his old friend, the veteran American codebreaker, William Friedman: 'Needless to say, the difficulties between our two countries over the Middle East are rather marring my trip home'. In 1957 NSA brought Friedman out of retirement and sent him to England to mend the fences with GCHQ damaged by the Suez fiasco.[25]

The fence-building exercise was assisted by changes at the top in SIS. 'Sinbad' Sinclair's downfall followed a bungled attempt to inspect the hull of the Soviet cruiser *Ordjonikidze* in Portsmouth harbour during a goodwill visit in April 1956. The ageing, out-of-condition frogman employed by SIS, Commander 'Buster' Crabb, failed to return from his underwater mission. After his headless body had been washed ashore, Eden was forced to make an embarrassed apology to the Commons in May, deny ministerial responsibility, and announce that those responsible had been disciplined. The chief casualty was Sinclair himself, who was succeeded as 'C' by Sir Dick White, head of MI5 since Sillitoe's retirement in 1953. With the encouragement of the cabinet secretary, Sir Norman Brook (later Baron Normanbrook), White tightened up the ground rules of SIS and specifically forbade assassination.[26] Though all did not instantly go smoothly, there were no more plots to kill foreign leaders and no more 'Buster' Crabb adventures. Unlike Menzies and Sinclair, White had long been convinced of Philby's guilt and was determined to track him down. The evidence which eventually made Philby confess and then defect from Beirut in 1963 came from two defectors: Michal Goleniewski, a Polish intelligence officer who had worked for the KGB, and Anatoli Golitsin, a major in the KGB itself. Goleniewski's evidence also led to the round-up in 1961 of the Portland spy ring which was passing submarine warfare secrets to the Soviet spymaster Konon Molody, *alias* Gordon Lonsdale. And, before Philby himself was finally cornered in 1963, Goleniewski's evidence had helped to uncover George Blake in 1961 who received the record jail sentence of forty-two years. To save itself embarrassment the Macmillan government tried to conceal the fact that Blake had worked for SIS. George Brown, who learned the truth under privy council rules, was understandably outraged by the attempted cover-up and gave the story to the journalist Chapman Pincher who produced the banner headline in the *Daily Express*: '40 AGENTS BETRAYED – and all by this man'.[27]

While Blake, Philby and the Portland spy ring were being uncovered, SIS was simultaneously receiving the best Soviet intelligence in its history. In 1960 Colonel Oleg Penkovsky of the GRU (Soviet Military Intelligence) started handing over the first of thousands of photographs of classified Soviet documents. During secret meetings with SIS in London, and once in Paris, Penkovsky also answered questions long into the night in hotel bedrooms. Though the CIA had rebuffed an earlier overture from Penkovsky, suspecting a plant, SIS agreed to make the case 'practically a joint operation' with the Americans picking up the films on which Penkovsky photographed secret documents with a Minox camera. According to Ray Cline, then deputy director of the CIA:

> It was a very risky and far from certain pay-off activity when it began. That may have motivated the British willingness to share in probably the most successful Soviet penetration in the post-war period.[28]

Penkovsky's intelligence 'allowed the CIA to follow the progress of Soviet missile emplacement in Cuba by the hour'. It also helped Washington grasp the extent of the American strategic advantage in nuclear missiles.[29] So valuable did the CIA consider Penkovsky's intelligence that during one of his visits to London with a Soviet trade delegation he was flown on a day trip to the White House to receive the personal thanks of President Kennedy. Penkovsky was even more anxious to meet the Queen but had to be content with a close view of Her Majesty in Windsor Great Park and a day with Earl Mountbatten. Penkovsky's moment of triumph was also the moment of his downfall. In October 1962, during the missile crisis on which his intelligence had such an important influence, he was arrested by the KGB.[30] When the crisis was over Sir Dick White summoned his staff to the cinema in the new SIS headquarters at Century House in Lambeth and passed on to them the thanks of the CIA. The professional skill shown in the handling of the Penkovsky case, and other intelligence successes against the Soviet Union of the same period which have yet to be revealed, left most in Century House convinced that the 'horrors' of the 'Sinbad' Sinclair era were behind them.[31]

Even more important in the longer term than the intelligence from Penkovsky was an almost simultaneous revolution in aerial reconnaissance. In 1955 President Eisenhower had proposed to the Soviet Union an 'open skies' policy by which each side would be free to monitor the other's military capacity from the air. Russia refused as she was bound to: the Gulag archipelago was not to be inspected even from the air. The United States went ahead unilaterally with overflights of Soviet territory by U2 aircraft capable of cruising at 70,000 feet.[32] In 1960 Russia scored a temporary victory by shooting down a U2 and staging a show trial of its captured pilot, Gary Powers. But Powers's capture was only a temporary setback. Within a few months the USA had launched its first spy satellite, though the early satellite photographs lacked the definition of those taken by the U2s. By 1963 satellite surveillance was tacitly accepted by the Soviet Union. Aerial reconnaissance became for the first time, and has since remained, the most important form of intelligence gathering. A similar system in the 1930s would have solved many, if not most, of the problems encountered by Whitehall in monitoring German rearmament. Thanks to spy satellites, Eisenhower's Open Skies proposal has become a reality. By signing the Anti-Ballistic Missile Treaty of 1972, which provides for verification by what are euphemistically termed 'national technical means', Russia formally sanctioned the principle of aerial inspection which it had violently opposed in 1955.[33]

The primacy of the spy satellite, increasingly used for signals interception as well as photographic reconnaissance, gave the two superpowers, as the only satellite-owners, an unassailable intelligence lead over all other states for more than two decades. In the process it inevitably confirmed the relegation of the United Kingdom to the status of junior partner in the intelligence alliance with the United States. According to Ray Cline, deputy director of the CIA at the beginning of the satellite era:

... It was only because of our tradition of close collaboration with British Intelligence in cryptanalysis, espionage and general exchange of finished intelligence that we felt we should share with the British in the U2 and satellite processes.[34]

As the superpowers lose their monopoly of satellites during the 1980s, they are bound also to lose their monopoly of satellite intelligence. But for the foreseeable future all systems of arms control will continue to depend on satellite surveillance.

The enormous post-war expansion of sigint under the UKUSA pact and the revolution in aerial reconnaissance produced by the U2 and the satellite have faced the British intelligence community, like many others, with an information explosion of unprecedented dimensions. Though it is unlikely that any major power now employs code and cipher systems for its high-grade traffic as vulnerable as those of the Russians during the decade after the Bolshevik Revolution or the Axis powers during the Second World War, the total amount of communications traffic accessible to GCHQ and NSA must surely exceed their capacity to process it. The intelligence community nowadays faces what one CIA analyst has called 'an all-source glut: millions of words daily from foreign radio broadcasts, thousands of embassy and attaché reports, a stream of communications intercepts, cartons of photographs, miles of recorded electronic transmissions – and a handful of agent reports'.[35]

Despite far better systems of assessment than between the wars, the information explosion has posed once again, sometimes in an acute form, the old problem of distinguishing the really significant intelligence signals from misleading or irrelevant background noise. The hardest thing to judge, as always, remains political intention. SIS concluded in 1968 from intelligence on the movement of Soviet armed forces that the Russians intended to invade Czechoslovakia. The Foreign Office believed, however, that there would be no invasion because of the international repercussions for the USSR.[36] The problems of assessment led Sir Dick White to propose the new post of Intelligence Coordinator in the Cabinet Office. On his retirement as head of SIS in 1968 he became the first holder of the post. Within the Cabinet Office a Joint Intelligence Organisation (JIO) was created to prepare assessments for consideration by the JIC and circulation to ministers and officials. According to the Franks report of 1983:

[The JIO] draws for its assessments on all relevant information: diplomatic reports and telegrams, the views of Government departments and publicly available information, as well as secret intelligence reports. It also has a co-ordinating role in respect of the work of the security and intelligence agencies.[37]

Despite greater coordination within the Cabinet Office, the recent history of the intelligence community has provided further glimpses of some old problems. The lack of coordination between different branches of the intelligence community in Northern Ireland during the Troubles of the early and mid-seventies vividly recalled the confusion of British intelligence-gathering in Ireland over half a century earlier. There have been echoes too of the sometimes casual Whitehall attitude to security during the interwar years. The Security Commission reported in May 1981 'extensive breaches' of computer security at the Ministry of Defence. Of about a hundred secret MOD tapes found missing in 1979, some were later discovered to have been taken home by a defence official to record pop music and German lessons on the radio. The Geoffrey Prime case of 1982 and the Michael Bettaney case of 1984, each involving a bizarre, inadequate personality employed in a highly sensitive intelligence post, revealed continuing weaknesses in the security of GCHQ and MI5. Despite the improved system of intelligence assessment in the cabinet office, the Franks Committee found that before the Falklands conflict the JIC had inadequately collated secret and non-secret sources and paid too little attention to the latter: 'The changes in the Argentinian position were, we believe, more evident on the diplomatic front and in the associated press campaign than in the intelligence reports'. But the Committee found 'no reason to question the reliability of the intelligence that was regularly received from a variety of sources'.[38]

It is still too early to attempt any balanced assessment of the operational successes and failures of the British intelligence community since the era of Philby and Penkovsky. Most of its recent operational record remains, quite rightly, secret. Even those fragments of that record which have come to light necessarily give a distorted impression of the whole. Intelligence failures usually become public knowledge before intelligence successes. Ultra, the greatest success in British intelligence history, remained a secret until almost thirty years after the war was over. By the time that wartime secret came out, however, much of the post-war damage done by Soviet moles and atom spies was already public knowledge. Even the most spectacular post-war SIS success to have come to light so far, the Penkovsky case, has become known only because of its tragic conclusion. It is unsafe to conclude that there have been no Penkovskys since, simply because their names have yet to appear in the newspapers. Similarly, the recent failures of MI5, as exemplified by the Bettaney case and terrorist bombs, have been far more visible than its successes. Its success in helping to contain the terrorist offensives against British cities over the last decade has, however, almost certainly been very much greater than the limited number of terrorist trials would indicate.

But while the recent operational record of the intelligence community necessarily remains largely obscure, it is clear that government management of it has suffered in varying degree ever since the war from the inherited legacy of interwar confusion. The policy of all post-war governments has been conditioned by two highly questionable pre-war constitutional principles: that intelligence is undiscussable in public, and that parliament surrenders all its powers in intelligence matters to the executive. The classic formulation of the first principle is that by Austen Chamberlain, speaking to the Commons as foreign secretary in November 1924:

> It is of the essence of a Secret Service that it must be secret, and if you once begin disclosure it is perfectly obvious to me as to hon. members opposite that there is no longer any Secret Service and that you must do without it.[39]

So far from proceeding from long and careful cabinet deliberation, that doctrine, which led for the next half century to a refusal even to admit to the existence of SIS, was simply part of the more general confusion which characterised government management of intelligence between the wars. The intelligence services were held to require total secrecy not merely about their current and recent operations but also about their past record virtually without limit of time. Yet the government which formulated the doctrine of total secrecy in November 1924 was to commit only two and a half years later one of the biggest intelligence gaffes of modern times and compromise the most valuable British intelligence source – the Soviet intercepts – by a spectacular indiscretion.[40]

The simple fallacy behind the argument that total disclosure is the only alternative to total secrecy (roughly equivalent to saying that a nuclear holocaust is the only alternative to complete pacifism) escaped serious challenge for so long because the intelligence community acquired the status of an unmentionable taboo exempt from any process of rational public or parliamentary debate. Since 1924 successive governments have done their best to keep the taboo intact. Harold Macmillan told the Commons sternly after Philby's defection in 1963: 'It is dangerous and bad for our general national interest to discuss these matters'. That dictum is quoted with approval in Lord Wilson's book, *The Governance of Britain*, published soon after his resignation in 1976. The chapter in his book entitled 'The Prime Minister and National Security' is probably the shortest chapter ever written by a British prime minister. It is barely a page long and concludes thus:

> The Prime Minister is occasionally questioned on security matters. His answers may be regarded as uniformly uninformative. There is no further information that can usefully or properly be added before bringing this chapter to an end.

Edward Heath took an equally grim view. As prime minister he was even more secretive about intelligence matters than the Secret Service itself. On at least two occasions his intelligence chiefs tried to persuade him to publicise some of their successes. Mr Heath made it 'an inviolate rule' always to refuse.[41] It has usually been an almost equally 'inviolate rule' that M.P.s do not table questions about the intelligence services. Except in the immediate aftermath of security scandals, M.P.s attempting to do so have usually found their questions rejected by the Table Office. The Callaghan government stoutly maintained its predecessors' insistence on the omnipotence of the executive in the management of the intelligence community. 'Parliament', it declared, 'accepts that accountability must be to Ministers rather than to Parliament, and trusts Ministers to discharge that responsibility faithfully'.[42]

It is sometimes suggested, though rarely argued in public, that the twin intelligence principles of as near total secrecy as possible and the government's non-accountability to parliament, whatever their constitutional impropriety, at least make for efficient administration and good security. So far as the inter-war years are concerned, that argument is clearly ill-founded. All too often secrecy and non-accountability encouraged governmental neglect and malad-ministration. Government security was neglected and the intelligence services run down to levels which threatened national security as a whole and seriously hampered the British response to the rise of Nazi Germany. The machinery of intelligence assessment on the eve of war was so defective that Whitehall was frequently incapable of distinguishing good intelligence from bogus intelligence plants. It required remarkable last-minute improvisation, a major new recruitment and inspired leadership to fit the intelligence community for war. In a short war the intelligence renaissance evident by 1941 would have come too late.

It is unlikely that the management of the intelligence community by any post-war government has ever descended to the pre-war level of confusion. But there has been recurrent evidence, none the less, since 1945 of neglect and maladministration. A government which took its responsibilities to SIS seriously would scarcely have allowed the 'horrors' of the 'Sinbad' Sinclair era. In 1952 MI5 was made responsible to the Home Office rather than, as previously, to the War Office. But during the Profumo affair in 1963 the home secretary, Henry Brooke, appeared, as the Labour Opposition com-plained, confused about his responsibilities.[43] However, Labour was itself confused about its attitude to the intelligence community. Some of the Labour ministers who took office in 1964 after thirteen years out of power were highly suspicious. The lord chancellor, Lord Gardiner, later confessed that he 'thought it more likely than not that MI5 was bugging the telephones in my office'. When he had really confidential business which concerned the attorney general, he would order his chauffeur to drive them round while they discussed it, confident that 'she would never have allowed the car to be bugged without my knowledge'.[44] George Brown's suspicions of SIS when he became foreign secretary in 1966 were more modest. Soon after he took office he became the first foreign secretary ever to visit SIS headquarters, apparently convinced that he would find Century House full of snobbish ex-public schoolboys recruited from exclusive clubs. (Sir) Maurice Oldfield, later a distinguished head of SIS from 1973 to 1978, recalled George Brown's visit as 'a very funny day' when the foreign secretary roamed through the building fighting the class war (though his initial suspicions were afterwards allayed).[45]

Despite his reputation for reading intelligence reports with close attention, Harold Wilson kept his intelligence chiefs rather at arm's length. He later claimed that during his final term in office he had not known 'what was happening fully in security'. 'I saw so little of the heads of MI5 and MI6', he told Chapman Pincher, 'that I used to confuse their names' – a remarkable admission by a prime minister with a celebrated memory for detail. In 1977, a year after his resignation, Wilson disregarded the recent advice in his own book, *The Governance of Britain*, and began voicing suspicions of an improbable plot against him by MI5, possibly assisted by the CIA, during his final term. His successor, James Callaghan, was forced to issue a formal statement of confidence in 'the competence and impartiality of the Security Service', denying that any part of the intelligence community had ever bugged the prime minister's room.[46] The whole farcical episode inevitably raises doubts about the competence of government policy to the intelligence community during the Wilson years. A prime minister who after eight years in office entertains suspicions, however improbable, that his own security service is plotting against him scarcely merits confidence in his administration.

Though the evidence is inevitably scanty, the relations of the Callaghan and Thatcher governments with the intelligence community seem to have been much smoother.[47] As foreign secretary from 1976 to 1979, David Owen ordered a detailed check of the cases referred to him by SIS and GCHQ over a six-month period to see whether anything of importance had been held back:

> I found, I must confess, that they were scrupulous and that they had referred the right ones to me and they had been very good in sorting out what was technical detail and what was something which involved political content and required the authorisation of the democratic political leadership ... I didn't get the feeling that I was dealing with a reactionary bunch of people at all. Dealing with things like Southern Africa and race, I found them very broad minded and not by any means the sort of archetypal right wing figure.

Owen formed a particular respect for the head of SIS, Sir Maurice Oldfield, as 'a remarkable man ... modest, quiet, unassuming, with a great sense of humour ... an absolute model democrat'.[48]

Other Labour ministers were less complimentary. Roy Hattersley, whose posts included terms as minister of state responsible for the security divisions in both the Foreign Office and the MOD, considered the intelligence community, like the Establishment as a whole, lacking in the ability to look at itself 'in the open, objective way that makes for efficiency'. But he also observed 'a good deal of learning, an enormous amount of dedication and absolute integrity'. As secretary of state for defence, Denis Healey became unhappy with a system which gave those concerned with policy-making, particularly in the Foreign Office, responsibility for intelligence assessment also:

> Inevitably, once part of the Foreign Office has taken a view on an issue, it tries to interpret intelligence so as to confirm that view and tends to discount intelligence which disagrees with it.

Healey's views to some extent anticipated those of the Franks Committee, which in 1983 recommended removing chairmanship of the JIC from Foreign Office control. He went some way further than the Franks Committee and probably surprised some of his colleagues by proposing in 1982 the creation of a body independent of the Foreign Office, the MOD and the cabinet office, to interpret the raw intelligence collected by SIS and GCHQ.[49]

Mrs Thatcher is believed within Whitehall to take a close personal interest in the working of the intelligence community. She chairs the Ministerial Steering Committee on Intelligence (MIS) which supervises the community and fixes its budget priorities. A permanent secretaries' steering group on intelligence (PSIS) chaired by the cabinet secretary prepares briefs for the MIS.[50] But the Thatcher government's management of GCHQ has given rise to public controversy of an unprecedented kind. By 1981 the MIS had concluded that industrial disruption at GCHQ during and since the Russian invasion of Afghanistan in 1979 posed such a threat to national security that unions at GCHQ would have to be banned. But because the government could not yet bring itself to admit officially that GCHQ had an intelligence function it took no action for another three years. Whatever the merits of the government's decision in 1981, it was seriously lacking in credibility by the time it was announced in 1984. GCHQ remained for some months in the full glare of publicity as a substantial minority of GCHQ staff took part in public protests with the full backing of the TUC and challenged the government's decision in the courts. Even to many Conservative backbenchers the government's handling of the whole affair appeared a public relations disaster.

The GCHQ controversy of 1984 marked only one stage in the crumbling of the traditional taboos which have protected the intelligence community from both public discussion and parliamentary accountability. The early stages of that crumbling in the mid-seventies were assisted by growing public interest in intelligence history. The belated revelation of the wartime 'Ultra' secret in

1973 inevitably drew attention to Bletchley Park's successors at GCHQ Cheltenham of whose existence most people had hitherto been unaware. The historical mole-hunt which led to the unmasking of Anthony Blunt in 1979 focused even greater public attention on MI5, and forced the government to concede a full-scale Commons debate of the kind previously denounced by Macmillan and Wilson as 'dangerous and bad for our general national interest'. In the course of that debate the government publicly abandoned for the first time the ancient and eccentric fiction that SIS does not exist in peacetime, just as the Prime affair later forced it to admit, also for the first time, that GCHQ has an intelligence role.

Revelations about the mole-hunt also laid bare some of the tensions that hunt had produced within the intelligence community. The occupational disease inevitably contracted by some of those whose job it is to investigate conspiracy is an addiction to conspiracy theory. Some of the mole hunters who fell victim to this occupational disease became convinced that Soviet penetration had been much vaster than Whitehall realised, and in particular that Sir Roger Hollis, director-general of MI5 from 1956 to 1965, was a Soviet agent. Unconvinced by an enquiry by Lord Trend in 1974 which found the case against Hollis implausible, some of the conspiracy-theorists took their theories in the late seventies to a handful of politicians and to a sympathetic journalist, Chapman Pincher, who has since written two best-selling accounts of the case against Hollis. The first of these accounts, *Their Trade is Treachery*, drew a formal denial from the prime minister on its publication in March 1981. In 1984 one of Pincher's main sources, the former MI5 officer Peter Wright, took the unprecedented step of putting the case against his former chief on television and delivering a 140-page study of Soviet penetration to the chairman of the Commons Select Committee on Foreign Affairs. In its extreme form, first elaborated by the Soviet defector Anatoli Golitsin, the conspiracy theory of Soviet penetration asserts that the West has been the victim of a long-term deception campaign of unprecedented scope and sophistication, interprets even the Sino-Soviet split as a part of the deception, and dismisses apparent Western intelligence successes like Penkovsky as the product of a Soviet double cross system.[51]

One of the consequences of the Blunt, Hollis, Prime, Bettaney and other security scandals, real or alleged, of recent years has been to force the government to explain itself to parliament on intelligence matters more fully than ever before. In so doing it has helped to erode the traditional doctrine that parliament has simply to trust ministers to 'discharge their [intelligence] responsibilities faithfully' and not to question their competence. By the time that parliament debated the government's decision to ban unions at GCHQ in 1984, that doctrine was widely disregarded. The continuing government insistence that parliamentary accountability is incompatible with national security has also been undermined by the post-Watergate investigations of the American intelligence community by Congressional committees. Out of those investigations emerged select committees on intelligence in the Senate and the House of Representatives which, according to the former Director of Central Intelligence, William Colby, have shown that 'they can know the secrets and keep the secrets'. 'The effect', he believes, 'will be to spread the concept of intelligence working under the law and not outside it'.[52] The emergence of the Congressional committees has produced curious contradictions in the Anglo-American intelligence alliance. The committees were informed of the charges made against Sir Roger Hollis long before the Commons. They were also better briefed than British M.P.s on security problems at GCHQ.[53]

Most M.P.s accept that secret intelligence operations cannot be safely aired on the floor of the House. But there is no reason why a select committee at Westminster should be any less trustworthy than in Washington. As foreign secretary in the Callaghan government, David Owen came to favour the creation of an intelligence select committee composed of 'senior Members of Parliament, trusted on all sides' (probably privy counsellors) with the right to question *in camera* both the foreign secretary and intelligence chiefs: 'People have got to feel confident that a secret service has democratic accountability and that its powers and secrecy could never be abused'.[54] By the 1983 election Owen's views were broadly shared by the majority of Labour and Alliance M.P.s and a small, but growing, minority of Conservatives.

The Thatcher administration has stoutly resisted all proposals for a select committee on intelligence. But by establishing the Franks Committee of privy counsellors in 1982 to carry out the Falklands Islands Review, it came very close to conceding the principle it still opposes. The six privy counsellors included four members of the Lords and one of the Commons. They were subject to 'no reservations' in seeing 'intelligence assessments and reports' and taking oral evidence from intelligence officers. So far as the Falklands conflict was concerned they were thus allowed privileges at least as extensive as those of Congressional intelligence committees. The Thatcher government accepted not merely the Franks Committee's findings on the origins of the Falklands war but also its recommendations on the structure of the Joint Intelligence Organisation. As a result the JIC, chaired from 1939 to 1983 by a Foreign Office official, was given a new chairman, Sir Antony Duff, appointed directly by the prime minister, charged with giving the JIC – to quote the Franks report – 'a more critical and independent role' in intelligence assessment.[55]

Forty years after the end of the Second World War government policy towards the intelligence community remained riddled with internal contradictions which bore witness to the continuing strength of the traditional taboos which surrounded its early growth. The government released the three volumes of Professor F.H. Hinsley's magisterial official history of 'the part played by

British intelligence in allied strategy and operations in the Second World War', but banned publication of Professor Michael Howard's official history of the role of deception in the same strategy and operations. Wartime German intercepts of the early 1940s were released to the Public Record Office; peacetime Soviet intercepts of the early 1920s were withheld indefinitely, despite the fact that copies of many had already leaked out to other archives. When asked for an explanation by a Commons select committee, the cabinet secretary, Sir Robert Armstrong, replied after long delay that peacetime intelligence documents are much more secret than wartime documents, apparently irrespective of age[56] – an eccentric policy scarcely relevant to national security but clearly derived from the traditional taboo which inhibits any official admission of peacetime intelligence gathering.

The same taboo also helps to explain the insistence of successive governments that it is 'dangerous and bad for our general national interest' for the intelligence community to be discussed by parliament at all. The problems of reconciling parliamentary accountability, central to the working of the British constitution, with the secrecy of intelligence operations, essential to national security, have been evaded by every government since the founding of the Secret Service Bureau in 1909. But the experience of the Congressional intelligence committees in the United States and of the Franks Committee in Britain has demonstrated that these problems are not insoluble. At the time of writing, the Thatcher government appears to hope that the whole issue will simply go away. It will not do so.

# NOTES

## ABBREVIATIONS USED IN NOTES AND BIBLIOGRAPHY

BUL     Birmingham University Library
CCAC    Churchill College Archives Centre, Cambridge
CUL     Cambridge University Library
HLRO   House of Lords Record Office
ICM     Intelligence Corps Museum, Ashford, Kent
IOLR    India Office Library and Records, London
IWM     Imperial War Museum, London
LHC     Liddell Hart Centre for Military Archives, King's College, London
NAW    National Archives, Washington
NMM    National Maritime Museum, Greenwich
PRO     Public Record Office, Kew

The full titles of publications and theses cited in the notes are given in the bibliography.

## PREFACE

1   By F.H. Hinsley et al.
2   See below, p. 506.
3   Muggeridge, *Chronicles of Wasted Time*, vol. II, pp.122–3.
4   See the introduction to Andrew and Dilks, *Missing Dimension*.

## CHAPTER 1

1   *Numbers*, XIII. The Lord insisted on the choice of 'leading men' for intelligence work. Failure to heed His advice later contributed to the problems faced by British intelligence between the two world wars of the twentieth century.
2   *Joshua*, II.
3   Aston, *Secret Service*, pp.32–3.

4   Clark, *British Treasury*, p.44.
5   'Secret Service' [A history of the Secret Vote up to 1914], p.4, PRO TI 11689/25138.
6   Middleton, *British Foreign Policy*, appendix VIII. Cobban, *Ambassadors and Secret Agents*. Mitchell, *Underground War*.
7   Kahn, *Codebreakers*, pp.169–74, 187–8. Middleton, *British Foreign Policy*, pp.211–12.
8   'Secret Service', PRO TI 11689/25138. Middleton, *British Foreign Policy*, appendix VIII.
9   Henderson, 'Palmerston and the Secret Service Fund', pp.485–7.
10  Taylor, *Oliphant*, ch.5.
11  'Secret Service', PRO TI 11689/25183. Figures for the amount of money spent by individual ministries are not available before 1885.
12  Morgan, 'Myth and Reality in the Great Game'.
13  McLean, *Britain and her Buffer State*, chs.1, 4. Kamzadeh, *Russia and Britain in Persia*, pp.389–97. Morris, 'British Secret Service Activity in Khorassan'.
14  Jones, *British Diplomatic Service*. Steiner and Cromwell, 'The Foreign Office before 1914'.
15  Ramm (ed), *Correspondence of Mr. Gladstone and Lord Granville*, vol. II, pp.33–5. Monson to Lansdowne, 21 Feb. 1902, PRO FO 800/124.
16  Andrew, 'Déchiffrement et diplomatie', p.49.
17  Fergusson, *British Military Intelligence*, chs.1,2. Strachan, 'Soldiers, Strategy and Sebastopol', pp.307ff.
18  Jervis, *Jervis*, pp.323–4.
19  Ibid., pp.10, 201, 218, 270–1.
20  Parritt, *Intelligencers*, ch.8.
21  Jervis, *Jervis*, ch.13.
22  Watson, *Wilson*, ch.5. Fergusson, *British Military Intelligence*, chs.2, 3.
23  Watson, *Wilson*, chs.1–5.
24  Watson, *Wilson*, ch.1. Parritt, *Intelligencers*, ch.11. Fergusson, *British Military Intelligence*, ch.3. Brian Bond, *Victorian Army and Staff College*, pp.120–1.
25  Beaver, 'Development of the Intelligence Division', chs.2–4. Fergusson, *British Military Intelligence*, ch.4.
26  Repington, *Vestigia*, pp.88–9.
27  Beaver, 'Development of the Intelligence Division', pp.90–1.
28  Wells, 'Naval Intelligence and Decision-Making', pp.124–5. Aston, *Secret Service*, p.28.
29  Schurman, *Education of a Navy*, ch.2. Wells, 'Studies in British Naval Intelligence', pp.21–2.
30  Colomb, 'Naval Intelligence and Protection of Commerce', pp.553–73. By a curious coincidence one of the officers serving on the *Hecla* at the time of Colomb's lecture was Mansfield Smith (later Cumming), afterwards the first head of SIS.
31  Ranft (ed.), *Technical Change and British Naval Policy*, pp.3–5. Schurman, *Education of a Navy*, pp.30–1. Hall's obituary in *The Times*, 13 March 1895.
32  Aston, *Secret Service*, pp.30–1.
33  Ranft (ed.), *Technical Change and British Naval Policy*, p.5. Wells, 'Naval

Intelligence and Decision Making', pp.124–5. Idem, 'Studies in British Naval Intelligence', pp.22ff. *Pall Mall Gazette*, 13 Oct. 1886.

34   Beresford, *Memoirs*, vol. II, pp.344–7. On Salisbury and the IB see Beaver, 'The Development of the Intelligence Division', pp.87ff.

35   Beresford, *Memoirs*, vol. II, p.353. Mackay, *Fisher*, p.189. Beresford resigned in January 1888 to campaign for 'the necessity of strengthening the fleet'.

36   Marder, *British Naval Policy 1880–1905*, pp.127–8.

37   Aston, *Secret Service*, pp.35–41.

38   Royle and Walvin, *English Radicals and Reformers*, p.72.

39   Memo by Williamson, 22 Oct. 1880, PRO MEPO 2/134. Porter, 'Origins of Britain's Political Police'.

40   Short, *Dynamite War*, ch.1.

41   Ibid. Cole, *Prince of Spies*.

42   Porter, 'Origins of Britain's Political Police'. Police reports of 24 May, 15 June 1872, PRO HO 45/9303/11335.

43   Short, *Dynamite War*, chs.3–7. Porter, 'Origins of Britain's Political Police'.

44   Short, *Dynamite War*, pp.184–6.

45   Porter, 'Origins of Britain's Political Police'.

46   Short, *Dynamite War*, pp.232–3.

47   Ibid., pp.231, 234. Porter, 'Origins of Britain's Political Police'.

48   Porter, 'Origins of Britain's Political Police'. My account of the origins of the Special Branch also draws on my filmed report for 'Timewatch', BBC 2, 6 Feb. 1985 (producer Paul Lee), based chiefly on research by Dr Bernard Porter.

49   Fergusson, *British Military Intelligence*, pp.70–1, 83. Parritt, *Intelligencers*, pp.151–2. Beaver, 'Development of the Intelligence Division', ch.5.

50   Gleichen, *Guardsman's Memories*, pp.176, 142. Parritt, *Intelligencers*, p.152.

51   The Intelligence Division only formally became the Intelligence Department in 1901, but during the 1890s was already often called by its later title. Parritt, *Intelligencers*, pp.107n, 153–4. Fergusson, *British Military Intelligence*, p.85.

52   Gleichen, *Guardsman's Memories*, pp.49–50. Wingate, Kitchener's senior intelligence officer, was more forthcoming.

53   Beaver, 'Development of the Intelligence Division', p.303.

54   Ibid., chs.7–8. Gleichen, *Guardsman's Memories*, p.177.

55   Gleichen, *Guardsman's Memories*, pp.77–8. Cf. Callwell, *Stray Recollections*, vol. I, pp.311–12.

56   Beaver, 'The Intelligence Division Library'. Idem, 'Development of the Intelligence Division', ch.6. Curiously, Cromie was subsequently taken on by the Inspector General of Fortifications.

57   Gleichen, *Guardsman's Memories*, pp.145–6. Callwell, *Stray Recollections*, p.327. Beaver, 'Development of the Intelligence Division', ch.6.

58   Callwell, 'War Office Reminiscences', pp.158, 24.

59   Aston, *Secret Service*, p.49.

60   Brendon, *Eminent Edwardians*, pp.216–19.

61   Baden-Powell, *My Adventures as a Spy*, pp.88, 11–12, 159.

62   *Parliamentary Debates (Commons)*, 4th series, vol. CVIIIC, 13 July 1908, col. 393.

63  Aston, *Secret Service*, p.49.
64  Tulloch, *Recollections*, pp.222, 250.
65  Gleichen, *Guardsman's Memories*, p.325.
66  Callwell, *Small Wars*, pp.49–50.
67  Baden-Powell, *My Adventures as a Spy*, p.159.
68  Aston, *Secret Service*, p.142.
69  Tulloch, *Recollections*, p.267.
70  Baden-Powell, *Lessons from the 'Varsity' of Life*, p.115.
71  See below, p.76.
72  Report of Lord Hardwicke's Committee, 1903, p.56, PRO TI 10966/617/09.
73  Waters, *Secret and Confidential*, p.248.
74  Countess of Malmesbury, *Ardagh*, pp.282ff.
75  Brigadier-General Sir James E. Edmonds, Unpublished Memoirs, ch.16, p.5, LHC Edmonds MSS III/3.
76  Gleichen, *Guardsman's Memories*, p. 176.
77  Cited by Fergusson, *British Military Intelligence*, p.109.
78  Warwick, *South African War*, p.66.
79  Report of the Royal Commission on the War in South Africa, Cd. 1789 (1903), p.128. Countess of Malmesbury, *Ardagh*, pp.277–8.
80  Fergusson, *British Military Intelligence*, pp.113ff.
81  Ibid., pp.148, 114.
82  Edmonds, Unpublished Memoirs, ch.16, pp.3–5, LHC Edmonds MSS III/3. Fergusson, *British Military Intelligence*, pp.151–2.
83  Aston, *Secret Service*, p.22.
84  Fergusson, *British Military Intelligence*, ch.8.
85  'A Secret Service Agent in South-West Africa: Ironside's Story as told to me from notes he left behind, by Colonel R. Macleod', LHC Macleod MSS 2.
86  Fergusson, *British Military Intelligence*, ch.9.
87  Royal Commission on the War in South Africa, *Minutes of Evidence*, vol. I, Cd 1790 (1903), pp.216, 465.
88  Report of Lord Hardwicke's Committee, 1903, pp.10, 15, 21, 23, PRO TI 10966/617/09. Fergusson, *British Military Intelligence*, p.221.
89  Fergusson, *British Military Intelligence*, pp.202–3. Hinsley et al., *British Intelligence*, vol. I, p.9. Edmonds, Unpublished Memoirs, ch.20, LHC Edmonds MSS III/5.
90  Andrew, *Delcassé*, pp.284–5.
91  Edmonds, Unpublished Memoirs, ch.19, LHC Edmonds MSS III/4. Edmonds misremembered the date of his appointment to the 'Special Section'.
92  Gleichen, *Guardsman's Memories*, pp.314–16.

## CHAPTER 2

1  Howard, *Continental Commitment*, p.11. Kennedy, *Anglo-German Antagonism*, p.242.
2  Clarke, *Voices Prophesying War*, pp.136–8.
3  Le Queux, *England's Peril*, passim.

4   Ibid., p.42.
5   *Kim* was first published in 1901, a year after *England's Peril*.
6   Clarke, *Voices Prophesying War*, p.136.
7   Andrew, *Delcassé*, p.171.
8   Kennedy, *Anglo-German Antagonism*, pp.224, 82.
9   Childers, *Riddle of the Sands*, pp.264, 247, 217, postscript.
10  Kennedy, 'Riddle of the Sands'.
11  Gleichen, *Guardsman's Memories*, pp.344–5.
12  Boyle, *Erskine Childers*, p.113.
13  Kennedy, 'Riddle of the Sands'.
14  Le Queux, *Secrets of the Foreign Office*, pp.5, 13, 23, 29. The much later CIA scheme (never implemented) to interfere with Fidel Castro's cigars is reminiscent of Drew.
15  Ibid., pp.11, 45.
16  Le Queux, *Things I Know*, p.235: a story further elaborated later by Le Queux in *German Spies in England*.
17  See below, pp.51–8.
18  Le Queux, *Things I Know*, pp.235–6.
19  Ibid., pp.237.
20  Ibid., p.238.
21  Morris, 'And, Is the Kaiser Coming for Tea?', pp.43–4. Kennedy, *Anglo-German Antagonism*, p.371.
22  Kennedy, *Anglo-German Antagonism*, p.362.
23  Ferris, *House of Northcliffe*, pp.189, 265, 271–2, 64–5. Pound and Harmsworth, *Northcliffe*, pp.151–2.
24  Falk, *Bouquets for Fleet Street*, pp.64–5. Clarke, *Voices Prophesying War*, p.145.
25  Le Queux, *The Invasion of 1910*, pp.16, 28–9.
26  Le Queux, *Things I Know*, p.237.
27  Oppenheim, *Pool of Memory*, pp.27, 37.
28  Standish, *Prince of Storytellers*; quotation from p.149.
29  Oppenheim, *Maker of History*, pp.240, 251, 258, 311–12.
30  Surprisingly, *The Swoop*, probably alone of Wodehouse's books, has never been reprinted.
31  Le Queux, *Things I Know*, pp.238–9, 246.
32  Introduction by Stephen Gwynne to Pocock, *Chorus to Adventurers*.
33  Pocock, *Chorus to Adventurers*, pp.61–7.
34  I am grateful to Mr Geoffrey Pocock (no relation to Roger), who is writing a history of the Frontiersmen, for lending me a copy of this privately printed history.
35  Pocock, *Chorus to Adventurers*, ch.6 gives a confused account of fears of German spies within the Legion and of his own ousting.
36  *The Times*, 21 Aug. 1908, cited by Morris, 'And, Is the Kaiser Coming for Tea?', p.74.
37  'The Psychology of a Scare', *The Nation*, 27 March 1909; 'A Plague of Spying', ibid., 10 Sept. 1910.
38  Lowe, 'About German Spies', p.45. Maxse published a book in 1915 entitled *Germany on the Brain*.

39  'The German Peril', *Quarterly Review*, vol. CCIX (July 1908), p.296.
40  Lowe, 'About German Spies', pp.52–3. Morris, 'And, Is the Kaiser Coming for Tea?', p.78.
41  Le Queux, *Things I Know*, ch.16. Idem, *German Spies in England*, ch.2.
42  Le Queux, *Things I Know*, ch.16.
43  Le Queux, *German Spies in England*, foreword, ch.2.
44  Introduction by Gower to Sladen, *The Real Le Queux*, p.xv.
45  Sladen, *The Real Le Queux*, pp.124, 127.
46  Ibid., p.vii.
47  Felstead (ed.), *Steinhauer*, p.62.
48  See below, pp.51–2.
49  Baden-Powell, *My Adventures as a Spy*, p.52.
50  Bywater and Ferraby, *Strange Intelligence*, pp.59–60, 176–7.
51  Baden-Powell, *My Adventures as a Spy*, pp.52–7.
52  See below, p.83.
53  *Parliamentary Debates (Lords)*, 4th series, vol. CXCII, 13 July 1908, col. 393.
54  Le Queux, *Spies of the Kaiser*, introduction.
55  Ibid., p.87.
56  R.S. Churchill, *Winston S. Churchill*, vol.II, p.513.
57  Mackay, *Fisher*, p.385.
58  Morris, 'And, Is the Kaiser Coming for Tea?', pp.58–9. Gooch, *Plans of War*, pp.284–5. The subcommittee recommended, however, that the territorials should be bolstered by two divisions of regulars to repel small raids.
59  Morris, 'And, Is the Kaiser Coming for Tea?', pp.60–1.
60  Clarke, *Voices Prophesying War*, p.152.
61  Steiner, *Britain and the Origins of the First World War*, pp.53, 287n23.
62  Marder, *Dreadnought to Scapa Flow*, vol. I, ch.7.
63  Edmonds, 'Origins of MI5', LHC Edmonds MSS VII/3; idem, Unpublished Memoirs, ch.20, Edmonds MSS, III/5.
64  Ewart to CGS, 1 Feb. 1908, and accompanying memo, n.d., PRO WO 106/47B.
65  Slade to Asquith, 8 May 1909, 'Appendices to Proceedings of a Subcommittee of the Committee of Imperial Defence to enquire into certain questions of Naval Policy raised by Lord Charles Beresford', pp.193–5, PRO CAB 16/9B.
66  Hinsley et al., *British Intelligence in the Second World War*, vol. I, p.16n.
67  Edmonds, Unpublished Memoirs, ch.20, LHC Edmonds MSS III/5.
68  Hiley, 'Failure of British Espionage', p.872.
69  Waters, *'Secret and Confidential'*, p.36.
70  Hiley, 'Failure of British Espionage', pp.872–4. Slade to Asquith, 8 May 1909, 'Appendices to Proceedings of a Subcommittee of the Committee of Imperial Defence ...', p.195, PRO CAB 16/9B.
71  Thwaites to Gleichen, 7 May 1907, PRO WO 32/8873 (I am grateful for this reference to Nicholas Hiley). Hiley, 'Failure of British Espionage', p.874.
72  Edmonds, Unpublished Memoirs, ch.20, LHC Edmonds MSS III/5.
73  Lieut-Col. R.E. Lee, G2 report no.37878 (reporting discussion with Edmonds), 18 Feb. 1936, NAW RG 165 9944-A-187.

74 Ibid. Edmonds, Unpublished Memoirs, ch.20, LHC Edmonds MSS III/5.
75 Edmonds, Unpublished Memoirs, ch.20, LHC Edmonds MSS III/5.
76 'Report and Proceedings of a Sub-Committee of the Committee of Imperial Defence Appointed by the Prime Minister to Consider the Question of Foreign Espionage in the United Kingdom', Oct. 1909, appendix no.1, case no. 26, PRO CAB 16/8.
77 Edmonds, Unpublished Memoirs, ch.20, LHC Edmonds MSS III/5. Andrew, 'Mobilization of British Intelligence', pp.91–2.
78 Lady Kell, 'Secret Well Kept', p.113, IWM.
79 Spiers, *Haldane*, ch.8.
80 Edmonds, Unpublished Memoirs, ch.20, LHC Edmonds MSS III/5.
81 'Report and Proceedings of a Sub-Committee of the Committee of Imperial Defence ...', Oct. 1909, PRO CAB 16/8. (This important document was first analysed in French, 'Spy Fever in Britain'). Edmonds, Unpublished Memoirs, ch.20, LHC Edmonds MSS III/5.
82 Trumpener, 'War Premeditated?', pp.60–1, n.7.
83 Holt-Wilson, 'Security Intelligence in War. Lecture Notes', 1934, IWM Kell MSS.
84 Felstead (ed.), *Steinhauer*, esp. pp.6, 10–11, 50, 96. A foreword by Admiral 'Blinker' Hall confirms the general reliability of Steinhauer's account.
85 See below, p.70.
86 Edmonds, memo, 9 Feb. 1909, IWM Kell MSS.
87 'Report and Proceedings of a Sub-Committee of the Committee of Imperial Defence ...', minutes of 1st meeting, 30 March 1909, PRO CAB 16/8.
88 Ibid., appendix I, part I.
89 Ibid., appendix I, parts II, III.
90 Ibid., minutes of 1st meeting, 30 March 1909.
91 Brett (ed.), *Esher Journals and Letters*, vol. II, p.379.
92 'Report and Proceedings of a Sub-Committee of the Committee of Imperial Defence ...', minutes of 1st meeting, 30 March 1909, PRO CAB 16/8.
93 Koss, *Haldane*, pp.15–16, 65, 69.
94 'Report and Proceedings of a Sub-Committee of the Committee of Imperial Defence ...', minutes of 3rd meeting, 12 July 1909, PRO CAB 16/8.
95 Ibid.
96 Edmonds, Unpublished Memoirs, ch.20, p.4, LHC Edmonds MSS III/6.
97 'Report and Proceedings of a Sub-Committee of the Committee of Imperial Defence ...', appendix IX, PRO CAB 16/8.
98 See above, p.25.
99 'Report and Proceedings of a Sub-Committee of the Committee of Imperial Defence ...', appendix IX, PRO CAB 16/8.
100 Ibid., Report, pp.iii–iv.
101 Hinsley et al., *British Intelligence in the Second World War*, vol. I, p.16. Hiley, 'Failure of British Espionage', p.877.
102 Lady Kell, 'Secret Well Kept', ch.1, IWM.
103 Ibid., p.32.
104 Ibid., p.110.
105 Edmonds, Unpublished Memoirs, ch.19, p.7; ch.20, p.5. LHC Edmonds MSS

III 4–5.

106    Lady Kell, 'Secret Well Kept', pp.1, 22, 137, LWM. *Who's Who* entries for Holt-Wilson.

107    Holt-Wilson, 'Security Intelligence in War. Lecture Notes', 1934, p.9, IWM Kell MSS.

108    Thomson, *Scene Changes*, passim.

109    'Return of Aliens' form devised by Kell, approved by Sir Edward Troup (PUS Home Office), 1 Nov. 1910; Troup to Churchill, 14 Oct. 1911, with minute by Churchill, 15 Oct. 1911; Kell to Troup, 11 Dec. 1913, PRO HO 45/ 10629/199699. Churchill, *World Crisis*, vol. I, p.36. The early proceedings of the Aliens Committee may be followed in PRO CAB 17/90.

110    Churchill, 'Memorandum on the General Naval Situation', 26 Aug. 1912, p.382, PRO FO 800/87. I am grateful for this reference to Nicholas Hiley.

111    *The Times*, 16 Sept. 1910. Helm had made only 'rather futile sketches of the obsolete Portsmouth land defences'. Holt-Wilson, 'Security Intelligence in War. Lecture Notes', 1934, p.16, IWM Kell MSS.

112    *The Times*, 16 Sept. 1910.

113    Lady Kell, 'Secret Well Kept', pp.120–1, IWM.

114    *The Times*, 21 Sept. 1910.

115    *The Times*, 15 Nov. 1910.

116    Lady Kell, 'Secret Well Kept', pp.121–2, IWM. *The Times*, 29, 30 Aug., 4 Nov. 1911. File 32404, PRO FO 371/1126.

117    *Parliamentary Debates (Lords)*, 5th series, vol. IX, 25 July 1911, col. 642.

118    Williams, *Not in the Public Interest*, pp.24–8.

119    *Parliamentary Debates (Commons)*, 5th Series, vol. XXIX, 18 Aug. 1911, cols. 2252ff.

120    Williams, *Not in the Public Interest*, pp.132–3. Bywater and Ferraby, *Strange Intelligence*, p.177. *The Times*, 10 Feb. 1912.

121    Felstead (ed.), *Steinhauer*, ch.3, pp.18–19.

122    *The Times*, 23, 24 July 1912.

123    Graves, *Secrets of the German War Office*, p.136. Graves describes himself on the title page as 'Late Spy to the German Government'.

124    Lady Kell, 'Secret Well Kept', p.128.

125    Felstead (ed.), *Steinhauer*, p.19.

126    *The Times*, 23, 24 July 1912. Graves, *Secrets of the German War Office*, p.146.

127    Bulloch, *MI5*, ch.3. Bulloch provides no references but was given by Lady Kell 'all the help and assistance that she was able, within the limits of security'. Since his book is intended as 'a tribute' to Kell and is almost invariably uncritical, his account of Kell's fallibility on this occasion is all the more plausible. Graves predictably produced a highly embroidered version of his release according to which he was summoned before Sir Edward Grey prior to his departure for New York. *Secrets of the German War Office*, pp.147–54.

128    *The Times*, 17 Jan. 1913. Lady Kell, 'Secret Well Kept', p.135.

129    Felstead (ed.), *Steinhauer*, pp.69–70. Parrott's betrayal was admitted at his trial. *The Times*, 19 Nov. 1913.

130    *The Times*, 15, 16 Jan. 1913.

131    Holt-Wilson, 'Security Intelligence in War. Lecture Notes', 1934, p.14.

132   *The Times*, 17 Jan. 1913.
133   Felstead (ed.), *Steinhauer*, pp.67–8. Hentschel acknowledged at his trial that he had received money from Germany in August 1913. *The Times*, 10 Nov. 1913.
134   *The Times*, 10, 19 Nov. 1913.
135   *The Times*, 7, 14, 21 March 1913.
136   *The Times*, 5, 12 March, 4 April 1914. Felstead (ed.), *Steinhauer*, ch.7.
137   Holt-Wilson, 'Security Intelligence in War. Lecture Notes', 1934, p.16, IWM Kell MSS.
138   Felstead (ed.), *Steinhauer*, p.49.
139   Lady Kell, 'Secret Well Kept', p.140, IWM.
140   Holt-Wilson, 'Security Intelligence in War. Lecture Notes', 1934, p.17.
141   *The Times*, 6 Aug., 14 Nov. 1914.
142   Holt-Wilson, 'Security Intelligence in War. Lecture Notes', 1934, pp.14–15. Lady Kell, 'Secret Well Kept', p.126, IWM.
143   *The Times*, 13, 14 Nov. 1914.
144   Felstead (ed.), *Steinhauer*, p.6.
145   Lady Kell, 'Secret Well Kept', p.139, IWM.
146   *The Times*, 14 Nov. 1914.
147   Felstead (ed.), *Steinhauer*, pp.49–51.
148   Lady Kell, 'Secret Well Kept', pp.125, 141, IWM.
149   'Secret Paper A. B2068. For Chief Constables Only, Notes on the Work of Counter-Espionage', Oct. 1912, PRO CAB 17/90.
150   Diary entry, 21 Aug. 1911, CCAC Grant-Duff MSS 2.
151   'Confidential. Paper B. B2068. Notes on the Work and Methods of Foreign Secret Service Agents', Oct. 1912, PRO CAB 17/90. The main pre-war suspect was Baron Louis von Horst though it was thought 'practically certain' that he was not the only German agent encouraging industrial disruption. G173, 13 Nov. 1917, PRO CAB 24/4.
152   Tuchman, *August 1914*, p.269. Andrew, 'France and the German Menace'.
153   *The Times*, 15 Oct. 1914. See below, pp.177–81.
154   The date is suggested by Cumming's service record in PRO ADM 196/20, p.123.
155   Ibid. Cf. Cumming's entries in *Who's Who*. I am grateful for additional information to Cumming's great nephew, the late A.N.W. Saunders, and to his great niece, Miss Diana Pares.
156   Cumming's entries in the *Navy List*.
157   Payne Best transcripts.
158   Kirke to his wife, 14 July 1913, Kirke MSS.
159   Ibid. I am grateful for further information to Colonel Humphrey Quill.
160   Dukes, '*ST 25*', p.35.
161   Information from Miss Diana Pares.
162   Cumming's service record, PRO ADM 196/20, p.123.
163   Information from Colonel Humphrey Quill.
164   Merson, *Village School*, p.82. Information from Miss Diana Pares.
165   Kirke to his wife, 7, 14 July 1913, Kirke MSS.
166   Mackenzie, *Greek Memories*, p.309.

167   Dukes, '*ST 25*', p.35.
168   Williams, *World of Action*, pp.334–5.
169   Private information.
170   The swordstick still survives in private possession.
171   Williams, *World of Action*, p.334. Information from Miss Diana Pares.
172   Mackenzie, *Greek Memories*, p.324.
173   Day, 'The Basic Conception of Education of Kurt Hahn', pp.25, 176.
174   Information from Miss Diana Pares and Mrs Pippa Temple (née Pares). Brereton, *Gordonstoun*, p.222, identifies Lady Cumming as the school's first hostess but makes no reference to her late husband.
175   Private information.
176   Hinsley et al., *British Intelligence in the Second World War*, p.16.
177   Cabinet memorandum, 'Reduction of Estimates for Secret Services', 19 March 1920: withheld from PRO, but copy in HLRO Lloyd George MSS F/9/2/16.
178   Churchill to Secretary of Admiralty and First Sea Lord, 27 Oct. 1914, PRO ADM 137/965: cited by Hiley, 'Failure of British Espionage', p.886.
179   Andrew, 'France and the German Menace'.
180   'Reduction of Estimates for Secret Services', 19 March 1920, HLRO Lloyd George MSS F/9/2/16.
181   'A Former Member of the Service', 'Work of the Secret Service', Part I.
182   *The Times*, 14 Dec. 1911.
183   Bywater and Ferraby, *Strange Intelligence*, p.37. The credibility of this source is strengthened by the foreword by Admiral 'Blinker' Hall. Cf. 'A Former Member of the Service', 'Work of the Secret Service', part IV.
184   A number of Rotter's logbooks are in PRO ADM 137 series.
185   Ibid. Hiley, 'Failure of British Espionage', p.884.
186   Raleigh, *War in the Air*, vol. I, pp.180ff.
187   Information from Spottiswoode's son, Mr John Spottiswoode. Spottiswoode was always reluctant, and usually refused, to talk about his brief intelligence career. His son first discovered the outline of his father's experiences only after his nightmares in the 1930s. Spottiswoode's few surviving pre-1914 papers concern chiefly his interest in aviation. Because of the lack of corroborative written evidence, Spottiswoode's account of his role as a 'casual agent' has necessarily to be treated with caution. But his knowledge of Cumming (whom he described to his son not by name but as captain of the *Victory*), their joint involvement in the Royal Aero Club and the genuine horror with which he later relived his German experiences make it unlikely that they were mere fantasy.
188   'A Former Member of the Service', 'Work of the Secret Service'.
189   'Reggie' was Captain Cyrus Regnart of NID. James, *Eyes of the Navy*, p.8.
190   *The Times*, 22, 23 Dec. 1910.
191   Information kindly supplied by the late Captain Stephen Roskill, based on his conversations with Trench.
192   James, *A Great Seaman*, pp.123–4.
193   Information from Captain Roskill.
194   *The Times*, 11 Dec. 1911.

195 Drake to Payne Best, 25 July 1947, enclosing account of the Bertrand Stewart case, IWM Payne Best MSS 79/57/1. Drake, then working as Kell's assistant, had been 'told the whole story from the inside by old "C"' shortly after Stewart's arrest.

196 Ibid. Hiley, 'Failure of British Espionage', p.881. *The Times*, 1, 5, 7 Feb. 1912. Stewart was released at the same time as Brandon and Trench.

197 Kirkpatrick, 'The War 1914–1918', p.150, IWM. See below, p.000.

198 DMO to military attaché, Brussels, no. 33, 8 Aug. 1914, PRO FO 371/2163. Hiley, 'Failure of British Espionage', p.881.

199 See below, p.87. On the Brussels spy bureaux see also Villiers to Grey, 26 Feb. 1914, PRO FO 371/1909.

200 Oliver, Unpublished Recollections, pp.96–7, NMM Oliver MSS OLV/12.

201 'Deacon', *British Secret Service*, pp.139–42, 175.

202 Kettle, *Sidney Reilly*, ch.1.

203 See above, p.50.

204 Kettle, *Sidney Reilly*, ch.1.

205 Young (ed.), *Lockhart Diaries*, vol. I, p.183.

206 Lockhart, *British Agent*, pp.322–3. Bailey, *Conspirators*, pp.20ff. Kettle, *Sidney Reilly*, pp.18–20.

207 Lockhart, *Ace of Spies*, p.54.

208 See above, p.78.

209 Lockhart, *Ace of Spies*, pp.51–5. Kettle, *Sidney Reilly*, pp.19–20.

210 Andrew, 'Déchiffrement et diplomatie'. Idem, 'British Secret Service and Anglo-Soviet Relations', pp.678–9. Neilson and Andrew, 'Tsarist Codebreakers and British Codes'.

## CHAPTER 3

1 A.G. Denniston, Untitled MS memoir on Room 40, n.d., CCAC Denniston MSS DENN 1/3. Admiral of the Fleet Sir Henry Oliver, 'Notes about Room 40 and Sir Alfred Ewing in the 1914–18 War'; Oliver to Secretary of the Admiralty, 7 March 1919, NMM Oliver MSS OLV/8.

2 James, *Eyes of the Navy*, p. 26. Churchill, *World Crisis*, vol. I, pp.322–7.

3 Denniston, MS memoir on Room 40, n.d.; idem, TS memoir on Room 40, [1917], CCAC, Denniston MSS DENN 1/3, DENN 1/2. Ewing, *Man of Room 40*, pp.173–5. According to a later recruit, W.F. Clarke, Herschell was 'not a good German scholar'; Clarke, '40 O.B. Early Memories', CCAC Clarke MSS CLKE 3.

4 Denniston, MS memoir on Room 40, n.d., CCAC Denniston MSS DENN 1/3. Andrew, 'Déchiffrement et diplomatie', pp.131–2. Kahn, *Codebreakers*, p.304. Denniston is wrong in suggesting, from memory, that the French cracked the main German code 'about the middle of September'; they may, however, have produced a partial solution then.

5 Denniston was still on leave from Osborne. The other language teachers had gone back to their colleges, though Anstie was later to return to Room 40.

6   Denniston, MS and TS memoirs on Room 40, CCAC Denniston MSS, DENN 1/3, DENN 1/2.

7   Ibid. Beesly, *Room 40*, pp.3–4.

8   Churchill, *World Crisis*, vol. I, p.462. Beesly, *Room 40*, pp.4–6.

9   W.F. Clarke, '40 O.B. & GC & CS 1914 to 1945', ch.4, CCAC Clarke MSS CLKE 3. Clarke's sometimes harsh judgments fail to give due weight to the general ignorance of cryptography in the early months of the war. Denniston's judgments are more charitable.

10  Denniston, MS memoir on Room 40, n.d., CCAC Denniston MSS DENN 1/3. Churchill, *World Crisis*, vol. I, p.462, dates the breaking of the HVB at the beginning of November.

11  Beesly, *Room 40*, p.7.

12  W.F. Clarke, '40 O.B. & GC & CS 1914 to 1945', ch.4, CCAC Clarke MSS CLKE 3.

13  Ibid. Denniston, MS memoir on Room 40, n.d., CCAC Denniston MSS DENN 1/3.

14  Mackenzie, *Life and Times, Octave Five*, p.113.

15  James, *Eyes of the Navy*, p.xvii.

16  Ewing, *Man of Room 40*, p.179.

17  'Narrative of Captain Hope', according to Clarke 'written before June 1926'; Clarke, '40 O.B. & GC & CS 1914 to 1945', ch.3, CCAC Clarke MSS CLKE 3.

18  'Narrative of Captain Hope', ibid.

19  Korvettenkapitän Kleikamp, 'Der Einfluss der Funkaufklärung auf die Seekriegsführung in der Nordsee 1914–1918' (Kiel, 1934), Bibliothek für Zeitgeschichte, Stuttgart. I am grateful to Patrick Beesly for lending me a copy of this document.

20  'Narrative of Captain Hope', CCAC Clarke MSS CLKE 3.

21  Denniston, MS memoir on Room 40, n.d., CCAC Denniston MSS DENN 1/3.

22  Oliver, 'Recollections', vol. II, p.164, NMM Oliver MSS OLV/12. Beesly, *Room 40*, p.134.

23  Ewing, *Man of Room 40*, pp.198–9.

24  Clarke, '40 O.B. & GC & CS 1914 to 1945', ch.1, CCAC Clarke MSS CLKE 3.

25  Ewing, *Man of Room 40*, p.198.

26  Beesly, *Room 40*, ch.11.

27  Andrew, 'Mobilization of British Intelligence'. Fitzgerald, *Knox Brothers*, pp.90–2, 137.

28  Professor E.R. Vincent, Unpublished Memoirs, p.107, Corpus Christi College Archives, Cambridge.

29  Clarke, '40 O.B. & GC & CS 1914 to 1945', ch.1, CCAC Clarke MSS CLKE 3. Denniston also met his wife Dorothy (née Gilliat) in Room 40.

30  Fitzgerald, *Knox Brothers*, p.93.

31  Copy in CCAC Denniston MSS DENN 3/3. The title page reveals that the verses are by Knox.

32  Clarke, '40 O.B. & GC & CS 1914 to 1945', chs.1, 2, CCAC Clarke MSS

CLKE 3. Beesly, *Room 40*, passim.
33   Army Security Agency, 'Historical Background of the Signal Security Agency', vol. II, pp.17–18, NAW RG 457, NC3-457-77-1.
34   Clarke, '40 O.B. & GC & CS 1914 to 1945', chs.1, 2, CCAC Clarke MSS CLKE 3. Denniston, MS memoir on Room 40, n.d., CCAC Denniston MSS DENN 1/3. Beesly, *Room 40*, passim.
35   Birch, 'Alice in ID 25', pp.10–14, CCAC Denniston MSS DENN 3/3.
36   Ibid., pp.35ff.
37   Beesly, *Room 40*, ch.5.
38   Churchill, *World Crisis*, vol. I, p.466.
39   The most vivid account of the engagement is in Churchill, *World Crisis*, vol. I, ch.20; the most judicious analysis is probably in Roskill, *Beatty*. My account derives chiefly from theirs.
40   Marder, *Dreadnought to Scapa Flow*, vol. III, p.142.
41   Naval Staff Monograph, vol. XII (1925), pp.120–1, MOD Naval Historical Branch.
42   Marder, *Dreadnought to Scapa Flow*, vol. III, pp.143–4.
43   Naval Staff Monograph, vol. XII (1925), p.144, MOD Naval Historical Branch.
44   Churchill, *World Crisis*, vol. I, pp.477–8.
45   Ibid., vol. II, pp.128ff.
46   Marder, *Dreadnought to Scapa Flow*, vol. III, p.161.
47   Roskill, *Beatty*, pp.115–16.
48   Ibid., pp.114–15. Marder, *Dreadnought to Scapa Flow*, vol. III, pp.140, 167.
49   Marder, *Dreadnought to Scapa Flow*, vol. III, p.172.
50   Roskill, *Beatty*, pp.120–1.
51   Ibid., pp.145–6. Churchill, *World Crisis*, vol. I, p.466.
52   Denniston, MS memoir on Room 40, n.d., CCAC Denniston MSS DENN 1/3.
53   Clarke, '40 O.B. & GC & CS 1914 to 1945', ch.4, CCAC Clarke MSS CLKE 3.
54   Denniston, MS memoir on Room 40, n.d., CCAC Denniston MSS DENN 1/3.
55   Fraser, *All to the Good*, p.56.
56   Marder, *Jutland and After*, p.47.
57   'Narrative of Captain Hope', CCAC Clarke MSS CLKE 3.
58   Churchill, *World Crisis*, vol. II, p.147.
59   Save where otherwise indicated, my account of Jutland is based on Marder, *Jutland and After*, and Roskill, *Beatty*.
60   Marder, *Jutland and After*, pp.172–86. Roskill, *Beatty*, pp. 179–83. Clarke, '40 O.B. & GC & CS 1914 to 1945', ch.4, CCAC Clarke MSS CLKE 3. Clarke, 'Jutland 31.5.16', 16 Feb. 1958, CCAC Roskill MSS ROSKILL 3/6.
61   Marder, *Jutland and After*, pp.176–8.
62   Roskill, *Beatty*, p.191.
63   Marder, *Jutland and After*, pp.176, 269–70.
64   Clarke to Roskill, 17 Feb. 1959, CCAC Roskill MSS ROSKILL 3/6.
65   Tuchman, *Zimmermann Telegram*, pp.17–19.
66   Boucard, *Revelations from the Secret Service*, pp.66–76. Boucard's sources appear

to have included Szek's father and several Belgians who assisted his escape to Holland.

67   Roskill, *Beatty*, p.87n.
68   Hall's own account of the episode is in his notes on 'Intelligence in Wartime', pp.3–4, CCAC HALL 2/1. For an alternative version see Beesly, *Room 40*, pp.131–2. James dates the windfall as April 1915 (*Eyes of the Navy*, p.69). Tuchman suggests 'sometime between June and September 1915' (*Zimmermann Telegram*, p.21). Hall's own notes do not mention the month.
69   Kahn, *Codebreakers*, p.284.
70   Ibid., p.285.
71   Ibid., p.351. Baker, *Woodrow Wilson, Life and Letters*, vol. V, pp.204ff, 307, 317–18; vol. VI, pp.52–3, 143ff.
72   It was indeed 'Neptune'.
73   For evidence that Room 40 decrypted American telegrams, see Roskill, *Hankey*, vol. I, p.247.
74   James, *Eyes of the Navy*, p.71.
75   Roskill, *Hankey*, vol. I, p.247.
76   Note by Ralph Strauss (Hall's collaborator in an unfinished, banned autobiography), 29 Nov. 1932, recording account given him by de Grey, CCAC HALL 1/4. De Grey's account differs from the reconstruction in Tuchman, *Zimmermann Telegram*, ch.I.
77   James, *Eyes of the Navy*, pp.136–7.
78   Kahn, *Codebreakers*, pp.284–7.
79   Strauss, Notes on conversation with de Grey, 29 Nov. 1932, CCAC HALL 1/4.
80   They eventually did. See W.F. Friedman and C.J. Mendelsohn, 'The Zimmermann telegram of January 16, 1917, and its cryptographic background', 1936, p.26, NAW RG 165 9140–5953. Cf Kahn, *Codebreakers*, p.288.
81   Strauss, Notes on conversation with de Grey, 29 Nov. 1932, CCAC HALL 1/4.
82   Kahn, *Codebreakers*, pp.288–91. Tuchman, *Zimmermann Telegram*, ch.10. James, *Eyes of the Navy*, pp.140–1. All three authors identify Hall's agent in Mexico only as 'T'. A covering note to Strauss's draft chapter for Hall's banned autobiography reveals that 'T' was Thurston. As well as being checked by Hall, the draft is marked 'Chapter seen by N. de Grey'. Draft 'D', CCAC HALL 3/6.
83   James, *Eyes of the Navy*, p.141.
84   Strauss, Draft 'D', pp.19–20, CCAC HALL 3/6. James used this as the basis of the briefer account in *Eyes of the Navy*, p.142.
85   Memorandum by R.H. Campbell, 20 Feb. 1917, with minutes by Hardinge and Balfour. Reproduced in Strauss, Draft 'D', pp.21–2, CCAC HALL 3/6.
86   Tuchman, *Zimmermann Telegram*, pp.164–6.
87   *Papers Relating to the Foreign Relations of the United States*, 1917, Supplement I, pp.147–8.
88   Link, *Wilson 1916–1917*, pp.345ff.
89   Ibid., p.354.
90   *Papers Relating to the Foreign Relations of the United States*, 1917, Supplement

I, pp.155, 158. Kahn, *Codebreakers*, p.294.

91    Strauss, Notes on conversation with de Grey, 29 Nov. 1932, CCAC HALL 1/4. Misled by a slip in the draft chapter based on this conversation, James wrongly located the decoding in the American embassy.

92    *Papers Relating to the Foreign Relations of the United States*, 1917, Supplement I, p.158.

93    James, *Eyes of the Navy*, pp.152–4. Kahn, *Codebreakers*, pp.294–6. Tuchman, *Zimmermann Telegram*, pp.183, 189–90.

94    James, *Eyes of the Navy*, p.153.

95    Strauss, Draft 'D', pp.33–4, 37, quoting Hall to Captain Guy Gaunt, 22 March 1917, CCAC HALL 3/6.

96    The fullest account of the *Sayonara* episode is Strauss, Draft 'C' (checked by the *Sayonara's* captain), CCAC HALL 3/3. See also O'Halpin, 'British Intelligence in Ireland', p.58, and Beesly, *Room 40*, pp.185–6.

97    Kirke diary, 27 Nov. 1916, IWM.

98    Beesly, *Room 40*, p.186.

99    Green, *Mason*, ch.8.

100    Thomson, *Scene Changes*, p.294.

101    Beesly, *Room 40*, pp.190–1.

102    'Some Services Rendered by Our Organisation in the South of Spain', [Jan. 1917], A.E.W. Mason MSS, Walter L. Pforzheimer Collection on Intelligence Service.

103    Kirke diary, 27 Nov. 1916, IWM.

104    Bell to Leland Harrison, 2 May 1919, Leland Harrison MSS box 102, Library of Congress. (I am grateful for this reference to David Kahn.)

105    Godfrey, Unpublished Memoirs, vol. V, pp.136–7.

106    Birch and Clarke, 'Naval Intelligence Organisation (based on an historical analysis of the 1914–18 War)', p.8 (NID document in the possession of the late Captain Stephen Roskill).

107    Beesly, *Room 40*, pp.191–8.

108    Green, *Mason*, pp.161–2, 147.

109    Mason, Report no. 7, 3 Oct. 1916, A.E.W. Mason MSS, Walter L. Pforzheimer Collection.

110    Green, *Mason*, pp.150–4. Beesly, *Room 40*, pp.241–2.

111    Green, *Mason*, p.147. Cf. Beesly, *Room 40*, pp.200–2.

112    There is no documentary evidence on the reasons for placing Room 40 under Hall's control in May 1917. But the date at which it happened surely indicates official recognition of Hall's brilliant handling of the Zimmermann telegram, in contrast to Oliver's and Jackson's less than brilliant handling of German intercepts during Jutland.

113    Beesly, *Room 40*, pp.35n., 176ff.

114    Roskill, *Hankey*, vol. I, pp.356–7, 380–4. Marder, *Dreadnought to Scapa Flow*, vol. IV, chs.6, 7, 10.

115    Marder, *Dreadnought to Scapa Flow*, vol. IV, pp.264–8.

116    The 'special telegrams' are in PRO ADM 137/203, 451, 645, 868, 869, 964. They total: 1915: 333; 1916: 321; 1917 (Jan.–April): 156; 1917 (May–Dec.): 530; 1918 (Jan.–Oct): 1723. These totals include 'special telegrams' both sent

(the majority) and received by the Admiralty.

117   Marder, *Dreadnought to Scapa Flow*, vol. IV, pp.265–6.
118   Ibid., pp.266–7. Marder wrongly identifies Willoughby as from Sheffield University.
119   Clarke, '40 O.B. Achievements', CCAC Clarke MSS CLKE 3.
120   Korvettenkapitän Kleikamp, 'Der Einfluss der Funkaufklärung auf die Seekriegsführung in der Nordsee 1914–1918', pp.34–5 (see note 19 above).
121   Clarke, '40 O.B. Part' [*sic*], CCAC Clarke MSS CLKE 3.
122   James, *Eyes of the Navy*, pp.115–16. James is vague on the identity of the codebook discovered but identifies it as a recent introduction. Cf. Hall, 'Rough Notes', 10 Jan. 1936, pp.1–2, CCAC HALL 2/1.
123   Hall, 'Rough Notes', 10 Jan. 1936, p.2, CCAC HALL 2/1.
124   E.C. Miller, 'A War Secret', *Saturday Evening Post*, 23 Oct. 1926: cited by Kahn, *Codebreakers*, pp.273–4.
125   Hall to Captain Kelly, 7 Aug. 1917, PRO ADM 137/645.
126   James, *Eyes of the Navy*, p.116. James is once again vague on the identity of the codebook recovered. Cf. Kahn, *Codebreakers*, p.274.
127   DCNS to C-in-C Grand Fleet, no. 50, 1 Nov. 1918, PRO ADM 137/964.
128   Roskill, *Beatty*, pp.258–9. Marder, *Dreadnought to Scapa Flow*, vol. V, pp.147–56.
129   Cf. ID 25 to Gallatly (Rome), 16 March 1918, PRO ADM 137/868.
130   Andrew, 'Déchiffrement et diplomatie', pp.53–8.
131   'Souvenirs du général Cartier', part 2, pp.34–6.
132   Roskill, *Beatty*, p.273.
133   Toye, *For What We Have Received*, pp.153–5. Toye mistakenly places the date as 'early November'.
134   Marder, *Dreadnought to Scapa Flow*, vol. V, pp.172–5.
135   The intercepts may be followed in PRO ADM 137/964.

## CHAPTER 4

1   Details of Macdonogh's responsibilities are given in 'Historical Sketch of the Directorate of Military Intelligence during the Great War 1914–1919', p.1, PRO WO 32/10776.
2   Hawker, 'Intelligence Corps', p.75.
3   'Journal of 2nd Lieut. R.R.F. West DSO', pp.3–5, ICM. There is a list of early recruits on pp.12–13.
4   Payne Best transcripts.
5   Spears, *Liaison 1914*, p.31.
6   Hawker, 'Intelligence Corps', p.75.
7   Kirke to his wife, 10 & 19 Sept. 1914, IWM, Kirke MSS.
8   Payne Best transcripts.
9   Kirke to his wife, 12 Oct. 1914, IWM Kirke MSS.
10  Mackenzie, *Greek Memories*, pp.73–4.
11  Payne Best transcripts.
12  Dukes, '*ST 25*', p.35. This passage was 'read and approved' by C himself.

13 Spears, *Liaison 1914*, pp.31, 27, 42.
14 Holmes, *Little Field-Marshal*, p.205.
15 Raleigh, *War in the Air*, vol. I, pp.10, 329. Edmonds, *France and Belgium 1914*, p.48.
16 Kirke, 'Lecture on Secret Service', 1925, ICM Kirke MSS.
17 Edmonds, *France and Belgium 1914*, pp.50–1. Spears, *Liaison 1914*. Raleigh, *War in the Air*, vol. I, pp.298–301.
18 Kirke, obituary notice on Macdonogh, 29 July 1947, Kirke MSS.
19 Holmes, *Little Field-Marshal*, ch.7. Raleigh, *War in the Air*, vol. I, pp.302–3.
20 Holmes, *Little Field-Marshal*, ch.7. Taylor, *English History 1914–1945*, p.34.
21 Holmes, *Little Field-Marshal*, ch.7.
22 Hawker, 'Intelligence Corps', pp.76–7. Payne Best transcripts.
23 Payne Best transcripts.
24 Hawker, 'Intelligence Corps', p.82.
25 Churchill, *World Crisis*, vol. II, p.19.
26 Kirke diary, 8 Dec. 1914, 30 Jan. 1915; Kirke, 'Lecture on Secret Service', 27 Nov. 1925, IWM Kirke MSS.
27 Jones, *War in the Air*, vol. II, pp.87–90. Marshall-Cornwall, Unpublished Memoirs, ch.2, pp.8–9, ICM.
28 Raleigh, *War in the Air*, vol. I, p.9. Jones, *War in the Air*, vol. II, pp.149–60; vol. III, pp.307, 314.
29 Kirke, 'Lecture on Secret Service', 27 Nov. 1925, IWM Kirke MSS.
30 Priestley, *Signal Service*, pp.88–9, 100–10. Kirke diary, 7 Sept. 1916, IWM.
31 Kahn, *Codebreakers*, pp.310–11. Kirke diary, 15 Oct. 1916, 7 Jan. 1917, IWM.
32 On the reorganisation of January 1916 see 'Historical Sketch of the Directorate of Military Intelligence ...', PRO WO 32/10776.
33 Lieut-Col. R.F. Drake, 'History of Intelligence (B), British Expeditionary Force, France, from January, 1917, to April, 1919', 8 May 1919, PRO WO 106/45.
34 Winter, *Winter's Tale*, ch.6. Payne Best transcripts.
35 Payne Best transcripts. Kirke diary, 12 April 1915, IWM.
36 Payne Best transcripts. Decock, 'La Dame Blanche', pp.7, 129–30.
37 Priestley, *Signal Service*, p. 90. 'St George', 'Mervyn Lamb's [Kirke's] Diary', part I, p.442.
38 Kirke diary, 27 Nov. 1914, 27 May 1915, IWM.
39 'Mervyn Lamb' [Kirke], 'On Hazardous Service', part I, pp.752–3. 'St George', 'Mervyn Lamb's Diary', Part I, p.444.
40 'Mervyn Lamb' [Kirke], 'On Hazardous Service', passim. 'St George', 'Mervyn Lamb's Diary', part I, pp.445–6. Kirke diary, 12 Feb., 11, 20 June, 7 Oct., 2, 6 Nov., 1915, IWM.
41 Kirke, 'Lecture on Secret Service', 27 Nov. 1925, p.10; Kirke, obituary notice on Macdonogh, 29 July 1947, pp.6–7, Kirke MSS.
42 Marshall-Cornwall, Unpublished Memoirs, ch.2, pp.10–12, ICM.
43 Kirke diary, 1 April 1915, IWM.
44 Drake, 'History of Intelligence (B) ...', 8 May 1919, pp.1–3, PRO WO 106/45.
45 Oppenheimer, *Stranger Within*, pp.266–7, 289. See below, p.155.

46   Landau, *Spy Net*, pp.31–3. Kirke diary, 29 Nov. 1915, IWM. Payne Best transcripts.
47   Landau, *Spy Net*, p.37.
48   Kirkpatrick, 'The War 1914–1918', p.59, IWM. M.K. Burge, 'The History of the British Secret Service in Holland', 14 Feb. 1917, Part I, p.18, ICM.
49   Burge, 'Secret Service in Holland', Part I, ICM. Kirke diary, 3 Dec. 1915, IWM.
50   Kirke diary, 12, 18 Feb., entry for period 25 Feb. to 3 March, 22, 23 March, 3, 10 April, 20, 22 June, 14 July 1915, IWM. Entry on Pollitt in *Dictionary of National Biography 1961–1970*. Though the consuls in Switzerland, as in Holland, were forbidden all direct contact with agents, they were allowed to recommend the names of likely agents and forward their reports to London.
51   Kirke diary, entries for period 25 Feb. to 3 March 1915, 17 March 1915, IWM. Some of John Wallinger's reports on Indian nationalists are listed in catalogues at the India Office Library and Records, but many appear to have been destroyed.
52   Maugham, *Collected Short Stories*, vol. III, pp.79–80, 42, 20–1. Wallinger appears in both Maugham's reminiscences, 'Looking Back', part I, and the Ashenden stories as 'R'; private information confirms this identification. Bernard's name is unchanged in the Ashenden stories. See below, p.152.
53   Kirke diary, 24 March, 9 April, 23 May, 3, 13 June 1915, IWM.
54   Ibid., 14 July 1915, Foulkes, *Gas!*, p.47.
55   Kirke diary, 27 July, 2 Aug., 4 Aug., 11 Dec. 1915, IWM.
56   Ibid., 22 Feb., 17, 27 July, 2, 19 Aug., 5, 8 Oct. 1915.
57   Ibid., 23, 27 Aug. 1915.
58   Ibid., 15 Nov., 22 June, 11 Oct. 1915.
59   Morgan, *Somerset Maugham*, pp.206, 313.
60   Maugham, *Collected Short Stories*, vol. III, pp.24, 41–2, 78–9.
61   Kirke diary, 3 Dec. 1915, IWM.
62   Ibid., 23 Aug., 15, 29, 30 Nov. 1915, 10 Jan. 1916.
63   Ibid., 28 Feb. 1916.
64   Maugham, *Collected Short Stories*, vol. III, pp.20–3, 113–17.
65   Calder, *Somerset Maugham*, pp.206–9. Morgan, *Somerset Maugham*, p.313.
66   Kirke diary, 8 Feb. 1916, IWM. Maugham, 'Looking Back', part I.
67   Maugham, 'Looking Back', part I.
68   Kirke diary, 11, 19, 28 July 1916, IWM.
69   Ibid., 24 July, 13, 16 Aug. 1916. L.G. Campbell to Kirke, 6 Dec. 1916, IWM Kirke MSS.
70   Kirke diary, 30 May, 9–10 June, 23, 28 July, 17 Aug. 1916, IWM. Landau, *Spy Net*, pp.31–3. Burge, 'The History of the British Secret Service in Holland', 14 Feb. 1917, Part II, p.2, ICM.
71   Kirkpatrick, 'The War 1914–1918', p.65, IWM.
72   Burge, 'The History of the British Secret Service in Holland', 14 Feb. 1917, Part II, ICM. Kirkpatrick, 'The War 1914–1918', p.106, IWM.
73   Marshall-Cornwall, Unpublished Memoirs, ch.2, pp.14ff, ICM. Kirke, obituary notice on Macdonogh, 29 July 1947, Kirke MSS.
74   Burge, 'The History of the British Secret Service in Holland', 14 Feb. 1917,

Part II, p.21 and appendix, ICM.

75 Oppenheimer, *Stranger Within*, pp.266–7, 286–9.

76 Payne Best transcripts.

77 Ibid.

78 Ibid. Kirkpatrick, 'The War 1914–1918', pp.150–1, IWM.

79 Kirkpatrick, 'The War 1914–1918, p.108, IWM. During the autumn of 1917 Best fell out with Kirkpatrick and others, according to Kirkpatrick, 'owing to his relationship with the wife of a Belgian'. Ibid., p.111.

80 Ibid., pp.128ff. Kirkpatrick, *Inner Circle*, pp.17–18.

81 Kirkpatrick, 'The War 1914–1918', pp.128–35, IWM.

82 Landau, *Spy Net*, pp.9–35.

83 Decock, 'La Dame Blanche', pp.65–72.

84 Landau, *Spy Net*, chs.24, 27. SIS reaction to the publication of Landau, *Secrets of the White Lady* (New York, 1935) is described in the Payne Best transcripts.

85 See below, p.378.

86 Decock, 'La Dame Blanche', pp.70–4.

87 Landau, *Spy Net*, p.49.

88 Decock, 'La Dame Blanche', pp.78ff. Landau, *Spy Net*, ch.7.

89 Decock, 'La Dame Blanche', pp.102ff, 120ff. Cf. Landau, *Spy Net*, pp.46–8, 64.

90 Drake, 'History of Intelligence (B) ...', 8 May 1919, p.23, PRO WO 106/45.

91 Payne Best transcripts. Kirkpatrick, 'The War 1914–18', pp.69–70, IWM.

92 Kirkpatrick, 'The War 1914–18', pp.75–6, IWM. Idem, *Inner Circle*, p.12.

93 Kirkpatrick, 'The War 1914–18', pp.76–8, IWM. Drake, 'History of Intelligence (B) ...', 8 May 1919, pp.24–6, PRO WO 106/45.

94 Kirkpatrick, 'The War 1914–18', pp.78–88, IWM. Drake, 'History of Intelligence (B) ...', 8 May 1919, pp.26–7, PRO WO 106/45. Payne Best transcripts.

95 Ibid.

96 Greene and Greene, *Spy's Bedside Book*, p.223.

97 Payne Best transcripts.

98 Priestley, *Signal Service*, p.53. Drake, 'History of Intelligence (B) ...', 8 May 1919, p.27, PRO WO 106/45.

99 Drake, 'History of Intelligence (B) ...', 8 May 1919, pp.27–8, PRO WO 106/45. Kirkpatrick, 'The War 1914–1918', pp.91–5, IWM.

100 Marshall-Cornwall, Unpublished Memoirs, ch.2, p.10, ICM. Hawker, 'Intelligence Corps', p.81.

101 Terraine, *Douglas Haig*, ch.8. Kirke diary, 31 Aug., 3, 26 Sept., 2 Dec. 1916, IWM. 'St George', 'Mervyn Lamb's Diary', part II, pp.33, 36.

102 Drake, 'History of Intelligence (B) ...', 8 May 1919, pp.30–2, PRO WO 106/45. Drake insisted that the scheme could have worked 'but, for lack of the necessary information and of the word to go ... opportunities were not taken advantage of.'

103 Charteris, 'Lecture on Intelligence', 4 Feb. 1916, p.5, ICM. Marshall-Cornwall, Unpublished Memoirs, ch.2, pp.14ff, ICM. Terraine, *Douglas Haig*, pp.208, 234.

104 Marshall-Cornwall, Unpublished Memoirs, ch.2, pp.16ff, ICM. Strong, *Men of Intelligence*, pp.26–30. Blake (ed.), *Papers of Douglas Haig*, pp.236, 240.

105   Morton to Liddell Hart, 17 July 1961, LHC Liddell Hart MSS 1/531.
106   Marshall-Cornwall, Unpublished Memoirs, ch.2, pp.21–4, ICM. Payne Best transcripts. Strong, *Men of Intelligence*, pp.31–2. Blake (ed.), *Papers of Douglas Haig*, p.324.
107   Decock, 'La Dame Blanche', chs.5–8 (quotations from p.149).
108   Kirkpatrick, 'The War 1914–1918', pp.129–35, appendix 2, IWM.
109   Ibid., p.114. Decock, 'La Dame Blanche', p.8.
110   Kirkpatrick, 'The War 1914–1918', p.114.
111   Decock, 'La Dame Blanche', pp.132ff.
112   Ibid., p.151.
113   Kirkpatrick, 'The War 1914–1918', pp.137–9, IWM. Edmonds, *France and Belgium 1918*, vol. I, pp.104n, 108–9, 111; vol. II, pp.116–18. Payne Best transcripts. Blake (ed.), *Papers of Douglas Haig*, pp.285, 291.
114   Edmonds, *France and Belgium 1918*, vol. I, p.109. Gough, *Fifth Army*, p.259.
115   Kirkpatrick, 'The War 1914–1918', pp.139, 148, IWM. Idem, *Inner Circle*, p.18.
116   Terraine, *Douglas Haig*, pp.414ff.
117   Major-General S.S. Butler, 'France 1916–1918', unpaginated microfilm, IWM.
118   Liddell Hart, *World War 1914–1918*, pp.516–17. Edmonds, *France and Belgium 1918*, vol. III, pp.20–4.
119   Marshall-Cornwall, Unpublished Memoirs, ch.4, p.7, ICM.
120   'Souvenirs du général Cartier', pp.19–20. 'Conférence de M. Georges Jean Painvin', p.50.
121   Butler, 'France 1916–1918', IWM.

## CHAPTER 5

1   See above, p.70.
2   'Historical Sketch of the Directorate of Military Intelligence during the Great War, 1914–1919', 6 May 1921, PRO WO 32/10776. In April 1915 MO5g became a full War Office section as MO5, but continued until January 1916 to use its old designation because, wrote Kell, 'we are better known to the Police under this "nom de guerre"'. Kell to Dixon, 10 Sept. 1915, PRO HO 45/10779/277334.
3   Kell to Edmonds, 29 March 1917, LHC Edmonds MSS II/2. Lady Kell, 'Secret Well Kept', p.156, IWM.
4   Kell to Home Office, 11 Dec. 1913, PRO HO 45/10629/199699. 'Historical Sketch of the Directorate of Military Intelligence ...', PRO WO 32/10776.
5   Dansey to Major Van Deman, 1 May 1917; lecture by Dansey, 4 May 1917, NAW RG 165, 9944-A-4/5.
6   MI5f, 'Notes on Preventive Intelligence Duties in War', April 1918; copy in NAW RG 165, 11013-21.
7   'Historical Sketch of the Directorate of Military Intelligence ...', PRO WO 32/10776.
8   Strauss, draft chapter C, CCAC Hall MSS HALL 3/2.
9   'Historical Sketch of the Directorate of Military Intelligence ...', PRO WO

32/10776.

10 Thomson, *Queer People*, p.36. The size of the Special Branch is given in a minute of 20 Nov. 1914, PRO MEPO 2/1643/ON856720.

11 *The Times*, 15 Aug. 1914.

12 Thomson, *Queer People*, p.37.

13 Ibid., p.38. *The Times*, 8 Sept. 1914.

14 Thomson, *Queer People*, p.39.

15 *Parliamentary Debates (Lords)*, 5th series, vol. XVIII, 11 Nov. 1914, cols.41–2.

16 Thomson, *Queer People*, pp.43–4.

17 Le Queux, *German Spies in England*, passim.

18 Hazlehurst, *Politicians at War*, p.145.

19 Ibid., p.146. Gillman, *Collar the Lot*, p.10.

20 Bird, 'Control of Enemy Alien Civilians', pp.2, 19–20, 46–9, 94, 116, 132, 203, 236.

21 Cubitt (WO) to Troup (HO), 24 Oct. 1917; J.F. Moylan, memo, 10 Nov. 1917, PRO HO 45/10881/338498. Bird, 'Control of Enemy Alien Civilians', pp.204–8, 216.

22 Felstead (ed.), *Steinhauer*, pp.39–40. The introduction by 'Blinker' Hall commends Steinhauer's memoirs as 'extremely interesting and informative'.

23 Lady Kell, 'Secret Well Kept', p.144, IWM. Thomson, *Queer People*, pp.122–6. Felstead, *German Spies at Bay*, ch.3. The title page of Felstead's book claims that it was 'compiled from official sources'. These appear to have included MI5 as well as Special Branch reports. Drake later told Hall: 'B[asil] T[homson] gave him [Felstead] my reports to read, I understand'. Drake to Hall, 1 Nov. 1932, CCAC HALL 1/3.

24 Baden-Powell, *Adventures as a Spy*, p.11. Felstead (ed.), *Steinhauer*, p.40.

25 Thomson, *Queer People*, pp.126–9. Felstead, *German Spies at Bay*, ch.3.

26 Lady Kell, 'Secret Well Kept', p.144, IWM. Thomson, *Queer People*, pp.125–6.

27 Felstead, *German Spies at Bay*, pp.44–52.

28 Ibid., pp.53–6.

29 Kirke diary, 13 June 1916, IWM.

30 Felstead, *German Spies at Bay*, p.56.

31 Ibid., pp.102–8.

32 Kirke diary, 15 June 1915, IWM. Whether Room 40 decrypted the same signals is unclear. It had, however, broken off direct contact with the War Office. See above, p.88.

33 Felstead, *German Spies at Bay*, p.109.

34 Ibid., ch.4. Lady Kell, 'Secret Well Kept', p.154, IWM.

35 Felstead, *German Spies at Bay*, pp.110, 139, 150, 209–15, 284.

36 Kirke diary, 26 May 1916, IWM.

37 HO circulars (drafted by MI5) to chief constables, 10 June, 6 July 1916, PRO HO 45/10779/277334.

38 Felstead, *German Spies at Bay*, ch.15.

39 Walker-Smith, *Lord Darling*, pp.206–24. The confusion surrounding the Pemberton Billing trial extends to the court records. I have followed the sequence of evidence in Walker-Smith's official biography. Cf. Kettle, *Salome's*

*Last Veil.*
40  Thomson, *Scene Changes*, p.374.
41  Felstead, *German Spies at Bay*, p.154. See above, note 23.
42  Ibid., pp.161–3.
43  Drake to Hall, 1 Nov. 1932, CCAC HALL 1/3.
44  Bell to Leland Harrison, 2 May 1919, enclosing memo on British intelligence, Library of Congress, Leland Harrison MSS, box 102 (I am grateful for this reference to David Kahn).
45  Newman, *Speaking from Memory*, p.93.
46  See, e.g. Kell to Home Office, 14 Dec. 1917, enclosing 'Return no. 2' of 41 cases (involving, inter alia, Ramsay MacDonald, Philip Snowden and Mrs Pankhurst) in which it was decided not to prosecute. PRO HO 45/10743/263275.
47  Kell to Home Office, 2 May 1918, ibid. A rather stronger case was eventually assembled. On 3 September 1918 Goulding was fined £100 and sentenced to 6 months' imprisonment.
48  Lady Kell, 'Secret Well Kept', pp.149–50, IWM.
49  Home Office to Chief Constable, Norwich, 1 April 1915, PRO HO 45/10741/263275. Carsten, *War against War*, pp.52–6.
50  F.B. Booth, memo for Kell, 27 July 1915, PRO HO 45/10741/263275. Carsten, *War against War*, p.56.
51  Acting Chief Constable, Cheshire, to Home Office, forwarding report by Superintendent A.J. Dutton, 9 Aug. 1915, PRO HO 45/10741/263275. Carsten, *War against War*, p.56.
52  Thomson, *My Experiences*, pp.124–5.
53  Sir E. Carson to Sir J. Simon, 15 Sept. 1915; Thomson to Sir E. Troup, 18 Sept. 1915; Thomson to W. Meredith, 30 Sept. 1915, PRO HO 45/10741/263275.
54  Carsten, *War against War*, pp.55–6.
55  Thomson, *Queer People*, p.266.
56  Carsten, *War against War*, pp.58–9.
57  Thomson, *Queer People*, p.269.
58  Carsten, *War against War*, p.68.
59  Ibid., pp.65–6.
60  Thomson, *Queer People*, p.269.
61  On Clydeside's reputation see McLean, *Legend of Red Clydeside*.
62  Ibid., ch.7.
63  'Historical Sketch of the Directorate of Military Intelligence …', p.13, PRO WO 32/10776.
64  Macassey to Llewellyn Smith, 20 Feb. 1916, Bodleian Library, Addison MSS, box 56: cited by McLean, *Legend of Red Clydeside*, p.83.
65  Thomson, *Scene Changes*, p.312.
66  McLean, *Legend of Red Clydeside*, p.84.
67  Turner, *Dear Old Blighty*, pp.244–5. Clark (ed.), *Papers of Viscount Lee*, pp.164–5.
68  Thomson, *Scene Changes*, p.314.
69  Ibid., p.312. E.F. Wodehouse (New Scotland Yard) to Home Office, 23 April

1917, PRO HO 45/11000/223532. 'Historical Sketch of the Directorate of Military Intelligence ...', PRO WO 32/10776.

70 GT 733, 15 April 1917, PRO CAB 24/13.
71 GT 832, 24 May 1917, PRO CAB 24/14.
72 Thomson, *Scene Changes*, p.337.
73 Carsten, *War against War*, pp.172–4.
74 Kirkwood, *Life of Revolt*: cited by Gilbert, *Winston S. Churchill*, vol. IV, pp.35–7.
75 Carsten, *War against War*, p.102.
76 Thomson, *Queer People*, p.273.
77 GT 832, 24 May 1917, PRO CAB 24/14.
78 Thomson, *Queer People*, pp.272–3. Idem, *Scene Changes*, pp.336–7. Cf. GT 832, 24 May 1917, PRO CAB 24/14.
79 Lloyd George, *War Memoirs*, vol. II, p.1156. Taylor, *English History 1914–1945*, p.71.
80 Swartz, *Union of Democratic Control*, p.175. Taylor, *English History 1914–1945*, p.128.
81 Thomson, *Scene Changes*, p.383.
82 Challinor, *British Bolshevism*, p.183. GT 2139, PRO CAB 24/27.
83 Swartz, *Union of Democratic Control*, pp.178–80. Cline, *E.D. Morel*, pp.111–13. G 173, 13 Nov. 1917, PRO CAB 24/4.
84 Carsten, *War against War*, pp.168–71. Three Labour ministers remained in the government.
85 Swartz, *Union of Democratic Control*, p.164.
86 G 157, 3 Oct. 1917, PRO CAB 24/4.
87 WC 245 (20), 4 Oct. 1917, PRO CAB 23/4.
88 Thomson, *Scene Changes*, p.357.
89 With their usual discretion the cabinet minutes do not refer to Kell by name. But the reference to 'the War Office' almost certainly refers to MI5. In a cabinet memorandum of 13 Nov. (see above, note 83) Cave confirmed that Kell and Thomson were 'in close communication'.
90 WC 253 (1), 19 Oct. 1917, PRO CAB 23/4.
91 Thomson, *Scene Changes*, p.359.
92 Thomson, 'Pacifist and Revolutionary Organizations in the United Kingdom', included in G 173, 13 Nov. 1917, PRO CAB 24/4.
93 'Report on Labour in Great Britain, November 1917', 11 Dec. 1917, PRO MUN 5/56.

## CHAPTER 6

1 Neilson, 'Joy Rides?'
2 Except where other references are given my analysis of British intelligence organisation in Tsarist Russia is based on Neilson, 'Joy Rides?', and M.K. Burge, 'History of the British Intelligence Organization in Russia', 26 Feb. 1917, ICM, which was unavailable to Dr Neilson.
3 Nabokoff, *Ordeal of a Diplomat*, p.121 (cited by Neilson, 'Joy Rides?', p.900n).

4  Lockhart, *British Agent*, p.137.
5  Hoare, *Fourth Seal*, chs.1, 2.
6  Ibid., ch.2.
7  Burge, 'History of the British Intelligence Organization in Russia', 26 Feb. 1917, ICM.
8  Hoare to wife, 25 May 1916, CUL Templewood MSS II/5.
9  Burge, 'History of the British Intelligence Organization in Russia', 26 Feb. 1917, p.7, ICM.
10  Ibid.
11  Hoare, *Fourth Seal*, pp.53–4.
12  Ibid., p.88.
13  Cross, *Hoare*, pp.49–51. On Alley see Lockhart, *Ace of Spies*, pp.67, 84, 91–2.
14  Neilson, 'Joy Rides?', p.900.
15  Cross, *Hoare*, pp.44–8. Hoare, *Fourth Seal*, p.118.
16  Cross, *Hoare*, pp.47–8. Hoare, *Fourth Seal*, ch.7.
17  Hoare, *Fourth Seal*, p.126.
18  Cross, *Hoare*, pp.50–1.
19  Ullman, *Anglo-Soviet Relations*, vol. I, pp.11–12.
20  On Barter see Neilson, *Strategy and Supply*, pp.283–7.
21  Ullman, *Anglo-Soviet Relations*, vol. I, pp.11–12.
22  Maugham, 'Looking Back', *Sunday Express*, 30 Sept. 1962.
23  Fowler, *Sir William Wiseman*, pp.16–18.
24  Ibid., pp.114ff. Maugham, 'Looking Back', *Sunday Express*, 30 Sept. 1962.
25  Maugham, *Collected Short Stories*, vol. III: 'His Excellency' and 'Mr Harrington's Washing'.
26  Wiseman to Drummond, 24 Sept. 1917; Wiseman, memo, 21 Oct. 1917. Calder, *Maugham*, pp.283–5.
27  Morgan, *Maugham*, p.231.
28  Maugham, 'Looking Back', *Sunday Express*, 7 Oct. 1962.
29  Morgan, *Maugham*, p.231.
30  Maugham, 'Looking Back', *Sunday Express*, 7 Oct. 1962.
31  Hoare, *Fourth Seal*, p.253.
32  Lockhart, *British Agent*, pp.191–201.
33  Sisson, *One Hundred Red Days*, p.294.
34  Lockhart, *British Agent*, p.231.
35  Ullman, *Anglo-Soviet Relations*, vol. I, p.121.
36  Debo, *Revolution and Survival*, pp.239, 242.
37  Maugham, 'Looking Back', *Sunday Express*, 7 Oct. 1962.
38  Debo, 'Lockhart Plot or Dzerzhinskii Plot?', pp.426–7.
39  Ullman, *Anglo-Soviet Relations*, vol. I, pp.134–5.
40  Lockhart, *British Agent*, pp.276–7.
41  Thwaites, *Velvet and Vinegar*, ch.17.
42  Lockhart, *Ace of Spies*, chs.6, 7. The author provides much valuable information on Reilly but credits his tale of his wartime meeting with the Kaiser as well as other improbable exploits.
43  Lockhart, *British Agent*, pp.276–7.
44  Philby, *My Secret War*, p.30.

45  Hill, *Go Spy the Land*, passim.
46  Ibid., p.179.
47  Ibid., p.193.
48  Hill, Secret 29 page 'Report on Work Done in Russia', 26 Nov. 1918, PRO FO 371/3350.
49  Hill, *Go Spy the Land*, pp.196–7.
50  Hill, 'Report on Work Done in Russia', 26 Nov. 1918, pp.12–16, PRO FO 371/3350.
51  Philby, *My Silent War*, p.30.
52  Debo, 'Lockhart Plot or Dzerzhinskii Plot?', p.423n. Lockhart himself 'was afraid that the Bolsheviks had a key to our ciphers'; *British Agent*, p.278.
53  Leggett, *Cheka*, p.281.
54  Ullman, *Anglo-Soviet Relations*, vol. I, ch.8.
55  Ibid., vol. II, p.23n.
56  Ibid., vol. I, pp.285–6.
57  Leggett, *Cheka*, pp.281–4.
58  Hill, 'Report on Work Done in Russia', 26 Nov. 1918, pp.17–19, PRO FO 371/3350. Hill was in close touch with Reilly, who kept him 'fully' informed. Ibid., p.17.
59  Lockhart, *Secret Agent*, p.322. Hill, *Go Spy the Land*, p.238.
60  Hill, 'Report on Work Done in Russia', 26 Nov. 1918, p.23, PRO FO 371/3350.
61  Lockhart, *Ace of Spies*, pp.81–3. Hill, *Go Spy the Land*, pp.231, 253. Neither Reilly nor Hill ever realised the extent to which their operations had been penetrated by Soviet agents. They continued to believe for the remainder of their lives that the Cheka agent-provocateur, Colonel Berzin, had been genuinely willing to lead a coup against Lenin. In fact he was decorated with the Order of the Red Banner for his deception of the British, moved into a full-time career with the Cheka and its successors, and later became head of the Magadan forced labour gold-fields. Leggett, *Cheka*, p.417n.21.
62  Young (ed.), *Lockhart Diaries*, vol. I, p.49.
63  Dukes, *'ST 25'*, ch.1.
64  Lockhart, *Ace of Spies*, p.98n.
65  Dukes, *'ST 25'*, pp.35–6.
66  Ibid., pp.280–1.
67  Ibid., pp.221, 263.
68  Leggett, *Cheka*, pp.284–6.
69  Dukes, *'ST 25'*, ch.22, p.339.
70  Ibid., pp.340–1. Agar, *Baltic Episode*, p.209.
71  Dukes, *'ST 25'*, pp.282, 340.
72  Agar, *Baltic Episode*, pp.214–17.
73  Ullman, *Anglo-Soviet Relations*, vol. II, pp.173–4.

## CHAPTER 7

1  Ullman, *Anglo-Soviet Relations*, vol. I, p.3.
2  Swartz, *Union of Democratic Control*, p.188.

3    See illustration between pp.270 and 271. 'Hidden Hand' was also used to designate German-inspired subversion.

4    G 173, 13 Nov. 1917, PRO CAB 24/4. GT 2809, 24 Nov. 1917, PRO CAB 24/34.

5    Thomson, *Scene Changes*, p.361.

6    GT 2980, 13 Dec. 1917, PRO CAB 24/35.

7    Ullman, *Anglo-Soviet Relations*, vol. I, p.20. Carsten, *War against War*, pp.109–11.

8    GT 3424, 22 Jan. 1918, PRO CAB 24/40.

9    Taylor, *English History 1914–1945*, pp.135–7.

10   GT 3424, 22 Jan. 1918, PRO CAB 24/40.

11   Carsten, *War against War*, p.202.

12   GT 3424, 22 Jan. 1918, PRO CAB 24/40.

13   GT 3502, report for week ending 30 Jan. 1918, PRO CAB 24/41.

14   GT 4624, 23 May 1918, PRO CAB 24/52.

15   GT 4199, 10 April 1918, PRO CAB 24/47.

16   Swartz, *Union of Democratic Control*, pp.188–91. Minute by Thomson, 26 Nov. 1917, PRO HO 45/10743/263275.

17   GT 4624, 23 May 1918, PRO CAB 24/52.

18   GT 5407, 12 Aug. 1918 PRO CAB 24/61.

19   GT 6079, 21 Oct. 1918, PRO CAB 24/67.

20   Thomson, *Scotland Yard*, ch.20. Jeffery and Hennessy, *States of Emergency*, p.5.

21   GT 6079, 21 Oct. 1918, PRO CAB 24/67.

22   GT 6085, 24 Oct. 1918, PRO CAB 24/67.

23   GT 6079, 21 Oct. 1918, PRO CAB 24/67. GT 6425, 2 Dec. 1918, PRO CAB 24/71.

24   GT 6328, 18 Nov. 1918, PRO CAB 24/70.

25   Ullman, *Anglo-Soviet Relations*, vol. II, pp.62–3. GT 7195, 30 April 1919, PRO CAB 24/78.

26   Major Hall-Dalwood, 'Suggested Scheme for the Formation of a National Intelligence Service', 1 Jan. 1917; minute by Basil Thomson, 10 Jan. 1917; Thomson to Troup, 4 April 1917, PRO HO 45/22901/446727.

27   Thomson, *Scene Changes*, pp.358, 377.

28   Untitled secret memo by Thomson on Irish Intelligence, Sept. 1916: copy enclosed in Thomson to French, 8 May 1918, IWM French MSS 75/46/12.

29   C.E. Russell to Thomson, 14 Oct. 1918, enclosing memo by Long, Wiltshire Record Office Long MSS (I am grateful for this reference to Eunan O'Halpin). On the Pemberton Billing case see above, pp.188–90.

30   Thomson to Long, 15 Oct. 1918, enclosing 'Comments on the Attached Memorandum. Scheme for the Reorganisation and Coordination of Intelligence', Wiltshire Record Office, Long MSS.

31   Long to Thomson, 16 Oct. 1918; Long to Lloyd George, n.d., Wiltshire Record Office, Long MSS.

32   Long to Lloyd George, 18 Nov. 1918, Wiltshire Record Office, Long MSS.

33   Long to Lloyd George, 9 Jan. 1919, HLRO Lloyd George MSS F/33/2/3.

34   Curzon to Long, 18 Feb. 1919, Wiltshire Record Office, Long MSS. Long

to Austen Chamberlain, 2 Nov. 1921, BUL Chamberlain MSS AC 23/2/1. The proceedings of the Secret Service Committee are still classified.

35 PRO CAB 24 series.
36 Cabinet memorandum, 'Reduction of Estimates for Secret Services', 19 March 1920: withheld from PRO but available in HLRO Lloyd George MSS F/9/2/16.
37 McLean, *Legend of Red Clydeside*, part II.
38 GT 6816, 10 Feb. 1919, PRO CAB 24/75.
39 Jeffery and Hennessy, *States of Emergency*, p.10.
40 Ibid., pp.6–7. McLean, *Legend of Red Clydeside*, pp.237–9.
41 Ullman, *Anglo-Soviet Relations*, vol. II, pp.130–1. Thomson, 'A Survey of Revolutionary Feeling in the Year 1919', CP 462, PRO CAB 24/96.
42 Sinclair to Long, 20 June 1919, Wiltshire Record Office Long MSS.
43 GT 6857, 28 Jan. 1919, PRO CAB 24/75. Kell also claimed that Germany 'remained very active in matters of espionage' throughout 1919: 'Reduction of Estimates for Secret Services', 19 March 1920, HLRO Lloyd George MSS F9/2/16.
44 GT 6816, 10 Feb. 1919, PRO CAB 24/75.
45 CP 462, PRO CAB 24/96.
46 Kendall, *Revolutionary Movement*, ch.13.
47 Fitch, *Traitors Within*, pp.76–9, 249.
48 Ibid., pp.83–4.
49 Kendall, *Revolutionary Movement*, pp.248–9.
50 On its demise a small War Office department, MO4x, was set up with a watching brief for liaison with civil intelligence but was disbanded in 1922. Jeffery and Hennessy, *States of Emergency*, pp.13–14. Jeffery, 'British Army and Internal Security'.
51 CP 462, PRO CAB 24/96.
52 GT 6816, 10 Feb. 1919, PRO CAB 24/75. Jeffery and Hennessy, *States of Emergency*, pp.15–20.
53 GT 6816, 10 Feb. 1919, PRO CAB 24/75.
54 CP 462, PRO CAB 24/96.
55 Minutes of Aliens and Nationality Committee, 3 Oct. 1919; minutes of Passport Control Subcommittee, 27 Feb. 1919; report of Passport Control Subcommittee, 15 Sept. 1919. PRO HO 45/19966/31848.
56 Ibid. Minutes of Aliens and Nationality Committee, 10 June 1921, PRO T161/501/S9242/1. F.H. Mugliston, 'The Visa System', Oct. 1921, PRO FO 371/10480 N 1747.
57 Captain McConville, 'The British Intelligence System', 20 June 1921, NAW RG 165, 11013–19.
58 'Reduction of Estimates for Secret Services', 19 March 1920, HLRO Lloyd George MSS F9/2/16. Minutes of Aliens and Nationality Committee, 10 June 1921, PRO T161/501/S9242/1.
59 Memo by Thomson, 28 April 1921, PRO FO 372/1624.
60 Note by G.W. Rendel, 17 May 1921, PRO T5549/16/350.
61 'War Book 1926. War Office Chapter', p.70, PRO WO 33/1077. 'Field Security Police ...', 1923, pp.22–3, PRO WO 33/1025 (I am grateful to

Nicholas Hiley for these references). Kell, lecture to Scottish chief constables, 26 Feb. 1925, Kell MSS.

62 'Reduction of Estimates for Secret Services', 19 March 1920, HLRO Lloyd George MSS F9/2/16.

63 Mugliston, 'The Visa System', Oct. 1921, PRO FO 371/10480 N1747.

64 Aliens and Nationality Committee, memo no. 67; Report of Passport Control Subcommittee, 15 Sept. 1919 (enclosing Kell to Haldane Porter, 28 Aug. 1919), PRO HO 45/19966/31848.

65 Kell, Lecture to Scottish chief constables at Edinburgh, 26 Feb. 1925, Kell MSS. This lecture seems to have been typical of many.

66 Ibid.

67 Illustration between pp.270 and 271.

68 White, *Britain and the Bolshevik Revolution*, p.3.

69 Directorate of Intelligence, 'A Survey of Revolutionary Movements in Great Britain in the Year 1920', GT 6323, Jan. 1921, pp.1–11, PRO CAB 24/118.

70 Ibid., pp.12–14.

71 Ullman, *Anglo-Soviet Relations*, vol. III, pp.44–52.

72 Ibid., ch.3.

## CHAPTER 8

1 Choille (ed.), *Intelligence Notes*, p.xx.

2 Thomson to Lord French, 8 May 1918, enclosing copy of Thomson's secret memo of Sept. 1916, IWM French MSS 75/46/12. O'Halpin, 'British Intelligence in Ireland', pp.54–61.

3 Ibid.

4 O'Halpin, 'British Intelligence in Ireland', pp.59–61. Bayly, *Pull Together*, ch.9.

5 O'Halpin, 'British Intelligence in Ireland', pp.59–61.

6 Reid, *Casement*, passim. James, *Eyes of the Navy*, pp.112–14. Reid demolishes the theory that the Casement diaries were forged.

7 Townshend, *British Campaign in Ireland*, pp.6–7.

8 GHQ Ireland, 'Record of the Rebellion in Ireland in 1920–21 and the Part Played by the Army in Dealing with it. II: Intelligence', May 1922, p.5, ICM.

9 O'Halpin, 'British Intelligence in Ireland', pp.63–5. Telegrams from the German embassy in Madrid continued to be decrypted but provided only fragmentary intelligence on German policy to Ireland.

10 Ibid., pp.65ff.

11 Ibid. Townshend, *British Campaign in Ireland*, pp.8–12.

12 O'Halpin, 'British Intelligence in Ireland', pp.67–9.

13 Holmes, *Little Field-Marshal*, p.339.

14 Ibid., p.348.

15 O'Halpin, 'British Intelligence in Ireland', pp.69–70.

16 French to Londonderry. 3 Jan. 1920, IWM French MSS 75/46/12.

17 O'Halpin, 'British Intelligence in Ireland', pp.70–1.

18 French to Churchill (copy), 10 April 1919, IWM French MSS 75/46/11.

19 Neligan, *Spy in the Castle*, p.82.

20   GHQ Ireland, 'Record of the Rebellion in Ireland ...', II, p.24, ICM.
21   Ibid., p.25.
22   Kee, *Ireland*, ch.10. O'Connor, *Terrible Beauty*, p.119.
23   GHQ Ireland, 'Record of the Rebellion in Ireland ...', II, p.33, ICM.
24   O'Connor, *Terrible Beauty*, p.120.
25   O'Broin, *Revolutionary Underground*, p.189.
26   O'Connor, *Terrible Beauty*, p.124.
27   O'Halpin, 'British Intelligence in Ireland', pp.70–1.
28   French to Londonderry, 3 Jan. 1920, IWM French MSS 75/46/12.
29   GHQ Ireland, 'Record of the Rebellion in Ireland ...', II, pp.33–4, ICM.
30   O'Halpin, 'British Intelligence in Ireland', p.72.
31   Neligan, *Spy in the Castle*, pp.55–6, 64–6. Neligan remembered Redmond's 'pep talk', probably wrongly, as taking place in November 1919. Broy's recollections differ on some points of detail from Neligan's. O'Connor, *Terrible Beauty*, p.122.
32   O'Connor, *Terrible Beauty*, p.122.
33   GHQ Ireland, 'Record of the Rebellion in Ireland ...', II , p.5, ICM.
34   Neligan, *Spy in the Castle*, p.66.
35   O'Halpin, 'British Intelligence in Ireland', pp.72–3.
36   On the statistics of destruction see Townshend, *British Campaign in Ireland*.
37   Ibid., pp.73–6.
38   Ibid., pp.82, 126–7.
39   GHQ Ireland, 'Record of the Rebellion in Ireland ...', II, pp.13, 20, ICM.
40   O'Halpin, 'British Intelligence in Ireland', p.73.
41   Winter, *Winter's Tale*, p.296.
42   The Special Intelligence Branch only formally came under O's direct control in 1921 but its chief 'courteously and clearly' acknowledged his subordination to O a year earlier. Townshend, *British Campaign in Ireland*, p.127.
43   Referred to in Winter's memoirs simply as 'the War Office'.
44   Winter, *Winter's Tale*, p.297.
45   O'Connor, *Terrible Beauty*, pp.165–6.
46   Winter, *Winter's Tale*, p.345.
47   GHQ Ireland, 'Record of the Rebellion in Ireland ...', II, p.18, ICM.
48   O'Halpin, 'British Intelligence in Ireland', pp.74–5.
49   Winter, *Winter's Tale*, p.304.
50   GHQ Ireland, 'Record of the Rebellion in Ireland ...', II, p.18, ICM.
51   Winter, *Winter's Tale*, pp.302–5.
52   GHQ Ireland, 'Record of the Rebellion in Ireland ...', II, p.13, ICM.
53   Ibid., p.33.
54   Predictably, the IRA now blames his murder on British Intelligence.

CHAPTER 9

1   On the early history of GC & CS see: A.G. Denniston, Untitled memoir on GC & CS, 2 Dec. 1944, CCAC Denniston MSS DENN 1/4; W.F. Clarke,

'The Years Between', CCAC Clarke MSS CLKE 3; Report of the Inter-Service Directorate Committee, 9 April 1923, PRO WO 32/4897.

2   *Dictionary of National Biography, 1961–1970.* See below, pp.451–4.

3   Denniston, Untitled memoir, 2 Dec. 1944, CCAC Denniston MSS DENN 1/4.

4   Ibid.

5   Andrew, 'Codebreakers and Foreign Offices'. Idem, 'Déchiffrement et diplomatie'.

6   Denniston, Untitled memoir, 2 Dec. 1944, CCAC Denniston MSS DENN 1/4. *Who Was Who.*

7   Denniston, Untitled memoir, 2 Dec. 1944, CCAC Denniston MSS DENN 1/4/.

8   Recollections of Fetterlein kindly supplied to the author by Professor F.H. Hinsley, Mr Christopher Morris and Mr Robin Denniston.

9   W.F. Friedman, 'Six lectures on Cryptology', April 1963, p.18, NAW RG 457 SRH-004.

10   Ullman, *Anglo-Soviet Relations*, vol. III, ch.3.

11   'A Survey of Revolutionary Movements in Great Britain in the Year 1920', Jan. 1921, PRO CAB 24/118.

12   Ullman, *Anglo-Soviet Relations*, vol. III, p.272. Though claiming that the version of the telegram later published had been doctored, Meynell acknowledged that the substance was accurate and that 'the Secret Service obtained copies of telegrams passed between Litvinoff in Copenhagen and Chicherin in Russia'. Meynell, *My Lives*, p.118.

13   Meynell, *My Lives*, pp.119–22.

14   'Report on the disposal of gems believed to have been brought over by Kameneff and Krassin for propaganda purposes. Vide cable 20th August', 8 Sept. 1920, HLRO Lloyd George MSS F/203/1/12. Ullman, *Anglo-Soviet Relations*, vol. III, pp.272–3.

15   Cited in Curzon, 'Very secret. Krassin & Klishko', 16 Sept. 1920, IOLR Curzon MSS Eur F 112/236.

16   Pelling, *British Communist Party*, pp.11, 17–18, 29.

17   Kell, memo, 24 Nov. 1922, PRO WO 32/3948 5/Bills/1873. 'Seditious Literature etc.', Jan. 1932, PRO WO 32/3948 110/Gen/4638. The MI5 campaign for new legislation can be partly followed in several files in WO 32/3948.

18   'A Survey of Revolutionary Movements in Great Britain in the Year 1920', June 1921, PRO CAB 24/118.

19   Ullman, *Anglo-Soviet Relations*, vol. III, pp.210–22, 244–5, 253–62.

20   'A Survey of Revolutionary Movements in Great Britain in the Year 1920', Jan. 1921, PRO CAB 24/118.

21   Ullman, *Anglo-Soviet Relations*, vol. III, p.266.

22   Ibid., p.279.

23   Ibid., pp.275–7.

24   Lloyd George, 'Memorandum on the proposal to expel Messrs Kameneff & Krassin', 2 Sept. 1920, HLRO Lloyd George MSS F/203/1/4.

25   Ullman, *Anglo-Soviet Relations*, vol. III, pp.283–4.

26 Ibid., pp.286–9.
27 Curzon, 'Kameneff and Krassin', 2 Sept. 1920, HLRO Lloyd George MSS F/203/1/3. Soviet wireless communications with Afghanistan and the Middle East were intercepted by a British wireless station at Constantinople (moved to Sarafand in 1922) as well as in India.
28 Ullman, *Anglo-Soviet Relations*, vol. III, pp.302–7.
29 Ibid., p.307.
30 Cabinet conclusions, 15 Sept. 1920, PRO CAB 23/23. This leak is not discussed by Ullman.
31 Diary entry by Hankey, 15 Sept. 1920, CCAC Hankey MSS 1/5.
32 Jeffery and Hennessy, *States of Emergency*, pp.54–5. Most of the detailed planning was done by the civil servants of the Supply and Transport Organisation (STO) which reported to the STC.
33 'A Survey of Revolutionary Movements in Great Britain in the Year 1920', Jan. 1921, PRO CAB 24/118.
34 Jeffery and Hennessy, *States of Emergency*, pp.55–8. Taylor, *English History 1914–1945*, p.194.
35 'A Survey of Revolutionary Movements in Great Britain in the Year 1920', Jan. 1921, PRO CAB 24/118. Kendall, *Revolutionary Movement in Britain*, pp.246–7. Fitch, *Traitors Within*, pp.87–9.
36 Major O.N. Solbert to DMI Washington, 30 Oct. 1920, NAW RG 165 9944-A-165.
37 Major R.F. Hyatt to DMI Washington, 15 Dec. 1920, NAW RG 165 9944-A-166.
38 Ullman, *Anglo-Soviet Relations*, vol. III, ch.10.
39 Ibid., pp.426–7.
40 Frunze to Lenin and others, 19 Dec. 1920, Meijer (ed.), *Trotsky Papers*, vol. II, p.369. Ullman (*Anglo-Soviet Relations*, vol. III, pp.308–9) implies that British indiscretions in September alerted the Russians to the breaking of their codes. This appears unlikely. The Russians did not decide to change their codes until after Frunze's warning three months later.
41 Ullman, *Anglo-Soviet Relations*, vol. III, pp.309–10. Though providing an excellent analysis of Soviet intercepts in 1920, Ullman wrongly suggests that these were now 'to dry up' for a considerable period.
42 SIS report no. 86, 14 March 1921, PRO FO 371/6847 N 3296. Leggett, *Cheka*, pp.325–7.
43 Ullman, *Anglo-Soviet Relations*, vol. III, pp.443–53.
44 Ibid., p.429.
45 Foreign Office Confidential Print no. 11861, 'Violations of the Russian Trade Agreement, 1921', p.5, CUL.
46 Ibid., file 7.
47 Jeffery and Hennessy, *States of Emergency*, pp.58–61.
48 Meynell, *My Lives*, pp.128–31.
49 Jeffery and Hennessy, *States of Emergency*, p.63.
50 Thomson, memo, 28 April 1921, PRO FO 372/1624.
51 Jeffery and Hennessy, *States of Emergency*, pp.63–6.

52    White, *Britain and the Bolshevik Revolution*, p.102.
53    *Parliamentary Debates (Commons)*, 5th series, vol. CXXXIX, 23 March 1921, cols.895–6.
54    On informers see Griffiths, *To Guard My People*, ch.18.
55    Kaye, *Communism in India [1920–24]*, pp.1–5. Petrie, *Communism in India 1924–27*, pp.5–9. The first editions of these works, originally distributed only to intelligence and government personnel, are available in the Indian National Archives. Significantly, the Communist editor of the Indian reprints does not suggest that any of the intercepted Comintern and other communications cited by Kaye and Petrie are forgeries.
56    Foreign Office Confidential Print no. 11861, 'Violations of the Russian Trade Agreement', 1921, pp.21–2, 25, 45–7, CUL. This document was first analysed in Andrew, 'British Secret Service and Anglo-Soviet Relations'. West, *MI6*, p.27 identifies B.P.11 as Gregory but, as usual, gives no source.
57    Foreign Office Confidential Print no.11861, 'Violations of the Russian Trade Agreement 1921', pp.21, 24–5, 27, 45–7, CUL.
58    Ibid., pp.47–8, 63, 75–7.
59    Ibid., pp.45, 70–2.
60    Ibid., pp.90–6.
61    Ibid., pp.113–17.
62    Ibid., pp.108–11.
63    Ibid., pp.153–4.
64    Printed memo on 'classification of reports', attached to intelligence report of 10 May 1922, HLRO Lloyd George MSS F/26/1/30.
65    Austen Chamberlain to Curzon, 7 Nov. 1921, BUL Chamberlain MSS AC 23/2/4.
66    O'Halpin, 'Sir Warren Fisher', p.923.
67    Horwood, memo, 26 Oct. 1921, HLRO Lloyd George MSS F/28/1/6. O'Halpin, 'Sir Warren Fisher', p.924.
68    O'Halpin, 'Sir Warren Fisher', p.924.
69    Curzon to Austen Chamberlain, 5 Nov. 1921, BUL Chamberlain MSS AC 23/2/11.
70    Long to Austen Chamberlain, 2 Nov. 1921, BUL Chamberlain MSS AC 23/2/1.
71    *Parliamentary Debates (Commons)*, 5th series, vol. CXXXXVII, 3 Nov. 1921, cols. 2041–86.
72    Major O.N. Solbert to Major M. Churchill, 9 May 1922, NAW RG 165 11013–9.
73    Deacon, *British Secret Service*, p.243.
74    Long to Austen Chamberlain, 2 Nov. 1921, BUL Chamberlain MSS AC 23/2/1.
75    Private information.
76    *Parliamentary Debates (Commons)*, 5th series, vol. CXXXXVII, 3 Nov. 1921, col. 2057; 8 Nov. 1921, col. 2201. See above, pp.240–1.
77    Hinsley et al., *British Intelligence in the Second World War*, vol. I, p.17.
78    Foreign Office to Treasury, 9 July 1920, PRO T161/25/S1400. Foreign Office minutes of interdepartmental meeting to discuss passport control, 9

March 1923, PRO T161/50/S9242/2.

79    European passport control offices at the end of 1921 were situated in Antwerp, Athens, Berlin, Brussels, Bucharest, Budapest, Christiana, Copenhagen, Helsinki, Kovno (Kaunas), Libau (Liepaja), Madrid, Paris, Prague, Reval (Tallinn), Riga, Rome, Rotterdam, Sofia, Stockholm, Vienna, Warsaw, Zurich. Details of passport control offices and their budgets are given in Montgomery (Foreign Office) to Treasury, 4 Feb. 1922; Foreign Office to Treasury, 4 Jan. 1923, PRO T162/76 E7483/1.

80    'Reduction of Estimates for Secret Services', 19 March 1920, HLRO Lloyd George MSS F/9/2/16.

81    See below, pp.349, 407. Private information.

82    Philby, *My Secret War*, pp.51ff. Private information. See below, pp.343–9. The date of Menzies's entry to SIS is given in the *Dictionary of National Biography 1961–1970*. The late David Footman told me that Russel was also 'an original member of the club'. The date of Woollcombe's appointment may be deduced from his *Who's Who* entries ('1921–44 employed under Foreign Office').

83    O'Malley, 'Memorandum on Soviet policy, March 1921 – December 1922 (secret)', 6 Feb. 1923, p.11, IOLR Curzon MSS Eur. F112/236.

84    Lockhart, *Ace of Spies*, pp.98–9.

85    Churchill, *Great Contemporaries*, pp.93–9. Gilbert, *Winston S. Churchill*, vol. IV, p.422.

86    Gilbert, *Winston S. Churchill*, vol. IV, companion vol. III, p.1703; ibid., vol. IV, pp.431–2.

87    Golinkov, *Secret War Against Soviet Russia*, pp.90–1.

88    Spears to Churchill, draft, n.d.; Savinkov to unnamed French minister, copy, 25 Feb. 1920, CCAC Spears MSS SPRS 1/301.

89    Lockhart, *Ace of Spies*, p.105.

90    Spears diary, 1, 26 April, 6 June, 17 July, 5 Aug., 5, 17, 22 Nov., 14 Dec. 1921, CCAC Spears MSS SPRS 2/4.

91    Ibid., 26 May, 20 Sept., 23 Nov. 1921.

92    Golinkov, *Secret War Against Soviet Russia*, pp.90–1.

93    Lockhart, *Ace of Spies*, pp.101–8. Spears diary, 1 Oct. 1921, CCAC Spears MSS SPRS 2/4.

94    Spears diary, 21, 25 Oct., 17, 24 Nov. 1921, CCAC Spears MSS SPRS 2/4.

95    White, *Britain and the Bolshevik Revolution*, p.55.

96    Reilly, 'Memorandum on the Situation in Russia', copy no. 9, 5 Aug. 1921, HLRO Lloyd George MSS F/203/3/6. Andrew, 'British Secret Service and Anglo-Soviet Relations', p.681.

97    Fink, *Genoa Conference*. White, *Britain and the Bolshevik Revolution*, p.55.

98    Spears diary, 23 Nov. 1921, CCAC Spears MSS SPRS 2/4.

99    Crowe to Curzon, 28 Dec. 1921, in Gilbert, *Winston S. Churchill*, vol. IV, companion vol. III, pp.1703–5. Crowe does not identify the PCO by name but Field-Robinson was a close friend of Reilly and visited him in London in November 1921. Spears diary, 24 Nov. 1921, CCAC Spears MSS SPRS 2/4.

100   Spears to Churchill, copy, 3 Jan. 1922, CCAC Spears MSS SPRS 1/301.

101    Crowe to Curzon, 28 Dec. 1921, in Gilbert, *Winston S. Churchill*, vol. IV, companion vol. III, pp.1703–5.
102    Churchill, *Great Contemporaries*, pp.99–100.
103    Crowe to Curzon, 28 Dec. 1921, in Gilbert, *Winston S. Churchill*, vol. IV, companion vol. III, pp.1703–5.
104    Kettle, *Sidney Reilly*, pp.104–5.
105    Fink, *Genoa Conference*, p.105n.
106    Lockhart, *Ace of Spies*, p.113.
107    Golinkov, *Secret War Against Soviet Russia*, p.91.
108    Spears diary, 20 April, 30 June, 2 Aug. 1922, CCAC Spears MSS SPRS 2/5.
109    Lockhart, *Ace of Spies*, pp.114–15. Spears to Reilly, 19 July 1923 (enclosing references), copy, CCAC Spears MSS SPRS 1/301.
110    O'Malley, 'Memorandum on Soviet policy, March 1921 – December 1922 (secret)', 6 Feb. 1923, pp.18–20, 29–32, IOLR Curzon MSS Eur. F 112/236.
111    Cabinet conclusions, 3 May 1923, PRO CAB 23/45. Cf. Curzon to Bonar Law, 5 May 1923, HLRO Davidson MSS.
112    Cmd. 1869 (1923).
113    Cmd. 1874 (1923).
114    Report of Inter-Service Directorate Committee, Most Secret, 9 April 1923, PRO WO 32/4897.
115    Curzon to Amery, 7 July 1923, enclosing Foreign Office comments on report, PRO WO 32/4897.
116    Cumming to Hoare, 24 Jan. [1923], CUL Templewood MSS V:I.
117    Williams, *World of Action*, pp.338–9.
118    'Control of Interception', n.d. [1924]; Sinclair to DMO & I, 9 May 1924, PRO WO 32/4897.
119    Hinsley et al., *British Intelligence in the Second World War*, vol. I, p.22. Army and air sections followed in 1930 and 1936.
120    W.F. Clarke, 'Foundation and building up of Naval Section 1924–33', CCAC Clarke MSS CLKE 3.
121    Sinclair's service record, PRO ADM 196/43, p.368; ADM 196/53, p.199. Private information.
122    Private information.
123    Winterbotham, *Nazi Connection*, pp.28–9.
124    Young (ed.), *Lockhart Diaries*, vol. I, p.97.
125    Inside Europe the passport control offices at Antwerp, Bucharest, Christiana, Libau, Lisbon, Madrid and Zurich disappeared. A new office was opened in Oslo. 'Passport Control Organization, Schedule of rates of pay for 1925–1926', PRO T162/76 E7483/1.
126    J.D. Gregory, Untitled memorandum on Russia, 8 Jan. 1924, IOLR Curzon MSS Eur. F112/236. Gregory believed that one reason for the 'almost complete lack of evidence of hostile activity by Soviet representatives in the East' was 'the fact that we are perhaps not now in a position to interpret the wireless messages which were the chief source for our charges in May last'.
127    Gilbert, *Winston S. Churchill*, vol. IV, p.429.

128 Minute by Thwaites, 30 July 1920, PRO WO 106/64. Harrington to Wilson, 13 July 1921, IWM Wilson MSS HHW 2/46B/16. I am grateful for these references to Keith Jeffery.

129 Curzon to Crewe, 2 Feb. 1923, CUL Crewe MSS 12.

130 Andrew and Kanya-Forstner, *France Overseas*, p.232.

131 Title written by Curzon on an envelope containing French intercepts, IOLR Curzon MSS Eur. F 112/320.

132 Curzon to Crewe, 13 Oct., 12 Nov., 12 Dec. 1923, CUL Crewe MSS 12. Curzon to Baldwin, 9 Nov. 1923, IOLR Curzon MSS Eur. F 112/320.


CHAPTER 10

1 Taylor, *English History 1914–1945*, pp.269–70. Nicolson, *George V*, p.403.

2 Roskill, *Hankey*, vol. II, pp.353–4. Chester, Fay and Young, *Zinoviev Letter*, p.108. Jeffery and Hennessy, *States of Emergency*, p.78.

3 Kell to Troup (Home Office), 2 May 1918, enclosing 'Return no. 2' of cases considered for prosecution with 'remarks by MI5', PRO HO 45/10743/263275.

4 Hankey to Lloyd George, 8 Sept. 1920, HLRO Davidson MSS.

5 Yardley, *Black Chamber*, pp.262–3.

6 Churchill to Austen Chamberlain, 21 Nov. 1924, BUL Chamberlain MSS AC 51/58.

7 *Parliamentary Debates (Commons)*, 5th series, vol. CCVI, 26 May 1927, cols. 2257–8.

8 Childs, *Episodes and Reflections*, p.209.

9 Marquand, *Ramsay MacDonald*, pp.314–15.

10 Taylor, *English History 1914–1945*, p.275n.

11 Roskill, *Hankey*, vol. II, p.358. Jeffery and Hennessy, *States of Emergency*, pp.76–8.

12 Barnes, 'Special Branch and the First Labour Government', p.37.

13 Jeffery and Hennessy, *States of Emergency*, pp.79–86.

14 Industrial Unrest Committee Interim Report (with memorandum by Home Secretary summarising intelligence on the CPGB), 30 April 1924, CP 273 (24), PRO CAB 24/166.

15 Ibid.

16 Cabinet conclusion 32 (24) 5, 15 May 1924, PRO CAB 23/48.

17 See the editions of Kaye, *Communism in India [1920–4]* and Petrie, *Communism in India 1924–1927* edited by M. Saha.

18 See above, pp.281–2.

19 'Report on Revolutionary Organizations in the United Kingdom', 1 May 1924, Ramsay MacDonald MSS PRO 30/69/220. Sir John Anderson to the Foreign Office, 3 May 1924, makes clear that the source of the letter was SIS; PRO PREM 1/49.

20 Minute by Maxse, 3 May 1924; Mounsey (Foreign Office) to Home Office, 12 May 1924, PRO FO 371/10478.

21 Marquand, *Ramsay MacDonald*, pp.361–3. Cline, *E.D. Morel*, pp.141–3.

22 *Parliamentary Debates (Commons)*, 5th series, vol. CCXV, 19 Mar. 1928, col.

60.

23    The original intercept of the Zinoviev letter of 15 Sept. 1924 has disappeared from Foreign Office files. The earliest copies are in PRO FO 371/10478.

24    Bland to Lord Stamfordham, 27 Oct. 1924, PRO FO 371/10478.

25    *Parliamentary Debates (Commons)*, 5th series, vol. CCXV, 19 Mar. 1928, col. 62.

26    Gorodetsky, *Precarious Peace*, p.46.

27    Kettle, *Sidney Reilly*, pp.121ff.

28    Petrie, *Communism in India 1924–1927*, pp.72–3. For examples of Comintern intercepts during 1925 see ibid., pp.73–4.

29    Calhoun, *United Front*, pp.64–5. Cf. weekly Special Branch reports of 3 July 1924 onwards, Ramsay MacDonald MSS PRO 30/69/220.

30    MacDonald diary, 31 Oct. 1924, cited in Marquand, *Ramsay MacDonald*, p.383.

31    'History of the Zinoviev incident', 2nd revise, 11 Nov. 1924, PRO FO 371/10479.

32    Crowe, 'Zinoviev Letter', pp.420–4.

33    Gregory, *Edge of Diplomacy*, p.221. Marquand, *Ramsay MacDonald*, p.381.

34    'History of the Zinoviev incident', 2nd revise, 11 Nov. 1924, PRO FO 371/10479.

35    MacDonald diary, 31 Oct. 1924, cited in Marquand, *Ramsay MacDonald*, p.384.

36    Crowe to MacDonald (copy), 25 Oct. 1924, PRO FO 371/10478.

37    Chester, Fay and Young, *Zinoviev Letter*, pp.95–100. Hall considered Marlowe 'one of the greatest patriots ever'. Hall, 'Rough Notes', 10 Jan. 1936, p.5, CCAC HALL 2/1.

38    Gilbert, *Winston S. Churchill*, vol. III, p.359.

39    See above, pp.247–8.

40    *Parliamentary Debates (Commons)*, 5th series, vol. CXXXXVII, 3 Nov. 1921, col. 2044.

41    Chester, Fay and Young, *Zinoviev Letter*, pp.99–100.

42    Letter from Marlowe published in *The Observer*, 4 Mar. 1928.

43    Chester, Fay and Young, *Zinoviev Letter*, pp.95–6, 100–8.

44    Ibid., passim. Kettle, *Sidney Reilly*, pp.122–4. Im Thurn seems a shadier character than these authors suggest. He may have been, at least in part, a confidence trickster. He later extracted large sums from Conservative Central Office, allegedly to recompense the unidentified source who had informed him of the letter and had – he implausibly claimed – subsequently taken refuge in Argentina. Im Thurn also sought a knighthood for himself.

45    It is impossible to reconstruct the precise pattern of contacts by which retired intelligence personnel sometimes received classified information from serving officers. Hankey's diary for 28 Nov. 1920, however, gives one example: a dining club of past and present intelligence officers at which current espionage by Germany and Japan was among the subjects discussed. CCAC Hankey MSS 1/5.

46    Wilson, *Leonard Woolf*, p.160.

47    Taylor, *Beaverbrook*, pp.223–41.

48 W. Strang, 'Note on arguments used to support the contention that the Zinoviev letter is a forgery', 17 Nov. 1924, PRO FO 371/10479. Crowe, 'Zinoviev Letter'.

49 See below, p.319.

50 Peters to MacDonald, no. 1027, 4 Nov. 1924, PRO FO 371/10479.

51 *Parliamentary Debates (Commons)*, 5th series, vol. CCXV, col.63. Grant, 'Zinoviev Letter', pp.274–5.

52 Chester, Fay and Young, *Zinoviev Letter*, ch.5.

53 *Parliamentary Debates (Commons)*, 5th series, vol. CLXXXIX, col. 674.

54 See above, pp.278–81.

55 'History of the Zinoviev incident', 2nd revise, 11 Nov. 1924, PRO FO 371/10479.

56 Childs, *Episodes and Reflections*, pp.224–5. Petrie, *Communism in India 1924–1927*, pp.77–82.

57 *Parliamentary Debates (Commons)*, 5th series, vol. CLXXXIX, cols. 673–4.

58 Crowe to MacDonald (copy), 26 Oct. 1924, PRO FO 371/10478. 'History of the Zinoviev incident', 2nd revise, 11 Nov. 1924, PRO FO 371/10479. Special Branch also had informers but, according to Childs, played no part in the Zinoviev letter affair; *Episodes and Reflections*, p.246.

59 See, e.g. 'Report on Revolutionary Organizations in the United Kingdom', 22 Nov. 1923, PRO CAB 24/162; 'Report on Revolutionary Organizations in the United Kingdom', 26 June 1924, Ramsay MacDonald MSS PRO 30/69/220; Industrial Unrest Committee, Interim Report, 30 April 1924, PRO CAB 24/166; and below, p.319.

60 See above, p.272.

61 Private information. See below, pp.334–5, 368–9.

62 See above, pp.283–4.

63 *Parliamentary Debates (Commons)*, 5th series, vol. CLXXXIX, cols. 673–4.

64 Sinclair to Crowe, 6 Nov. 1924, PRO FO 371/10479. Austen Chamberlain, 'The Zinoviev Letter', 22 Dec. 1924, PRO FO 371/10480.

65 Ibid. Kuusinen, *Before and After Stalin*, pp.50–1.

66 Childs, *Episodes and Reflections*, p.246. Marquand, *Ramsay MacDonald*, p.388.

67 Denniston's brief summary of GC & CS's 'success' in decrypting Soviet traffic appears to indicate that until 1927 no changes in Soviet codes and ciphers defeated GC & CS for more than a few months. Denniston, Untitled memoir on GC & CS, 2 Dec. 1944, p.8, CCAC Denniston MSS DENN 1/4.

68 Kuusinen, *Before and After Stalin*, ch.2.

69 This possibility occurred to the late Sir Maurice Oldfield.

70 Golinkov, *Secret War Against Soviet Russia*, pp.90–6. Kettle, *Sidney Reilly*, ch.7.

71 Lockhart, *Ace of Spies*, pp.131–5. Kettle, *Sidney Reilly*, pp.131–6. On Reilly's business dealings see also Spears to Reilly (copy), 1 March 1925, CCAC Spears MSS SPRS 1/301.

72 Golinkov, *Secret War*, pp.99.

73 Ibid., pp.96–101. Kettle, *Sidney Reilly*, pp.136–41. Lockhart, *Ace of Spies*, chs.10–13.

74 Churchill to Austen Chamberlain, 22 Nov. 1924, BUL Chamberlain MSS AC 51/61.

75 Denniston, Untitled memoir on GC & CS, 2 Dec. 1944, p.2, CCAC Denniston MSS DENN 1/4.

76 Mrs Caroline Oliver, interviewed by the author in 'The Profession of Intelligence', part 2, BBC Radio 4, 9 Aug. 1981 (producer Peter Everett).

77 Private information. Payne Best transcripts.

78 Austen Chamberlain, memo for Baldwin (copy), 24 July 1925 (with addendum by Chamberlain of 30 July), BUL Chamberlain MSS AC 52/81.

79 Carr, *Foundations of a Planned Economy*, vol. III, part I, p.21. J.D. Gregory, 'Russia', 10 Dec. 1926, CUL Baldwin MSS 113.

80 CP 250 (26), 16 June 1926, PRO CAB 24/180.

81 Austen Chamberlain to Tyrrell (copy), 18 Oct. 1925, BUL Chamberlain MSS AC 52/769.

82 Austen Chamberlain to Churchill (copy), 5 Nov. 1925, BUL Chamberlain MSS AC 52/171.

83 Taylor, *Jix*, p.180. Childs, *Episodes and Reflections*, p.209.

84 Calhoun, *United Front*, pp.45, 136, 140–9, 173–83. Renshaw, 'Anti-Labour Politics', pp.699–700.

85 Jeffery and Hennessy, *States of Emergency*, p.93. Cabinet conclusions 47 (25) 2, 7 Oct. 1925, PRO CAB 23/51.

86 Taylor, *Jix*, pp.193–5.

87 See below, p.322.

88 Minute by Kell, 29 July 1925, PRO WO 32/3948 110/Gen/4399. 'Report on Revolutionary Organizations in the United Kingdom', no. 317 (including copy of Comintern letter of 20 July), 13 Aug. 1925; 'Notes on Subversive Propaganda in the Fighting Services', 25 April 1926 (citing Zinoviev to Pollitt, 22 May 1925, and memos by Kell, 1 Sept. 1925, 12 April 1926), PRO WO 32/3948 110/Gen/3996.

89 Minute by Kell, 29 July 1925, PRO WO 32/3948 110/Gen/4399. (The same file contains references to reports by Kell of Sept. 1925 and April 1926 which are missing – doubtless 'weeded' – from the file.) Cab. 48 (25) 2A, 13 Oct. 1925, PRO CAB 23/51.

90 *The Times*, 17, 26 Nov. 1925. Taylor, *English History 1914–1945*, p.308.

91 Memo by Kell of 12 April 1926 cited in 'Notes on Subversive Propaganda in the Fighting Services', 25 April 1926, PRO WO 32/3948 110/Gen/3996.

92 A summary of the intelligence which most impressed Jix appears in his cabinet memorandum, 'Russian Money', CP 236(26), 11 June 1926, PRO CAB 24/180. Jix included 'the most secret information in the possession of the Foreign Office' (i.e. that supplied by SIS and GC & CS).

93 Gorodetsky, *Precarious Truce*, pp.123–4. Calhoun, *United Front*, pp.223–4.

94 Calhoun, *United Front*, p.237.

95 Jix, 'Russian Money', CP 236(26), 11 June 1926, PRO CAB/180.

96 Jeffery and Hennessy, *States of Emergency*, pp.108–24.

97 Jix, 'Russian Money', CP 236(26), 11 June 1926; second memorandum by Jix also entitled 'Russian Money', CP 244(26), 15 June 1926, PRO CAB 24/180.

98   *Parliamentary Debates (Commons)*, 5th series, vol. CLXXXIX, 1 Dec. 1925, cols. 2094ff. 'Communist Papers', Cmd. 2682 (1926). Pelling, *Communist Party*, pp.33–7.
99   Gorodetsky, *Precarious Truce*, p.157.
100  Kuusinen, *Before and After Stalin*, pp.71–2.
101  Calhoun, *United Front*, pp.250–1.
102  Among the most valuable intelligence reports are three volumes originally printed solely for Indian government and intelligence use: Kaye, *Communism in India [1920–4]*; Petrie, *Communism in India 1924–1927*; Williamson, *India and Communism [1927–33]*. The volumes by Kaye and Petrie are now available in Indian reprints (ed. M. Saha, Calcutta, 1971 and 1972) and my references are to these editions. I have used the privately printed edition of the volume by Petrie's successor, Sir Horace Williamson, in the IOLR MSS Eur. E251/33. Decrypts were considered too sensitive to include in these volumes.
103  Petrie, *Communism in India 1924–1927*, pp.95–6.
104  Ibid., pp.103–5.
105  Spratt, *Blowing Up India*, pp.4, 9–14, 22–9. I am grateful to the Tutors Office at Downing College for details of Spratt's academic record. Sadly, his college file has been destroyed.
106  Petrie, *Communism in India 1924–1927*, pp.108–9.
107  Ibid. Carr, *Foundations of a Planned Economy*, vol. III, part III, pp.915–17.
108  Petrie, *Communism in India 1924–1927*, pp.109–10, 336.
109  Ibid., pp.86–8, 330. Misra, *Indian Political Parties*, pp.202–8.
110  CP 234(26), June 1926, PRO CAB 24/180.
111  Petrie, *Communism in India 1924–1927*, p.171.
112  Note by Political Department, 15 Dec. 1925, IOLR L/P & S/18-A.200: cited by Jackman, 'Lord Birkenhead's Paper Tiger'. See also Dr Jackman's thesis, 'Afghanistan in British Imperial Strategy and Diplomacy 1919–1941'.
113  Petrie, *Communism in India 1924–1927*, pp.172–9.
114  Jackman, 'Lord Birkenhead's Paper Tiger'.
115  Minutes of Inter-Departmental Committee on Eastern Unrest, 23 July 1926, PRO FO 371/11678.
116  Birkenhead, *F.E.*, p.535.
117  Memorandum by J.D. Gregory, 10 Dec. 1926, CUL Baldwin MSS 113. Tyrrell to Austen Chamberlain, 6 Dec. 1926, BUL Chamberlain MSS AC 53/566. Davidson to Baldwin, 10 Jan. 1927, CUL Baldwin MSS 115; Davidson vainly asked the prime minister: 'Please burn this letter'.
118  Cab. 2(27), PRO CAB 23/54.
119  CP 24(27), CP 25(27), PRO CAB 24/184. Cab. 12(27), PRO CAB 23/54.
120  Cab. 14(27)1A, PRO CAB 23/90B.
121  Cab. 17(27)4, PRO CAB 23/90B.
122  Prologue by Compton Mackenzie to Macartney, *Walls Have Mouths*. Macartney, *Zigzag*, chs.15–17 (quotation from pp.344–5).
123  Reports of Macartney's trial in *The Times*, 5, 6 Dec. 1927; 17, 18, 19 Jan. 1928.
124  Cab. 17(27)4, PRO CAB 23/90B.

125 *Parliamentary Debates (Commons)*, 5th series, vol. CCVI, 26 May 1927, cols. 2302–3.

126 Intercepted telegrams from Yakoklev to Moscow, 13 April, 18 May 1927, published in Cmd 2874 (1927), *Documents Illustrating the Hostile Activities of the Soviet Government and Third International against Great Britain*, p.31. Yakoklev doubtless used 'friends, "neighbours" and so forth' as euphemisms for agents of various kinds.

127 *The Times*, 5 Dec. 1927.

128 Cab. 23(27), PRO CAB 23/55.

129 *Parliamentary Debates (Commons)*, 5th series, vol. CCVI, 24 May 1927, cols. 1842–54.

130 Ibid., 26 May 1927, cols. 2207–22, 2299–2306.

131 Chamberlain to Rosengolz, 26 May 1927, *Documents on British Foreign Policy*, series IA, vol. III, no. 215.

132 Cmd. 2874.

133 Denniston, Untitled memoir on GC & CS, 2 Dec. 1944, p.8, CCAC Denniston MSS DENN 1/4. Research in progress suggests that in 1928 GC & CS was able to decrypt some Soviet diplomatic traffic with Afghanistan, probably sent in old ciphers.

134 See above, p.269.

135 Cave Brown and MacDonald, *Field of Red*, pp.236ff. *The Times* trial reports.

136 See above, p.314.

137 Lockhart, *Ace of Spies*, pp.134ff, 171–6.

138 Monthly report by C.B. Follmer (American vice-consul at Reval), 17 Aug. 1927, NAW RG 59 800i.00/155. There are press reports of the arrest of Boyce's Russian network in NAW RG 165 9944-A-183, but a military intelligence report on the same subject was 'removed from the file on security grounds' in 1974. The date of Harry Carr's appointment as PCO is given in his *Who's Who* entries.

139 Memo by Kell, 27 July 1927, PRO WO 32/3948 110/Gen/4036.

140 'Internal Security of H.M. Forces during 1929' (with statistics for 1928), 3 Feb. 1930, PRO WO 32/3948 110/Gen/4399.

141 The two main sources for Knight's career are the interview with his wartime assistant Joan Miller in *The Sunday Times Magazine*, 18 Oct. 1981, and Masters, *The Man Who Was M*. Both contain valuable new information but should be used with caution.

142 Knight, *Pets Usual and Unusual*, pp.13–14, 78–9. Obituary notices in *The Times*, 27, 31 Jan. 1968.

143 Matthews and Knight, *Senses of Animals*, p.13.

144 Interview with Joan Miller, *Sunday Times Magazine*, 18 Oct. 1981. Masters, *The Man Who Was M.*, chs.2–5. On the other Captain King see below, p.432.

145 Misra, *Indian Political Parties*, p.208.

146 Petrie, *Communism in India 1924–1927*, pp.70–1.

147 Carr, *Foundations of a Planned Economy*, vol. III, part III, pp.922–3.

148 Sir Horace Williamson, *India and Communism [1927–33]*, printed for Government of India, 1935 edition, pp.153–4, 158, IOLR MSS Eur. E251/33.

149  Carr, *Foundations of a Planned Economy*, vol. III, part III, pp.919–20.
150  Williamson, *India and Communism [1927–33]*, p.152, IOLR MSS Eur. E251/33.
151  Carr, *Foundations of a Planned Economy*, vol. III, part III, pp.929n, 939–40.
152  Williamson, *India and Communism [1927–33]*, pp.156–8, IOLR MSS Eur. E251/33. Cf. Misra, *Indian Political Parties*, pp.254ff.
153  CP 54 (34), PRO CAB 24/247.
154  Pelling, *British Communist Party*, pp.45ff.
155  Petrie, *Communism in India, 1924–1927*, pp.136–7, 286.

## CHAPTER 11

1  Taylor, *English History 1914–1945*, p.371.
2  Davidson, *Memoirs of a Conservative*, p.272. On Ball's earlier career in MI5 see Cubitt (War Office) to Treasury, 12 Jan. 1923, and minute by Cleary (Treasury), 5 Jan. 1927, PRO T162 982/E10034.
3  Ramsden, *Making of Conservative Party Policy*, chs.3, 4. Entry on Ball by Lord Blake in *Dictionary of National Biography 1961–1970*.
4  Hawker, 'Intelligence Corps', p.85.
5  Hinsley et al., *British Intelligence in the Second World War*, vol. I, pp.10, 13–14.
6  Bond, *British Military Policy*, pp.69–70 and passim.
7  Godfrey, Unpublished Memoirs, vol. VIII, p.156.
8  Domville, *By and Large*, pp.175–80.
9  Godfrey, Unpublished Memoirs, vol. VIII, p.156. Griffiths, *Fellow Travellers of the Right*, passim.
10  Hinsley et al., *British Intelligence in the Second World War*, vol. I, pp.9, 11, 22. See below, pp.388ff.
11  The Air Ministry was, however, permitted an intelligence staff to study Iraq and Aden where military control was vested in the RAF. Air Marshal Sir Victor Goddard, 'Epic Violet', part I, ch.1, p.30, LHC.
12  Ibid., pp.29–30.
13  Hinsley, et al., *British Intelligence in the Second World War*, vol. I, p.26.
14  Vansittart, *Mist Procession*, p.397.
15  Dalton to Mounsey, 3 Dec. 1929, PRO FO 372/2563.
16  Bialer, *Shadow of the Bomber*, pp.18–19.
17  Vansittart, *Mist Procession*, p.397. Private information.
18  Young (ed.), *Lockhart Diaries*, p.328.
19  See below, pp.402–9.
20  See above, pp.284–5.
21  Entry on Menzies in *Dictionary of National Biography 1961–1970*. Kirke diary, 13, 31 Dec. 1915, IWM. Page, Leitch and Knightley, *Philby*, pp.143–5. Boyle, *Climate of Treason*, p.219. Private information.
22  Private information.
23  Winterbotham, *Nazi Connection*.
24  Private information.
25  Private information.

26    The entry in the *Dictionary of National Biography 1961–1970* makes no reference to Fletcher's intelligence career but provides a useful summary of his other activities.

27    Private information. Peel's career in SIS overlapped with that of Colonel Edward R. Peal. It is possible that both were, at different times, responsible for Far Eastern operations. My identification of Peel as the G officer responsible for the Far East in the early 1930s is based on private information from an intelligence officer who knew him at the time.

28    *Dictionary of National Biography 1961–1970*. Private information.

29    *Who's Who* entries for Spencer.

30    Philby, *My Silent War*, p.71. Joan Davis, Vivian's wartime secretary, interviewed by the author on 'Timewatch', BBC 2, 10 July 1984. Further information kindly provided by Mrs Davis and Malcolm Muggeridge.

31    Private information. Cf. Chilston to Collier, 10 March 1936, PRO FO 372/3180.

32    I owe this information to the former diplomat and wartime personal assistant to 'C', Robert Cecil.

33    SIS memorandum, Dec. 1925, PRO FO 372/2706. Foreign Office memorandum, 22 Nov. 1933, PRO FO 372/2975.

34    *Foreign Office Index*, 1922, p.1641, PRO. Some of the documents here referred to, like many dealing with passport control, appear to have been 'weeded'.

35    SIS memorandum, Dec. 1925, PRO FO 372/2706. Foreign Office minute, 28 Jan. 1931, ibid. Minute by Major H.E. Spencer, 18 Nov. 1932, PRO 372/2799. Foreign Office minutes, Nov. 1933, PRO FO 372/2975. Foreign Office minutes, Dec. 1933, PRO T5921/5774/373.

36    'John Whitwell', *British Agent*, chs.1–3. I am grateful to Malcolm Muggeridge for identifying 'Whitwell' as Nicholson and for further information about him.

37    Vansittart, *Mist Procession*, p.398.

38    Hinsley et al., *British Intelligence in the Second World War*, vol. I, p.51.

39    'John Whitwell', *British Agent*, pp.40–2.

40    See, e.g. Sykes to Payne Best, 13 May 1946, IWM Payne Best MSS 79/57/1.

41    See entries for 'Passport Control Offices' in the PRO *Foreign Office Index* for the years 1929 to 1937. The relevant PRO files have been heavily, but incompletely, weeded. Cf. West, *MI6*, pp.43–4. On the 1936 scandals see below, pp.377–8.

42    Private information. See below, pp.357–9.

43    Group-Captain F.W. Winterbotham, interviewed by the author in 'The Profession of Intelligence', part 2, BBC Radio 4, 9 Aug. 1981 (Producer Peter Everett); and further information kindly provided by Group-Captain Winterbotham.

44    Private information.

45    Rose, *Vansittart*, p.74.

46    Young (ed.), *Lockhart Diaries*, vol. I, pp.204, 319, 356. Fletcher, 'Britain's Air Strength', pp.170, 209.

47    Marquand, *Ramsay MacDonald*, pp.700–1.

48    Roskill, *Hankey*, vol. III, p.162n mentions this episode but Captain Roskill was not then free to identify Selby as his source. He authorised me to do so not long before his death in 1982, and also to reveal that Selby's story was confirmed to him by Wing-Commander Sir Archibald James M.P., who may have learned it from Fletcher or other intelligence contacts while campaigning for aerial rearmament in the 1930s. MacDonald's biographer, David Marquand, who does not seem to have had access to Captain Roskill's sources, finds the story 'not proven'. He believes it 'quite conceivable' that MacDonald did have an affair with a continental mistress and wrote compromising letters to her, but considers it would have been 'wholly out of character for MacDonald himself to have authorised – and still more out of character for him to have ordered – public money to be used' for the letters' recovery (Marquand, *Ramsay MacDonald*, pp.700–1). Any money used, however, could well have been MacDonald's own, with SIS acting simply as intermediary.

49    Young (ed.), *Lockhart Diaries*, p.240.

50    Liddell Hart, Notes of a talk with Compton Mackenzie, 29 Nov. 1932, LHC Liddell Hart MSS 11/1932/42. Mackenzie, *Life and Times: Octave Five*, pp. 86–8.

51    Ibid.

52    Published in 1933.

53    Denniston, Untitled memoir on GC & CS, 2 Dec. 1944, CCAC Denniston MSS DENN 1/4.

54    Private information.

55    Denniston, Untitled memoir on GC & CS, 2 Dec. 1944, CCAC Denniston MSS DENN 1/4.

56    Private information.

57    Denniston, Untitled memoir on GC & CS, 2 Dec. 1944, CCAC Denniston MSS DENN 1/4.

58    Rose, *Vansittart*, pp.105–7.

59    Denniston, Untitled memoir on GC & CS, 2 Dec. 1944, CCAC Denniston MSS DENN 1/4.

60    Hinsley et al., *British Intelligence in the Second World War*, vol. I, p.52.

61    Dilks, 'Appeasement and Intelligence', p.151. See below, pp.402–7.

62    Private information.

63    See below, pp.402–9, 432, 441–2.

64    Bell, *Blockade of Germany*.

65    Hinsley et al., *British Intelligence in the Second World War*, vol. I, p.30.

66    Churchill, *Second World War*, vol. I, pp.62–3. Hinsley et al., *British Intelligence in the Second World War*, vol I, pp.30–1. Roskill, *Hankey*, vol. II, pp.464–5. Young, 'Spokesmen for Economic Warfare'.

67    Hinsley et al., *British Intelligence in the Second World War*, vol. I, pp.30–4.

68    Morton to Liddell Hart, 9 July 1961, 9 May 1963, LHC Liddell Hart MSS 1/152.

69    Thompson, *Churchill and Morton*, pp.21, 148.

70   Royal Commission on the Private Manufacture of, and Trading in, Arms, *Minutes of Evidence*, 1935, pp.311–14, 748–51. Entry on Sir Arthur Dawson in *Dictionary of Business Biography*, vol. II.

71   Davenport-Hines, 'Vickers' Balkan Conscience', pp.302–3.

72   Minutes by Roberts, 16 Feb. 1932, and O'Malley, 17 Feb. 1932, PRO FO 371/15853 A969/169/35. Appropriately, Ian Fleming made James Bond's father a Vickers foreign representative.

73   Royal Commission on the Private Manufacture of, and Trading in, Arms, *Minutes of Evidence*, 1935, p.382.

74   Jones and Trebilcock, 'Russian Industry and British Business', p.91. Strang, *Home and Abroad*, p.102. I am grateful to Clive Trebilcock for further information on Metro-Vic reports. Vickers sold a controlling interest in Metro-Vic to the U.S. General Electric Co. in 1928 but retained a minority holding.

75   Wark, 'British Military and Economic Intelligence on Nazi Germany', p.234.

76   COS 326, 23 Feb. 1934, CP 54 (34), PRO CAB 24/247.

77   Wark, 'British Military and Economic Intelligence on Nazi Germany', p.231.

78   Read and Fisher, *Colonel Z.*

79   Private information.

80   Dansey to Payne Best, 14 Dec. 1945, 18 Aug. 1946, IWM Payne Best MSS 79/57/1.

81   Philby, *My Silent War*, p.57.

82   Read and Fisher, *Colonel Z*, ch.15.

83   Ibid., chs.15, 16. Payne Best transcripts. See below, pp.380–2.

84   Most of MI5 headquarters officers appear in the official *War Office List* for 1930; the remainder appear in a 'Supplementary List' in IWM Kell MSS. Details of the appointment of the civil assistants are to be found in PRO T162 982/E10034. On the subsequent careers of Butler and Bacon see West, *MI5.*

85   Creedy (War Office) to Treasury, 17 Dec. 1938, and Treasury minutes, PRO T162 982/E10034. Details of Kell's and Holt-Wilson's salaries are to be found in PRO T161 211/S20779.

86   'Internal Security of H.M. Forces during 1929', 3 Feb. 1930, PRO WO 32/3948 110/Gen/4399.

87   Roskill, *Naval Policy*, vol. II, ch.4. Idem, *Hankey*, vol. II, p.556. Ereira, *Invergordon Mutiny*, ch.10.

88   'Most Secret' cabinet minute, 21 Sept. 1931, PRO CAB 23/90B. Cf. Ereira, *Invergordon Mutiny*, p.160.

89   *The Times*, 17 Oct., 27 Nov. 1931. H.G.E. Hutchings, who was arrested on 23 Oct., maintained that he was a victim of mistaken identity and had never been to Portsmouth. *The Times*, 26 Oct., 3 Nov. 1931. On Allison's early career as a Comintern agent see above, p.324.

90   Ereira, *Invergordon Mutiny*, ch.11.

91   Holt-Wilson, 'Security Intelligence in War', 1934, and attached note by Kell, IWM Kell MSS.

92   Philby, *My Silent War*, p.74.

93   Private information.

94   Allason, *The Branch*, pp.94–5.
95   Holt-Wilson, 'Security Intelligence in War', 1934, IWM Kell MSS.
96   Roskill, *Naval Policy*, vol. II, pp.115n. 116n.
97   Wincott, *Invergordon Mutineer* (quotations from pp.161, 175).
98   Copeman, *Reason in Revolt*.
99   *Parliamentary Debates (Commons)*, 5th series, vol. CCXXVIII, 16 April 1934, cols. 740–3. Anderson, *Fascists, Communists and the National Government*, p.70.
100  Hyde, *I Believed*, pp.42–3.
101  The MI5 memorandum of Oct. 1932 has been removed from the files in the PRO but is quoted and summarised in a secret untitled memorandum, 16 March 1933, PRO WO 32/3948 110/Gen/4771.
102  Ibid.
103  Denniston, Untitled memoir on GC & CS, p.10, 2 Dec. 1944, CCAC Denniston MSS DENN 1/4.
104  Secret untitled memorandum, 16 March 1933, PRO WO 32/3948 110/Gen/ 4771.
105  Cab. 52(33)4, 9 Oct. 1933, PRO CAB 23/77.
106  Cab. 53(33)6, 18 Oct. 1933, PRO CAB 23/77.
107  CP 53(34), 23 Feb. 1934, PRO CAB 24/247. Cab. 8(34)6, 7 March 1934, PRO CAB 23/78.
108  *Parliamentary Debates (Commons)*, 5th series, vol. CCXXVIII, 16 April 1934, col. 763.
109  Anderson, *Fascists, Communists and the National Government*, p.96.
110  Harker (MI5) to Rae (Treasury), 9 Oct. 1936, enclosing MI5 reports on Trebilcock and other Communists 'employed in Civil Establishments under the Admiralty'; Secret report by Carter committee on 'Undesirable Employees in Naval Establishments', 4 Nov. 1936; Macleod (Admiralty) to Rae (Treasury), 7 Jan. 1937; Notes prepared for Baldwin's meeting with Bevin, Feb. 1937, PRO T162 424/E13264/04. Notes by Sir Horace Wilson on meeting between Baldwin, Bevin and First Sea Lord, 9 Feb. 1937, PRO PREM 1/206.
111  Ibid.
112  Masters, *The Man Who Was M*, pp.30–4. Reports of Glading's trial in *The Times*, 4, 8 Feb., 15 Mar. 1938.
113  Private information.
114  Masters, *The Man Who Was M*, chs.2–5.
115  Pincher, *Their Trade is Treachery*, pp.96–7.
116  Interview with Joan Miller, *Sunday Times Magazine*, 18 Oct. 1981. Masters, *The Man Who Was M*, ch.9. Driberg is less forthcoming in his memoirs about his Communism than about his lovemaking, but mentions his friendship with Springhall and his expulsion from the CPGB. Driberg, *Ruling Passions*, pp.50, 75, 102, 105, 150.
117  Knight, *Crime Cargo*, pp.1, 22–3, 165, 272, 279, 309, 311.
118  Private information.
119  Masters, *The Man Who Was M*, ch.4. Brook-Shepherd, *Storm Petrels*, pp.176, 181–2.

120 On Maly see Brook-Shepherd, *Storm Petrels*, p.176.
121 Trial reports in *The Times*, 4, 8 Feb., 15 Mar. 1938. Masters, *The Man Who Was M*, ch.4.
122 See, e.g., Childs to Gower, 2 Feb. 1924, Ramsay MacDonald MSS PRO 30/69/221.
123 Kell to Scott (Home Office), 18 June 1934, enclosing Report no. 1 on the BUF, PRO HO 144/20141.
124 Anderson, *Fascists, Communists and the National Government*, chs.6, 7.
125 Kell to Scott, 1 Aug. 1934, enclosing report no. 2 on the BUF, PRO HO 144/20142.
126 Kell to Scott, 8 Oct. 1934, enclosing report no. 3 on the BUF, PRO HO 144/20142.
127 Kell to Scott, 11 Mar. 1935, enclosing report no. 5 on the BUF, PRO HO 144/20144.
128 Mosley, *Beyond the Pale*, pp.30–1.
129 Rome Chancery to Foreign Office, 27 April 1935, PRO HO 144/20144. 'Home Office information concerning the present source of BUF funds', 27 Nov. 1936; Kell to Home Office, enclosing report no. 9 on the BUF, 27 Nov. 1936; Special Branch report, 2 Nov. 1936, PRO HO 144/20162. A note of MI5 triumph at the discovery of the Italian subsidies is clearly detectable in, e.g., a minute by Liddell of 10 Dec. 1936, ibid.
130 Mosley, *Beyond the Pale*, pp.174–5.
131 Kell to Scott, 10 July 1936, enclosing report no. 8 on BUF, PRO HO 144/21060.
132 Kell to Scott, 27 Nov. 1936, enclosing report no. 9 on BUF, PRO HO 144/21062.
133 Kell to Scott, 10 July 1936, enclosing report no. 8 on BUF, PRO HO 144/21060.
134 Anderson, *Fascists, Communists and the National Government*, chs.10, 11.
135 Kell to Scott, 27 Nov. 1936, enclosing report no. 9; minute by Liddell, 10 Dec. 1936; minute by Harker, 10 July 1937, PRO HO 144/21062.
136 Anderson, *Fascists, Communists and the National Government*, ch.11.

## CHAPTER 12

1 CP 85(35), 15 April 1935, PRO CAB 24/254.
2 Gilbert, *Winston S. Churchill*, vol. V, p.630.
3 Formerly the Ministerial Disarmament Committee (a title not finally abandoned until June 1935).
4 CP 100(35), 13 May 1935, PRO CAB 24/255.
5 Hinsley et al., *British Intelligence in the Second World War*, vol. I, pp.50–1.
6 Details of the secret service vote are contained in PRO T160 787/F6139/053.
7 Hinsley et al., *British Intelligence in the Second World War*, vol. I, p.57.
8 See above, p.349.
9 Payne Best to Drake, 25 Sept. 1947, IWM Payne Best MSS 79/57/1. Farago, *Game of the Foxes*, ch.11. West, *MI6*, pp.44, 48–61. Private

  information.
10  Farago, *Game of the Foxes*, p.109. West, *MI6*, p.52. Foot, *SOE*, p.15.
11  Payne Best to Drake, 25 Sept. 1947, IWM Payne Best MSS 79/57/1.
12  Farago, *Game of the Foxes*, ch.11. West, *MI6*, pp.49–51.
13  See below, pp.433–9.
14  Payne Best to Walter Leschander, 5 Nov. 1958, Payne Best MSS.
15  Farago, *Game of the Foxes*, p.109.
16  Interview with the late David Footman, 18 May 1981. Private information.
17  Sherman, *Island Refuge*, pp.29, 57, 134, 210. Sherman does not mention the covert role of PCOs.
18  Shepherd, *Wilfrid Israel*, pp.90, 107–8, 129–31, 156–8, 264n31.
19  Philby, *My Silent War*, p.143. Muggeridge, *Chronicles of Wasted Time*, vol. II, p.132.
20  Jeffes to Howard Smith, 13 June 1939, PRO FO 366/1057 X5917.
21  See above, pp.357–9.
22  Private information.
23  See the passport control entries in the PRO *Foreign Office Index*.
24  Interview with David Footman, 18 May 1981.
25  Read and Fisher, *Colonel Z*, chs.16, 17.
26  Langley, *Fight Another Day*, p.127.
27  Interview with the late Commander Kenneth Cohen, 19 Oct. 1981.
28  See above, p.346.
29  Read and Fisher, *Colonel Z*, chs.16, 17.
30  Ibid., pp.184–5.
31  Payne Best to Stewart Menzies (copy), 11 Oct. 1946, IWM Payne Best MSS 79/57/1. Payne Best transcripts.
32  Read and Fisher, *Colonel Z*, chs.16, 17. Further information from Group-Captain Winterbotham.
33  Interview with the late Commander Kenneth Cohen, 19 Oct. 1981.
34  The Z organisation and Van's 'detective agency' were probably more distinct than suggested by Read and Fisher, *Colonel Z*, but may have overlapped.
35  Rose, *Vansittart*, pp.135ff. Wark, 'British Intelligence on the German Air Force', pp.636ff. CCAC Christie MSS.
36  'Timewatch' report on Goering and Christie, BBC2 7 Nov. 1984 (Producer Peter Maniura). See below, p.391.
37  Christie MSS CCAC CHRS 1/17. Wark, 'British Intelligence on the German Air Force', p.637. Rose, *Vansittart*, pp.135ff (Rose misidentifies 'X'). Neither author identifies 'Johnnie', on whom see below, pp.426–7.
38  Wark, 'British Intelligence on the German Air Force', p.636. Rose, *Vansittart*, pp. 136–8, 222.
39  Private information from several sources. On intelligence gained by MI5 from the Deutsche Nachrichten Büro, cf. F.R. Roberts, 'Evidence of German Measures and Preparations for Supporting Italy', 14 Feb. 1939, PRO 371/22958 C2058, and see below, pp.387, 420.
40  Rose, *Vansittart*, pp.104, 164, 182.
41  Ibid., pp.205–6, 210.
42  Colvin, *Vansittart*, pp.171–2.

43  Dilks (ed.), *Cadogan Diaries*, p.43. Cadogan, MS diary, 6 June 1938, CCAC ACAD 1/7.

44  Dingli's version of events is given in his unpublished memoirs, quoted extensively in Quartararo, 'Il Canale Segreto di Chamberlain'; see also the valuable critique of this article in Stafford, 'Chamberlain–Halifax Visit to Rome'. Ball's much briefer recollections are summarised in notes by Templewood, 26 Jan. 1949, 28 Dec. 1951, CUL Templewood MSS XIX(B)5.

45  Rose, 'Resignation of Sir Anthony Eden', p.928n.

46  Notes by Templewood, 26 Jan. 1949, 28 Dec. 1951, CUL Templewood MSS XIX(B)5.

47  Stafford, 'Chamberlain–Halifax Visit to Rome', pp.83–5.

48  Notes by Templewood, 26 Jan. 1949, 28 Dec. 1951, CUL Templewood MSS XIX(B)5.

49  Gorodetsky, *Cripps' Mission to Moscow*, p.9.

50  Cadogan, MS diary, 28, 29 Nov., 1, 6 Dec. 1938, CCAC ACAD 1/7. On the informant in Hesse's office, see above, p.384.

51  Wark, 'British Economic and Military Intelligence on Nazi Germany', pp.78–9.

52  Bialer, *Shadow of the Bomber*.

53  Overy, 'German Air Strength'.

54  Goddard, 'Epic Violet', ch.3, p.27, LHC.

55  Cross, *Lord Swinton*, p.139.

56  Goddard, 'Epic Violet', ch.3.

57  Wark, 'British Intelligence on the German Air Force'.

58  Ibid. Wark, 'British Economic and Military Intelligence on Nazi Germany', ch.1.

59  Overy, 'German Air Strength'.

60  Wark, 'British Military and Economic Intelligence: Assessments of Nazi Germany', pp.84–9.

61  Watt, 'British Intelligence and the Coming of the Second World War', p.254.

62  Record of a telephone conversation c.12.45 a.m., 7 March 1936, CCAC Christie MSS CHRS 1/17. Rose, *Vansittart*, p.192.

63  Goering to Christie, 9 Jan. 1937; Christie, 'Most Secret. Private Interview with General Göring in Berlin Feb. 3rd 1937', CCAC Christie MSS CHRS 180/1/5.

64  Knowles-Cutler, 'British Secret Intelligence about Germany 1938–1939', quoting FO file N3085.

65  Ibid.

66  Christie, Untitled memorandum based on 'first hand information' from his German sources, March 1938, CCAC Christie MSS CHRS 150/1/26.

67  Hauner, *Hitler*, provides a useful chronology.

68  Moravec, *Master of Spies*, chs.5, 6. Amort and Jedlicka, *Canaris File*, passim. Piekalkiewicz, *Secret Agents*, pp.132ff. Hinsley et al., *British Intelligence in the Second World War*, vol. I, p.58.

69  Amort and Jedlicka, *Canaris File*, pp.32–3.

70  Ibid., pp.33–4. Moravec, *Master of Spies*, pp.126ff.

71  Watt, 'British Intelligence and the Coming of the Second World War', pp.247, 262.
72  Moravec, *Master of Spies*, p.126. Duroselle, *La décadence*, p.337.
73  Stronge, 'The Czechoslovak Army'.
74  Bond (ed.), *Chief of Staff*, pp.146–7.
75  Douglas, *Year of Munich*, p.34.
76  See below, pp.414–20.
77  Weinberg, *Foreign Policy of Hitler's Germany 1937–1939*, p.393.
78  See below, pp.398–9.
79  Hinsley et al., *British Intelligence in the Second World War*, vol. I, pp.55–6. On Krueger see below, pp.433–4.
80  Weinberg, *Foreign Policy of Hitler's Germany 1937–1939*, p.394.
81  Ibid., pp.394–7.
82  *The Times*, 19, 20, 22, 24 Aug. 1938.
83  My own sources largely confirm the account of Kendrick's arrest and its consequences in 'West', *MI6*, pp.58–9. Mr 'West' does not, however, relate the Kendrick affair to the coming of the Munich crisis.
84  Dilks (ed.), *Cadogan Diaries*, pp.94–7. Weinberg, *Foreign Policy of Hitler's Germany 1937–1939*, pp.394, 396, 421, 428.
85  Rose, *Vansittart*, p.228. Dilks (ed.), *Cadogan Diaries*, p.95.
86  Bond, *British Military Policy*, p.277.
87  Memorandum entitled 'What Should We Do?', marked 'Views of SIS', 18 Sept. 1938, PRO FO 371/21659 C14471/42/18.
88  Wark, 'British Military and Economic Intelligence: Assessments of Nazi Germany', p.89.
89  Strong, 'The Czechoslovak Army', pp.171–2.
90  Bond, *British Military Policy*, p.281.
91  Memorandum entitled 'What Should We Do?', marked 'Views of SIS', 18 Sept. 1938, PRO FO 371/21659 C14471/42/18. Dilks, 'Flashes of Intelligence', pp.118ff.
92  Dilks, 'Flashes of Intelligence', p.122.
93  Hauner, 'Czechoslovakia as a Military Factor in British Considerations'.
94  Bialer, *Shadow of the Bomber*, pp.157–8.
95  Taylor, *Munich*, pp.804, 853, 872. Dilks, 'Appeasement and Intelligence', pp.150–1.
96  Templewood, notes on conversations with Cadogan (14 Nov. 1951) and Halifax (5 Dec. 1951), CUL Templewood MSS XIX(B)5.
97  Hinsley et al., *British Intelligence in the Second World War*, vol. I, p.199.
98  Ibid., pp.52–3.
99  W.F. Clarke, 'Wars and Rumours of Wars 1934–37', CCAC Clarke MSS CLKE 3.
100  'What Should We Do?', 18 Sept. 1938, PRO FO 371/21659 C14471/42/18.
101  Gretton, 'Nyon Conference'.
102  Major Vivian, 'Security of Documents in H.M. Embassy, Rome', 20 Feb. 1937, PRO FO 850/2 Y775. This report, though not its authorship, was discovered by David Dilks and is discussed in his article, 'Flashes of Intelligence', pp.107ff. Fol. 73 in FO 850/2 identifies the author as Major

Vivian. His authorship has been confirmed to me by Sir Andrew Noble, then head of chancery in the Rome embassy.

103   *Documents on British Foreign Policy*, 2nd series, vol. XV, p.693n. Lord Gladwyn, interviewed by the author on 'Timewatch', BBC2, 10 July 1984.

104   Dilks, 'Appeasement and Intelligence', pp.151–4.

105   Toscano, *Designs in Diplomacy*, pp.412–13.

106   See, e.g., *Documents on British Foreign Policy*, 2nd series, vol. XV, no. 539.

107   Vivian, 'Security of Documents in H.M. Embassy, Rome', 20 Feb. 1937, PRO FO 850/2 Y775.

108   Ibid. Interview with Sir Andrew Noble on 'Timewatch', BBC2, 10 July 1984.

109   Vivian, 'Security of Documents in H.M. Embassy, Rome', 20 Feb. 1937, PRO FO 850/2 Y775.

110   Drummond to Howard Smith, 18 May 1937, PRO FO 850/2 Y777.

111   Vivian, 'Security of Documents in H.M. Embassy, Rome', 20 Feb. 1937, PRO FO 850/2 Y775.

112   Ibid.

113   Memorandum by C. Howard Smith, 24 Feb. 1937, with marginal comments by Vansittart, PRO FO 850/2 Y777/G.

114   Watt, introduction to Irving, *Breach of Security*, p.32.

115   Vivian, 'Security Measures at H.M. Embassy, Berlin', 22 July 1937, PRO FO 850/2 Y832. Dilks, 'Flashes of Intelligence', p.112, discusses this document but does not identify the author.

116   Vivian, 'Security of Documents in H.M. Embassy, Rome', 20 Feb. 1937, PRO FO 850/2 Y775.

117   Dilks, 'Flashes of Intelligence', p.113.

118   'Security Measures in His Majesty's Diplomatic Missions and Consulates', 1 Apr. 1937, PRO FO 850/2 Y414/414/650.

119   Minute by C. Howard Smith, 28 May 1937, PRO FO 850/2 X3965.

120   Drummond responded to Vivian's report by declaring the need for 'the replacement of the Head Chancery Servant [Picton] and ultimately of the remaining Chancery Servants'. Had he entertained any serious suspicion about Constantini, he would scarcely have given his replacement such low priority. Drummond to C. Howard Smith, 18 May 1937, PRO FO 850/2 X777.

121   *Documents on British Foreign Policy*, 2nd series, vol. XV, p.693n. Dilks, 'Flashes of Intelligence', pp.117–18.

122   Dilks, 'Flashes of Intelligence', pp.114–15.

123   Hinsley, *British Intelligence in the Second World War*, vol. I, p.46.

124   Chilston to Collier (Foreign Office), 10 Mar. 1936, PRO FO 372/3180.

125   See below, p.432.

126   Mrs Jenifer Hart, interviewed by the author on 'Timewatch', BBC2, 27 July 1983.

127   Lord Gladwyn, interviewed by the author on 'Timewatch', BBC2, 10 July 1984. Andrew, 'F.H. Hinsley and the Cambridge Moles', pp.27–30.

128   Hinsley, *British Intelligence in the Second World War*, vol. I, pp.34–6.

129   Ibid., pp.37–8.

130   Ibid., p.42. The Foreign Office was also concerned by plans for a Middle

East Intelligence Centre.

131 Beaumont-Nesbitt to Oliphant (Foreign Office), 12 Jan. 1939, enclosing copy of memorandum written at least a month before, PRO FO 371/23994.
132 Memorandum by Menzies, 14 Dec. 1938, ibid.
133 Minute by Cadogan, 14 Feb. 1939, ibid.


CHAPTER 13

1 Weinberg, *Foreign Policy of Hitler's Germany 1937–1939*, pp.462–3.
2 Sinclair to Ismay, 15 Nov. 1938, enclosing 12 page summary of SIS intelligence received up to 11 Nov. ('for the greater part already issued in detail'), PRO CAB 104/43.
3 Gladwyn Jebb, 'Summary of Information from Secret Sources' (summarising intelligence up to mid-Dec. 1938), 19 Jan. 1939, annex to FP (36) 74, PRO CAB 27/627.
4 Aster, *1939*, p.41.
5 Godfrey, Unpublished Memoirs, vol. V, part I, p.7: vol. VIII, pp.41–2. Private information.
6 Watt, *Too Serious a Business*, pp.124–9. Kahn, *Hitler's Spies*, pp.226–36. It has been alleged that during the war Canaris fed a stream of 'top grade political intelligence' to the Allies through the wife of a former Polish military attaché in Berlin, Madame Halina Szymanska, resident in Berne (West, *MI6*, pp.116–17). This story remains at best unproven and is unsupported by any evidence in SIS or other closed files. Hinsley et al., *British Intelligence in the Second World War*, vol. I, p.58n.
7 Hinsley et al., *British Intelligence in the Second World War*, vol. I, pp.113–14, 117, 134–5.
8 Beaumont-Nesbitt to Jebb, 30 June 1939, enclosing 'records of conversations and other details' of von Schwerin, PRO FO 371/22974. Some of these documents have been published in *Documents on British Foreign Policy*, 3rd series, vol. VI.
9 Dilks (ed.), *Cadogan Diaries*, pp.94, 178. Cadogan, MS diary, 23 May 1940, CCAC ACAD 1/9.
10 Aster, *1939*, p.51.
11 Kirkpatrick, *Inner Circle*, pp.136–7.
12 Ibid. Dilks (ed.), *Cadogan Diaries*, p.130.
13 Memorandum by Vansittart, 16 Jan. 1939; Jebb, 'Summary of Information from Secret Sources', 19 Jan. 1939, FP(36)74, PRO CAB 27/267.
14 Memorandum by Vansittart, 16 Jan. 1939; Cadogan, 'Possibility of a German Attack in the West', 19 Jan 1939, FP(36)74, PRO CAB 27/267.
15 FP(36)35, 23 Jan. 1939, PRO CAB 27/264.
16 Bond, *British Military Policy*, pp.298–9. On the background to this policy change see Howard, *Continental Commitment*.
17 Jebb to Cadogan, 21 Feb. 1939, PRO FO 371/22965 C2431/G.
18 Dilks (ed.), *Cadogan Diaries*, p.151.
19 Cadogan to Henderson, 28 Feb. 1939, PRO Henderson MSS FO 800/270. Aster, *1939*, pp.53–4.

20    Feiling, *Neville Chamberlain*, p.396.
21    Rose, *Vansittart*, pp.232–3.
22    Dilks (ed.), *Cadogan Diaries*, pp.153–7, 163. Rose, *Vansittart*, p.233.
23    Newman, *March 1939*, pp.110–11, 115n. Jebb, 'Summary of SIS military information re Germany', 18 Mar. 1939, PRO FO 371/22958 C3565/G. Cf. Harvey (ed.), *Harvey Diaries*, p.263.
24    Newman, *March 1939*, pp.112–13. Newman does not mention the possibility that Tilea's communications were intercepted. The Rumanian embassy was, however, one of those whose diplomatic bags were sometimes opened. GC & CS was frustrated for much of the interwar period by a shortage of Balkan traffic on which to work, much of it being carried on continental landlines which could not be tapped. However, Denniston noted that in the final years of peace 'an increase in the use of W/T and the troublous political situation did enable us to read some of the traffic'. One diplomat remembers intermittent 'floods' of Balkan intercepts in the 1930s. It is uncertain whether Tilea's telegrams of March 1939 were among them. Private information. Denniston, Untitled memoir on GC & CS, 2 Dec. 1944, p.9, CCAC DENN 1/4.
25    Newman, *March 1939*, pp.113–18.
26    Ibid., chs.6–8. Bond (ed.), *Chief of Staff*, p.197.
27    Colvin, *Vansittart*, pp.303–10. Newman, *March 1939*, ch.9. Dilks (ed.), *Cadogan Diaries*, pp.164–5. Aster, *1939*, pp.99ff.
28    Aster, *1939*, p.103.
29    Wark, 'Baltic Myths', pp.75–6.
30    Hinsley et al., *British Intelligence in the Second World War*, vol. I, p.84.
31    Ibid., p.64. Dilks (ed.), *Cadogan Diaries*, p.169. Harvey (ed.), *Harvey Diaries*, pp.273–4.
32    Aster, *1939*, pp.128–32. Dilks (ed.), *Cadogan Diaries*, p.170. Private information.
33    Douglas, *Advent of War*, pp.11–12.
34    Hinsley et al., *British Intelligence in the Second World War*, vol. I, pp.41, 84–5.
35    FP(36)35, PRO CAB 27/624.
36    Dilks (ed.), *Cadogan Diaries*, p.158. Cadogan, MS diary, 21 April 1939, CCAC ACAD 1/8.
37    Hinsley et al., *British Intelligence in the Second World War*, vol. I, pp.42–3.
38    Dilks (ed.), *Cadogan Diaries*, p.182. Strang, *Home and Abroad*, p.174.
39    Drax, 'Mission to Moscow', p.7, CCAC DRAX 6/5.
40    Ibid., p.10. Minute by Oliphant, 29 March 1939, reporting conversation with Sinclair, PRO FO 371/23061 C3968/3356/18.
41    Drax, 'Mission to Moscow', p.5, CCAC DRAX 6/5. I have added slightly to Drax's sparing punctuation.
42    Brook-Shepherd, *Storm Petrels*, ch.10. 'Who Killed Krivitsky?', *Washington Post*, 13 Feb. 1966. Much of the FBI file on Krivitsky (FBI 110–11146) still remains classified.
43    Minutes and correspondence in PRO FO 371/23697. I am grateful to Donald Cameron Watt and Angus Knowles-Cutler for these references.
44    Ibid.

45 Aster, *1939*, pp.181–4. Rose, *Vansittart*, pp.235-6. Dilks (ed.), *Cadogan Diaries*, pp.180–1.
46 Rosc, *Vansittart*, pp.236–7. Aster, *1939*, p.275.
47 Aster, *1939*, pp.273–6, 281. Dilks (ed.), *Cadogan Diaries*, p.201.
48 Bond (ed.), *Chief of Staff*, p.219.
49 R.A. Butler, minute to Cadogan, 25 Aug. 1939, PRO FO 371/23686 N3335/243/38.
50 Memorandum by Collier, 26 Aug. 1939, PRO FO 371/23686 N4146. Aster, *1939*, pp.317–18.
51 Minute by Sargent, 3 Sept. 1939, ibid.
52 Bohlen, *Witness to History*, ch. 5. Herwarth, *Against Two Evils*, ch.11. These two accounts are in close agreement.
53 Herwarth, *Against Two Evils*, pp.152–3.
54 Bohlen, *Witness to History*, pp.79–80.
55 Aster, *1939*, pp.316–17.
56 Bohlen, *Witness to History*, p.82.
57 Wark, 'British Military and Economic Intelligence: Assessments of Nazi Germany', p.97.
58 Hinsley et al., *British Intelligence in the Second World War*, vol. I, p.68.
59 FP(36)35, 23 Jan. 1939, PRO CAB 27/624.
60 Hinsley et al., *British Intelligence in the Second World War*, vol. I, pp.64–71.
61 Aster, *1939*, p.208. Irving, *War Path*, p.239.
62 Woollcombe to Jebb, 15 June 1939, PRO FO 371/23020 C8336. On Sinclair's holiday plans see Colvin, *Vansittart*, p.334.
63 Rosc, *Vansittart*, pp.237–8.
64 Dilks (ed.), *Cadogan Diaries*, pp.196–8.
65 Douglas, *Advent of War*, p.49. Jebb, 'Summary of Information from Secret Sources', 19 Jan. 1939, FP(36)74, PRO CAB 27/627.
66 Halifax, 'A Record of Events Before the War, 1939', Halifax MSS PRO FO 800/317. Dilks (ed.), *Cadogan Diaries*, p.199.
67 Dilks (ed.), *Cadogan Diaries*, p.200.
68 *Documents on British Foreign Policy*, 3rd series, vol. VII, no. 314. Adamthwaite, *Making of the Second World War*, pp.220–1.
69 Adamthwaite, *Making of the Second World War*, pp.92–3.
70 Dilks (ed.), *Cadogan Diaries*, p.203.
71 Aster, *1939*, p.345.
72 Cadogan, MS diary, 27 Aug. 1939, CCAC ACAD 1/8.
73 Ibid., 29 Aug. 1939.
74 Secret memorandum by Gwatkin, 29 Aug. 1939, PRO FO 371/22981 C12878.
75 'Telegram received from Dr Goerdeler in Stockholm dated 22.49 p.m. Aug. 30', PRO FO 371/22981 C12789.
76 Dilks (ed.), *Cadogan Diaries*, pp.204–5.
77 Henderson to Foreign Office, no. 521, 31 Aug. 1939; minutes by Sargent and Cadogan, 31 Aug. 1939, PRO FO 371/23010 C12519.
78 Dilks (ed.), *Cadogan Diaries*, p.206.
79 Bond (ed.), *Chief of Staff*, p.223n.

80   Cadogan, MS diary, 4 Sept. 1939, CCAC ACAD 1/8. Brook-Shepherd, *Storm Petrels*, ch.10.
81   Cadogan, MS diary, 4, 21, 25, 26, 27, 29 Sept. 1939. Cadogan wrongly uses the spelling 'Vyvyan'. By the time he had learned to spell Vivian's name correctly he was pressing for his removal.
82   Brook-Shepherd, *Storm Petrels*, ch.10.
83   Cadogan to Treasury, 2 Dec. 1939, PRO T162 574/E40411. Cadogan, MS diary, 26 Sept., 30 Nov. 1939, CCAC ACAD 1/8. Dilks (ed.), *Cadogan Diary*, p.235.
84   Jones, *Most Secret War*, ch.8. Hinsley et al., *British Intelligence in the Second World War*, vol. I, pp.99–100, 508–12. Collier, *Defence of the United Kingdom*, pp.331–2.
85   See above, p.378.
86   Farago, *Game of the Foxes*, pp.116–22. Wark, 'Baltic Myths', p.79n34.
87   See above, p.378.
88   Farago, *Game of the Foxes*, p.113. West, *MI6*, pp.49–50. Private information. There has been some confusion over the date of Putlitz's escape. I am reliably informed that it occurred before the Venlo incident.
89   The fullest account by Best of the events which led to his capture at Venlo is contained in his letter (marked 'Secret and Confidential') to the retired intelligence officer Colonel Reginald Drake, 25 July 1947, IWM Payne Best MSS 79/57/1. Cf. Farago, *Game of the Foxes*, pp.121ff.
90   Evidence of Walter Schellenberg to enquiry by Dutch States General, vol.Ib, exhibit no. 43. Extract in IWM Payne Best MSS 79/57/1.
91   Best to Drake, 25 July, 25 Sept. 1947, IWM Payne Best MSS 79/57/1. While it is quite possible that, in order to defend his own record, Best overstated his pre-war suspicions of Fischer, he repeated his claims to have reported these suspicions in writing when corresponding after the war with Menzies who was in a position to check these claims in SIS files.
92   Ibid. Farago, *Game of the Foxes*, pp.121ff.
93   Best, *Venlo Incident*, p.8.
94   Ibid. Best to Drake, 25 July 1947, IWM Payne Best MSS 79/57/1.
95   Best, *Venlo Incident*, p.8.
96   Schofield, Unpublished Memoirs, p.187.
97   Best, *Venlo Incident*, p.9.
98   Ibid., pp.9–11. Macdonald, 'Venlo Incident', pp.451–2.
99   Best to Drake, 25 July 1947, IWM Payne Best MSS 79/57/1.
100  Dilks (ed.), *Cadogan Diaries*, pp.226–8.
101  Best to Drake, 25 Sept. 1947, IWM Payne Best MSS 79/57/1.
102  Best, *Venlo Incident*, pp.11–12. Macdonald, 'Venlo Incident', pp.453–4.
103  Dilks (ed.), *Cadogan Diaries*, pp.228–9.
104  Cadogan, MS diary, 30 Oct., 5 Nov. 1939, CCAC ACAD 1/8.
105  Read and Fisher, *Colonel Z*, pp.191, 195–6. Beesly, *Very Special Admiral*, pp.139–40. Cadogan, MS diary, 4 Nov. 1939, CCAC ACAD 1/8.
106  Cadogan, MS diary, 4, 5 Nov. 1939, CCAC ACAD 1/8.
107  Dilks (ed.), *Cadogan Diaries*, pp.228–9. Macdonald, 'Venlo Incident', p.455.
108  Macdonald, 'Venlo Incident', pp.458–9.

109 Dilks (ed.), *Cadogan Diaries*, pp.230–33.
110 Cadogan, MS diary, 4, 5, 30 Nov. 1939, CCAC ACAD 1/8. Dilks (ed.), *Cadogan Diaries*, pp.232–4. Beesly, *Very Special Admiral*, pp.139–40. Read and Fisher, *Colonel Z*, pp.195–6, 230.
111 Masterman, *Chariot Wheel*, p.221. Private information.
112 Masterman, *Double Cross System*, ch.2. West, *MI5*, pp.171ff. Hinsley et al., *British Intelligence in the Second World War*, vol. I, p.120n.
113 Cadogan, MS diary, 29 Nov., 7 Dec. 1939, CCAC ACAD 1/8; 3, 4 10, 12 Jan. 1940, CCAC ACAD 1/9.
114 Lord Gladwyn, interviewed by the author on BBC2 'Timewatch', 10 July 1984.
115 Cadogan, MS diary, 26 Jan., 8 Feb. 1940, CCAC ACAD 1/9.
116 Cecil, 'Cambridge Comintern', pp.181–2.
117 Hinsley et al., *British Intelligence in the Second World War*, vol. I, pp.92–5. COS(40)241(JP), 14 Feb. 1940, PRO CAB 80/8.
118 Hinsley et al., *British Intelligence in the Second World War*, vol. I, pp.116–20. Dilks (ed.), *Cadogan Diaries*, pp.86–7.
119 Gilbert, *Winston S. Churchill*, vol. VI, pp.197, 213.
120 Hinsley et al., *British Intelligence in the Second World War*, vol. I, p.117.
121 Bond (ed.), *Chief of Staff*, p.319.
122 Butler, *Mason-Mac*, pp.100–1.
123 Ibid., p.104. Hinsley et al., *British Intelligence in the Second World War*, vol. I, p.146.
124 Watt, 'British Image of French Military Morale'.
125 Butler, *Mason-Mac*, pp.106–7.
126 Hinsley et al., *British Intelligence in the Second World War*, ch.4. Stengers, 'Notice sur Fernand Vanlangenhove', p.169. Moravec, *Master of Spies*, pp.189–90. Piekalkiewicz, *Secret Agents*, p.142.
127 Hinsley et al., *British Intelligence in the Second World War*, vol. I, pp.143ff. Bond, *France and Belgium 1939–1940* (London, 1975), ch.2.
128 Hinsley et al., *British Intelligence in the Second World War*, vol. I, pp.146–8. Butler, *Mason-Mac*, pp.113–17. Ellis, *France and Flanders 1939–1940*, pp.148–9.
129 Ellis, *France and Flanders 1939–1940*, pp.148–9.

CHAPTER 14

1 *Parliamentary Debates (Commons)*, 5th series, vol. CCCXLVI, cols. 33–4. Dilks, 'Appeasement and Intelligence', pp.140–1.
2 Hinsley et al., *British Intelligence in the Second World War*, vol. I, p.144.
3 Gilbert, *Winston S. Churchill*, vol. VI, pp.612–13, 814.
4 Cadogan, MS diary, 11 Jan. 1941, CCAC ACAD 1/10.
5 Gilbert, *Winston S. Churchill*, vol. VI, pp.611–12.
6 Garliński, *Intercept*, ch.2.
7 Ibid., chs.2, 3. Stengers, 'Enigma', pp.127–32.

8   It has been mistakenly suggested that 'Sandwith' or 'Sandwich' was a pseudonym for Stewart Menzies. But see Stengers, 'Enigma', pp.271–2,n46, and Beesly, *Very Special Admiral*, pp.19–20.

9   Denniston, Untitled memoir on GC & CS, 2 Dec. 1944, p.13, CCAC Denniston MSS DENN 1/4.

10  Unpublished memorandum by Sinclair, 17 Oct. 1938. The original is still, quite unnecessarily, withheld from the PRO; an extract from it has been made available to me by a retired intelligence officer.

11  Birch to Travis, 21 Aug. 1940; Birch to Denniston, 27 Dec. 1940: extracts communicated to the author by a retired intelligence officer.

12  See the authoritative account of the attack on Enigma in Hinsley et al., *British Intelligence in the Second World War*, vols. I and II.

13  The British 'Most Secret' classification caused confusion in dealings with American intelligence and was changed to the American 'Top Secret'.

14  Denniston, Untitled memoir on GC & CS, 2 Dec. 1944, p.5, CCAC Denniston MSS DENN 1/4.

15  E.R.P. Vincent, Unpublished Memoirs, pp.77–8.

16  Denniston, Untitled memoir on GC & CS, 2 Dec. 1944, p.5, CCAC Denniston MSS DENN 1/4.

17  Letter from Peter Twinn to the author, 29 May 1981.

18  Andrew, 'F.H. Hinsley and the Cambridge Moles', pp.34–5.

19  Ibid., pp.35–9.

20  Ibid., pp.38–40. F.H. Hinsley et al., *British Intelligence in the Second World War*, vol. I, pp.273–4. Hodges, *Alan Turing*, pp.193, 345, 479.

21  Godfrey, Unpublished Memoirs, vol. V, pp.7ff.

22  Ibid., p.173.

23  Hinsley et al., *British Intelligence in the Second World War*, vol. I, pp.105–7.

24  Hawker, 'Intelligence Corps', pp.86–7.

25  Shearer, 'Trader Crusader', pp.95–8.

26  Ibid. Hawker, 'Intelligence Corps', pp.86–7. According to Hawker, 'Some 50 per cent of the Intelligence Staff at GHQ were RARO or AOER. The percentage was smaller in front of GHQ but considerably larger on the lines of communication.'

27  Shearer, 'Trader Crusader', pp.97–106.

28  Brigadier T. Robbins, 'Random Recollections of Intelligence Training', included in Shearer, 'Trader Crusader'.

29  Ibid. The 'outstanding pupil' on the first course was Enoch Powell.

30  Private information.

31  Hawker, 'Intelligence Corps', pp.87–8.

32  Ibid. Private information.

33  Masterman, *Chariot Wheel*, p.219.

34  Private information.

35  The suggestion that Liddell was a Soviet mole is convincingly refuted by those of his former colleagues to whom I have spoken.

36  Masterman, *Chariot Wheel*, pp.218–19. Private information

37  Mrs Jenifer Hart, interviewed by the author on 'Timewatch', BBC2, 27 July 1983, and further information from Mrs Hart.

38  Private information. West, *MI5*, pp.332–3.
39  Masterman, *Chariot Wheel*, p.212.
40  Muggeridge, *Chronicles of Wasted Time*, vol. II, pp.122–33. Cf. Greene, *Our Man in Havana*, with introduction by author.
41  Trevor-Roper, *Philby Affair*, pp.28, 71. Lord Dacre, interviewed by the author in 'The Profession of Intelligence', part 2, BBC Radio 4, 9 Aug. 1981.
42  Trevor-Roper, *Philby Affair*, pp.37–9.
43  Ibid., pp.28–47, 71–2. Lord Dacre, interviewed by the author in 'The Profession of Intelligence', part 2, BBC Radio 4, 9 Aug. 1981.
44  Cadogan, MS diary, 11 Jan., 15 July 1941, CCAC ACAD 1/10. Ibid., 5 Nov. 1942, CCAC ACAD 1/11. Further information from Gordon Welchman. See above, p.449.
45  West, *MI6*, pp.81ff. Hinsley et al., *British Intelligence in the Second World War*, vol. I, pp.275–6. Beesly, *Very Special Admiral*, pp.143–4. Cadogan, MS diary, 25 Apr. 1941, CCAC ACAD 1/10.
46  See the accounts of Thümmel's career in Moravec, *Master of Spies*; Amort and Jedlicka, *Canaris File*; Piekalkiewicz, *Secret Agents*; Hinsley et al., *British Intelligence in the Second World War*, vol. I. Thümmel was arrested by the Gestapo in October 1941, released and rearrested in March 1942, spent three years in prison, and was executed in April 1945.
47  Hinsley et al., *British Intelligence in the Second World War*, vol. I, pp.276–7, 438, 445, 457–8, 462, 482.
48  Ibid., pp.276–7. West, *MI6*, pp.94, 162–4.
49  Hinsley et al., *British Intelligence in the Second World War*, vol. I, p.277. West *MI6*, pp.95–6.
50  Hinsley et al., *British Intelligence in the Second World War*, vol. I, p.277. West, *MI6*, pp.97–8.
51  Gilbert, *Winston S. Churchill*, vol. VI, pp.750–1.
52  Menzies to Spears, 19 Feb. 1941; Spears to Menzies, 20 Feb. 1941, St Antony's College Oxford, Middle East Studies Centre, Spears MSS box 2, file 5. I am grateful to Alex Gaunson for this reference.
53  De Gaulle, *Mémoires de Guerre*, vol. I, pp.157–60. Kersaudy, *Churchill and De Gaulle*, pp.120–3, 180–2. Dilks (ed.), *Cadogan Diaries*, pp.346–8. Cadogan, MS diary, 3, 9 Jan. 1941, CCAC ACAD 1/10.
54  Hyde, *Quiet Canadian*, ch.1.
55  Ibid., ch.2. Godfrey, Unpublished Memoirs, vol. V, p.129. Gilbert, *Winston S. Churchill*, vol. VI, p.738. Reynolds, *Anglo-American Alliance*, ch.5.
56  Godfrey, Unpublished Memoirs, vol. V, pp.131, 136–7. Hinsley et al., *British Intelligence in the Second World War*, vol. I, p.313.
57  Hinsley et al., *British Intelligence in the Second World War*, vol. I, pp.313, 444.
58  Reynolds, *Anglo-American Alliance*, p.219.
59  Hinsley et al., *British Intelligence in the Second World War*, vol. I, pp.90–1, 275. Roskill, *Hankey*, vol. III, pp.447–8.
60  Cadogan, MS diary, 25 May 1940, CCAC ACAD 1/9; 11 Mar. 1941, CCAC ACAD 1/10. Cecil, 'Cambridge Comintern', p.179. West, *MI6*, pp.138–9.

61   My account of the development of PR is based on Winterbotham, *Nazi Connection*, ch.19; interview by the author with Winterbotham in 'The Profession of Intelligence', part 2, BBC Radio 4, 9 Aug. 1981; Barker, *Aviator Extraordinary*, chs.12–18; Babington Smith, *Evidence in Camera*, chs.1, 2; Hinsley, *British Intelligence in the Second World War*, vol. I, pp.27–9, 104, 169–70, 279, 496–9.

62   Hinsley et al., *British Intelligence in the Second World War*, vol. I, pp.28–30, 496–9. Barker, *Aviator Extraordinary*, chs.13, 14.

63   Babington Smith, *Evidence in Camera*, chs.1, 2. Barker, *Aviator Extraordinary*, chs.16, 17. Hinsley et al., *British Intelligence in the Second World War*, vol. I, pp.496–9.

64   Babington Smith, *Evidence in Camera*, chs.2, 3. Barker, *Aviator Extraordinary*, chs.17–19.

65   Ibid. Group Captain Winterbotham interviewed by the author in 'The Profession of Intelligence', part 2, BBC Radio 4, 9 Aug. 1981.

66   Foot, *SOE in France*, pp.1–6. Sweet–Escott, *Baker Street Irregular*, pp.20–1. Philby, *My Silent War*, pp.26ff.

67   Foot, *SOE in France*, pp.2–5. Foot, *SOE*, ch.1.

68   Foot, *SOE*, p.15.

69   Sweet–Escott, *Baker Street Irregular*, pp.21–4. Philby, *My Silent War*, pp.29–34.

70   Foot, *SOE in France*, p.5.

71   Dilks (ed.), *Cadogan Diaries*, p.233.

72   Stafford, *Britain and European Resistance*, pp.12–13.

73   Churchill, *Second World War*, vol. I, ch.30.

74   Cadogan, MS diary, 8, 17 Jan. 1940, CCAC ACAD 1/9. Salmon, 'Problem of Swedish Iron Ore'. Hyde, *Quiet Canadian*, pp.17–23. West, *MI6*, p.122.

75   Household, *Against the Wind*, pp.101–8. Foot, *SOE*, p.16.

76   Foot, *SOE*, p.15.

77   'Interference with German oil supplies', 8 Jan. 1941, COS(41)3(0), PRO CAB 80/56; reprinted in Stafford, *Britain and European Resistance*, appendix 3. Wheeler, *Britain and the War for Yugoslavia*, p.61.

78   Minshall, *Guilt-Edged*, chs.23–32.

79   Dilks (ed.), *Cadogan Diaries*, p.295. Cadogan, MS diary, 19 Oct., 24 Nov. 1939, CCAC ACAD 1/8; 15 May, 8, 10 June, 2, 10 Dec. 1940, ACAD 1/9; 15 Jan. 1941, ACAD 1/10.

80   Wheeler, *Britain and the War for Yugoslavia*, p.161.

81   'Interference with German oil supplies', 8 Jan. 1941, COS(41)3(0), PRO CAB 80/56: reprinted in Stafford, *Britain and European Resistance*, appendix 3. Wheeler, *Britain and the War for Yugoslavia*, pp.24ff, 61. Dilks (ed.), *Cadogan Diaries*, p.370. Foot, *SOE*, p.15. Sweet–Escott, *Baker Street Irregular*, pp.22ff.

82   Foot, *SOE in France*, pp.6–9. Dilks (ed.), *Cadogan Diaries*, pp.312–13. Stafford, *Britain and European Resistance*, pp.16–17, 24–5.

83   Dalton, *Fateful Years*, pp.366–7. Foot, 'Was SOE Any Good?', p.241.

84   Foot, *SOE in France*, chs.1, 2. Stafford, *Britain and European Resistance*, chs.1, 2.

85 Stafford, *Britain and European Resistance*, p.38. Hinsley et al., *British Intelligence in the Second World War*, vol. I, pp.277–8.
86 Sweet–Escott, *Baker Street Irregular*, p.24.
87 Stafford, *Britain and European Resistance*, p.38.
88 Wasserstein, *Britain and the Jews of Europe*, p.88. Gilbert, *Winston S. Churchill*, vol. VI, p.342.
89 Cross, *Swinton*, p.225.
90 McLaine, *Ministry of Morale*, pp.74, 80–1. Calder, *People's War*, p.156.
91 McLaine, *Ministry of Morale*, pp.74–5. Calder, *People's War*, pp.149–57.
92 Cross, *Swinton*, p.244.
93 Cadogan, MS diary, 4, 6 June 1940, CCAC ACAD 1/9.
94 Kell diary (microfilm), 10 June 1940, IWM PP/MCR/120II.
95 Cross, *Swinton*, pp.225–9.
96 Private information. Cadogan, MS diary, 19 Mar. 1941, CCAC ACAD 1/10.
97 Stammers, *Civil Liberties in Britain*, pp.34–41.
98 War Cabinet 123(40)15, 15 May 1940, PRO CAB 65/7.
99 Cross, *Swinton*, pp.228–9.
100 In November there were still 3,695 enemy aliens interned in Britain and about 5,000 in the Dominions. Stammers, *Civil Liberties in Britain*, ch.2. Wasserstein, *Britain and the Jews of Europe*, pp.102–4. Cross, *Swinton*, pp.228–30.
101 Masterman, *Double Cross System*, chs.3, 4. West, *MI5*, chs.7, 8. Lewin, *Ultra Goes to War*, pp.299ff.
102 Ibid.
103 Masterman, *Chariot Wheel*, ch.21.
104 Masterman, *Double Cross System*, p.xii.
105 Cadogan, MS diary, 11, 19 Mar. 1941, CCAC ACAD 1/10; 29 Jan. 1942, ACAD 1/11. West, *MI6*, p.139. By the end of 1943 coordination between the service intelligence departments had improved to a point at which the appointment of 'deputy directors' was felt no longer necessary and was 'abandoned by mutual agreement'. The service intelligence departments continued, however, to have representatives at SIS headquarters. Hinsley et al., *British Intelligence in the Second World War*, vol. III, p.462.
106 Hinsley et al., *British Intelligence in the Second World War*, vol. I, pp.278–82; vol. II, pp.34–9.
107 See above, pp.442–3.
108 Davidson, Memoir G, part II, LHC Davidson MSS.
109 Ibid. Hinsley et al., *British Intelligence in the Second World War*, vol. I, pp.296–9; vol. II, pp.3–4.
110 Hinsley et al., *British Intelligence in the Second World War*, vol. I, ch.14.
111 *Dictionary of National Biography 1961–1970*, p.204.
112 Hinsley et al., *British Intelligence in the Second World War*, vol. I, p.160.
113 Churchill to Lloyd George and other ministers, Most Secret, 19 Mar. 1920, HLRO Lloyd George MSS F9/2/16.
114 Hinsley et al., *British Intelligence in the Second World War*, vol. I, p.291.
115 Stammers, *Civil Liberties in Britain*, p.56.
116 Hinsley et al., *British Intelligence in the Second World War*, vol. II, appendix 3.

117   Ibid., vol. I, pp.295–6; vol. II, p.4n.


EPILOGUE

1   Hinsley et al., *British Intelligence in the Second World War*, vol. II.
2   Masterman, *Double Cross System*, ch.11. Ambrose, *Ike's Spies*, chs.6, 7.
3   West, *Matter of Trust*, pp.28ff. Private information.
4   Verrier, *Through the Looking Glass*, p.63. Private information.
5   Alistair Horne, interviewed by the author on 'The Profession of Intelligence', part 4, Radio 4, 23 Aug. 1981.
6   Verrier, *Through the Looking Glass*, pp.2–3, ch.3.
7   Cockerill, *Sir Percy Sillitoe*, ch.17. Pincher, *Too Secret Too Long*, pp.133–4. West, *Matter of Trust*, ch.2.
8   Jeffery and Hennessy, *States of Emergency*, ch.7. Private information.
9   D.O.(47)25, COS report (based partly on MI5 intelligence), 13 Mar. 1947, PRO CAB 21/2554.
10   Miller, *Jungle War in Malaya*, chs.8, 9. Private information.
11   Hinsley et al., *British Intelligence in the Second World War*, vol. II, ch.16; vol. III, appendix I.
12   Ambrose, *Ike's Spies*, pp.125ff. Strong, *Intelligence at the Top*, pp.112ff.
13   Bamford, *Puzzle Palace*, ch.8. 'The Profession of Intelligence', part 4, BBC Radio 4, 23 Aug. 1981.
14   Yergin, *Shattered Peace*, pp.216–17.
15   Bethell, *Great Betrayal*, passim. Verrier, *Through the Looking Glass*, ch.3.
16   Philby, *My Silent War*, chs.11, 12.
17   Macmillan, *Tides of Fortune*, p.572.
18   Eveland, *Ropes of Sand*, pp.108–9. Private information.
19   Ambrose, *Ike's Spies*, pp.212–13. Roosevelt, *Counter-Coup*, pp.199–209.
20   *Dictionary of National Biography 1961–1970*, p.214.
21   Private information. There is a brief allusion to this incident in Baron Home, *Way the Wind Blows*, p.203. (I am grateful to Peter Hennessy for this reference.)
22   Eveland, *Ropes of Sand*, ch.14.
23   Jonathan Aitken, interviewed by the author on 'The Profession of Intelligence', part 4, BBC Radio 4, 23 Aug. 1981. Lapping, *End of Empire*, p.262
24   Ambrose, *Ike's Spies*, p.274.
25   Bamford, *Puzzle Palace*, pp.320ff.
26   Trevor-Roper, *Philby Affair*, pp.54–5. Pincher, *Inside Story*, pp.90–1. Private information.
27   Pincher, *Inside Story*, pp.87–96.
28   Ray Cline, interviewed by the author in 'The Profession of Intelligence', part 4, Radio 4, 23 Aug. 1981.
29   Ibid. Powers, *Man Who Kept The Secrets*, p.101.
30   Wynne, *Man From Odessa*.
31   Verrier, *Through the Looking Glass*, ch.6. My own sources dispute the accuracy of the quotation from White's speech on p.193.

32   Ambrose, *Ike's Spies*, pp.267–78.
33   Andrew, 'Whitehall, Washington and the Intelligence Services', pp.392–3.
34   Ray Cline, interviewed by the author in 'The Profession of Intelligence', part 4, Radio 4, 23 Aug. 1981.
35   Andrew, 'Whitehall, Washington and the Intelligence Services', p.395.
36   Private information.
37   Cmnd 8787 (1983), pp.94–5.
38   Ibid., pp.84–5.
39   *Parliamentary Debates (Commons)*, 5th series, vol. CLXXIV, 15 Dec. 1924, col. 674.
40   See above, pp.331–2.
41   *Parliamentary Debates (Commons)*, 5th series, vol. DCCCCLXXIV, 21 Nov. 1979, col. 467.
42   Ibid., vol. DCCCCXXXVI, 28 July 1977, col. 1223.
43   1963 interview with Harold Wilson rebroadcast in 'The Profession of Intelligence', part 5, BBC Radio 4, 30 Aug. 1981.
44   *Parliamentary Debates (Lords)*, 5th series, vol. CCCCXX, 19 May 1981, col. 858.
45   Chapman Pincher, recalling description by Sir Maurice Oldfield of George Brown's visit in 'The Profession of Intelligence', part 5, BBC Radio 4, 30 Aug. 1981. Cf. Pincher, *Inside Story*, pp.24–6. My own sources confirm Pincher's account.
46   Pincher, *Inside Story*, ch.3.
47   See, e.g., Callaghan's comments on the intelligence services during the Blunt debate. *Parliamentary Debates (Commons)*, 5th series, vol. DCCCCLXXIV, 21 Nov. 1979, cols. 501–11. According to David Owen (as reported in *The Guardian*, 6 Mar. 1985), however, Callaghan's appointment of the ex-ambassador Sir Howard Smith as director-general of the Security Service in 1979 reflected dissatisfaction with existing MI5 leadership.
48   David Owen interviewed by the author in 'The Profession of Intelligence', part 5, BBC Radio 4, 30 Aug. 1981.
49   Roy Hattersley and Denis Healey interviewed by the author in 'File on Four', BBC Radio 4, 4 and 11 Aug. 1982 (Producer Peter Everett).
50   Peter Hennessy, 'Whitehall's Real Powerhouse', *The Times*, 30 Apr. 1984.
51   Pincher, *Their Trade is Treachery*. Idem, *Too Secret Too Long*. Golitsyn, *New Lies for Old*.
52   William Colby interviewed by the author in 'The Profession of Intelligence', part 5, BBC Radio 4, 30 Aug. 1981.
53   Private information.
54   David Owen interviewed by the author in 'The Profession of Intelligence', part 5, BBC Radio 4, 30 Aug. 1981.
55   Cmnd 8787 (1983), p.86. Peter Hennessy, 'Whitehall's Real Powerhouse', *The Times*, 30 Apr. 1984. In 1985 Duff became director-general of MI5.
56   House of Commons Education, Science and Arts Committee (Session 1982–83), *Public Records: Minutes of Evidence*, pp.76–7.

# BIBLIOGRAPHY

## 1. UNPUBLISHED SOURCES

*a. Private Papers*

Viscount Addison MSS, Bodleian Library, Oxford
Earl of Balfour MSS, CUL
M.K. Burge, MSS, ICM
Major-General S.S. Butler, 'France 1916–1918', microfilm copy, IWM
Sir Alexander Cadogan MSS, CCAC
Sir Austen Chamberlain MSS, BUL
Neville Chamberlain MSS, BUL
Group-Captain Malcolm Christie MSS, CCAC
W.F. Clarke MSS, CCAC
Marquess of Crewe MSS, CUL
Marquess Curzon of Kedleston MSS, IOLR
Viscount Davidson MSS, HLRO
Major-General Francis Davidson MSS, LHC
A.G. Denniston MSS, CCAC
Admiral Sir R.A.A. Plunkett-Ernle-Erle-Drax MSS, CCAC
Brigadier-General Sir James Edmonds MSS, LHC
Field-Marshal Earl French of Ypres MSS, IWM
Air-Marshal Sir Victor Goddard, 'Epic Violet' [Memoirs], LHC
Admiral John H. Godfrey, Unpublished Memoirs, NMM and CCAC
Adrian Grant Duff MSS CCAC
Viscount Halifax MSS, PRO
Admiral Sir W. Reginald Hall MSS, CCAC
Baron Hankey MSS, CCAC
Leland Harrison MSS, Library of Congress
Sir Nevile Henderson MSS, PRO
Lady Constance Kell, 'A Secret Well Kept', IWM
Major-General Sir Vernon Kell MSS
  1) Microfilm copies, IWM
  2) Papers in possession of Mr and Mrs Robin Frost (Unless otherwise indicated my references are to the Frost collection)

Major-General Sir Walter Kirke MSS
1) Papers at IWM
2) Papers at ICM
3) Papers in possession of Colonel Richard Kirke (Unless otherwise indicated my references are to Colonel Kirke's collection)
Sir Ivone Kirkpatrick, 'The War 1914–1918' [Memoirs], IWM
Captain Sir Basil Liddell Hart MSS, LHC
Earl Lloyd George of Dwfor MSS, HLRO
Viscount Long MSS, Wiltshire Record Office
Ramsay MacDonald MSS, PRO
Colonel Roderick Macleod, 'Ironside's Life as Secret Agent in Africa 1899–1904', LHC
General Sir James Marshall-Cornwall, Unpublished Memoirs, ICM
A.E.W. Mason MSS, Walter L. Pforzheimer Collection, Washington
Admiral of the Fleet Sir Henry Oliver MSS, NMM
Sigismund Payne Best MSS
1) Papers in IWM
2) Transcripts (unpaginated at time of consultation) of tape-recorded reminiscences and other papers in the possession of Mrs Bridget Payne Best. (Unless otherwise indicated, my references are to Mrs Payne Best's collection. Her late husband was usually known by the single surname Best during his earlier career but by his retirement used the surname Payne Best.)
Captain Stephen Roskill MSS, CCAC
Vice-Admiral B.B. Schofield, Unpublished Memoirs (made available to me by Vice-Admiral Schofield)
Brigadier Eric Shearer, 'Trader Crusader' [Unpublished Memoirs], in the possession of Mrs Shearer
Admiral Sir Edmond Slade MSS, NMM
Major-General Sir Edward Louis Spears MSS
1) Papers in CCAC
2) Papers in Middle East Centre, St Antony's College, Oxford
John Herbert Spottiswoode MSS, in the possession of Mr John Spottiswoode
Viscount Templewood MSS, CUL
Professor E.R. Vincent, Unpublished Memoirs, Corpus Christi College, Cambridge, Archives
R.R.F. West, 'Journal of 2nd Lieutenant R.R.F. West DSO', ICM
Field-Marshal Sir Henry Wilson MSS, IWM

*b. Official Papers*

*Public Record Office*
Intelligence-related documents are scattered in small but significant quantities, often unpredictably, through a large part of the government archive, in particular in the files of the Cabinet (CAB) and the departments of state most concerned with the intelligence community: the Foreign Office (FO), the Home Office (HO), the Treasury (T) and the service ministries (ADM, AIR, WO). Precise references to some of the files I have found most useful are given in the notes. How much intelligence material survives

in any file depends on, inter alia, filing practices when it was compiled, 'weeding' regulations at the time of weeding, and the attentiveness and benevolence of the weeder(s) concerned. All are very variable. Documents weeded from the archive of one government department may sometimes be discovered in the files of another.

*Cambridge University Library*
Foreign Office Confidential Print

*Intelligence Corps Museum, Ashford, Kent*
Records of the Intelligence Corps and other papers on military intelligence.

*Ministry of Defence Naval Historical Branch*
'Naval Staff Monographs' on the First World War

*National Archives, Washington*
Due largely to the special Anglo-American intelligence relationship during the two World Wars and since the Second, the files of the CIA, FBI, MID, NID, NSA, OSS and State Department, among others, contain material relevant to the history of British intelligence. Some detailed references are given in the notes.

*Bibliothek für Zeitgeschichte, Stuttgart*
Korvettenkapitän Kleikamp, 'Der Einfluss der Funkaufklärung auf die Seekriegsführung in der Nordsee, 1914–1918', Kiel 1934


## 2.  PUBLISHED SOURCES AND THESES

The works listed below are limited to those cited in the notes. References to newspaper and magazine articles, to broadcasts and to parliamentary debates appear only in the notes.

Anthony Adamthwaite, *The Making of the Second World War* (London, 1977)
Captain Augustus Agar, *Baltic Episode* (London, 1963)
Rupert Allason, *The Branch* (London, 1983)
Stephen E. Ambrose, *Ike's Spies* (New York, 1981)
C. Amort and I.M. Jedlicka, *The Canaris File* (London, 1970)
G.D. Anderson, *Fascists, Communists and the National Government* (London, 1983)
C.M. Andrew, 'The Mobilization of British Intelligence for the Two World Wars', in
   N.F. Dreisziger (ed.), *Mobilization for Total War* (Waterloo, Ontario, 1981)
C.M. Andrew, *Théophile Delcassé and the Making of the Entente Cordiale* (London, 1968)
C.M. Andrew, 'Déchiffrement et diplomatie: le cabinet noir du Quai d'Orsay sous la
   Troisième République', *Relations Internationales*, vol. III (1976)
C.M. Andrew, 'The British Secret Service and Anglo-Soviet Relations in the 1920s.
   Part I', *Historical Journal*, vol. XX (1977)
C.M. Andrew, 'Codebreakers and Foreign Offices: The French, British and American
   Experience', in C.M. Andrew and D.N. Dilks (eds.), *The Missing Dimension:
   Governments and Intelligence Communities in the Twentieth Century* (London, 1984)
C.M. Andrew, 'France and the German Menace', in Ernest May (ed.), *Knowing One's
   Enemies* (Princeton, 1985)
C.M. Andrew, 'F.H. Hinsley and the Cambridge Moles: Two Patterns of Intelligence

Recruitment', in R.T.B. Langhorne (ed.), *Diplomacy and Intelligence during the Second World War: Essays in Honour of F.H. Hinsley* (Cambridge, 1985)

C.M. Andrew, 'Whitehall, Washington and the Intelligence Services', *International Affairs*, vol. LIII (1977)

C.M. Andrew and A.S. Kanya-Forstner, *France Overseas: The Great War and the Climax of French Imperial Expansion* (London, 1981). Published in the USA as *The Climax of French Imperial Expansion 1914–1924* (Stanford, 1981).

Sidney Aster, *1939: The Making of the Second World War* (London, 1972)

Sir George Aston, *Secret Service* (London, 1930)

Constance Babington Smith, *Evidence in Camera* (London, 1958)

Lieutenant-General Sir (later Baron) Robert Baden-Powell, *My Adventures as a Spy* (London, 1915)

Baron Baden-Powell, *Lessons from the 'Varsity' of Life* (London, 1933)

Geoffrey Bailey, *The Conspirators* (London, 1961)

R.S. Baker, *Woodrow Wilson, Life and Letters* (New York, 1928–39)

James Bamford, *The Puzzle Palace* (Boston, Mass., 1982)

Ralph Barker, *Aviator Extraordinary* (London, 1969)

Trevor Barnes, 'Special Branch and the First Labour Government', *Historical Journal*, vol. XXII (1979)

Admiral Sir Lewis Bayly, *Pull Together* (London, 1939)

W.C. Beaver, 'The Intelligence Division Library 1854–1902', *Journal of Library History*, July 1976

W.C. Beaver, 'The Development of the Intelligence Division and its Role in Aspects of Imperial Policymaking' (Oxford D. Phil. dissertation, 1976)

Patrick Beesly, *Very Special Intelligence* (London, 1977)

Patrick Beesly, *Very Special Admiral* (London, 1980)

Patrick Beesly, *Room 40* (London, 1982)

A.C. Bell, *A History of the Blockade of Germany*, 2nd edn (London, 1961)

Lord Charles Beresford, *The Memoirs of Lord Charles Beresford* (London, 1914)

Sigismund Payne Best, *The Venlo Incident* (London, 1950)

Nicholas Bethell, *The Great Betrayal* (London, 1984)

Uri Bialer, *The Shadow of the Bomber* (London, 1980)

Frank Birch, *Alice in I.D.25*, privately printed (copy in Denniston MSS, CCAC)

J.C. Bird, 'Control of Enemy Alien Civilians in Great Britain 1914–1918', London Ph.D. dissertation, 1981

Second Earl of Birkenhead, *F.E.: The Life of F.E. Smith, First Earl of Birkenhead* (London, 1960)

Robert Blake (ed.), *The Private Papers of Douglas Haig* (London, 1952)

C.E. Bohlen, *Witness to History 1929–1969* (London, 1973)

Brian Bond, *The Victorian Army and the Staff College 1854–1914* (London, 1972)

Brian Bond (ed.), *Chief of Staff: The Diaries of Lieutenant-General Sir Henry Pownall* (London, 1972)

Brian Bond, *France and Belgium 1939–1940* (London, 1975)

Brian Bond, *British Military Policy Between the Two World Wars* (Oxford, 1980)

Victor Bonham-Carter, *Soldier True* (London, 1963)

Robert Boucard, *Revelations from the Secret Service* (London, 1930)

Andrew Boyle, *The Riddle of Erskine Childers* (London, 1977)

Andrew Boyle, *The Climate of Treason* (London, 1979)

Piers Brendon, *Eminent Edwardians* (London, 1979)

H.L. Brereton, *Gordonstoun: Ancient Estate and Modern School* (London and Edinburgh, 1968)

M.V. Brett (ed.), *Journals and Letters of Reginald Viscount Esher* (London, 1934–8)

Gordon Brook-Shepherd, *The Storm Petrels* (London, 1977)

A. Cave Brown and C.B. MacDonald, *On a Field of Red* (New York, 1981)

John Bulloch, *MI5* (London, 1963)

Ewan Butler, *Mason-Mac* (London, 1972)

H. Bywater and H.C. Ferraby, *Strange Intelligence* (London, 1931)

Angus Calder, *The People's War*, paperback edn. (London, 1971)

R.L. Calder, *W. Somerset Maugham and the Quest for Freedom* (London, 1972)

D.F. Calhoun, *The United Front: The TUC and the Russians 1923–1928* (Cambridge, 1976)

Major-General Sir C.E. Callwell, 'War Office Reminiscences', *Blackwood's Magazine*, vol. CXC (1911)

Major-General Sir C.E. Callwell, *Small Wars*, 3rd edn. (London, 1906)

Major-General Sir C.E. Callwell, *Stray Recollections* (London, 1923)

E.H. Carr, *Foundations of a Planned Economy*, vol. III (London, 1976–8)

F.L. Carsten, *War against War* (London, 1982)

General François Cartier, 'Souvenirs du général Cartier', part 2, *Revue des Transmissions*, no. 87 (Nov–Dec. 1959)

Robert Cecil, 'The Cambridge Comintern', in C.M. Andrew and D.N. Dilks (eds.), *The Missing Dimension: Governments and Intelligence Communities in the Twentieth Century* (London, 1984)

R. Challinor, *The Origins of British Bolshevism* (London, 1977)

Lord Chandos, *Memoirs of Lord Chandos* (London, 1962)

L. Chester, S. Fay and H. Young, *The Zinoviev Letter* (London, 1967)

Erskine Childers, *The Riddle of the Sands*, Collins edn (London, 1955)

Sir Wyndham Childs, *Episodes and Reflections* (London, 1930)

B. MacGiolla Choille (ed.), *Intelligence Notes* (Dublin, 1966)

Randolph S. Churchill, *Winston S. Churchill*, 2 vols (London, 1966–7)

Winston S. Churchill, *The World Crisis, 1911–1918*, Hamlyn edn. (London, 1974)

Winston S. Churchill, *Great Contemporaries*, Odhams edn. (London, 1947)

Winston S. Churchill, *The Second World War* (London, 1948–54)

Alan Clark (ed.), *A Good Innings. The Private Papers of Viscount Lee of Fareham* (London, 1974)

D.M. Clark, *The Rise of the British Treasury* (Newton Abbot, 1960)

I.F. Clarke, *Voices Prophesying War, 1763–1984* (London, 1966)

C.A. Cline, *E.D. Morel 1873–1924* (Belfast, 1980)

A. Cobban, *Ambassadors and Secret Agents* (London, 1954)

A.W. Cockerill, *Sir Percy Sillitoe* (London, 1975)

J.A. Cole, *Prince of Spies: Henri Le Caron* (London, 1984)

Basil Collier, *The Defence of the United Kingdom* (London, 1957)

Captain J.C.R. Colomb, 'Naval Intelligence and Protection of Commerce in War', *The*

*Journal of the Royal United Service Institution*, vol. XXV (1881)

Ian Colvin, *Vansittart in Office* (London, 1965)

Fred Copeman, *Reason in Revolt* (London, 1948)

J.A. Cross, *Sir Samuel Hoare* (London, 1977)

J.A. Cross, *Lord Swinton* (Oxford, 1982)

Sibyl Crowe, 'The Zinoviev Letter: A Reappraisal', *Journal of Contemporary History*, vol. X (1975)

Hugh Dalton, *The Fateful Years* (London, 1957)

R.P.T. Davenport-Hines, 'Vickers' Balkan Conscience: Aspects of Anglo-Romanian Armaments 1918–39', *Business History*, vol. XXV (1983)

Viscount Davidson, *Memoirs of a Conservative*, ed. Robert Rhodes James (London, 1969)

J.H. Day, 'The Basic Conception of Education of Kurt Hahn and Its Translation into Practice', M.Ed. thesis (Queensland, 1980)

'Richard Deacon', *A History of the British Secret Service* (London, 1969)

R.K. Debo, *Revolution and Survival: The Foreign Policy of Soviet Russia 1917–18* (Liverpool, 1979)

R.K. Debo, 'Lockhart Plot or Dzerzhinskii Plot?', *Journal of Modern History*, vol. XLIII (1971)

P. Decock, 'La Dame Blanche', unpublished dissertation (Université Libre de Bruxelles, 1981)

D.N. Dilks (ed.), *The Diaries of Sir Alexander Cadogan O.M. 1938–1945* (London, 1971)

D.N. Dilks, 'Appeasement and Intelligence' in D.N. Dilks (ed.), *Retreat From Power*, vol. I (London, 1981)

D.N. Dilks, 'Flashes of Intelligence: The Foreign Office, the SIS and Security before the Second World War', in C.M. Andrew and D.N. Dilks (eds.), *The Missing Dimension: Governments and Intelligence Communities in the Twentieth Century* (London, 1984)

*Documents on British Foreign Policy 1919–1939* (London, 1949–   )

Admiral Sir Barry Domville, *By and Large* (London, 1936)

Roy Douglas, *In the Year of Munich* (London, 1977)

Roy Douglas, *The Advent of War 1939–40* (London, 1978)

Tom Driberg, *Ruling Passions*, paperback edn. (London, 1978)

Sir Paul Dukes, *The Story of 'ST 25'* (London, 1938)

J-B. Duroselle, *La décadence* (Paris, 1979)

Brigadier-General Sir J.E. Edmonds, *Military Operations: France and Belgium 1914* (London, 1922)

Brigadier-General Sir J.E. Edmonds, *Military Operations: France and Belgium 1918* (London, 1935–9)

Major L.F. Ellis, *The War in France and Flanders 1939–1940* (London, 1953)

A. Ereira, *The Invergordon Mutiny* (London, 1981)

Wilbur C. Eveland, *Ropes of Sand* (London, 1980)

A.W. Ewing, *The Man of Room 40: The Life of Sir Alfred Ewing* (London, 1939)

Bernard Falk, *Bouquets for Fleet Street* (London, 1951)

Ladislav Farago, *The Game of the Foxes* (London, 1972)

Keith Feiling, *The Life of Neville Chamberlain* (London, 1946)

S.T. Felstead, *German Spies at Bay* (London, 1920)

S.T. Felstead (ed.), *Steinhauer: The Kaiser's Master Spy. The Story as Told by Himself* (London, 1930)

T.G. Fergusson, *British Military Intelligence 1870–1914* (London, 1984)

Paul Ferris, *The House of Northcliffe* (London, 1971)

Carole Fink, *The Genoa Conference* (London, 1984)

H.T. Fitch, *Traitors Within* (London, 1933)

Penelope Fitzgerald, *The Knox Brothers* (London, 1977)

Reginald Fletcher, 'Britain's Air Strength', in R.E.O. Charlton, G.T. Garratt and R. Fletcher, *The Air Defence of Britain* (Harmondsworth, 1938)

M.R.D. Foot, *SOE in France* (London, 1966)

M.R.D. Foot, *SOE* (London, 1984)

M.R.D. Foot, 'Was SOE Any Good?' in Walter Laqueur (ed.), *The Second World War* (London, 1982)

'A Former Member of the Service', 'Work of The Secret Service', *Daily Telegraph*: part I, 24 Sept. 1930; part II, 25 Sept. 1930; part III, 26 Sept. 1930; part IV, 29 Sept. 1930.

Major-General C.H. Foulkes, *Gas!* (London, 1934)

W.B. Fowler, *British-American Relations 1917–1918. The Role of Sir William Wiseman* (Princeton, 1969)

W. Lionel Fraser, *All to the Good* (London, 1963)

David French, 'Spy Fever in Britain 1900–1915', *Historical Journal*, vol. XXI (1978)

Józef Garliński, *Intercept* (London, 1979)

Charles de Gaulle, *Mémoires de Guerre*, Livre de Poche edn. (Paris, 1969)

Martin Gilbert, *Winston S. Churchill*, vols. III (1914–16), IV (1917–22), V (1922–39), VI (1939–41) (London, 1971–83)

Peter and Leni Gillman, *Collar The Lot* (London, 1980)

Major-General Lord Edward Gleichen, *A Guardsman's Memories* (London, 1932)

David Golinkov, *The Secret War against Soviet Russia* (Moscow, 1982)

Anatoliy Golitsyn, *New Lies for Old* (London, 1984)

John Gooch, *The Plans of War* (London, 1974)

Gabriel Gorodetsky, *The Precarious Peace* (Cambridge, 1977)

Gabriel Gorodetsky, *Stafford Cripps' Mission to Moscow 1940–42* (Cambridge, 1984)

General Sir Hugh Gough, *The Fifth Army* (London, 1931)

N. Grant, 'The "Zinoviev Letter" Case', *Soviet Studies*, vol. XIX (1967–8)

A.K. Graves ('Late Spy to the German Government'), *The Secrets of the German War Office* (London, 1914)

R.L. Green, *A.E.W. Mason* (London, 1952)

Graham and Hugh Greene, *The Spy's Bedside Book* (London, 1957)

Graham Greene, *Our Man in Havana*, with introduction by author (London, 1970 edn.)

J.D. Gregory, *On the Edge of Diplomacy* (London, 1929)

Peter Gretton, 'The Nyon Conference – the Naval Aspect', *English Historical Review*, vol. XC (1975)

Sir Percival Griffiths, *To Guard My People* (London, 1971)

Richard Griffiths, *Fellow Travellers of the Right* (London, 1980)

J. Harvey (ed.), *The Diplomatic Diaries of Oliver Harvey, 1937–1940* (London, 1970)

Milan Hauner, 'Czechoslovakia as a Military Factor in British Considerations of 1938', *Journal of Strategic Studies*, vol. I (1978)

Milan Hauner, *Hitler* (London, 1983)

Major D.S. Hawker, 'An Outline of the Early History of the Intelligence Corps', *Rose & Laurel*, no. 27 (Dec. 1965)

G.C.L. Hazlehurst, *Politicians at War, July 1914 – May 1915* (London, 1971)

G.B. Henderson, 'Lord Palmerston and the Secret Service Fund', *English Historical Review*, vol. LIII (1938)

Johnnie von Herwarth, *Against Two Evils* (London, 1981)

Nicholas P. Hiley, 'The Failure of British Espionage Against Germany, 1907–1914', *Historical Journal*, vol. XXVI (1983)

G.A. Hill, *Go Spy the Land* (London, 1932)

F.H. Hinsley et al., *British Intelligence in the Second World War* (London, 1979–   )

Sir Samuel Hoare, *The Fourth Seal* (London, 1930)

Richard Holmes, *The Little Field-Marshal: Sir John French* (London, 1981)

Baron Home of the Hirsel, *The Way The Wind Blows* (London, 1976)

Geoffrey Household, *Against The Wind* (London, 1958)

Michael Howard, *The Continental Commitment* (London, 1972)

Douglas Hyde, *I Believed* (London, 1950)

H. Montgomery Hyde, *The Quiet Canadian* (London, 1962)

David Irving, *Breach of Security* (London, 1968)

David Irving, *The War Path* (London, 1978)

Lesley Jackman, 'Lord Birkenhead's Paper Tiger: The Soviet Military Threat to India in the 1920s', paper to Cambridge Commonwealth and Overseas History Seminar, 24 May 1979.

Lesley Jackman, 'Afghanistan in British Imperial Strategy and Diplomacy 1919–1941', Ph.D. thesis (Cambridge, 1980)

Admiral Sir William James, *The Eyes of the Navy* (London, 1955)

Admiral Sir William James, *A Great Seaman: The Life of Admiral of the Fleet Sir Henry F. Oliver* (London, 1956)

Keith Jeffery, 'The British Army and Internal Security 1919–1939', *Historical Journal*, vol. XXIV (1981)

Keith Jeffery and Peter Hennessy, *States of Emergency* (London, 1983)

W.F. Jervis, *Thomas Best Jervis* (London, 1898)

G. Jones and C. Trebilcock, 'Russian Industry and British Business 1910–1930: Oil and Armaments', *Journal of European Economic History*, vol. XI (1982)

H.A. Jones, *The War in the Air*, vols. II to V (London, 1928–1937)

R.A. Jones, *The British Diplomatic Service* (Waterloo, Ontario, 1983)

R.V. Jones, *Most Secret War*, paperback edn. (London, 1979)

David Kahn, *The Codebreakers* (London, 1968)

David Kahn, *Hitler's Spies* (London, 1978)

F. Kamzadeh, *Russia and Britain in Persia, 1864–1914* (London, 1968)

Sir Cecil Kaye, *Communism in India [1920–4]*, 2nd edn., ed. M. Saha (Calcutta, 1971)

Robert Kee, *Ireland* (London, 1980)

W. Kendall, *The Revolutionary Movement in Britain 1900–21* (London, 1969)
Paul Kennedy, *The Rise of the Anglo-German Antagonism 1860-1914* (London, 1980)
Paul Kennedy, 'Riddle of the Sands', *The Times*, 3 Jan. 1981.
François Kersaudy, *Churchill and De Gaulle* (London, 1981)
Michael Kettle, *Salome's Last Veil* (London, 1977)
Michael Kettle, *Sidney Reilly: The True Story* (London, 1983)
Rudyard Kipling, *Kim* (London, 1901)
Sir Ivone Kirkpatrick, *The Inner Circle* (London, 1959)
David Kirkwood, *My Life of Revolt* (London, 1935)
Maxwell Knight, *Crime Cargo* (London, 1934)
Maxwell Knight, *Pets Usual and Unusual* (London, 1951)
Brian Lapping, *End of Empire* (London, 1985)
S.E. Koss, *Lord Haldane: Scapegoat for Liberalism* (London, 1969)
Aino Kuusinen, *Before and After Stalin* (London, 1974)
'Mervyn Lamb' [Colonel Walter Kirke], 'On Hazardous Service', *Blackwood's Magazine*.
    Part I: vol. CCVIII (1920; part II: vol. CCIX (1921); part III: vol. CCX (1921)
Henry Landau, *Secrets of the White Lady* (New York, 1935)
Henry Landau, *Spreading the Spy Net* (London, 1938)
J.A. Langley, *Fight Another Day*, paperback edn. (London, 1980)
George Leggett, *The Cheka* (Oxford, 1981)
William Le Queux, *England's Peril: A Story of the Secret Service* (London, 1900)
William Le Queux, *Secrets of the Foreign Office* (London, 1903)
WIlliam Le Queux, *Things I Know* (London, 1923)
William Le Queux, *The Invasion of 1910* (London, 1906)
WIlliam Le Queux, *Spies of the Kaiser: Plotting the Downfall of England* (London, 1909)
William Le Queux, *German Spies in England* (London, 1915)
Sir Basil Liddell Hart, *A History of the World War 1914-1918*, 2nd edn. (London, 1934)
A.S. Link, *Wilson: Campaigns for Progessivism and Peace 1916-1917* (Princeton, 1965)
David Lloyd George, *War Memoirs*, Odhams edn. (London, 1938)
Robert Bruce Lockhart, *Memoirs of a British Agent*, 2nd edn. (London, 1934)
Robin Bruce Lockhart, *Ace of Spies* (London, 1967)
C. Lowe, 'About German Spies', *Contemporary Review*, vol. XCVII (1910)
Wilfred Macartney, *Walls Have Mouths* (London, 1936)
Wilfred Macartney, *Zigzag* (London, 1937)
R.F. Mackay, *Fisher of Kilverstone* (Oxford, 1973)
Compton Mackenzie, *Greek Memories*, 2nd edn. (London, 1939)
Compton Mackenzie, *Water on the Brain* (London, 1933)
Compton Mackenzie, *My Life and Times. Octave Five 1915-1923* (London, 1966)
Compton Mackenzie, *My Life and Times: Octave Seven 1931-1938* (London, 1968)
Ian McLaine, *Ministry of Morale* (London, 1979)
David McLean, *Britain and Her Buffer State* (London, 1979)
Iain McLean, *The Legend of Red Clydeside* (Edinburgh, 1983)
Harold Macmillan [Earl of Stockton], *Tide of Fortune 1945-1955* (London, 1969)
Susan Countess of Malmesbury, *The Life of Major-General Sir John Ardagh* (London, 1909)

A.J. Marder, *British Naval Policy 1880–1905* (London, 1941)

A.J. Marder, *From the Dreadnought to Scapa Flow*, 5 vols. (London, 1961–70)

A.J. Marder, *Jutland and After*, revised edn. (London, 1978)

David Marquand, *Ramsay MacDonald* (London, 1977)

J.C. Masterman, *The Double Cross System*, paperback edn. (London, 1973)

J.C. Masterman, *On the Chariot Wheel* (London, 1975)

Anthony Masters, *The Man Who Was M* (Oxford, 1984)

L. Harrison Matthews and Maxwell Knight, *The Senses of Animals* (London, 1963)

W. Somerset Maugham, 'Looking Back', *Sunday Express*; part I: 30 Sept. 1962; part II: 7 Oct. 1962.

W. Somerset Maugham, *Collected Short Stories*, Pan edn. (London, 1976)

Leo Maxse, *Germany on the Brain* (London, 1915)

E. Merson, *Once There Was ... The Village School* (Southampton, 1979)

Francis Meynell, *My Lives* (London, 1971)

Keith Middlemas, *Politics in an Industrial Society* (London, 1979)

C.R. Middleton, *The Administration of British Foreign Policy, 1782–1846* (Durham, North Carolina, 1977)

Harry Miller, *Jungle War in Malaya* (London, 1972)

Mervin Minshall, *Guilt-Edged* (London, 1975)

J.M. Meijer (ed.), *The Trotsky Papers 1917–22* (The Hague, 1971)

B.B. Misra, *The Indian Political Parties* (Delhi, 1976)

H. Mitchell, *The Underground War against Revolutionary France: The Missions of William Wickham, 1794–1800* (Oxford, 1965)

Frantisek Moravec, *Master of Spies* (London, 1975)

Gerald Morgan, 'Myth and Reality in the Great Game', *Asian Affairs*, vol. LX (new series, vol. IV part I (Feb. 1973))

Ted Morgan, *Somerset Maugham* (London, 1980)

A.J. Morris, 'And, Is the Kaiser Coming For Tea?', *Moirae*, vol. V (1980)

L.P. Morris, 'British Secret Service Activity in Khorassan, 1887–1908', *Historical Journal*, vol. XXVII (1984)

Nicholas Mosley, *Beyond the Pale* (London, 1983)

Malcolm Muggeridge, *Chronicles of Wasted Time, II: The Infernal Grove* (London, 1973)

C. Nabokoff, *The Ordeal of a Diplomat* (London, 1921)

Keith Neilson, '"Joy Rides"? British Intelligence and Propaganda in Russia 1914–1917', *Historical Journal*, vol. XXIV (1981)

Keith Neilson, *Strategy and Supply: The Anglo-Russian Alliance 1914–17* (London, 1984)

Keith Neilson and C.M. Andrew, 'Tsarist Codebreakers and British Codes', forthcoming in *Intelligence and National Security*

David Neligan, *The Spy in the Castle* (London, 1968)

Bernard Newman, *Speaking From Memory* (London, 1960)

S. Newman, *March 1939: The British Guarantee to Poland* (Oxford, 1976)

Harold Nicolson, *King George V* (London, 1952)

Liam O'Broin, *Revolutionary Underground* (Dublin, 1976)

Ulrick O'Connor, *A Terrible Beauty is Born* (London, 1975)

Eunan O'Halpin, 'Sir Warren Fisher and the Coalition, 1919–1922', *Historical Journal*, vol. XXIV (1981)

Eunan O'Halpin, 'British Intelligence in Ireland, 1914–21', in C.M. Andrew and D.N. Dilks (eds.), *The Missing Dimension: Governments and Intelligence Communities in the Twentieth Century* (London, 1984)

E. Phillips Oppenheim, *A Maker of History* (London, 1905)

E. Phillips Oppenheim, *The Pool of Memory* (London, 1941)

C. Francis Oppenheimer, *Stranger Within* (London, 1960)

R.J. Overy, 'German Air Strength 1933 to 1939: A Note', *Historical Journal*, vol. XXVII (1984)

B. Page, D. Leitch and P. Knightley, *Philby*, paperback edn. (London, 1977)

'Conférence de M. Georges Jean Painvin', *Bulletin de l'A.R.C.*, nouvelle série, vol. VIII, May 1961

*Papers Relating to the Foreign Relations of the United States* (Washington, 1862– )

B.A.H. Parritt, *The Intelligencers* (Ashford, 1971)

Henry Pelling, *The British Communist Party*, 2nd edn. (London, 1975)

Sir David Petrie, *Communism in India 1924–1927*, 2nd edn., ed. M. Saha (Calcutta, 1972)

Kim Philby, *My Silent War*, paperback edn. (London, 1969)

J. Piekalkiewicz, *Secret Agents, Spies and Saboteurs* (Newton Abbott, 1974)

Chapman Pincher, *Inside Story* (London, 1978)

Chapman Pincher, *Their Trade is Treachery* (London, 1981)

Chapman Pincher, *Too Secret Too Long* (London, 1984)

Roger Pocock, *Chorus to Adventurers* (London, 1931)

Bernard Porter, 'The Origins of Britain's Political Police', forthcoming in *Historical Journal*

A. Pound and G. Harmsworth, *Northcliffe* (London, 1959)

Thomas Powers, *The Man Who Kept The Secrets: Richard Helms and the CIA* (London, 1979)

R.E. Priestley, *The Signal Service in the European War of 1914 to 1918 (France)* (Chatham, 1921)

Rosaria Quartararo, 'Il Canale Segreto di Chamberlain', *Storia Contemporanea*, 1976

Sir W. Raleigh, *The War in the Air*, vol. I (London, 1922)

A. Ramm (ed.), *The Political Correspondence of Mr Gladstone and Lord Granville, 1876–1886* (Oxford, 1962)

J. Ramsden, *The Making of Conservative Party Policy* (London, 1980)

B. Ranft (ed.), *Technical Change and British Naval Policy 1860–1939* (London, 1977)

Anthony Read and David Fisher, *Colonel Z* (London, 1984)

B.L. Reid, *The Lives of Roger Casement* (London, 1976)

P. Renshaw, 'Anti-Labour Politics in Britain, 1918–27', *Journal of Contemporary History*, vol. XII (1977)

Lieutenant-Colonel Charles à Court Repington, *Vestigia* (London, 1919)

David Reynolds, *The Creation of the Anglo-American Alliance 1937–1941* (London, 1981)

Kermit Roosevelt, *Countercoup: The Struggle for Control of Iran* (New York, 1979)

Norman Rose, *Vansittart* (London, 1978)

Norman Rose, 'The Resignation of Sir Anthony Eden', *Historical Journal*, vol. XXV (1982)

Stephen Roskill, *Hankey: Man of Secrets* (London, 1970–4)

Stephen Roskill, *Naval Policy between the Wars* (London, 1976)

Stephen Roskill, *Admiral of the Fleet Earl Beatty* (London, 1980)

E. Royle and J. Walvin, *English Radicals and Reformers* (Brighton, 1984)

'Brian St. George', 'Mervyn Lamb's [Walter Kirke's] Diary', *Army Quarterly*. Part I: vol. CIX (1979); Part II: vol. CX (1980)

Patrick Salmon, 'British Plans for Economic Warfare against Germany 1937–1939: The Problem of Swedish Iron Ore', in Walter Laqueur (ed.), *The Second World War* (London, 1982)

D.M. Schurman, *The Education of a Navy* (London, 1965)

A.J. Sherman, *Island Refuge* (London, 1973)

Naomi Shepherd, *Wilfrid Israel* (London, 1984)

Anthony Short, *The Communist Insurrection in Malaya, 1948–1960* (London, 1975)

K.R.M. Short, *The Dynamite War* (Dublin, 1979)

E. Sisson, *One Hundred Red Days* (New Haven, 1931)

N. St. Barbe Sladen, *The Real Le Queux: The Official Biography of William Le Queux* (London, 1938)

Major-General Sir E.L. Spears, *Liaison 1914*, revised edn. (London, 1968)

E.M. Spiers, *Haldane: An Army Reformer* (Edinburgh, 1980)

Philip Spratt, *Blowing Up India* (Calcutta, 1955)

David Stafford, *Britain and European Resistance 1940–1945* (London, 1980)

Paul Stafford, 'The Chamberlain–Halifax Visit to Rome: A Reappraisal', *English Historical Review*, vol. CCCLXXXVI (1983)

Neil Stammers, *Civil Liberties in Britain during the Second World War* (London, 1983)

'R. Standish', *The Prince of Storytellers* (London, 1957)

*Statistics of the Military Effort of the British Empire during the Great War 1914–1920* (London, 1922)

Zara Steiner, *Britain and the Origins of the First World War* (London, 1977)

Zara Steiner and Valerie Cromwell, 'The Foreign Office before 1914', in G. Sutherland (ed.), *Studies in the Growth of Nineteenth-Century Government* (London, 1972)

Jean Stengers, 'Enigma, the French, the Poles and the British, 1931–1940', in C.M. Andrew and D.N. Dilks, *The Missing Dimension: Governments and Intelligence Communities in the Twentieth Century* (London, 1984)

Jean Stengers, 'Notice sur Fernand Vanlangenhove', in Académie Royale de Belgique, *Annuaire 1984* (Brussels, 1984)

H.F.A. Strachan, 'Soldiers, Strategy and Sebastopol', *Historical Journal*, vol. XXI (1978)

Lord Strang, *Home and Abroad* (London, 1956)

Major-General Sir Kenneth Strong, *Intelligence at the Top* (London, 1968)

Major-General Sir Kenneth Strong, *Men of Intelligence* (London, 1970)

Brigadier H.C.T. Stronge, 'The Czechoslovak Army and the Munich Crisis: A Personal Memorandum', in Brian Bond and Ian Roy (eds.), *War and Society*, vol. I (London, 1976)

M. Swartz, *The Union of Democratic Control in British Politics during the First World War* (Oxford, 1971)

Bickham Sweet-Escott, *Baker Street Irregular* (London, 1965)

A.J.P. Taylor, *Beaverbrook* (London, 1972)
A.J.P. Taylor, *English History 1914–1945*, Pelican revised edn. (London, 1975)
Anne Taylor, *Laurence Oliphant* (Oxford, 1982)
H.A. Taylor, *Jix – Viscount Beresford* (London, 1933)
Telford Taylor, *Munich* (London, 1979)
John Terraine, *Douglas Haig: The Educated Soldier* (London, 1963)
R.W. Thompson, *Churchill and Morton* (London, 1976)
Sir Basil Thomson, *Queer People* (London, 1922)
Sir Basil Thomson, *My Experiences at Scotland Yard* (New York, 1923)
Sir Basil Thomson, *The Story of Scotland Yard* (London, 1935)
Sir Basil Thomson, *The Scene Changes* (London, 1939)
Norman Thwaites, *Velvet and Vinegar* (London, 1932)
Mario Toscano, *Designs in Diplomacy* (London, 1970)
Charles Townshend, *The British Campaign in Ireland, 1919–1921* (Oxford, 1975)
Francis Toye, *For What We Have Received* (London, 1950)
H.R. Trevor-Roper [Lord Dacre], *The Philby Affair* (London, 1968)
Ulrich Trumpener, 'War Premeditated? German Intelligence Operations in July 1914',
    *Central European History*, vol. IX (1976)
Barbara Tuchman, *August 1914* (London, 1962)
Barbara Tuchman, *The Zimmermann Telegram* (London, 1959)
Major-General Sir Alexander Bruce Tulloch, *Recollections of Forty Years Service* (Edin-
    burgh and London, 1903)
E. S. Turner, *Dear Old Blighty* (London, 1980)
R. H. Ullman, *Anglo-Soviet Relations 1917–21* (London, 1961–72)
Lord Vansittart, *The Mist Procession* (London, 1958)
Anthony Verrier, *Through the Looking Glass* (London, 1983)
Derek Walker-Smith, *The Life of Lord Darling* (London, 1938)
W. K. Wark, 'British Military and Economic Intelligence on Nazi Germany 1933–
    1939', Ph.D. thesis (London, 1984)
W. K. Wark, 'British Intelligence on the German Airforce and Aircraft Industry 1933–
    1939', *Historical Journal*, vol. XXV (1982)
W. K. Wark, 'Baltic Myths and Submarine Bogeys: British Naval Intelligence and
    Nazi Germany 1933–1939', *Journal of Strategic Studies*, vol. VI (1983)
W. K. Wark, 'British Military and Economic Intelligence: Assessments of Nazi
    Germany before the Second World War', in C. M. Andrew and D. N. Dilks (eds.),
    *The Missing Dimension: Governments and Intelligence Communities in the Twentieth
    Century* (London, 1984)
Peter Warwick (ed.), *The South African War* (London, 1980)
B. Wasserstein, *Britain and the Jews of Europe* (Oxford, 1979)
Brigadier-General W. H. H. Waters, *Secret and Confidential* (London, 1926)
Sir C. M. Watson, *The Life of Major-General Sir Charles Wilson* (London, 1909)
D. Cameron Watt, *Too Serious a Business* (London, 1975)
D. Cameron Watt, 'The British Image of French Military Morale, 1939–40: An
    Intelligence Failure?', paper to Anglo-French Colloquium, 1975
D. Cameron Watt, 'British Intelligence and the Coming of the Second World War in
    Europe', in Ernest May (ed.), *Knowing One's Enemies* (Princeton, 1985)

G. Weinberg, *The Foreign Policy of Hitler's Germany. Starting World War II 1937–1939* (London, 1980)

A. R. Wells, 'Studies in British Naval Intelligence, 1880–1945' (London Ph.D. thesis, 1972)

A. R Wells, 'Naval Intelligence and Decision-Making in an Era of Technical Change', in B. Ranft (ed.), *Technical Change and British Naval Policy 1860–1939* (London, 1977)

'Nigel West', *MI5: British Security Service Operations 1909–1945* (London, 1981)

'Nigel West', *A Matter of Trust: MI5 1945–72* (London, 1982)

'Nigel West', *MI6: British Secret Intelligence Service Operations, 1909–45* (London, 1983)

M. C. Wheeler, *Britain and The War for Yugoslavia, 1940–1943* (Boulder, Colorado, 1980)

Stephen White, *Britain and the Bolshevik Revolution* (London, 1979)

'John Whitwell' [Leslie Nicholson], *British Agent* (London, 1966)

D. G. T. Williams, *Not in the Public Interest* (London, 1965)

Valentine Williams, *The World of Action* (London, 1938)

Baron Wilson of Rievaulx, *The Governance of Britain* (London, 1976)

Sir Duncan Wilson, *Leonard Woolf: A Political Biography* (London, 1978)

Len Wincott, *Invergordon Mutineer* (London, 1974)

Brigadier-General Sir Ormonde Winter, *Winter's Tale* (London, 1955)

F. W. Winterbotham, *The Nazi Connection,* paperback edn. (London, 1979)

P. G. Wodehouse, *The Swoop! Or How Clarence Saved England* (London, 1909)

Greville Wynne, *The Man from Odessa* (London, 1981)

Herbert Yardley, *The American Black Chamber* (New York, 1931)

Daniel Yergin, *Shattered Peace* (London, 1978)

Kenneth Young (ed.), *The Diaries of Sir Robert Bruce Lockhart, vol. I: 1915–1938* (London, 1973)

R. J. Young, 'Spokesmen for Economic Warfare: The Industrial Intelligence Centre in the 1930s', *European Studies Review,* vol. VI (1976)

# INDEX

Compiled by the late G.P. Bartholomew
Indexer's Note: The following abbreviations have been used:
WW1   First World War
WW2   Second World War
The abbreviations on pages xi–xiii are also used.